ISBN 978-1-332-78615-2
PIBN 10448069

1 MONTH OF
FREE
READING

at

www.ForgottenBooks.com

By purchasing this book you are eligible for one month membership to ForgottenBooks.com, giving you unlimited access to our entire collection of over 1,000,000 titles via our web site and mobile apps.

To claim your free month visit:
www.forgottenbooks.com/free448069

Clarendon Press Series

GREEK ACCENTUATION.

CHANDLER.

London

HENRY FROWDE

OXFORD UNIVERSITY PRESS WAREHOUSE

7 PATERNOSTER ROW

Clarendon Press Series

A

PRACTICAL INTRODUCTION

TO

GREEK ACCENTUATION,

BY

HENRY W. CHANDLER, M.A.,

WAYNFLETE PROFESSOR OF MORAL AND METAPHYSICAL PHILOSOPHY,
FELLOW OF PEMBROKE COLLEGE, OXFORD.

SECOND EDITION, REVISED.

Τὸ ἑκάστῃ λέξει τὴν δέουσαν προσῳδίαν τιθέναι συμπέρασμα σχεδὸν
πάσης τῆς γραμματικῆς τυγχάνει μεθόδου.
JOANNES ALEXANDRINUS.

Oxford:
AT THE CLARENDON PRESS.
1881.

Hæc si quis tempestatis prope ritu
Mobilia et cæca fluitantia sorte laboret
Reddere certa sibi, nihilo plus explicet, ac si
Insanire paret certa ratione modoque.

PREFACE TO THE FIRST EDITION.

THE greatest scholars have sanctioned the practice of accenting Greek by their example, a few have enforced it by their precept, but it is to be regretted that none have condescended to justify it by sound and conclusive reasons. Porson, as is well known, in language more vigorous than polite, denounces those who valued such matters less highly than he did himself; but none who can distinguish between assertion and proof will attach much importance to the bare word even of a critic so illustrious as Porson, while they may possibly suspect that his vehemence, though caused in part by zeal for this curious branch of knowledge, is attributable in some degree to his contempt for Wakefield, who happened to entertain a different opinion from his own. Whether a skilful advocate could convince, I do not say a mere verbal scholar, for that would be easy, but a man of sense, that a knowledge of the subject is worth the time and trouble which must be expended to acquire it, may or may not be doubtful, but it is certain that for the present all who pretend to a critical knowledge of the Greek language must yield perforce to a tyrannous custom, or refusing to do so, must expect to be rebuked for their ignorance by those who are unable to see the absurdity of perpetuating in writing a something to which they never attend in reading, and who persist in ornamenting their Greek with three small scratches, the very meaning of which is doubtful and perhaps unknown.

It is remarkable that we accent Homer and Hesiod, Lascaris and Gaza in substantially the same way; which is tacitly to assume that no material change in pronunciation took place for the space of more than two thousand years. If true, this is an interesting fact. To affix these signs correctly is a work of no small difficulty, and for our guidance we find either principles so vague that they cannot be applied, or rules so numerous that they cannot be remembered. We have to deal with a subject in which popular caprice has been complicated by scholastic pedantry, two elements of confusion, governed it may be by laws, but by laws mysterious as those which regulate English weather or Parisian fashions. We are environed by false theories and still falser facts, by erroneous analogies, absurd derivations, preposterous ideas of language, and by the puerile conceits of the grammarians, of whom it has been truly said, εἰ μὴ ἰατροὶ ἦσαν, οὐδὲν ἂν ἦν τῶν γραμματικῶν μωρότερον.

In treating the subject, two paths lie open to the writer. He may either construct a theory, and deduce, if he can, the practice from it, or he may confine himself to the humble employment of cataloguing facts. The former course is seductive, and appeals strongly to the imagination from the specious claims which it makes to a rational procedure ; the latter is repulsive, but bears with it the consoling assurance that it is impossible to fall any lower, and that, after all, the fairest theories must ultimately rest on the lowly foundation which it and it alone furnishes. But a theory of the subject would of itself fill a volume. In the first place it would be necessary to determine the nature of the accents, a point on which authorities are by no means agreed. Kreuser is of opinion that they indicate the length or shortness of syllables, Matthiä and others think that the acute marks a raising of the voice. and the grave its depression, while Göttling maintains that they are in Greek, what they are in German or English, nothing more than signs of the intension or stress laid upon a syllable in pronunciation. It would be impossible to establish or refute any one of these conflicting opinions without enquiring into the nature of accent in the cognate languages, an enterprise not without its difficulties. In the next place its relations to quantity, to rhythm, and to metre must be discussed, and here again opinions are divided. Some assert that accent and quantity are frequently at variance, others direct us invariably to observe both. It seems to be the opinion of many writers that he, who finds the least difficulty in reconciling Greek accent with Greek quantity, only exposes his lamentable ignorance of both. Sharpness of sound, we are properly reminded, is one thing, its duration another. An Englishman can and does throw the stress of his voice on the last syllable of *volunteer*, why then should he not do so in such a word as φιλικός?

It is unfortunate that those who ask such questions invariably exemplify their theories by words in which the written accent does not interfere with the quantity. It would have been more to the purpose had they told their readers how to preserve both accent and quantity in such words as φιλητέον, νυμφίος, πεδίον, σοφία, ἀμαθία, μωρία, and the like. But this they have prudently avoided. If with Kreuser we say that the ι in σοφία is long, and make it *sophéea*, as the modern Greeks do, the quantity is unquestionably sacrificed. If, as is usual in England, we pronounce it *sóphia*, what is meant by accent? If we raise the pitch of the voice and utter the first and last syllable, say in the note C, and the penultimate in D, we obey the directions of Matthiä, but experiment will prove it to be difficult, one might say ludicrous, to read a passage of Greek upon such a principle. If the opinion of this learned scholar be correct, it would be impossible to give any effect whatever to the Greek accents, if a sentence were pronounced in a monotone. But granting that it is difficult upon any theory to give due force to the acute and grave accents, it is to be feared that a proper enunciation of the circumflex will be found to present insuperable difficulties to all whose vocal endowments are not of the first order, for according to one of the highest grammatical authorities it indicates a 'prolonged rolling sound.' If this be true, only oriental gravity and sonorousness could do justice to a sentence in which this accent might recur, for instance, οὐκοῦν γελοῖον δεῖ ἡγεῖσθαι τοῦτον, ᾧ τὰ τοιαῦτα δοκεῖ ἀληθῆ εἶναι; the deep rumble of such a succession of 'prolonged rolling sounds' must have produced an indescribable effect.

The relations of accent to rhythm, of the *versus politici* to classical metres, would inevitably lead to a discussion of Greek pronunciation in general. After forcing a way through these problems and many others of equal interest, we should at last find ourselves face to face with the most puzzling question of all—upon what principle or principles does the position of the accent depend? Göttling's attempt at an answer is the only one that I have met with. He writes as follows [1]: 'The accent falls either on the syllable containing the principal idea of the whole word, or on the one which is the nearest to the syllable of the principal idea that the number of syllables in the word generally will permit. To find the syllable of the principal idea, the study of the etymological part of the language is indispensable. In a simple uncompounded word, that called the root, is the principal idea, as the first syllable in γράμμα. In compound words the added word forms for the accent the principal idea, because it gives to the whole its shade, its definiteness, its distinction. Thus in πρόγραμμα the principal idea is now in πρό, and γράμμα, in reference to the accent, becomes subordinate, because the preposition πρό gives to γράμμα its definite signification. In certain instances, therefore, the above second principal law is to be applied, as e. g. in γραμματιον. For γραμ is also the principal idea in this diminutive; the accentuation ought therefore to be γράμματιον; but this would be a violation of the first principal law: hence the accent can only fall on the syllable which is the nearest possible to that of the principal idea; consequently γραμμάτιον or προγραμμάτιον.' This law he considers sufficient to account for the accentuation of Æolic, and for that of verbs, neuters and proper names in the other dialects. But it is a law which labours under the treble defect of contradicting itself, misrepresenting the facts, and being practically useless. It contradicts itself; for it is distinctly implied that the principal idea in a word is that which gives it 'its shade, its definiteness, its distinction:' if so, why are not γράμ-μα, γράφ-ω, γράφ-ος oxytone, like γραμ-ματικός, γραμ-μικός, γραμ-μή, γραπ-τήρ, γραπ-τός, γραπ-τύς? The syllables μα, ω and ος ought, on this principle, to be considered the prominent idea, since they give to a common root 'its shade, its definiteness, its distinction.' In short, this law virtually denies the existence of oxytones, and professing to account for barytones, enunciates a principle which, if carried out, would place an acute accent on the last syllable of every simple word in the language. It misrepresents the facts, for, as Göttling himself allows, in all words except verbs,

---

[1] Greek Accent, p. 4.

neuters and proper names, the Attic, Doric and other dialects 'exhibit a remarkable deviation from the oldest or Æolic usage, all endeavouring to place the accent on the final syllable of words, even when these contain no principal idea[1].' The latter words are hardly intelligible, for upon his own showing the final syllable cannot contain the principal idea, unless indeed it be the root, but of such a case, an instance or two would have been desirable. It is practically useless, for allowing that the Greeks accented what they considered the principal idea or the syllable nearest to it, still it is only by the accent that we can discover what part of the word they chose to consider such. If the προ in πρόγραμμα is accented because it modifies the γράμμα, then we might reasonably have expected that the προ in προγραφή would have attracted the accent towards itself, which however is not the case. This general law then breaks down from inherent weakness. It accounts for facts the existence of which it denies; it does not account for facts the existence of which it asserts; it would smooth all difficulties if things were as they are not; and finally it is driven to the melancholy confession, that while utterly incompetent to deal with the actual accentuation of the great bulk of the Greek language, it can perhaps account for the phenomena presented by a single dialect, the whole extant remains of which would be no burden to a weak memory.

But although this law fails to accomplish its end, its learned and accomplished author deserves great praise for having tried, however unsuccessfully, to discover the principle upon which the position of the Greek accent depends. Perhaps indeed his failure may be owing to the preconceived notion that there must have been *one* principle at work, whereas a glance at the subject and a little reflection seem to show that the tangled disorder of these troublesome appendages springs, like other anomalies, not from one principle, but from the conflict of several, in which case any attempt at explaining it by reference to a single law must inevitably miscarry. Theorists also in general seem to underrate the influence of caprice and accident, and to attribute too much to reason, while they have a tendency to forget

[1] Greek Accent, p. 8.

that people have at all times persisted in violating as they found convenient all or any of the rules laid down for their guidance by academies and grammarians.

Seeing then that the theory of the subject might well claim a separate treatment, it was resolved to exclude it rigidly and totally from the present volume, while such a course is warranted by the further consideration, that the practice of accentuation does not flow either naturally or necessarily from any theory yet propounded ; and it therefore seemed unwise to complicate still further a matter already intricate enough by mixing hypothesis and fact, and so confusing in one heterogeneous whole things which may be kept asunder with convenience if not with propriety. The total exclusion of theory of course has its inconveniences. It was, for instance, difficult to give any intelligible rules for the accentuation of enclitics without trenching upon the forbidden subject : and it was still more difficult to avoid any assumptions as to the origin of various grammatical forms ; but as it appeared on the whole better to be consistent, no such assumptions have been made.

Adopting this course we necessarily restrict ourselves to the enunciation of mere empirical rules, which, objectionable as they may be in other respects, still possess this great advantage that, if properly constructed, they can be applied immediately, and without fear of error, by any one competently acquainted with the etymology and prosody of the language ; for it need hardly be said that accentuation is impossible without a considerable knowledge of the forms of words. The ancient grammarians, though occasionally in their feeble fashion appealing to principles (which by the way are frequently wrong), yet for the most part prudently confine themselves to the statement of rules without reasons. And it is fortunate that they had enough self-control to do so. For when a being professing to be rational gravely tells us that there are seven vowels in Greek because there are seven planets, and explains with equal felicity how A comes to stand at the head of the alphabet and Ω at the tail ; or when another writer, deemed learned in his own generation and worthy of publication in this, informs us that Σινά is a barbarous or un-Hellenic word, and then, without one trace of humour or irony, derives it from the Greek verb σίνομαι, one is almost tempted to think that the study of words, when not corrected by some more healthful pursuit, had a tendency, at least in ancient times, to infatuate its victims, and predisposed them to embrace the wildest fancies for incontrovertible verities. Of all the old grammatical authors extant, Apollonius and Herodian alone rise above the dullest mediocrity. And Herodian, the great authority on accentuation, was generally sane enough not to venture out of the region of fact, if, that is, we are at liberty to argue from the wretched compendium of his Καθολικὴ Προσῳδία, which has survived to modern times. The swarm of obscure writers who succeeded him did little more than copy his huge compilation. The rules also in the best modern treatises are in great part empirical; and should be wholly so, for the introduction of reasons which are liable to break down when used, (and all the reasons which they allege are liable to do so,) can only be defended on the weak plea of a necessity which does not exist. After burdening the memory with a number of petty directions, nothing can be more disheartening than to find either that they cannot be applied with ease, or that, if they can, no dependence is to be placed on their results. An instance will render this clear. Authorities, ancient and modern, conspire to teach that verbal nouns in α or η, especially when derived from the Second Aorist or Second Perfect, are oxytone, whilst nominal derivatives are barytone, as δείρω δορά, φθείρω φθορά, φέρω φορά, οἰμώζω οἰμωγή. A rule so expressed is obnoxious to several objections. In the first place, it assumes as an etymological fact something which is neither apparent in itself nor capable of proof; it makes a mere grammatical fiction the basis of a rule which cannot be applied with certainty, unless we possess much more knowledge than we have or are ever likely to have. In the next place, it offers no criterion by which to discriminate verbal from nominal derivatives or from primitive nouns. It may possibly be convenient to say that σιγή, ὄζη, ἀγορά, σόβη, μάχη, δορά, φορβή, πόρπη, and the like, are verbals, but nothing can be gained, while much may be lost, by resting an accentual precept on that supposition. Thirdly, no indication is given as to the area over which the rule is supposed to be valid. Is it, with the exceptions usually given, exhaustive, and if so, within what limits? If this question cannot be answered, the student has no assurance that his guide may not on a sudden fail him. Such a defect is the more to be regretted in a modern treatise, because classical Greek is now a fixed quantity, admitting of no further changes, unless new authors should be discovered; and a perfect induction is to us possible, whatever may have been the case when it was still a living language and capable of further development. That the usual exceptions to the rule in question are by no means all that occur, will be apparent to any one who will take the trouble to look over the lists in the present work. Again, it is stated that nouns in *as* (gen. *a* or *ov*) are perispomena when contracted from *έας* or *άας*; and this is unquestionably true, but we are not told what nouns are so contracted; and yet without that information the rule is almost useless. Again, it is said that synthesis does, and parasynthesis does not affect the accent; which is really tantamount to saying, that when the accent of a word is known, and not before, we shall be able to judge whether a Greek grammarian regarded that word as a synthetic or parasynthetic compound: as a rule for determining the accent, it is worthless, and presupposes the possession of the very knowledge which it professes to impart.

To avoid these and similar incongruities it was determined to reserve the consideration of the theory and its cognate questions for another volume, and to give such rules here as could be applied at once by all possessed of the requisite preliminary information. And it is confidently hoped that they will enable any one possessed of that knowledge to affix the traditional accent to every word contained in the excellent lexicon of Messrs. Liddell and Scott, and to all the proper names in Dr. Pape's Dictionary of Proper Names. While this is all that is professed, and all that the general classical scholar can possibly want, it is not all that has been done. A large number of words to be found for the most part only in the ancient grammarians, lexicographers, and other late writers have been included. Doubtless, however, many of these out-of-the-way forms have escaped detection, but it is hoped and believed that all ordinary Greek has been exhausted. If in the dreary task of hunting through dictionaries and grammarians some words have eluded observation, I can only throw myself on the indulgence of the reader, though few who have not tried the experiment can tell how hard it is to keep the attention fixed on such dry and petty details— on words rather than on things.

In constructing the multitudinous rules, the best authorities, ancient and modern, have been consulted. The former consist of special treatises on the subject, incidental notices scattered about the pages of scholiasts and grammarians, the practice of MSS., and that of printed books. Among the works upon accentuation the Καθολικὴ Προσῳδία of Herodian in twenty books held the foremost place. It is no longer extant, but we possess a corrupt and mutilated epitome, perhaps made by Arcadius, in which the voluminous original has dwindled down to two hundred octavo pages. There are also a few unimportant extracts from it by Porphyry, first published by Villoison in his Anecdota Græca, and numberless references to it in the scholiasts. The Τονικὰ Παραγγέλματα of Joannes Alexandrinus are also derived from the same source, while there can be little doubt that Theognostus had the work before him when writing his Canons. It consists of a string of empirical rules generalised from words of similar terminations, each of which is illustrated by examples, and finished off with the exceptions, for instance, Arc. p. 16, 17 : Τὰ εἰς ΩΝ δισύλλαβα ἐπὶ πόλεων ὀξύνονται· εἰ δέ τι βαρυνθῇ, ἐτέρῳ χαρακτῆρι, ἢ διαστολῇ σημαινομένου· Ἡιών Πλευρών Πυθών Σιδών. τὸ Ἴτων βαρύνεται, ὡς [ἐν] ἐτέρῳ χαρακτῆρι ὑποπεσόν· (καθόλου γὰρ τὰ εἰς ΤΩΝ δισύλλαβα φύσει μακρᾷ παραληγόμενα βαρύνεται μὴ ὄντα τοπικά, διὰ τὸ κοιτών. τὰ δὲ βαρύτονα· Πλούτων, γείτων Τρίτων) . . . Σούλμων πόλις Σικελίας, πλὴν τοῦ κροτών. The author seems to have had before him lists of words identical in form and termination ; these he reduces to the smallest number of classes that he can, generally looking at them, not with reference to their meaning or etymology, but as the schoolmen say *materialiter*. And for practical purposes there is no better method of constructing a rule. It is for this reason that the labours of Herodian have been made the foundation of the present treatise. When however it seemed possible to arrive at simpler results than his I have never hesitated to alter his canons, or even in one or two instances to reverse them; but such a liberty has never been taken without carefully examining every word affected by the rule, that is, every word that I could discover. And here great assistance has been derived from the Lexicon Analogicum of Hoogeveen, and in a lesser degree from the Etymologisches Wörterbuch der griechischen Sprache of Dr. Pape, though I never depended on either of them solely. Those who may be disposed to quarrel with any alterations that have been made are requested to test both the old rule and the new by putting them in practice; they will then be better able to judge how far the departure from ancient precedents is warranted.

The occasional passages in the grammarians and scholiasts are of some value, because they supplement the gaps in Arcadius or otherwise throw light on the corruptions of his text. Foremost in this class of authorities stand the Venetian Scholia on Homer, of which a new and more correct edition is sorely wanted, the Dictata and Epimerismi of George Chœroboscus, the Canons of Theognostus, the Lexicon of Ammonius, and the Commentaries of Eustathius. And here it may be as well to mention that the references to the lines of the last mentioned author may occasionally be found incorrect. The fact is that the greater part of the present work was written at hours when public libraries are closed; the Roman edition of Eustathius is not within the reach of all purses, and as I had only Stallbaum's reprint I was obliged to guess the exact lines as well as I could; the references will, however, never be found more than four or five lines out. It may also be noticed that in extracts from the grammarians and others, the accentuation of the particular edition employed has been retained even when it seemed to be erroneous.

Of the practice of manuscripts, except in so far as it is represented by printed books, few can know much, and I know nothing. But it may be safely assumed that the best modern editions, though occasionally caught tripping, do on the whole faithfully represent the peculiarities of their written originals. Yet it may be asked what the accentuation of a manuscript proves. Can it prove any more than that the scribe who wrote

it believed the accents which he affixed to be the correct ones?
and if so, what would be the value of such a belief? It may
be answered that the authority of a bad manuscript is next to
nothing, while that of a good one may be very great. If it is
found that all the accents in a manuscript, that can be verified
by reference to the grammarians, accord with their precepts,
there is a strong presumption that the remainder are correct
also. The accentuation, for instance, of the Venetian Codex of
the Iliad or of the Ambrosian scholia on the Odyssey may prove
much. For it is certain that the scribes were in these cases
men of more than ordinary learning, that they were fully im-
pressed with the importance of such trifles, and that they had
access to many ancient authorities which have since perished.
The scrupulous care of some copyists would no doubt faithfully
reproduce all the critical signs and all the peculiarities of their
archetype; nor is it very uncommon to find in manuscripts a
note deprecating the wrath of the reader on the plea that the
scribe had honestly copied what was before him, and was not
therefore responsible for barbarisms or other blunders, just as we
are accustomed to call attention to our literary accuracy by the
word *sic*. It is therefore by no means impossible that the accents in a good manuscript of the tenth or twelfth century may
have been copied from one of a much earlier date. Frail as are
its materials, a book, if properly taken care of, is almost im-
perishable. When we consider how large a number of really
ancient manuscripts have survived the perils of the last thousand
years, it is not extravagant to imagine that the book-worm of
the tenth century might have possessed an Iliad revised by
Aristarchus himself. There are manuscripts now existing which
were certainly written long before the famous dilemma was
proposed, which condemned the Alexandrian library to destruc-
tion. There appears then nothing absurd in supposing that the
accentuation of manuscripts may be of considerable authority.
But it may be objected that the oldest now in existence are
unaccented, or if not, that the accents have been inserted some
considerable time after the manuscript was first written. This
may be true, but it does not follow that there were no accented
books say in the first century before Christ. For it is incredible

that Aristophanes should have invented written signs for accents, and yet that they never should have been written. If he designed them for the purpose of preserving the ancient pronunciation, as is said to have been the case, they must have been used at least occasionally, but probably not in the best manuscripts, unless critical editions of the older poets. We accent school books, dictionaries of pronunciation, and works intended for foreigners, but should hardly think of disfiguring a library edition of Shakspeare with them. Just so it is probable that in ancient times books intended for barbarians or for degenerate Greeks or for the purposes of education had accents, but naturally the more sumptuous manuscripts, which would also have the best chance of being preserved, were destitute of them. The practice of accenting *every* word doubtless belongs to a late age, but as one of the avowed purposes of Aristophanes' invention was to distinguish words otherwise identical (see Arc. 186. 4), it is on every ground probable that such words were so distinguished at a very early period, at least in books intended for universities and schools. At the same time it must be admitted that the accentuation of many manuscripts is occasionally faulty, and strange to say this is sometimes the case in grammatical treatises, where we might reasonably expect the writer to be more than usually attentive to such minute details. A remarkable instance is furnished by a manuscript in the Bodleian Library, containing among other treatises a transcript of the Canons of Theognostus. In it the accents are frequently interchanged, and examples are repeatedly given which not only violate all analogy, but the very rule which they are intended to illustrate. The scribes too in many instances seem to have been ignorant or forgetful of the older mode of accenting certain words, e. g. γελοῖος is not unfrequently written γέλοιος in authors who certainly never pronounced it so. In short, they frequently modernised their transcripts both in accent, spelling, and dialectic forms. The proneness to such errors is also evident from the fact, that the fragments of Sappho, Alcæus, and other Æolic writers do not, as it is said, occur in any manuscript with the proper Æolic accentuation, though the grammarians are never weary of repeating that οἱ Αἰολεῖς βαρυντικοί εἰσι; yet such a mistake is analogous to that of representing a Scotchman as talking English, or of making a native of Cork speak the dialect of London. These and similar instances of disregard for grammatical propriety should make us cautious how far we admit the accentuation of MSS. as conclusive evidence, but they should not induce us to discredit it altogether.

Of modern authorities the best by far is Dr. Carl Göttling, who, in his Allgemeine Lehre vom Accent der griechischen Sprache, has collected from the ancient writers, with true German diligence and accuracy, very nearly all that is worth collecting. His book has been of the greatest service to me, as the frequent references to it will show; and if I have occasionally been compelled to dissent from his conclusions, I trust that the reasons given for doing so will prove that no alteration has been made from a mere love of change. Wagner's[1] essay possesses much less merit, and is defective both in plan and execution. In English there is nothing on the practical part of the subject except a translation of Göttling's smaller treatise, published more than thirty years ago, and a few scattered rules in grammars and exercise books, which, whatever other value they may have, are necessarily incomplete. Those in Mr. Jelf's Greek Grammar are the best that I have seen in any English work. All these aids, however, as well as many others, have been used, and I take this opportunity of expressing my general acknowledgments for any assistance which they may have afforded. For most of the references appended to proper names I am indebted to Dr. Pape's Lexicon. They have all been verified, a process always necessary, but particularly so in Dr. Pape's case. Though the rules, with their exceptions, provide for all the names in his dictionary, amounting to between 20,000 and 30,000, still much more remains to be done before this part of the subject is nearly complete. I discovered only too late that he omits a large number of names occurring in Ptolemy, Strabo, and other geographers. The last, though not the least, debt to be acknowledged is that to Hase and Dindorf's edition of Stephens' Thesaurus. The letters H. D. after a reference

---

[1] [Die Lehre von dem Accent der griechischen Sprache ausführlich entwickelt von K. F. C. Wagner. 8vo. Helmstädt. 1807.]

show that I owe the knowledge of it to this magnificent publication. The list of words distinguished by their accent has been enlarged, but is still very far from being complete. [This has been omitted in the present edition.]

To meet the wants of the general classical student the important rules and all their ordinary exceptions have been printed in a large type: the paragraphs in smaller letter contain references to the original authorities, additional but rare exceptions, and such other information as appeared either necessary or useful.

To conclude—in dealing with such a mass of petty and uninteresting details, blunders arising from weariness and inadvertence, or more often from downright ignorance, must have been committed. I find, for instance, that I have carelessly used noun and substantive as convertible terms, and also that in several passages polysyllable has been used to mean any word of more than one syllable. Notices of such other errors as may be discovered, as well as suggestions for the improvement of the work, will be thankfully received.

To the Delegates of the Oxford University Press my best thanks are due for their liberality in printing a book which is hardly likely to repay the money spent upon it.

OXFORD, MAY 23, 1862.

PREFACE TO THE SECOND EDITION.

Among the lesser evils of existence must surely be numbered the necessity of turning once again to an insipid subject long since thrown aside and forgotten. This I have been obliged to do, and to perform the dismal duty of revision under some considerable disadvantages. All my original notes and collections were consigned to the flames years ago, in the firm belief that they would never more be wanted ; and the loss of such materials it is now impossible to repair. In circumstances so embarrassing real help is hard to get. The indefatigable Lobeck is the only man who collected words of like form on a large scale, and his works were pretty freely used in the first edition. A few more references to them are now added. Beyond consulting Lobeck and the Paris Thesaurus, I could do little more than read the grammarians and scholiasts over again and glean a few fresh facts. In this way, however, considerable additions have been made to the book, though, by enlarging the page and practising the arts of typographical compression, the original number of pages has barely been exceeded. Some parts have been re-written, and scarcely a single paragraph reappears without some change, and, it is hoped, improvement. That all defects have been made good it would be unreasonable to expect, for in the first place, he who deals with Greek accentuation independently, as I have done, has to contend with hosts of petty details which distract his attention, and not unfrequently exhaust his patience. Every alteration has to be made with the greatest circumspection, and it would be wonderful indeed, where the chances of error are so great, if I have not sometimes gone astray. In the next place, it is proverbially difficult to detect one's own mistakes, and here let it be remembered that, though I invited criticism and correction, I have received no assistance of any sort or kind.

Let those who noticed faults in the first edition know that they alone are answerable if those faults are repeated in the second. They had but to speak, and whatever was false or misleading would have been corrected. All censure now comes too late to be of any use to me.

The references to the Venetian Scholia were originally made to Villoison's edition: all of them I hope have now been adapted to the Oxford text, in which the scholia of codex A are at length accurately separated from those of codex B. Lentz's Herodian (Herodiani Technici Reliquiæ collegit disposuit emendavit explicavit præfatus est Augustus Lentz, Tom. 2· 8vo. Lipsiæ, 1867–71) has not been quoted as an authority, and for obvious reasons. A new edition of the epitomator of Herodian, corrected from the best manuscripts, and illustrated by all the more important parallel passages of the scholiasts and grammarians, would have been a valuable addition to our knowledge. Such a scheme was far too modest and too practical to find favour in the eyes of Dr. Lentz. He thought himself able to reconstruct the Καθολικὴ Προσῳδία, and the result is an astounding mosaic of bits laboriously fitted together—a paragraph from Arcadius—a line or two from Theognostus or Chœroboscus—a few words from somebody else—often with the accents violently changed, and the gaps in the text filled up by rules written by Dr. Lentz himself in Greek. A book so manufactured possesses no authority whatever beyond that which belongs to the fragments and splinters of which it is composed. I have therefore left my former references to the original sources untouched. Dr. Lentz indulges in conjectural emendation, but never once does he have recourse to manuscripts, although it is well known that a better copy of Chœroboscus exists than that from which Dr. Gaisford printed his edition.

Most of the references to Göttling's treatise on Accentuation have been omitted as unnecessary. Any one who cares to compare the present work with his will discover that many hundreds of words are here noticed which he wholly neglected. The list of words distinguished by their accent has also been suppressed as useless. No one who uses this book is likely to need it.

Beyond reading Stephanus Byzantius again, and registering

the results, little has been done for the accentuation of proper names. The truth is that these words follow no rule. Even the Greeks, who could consult the complete Herodian, are obliged incessantly to refer to him, because they are unable to remember either his rules or his exceptions. Of a comparatively small number of familiar names the scribes knew the accent, but outside that little circle they perpetually make mistakes.

Lastly, let it always be remembered that the present work does not profess to be more than what its title indicates. It is not a treatise on the principles of Greek accentuation. If it were, very different rules would have been given, but they would have been rules which would have left the reader in constant doubt and perplexity. Those here given aim above all things at simplicity, and their number has been reduced as much as was possible. It has been assumed that most men find it easier to remember one rule with thirty exceptions, than five rules with an average of six exceptions each. Occasionally perhaps the desire for simplicity has been indulged in rather to excess, but to any rules there are always some objections, and I have done as well as I could. It may occur to some minute critics that the exceptions, counting in those mentioned in the notes, outnumber in many cases the examples which conform to rule. Let any one who thinks so read over the words in the note, and see how many of them he is acquainted with ; let him ask himself their meanings, in what authors, and how often he has met with them, he will then find that there is much less force in his objection than there seems to be at first sight : for it will be generally allowed that if a rule embraces all the usual words, all the words that a man is likely to meet with in classical authors, it embraces quite enough for practical purposes. Other words find their proper place in a note, and it would be mere pedantry to split one rule into two or more merely to accommodate forms of very rare occurrence. If we possessed more than the mere fragments of Greek literature the case might be different. It might then be desirable to increase the number of rules, and to include many words which are now excluded. But since we have nothing but a few odd volumes, so to speak, saved from the great libraries of antiquity, since no good-natured fairy

gives us the joyful opportunity of exchanging some tons of
Byzantine theology for as many pounds' weight of the lyric and
dramatic poetry of Greece, common sense shows that we had
better accommodate our rules to what we do possess. From
a practical point of view, those rules are best which can be
applied with the least possible thought and trouble. Consider,
for example, the rule for the accentuation of compound adjectives in αιος, § 534, p. 152. A philosopher, or some one
equally sapient—a modern grammarian, for instance—may protest that it is completely irrational. Let him protest. The
rule will enable anybody to accent correctly, and without the
least trouble, every one of these puzzling words that he is
likely to meet with, even should his reading be more extensive
than usual; and what reasonable being can ask for more? A
rule, or rather a set of rules (for many there must be), based on
theory, would leave the reader in constant bewilderment. He
would have to settle all sorts of difficult and obscure questions
before he could apply his rule, and even then his chances of
going wrong would be considerable. With a merely empirical
rule he cannot go wrong, and is under no necessity of plunging
into a sea of grammatical troubles.

One serious omission there is which I much regret, and for
which, in any country governed rationally, I should incur a heavy
penalty. To make the present work really useful, it ought to
have a complete index of all the Greek words mentioned in it,
amounting on a rough estimate to some twenty thousand. I
would have constructed one myself, only the fact is that it
requires keener eyesight and greater patience than I possess.
A hundred years ago it would have been easy enough to find
in this place a score of mere schoolboys, anyone of whom would
have been willing and able to execute such a task with neatness,
quickness, and accuracy; but nowadays, thanks to the spread of
omniscience, it is difficult to meet with a young scholar who is
sufficiently acquainted with his Greek grammar to be entrusted
with such a work as an index; and as to zeal, industry, and
accuracy, where are they to be discovered?

In bidding a last farewell to a subject in which I never took
more than a languid interest, I may be permitted to say that in

England, at all events, every man will accent his Greek properly who wishes to stand well with the world. He whose accents are irreproachable may indeed be no better than a heathen, but concerning that man who misplaces them, or, worse still, altogether omits them, damaging inferences will certainly be drawn, and in most instances with justice. Unquestionably the shortest way of learning how to affix them correctly is to pronounce according to accent, as nearly all Englishmen did till comparatively recent times. There is, to be sure, the great difficulty of preserving quantity; but perhaps, if our ears and lips were a little better trained than they are, the difficulty might not be insuperable. Whether the art of accenting Greek can be learnt from rules may indeed be doubted. Herodian is said to have investigated the accents of about sixty thousand words in his Universal Prosody, and nothing less than a miraculous memory could retain the results at which he arrived. Even when rules are simplified to the utmost, it requires a very strong and a very tenacious memory to remember them. How difficult the thing is may be seen from the fact that few Greek books are quite free from false accents. Scribes, editors, even scholars, all err, and err frequently. I do not recollect to have ever caught Porson tripping, but then Porson's memory was prodigious; the two Dindorfs are generally accurate, yet both have their moments of forgetfulness. Dr. Gaisford certainly knew Greek, and was a minute and laborious student, yet in one and the same line of his Hephæstion (p. 456), may be found Τρώϊλον and Λήμνον, both accents being wrong, and one impossible. No one knew this better than he did, but his attention sometimes flagged. Those who pronounce according to accent rarely or never make such mistakes. A modern Greek newspaper might be searched in vain for what can easily be found in Greek books edited by professed scholars. If pronouncing according to accent be thought too violent, or too difficult, a proceeding, the next best expedient is, from the very first moment of learning Greek, to regard the accent as being quite as much part and parcel of the word as its breathing or its spelling. He who never writes a Greek word without its proper accent will (provided he only writes enough) gradually associate the two together, and thus render himself independent of all rules and all guides to a tiresome though necessary accomplishment.

OXFORD,
August 2, 1881.

POSTSCRIPT.

When one's attention is turned to accents, it is hardly possible to open a Greek book of any kind without seeing something to be noted. The following observations ought to have been made in the text of the work :—

§ 36. Συγκρίτης, E. M. 779. 17, is contrary to all rule and analogy; it should be συγκριτής, if not altogether corrupt.

§ 55. On the distinction between φιλητής, *a lover*, and φιλήτης, *a thief*, see Eust. 781. 12; 793. 57; 1967.35.

§ 87. Σπάθη, Eust. 1967. 33: σπάθη μὲν, ξίφος· σπαθὴ δὲ ναυτικὸν ξύλον, if he means by ναυτικὸν ξύλον, *an oar*, he must have found a different accent in his copy of Lycophron (v. 23) from that which our editions print.

§ 228. Κομβάβος, Lucian de dea Syria, c. 21, a strange accent, which may mean no more than the scribe's belief that the penultimate is long.

§ 275. Τύλλος (?) Dio Cass. 79. 20, a word of unknown meaning; comparing Lamprid. Heliogab. 17, it might perhaps be equivalent to *latrina*, if not altogether corrupt.

§ 279. Ἀγχίαλος, Eust. 1396. 22: δῆλον δὲ ὡς τὸ μὲν κύριον ὁ Ἀγχίαλος καὶ τὸ ἐπίθετον ὁ ἀγχίαλος τόπος, καὶ πόλις δὲ Θράκης Ἀγχίαλος ἡ καὶ Ἀγχιάλη, προπαροξύνονται, ἀγχιαλὸς δέ φασι σχοῖνος πλοίου, ὀξύνεται.

§ 292. Γόνος, Eust. 1410. 9: γουνὸς δὲ, ὁ γόνιμος τόπος καὶ κάρπιμος, ἀπὸ τοῦ γονὸς ὀξυτόνου ὀνόματος, Ἰωνικῇ ἐπενθέσει τοῦ Υ. γόνος μὲν γὰρ βαρυτόνως, ὁ γεννώμενος. γονὸς δὲ πρὸς διάφορον σημασίαν ὀξυτόνως, ὁ γόνιμος: cf. Eust. 1412. 27: ἐρινός = ἐρινεός is oxytone in the books: ἰπνός, Eust. 16. 42: καὶ ὁ ἴπνος βαρυτόνως ἢ ἰπνός ὀξυτόνως δι' οὗ δηλοῦται ἡ ἑστία ἢ ὁ κλίβανος: to Eustathius therefore, and probably to Herodian, ἴπνος was the accent which naturally presented itself.

§ 295. Ἡρκλανός, Plut. 2. 539 A, is singular ; the scribe, probably regarding it as a syncopated form of Ἡρκυλανός, threw the accent back in accordance with a general rule of the grammarians, one version of which is quoted in § 793, but Ἡρκλανός is probably the more correct accent.

§ 312. Κόπρος, Eust. 1165. 17: τινὲς δὲ γράφουσι κοπροῦ μετὰ περισπωμένης, διαστολῆς χάριν ὡς ἐν τύπῳ περιεκτικῷ.

§ 316. Θύρσος, Eust. 629. 50: οἱ περὶ τὸν Διόνυσον βακχικοὶ θύρσοι οἱ βαρυτονούμενοι, οἱ γάρ τοι ὀξυνόμενοι θυρσοί, γαμικὰ δηλοῦσι στέμματα.

§ 351. Ὕδιον, Aristoph. Vesp. 1356.

§ 354. Κουρεῖον, E. M. 533. 29: τὰ διὰ τοῦ ΕΙΟΝ τρισύλλαβα ἰδιάζοντα, τουτέστιν ἐνὶ τόπῳ μόνον λεγόμενα, διὰ τῆς ΕΙ διφθόγγου γράφεται καὶ προπαροξύνεται· οἷον, Λάγειον, τὸ ἱπποδρόμιον Ἀλεξανδρείας, ἀπὸ Λαγοῦ τινός· χλούνειον, τόπος ἐν Αἰτωλίᾳ, ὅπου ἦν ὁ χλούνης· Λαύρειον, τόπος ἐν Ἀττικῇ ἔχων μέταλλα. Οὕτω καὶ κούρειον· οὕτω δὲ καλεῖται ἐν Ἀττικῇ τὸ ἱερεῖον τὸ θυόμενον, ἡνίκα ἐγράφοντο οἱ κοῦροι εἰς τοὺς φράτορας.

§ 386. Ἀγανός, Eust. 200. 1: ἐν δὲ ῥητορικῷ λεξικῷ γράφεται ταῦτα. ἀγανὸν τὸ καλὸν καὶ ἡδὺ καὶ προσηνές· ποτὲ δὲ καὶ κατὰ ἀντίφρασιν, τὸ χαλεπόν. ἐν ἑτέρῳ δὲ ὅτι ἔστι καὶ ἄγανον προπαροξυτόνως· καὶ δηλοῖ τὸ κατεαγός.

§ 443. Συνεργός, Eust. 1967. 32: σύνεργος μὲν, ὁ συγκάμνων τεχνίτης· συνεργὸς δὲ, ὁ βοηθός.

§ 568. Although what is there said about the accentuation of the cases of Πάν fairly represents, I think, the general practice of the books, yet, on second thoughts, I am a little inclined to doubt whether it is quite correct. About the cases of the singular there is no question; the books are unvarying; in Schol. Eurip. Rhes. 36 we have Πάν, Πανός, Πανί, Πᾶνα, Πᾶνας, and Chœroboscus (C. 271. 15; 24) expressly says that the nominative and genitive singular are oxytone, but neither he nor any other grammarian tells us in plain words how the other cases are to be accented. The dual probably nowhere occurs; the doubtful cases therefore are the genitive and dative plural. According to the rules given by Chœroboscus they ought to be respectively perispomenon and oxytone. Πᾶνες is common enough, e. g. Moschus 3. 27; Πάνων, paroxytone, occurs in Heraclitus de Incred. c. 25, ed. Gale, Amstd. 1688; in the Cambridge edition of 1670 it is unaccented, but Πανῶν perispomenon, Plut. 2. 356 D, in the editions of Xylander, Wyttenbach, and Tauchnitz; and Strab. 813, ed. Meineke. Πᾶσι properispomenon, Diod. Sic. 5. 28, ed. Bekker; I cannot at the moment find another example, though tolerably confident that there is one. Πάνεσσι, Theocr. 4. 63, is certainly right; see § 574, and the authorities there referred to.

§ 680. Cf. Ammon. p. 148, and Valckenaer Animadv. ad Ammon. pp. 233 sqq.

§ 719. Ὀμφακόραξ, Auth. Pal. 6. 561. 5, is false for ὀμφακόραξ, and πυκνορρώξ, Auth. Pal. 6. 22. 3, should be πυκνόρρωξ, as it is in Strab. 726, ed. Meineke. Οἰνοχρώς, Theophr. H. P. 9. 13. 4, is a mistake for οἰνόχρως.

§ 743. Ὅτεως and ὅτεῳ are both of them proparoxytone, Chœrob. C. 414. 6.

I hoped that my own vigilance and that of the printers had wholly banished those odious intruders—misprints, but I have noticed two: § 405, p. 126, Ἡρωδώρου for Ἡροδώρου, and § 425, p. 132, ὄντως for οὕτως.

CONTENTS.

CHAPTER I.

GENERAL RULES AND OBSERVATIONS.

CHAPTER II.

ACCENTUATION OF WORDS BELONGING TO THE FIRST DECLENSION.

CHAPTER III.

ACCENTUATION OF WORDS BELONGING TO THE SECOND DECLENSION.

III. Compound Substantives.

IV. Compound Adjectives.

CHAPTER IV.

ACCENTUATION OF WORDS BELONGING TO THE THIRD DECLENSION.

CHAPTER V.

ACCENTUATION OF PRONOUNS AND NUMERALS.

CHAPTER VI.

ACCENTUATION OF VERBS AND PARTICIPLES.

c

CHAPTER VII.

ACCENTUATION OF INDECLINABLE WORDS.

CHAPTER VIII.

THE ACCENTUATION OF WORDS WHEN STANDING IN A SENTENCE;
MODIFICATIONS OF ACCENT ARISING FROM ELISION, ANASTROPHE,
AND CRASIS.

CHAPTER IX.

PROCLITICS AND ENCLITICS.

TABLE OF THE CORRESPONDENCE BETWEEN THE SECTIONS OF THE FIRST AND SECOND EDITIONS.

Ed. 1.	Ed. 2.	Ed. 1.	Ed. 2.	Ed. 1.	Ed. 2.	Ed. 1.	Ed. 2.	Ed. 1.	Ed. 2.
1	3	44	39	87	87	127	{ 132 / 133 }	167	176
2	4	45	40	88	88	128	134	168	177
3	6	46	41	89	89	129	135	169	178
4	5	47	{ 43 / 44 }	90	{ 90 / 91 / 92 / 93 / 94 }	130	136	170	179
5	6	48	45			131	137	171	180
6	8	49	46			132	{ 138 / 139 }	172	181
7	6	50	47			133	140	173	182
8	6	51	48	91	95	134	141	174	183
9	7	52	49	92	96	135	142	175	184
10	11	53	50	93	97	136	143	176	185
11	14	54	51	94	98	137	144	177	186
12	16	55	52	95	99	138	145	178	187
13	17	56	53	96	100	139	146	179	188
14	18	57	54	97	101	140	147	180	189
15	19	58	55	98	102	141	148	181	190
16	om.	59	56	99	103	142	149	182	191
17	12	60	57	100	104	143	150	183	192
18	13	61	58	101	105	144	151	184	193
19	15	62	65	102	106	145	152	185	194
20	20	63	{ 62 / 63 }	103	107	146	153	186	195
21	21	64	64	104	108	147	154	187	196
22	22	65	62	105	109	148	155	188	197
23	206	66	66	106	110	149	156	189	198
24	9	67	67	107	111	150	157	190	199
25	{ 9 / 10 }	68	68	108	112	151	158	191	200
26	9	69	69	109	113	152	159	192	201
27	23	70	70	110	114	153	160	193	202
28	25	71	71	111	{ 115 / 116 }	154	161	194	203
29	26	72	72	112	117	155	162	195	204
30	27	73	73	113	118	156	163		{ 205 / 206 / 207 / 208 / 209 }
31	{ 28 / 29 }	74	74	114	119	157	164	196	
32	30	75	75	115	120	158	165		
33	31	76	76	116	121	159	64	197	210
34	32	77	77	117	122	160	166	198	211
35	33	78	78	118	123	161	167	199	212
36	59	79	79	119	124	162	168	200	213
37	60	80	80	120	125	163	{ 169 / 170 / 171 }	201	214
38	61	81	81	121	126			202	215
39	34	82	82	122	127			203	216
40	37	83	83	123	128	164	172	204	217
41	38	84	84	124	129	165	173	205	218
42	35	85	85	125	130	166	{ 174 / 175 }	206	219
43	36	86	86	126	131			207	220

Ed. 1.	Ed. 2.	Ed. 1.	Ed. 2.	Ed. 1.	Ed. 2.	Ed. 1.	Ed. 2.	Ed.
208	221	265	276	322	330	379	386	437
	222	266	277	323	331	380	387	438
209	223	267	278	324	332	381	388	439
210	224	268	279	325	333	382	389	440
211	225	269	280		334	383	390	441
212	226	270	281	326	335	384	391	442
213	227	271	282	327	336	385	392	443
214	228	272	283	328	337	386	393	444
215	229	273	284	329	338	387	394	445
216	230	274	285	330	339	388	395	446
217	231	275	286	331	340	389	396	447
218	232	276	287	332	341	390	397	448
219	233	277	288	333	342	391	398	449
220	234	278	288	334	343	392	399	450
221	235	279	289	335	344	393	400	451
222	236	280	290	336	345	394	401	452
223	237	281	291	337	346	395	402	453
224	238	282	292	338	347	396	403	454
225	239	283	293	339	348	397	404	455
226	240	284	294	340	349	398	405	456
227	241	285	295	341	350	399	406	457
228	242	286	296	342	351	400		458
229	243	287	297	343	352	401	407	459
230	244	288	298	344	om.	402	408	460
231	245	289	299	345	353	403	409	461
232	246	290	300	346	354	404	410	462
233	247	291	301	347	355	405	411	463
234	248		302	348	356	406	412	464
235	249	292	303	349	357	407	413	465
236	250	293	304	350	359	408	414	466
237	251	294	305	351	358	409	415	467
338	252	295	306	352	360	410	416	468
239	253	296	307	353	361	411	417	469
240	254	297	308	354	362	412	418	470
241	254	298	309	355	363	413	419	471
242	255	299	310	356	364	414	420	472
243	256	300	311	357	365	415	421	473
244	257	301	312	358	366	416	422	474
245	257	302	313	359	367	417	423	475
246	258	303	314	360	368	418	424	476
247	259	304	315	361	369	419	425	477
248	259	305	316	362	370	420	426	478
249	260	306	317	363	371	421		479
250	261	307	318	364	372	422	428	480
251	262	308	319	365		423	429	481
252	263	309	320	366	373	424	430	482
253	264	310	321	367	374	425	431	483
254	265	311	322	368	375	426	432	484
255	266	312	322	369	376	427	433	485
256	267	313	323	370	377	428	434	486
257	268	314	324	371	378	429	435	487
258	269	315	325	372	379	430	436	488
259	270	316	326	373	380	431	437	489
260	271	317	327	374	381	432	438	490
261	272	318	327	375	382	433	439	491
262	273	319	328	376	383	434	440	492
263	274	320	328	377	384	435	441	493
264	275	321	329	378	385	436	442	494

Ed. 1.	Ed. 2.	Ed. 1.	Ed. 2.	Ed. 1.	Ed. 2.	Ed. 1.	Ed. 2.	Ed. 1.	Ed. 2.
495, 496 }	493	552	547	608	647	666	640	723	727
		553	548	609	648	667	668	724	{ 724, 725, 726
497	494	554	549	610	649	668	620		
498	495	555	552	611	650	669	{ 621, 622		
499	496	556	553	612	651			725	725
500	497	557	554	613	652	670	669	726	729
501	498	558	555	614	653	671	670	727	730
502	499	559	556	615	656	672	671	728	731
503, 504 }	500	560	557	616	657	673	672	729	732
		561	558	617	583	674	673	730	733
505	501	562	559	618	628	675	674	731	734
506	502	563	560	619	658	676	675	732	735
507, 508 }	504	564	561	620	659	677	676	733	736
		565	562	621	660	678	677	734	737
509	505	566	563	622	661	679	678	735	738
510	506	567	564	623	662	680	679	736	739
511	507	568	565	624	663	681	680	737	740
512	508	569	566	625	664	682	681	738	741
513	509	570	567	626	584	683	682	739	742
514	510	571	568	627	585	684	683	740	743
515	511	572	{ 569, 570	628	586	685	684	741	744
516	512			629	587	686	685	742	745
517	513	573	571	630	588	687	686	743	746
518	514	574	572	631	589	688	688	744	747
519	515	575	573	632	590	689	689	745	{ 748, 749
520	516	576	574	633	591	690	690		
521	517	577, 578 }	575	634	592	691	691	746, 747 }	750
522	518			635	593	692	692		
523	519	579	576	636	594	693	693	748	751
524	520	580	577	637	595	694	694	749	752
525	521	581	578	638	596	695	695	750	753
526	522	582	579	639	597	696	696	751	754
527	523	583	623	640	598	697	697	752	755
528	524	584, 585 }	630	641	599	698	698	753	756
529	525			642	600	699	699	754	757
530, 531 }	526	586	631	643	601	700	700	755	758
		587	632	644	602	701	701	756	759
532	527	588	633	645	603	702	702	757	760
533	528	589	627	646	604	703	703	758	761
534	529	590	655	647	605	704	704	759	762
535	{ 530, 531	591	580	648	606	705	705	760	763
		592	581	649	607	706	706	761	764
536	532	593	624	650	608	707	707	762	{ 765, 766
537	533	594	625	651	609	708	708		
538	534	595	626	652	610	709	709	763	769
539	535	596	634	653	611	710	710	764	767
540	536	597	{ 635, 636	654	612	711	711	765	770
541	537			655	613	712	712	766	771
542	538	598	637	656	614	713	713	767	772
543	539	599	638	657	615	714	716	768	773
544	540	600	639	658	616	415	717	769	774
545	541	601	654	659	617	716	718	770	775
546	542	602	641	660	618	717	719	771	776
547	543	603	642	661	619	718	720	772 }	
548, 549 }	544	604	643	662	629	719	721	773, 774 }	777
		605	644	663	665	720	722	775 }	
550	545	606	645	664	666	721	723		
551	546	607	646	665	667	722	725	776	778

Ed. 1.	Ed. 2.	Ed. 1.	Ed. 2.	Ed. 1.	Ed. 2.	Ed. 1.	Ed. 2.	Ed. 1.	Ed. 2.
777, 778, 779, 780 } ...	779			836 ...	836	876 ...	876	914 ...	915
781 ...	780			837 ...	837	877 ...	877	915 ...	917
782 ...	781			838 ...	838	878 ...	878	916 ...	918
783 ...	782	812 ... {	804, 805, 806, 807, 808, 809, 810	839 ...	839	879 ...	879	917 ...	920
784 ... {	783 / 784			840 ...	840	880 ...	880	918 ...	921
785, 786 } ...	785	813 ...	811	841 ...	841	881 ...	881	919 ...	922
		814 ...	813	842 ...	842	882 ...	882	920 ...	924
787, 788 } ...	786	815 ...	814	843 ...	843	883 ...	883	921 ...	925
		816 ...	815	844 ...	844	884 ...	884	922 ...	931
		817 ...	816	845 ...	845	885 ...	885	923 ...	932
789, 790, 791, 792 } ...	787	818 ...	817	846 ...	846	886 ...	886	924 ...	933
				847 ...	847	887 ...	887	925 ...	935
				848 ...	848	888 ...	888	926 ...	936
		819 ... {	804, 805, 806, 807, 808, 809, 810	849 ...	849	889 ...	889	927 ...	937
793 ...	788			850 ...	850	890 ...	890	928 ...	938
794 ...	789			851 ...	851	891 ...	891	929 ...	939
795 ...	790			852 ...	852	892 ...	892	930 ... {	943 / 944
796 ...	768			853 ...	853	893 ...	893	931 ...	945
797 ...	791	820 ...	818	854 ...	854	894 ...	894	932 ...	949
798 ...	792	821 ...	819	855 ...	855	895 ...	895	933 ...	950
		822 ...	820	856 ...	856	896 ...	896	934 ...	953
799 ... {	765 / 766 / 767	823 ...	821	857 ...	857	897 ...	897	935 ...	955
		824 ...	822	858 ...	858	898 ...	898	936 ...	956
800 ...	793	825 ...	823	859 ...	859	899 ...	899	937 ...	957
801 }		826 ...	824	860 ...	860	900 ...	900	938 ...	958
802 } ...	794	827 ...	825	861 ...	861	901 ...	901	939 ...	960
803 }				862 ...	862	902 ...	902	940 ...	961
804 ...	795			863 ...	863	903 ...	903	941 ...	962
805 ...	796	828 ... {	826 / 827	864 ...	864	904 ...	904	942 ...	963
806 ...	797	829 ...	828	865 ...	865	905 ...	905	943 ...	964
807 ...	798	830 ...	829	866 ...	866	906 ... {	906 / 907	944 ...	965
808 ...	799	831 ... {	830 / 831	867 ...	867	907 ...	908	945 ...	966
809 ...	801	832 ...	832	868 ...	868	908 ...	om.	946 ...	967
810 ...	802	833 ...	833	869 ...	869	909 ...	909	947 ...	969
811 ...	803	834 ...	834	870 ...	870	910 ...	910	948 ...	970
		835 ...	835	871 ...	871	911 ... {	911 / 912	949 ...	971
				872 ...	872	912 ...	913	950 ...	972
				873 ...	873	913 ...	914	951 ...	973
				874 ...	874			952 ...	974
				875 ...	875				

ABBREVIATIONS.

A. G. .... Immanuelis Bekkeri Anecdota Græca. 3 vols. 8vo.
                         Berolini, 1814.

A. G. Oxon. .... Anecdota Græca Oxoniensia, edidit J. A. Cramer, S.T.P.
                         4 vols. 8vo. Oxon. 1834-1837.

A. G. Paris. .... Anecdota Græca e Codd. MSS. Bibliothecæ Regiæ
                         Parisiensis, edidit J. A. Cramer, S. T. P. 4 vols.
                         8vo. Oxon. 1839-1841.

Ammon. .... Ammonius de adfinium vocabulorum differentia, ed.
                         L. C. Valckenaer. 4to. Ludg. Bat. 1739.

Apoll. de Adv. .... Apollonii Alexandrini de Adverbiis liber, in Bekker's
                         Anecdota Græca, vol. 2. pp. 527 sq.

Apoll. de Conj. .... Apollonii Alexandrini de Conjunctionibus liber, in Bek-
                         ker's Anecdota Græca, vol. 2. pp. 477 sq.

Apoll. de Syut. .... Apollonii Alexandrini de Constructione Orationis libri
                         quatuor ex rec. I. Bekkeri. 8vo. Berolini, 1817.

Apoll. de Pron. .... Apollonii Dyscoli de Pronomine liber ed. I. Bekker.
                         8vo. Berolini, 1813.

Arc. .... Ἀρκαδίου περὶ τόνων e cod. Paris. primum edidit E. H.
                         Barker. 8vo. Lipsiæ, 1820.
                         Ἐπιτομὴ τῆς καθολικῆς προσῳδίας Ἡρωδιάνου, recognovit
                         Mauricius Schmidt. 8vo. Jenæ, 1860.
                         The references are to the pages and lines in Barker's
                         edition.

Charax. .... Ἰωάννου γραμματικοῦ τοῦ Χάρακος περὶ ἐγκλινομένων, in
                         Bekker's Anecdota Græca, vol. 3. pp. 1149 sq.

Chœrob. C. .... Chœroboscus on the Canons of Theodosius, in Georgii
                         Chœrobosci Dictata in Theodosii Canones, necnon
                         Epimerismi in Psalmos ed. T. Gaisford, S. T. P.
                         3 vols. 8vo. Oxon. 1842.

Chœrob. E. .... The Epimerismi of Chœroboscus on the Psalms, in the
                         same edition.

Draco .... Draconis Stratonicensis liber de Metris Poeticis, ed.
                         G. Hermannus. 8vo. Lipsiæ, 1812.

E. M. .... Etymologicum Magnum, ed. F. Sylburg. fol. 1594.

Eust. . ... Eustathii Commentarii ad Homeri Iliadem et Odysseam,
                         ed. Stallbaum. 4 vols. 4to. Lipsiæ, 1827.

Eust. Dion. Per. .... Eustathii Commentarii in Dionysii περιήγησιν, in the
                         second vol. of the Geographi Græci minores, ed.
                         C. Müller. 8vo. Paris. 1861.

Göttling, Accent . ... Allgemeine Lehre vom Accent der griechischen Sprache.
                         Von D. Carl Göttling. 8vo. Jena, 1835.

Göttling, Greek Accent.   Elements of Greek Accentuation, translated from the German of Dr. Karl Göttling, by a member of the University of Oxford. 8vo. London, 1831.

H. D. ....   Stephani Thesaurus Græcæ Linguæ. Ed. C. B. Hase, G. Dindorf et L. Dindorf. fol. Paris. 1831–1865.

Herod. π. μ. λ. ....   Herodianus περὶ μονήρους λέξεως, in G. Dindorfii Grammatici Græci. Vol. 1. 8vo. Lipsiæ, 1823.

Herod. π. ε. μ. ....   Herodianus περὶ ἐγκλινομένων καὶ ἐγκλιτικῶν καὶ συνεγκλιτικῶν μορίων, in Bekker's Anecdota Græca, vol. 3. pp. 1142 sq.

Joh. Alex. ....   Ἰωάννου Ἀλεξανδρέως Τονικὰ Παραγγέλματα, ed. G. Dindorf. 8vo. Lipsiæ, 1825.

Joh. Philop. ....   Collectio vocum quæ pro diversa significatione accentum diversum accipiunt, in the Oxford edition of Scapulæ Lexicon.

Kühner, G. G.............   Ausführliche Grammatik der griechischen Sprache von Dr. Raphael Kühner. Zweite Auflage. 2 vols. 8vo. Hanover, 1869–72.

L. S......................   A Greek-English Lexicon compiled by Henry George Liddell, D.D., and Robert Scott, D.D. Fifth edition. 4to. Oxford, 1861.

Lob. Par..................   Paralipomena Grammaticæ Græcæ, scripsit C. A. Lobeck. 8vo. Lipsiæ, 1837.

Lob. Phryn. ....   Phrynichi Eclogæ nominum et verborum Atticorum. Ed. C. A. Lobeck. 8vo. Lipsiæ, 1820.

Lob. Ajax................   Sophoclis Aiax. Commentario perpetuo illustravit C. A. Lobeck. Editio Tertia. 8vo. Berolini, 1866.

Lob. Prol. ....   Pathologiæ Sermonis Græci Prolegomena scripsit C. A. Lobeck. 8vo. Lipsiæ, 1843.

Lob. Path. ....   Pathologiæ Græci Sermonis Elementa scripsit C. A. Lobeck. 2 vols. 8vo. Regimontii Borussorum, 1853–62.

Lob. Rhem...............   Ῥηματικὸν sive verborum Græcorum et nominum verbalium Technologia scripsit C. A. Lobeck. 8vo. Regimontii, 1846.

Matthiä Gr. Gr.........   A copious Greek grammar by A. Matthiæ, translated by E. V. Blomfield, M. A. Fifth edition. 2 vols. 8vo. Lond. 1832.

Phav. ....   Dictionarium Varini Phavorini Camertis. fol. Basileæ, 1538.

Philem. Lex. ....   Φιλήμονος Λεξικὸν τεχνολογικόν. 8vo. Londini, 1812.

Schol. Ambros. ....   Scholia in Homeri Odysseam, maximam partem e codd. Ambrosianis, ed. P. Buttmann. 8vo. Berolini, 1821.

Schol. Ven. ....   Scholia Græca in Homeri Iliadem, edidit Gulielmus Dindorfius. 8vo. Oxonii. 1875. Tom. 1 and 2, containing the scholia of codex Venetus A.

S. V. ....   Scholia Græca in Homeri Iliadem, edidit Gulielmus Dindorfius. 8vo. Oxonii. 1877. Tom. 3 and 4, containing the Scholia of Codex Venetus B.

St. Byz.	Stephani Byzantii Ἐθνικῶν quæ supersunt. Ed. A. Westermann. 8vo. Lipsiæ, 1839.
Theog. Can...............	Theognosti Canones, in Cramer's Anecdota Græca Oxoniensia, vol. 2.
Theodos. Gramm.	Theodosii Alexandrini Grammatica. Ed. C. G. Göttling. 8vo. Lipsiæ, 1822.
Theodos. Can.............	Theodosii Canones, in Bekker's Anecdota Græca, vol. 3.
Zonar.	Joannis Zonaræ Lexicon, ed. J. A. H. Tittman. 2 vols. 4to. Lipsiæ, 1808.

Unless the contrary is expressly indicated, all references to the above mentioned works are to volumes and pages, or to pages and lines.

The remaining abbreviations are those in common use.

GREEK ACCENTUATION.

CHAPTER I.

GENERAL RULES AND OBSERVATIONS.

1. In speaking their language the Greeks of the classical period distinguished accent from quantity. How they did so, or in what the spoken accent consisted, we do not here enquire. The native grammarians by degrees devised a system of marks by which to indicate Accent, Quantity, and other affections of speech. By Accent in the present work is always meant not the accent as pronounced, but the written sign of it.

2. NOTE.—Arcadius 186. 4 expressly attributes the invention of the written accents and other like signs to Aristophanes of Byzantium. Since this testimony occurs in a book which is known to be derived from Herodian's Universal Prosody it is natural to conclude that Arcadius drew his information from that source. Yet with strange perversity several German scholars have questioned the accuracy of the statement mainly on the strength of a very interesting passage in Servius (Analecta grammatica edd. Eichenfeld et Endlicher, pp. 530-534). But anyone who reads that passage with common attention will see that from § 18 to § 26 inclusive there is no question at all about *written* accents, all that is there said refers simply and solely to *spoken* accent; nowhere does Servius allude to the invention of the written signs of accent. Every educated Greek must have been aware that προσῳδία was matter for discussion long before the existence of what we call Grammar. Every educated Greek must have known, for instance, that there was such a thing as the *fallacia accentûs*. But to discuss the nature and the various species of προσῳδία is one thing, to devise written signs for them is another. No doubt Herodian knew all the facts stated by Servius, but all the evidence we possess shows that Herodian in his Καθολικὴ προσῳδία was mainly if not exclusively concerned with the question how the *written* accents were to be placed: he was not there interested in the wider question which asked how many spoken accents there were or in what way they could be best expressed. Herodian was dealing with certain well-known signs which when he wrote had been in general use for centuries. There was no reason why he should relate the opinions of his countrymen as to the nature and number of the spoken accents; there was a reason why he should mention

the inventor of the written accents.　See Herodiani reliquiae, ed. A. Lentz, I.
pp. xxxvii sqq.

3. The Greek accents (προσῳδίαι, τόνοι) are three in number,
the Acute (προσῳδία ὀξεῖα), as ή ; the Grave (προσῳδία βαρεῖα),
as ὴ ; and the Circumflex (προσῳδία περισπωμένη), as ῆ.

4. NOTE I.—Προσῳδία has generally a far wider meaning than τόνος; Schol.
Dion. Thrac. 674. I : προσῳδίαι εἰσὶ δέκα, ὀξεῖα, βαρεῖα, περισπωμένη, μακρά, βραχεῖα,
δασεῖα, ψιλή, ἀπόστροφος, ὑφὲν καὶ ὑποδιαστολή.　Cf. Arc. 191. 5 ; 186 sqq.　Herodian
(ap. Schol. Dion. Thrac. 676. 16) in his Καθολικὴ προσῳδία defined προσῳδία to be,
ποιὰ τάσις ἐγγραμμάτου φωνῆς ὑγιοῦς (or ὑγιής), κατὰ τὸ ἀπαγγελτικὸν τῆς λέξεως,
ἐκφερομένη μετά τινος τῶν συνεζευγμένων περὶ μίαν συλλαβήν, ἤτοι κατὰ συνήθειαν
διαλέκτου ὁμολογουμένης, ἤτοι κατὰ τὸν ἀναλογικὸν ὅρον καὶ λόγον.　Schol. Dion.
Thrac. 678. 27 : ἰστέον δὲ ὅτι οὐ τοὺς τόνους μόνον ὡρίσατο, καὶ τούτους προσῳδίας
ἐκάλεσεν, ὥς τισιν ἔδοξε, πλανηθεῖσιν ἐκ τοῦ εἰπεῖν ποιὰ τάσις, ἀλλὰ καὶ τοὺς χρόνους
καὶ τὰ πνεύματα.

5. NOTE 2.—That there are three accents in Greek is a statement which is true
only if by accent be meant the written sign of some peculiar mode of pronunciation :
even in that case some denied the fact.　Arc. 191. 14 : τόνοι μὲν τρεῖς, ὀξεῖα, βαρεῖα,
περισπωμένη.　Porphyrius ap. A. G. 757. 13 : τῶν τόνων γνήσιοι μέν εἰσι δύο, ὅ τε
ὀξὺς καὶ ὁ περισπώμενος· ἀλλ' ὁ μὲν κατ' ἀπαθοῦς λέξεως τίθεται, ὁ δὲ κατὰ πεπονθυίας,
ὁ περισπώμενος, καὶ ἔστι σύνθετος ἐκ τῆς ὀξείας καὶ βαρείας συντεθειμένης εἰς τὸν
περισπώμενον . . . . ὁ δὲ ἕτερος τόνος νωθὴς καὶ βραδύς.　Schol. Dion. Thrac. 663. 26 :
ἡ γὰρ βαρεῖα οὐκ ἔστι κύριος τόνος λέξεως, ἀλλὰ συλλαβῆς· ἡ δὲ ὀξεῖα κύριός ἐστι
τόνος.　κύριοι γὰρ τόνοι τῶν λέξεων δύο εἰσίν, ἡ ὀξεῖα καὶ ἡ περισπωμένη.　Schol.
Dion. Thrac. 705. 26 : ἰστέον δὲ ὅτι ἁπλοῖ μὲν τόνοι εἰσὶ δύο· ἡ ὀξεῖα καὶ ἡ βαρεῖα,
σύνθετος δὲ τόνος εἷς.　Καὶ λέγουσί τινες ὅτι διὰ τοῦτο ἡ περισπωμένη σύνθετος λέγεται,
ἐπειδὴ κ.τ.λ.

6. The Acute accent is restricted to the last, the penultimate, or
the antepenultimate syllable of a word ; the Circumflex, to the
last or penultimate syllable.　No word has more than one written
accent except under special circumstances hereafter to be described : see chap. 9.　The Grave accent is of no practical
importance till we come to consider words as connected together
in the sentence.

7. NOTE I.—That the acute accent can never recede beyond the antepenultimate
syllable is a rule which in ordinary Greek has no exceptions though Joh. Alex. 4. 29
mentions the fact that Μήδεïα was found in Sappho for Μήδεια.　Cf. Schol. Dion.
Thrac. 685. 18.

8. NOTE 2.—According to the ancient grammarians every syllable except that
marked with the acute or circumflex has the grave accent ; thus Θεόδωρος was sometimes written Θεὸδὼρὸς.　But this practice if it was ever general was at length
abandoned as Joh. Alex. 6. 18 says ' διὰ τὸ μὴ καταστίζειν τὰ βιβλία.'　Cf. A. G. 674.
31 ; 686. 5 ; Chœrob. C. 18. 17.　That the practice did prevail we know, for the
famous fragment of Alcman is so accented ; see Gardthausen, Griechische Palaeo-
graphie, p. 283.

9. A word with the acute on the last syllable is called Oxytone ;
on the penultimate, Paroxytone ; on the antepenultimate, Pro-

paroxytone. A word with the circumflex on the last syllable is called Perispomenon; on the penultimate, Properispomenon. A Barytone word is one which has not the acute accent on its last syllable.

Every word having an independent accent is called Orthotone in contradistinction to Proclitics and Enclitics : see chap. 9.

10. NOTE.—Chœrob. C. 17. 18 : ὀξύτονον γὰρ λέγομεν τὸ ἐπὶ τέλους ἔχον τὴν ὀξεῖαν, οἷον καλὸς, καὶ παροξύτονον τὸ πρὸ μιᾶς συλλαβῆς τοῦ τέλους ἔχον τὴν ὀξεῖαν, οἷον ἀνθρώπου, καὶ πάλιν περισπώμενον φαμὲν τὸ ἐπὶ τέλους ἔχον τὴν περισπωμένην, οἷον Ἑρμῆς, προπερισπώμενον δὲ τὸ πρὸ μιᾶς συλλαβῆς τοῦ τέλους ἔχον τὴν περισπω- μένην, οἷον μῆλον, τούτου χάριν τὰ παροξύτονα καὶ προπαροξύτονα καὶ προπερισπώμενα καλοῦμεν βαρύτονα τῷ κοινῷ ὀνόματι, ὡς ἔχοντα τὴν βαρεῖαν ἐν τῇ τελευταίᾳ συλλαβῇ, οἷον, φίλὸς, ἄνθρὼπὸς, μῆλόν. Perispomena are said to be potentially barytone because the circumflex on the last syllable implies according to the theories of the gram- marians, an acute followed by a grave accent; Joh. Alex. 6. 15 ; E. M. 684. 53 ; Theodos. Gram. 71. 29 ; Chœrob. C. 98. 12 ; 494. 5. Joannes Charax ap. Chœrob. C. 19. 20 : ὀρθοτονεῖσθαι μέν φαμεν, ὅτε τὸν ἀνάλογον κατὰ φύσιν τόνον φυλάττει· ἐγκλίνεσθαι δὲ, ὅτε τὸν τόνον ἀναβιβάζει τῇ πρὸ αὐτῶν λέξει, ὡς ἀπὸ μεταφορᾶς τῶν ἐγκλινόντων ἑαυτῶν τὰ σώματα ἐπὶ τὰ ὀπίσω.

11. No word with a final syllable long by nature can be proparoxytone or properispomenon.

12. The circumflex can only stand on a naturally long syllable, as σῶμα, οὐρανοῦ; and never on the antepenultimate.

13. A word with a trochaic ending and accented penultimate must be properispomenon: as μοῦσᾰ, βαλοῦσᾰ, ὀξεῖᾰ.

14. NOTE I.—Jo. Alex. 4. 28 sqq. In the Bœotian dialect forms are found which are proparoxytone although the last syllable is long, as τύπτομη = τύπτομαι ; Ὅμηρῦ =Ὅμηροι, Chœrob. C. 403. 10 ; Eust. 365. 29. Göttling (Accent. p. 25) observes that Bœckh. Corp. Inscr. 1. p. 723 accents ἴαρυ for ἴαρυ, and μειλιχίυ for μειλίχιυ : he is also of opinion that in A. G. 1187 we should write τῇ Ἑλένη and τῇ Πηνελόπη for Ἑλένη and Πηνελόπη. In like manner the long α = η in Æolic seems to have been reckoned short for the accent, Joh. Alex. 3. 17 : τὸ Ἀφρόδιτα παρὰ μὲν Αἰολεῦσι πρὸ δύο ἔχει τὸν τόνον. This remark he would hardly have made unless he held the α to be long, yet it is asserted to be short by Chœrob. C. 325. 28 : οἱ δὲ Αἰολεῖς τὸ Η εἰς Α βραχὺ τρέπουσιν, οἷον Ἀφροδίτη Ἀφροδίτα (sic). Hephæstion p. 83 ed. Gais- ford quotes from Sappho ποικιλόθρον᾽ ἀθάνατ᾽ Ἀφροδίτα and seems beyond all doubt to consider the final α long, and again p. 87. 5 : Ψάφοι τί τὰν πολύολβον Ἀφροδίταν, where one of the scholiasts says μακρὸν γάρ ἐστι τὸ ΤΑΝ.

15. NOTE 2.—Joh. Alex. 5. 18 : πᾶσα φύσει μακρὰ πρὸ βραχείας ληκτικῆς ἐφ᾽ ἑαυτῆς ἔχουσα τὸν τόνον περισπᾶται, οἶκος, ἦθος, ὦμος : Chœrob. C. 398. 15. This rule does not apply to those cases where the length of the vowel is caused by *arsis*, as in Hom. Il. 4. 155 : φίλε κασίγνητε ; cf. Eust. ad loc., nor to parathetic compounds as τοιῶδε, Πυθῶδε, μῆτις, οὔτις, but Οὖτις, the fictitious name of Ulysses, follows the rule. In many editions we find Hom. Il. 5. 31 : Ἄρες Ἄρες βροτολοιγέ : in Draco 24. 10 it is thus printed, though in the same author, 154. 18, it stands Ἄρες Ἄρες βροτολοιγέ, one out of ten thousand proofs of the singular carelessness of scribes or editors or both.

The circumflex may stand on the penultimate though the last syllable is long by position, as Δημῶναξ. The accentuation of such words as κῆρυξ, φοῖνιξ is discussed in chap. 4. The Epic τοῖσδεσι and τοῖσδεσσι is remarkable as violating the common rule.

16. The diphthongs αι and οι at the end of a word are accounted *short* for the accent : as ἄνθρωποι, τράπεζαι, ἅμαξαι, ἄελλαι, Ὁμήρου Ἀρίσταρχοι, τύπτονται, πεποίηνται, τύπτεσθαι λέγεσθαι, ἄσπασαι ; except in the Optative Mood and in Adverbs in οι; as ποιήσαι *he might make*, ὁμολογήσαι, οἴκοι, ἁρμοῖ. Yet the αι in πάλαι and its compounds is reckoned short; as ἔκπαλαι, πρόπαλαι. If followed by a consonant αι and οι are accounted long, as ἀνθρώποις, τραπέζαις. Hence may be distinguished ποιήσαι third person singular Optative Aorist active ; ποίησαι, second person singular Imperative Aorist middle ; ποιῆσαι, Infinitive Aorist active.

17. NOTE.—Apoll. de Adv. 537. 22 ; Chœrob. C. 400. 7 sqq. ; Schol. Ven. A. 255 ; 302 ; E. M. 647. 9. In Doric the final οι in the nominative plural of nouns and participles was regarded as long ; e. g. they wrote φιλοσόφοι, Μενελάοι, πωλούμενοι, καλουμένοι, δωρουμένοι, Greg. Cor. § 123, p. 314 ed. Schäfer. It does not appear whether they treated αι in the same way. Cf. Ahrens, de Dialect. ling. Gr. 2. p. 27.

18. The Ionic and Attic case-vowel ω is accounted short for the accent ; as Μενέλεως, ἀνώγεων, δύσερως (genitive δύσερω), φιλόγελως, βαθύγηρως, ἔμπλεως, πόλεως, πράξεως, πράξεων, Πηλείδεω.

19. NOTE.—Chœrob. C. 399. 25 : φύσει μακρᾶς οὔσης τῆς τελευταίας συλλαβῆς τρίτη ἀπὸ τέλους οὐδέποτε πίπτει ἡ ὀξεῖα, 'χωρὶς εἰ μὴ εὑρεθῇ τὸ Ω ἐν τῇ τελευταίᾳ συλλαβῇ παραληγοντος τοῦ Ε,' τουτέστιν, ὅταν τὸ Ω ἐν τῇ τελευταίᾳ συλλαβῇ παραλήγοντος τοῦ Ε εὑρεθῇ, τρίτη ἀπὸ τέλους τότε πίπτει ἡ ὀξεῖα, ὡς ἐπὶ τοῦ πόλεως, μάντεως, πράξεως, πόλεων, μάντεων, πράξεων, καὶ ὡς ἐπὶ τῶν παρὰ ταῖς διαλέκτοις, οἷον Ἀτρείδεω, Πηλείδεω. Ἰστέον ὅτι ταῦτα προπαροξυνόμενα οὐ θέλουσιν ἔχειν μεταξὺ τοῦ Ε καὶ τοῦ Ω σύμφωνον, ὡς ἐπὶ τῶν προλεχθέντων παραδειγμάτων· ἐὰν δὲ ἄρα καὶ ἔχωσι πάντως εὑρίσκεται ἢ τὸ Λ ἢ τὸ Ρ, ὡς ἐπὶ τοῦ χρυσόκερως, φιλόγελως. Cf. Theodos. Gram. 200. 3. In such words as δύσερως it must be noticed that the above accentuation holds of them only so far as they belong strictly to the Attic declension ; if they are inflected like δυσέρως, genitive δυσέρωτος, the vowel ω being no long casal (πτωτικόν, cf. Theodos. l. l.) the ordinary accentuation obtains. Special rules for these forms will be given hereafter.

20. The long syllable resulting from the contraction of an accented vowel or diphthong with another vowel is itself accented. When by the operation of this rule the *last syllable* should be accented, it is to be observed that words oxytone prior to contraction remain unchanged, but paroxytones become perispomena ; as φιλέομεθα φιλούμεθα, φιλέω φιλῶ, φιλέετε φιλεῖτε (§ 13), μουσάων μουσῶν, αἰδόος αἰδοῦς, ζωός ζώς, ἑσταώς ἑστώς, βεβαώς βεβώς, Νηρεΐς Νηρίς. To this rule there are some exceptions which are mentioned in their proper places.

21. NOTE.—In theory the Circumflex is supposed to represent the union of the Acute and Grave accents *in that order*; for example in φιλέδμεν, when ε and ο coalesce, the resulting syllable retains the old accents melted as it were into one, φιλοῦμεν; in like manner σόδμα becomes σῶμα; but ζὼός can only become ζώς because the grammarians have not devised an inverted circumflex ν to denote the fusion of the Grave and Acute. This theory is of course subject to the general rules; τριακον- ταέτις cannot produce τριακοντούτἴς; in accordance with the rule given above, § 13, the word must necessarily be written τριακοντοῦτις.

22. The different forms which a word assumes in the course of inflexion may require sometimes a change in the accent, some- times a shifting of its place, and occasionally both; for example ἄνθρωπος becomes ἀνθρωπου, ἀνθρωπῳ, ἀνθρωπων, ἀνθρωποις. Now the acute accent cannot stand on the antepenultimate when the last syllable is long (§ 11), though it may on the penultimate to which syllable it is accordingly shifted, and the cases mentioned are written ἀνθρώπου, ἀνθρώπῳ, ἀνθρώπων, ἀνθρώποις: μοῦσα becomes μουσης, μουσῃ, but as the circumflex cannot stand on the penultimate when the last syllable is long, it is superseded by the acute, and we therefore write μούσης, μούσῃ: ἐπιστήμη becomes in the nominative plural ἐπιστημαι where the final αι is considered short for the accent (§ 16); but the acute cannot stand on a naturally long penultimate when the last syllable is short, and therefore the circumflex takes its place (§ 13), and the word is written ἐπιστῆμαι; λαῖλαψ becomes λαιλαπος, λαιλαπι, λαιλαπων, and consequently by §§ 11, 12, λαίλαπος, λαίλαπι, λαιλάπων.

23. The accent is said to be *retracted* or *thrown back* when it is placed as far from the end of the word as the general laws permit.

24. In the rules which follow the accent for Substantives is that of the Nominative Case Singular; for Adjectives of three or two terminations, that of the Nominative Case Singular Masculine; for all others, that of the Nominative Case Singular Masculine, Feminine, or Neuter, as the case may be, and unless special rules to the contrary are given, it is to be understood that the accent remains, subject to the general rules, throughout all inflexions on the same syllable, counting from the beginning of the word, as that on which it stood in the Nominative singular. For example, πῆχυς is properispomenon, and the accent stands on the first syllable; hence πήχεως (§ 18), πήχεος (§ 12), πήχεϊ or πήχει (§§ 11, 12), πῆχῦν, πῆχὔ: πῆχεε, πηχέοιν

(§ 11), πήχεες, or πήχεις, πήχεων (§ 18), πήχεσι, πήχεας, or πήχεις : βασιλεύς is oxytone, and the accent stands on the third syllable, therefore βασιλέος βασιλέως βασιλῆος (§ 13), βασιλέι βασιλεῖ (§ 20), βασιλῆι (§ 13), βασιλέα βασιλῆ (§ 20), βασιλῆα (§ 13), βασιλέες βασιλεῖς βασιλῆς (§ 20), βασιλῆες (§ 13), βασιλέων βασιλήων, βασιλεῦσι (§ 13), βασιλέας βασιλεῖς (§ 20), βασιλέες βασιλεῖς (§ 20). Καλός is oxytone; hence καλή, καλόν; ὀξύς is oxytone, therefore ὀξεῖα (§ 13), ὀξύ.

To this general rule there are several exceptions which will be found in the special rules for oblique cases under the several declensions.

25. If we may argue from the silence of the native grammarians, all the Greek dialects with the single exception of the Æolic were accented in substantially the same manner; the known instances in which they vary from the ordinary rules are noticed in their respective places. Æolic however differs wholly from the other dialects in having no oxytone words except dissyllabic prepositions and conjunctions, and some monosyllables. For example, the Æolians pronounced σόφος for σοφός; Ποσείδαν, or Ποτίδαν, for Ποσειδῶν; ὤρανος, or ὄρανος, for οὐρανός; 'Ρώμαος, or 'Ρωμάος, for 'Ρωμαῖος; πάλαος, or παλάος, for παλαιός; σφρᾶγιν for σφραγῖδα.

26. Note.—Chœrob. C. 333. 26 : Πᾶσα γὰρ λέξις ὑπὲρ μίαν συλλαβὴν παρ' ἡμῖν ὀξυνομένη παρὰ τοῖς Αἰολεῦσι βαρύνεται, οἷον 'Ατρεὺς, 'Ατρευς, σοφὸς σόφος, χωρὶς τῶν προθέσεων καὶ τῶν συνδέσμων· ἐπὶ γὰρ τούτων φυλάττουσι τὴν ὀξεῖαν τάσιν, οἷον ἀνὰ κατὰ διὰ μετὰ αὐτὰρ ἀτὰρ πρός. ' Ὑπὲρ μίαν συλλαβήν.' Διὰ τὰ μονοσύλλαβα· ἐπὶ τούτων γὰρ φυλάττουσι τὴν ὀξεῖαν τάσιν, οἷον νύξ, Στύξ· πῶς γὰρ δύνανται τὰ μονοσύλλαβα βαρύνεσθαι; Chœrob. C. 70. 13 : οἱ γὰρ Αἰολεῖς βαρυντικοί εἰσιν· τὸ γὰρ Πήλευς καὶ 'Ατρευς λέγουσιν βαρυτόνως. Cf. Chœrob. C. 283. 7. Yet we find Gramm. Meerm. § 27. p. 331. ed. Koen. saying, περισπῶσιν ὡς ἐπίπαν τὰ μονοσύλλαβα ὀνόματα· ῥῶξ, πτῶξ, δρῶψ, χροῦς, ῥοῦς, θροῦς, βοῦς, χνοῦς, νοῦς, χῆν, Ζεῦς. Apoll. de Pron. 93 B: ἀδύνατον πρόθεσιν βαρύνεσθαι, χωρὶς εἰ μὴ ἀναστρέφοιτο· οὐδὲ γὰρ Αἰολεῖς τὸν ἐπὶ ταύταις τόνον ἀναβιβάζουσιν. Aristoph. Byzant. ap. Apoll. de Syut. 309. 15. Eust. 75. 36 : προπαροξυντικοὶ γάρ εἰσιν οἱ Αἰολεῖς ἐν πολλοῖς, ὡς δηλοῖ καὶ τὸ δύνατος παρ' αὐτοῖς προπαροξυνόμενον καὶ ἄλλα μυρία. Eust. 265. 16; 518. 37; Ahrens de Gr. ling. dialect. I. p. 10 sq.

The Bœotian accentuation seems to have differed from the Æolic, for it had polysyllabic oxytones, as εὐγενείς = εὐγενής, ἀγενείς = ἀγενής, ἐμύ, καλύ, etc. Arc. 92. 24; Apoll. de Pron. 104 B.

CHAPTER II.

ACCENTUATION OF WORDS BELONGING TO THE FIRST DECLENSION.

27. The rules for the accentuation of words belonging to the first declension apply to substantives and adjectives indifferently.

28. ACCENT OF COMPOUND WORDS. Compound words of the first declension, with a *long* final syllable, retain the accent of their last factor, as, πειρατής ἀρχιπειρατής, λεία ἀγελεία, ἐρανιστής ἀρχερανιστής, λῃστής ἀρχιλῃστής, Ἀπελλῆς φιλαπελλῆς, except dissyllabic oxytones, which, when compounded with any other word than a preposition, become paroxytone, as κριτής ὀρνιθοκρίτης, ὀνειροκρίτης, but ἐπικριτής, ὑποκριτής; δοκή ἱστοδόκη, καπνοδόκη, but προδοκή: ῥοή ὑδρορρόη, χοή οἰνοχόη, but ἀπορροή, προχοή. Compounds, with a *short* final syllable, throw their accent as far back as possible, as μυῖα χαλκόμυια, κυνάμυια; παῦλα ἀνάπαυλα, οὐρά κυνόσουρά, πεῖρα ἀνάπειρα, πρόπειρα. This rule has some few exceptions, which are mentioned under their respective terminations. Κατάρα is always paroxytone, though the simple ἀρά is oxytone. Words beginning with αὐτ- or αὐτο- retain the accent of the last factor unchanged, as αὐτοαρετή, αὐτοαρχή, αὐταρχή, αὐτοπηγή, αὐτοβουλή, αὐτοζωή, αὐτομετοχή, αὐτοδόξα, αὐτοφθορά, αὐτοψυχή; for such accents the sole authority is the practice of the scribes, the grammarians give no rule for such words, and it is somewhat doubtful whether they would regard them as synthetic compounds.

29. NOTE.—Schol. Ven. Ξ. 372; Arc. 102. 15; A. G. Oxon. I. 212. 1; E. M. 435. 26; Philem. Lex. p. 110. § 262; Eust. 897. 38. Although these passages as well as the actual practice of the scribes fully justify the rule given above, it will be discovered by anyone who consults them that the grammarians have a sad habit of mixing together words which have no possible analogies with each other.

Words in ας and ης.

30. Monosyllables in ας and ης are perispomena, as Βᾶς, Γρᾶς, Δᾶς, Θᾶς, Χνᾶς, Πᾶς, Δρῆς, Τρῆς.

NOTE.—Arc. 125. 15; 126. 16; 126. 11; concerning the latter passage Lobeck, Par. 82, is clearly mistaken. Joh. Alex. 7. 29; Chœrob. C. 43. 11.

31. All words of more than one syllable in ας are paroxytone, as βύας, κοχλίας, νεανίας, ὀρνιθοθήρας, πωγωνίας, ταμίας, ταραξίας, τραυματίας, Αἰνείας, Βορέας, Ἐπαμεινώνδας, Λεωνίδας, Λυσίας, Μίδας, Νικίας, Σιμμίας, except those contracted from ααϲ, or εας, which are perispomena, as Βορρᾶς, φιλοβορρᾶς, Δημᾶς, Ἑρμᾶς, Μαρικᾶς, Φιλωτᾶς, ἐλασᾶς, κερατᾶς, together with ἀτταγᾶς (or ἀττάγας).

32. NOTE.—Arc. 21. 22. The nouns in ᾶς are for the most part late, vulgar, or foreign words. (Lob. Phyrn. 433.) For the purposes of reference, a list of such as have been noted is appended.

Proper Names. Ἀγαθᾶς, Inscr. : Ἀζηνᾶς, Suid. : Ἀηδᾶς, Suid. : Αἰλουρᾶς, Sturz. de Dial. Maced. 136, quoted by *H. D.* : Ἀκεσᾶς, Athen. 48 B. Anthol. Gr. Brunck. T. 3. 192 : Ἀκοχᾶς, A. G. Paris. 2. 145. 12 : Ἀκριβᾶς (?) Arc. 21. 10 · Ἀλβᾶς, Diod. Sic. 7. 3 : Ἀλεξᾶς, Plut. 1. 947 ; 949 : Ἀμησινᾶς, A. G. Paris. 2. 145. 30 : Ἀμπελᾶς, Anna Comnena, 14. p. 442 B. *H. D.* : Ἀμυνᾶς, (?) Polyb. 4. 16. 9 : Ἀναφᾶς, Phot. Bib. 382. 31 : Ἀνεμᾶς, Leo Dial. p. 92 B. H. *D.* : Ἀπελλᾶς, Diog. Laert. 9. 106 ; Chœrob. C. 443. 32 : Ἀπολλᾶς (?) Pape. : Ἀργᾶς, Athen. 131 B : Ἀρκᾶς (perhaps for Ἀρκέας, which occurs in Iambl. Vit. Pyth. ad fin.), Arc. 21. 1, where Lobeck (Par. 222) would, as it seems without reason, read Μαρικᾶς : Ἀρκεσᾶς (?) : Ἀρποκρᾶς (?) Suid. s. v. is Ἀρπόκρας, in Galen ; wrongly as Dindorf thinks : Ἀρτεμᾶς, Arc. 22. 6 : Ἀρτεμιδωρᾶς, *H. D.*, there is no authority for such an accent : Ἀσκιδᾶς, Cyril. Vit. Sabæ. c. 86. H. *D.* : Ἀσκληπᾶς, Sozom. H. E. 3. 8. 11. *H. D.* : Ἀτταγᾶς, Diog. Laert. 9. 12. § 114 : Ἀττιλᾶς (?) : Ἀτ·τινᾶς, Inscr. : Ἀφροδᾶς, Galen. t. 13. p. 858 A : Ἀχιλλᾶς, Phot. Bib. 470. 11 : Ἀψεφᾶς, Schol. Dio Chrys. 1. p. 49. H. *D.* : Βαβυλᾶς, Suid. Βαβύλας, Zonar. 367 : Βαδᾶς, Strab. 728 : Βαλλαντᾶς, Synes. Ep. 127, H. *D.* : Βαραββᾶς, N. T. Matt. 27. 16 : Βαρσαβᾶς, N. T. Acts 1. 23 : Βᾶς, Arc. 125. 17 ; Chœrob. C. 16. 7 ; Phot. Bib. 228. 17. In Æschyl. Suppl. 869 = 892. ed. Didot. ὦ Βᾶ, Γᾶς παῖ, Ζεῦ, it is an old form for βασιλεύς : Βασιλᾶς, Soph. Gloss. : * Βαΰθλᾶς (?) : Βελιτανᾶς, Phot. Bib. 39. 5 : Βησᾶς, so Pape, who quotes an epigram in the Anthol. Gr., where, in Jacob's edn., Βήσας stands. In the following passage of Suid. it seems to be either an adverb or adjective : Βησᾶς ἕστηκεν οἷον ἀχανής. οὖτος ἕστηκεν ἀχανὴς καὶ παταγώδης καὶ ὑπόμωρος : Βορρᾶς, Arc. 22. 15 : Βουσᾶς, Phot. Bib. 28. 12 : Βρανᾶς, Cinnamus 6. 7 ; 2. 1 : Βυβλᾶς, or Βιβλᾶς, Galen. Comment. 2. in Hippocrat. Epidem. 3. § 5, tom. 9. p. 244. ed. Chart. : Γαβρᾶς, Cinnamus 2. 8. Γαρουνᾶς, Pape, but in Strabo, 4. p. 177 F. ed. Meineke, it is Γαρούνας, though some MSS. of that author do read Γαρουνᾶς : Γλισσᾶς (ᾶ, but generally ᾶντος), Chœrob. ap. Eust. 269. 21 : Γλυκᾶς or Γλύκας (?) : Γονατᾶς, Polyb. 2. 41. 10. St. Byz. s. v. Γόννοι has Γονατᾶς, and Eusebius Γονάτας : see *H. D.* s. v. : Γοργοσᾶς (?) Γουνᾶς (?) Pape : Γρᾶς, Arc. 125. 15 ; Joh. Alex. 7. 29 ; Chœrob. C. 15. 26 : Γρηγορᾶς, A. G. 1441, note, et alibi : Δαμᾶς, E. M. 247. 16 ; Zonar. 465 ; also Δάμα, gen. -α and -αντος : Δᾶς, Arc. 125. 16 ; Chœrob. C. 16. 7 : Δελφινᾶς, Leo Diac. 10. 9. H. *D.* : Δημᾶς, A. G. 714. 24 : Διογᾶς (?) : Διονυσᾶς (?) : Διονυτᾶς (?) : Εἰσᾶς, Inscr. : Ἐλεσβαᾶς, Phot. Bib. 2. 2 : Ἐπαφρᾶς, N. T. Coloss. 4. 12 : Ἐπικ·τᾶς (gen. ᾶ and οῦ), Inscr. : Ἐργωνᾶς (?) E. M. 422. 36 : Ἑρμᾶς, Arc. 22. 5 : Εὔκαρπᾶς, Inscr. : Εὔκτᾶς, Inscr. : Εὔπορᾶς, Inscr. : Εὔτυχᾶς, Inscr. : Εὔφρατᾶς, Theodoret. H. E. 2. 9, quoted by H. *D.* : Ζηνᾶς, Arc. 21. 19 ; Chœrob. C. 42. 33 ;

---

* I. e. A Glossary of later and Byzantine Greek, by E. A. Sophocles, forming Vol. VII. of the New Series of Memoirs of the American Academy of Arts and Sciences. Cambridge and Boston. 4to. 1860.

A. G. 857. 2 : Ζοναρᾶς : Ζωνᾶς, Anthol. Gr. Brunck. 2. 211 : Ζωπυρᾶς, Inscr. : Ζωσᾶς, Inscr. : Ζωσιμᾶς, Suid. : Ἡρακλᾶς, Georg. Syncell. p. 363 B., quoted by H. *D.* s. v. : Ἡρᾶς, Arc. 22. 15 : Θαδᾶς, Arc. 21. 18, where Schmidt reads Θευδᾶς with Cod. Hav. : Θᾶς, Arc. 125. 16. ; Joh. Alex. 7. 29 ; Chœrob. C. 16. 4 : Θαυμᾶς, E. M. 247. 17 ; Zonar. 465 : Θεοδᾶς, Galen. Method. Medend. 10. c. 7. tom. 10. p. 49 A. ed. Chart. : Θευδᾶς, E. M. 448. 30 : Θεωνᾶς, A. G. Paris. 2. 152. 9 : Θωμᾶς, Chœrob. E. 49. 23 ; Chœrob. C. 42. 34 ; A. G. 674. 28 ; Theodos. Gramm. 88. 24 : Ἰηνᾶς (?) Ptol. 2. 3. 2 : Ἰστᾶς, Chœrob. A. G. Oxon. 2. 270. 32 : Ἰωνᾶς, N. T. ; Phot. Bib. 116. 1 : Καναχᾶς, Anthol. Gr. Brunck. 2. 15 : Κερκιδᾶς, Arc. 21. 19 : Κερᾶς, Euseb. p. 153. ed. Mai. H. *D.* : Κεφαλᾶς, Leo Grammat. 234. 15 ; Cf. Soph. Gloss. s. v. : Κηφᾶς, N. T. Galat. 2. 14 ; Suid. s. v. has Κηφάς : Κιδηνᾶς, Theod. Melit. Procem. in Astronom. c. 11 : Κλειδᾶς, Georg. Acropol. Annal. p. 102 C. H. *D.* : Κλεοπᾶς, N. T. Luke 24. 18, and Κλεόπας : Κλεωπᾶς (?) : Κλονᾶς, Plut. 2. 1132 C. and 1133 A : Κλοπᾶς, *H. D.* Κλωπᾶς, Suid. and N. T. : Κοθυλᾶς (?) Jo. Mosch. Prat. Spir. p. 1077 A ; Hase. ap. H. *D.* : Κοκκωνᾶς, Lucian. Alex. § 6 : Κομητᾶς, Chœrob. C. 42. 34 : Κοννᾶς, Aristoph. Eq. 534 = 532 : Κοσμᾶς, Suid. s. v. Ἰωάννης : Κοτοκᾶς, Strab. 660 : Κοτυλᾶς, Joseph. B. J. 1. 2. 4 : Κουζινᾶς, Eust. 1367. 54 : Κρυτιδᾶς, Diod. Sic. 4. 23 : Κτησᾶς (?) Inscr. : Κυθηνᾶς (?) Diog. Laert. 9. 12. § 116 : Κωκαλᾶς, Cantacuz. Hist. 3. 93, 94 : Κωμᾶς, Suid. s. v. Ἱππῶναξ : Λαγγαδᾶς, Georg. Acrop. Chron. c. 63, quoted by H. D. s. v. λαγκάδιον : Λαχᾶς, Herod. π. μ. λ. 8. 16 ; Vid. inf. : Λεοντᾶς, Inscr. : Λεωνᾶς, Suid. : Λιχᾶς, Chœrob. C. 423. 14. Perhaps we should read Λαχᾶς here or Λιχᾶς in Herod. π. μ. λ. 8. 16 : Λίχας, Apollod. 2. 7. 7 : Λουκᾶς, Chœrob. E. 49. 23 ; Chœrob. C. 43. 34 ; A. G. 674. 28 : Λυγγᾶς, cf. Brunck. ad Ranas, vol. 1. p. 147, *H. D.* : Λυκιτᾶς (?) Pollux, 5. 47. H. *D.*, where Bekk. reads Λυκόττας : Μαλανᾶς, H. *D.* : Μαρᾶς (?) Phot. Bib. 475. 38 ; Μάρας, Suid. : Μαρικᾶς, name of a play of Eupolis (gen. ᾶ, οῦ, and ᾶντος), Eust. 300. 22 : Μαρουθᾶς Phot. Bib. 12. 17 : Μασινισσᾶς (?) Pape, generally Μασσανάσης, Μασανάσσης, etc. : Μασκᾶς, Xen. An. 1. 5. 4 : Μαχατᾶς, Polyh. 4. 34. 4, and Μαχάτας : Μελανθᾶς, Suid. s. v. Φρύνιχος : Μελεᾶς, N. T. Luke 3. 31 : Μεριδᾶς, Alciph. 3. 61 : Μετωπᾶς, Athanas. T. I. p. 192 C, quoted by H. *D.* s. v. : Μηνᾶς, Arc. 22. 9 ; Chœrob. C. 42. 27 ; Thucyd. 5. 19 : Μητρᾶς, Arc. 22. 14 ; Chœrob. C. 42. 33 ; Joh. Alex. 8. 16 : Μολπᾶς (?) Inscr. : Μονᾶς, "Theophr. fr. 9 ; De Sudor. 12. p. 814." H. *D.* ; Lob. Phryn. 765 : Μουσᾶς, Paul. Æginet. 7. 12. p. 274. 1, quoted by H. *D.* : Νασικᾶς, Plut. 1. 834 B. : Νειλαρᾶς, Athanas. vol. 1. p. 190 B, ubi olim Νειλᾶς, L. Dindorf ap. H. *D.* : Νικανδᾶς, Plut. frag. 3, tom. 10. p. 719, ed. Wyttenb. 8°. : Νικομᾶς, Lob. Phryn. 435 : Νομᾶς and Νουμᾶς, A. G. 714. 24. This is the constant accent of our books, yet Dion. Hal. Ant. Rom. 2. 58 = p. 120. 24. Sylb. expressly says it is barytone, and therefore we should probably write Νόμας or Νούμας. Cf. H. *D.* s. v. : Νυμφᾶς, N. T. Col. 4. 15 : Νωνᾶς, Suid. : Ξηνᾶς, Chœrob. A. G. Oxon. 2. 270. 31 : Οἰνωνᾶς, Athen. 1. p. 20 A. : Ὀλυμπᾶς, N. T. Rom. 16. 15 : Ὀνᾶς (?) Hesych. : Ὀνατᾶς, Anthol. Gr. Brunck. 3. 178, or Ὀνάτας, Phot. Bib. 114. 13, and Paus. 5. 27. 8 : Ὀνησᾶς, Inscr. : Ὀργᾶς, Strab. 577 ; Dindorf conjectures Ὀρβας : Οὐλφιλᾶς, Phot. Bib. 58. 10 : Ὀφελλᾶς, Phot. Bib. 70. 25 : Παλλαδᾶς, Tzetzes, Proleg. ad Lycoph. : Ηαννᾶς or Παννυάς, Euseb. Chron. p. 42. 45, ed. Mai. H. *D.* : Παλμᾶς, Auth. Plan. 4. 35. : Παραδαλᾶς (?) H. *D.* : Παρμενᾶς, N. T. Acts 6. 5 : Πασακᾶς, Plut. 1. 1015 : Πετρωνᾶς, Galen. T. 13. p. 731 F. : Πηγᾶς, Demetr. Procop. de Erudit. Græcis. c. 4 : Πιθηκᾶς, Nicet. Chon. Hist. p. 36 D. H. *D.* : Πλατανιστᾶς, Paus. 3. 11. 2 ; 3. 14. 8 : Ποπλᾶς, Joseph. B. J. 2. 2. 1. H. *D.* : Προβατᾶς, Eustath. Opusc. p. 290. 63. H. *D.* : Προσδοκᾶς, Inscr. : Πρωτᾶς, H. *D.* : Πτερᾶς, Paus. 10. 5. 10 : Πυθᾶς (?) Arc. 21. 19 : Σαβανᾶς (?) : Σακκᾶς, Suid. s. v. Ἀμμώνιος : Σαλᾶς (?) Inscr. : Σάλας, a river, Strab. 291 : Σαλκᾶς, (?) H. *D.* : Σαμωνᾶς, Suid. : Σατανᾶς, Phot. Bib. 63. 41. N. T. : Σελενᾶς, Suid. s. v. Ἀρειανοί : Σεραπᾶς (or Σαραπᾶς), Athanas. 1. 192 C. H. *D.* : Σερᾶς, Inscr. : Σευ-

θᾶς, Plut. 1. 1029: Σιλᾶς, *H. D.*: Σιλουρᾶς, *H. D.*: Σιμᾶς, Inscr.: Σιμωνᾶς (?)
H. D.: Σιννᾶς, Strab. 755: Σισεννᾶς, Plut. 1. 492: Σκευᾶς, Acts 9. 14, and Iuscr.:
Σκοτινᾶς, St. Byz. s. v. *Σκοτινά* where Göttling would read Σκοτίτας: Σολυμᾶς,
Suid.: Σουχᾶς, *H. D.*: Στεφανᾶς, N. T. 1 Cor. 16. 17: Στρογγυλᾶς, Fabric. Bib.
Græca, 11. p. 716, ed. Harles. *H. D.*: Σωζᾶς, Inscr.: Σωσηνᾶς, Synes. Ep. 43.
102: Σωτᾶς (and Σώτας), Eusch. H. E. 5. 19.: Σωτηρᾶς, Schol. Ven. Δ. 412:
Τατᾶς (?) Inscr.: Τριχᾶς, Append. ad Dracon.: Τροφιμᾶς (?) *H. D.*: Ὑψᾶς, Arc.
21. 22: Φαλερνᾶς, Joseph. B. J. 13. 9. 2: Φανᾶς, A. G. Paris. 2. 145. 15: Φαννᾶς,
Inscr.: Φελδᾶς, Joseph. A. J. 1. 6. 5. *H. D.*: Φιδιτᾶς, Chœrob. C. 42. 34: Φιλᾶς (?)
Bentl. Epist. ad Mill. p. 346, sqq. ed. Dyce: Φιλητᾶς, Joh. Alex. 9. 22; Theoc.
7. 40; in Ælian, V. H. 9. 14, it is falsely paroxytone: Φιλωνᾶς, Inscr.: Φιλωτᾶς,
Strab. 633, 636: Φῶκας, Phot. Bib. 32. 11: Χαμβδᾶς, Anth. Pal. App. 134: Χα-
ρανδαμᾶς, *H. D.*: Χαρωνᾶς (?) *H. D.*: Χιλᾶς, Iamb. de Vit. Pyth. ad fin.: Χνᾶς,
Arc. 125; Chœrob. C. 16. 5: Χουζᾶς, N. T. Luke 8. 3: Χρυσολωρᾶς. For the accent
of many of these words, especially of those which occur only on coins or inscrip-
tions, there is no real authority; Dindorf, and other scholars, imagine that they
are following the teaching of the old grammarians in making words in *as* (genitive
a) perispomena, but in fact the grammarians teach no such doctrine.

33. *Common Substantives and Adjectives.* ἀββᾶς, voc ἀββᾶ, N. T. Zonar. 2:
ἀηδᾶς (?) Suid.: ἀτταγᾶς, Eust. 854. 26; Chœrob. C. 43. 6: on the various forms
of this word see Lob. Phryn. 117: ἀμηρᾶς, Soph. Gloss.: ἀμπελᾶς, Leo Diac. Hist.
6, p. 69 C. quoted by H. D.: ἀργᾶς, *a kind of serpent:* ἀσβεστᾶς, Soph. Gloss.:
βακχᾶς = βακχευτής, Schol. Soph. Philoct. 1199: βασκᾶς, Matthiä Greek Grammar,
1. p. 122.　In Aristoph. Av. 885, it is written βάσκας:

> καὶ τέτρακι, καὶ ταῶνι
> καὶ ἐλεᾷ καὶ βάσκᾳ
> καὶ ἐλασᾷ, καὶ ἐρωδιῷ.

It is sometimes erroneously referred to the third declension: the cognate βασκάς
is oxytone in the text of Eust. 978. 5, and elsewhere: βελονᾶς, Soph. Gloss.:
βησσᾶς, Lob. Aglaoph. 27: βιλλᾶς (?) Arc. 22: βοϊλᾶς = βολιᾶς, Soph. Gloss.:
βροντᾶς = βροντήσας, Schol. Soph. Philoct. 1199, said to be a mere blunder: γουβᾶς,
Soph. Gloss.: δακνᾶς, probably an adjective, A. G. 36. 17. δακνᾶς ἵππος, δακνᾶς ὄνος
περισπᾶται, Chœrob. C. 43. 2: ἐλαδᾶς, Soph. Gloss.: ἐλασᾶς, Aristoph. Av. 886:
ἐλεᾶς, Aristoph. Av. *l. l.* (ἐλέας, Hesych.)　The lexicons are sometimes in error
with regard to this word, in making it of the third declension. Ἐλέας (gen. αντος)
is a proper name; Chœrob. C. 32. 6; 119. 26: ζελᾶς (?) Chœrob. C. 124. 11: Ἔτι
δεῖ προσθεῖναι ‘ καὶ χωρὶς τῶν διὰ τὸ μέτρον.’　Ἔστι γὰρ ὁ ζελᾶς τοῦ ζελᾶ, (οὕτως δὲ
λέγεται κατὰ Θρᾷκας ὁ οἶνος,) καὶ τούτου ἡ δοτικὴ εὑρίσκεται παρ’ Εὐριπίδῃ χωρὶς τοῦ Ι.
Συστεῖλαι γὰρ βουλόμενος τὸ Α, οὐ προσέγραψε τὸ Ι, οἷον

> ταὐτὸν ποιεῖ τό τ’ Ἀττικὸν τῷ ζελᾶ, σὺν γὰρ κεραννοῖς.

Phot. Lex. 51. 22. Ζειλα: τὸν οἶνον οἱ Θρᾷκες, where, according to the Cambridge
editor, the accent is omitted: in Hermann's edition it is printed Ζείλα: καπηλᾶς,
H. D.: καραβιᾶς, Soph. Gloss.: καρτζιμᾶς, Soph. Gloss.: κασᾶς = κασῆς, in Xen.
Cyrop. 8. 3. 6, and Pollux. 7. 68, it is κάσας or κάσσας: καταβλατᾶς, Soph. Gloss: καταφαγᾶς, Lob. Phryn. 434; καταφαγάς is wrong: καταφυγᾶς occurs in Chœrob. C. 43.
2, but in Gaisford's index it is rightly printed καταφαγᾶς: κατωφαγᾶς, according to
Schol. in Aristoph. Av. 288, κατωφάγας is an adjective, Κατωφαγᾶς a proper name:
κερατᾶς, Psellus, *H. D.*: κερνᾶς, Lob. Aglaoph. p. 27: κορβανᾶς, N. T. Matth.
27. 6: κορυζᾶς, Suid. s. v. βουκόρυζαν: κοχλιᾶς, Soph. Gloss.: κρασᾶς, Soph. Gloss.:
κτενᾶς, Soph. Gloss.: λαρυγγᾶς, Lob. Phryn. 434: λᾶς, Arc. 125; Joh. Alex. 7. 29:
Chœrob. C. 27. 29, 15. 27; E. M. 553. 2; Paus. 3. 24. 10: λαχανᾶς, Chœrob. C. 43. 1:

λαχᾶς=στίμμι, Chœrob. C. 373. 15: should it not be χολᾶς? cf. Eust. 728. 48: μαῖουμᾶς, Suid.: μασουχᾶς, Alex. Trall. 7. p. 322 D, *H. D.*: μυρικᾶς, Hesych.: ὀξυγαλατᾶς, Soph. Gloss.: ὀστρακᾶς, Chœrob. C. 42. 35: παξαμᾶς, Soph. Gloss.: πᾶς, ὁ πατήρ, Arc. 125; E. M. 655. 13: παπᾶς, A. G. 674. 28; cf. Soph. Gloss. s. v. and παππᾶς. This is the Greek accent: the Romans wrote πάπας, E. M. 655.14: πελεκᾶς, Arc. 21. Also gen. ἄντος and πελέκας, Lob. Par. 139: πελλᾶς, ὁ γέρων and φιλοπελλᾶς, Arc. 22: πεταλᾶς, Soph. Gloss.: πινακᾶς, Ducange ap. H. *D.*: πινακιδᾶς, Chœrob. C. 43. 1: στοματᾶς, Soph. Gloss.: σχοινᾶς, Lob. Phryn. 435: ταμᾶς, γαμβρός, Hesych.: τηθελᾶς (?) Lob. Phryn. 299: τραχηλᾶς, Soph. Gloss.: τρεσᾶς, Chœrob. C. 43. 3, where for τρέσας, τρέσα, we should probably read τρεσᾶς, τρεσᾶ: cf. Eust. 1000. 11: ὅθεν καί τις ἐν Ἀθηναίοις ἐπὶ δειλίᾳ κωμῳδούμενος τρεσᾶς ἐκα. λεῖτο, καθὰ καί τις ἕτερος διάρροιαν πάσχων γαστρὸς, χεσᾶς ἐλέγετο. The form τρεσᾶς, τρεσᾶντος, is also to be found in the lexicons. Hesych. s. v. Τρεσάντων has τρέσας, τρέσαντος: ὑψᾶς, Kühner, G. G. 1. 383: φαγᾶς, Arc. 21. 12; Lob. Phryn. 434: φακᾶς, Suid. s. v. φακαῖ: φλασκᾶς (?) Reg. Pros. 61. p. 433, where Lobeck would read φασκᾶς. His conjecture is improbable, since the only φασκας in Greek is oxytone, and of the third declension: χεσᾶς, Eust. 1000. 12: χολᾶς, Eust. 728. 48: χηλᾶς, Lob. Phryn. 434. Hesych. s. v.: ψευδαββᾶς, Soph. Gloss.: ψηνᾶς (?) Zonar. 1871. ψηφᾶς, see Ducange, s. v.: ψιλᾶς (?) Paus. 3. 19. 6, where in the editions ψίλας is read. Lob. Phryn. 434. To this head Göttling, Accent. p. 117, refers the Aristophanic forms μαμμᾶν and κακκᾶν, Nub. 1365-6. Cf. Phot. Lex. 245. 13. μαμμᾶν: Ἀργεῖοι τὸ ἐσθίειν· οὕτω Καλλίας. Schol. ad Aristoph. *l. l.* μαμμᾶν, ἄσημος φωνὴ τῶν παιδίων λαλούντων.

34. Words in ης, not preceded by τ, are paroxytone, as ἀγκυλοχείλης, ἀράχνης, γεωμέτρης, ἑλλανοδίκης, ἐογομίσης, ἡμερίδης, κλυτοτέχνης, μισογύνης, παιδοτρίβης, παρθενοπίπης, πωλοδάμνης, τελώνης, χρεωφείλης.

35. All dissyllables in της, with their compounds, are paroxytone, as ἀμυγδαλοκατάκτης, ἀπογνώστης, γλύπτης, διαλύτης, δότης, μεταίτης, μετανάστης, μνήστης, πεύστης, πλύτης, προσωπολήπτης, προφήτης, πυραύστης, σβέστης, ὠμήστης, except κριτής oxytone, and ψαλτής oxytone in Attic, though paroxytone in the common dialect: the oxytone λῃστής is not a real exception since it stands for λῃϊστής.

36. NOTE.—Herod. π.μ.λ. 40. 16; Arc. 23 sqq.; Chœrob. C. 176. 22; E. M. 435. 47. False accents are not at all uncommon in this class of words. Ἀκτής, though quite contrary to analogy, is found in Eust. 868. 31. ἀμαλλοδετής and μαλλοδετής are errors; in Theocr. 10. 44 the former is rightly paroxytone, like ἀμφιδέτης, ἀσκοδέτης, ζυγοδέτης, ἰοδέτης, ἱπποδέτης, κηροδέτης: ἀναγνωστής Schol. Ven. Z. 511 = vol. 1. p. 248. 31 is probably a mere oversight of the editor: ἀποθέται, Plut. 1. 49 E, is in some lexicons erroneously entered as ἀποθετής: ἀργοναυτής is contrary to all analogy and certainly false, cf. Ἀργοναύτης, δεσποσιοναύτης· καρυοναύτης, σωοναύτης· χιλιοναύτης: ἀφεστής is sometimes quoted from Plut. 2. 292 A, where it does not occur, but ἀφεστήρ; but ἀφεστής, ἀγαθός is found in Hesych. Lob. Par. 430: γλύπτης not γλυπτής is the right accent, Lob. Par. 135: δερμηστής A. G. 240. 14: δερμηστής: οἱ μέν φασιν εἶδος σκώληκος, ὁ κατεσθίει τὰ δέρματα· Ἀρίσταρχος δὲ ὄφεως εἶδος, the accent of this word, though contrary to analogy, finds a parallel in that of ὠμήστης mentioned below: διαλυτής is found in Thuc. 3. 82. 5, the codex Palat. is said to read διαλύτης, which is doubtless the correct form, Lob. Par. 548; 432 : διασωστήs should be διασώστης, Lob. Par. 448. note 72 : ἐγκαυστής, Plut. 2. 348 F, but Zonar. 68 has the right accent ἐγκαύστης : ἐκτιστής, Basil. Or. vol. 1. p. 437 A, *H.D.* is almost certainly wrong : ἐντευκτής, Pamphil. Abyd. Epist. p. 26. 30. H. *D.* : ἐπᾳστής which is quoted by H. *D.* from the Septuagint, may be correct, it is parallel with λῃστήs which is certainly oxytone : ἐπιρρυτής, H. *D.* cannot be right : ζευκτής, Hesych. s. v. Ζευξίλεως ought to be ζεύκτης, and the same remark is true of συζευκτής, Nomocanon. Coteler. n. 520. H. *D.* : καταλυτής, *a destroyer,* is in several places made oxytone ; καταλύτης, *a guest,* paroxytone, but in Hesychius both are written καταλύτης, and no doubt rightly : καταστρωτής, H. *D.* is a mere blunder : καταυσ-τής· καταδύστης Hesych., the last editor has changed the accent of καταδύστην and if καταυστής belongs to the first declension, it would be as well to alter its accent likewise : κατεντευκτής, Suid., should be altered : κλωστής, H. *D.*, is a mistake, the word is paroxytone in E. M. 495. 27 : κοστής, Athen. 357 A, if not altogether cor-rupt, should be κόστης : κριτής, Chœrob. C. 176. 14, the compound ψευδοκριτής quoted by H. *D.* from Achmes, Onirocr. p. 149. 11, is a monstrous error ; all the compounds of κριτής follow the general rule without an exception : κτιστής, H. *D.* is an oversight, in every passage which they quote the word is paroxytone : κυνακτής should be paroxytone, like other words of the same termination, ἀμυγ-δαλοκατάκτης, κατάκτης, καρυοκατάκτης, etc. : μεταφράστης is sometimes, though erroneously, made oxytone : μνηστής is false for μνήστης, Athen. 147 B. : παρα-σχίστης, ·Diod. Sic. 1. 91, is improperly oxytone in some lexicons : προγευστής ought to be προγεύστης, Herodian ap. Herm. de emend. rat. Gr. gr. p. 324 ; E. M. 315. 38 ; Athen. 171 B. : πτιστής for πτίστης is probably a mere misprint. With regard to the word ῥαιστής and its compounds some doubt exists, but it appears that it is paroxytone as a dissyllable, and oxytone as a trisyllable, hence we should write ῥαίστης, but ῥαϊστής, in like manner κυνοραϊστής, Arist. H. A. 5. 31. 6 ; Rhet. 2. 20. 6, and the manuscript readings there ; S. V. Π. 414 : θυμοραϊστής τετρασυλ-λάβως καὶ βαρυτόνως ὁ Γλαῦκός φησιν, ἵν' ᾖ θυμοραίστης, ἀλλὰ κακῶς· ἀντίκειται γὰρ αὐτῷ τὸ θυμοραϊστέων, the reference is to Hom. Od. 17. 300, and I cannot help thinking that Glaucus was right ; the form Ἰλιορραίστης can hardly be correct, cf. ἁλιρραίστης, ἀνθρωπορραίστης, βουρραίστης, λυκορραίστης, μητρορραίστης, πατρορραίστης, τεκνορραίστης : σειστής, Lydus de Ostentis, p. 188 = p. 104, 12 ed. Wachsmuth. is a very doubtful accent, it should most probably be paroxytone like κατασείστης, Georg. Pachym. Mich. Pal. p. 308 B, H. *D.* ; though they cite ἀνασειστής from late authors : συμπαιστής, Plat. Minos, 319 E., is rightly paroxytone in Phot. Bib. 100. 21 : τμήτης not τμητής is the proper accent, Lob. Par. 135 ; 548 : ὑπερεκτιστής, Basil. t. i. p. 165 D, can hardly be correct : ὑψιπέτης (not to be confounded with ὑψιπετής of the Third Declension) Schol. Ven. M. 201 : Ἀρίσταρχος ἐβάρυνεν εὑρὼν τὸ 'ὠκυπέτα χρυσέῃσιν ἐθείρῃσιν' οὕτως κεκλιμένον, ὡσεὶ καὶ ἀπὸ τοῦ παντοπώλης παντοπώλα ... τινὲς μέντοι ἐτόλμησαν τὸ ὑψιπέτης περισπάσαι, ἐπεὶ ἐν ἑτέροις ἔφη 'ὥστ' αἰετὸς ὑψιπετήεις.' ὡς οὖν τὸ τιμήεις ... ἐγένετο τιμῆς ... οὕτω ὑψιπετήεις ὑψιπετῆς : ψάλτης, Chœrob. C. 176. 24 ; in the common dialect this was paroxytone, 'in codd. constanter ψάλτης scribi vide-tur,' *H. D.*, but that it was oxytone in Attic is perpetually stated by the gram-marians Arc. 24. 7 ; Schol. Soph. Elect. 70 : ὠμήστης, this was the accent of Tyrannion, and it is in accordance with analogy, but Aristarchus wrote ὠμηστής, Schol. Ven. Λ. 454 ; Χ. 67 ; Eust. 855. 39.

37. All words in της with a short penultimate are paroxytone, as αἰνέτης, ἐπαινέτης, ἀρότης, γειαρότης, γαμέτης, δεσπότης, δραπέτης, ἑκατηβελέτης, ἐλάτης, αἰγελάτης, ἐργάτης· ἐρέτης, εὐεργέτης, ἱκέτης, ἱππότης, κυνηγέτης, μουσαγέτης, νεηλάτης, οἰκέτης, ὁμότης, ὁρκαπάτης, πανδακέτης, πελάτης, περιναιέτης, τηλυγέτης, τοξότης, ὑδραλέτης, ὑπηρέτης, φρεναπάτης, φυλέτης, χρεωφειλέτης, except εὑρετής oxytone, and its compounds as ἐφευρετής, which follow the general rule.

38. NOTE.—Arc. 26; Eust. 340. 45; Apoll. de Adv. 545. 25; S.V. B. 763, where εὑρετής is asserted to be the only exception to the rule. Εὑρέτης (*sic*) in Schol. Ven. Δ. 219 = vol. 1. p. 180. 25, is I presume an editorial oversight, for no Greek could have written it. According to Buttmann (Ausf. Gr. Gr. § 119. 31 quoted by *L. S.*) the feminine of εὑρετής is εὑρέτις; Lobeck, Phryn. 256, however, quotes εὑρετίς from Diod. Sic. 5. 76, where Bekker prints εὑρέτις, and such must be the proper accent because the accusative is εὑρέτιν, Diod. Sic. 1. 25. Αἰνετής and γειαροτής are errors, E. M. 258. 4; Philem. Lex. p. 23. § 57; Lob. Par. 236. Göttling also has γαμετής, the word is expressly made paroxytone in A. G. Oxon. 2. 357. 24; S. V. B. 763; E. M. 794. 8. Μικροτελετής in Eust. Opusc. 25. p. 281. 58 is a mistake for μικροτελεστής, Lob. Par. 431; and νεμετής in Synes. de Regno, p. 30 C should be νεμητής, Lob. Par. 447, note 69.

Such words as ὑποκριτής, διαλυτής or διαλύτης belong to the rule above, § 35.

39. All words in ῑτης (αιτης, ειτης, οιτης) are paroxytone, as ἀλείτης, ἀλοίτης, βαθυρρείτης, βαλανείτης, θαλαμίτης, κυανοχαίτης, λιμενίτης, μεσίτης, πολίτης, στυλίτης, σωρείτης, τραπεζίτης, τυμπανίτης.

40. NOTE.—In Plut. 2. 1113 B, ἀλοίτης is oxytone, but wrongly, for the word is expressly stated to be paroxytone by Theognostus, Can. 46. 4, cf. E. M. 61. 44; 69. 51; 85. 26, Arc. 27. 1.

41. Words of more than two syllables in ˙της preceded by any consonant but Σ are paroxytone, as ἀγύρτης, ἀλείπτης, ἀσκάντης, αὐθέντης, αὐτοέντης, διώκτης, κεκράκτης, κολάπτης, μιάντης, νυστάκτης, παραμασύντης, ὑφάντης, except oxytone, 1. ἐθελοντής, ἑκοντής, and in Attic ποικιλτής, and καθαρτής; 2. the following in ντης from verbs in αίνω and ύνω; ἀβρυντής, ἀμυντής, εὐθυντής, διευθυντής, ἰθυντής, διιθυντής, καλλυντής, κατιλλαντής, λαμπρυντής, λευκαντής, λυμαντής, ὀσφραντής, καπνοσφραντής, πραϋντής, φαιδρυντής; 3. several in κτης from verbs in άζω, ίζω, ύζω, and σσω, as αἰνικτής, ἁρπακτής, θωρηκτής, ἰύκτης, νυστακτής, σαλπιγκτής, or σαλπικτής, ἀριστοσαλπιγκτής, ἱεροσαλπιγκτής, συρικτής, φορμικτής, and φορμιγκτής, φρυακτής.

42. NOTE I.—The grammarians and the scribes, assisted by the carelessness of modern editors, have brought these words into great confusion, but the above rule with the exceptions mentioned in it embraces all the words of this class which occur in the lexicon of Messrs. Liddell and Scott. E. M. 435. 57: τὰ εἰς ΤΗΣ ἔχοντα τὴν παραλήγουσαν εἰς ἀμετάβολον λήγουσαν, ἀπρόσληπτα ὄντα τοῦ Σ κατὰ τὴν γενικὴν, βαρύνεται, εἰ μὴ εἴη μετοχικά, ὑφάντης, ἀγύρτης, εὐφραντής· τὸ δὲ ἑκοντὴς, ἐθελοντὴς, μετοχικά. Παρὰ δὲ ᾿Αττικοῖς ὀξύνεται τὸ καθαρτής· ἀμυντὴς ἐπὶ τοῦ βοηθοῦ·

φαιδρυντής, ποικιλτής, καλλυντής, πραϋντής· ὅτι οὐκ ἔχει τὴν πρώτην συλλαβὴν εἰς
φωνῆεν λήγουσαν. A. G. Oxon. 2. 419. 29 : ὑφάντης : παροξυτόνως· ἐπειδὴ τὰ εἰς
ΤΗΣ ἀρσενικὰ ἔχοντα τὴν παραλήγουσαν εἰς ἀμετάβολον λήγουσαν παροξυτόνως· οἷον
Λαέρτης· ὑφάντης· σεσημείωται τὸ ποικιλτής. Schol. Soph. Elect. 70 : τὰ εἰς ΤΗΣ,
ἔχοντα τὴν παρατέλευτον εἰς ἀμετάβολον λήγουσαν, ἀπρόσληπτα ὄντα τοῦ Σ κατὰ
τὴν γενικὴν, βαρύνονται, εἰ μὴ εἴη μετοχικά, ὑφάντης, ἀγύρτης, Εὐφράτης [leg.
εὐφράντης] τὸ δὲ ἑκοντὴς καὶ ἐθελοντὴς, μετοχικά· παρὰ δὲ Ἀττικοῖς ὀξύνεται τό
τε καθαρτὴς, καὶ ἀμυντὴς ἐπὶ τοῦ βοηθοῦ, φαιδρυντὴς, ποικιλτὴς, ψαλτὴς, πραϋντής.

43. NOTE 2.—As to the verbal derivatives in κτης I find no rule in the old grammarians ; as verbals they ought to be oxytone, but in the books the majority of
them are not so. Pape (Etymolog. Wörterb. d. Griech. Sprache, p. 54) lays down
the rule that polysyllables in κτης are *oxytone*, except κεκράκτης, ὀρύκτης, προΐ
κτης and φυλάκτης : but his list of exceptions may be much extended, for the following should be added ἀλλάκτης, Chrysost. Hom. 126. t. 5. p. 820. *H. D.*:
διαλλάκτης, Pollux. 1. 153 ; but διαλλακτής, Thucyd. 4. 60 ; Plut. 1. 83 ; 1. 1033 ;
ἐξαλλάκτης, Hesych. s. v. Διαμέσταν : καταλλάκτης seems to be always paroxytone :
συναλλακτής, *L. S.*, but συναλλάκτης, Eustath. Opusc. p. 93. 38. *H. D.* : καταρρά
κτης, βαβάκτης, E. M. 183 : βαστακτής, *H. D.*, yet they quote φορτοβαστάκτης·
from Schol. Plat. p. 421, ed. Bekk. : βρυάκτης, Stob. Ecl. Phys. vol. 1. p. 68 :
διδάκτης does not seem to occur, but there is αἰσχροδιδάκτης, Manetho, 4. 307,
H. D. : νομοδιδάκτης or νομοδιδακτής, Plut. 1. 348 A : ὁπλοδιδακτής (?) H.*D.*
διώκτης, is always paroxytone together with its compounds γνωμιδιώκτης, ἐκτο
διώκτης ˙ἐπιδιώκτης, θηριοδιώκτης, ληστοδιώκτης, Περσοδιώκτης : ἐρέκτης,
Orion. 54: 8 : λαβράκτης : λαφύκτης, Eust. 1246. 33, is elsewhere oxytone,
though wrongly : μαιμάκτης, Plut. 2. 458 B : δερματομαλάκτης, Schol. Plat.
Gorg. 517 E : ὀρέκτης : ὀρύκτης, Strab. 692, διορυκτής, *L. S.*, νεκρορύκτης,
ῥιζορυκτής (?) *H. D.*, τοιχορύκτης, φρεατορύκτης, E. M. 799. 41 : παντορέκτης :
προΐκτης, Hom. Od. 17. 449 : σαβάκτης : σκαρδαμυκτής is quoted from Arist.
Physiog. 6. 47, where, however, it is rightly paroxytone, like ἀσκαρδαμύκτης :·
σπαράκτης : τινάκτης, παντοτινάκτης : τρηματίκτης : φαρμάκτης : φοινικελίκτης :
χαράκτης, Manetho, 6. 388, *H. D.* : παραχαράκτης, Schol. Aristoph. Ach. 516,
H. D. : χειρονάκτης or χειρωνάκτης and others. Words like ἐπείκτης, ἐργε
πείκτης, θυρεπανοίκτης, παρατρώκτης, are naturally paroxytone as compounds of
dissyllables.

44. NOTE 3.—Αἰνικτής, Diog. Laert. 9. 1. 6 : ἁρπακτής, *L. S.* : δαϊκτής, *L. S.*,
ψυχοδαϊκτής Auth. Pal. 9. 524. 24 : ξενοδαϊκτής, *L. S.*, is ξενοδαίκτης in Eurip.
Herc. F. 391 : ἐλεγκτής, yet the compounds ἐχθρελέγκτης, Λατινελέγκτης, μοι
χοελέγκτης, are paroxytone in the passages quoted by H. D. ; ἀπελεγκτής is
oxytone in Euseb. Præp. Evan. 256 D : θωρηκτής, Hom. Il. 12. 317 ; Eust. 907.
48, this is an extraordinary accent, according to all principles of analogy the
word ought to be paroxytone, but the scribes have determined otherwise : ἰϋκτής
(άς), Theocr. 8. 30 : κηληκτής, Plut. 2. 220 F. H. *D.* : μειλικτής (?), μελικτάς,
Theocr. 4. 30 : μουσικτάς, Hesych. : νυστακτής, Aristoph. Vesp. 12 : σαλπιγκτής
(or σαλπικτής), Pollux. 4. 87 : ἀριστοσαλπιγκτής, ληστοσαλπιγκτής, ἱεροσαλ
πιγκτής, Pollux. 4. 87 : συρικτής, Arist. Prob. 18. 6. 1 : ταρακτής, Eust. 873. 16,
is paroxytone in Schol. Æschyl. Pers. 79 : φορμικτής and φορμιγκτής, E. M. 798.
45 : φρυακτής, see *L. S.* s. v.

45. NOTE 4.—On ποικιλτής as an Attic form, see E. M. 436. 6 ; Suid. s. v.
ψάλτης ; A. G. Oxon. 2. 419. 31 : βελονοποικιλτής, Hesych. For καταγγελτής
and προσαγγελτής the evidence is weak.

46. NOTE 5.—The chief Attic oxytones in ντης are enumerated in the rule
above : διθυντής is oxytone in Hesych. and paroxytone in Suid. : καπνοσφραντής

is also found paroxytone : ὑδροσφράντης only occurs as a proper name.　On ἐθελοντής and ἑκοντής, see E. M. 436. 4; Arc. 25. 25; and on θελοντής, Lob. Phryn. 7.　Ὀτρύντης and παραμασύντης do not seem ever to be oxytone : κηραμύντης, Lycoph. 663.

47. NOTE 6.—Ἀορτής, Suid., or ἀόρτης, Hesych., for which ἀβερτής, Suid., is a later form : καθαρτής, *Attic*, E. M. 436. 5.

48. All words of more than two syllables in ευτης are oxytone, as ἁλιευτής, βουλευτής, βραβευτής, εἰρωνευτής, ἑρμηνευτής, ἠπεροπευτής, θεραπευτής, θηρευτής, κυβευτής, νυμφευτής, πορθμευτής, πρεσβευτής, συνθηρευτής, χορευτής.

49. All words of more than two syllables in στης are oxytone, as ἀγωνιστής, ἀντεραστής, ἀσπιστής, γυμναστής, δικαστής, δοκιμαστής, ἐγκωμιαστής, ἐκκλησιαστής, ἐξεταστής, ἡλιαστής, κηδεστής, κιθαριστής, κωμαστής, λογιστής, οἰκιστής, ὀρχηστής, σοφιστής, συγγυμναστής, except δυνάστης, κεράστης, *horned* and χρεώστης, which are paroxytone.　Πενέστης is probably a proper name, and therefore paroxytone.

50. NOTE.—Apoll. de Adv. 545. 23; Arc. 26; 27; 28; Schol. Ven. Λ. 454; Eust. 533. 38; 596. 23; 855. 39.　According to Schol. Ven. E. 158, ἀγρώστης is paroxytone when it is an adjective; in the sense of *hunter* it is oxytone in E. M. 14. 12, paroxytone in A. G. 213. 6; cf. Eust. 533. 40: ἀκέστης, Eust. 1254. 2 : Φρύγες ἀκέστην (*sic*) καλοῦσι τὸν ἰατρὸν ὧς φασιν οἱ παλαιοί; S. V. X. 2 : ὅθεν Φρύγες ἀκεστήν (*sic*) τὸν ἰατρόν : there can be no doubt that as a common substantive or adjective the word is oxytone according to rule ; E. M. 46. 20; Pollux. 4. 177; Lob. Par. 448 : ἀλκήστης (?) Suid. s. v. ἀμύντης : ἀνακτοτελέσται, Clem. Alex. Protrep. should either be oxytone or ἀνακτοτελετής : ἀργεστής as an adjective is oxytone, Schol. Ven. Λ. 306; as a substantive it is paroxytone, E. M. 136. 25; Eust. 845. 61; Arc. 27. 8 : βειλαρμόστης, Hesych., has been changed by the last editor into βειλαρμοστής : γενούστης is a fanciful word invented by Plato, Phileb. 30. D, E; E. M. 226. 24 : δυνάστης, Lob. Par. 448, and παντοδυνάστης : ἐπαλώστης is found as well as ἐπαλωστής, Lob. Phryn. 254; Par. 450 : εὐάστης should be εὐαστής, Lob. Par. 448, note 72 : θυέστης, Phot. Bib. 532. 33; Lob. Par. 448 : κακοδαιμονίστης should be oxytone, Athen. 551 F.　We have ἀγαθοδαιμονιστής read by one MS. in Arist. Eth. Eud. 3. 6. 3 : κεράστης, Eur. Cycl. 52; κερστής, oxytone means *a mixer* and is regular; it is quoted by H. *D.* from Orph. fr. 28. 13 : κηλέστης (?) Suid.; Zonar. 1202. H. *D.* should be corrected : μονώστης, Theog. Can. 45. 1 : πενέστης, cf. Steph. Byz. s. v. Πενέσται, ἔθνος Θεσσαλικόν ὃ τόνος βαρύς· ὧς Ὀρέστης Θυέστης : ῥητοροσοφίστης, H. *D.* is a mere blunder : ῥινοκολούστης, a name of Hercules, Paus. 9. 25. 4, ought to be corrected : χρεώστης, Plut. 2. 828 D, *et alibi*.　Heracleides at one time wrote χηρώστης, but afterwards altered his mind; the word is oxytone, Eust. 533. 38; Schol. Ven. E. 158; Eust. 1724. 36: ὠμήστης, Tyrannion : ὠμηστής, Aristarchus : Schol. Ven. Λ. 454; X. 67; Eust. 855. 39; this strictly belongs to the dissyllables.

51. All words of more than two syllables in ᾱτης, ητης, ῡτης, and ωτης, are oxytone when they are derived from verbs; they are paroxytone when they are derived from nouns, or are passive in meaning.　The words ἀήτης, αἰσυμνήτης, ἀλήτης, εὐνήτης, κορυνήτης, κυβερνήτης, πλανήτης, σφενδονήτης, are paroxytone; and αἰχμητής, ἀστεροπητής, ἐπητής, oxytone. Examples of verbal derivatives are ἀγορητής, ἀθλητής, αἰσθητής, αἰτητής, ἀκροατής, ἀναλωτής, αὐλητής, *a flute player,* but αὐλήτης (αὐλή) *a steward,* βεβαιωτής, βελτιωτής, βιατής (βιατάς), γεννητής *a parent,* but γεννήτης *a clansman,* διαιτητής, διορθωτής, ἡβητής (ἡβάω), θεατής, θηρατής, κηλητής *a charmer,* but κηλήτης (κήλη) *herniosus,* κομμωτής, κωλυτής, λωβητής, μαθητής, μηνυτής, μιμητής, ὁμοιωτής, πεδητής *one who fetters,* but πεδήτης *one who is fettered,* πειρατής, περιηγητής, ποιητής, φιλητής *a lover* is by the grammarians distinguished from φιλήτης *a thief.* The following are examples of words said to be derived from nouns: ἀγυιάτης, ἀγωνιάτης *a nervous man* from ἀγωνία, not from ἀγωνιάω, ἀργήτης *white,* ἀσπιδιώτης, ἀχάτης, Βακχιώτης, γενειάτης, γενειήτης, δεσμώτης *a prisoner,* ἑστιώτης from ἑστία, ἡλικιώτης, ἠπειρώτης, θιασώτης, ἰδιώτης, κλαρῶται, κομήτης, from κόμη, not from κομάω, κορυνήτης, κωμήτης, λεσχηνώτης, λιμνήτης, μονώτης, οἰήτης (οἴη), πρυμνήτης, πρωράτης, πωγωνιάτης, σκοπιήτης, στασιώτης, στρατιώτης.

52. Note 1.—The accentuation of these nouns is far from easy. According to the old grammarians, all hyperdissyllabic derivatives from verbs in της with a naturally long penultimate are oxytone, except κυβερνήτης ἀήτης, and ἀγρώστης, Schol. Ven. E. 158; N. 382; E. M. 40. 38; 436. 12; Eust. 533. 36; 1724. 25; Philem. Lex. p. 5. § 12; p. 23. § 57; Arc. 26. 27. But in a large number of cases we can only tell from the accent whether the Greeks regarded the word as a verbal or nominal derivative. Bearing in mind however the examples and exceptions mentioned above, the following rule will hold good for all the Greek words of this class which have as yet found their way into dictionaries, and I doubt not for nine-tenths of those which have not. If the substitution of σω or σομαι for the final της yields a future of an actual verb of like root and signification with the substantive, then such substantive is a verbal derivative in the sense intended by the rule. The words about which a doubt might be felt have been inserted as exceptions. If δεσμώτης for example ever meant *one who imprisons,* then it is certain that the Greek grammarians would in that sense have made it oxytone. Such a word as ἐπητής puzzles them. Κυβερνήτης was to the Greeks *a helmsman* rather than *one who steers;* αἰχμητής, *one who fights with a spear* rather than *one who is armed with a spear.* The lists which follow comprise all the doubtful words that I have noted.

53. Note 2.—*Oxytones which should by the rule be paroxytone.* Αἰχμητής, E. M. 40. 38; Philem. Lex. p. 5. § 12: ἀστεροπητής, A. G. Oxon. 2. 321. 16: βυκανητής, probably from βυκανάω, on which see L. S. s. v.: δρυατής (?) Hesych.: ἐπητής or ἐπήτης, Schol. Odyss. N. 332: τῇ δὲ προσῳδίᾳ ὡς ἀεικής, φησὶν Ἀρίσταρχος. οὕτω δὲ καὶ Ἡρωδιανός. Eust. 1742. 59: ἔστι δὲ ἐπητὴς ἢ ὁ λόγιος παρὰ τὸ ἔπος, ἢ ὁ χαίρων τῇ ἀληθείᾳ παρὰ τὴν ΕΠΙ πρόθεσιν καὶ τὸ ἐτεόν. ὀξύνεται δέ φασιν ἡ λέξις παρὰ τοῖς παλαιοτέροις. οἱ δὲ ὕστερον, παροξύνουσι αὐτό, λέγοντες ἐπήτην, τὸν φρόνιμον: θηπητής (θηπέω?) Hesych.: θυητής, as if from θυέω: μηλατάς, Hesych., is very doubtful.

54. Note 3.—*Paroxytones which should by rule be oxytone.* ἀγωνιάτης, Diog.

Laert. 2. § 131. On ἀήτης, if it be an exception, see Schol. Ven. E. 158; Eust.
533. 39; 1724. 33: ἀλήτης, E. M. 40. 45; Schol. Ven. A. 540: βακχιώτης, Soph.
Œd. Col. 678: βαρυβρομήτης (?) Anth. Pal. 7. 394: βιατάς, Pind. Pyth. 4. 420;
Olymp. 9. 114; H. *D.*: βιοκωλύτης, which is quoted by H. D., is falsely accented :
γεννήτης is found both in the sense of ·*parent* and *member of a clan:* although in
the former signification γεννητής is the correct form, like ἀειγεννητής (not ἀειγεν-
νήτης) in Macrob. Sat. 1. 17: δειπνήτης (?) *L. S.*; δειπνητής, H. *D.*, who quote
Polyb. 3. 57. 7, a place which proves nothing as to the accent: δεσμώτης, Philem.
Lex. p. 23. § 57: ἑστιώτης is implied by the feminine ἑστιῶτις, Soph. Tr. 954:
εὐνήτης, Eurip. Med. 160, cf. κατευηντής, *L. S.*; ἐπευναταί (?): on this doubtful
form see H. *D.*: μονοθελήτης or μονοθελητής, cf. Soph. Gloss. s. v.: κηλήτης
(and καλήτης), *herniosus*, Anth. Pal. 11. 404: κηλητής (from κηλέω), *a charmer*,
Diog. Laert. 8. 67: κλοιώτης, Hesych.: κομήτης, Schol. Ven. Λ. 454; E. M.
40. 45: κονήτης (?) Hesych.: κορυνήτης, E. M. 40. 41; A. G. Oxon. 2. 321.
18: κυβερνήτης, Schol. Ven. E. 158; N. 382; Eust. 533. 39: λαλαγήτης in
Hesych. should be oxytone: θεολωβήτης, Manetho 4. 234; *H. D.* requires correction, cf. λωβητής, and E. M. 40. 44: παραμασητής (?) Athen. 242 C: μωλύ-
της, Diog. Laert. 7. 170: μεγαλομυκήτης in Hesych. is undoubtedly an error; the
word should be oxytone, like the simple μυκητής: πεδήτης, E. M. 40. 40 = *one who
is bound*, Lucian Jup. conf. c. 8; Hesych.; πεδητής, *one who binds*, Anth. Pal. 9.
756: περάτης, Philo Jud. vol. 1. p. 439. 25, should be oxytone: πλανήτης, Schol.
Ven. A. 540; Soph. Œd. Col. 3, etc.: ψευδοπλανήτης, Eust. 1742. 23: σαώτης,
Paus. 9. 26. 7: σκηνήτης (?): the proper form of this word is σκηνίτης: σκοπιήτης and σφενδονήτης are nominal derivatives: συνουσιώτης, Theophyl. Bulg. vol.
3. p. 562 B; *H. D.* almost certainly a false accent: χορωφελήτης, Aristoph. Lys.
1319, should be oxytone.

55. NOTE 4.—Tyrannion wished to paroxytone ἑεδνωτής, Schol. Ven. N. 382.
Φιλήτης, *a thief*, is distinguished from φιλητής, *a lover*, E. M. 793. 57. Καλα-
μαυλήτης, in Athen. 176 D, should undoubtedly be oxytone.

56. Masculines in ᾰ, as αἰχμητά, ἱππηλάτα, ἱππότα, retain the
accent on the same syllable as the corresponding forms in ηs;
except proparoxytone, ἀκάκητα, δέσποτα, εὐρύοπα᾽ and μητίετα.

57. NOTE 1.—Eust. 75. 37; Chœrob. C. 431. 5; 432. 16; Schol. Ven. A. 175;
Lob. Par. 183. They are frequently called Æolic, though it is clear that αἰχμητά
or πολεμιστά cannot be so, at least as far as the accent is concerned. The following are the more important nouns of this class: ἀγκυλομήτα, Phil. Lex. p. 24.
§ 60: αἰχμητά, Eust. 75. 20: ἀκάκητα, this was Aristarchus' accent, ἀκακῆτα
being the usual one, Schol. Ven. Π. 185; Chœrob. C. 431. 5; Eust. 75. 20; 1053.
55. 60; Joh. Alex. 13. 21: βαθυμήτα: δέσποτα, the vocative of δεσπότης, Schol.
Ven. A. 175; Chœrob. C. 431. 5: δολομήτα, E. M. 282. 42: εὐρύοπα, Schol. Ven.
A. 508: ἠπύτα, Eust. 75. 21: ἠχέτα, ἱππηλάτα, Schol. Ven. A. 508: ἱππότα᾽
Eust. 75. 21: κυανοχαῖτα, Eust. 75. 21: this also occurs as a dative in Antima-
chus ap. A. G. 1187: μητίετα, Aristarchus, Horus, Apollonius; Schol. Ven. A.
175; 508: νεφεληγερέτα, Schol. Ven. A. 175: πεδῆτα, Philem. Lex. p. 24. § 60:
ποικιλομήτα, πολεμιστά, πολυμῆτα, στεροπηγερέτα, χρυσῶπα.

58. NOTE 2.—The Lacedæmonian forms in ηρ or αρ (gen. ου) = ηs, seem to
have the same accent as those in ηs, at least in our books, as ἐπιγελαστάρ for
ἐπιγελαστής (?), καλλίαρ for καλλίας, and the like; Ahrens de Græcæ Linguæ
Dialectis, 2. p. 71. Kühner, G. G., does not appear to mention such forms at all.

C

59. Proper names in ης are paroxytone, as Αἰσχίνης, Ἀλκι-
βιάδης, Ἀτρείδης, Γράδης, Γύγης, Θουκυδίδης, Καππαδόκης, Λεπ-
τίνης, Μιλτιάδης, Νικήτης, Ξέρξης, Ὀζόλης, Ὀρέστης, Πέρσης,
Πηλείδης, Σκύθης, Χρύσης, except those contracted from έας,
which are perispomena, as Βορρῆς, Θαλῆς, Ἑρμῆς.

60. NOTE 1.—*Proper Names in ῆs.* Ἀπελλῆς, Herodian ap. Eust. 1951. 14;
Chœrob. C. 46. 34: Ἀρτεμῆς, Arc. 25: Αὐγῆς, Arc. 23: Βορῆς, a form, the ex-
istence of which is doubted by Eust. 1538. 34: Δρῆς, vide sup. § 30: Δρογῆς (?)
Arc. 23: Ἑρμῆς, Herodian ap. Eust. 1951. 13, and Aristarchus ap. Eust. 1118.
62: Ζαβρῆς, Zonar. 947: Ζαμβρῆς, Suid.: Θαλῆς, when barytone its genitive is
Θάλητος, Herodian ap. Eust. 1951. 13; Chœrob. C. 44. 14; 136. 25; Schol. Ven.
O. 302: Θυῆς, Arc. 23. 25: Ἰαμβρῆς, N. T.; Suid.: Ἰαννῆς, N. T.; Suid.
Ἰωσῆς: κασῆς or κασᾶς = τὸ πιλωτὸν ἱμάτιον. Κασης as a proper name is oxytone
in Chœrob. C. 413. 12, and paroxytone in Arc. 24: Καυσῆς, Herodian ap. A. G.
Oxon. 3. 288. 19: Κιβῆς, Arc. 23: Κισσῆς, Aristarchus ap. Eust. 840. 30; Schol.
Ven. Λ. 223: Κυῆς, Arc. 23. 25; also Κύης, gen. ητος: Μανῆς, Aristoph. Av.
1311: Μάνης, Aristoph. Ran. 963; on the accent of this word, which has a
double inflexion, see H. D. s. v.: Μεγῆς, so accented by Ptolemæus Ascalonites;
Aristarchus wrote Μέγης: the word has a double inflexion, Eust. 1017. 1; Schol. Ven.
O. 302, where it is observed that the accentuation of Aristarchus was generally
followed; cf. Arc. 23: Μιμνῆς (?) Tzetz. ad Lycoph. 424. p. 596; H. *D.*: Μογῆς,
Arc. 23. 23: Μυῆς, Arc. 25. 7, and Μύης (gen. ητος), St. Byz.: Μωϋσῆς, Chœrob. C. 46. 34; this word also follows the third declension: Ναρσῆς, Chœrob. C.
46. 33: Ναυῆς, Sept.: Ποδῆς, Aristarchus ap. Eust. 1118. 62; Herodian ap. Eust.
1951. 14; 182. 20; 840. 30; 1538. 33; Arc. 24: Πυθῆς, Herod. 7. 137; 8. 92;
not Πυθής, as it is wrongly written in St. Byz. s. v. Πυθόπολις, where it is
expressly said that the genitive Πυθοῦ is perispomenon, and the genitive Πυθέω
occurs more than once in Herodotus: Πυλῆς, Arc. 25. 11: Ῥαζῆς, the renowned
Arabian physician: Ῥοδῆς, Arc. 24: Στιλβῆς (?) H. *D.*: Στυπῆς or Στυπῆς,
Tzetz. Hist. 9. 970; *H.D.*: Σωσῆς, Chœrob. C. 46. 34; Eust. 182. 20; 1538. 34:
Τιμῆς, Iuscr.: Ὑῆς, Arc. 23. 9, though it is perpetually written Ὕης in our books:
Φαλῆς (and Φάλης, gen. ητος), Schol. Ven. O. 302; Schol. Aristoph. Ach. 251 = 262,
περισπωμένως δὲ τὸ Φαλῆς ἀναγνωστέον, ὡς Ἑρμῆς. οὕτως δὲ Ἀττικοί· παρὰ Δωριεῦσι
δὲ βαρυτόνως, ‘ὁ δ᾽ αὖ Φάλης κατακυπτάζει·’ οὕτω Σώφρων ἐχρήσατο: Φανῆς, Arc.
24: the common form for the name of the Orphic deity is Φάνης, gen. ητος.

It has not been thought advisable to insert such very late forms as Τζιμισκῆς,
Leo Diac., Φρανζῆς, Φουρνῆς, etc.

61. NOTE 2.—The following national names, if correct, which may be reasonably doubted, violate the general rule: Ἀδρησταί or Ἀδραϊσταί, Arrian Anab.
5. 22. 3: Ἀσταί, St. Byz.; Strab. 319: Ἀστρυβαί, Arrian Ind.: Βίθναι,
St. Byz.; Βουσαί, Herod. 1. 101, is correctly Βοῦσαι in St. Byz.: Δισοραί, St. Byz.:
Ἐντρυβαί, St. Byz.: Κορδιοταί, Athen. 234 A. B.   For Λυγχησταί, in Thucyd.
2. 99, 4. 124, Strabo 326 has Λυγκισταί, St. Byz. s. v. Λύγκος Λυγκισταί, and
others Λυγχεσταί: Μάραθαι, *H. D.*; but the passage in Athen. 575 B. does not
justify this accent: Σάννιγαι, St. Byz., for which Σαννίγαι is also found. In Strab.
296, καὶ τοὺς Ταυρίσκους δὲ Τευρίσκους καὶ Ταυρίστας φασί, some read Ταυριστάς.
A few names of men are also met with, e. g. Διοκορυστής, Apollod. 2. 1. 5: Κυρ-
ρεστής (and Κυρρέστης), Lob. Par. 443: Ὡριστής, Schol. Plat. Menex. 235 E.

Words in α and η.

62. In the accentuation of words in α and η a few general principles are dimly discernible. Substantives which express in a general and abstract manner the notion of the verb with which they are etymologically connected are frequently oxytone, and this is especially the case when they substitute another vowel sound for that of the verb, as στέλλω στολή, τέλλω τολή, ΦΕΝΩ φονή, δείρω δορά, φέρω φορά, ἀμείβω ἀμοιβή. Collectives (περιεκτικά) are commonly oxytone; for example, such words as ἰωνιά, ῥοδωνιά, and plural names of towns. Supposing the quantity of the word known, it is generally true that the accent is thrown as far back as possible, except common substantives in γη, δη, μη,·φη, χη and ωη, which are oxytone. The great majority of proper names retract the accent. But to all rules so general as these there are such hosts of exceptions that they are of little or no use in practice.

63. NOTE.—Schol. Ven. E. 202, τὰ γὰρ εἰς Η λήγοντα θηλυκὰ μετὰ συμφώνου δισύλλαβα ὀξύνεται τῷ Ο παραληγόμενα, εἰ γένοιτο ἀπὸ ῥημάτων τῷ Ε παραληγομένων μόνῳ, οἷον στρέφω, στροφή, τροπή, τροφή, ῥοπή, σπονδή, νομή, ὁλκή, πλοκή, οὕτως καὶ φορβή. προσέθηκα τῷ Ε παραληγομένων μόνῳ, ἵνα νῦν ἐκφύγω τὸ πόρπη· τοῦτο γὰρ παρὰ τὸ πείρω.

64. Though it does not fall within the province of the present work to determine the quantity of final syllables, yet it may be remarked that, subject to many exceptions, the final α is short when the genitive ends in ης, and long when it ends in ας, except 1. hyperdissyllabic words in εια with a corresponding adjective in ης, as ἀλήθειᾰ ἀληθής, ἀσάφεια ἀσαφής, ὑγίεια ὑγιής; 2. feminine forms like εὐπατέρεια, ἠριγένεια, τριτογένεια, δυσαριστοτόκεια, with no corresponding masculines; 3. feminines in εια corresponding to masculines in ευς, as βασίλεια βασιλεύς, ἱέρεια ἱερεύς, πανδόκεια πανδοκεύς, though this last word is by some derived directly from πανδοκεύω, and consequently written πανδοκειᾱ; the words βοήθειᾰ, θάλειᾰ, κράνειᾰ, and κώδειᾰ, have a short final syllable; 4. common names of women in τρια, as μαθήτρια, ποιήτρια, πλύντρια; 5. hyperdissyllables in οια, as εὔνοια, Εὔβοια; 6. those in υια, as μυῖα, χαλκόμυια, but θυιᾱ, μητρυιά and ἀγυιά are long. The termination ρα is *short* in all simple hyperdissyllables with a *naturally* long penultimate, as ἄρουρᾰ, γέφῡρᾰ, μάχαιρᾰ (except words in ωρα with τιάρα and κολλύρα); in all words ending in ιρα (except ζειρά, σειρά, χοίρα, ἑταίρα), and in

σφῦρα and κραῦρα, Κίρρα and Πύρρα : elsewhere it is *long*. All
in δρα, θρα, and τρα, are long, except σκολόπενδρᾰ. No notice is
here taken of the Doric forms in ᾱ = η.

65. Monosyllables in α and η are perispomena, as δᾶ, μνᾶ, Λᾶ,
Μᾶ, Χνᾶ, βῆ, γῆ.

Note.—Herod. π. μ. λ. 8. 7 ; St. Byz. s. v. Μάσταυρα. Λᾶ and Μᾶ are wrongly
written Λά, Μά, in St. Byz. For φλᾶ νῆσος in Joh. Alex. 8. 4, Göttling rightly
conjectures Φλᾶ νῆσος, quoting Herodot. 4. 178, where however our editions read
Φλά.

-ΑΑ and -ΑΗ.

66. All substantives in αα or αη are paroxytone, as ἐλάα, μνάα,
Κρανάα, Ναυσικάα, δάη, Δανάη, Κρανάη.

67. Note.—When contracted they become perispomenon, as μνᾶ, Ἀθηνᾶ, Herodian π. μ. λ. 7. 33. Hecatæus, ap. Herod. π. μ. λ. 8. 1, has τῇ Δανᾷ μίσγεται Ζεύς
for Δανάη. Lob. Prol. 75, ' Δανααί hoc est Danai filiæ oxytonon est in Hesiod.
Fr. 72, Goettl. ut Cranai filia Κρανάη eodem quo adjectivum accentu Apollod.
3. 14. 5, fortasse ut a gentilicio distingueretur quasi patronymicum.' Cf. Lob.
Rhem. 253.

-ΒΑ and -ΒΗ.

68. All substantives in βα and βη are paroxytone, as Ἄβα,
Ἄλβα, ἀλάβη, ἀρτάβη, βλάβη, βόλβα, ἑκατόμβη, ἐρυσίβη, ἥβη,
καλύβη, κύμβη, λώβη· σόβη, στίβη, στίλβη, φόβη, Ἄλβη, Ἀλύβη,
Ἀρίσβη, Βοίβη, Βόλβη, Δέρβη, Ἑκάβη, Θήβη, Θῆβαι (§ 13),
Θίσβη· Κύρβη, Νιόβη, Ὑσβη, Φοίβη ; except oxytone, ἀμοιβή,
λαβή, λοιβή, στοιβή, τριβή, φορβή, and ὠβή.

69. Note 1.—A. G. Oxon. 1. 257. 16 : Ἀβά = βοή appears in Cyril. Lex. ap.
Zonar. p. 99 : ἄλαβα, in Hesych. and elsewhere, should probably be paroxytone :
ἀμοιβή, Arc. 104. 10 : ἀνασοβή, Socr. H. E. 2. 23. p. 115 ; *H. D.* ; yet μυιοσόβη and
σόβη are paroxytone, a fair test of the reliance to be placed on the rule which
declares that verbals in η are oxytone : ἀποκρυβή, Eust. 974. 45 ; *H. D.* : βηβή (?)
= πρόβατον, Hesych. : γραβά, *pit*, Hesych. : δολβαί, Hesych. : ἐκθλιβή (?) Sept. :
κολοβή (sc. χλαῖνα) is an adjective used substantively ; Chœrob. ap. A. G. Oxon.
2. 227. 11, κολοβὴν βαρύνεται, Ἀττικοὶ δὲ ὀξύνουσιν. A distinction (it is to be
suspected a vain one) is sometimes made between λαβή, *hold*, and λάβη, *excuse*.
' Λάβη, paroxytonως e Cyrillo affertur pro Excusatio,' Steph. Thes. p. 5590. ed. Lond.
I have been unable to discover the passage alluded to. λοιβή, Arc. 104. 13 :
στοιβή, Arc. 104. 13 ; Lob. Rhem. 260, note 14 : τριβή, Arc. 104 : φορβή, Arc. 104 ;
Schol. Ven. E. 202 ; Eust. 539. 13. 19 : ὠβή, Plut. 1. 43 A ; Suid. s. v. ὠβάς.

70. Note 2.—*Proper Names.* Ἄβη, Arc. 104. 11 : Ἄβαι is occasionally found
oxytone in the books, e. g. Soph. Œd. R. 894 = 900 ; Eust. 279. 1, παρ᾽ ἐκείνῳ δὲ
(sc. Sophocles) καὶ ὀξύνονται κατά τινα τῶν ἀντιγράφων αἱ Ἀβαί. Ἄλαβα (?) Ptol.
2. 6. 58 : Ἀλβή in St. Byz. s. v. Ἄλβα is certainly an error : Ἄρυββα (?) St. Byz. :
Βάβυβα (?) Ptol. 4. 6. 6 : Δαραβά (?) Strab. 771, where Meineke reads Δάραβα :
Ἐντριβαί, St. Byz. : Κοβή, Ptol. 4. 7. 10 : Κόρδυβα, Strab. 141, yet Κορδύβη, Ptol.

2. 4. 11; 8. 4. 4 : Μαίνοβα, Strab. 143 : Μαρίαβα, St. Byz. : Μέσσαβα (?) St. Byz. : Μοναβαί, St. Byz. : Ὄνοβα, Strab. 143 ; Ptol. 2. 4. 11 : Ὀσσόνοβα, Strab. *l. l.* ; Ptol. 2. 5. 3 : Σαβά, Strab. 770 : Σάβαι, Ptol. 4. 6. 30 ; Σαβαί, Strab. 771, and St. Byz., but he observes s. v. Τάβαι, βαρύνεται δέ, ὡς Σάβαι ; hence Σαβή should probably be paroxytone, cf. St. Byz. s. v. Σάβοι : Σίσυρβα, St. Byz. : Τούκαβα (?) Ptol. 4. 6. 25. As to those marked with a note of interrogation, I do not know whether they belong to this declension or not : they may be neuter plurals, or barbarous and indeclinable altogether, like Ἀγίσυμβα, Ptol. 4. 6. 3 ; 1. 7. 2.

-ΓΑ and -ΓΗ.

71. Common substantives in γα and γη are oxytone, as ἀναζυγή, ἀναφυγή, ἁρμογή, ἀρωγή, δημιουργή, κλαγγή, κραυγή, μαρμαρυγή, οἰμωγή, ὀλολυγή, ὀργή, πληγή, ῥωγή, σιγή, στοργή, σφαγή; except paroxytone, ἄγη, *wonder*, ἀμόργη, ἁρπάγη, *a hook*, ἠλύγη, λύγη, πάγη, *a snare*, στέγη, τέγη, τρύγη, and the contracted nouns γῆ, αἰγῆ, τραγῆ, which are perispomena.

72. NOTE.—A. G. Oxon. 2. 412. 4 : Ἀγή, *breakage*, ἀπόκλασις τοῦ κύματος : ἄγη, *wonder*, E. M. 8. 35 : αἶγα = αἴξ, a late form, Valckn. ad Ammon. p. 230 : αἰγῆ = αἰγέα, Arc. 105. 2 : ἀμόργη, Arc. 105. 12 : ἀράγγη, *H. D.* : ἁρπαγή, *rapine* : ἁρπάγη, *a hook*, Arc. 102. 7 ; A. G. 446. 10 ; Ammon. 22 ; E. M. 87. 38 ; Eust. 906. 48 ; 1390. 52 : γᾶ, Dor. = γῆ : γῆ = γέα, Herod. π. μ. λ. 7. 3 : γέλγη, Eust. 927. 53 ; it is a plural neuter in Pollux 7. 8 ; Lucian Lexiph. 3 : γόγγα, a barbarous word, Georg. Sync. p. 28 C ; *H. D.* : γύγγη (?) Arc. 105. 1 : ἑόργη and εὐέργη, Pollux 6. 88 ; ἠλύγη, Arc. 105. 7 : θήγη (?) or θηγή, Lob. Rhem. 258 : κρηνάγγη (?) Hesych., is corrupt : κρίγη (?) and κριγή, the latter being better attested, E. M. 539. 2 : λάγγα, Hesych. : λαλάγγη, Suid. s. v. κολλύρα : λατάγη, Eust. 1170. 55 ; L. S. have λαταγή, which seems the better way of writing the word : λεύγη, Hesych. : for λιβύργη in Arc. 105 the last editor has rightly substituted Ἐλιβύργη : λόγγη, Hesych. ; 'Verum est λοίτη,' *H. D.* : λύγη, Eust. 689. 18, 809. 44 ; E. M. 91. 27 : λώγη, Hesych., but λωγή, Zonar. 1325 : μάργη, Lob. Par. 346 ; Hesych. : ὀλίγγη (?) Arc. 105. 12 : ὀξύγη, *a toad* : παγῆ (?) Herod. π. μ. λ. 6. 23 : πάγη, Arc. 104. 24 : πανάγη, Arc. 105. 8, who says it means ἡ ἁγνὴ ἱέρεια : Meineke (cf. Lob. Prol. 44) thinks it a contracted form for πανάγεια, but this is doubtful : παταγή, Eust. Dion. Per. 566, τὸ δὲ παταγή κοινότερον μὲν ὀξύνεται, ὡς τὸ ἀλαλαγή, ὁ δὲ Ἡρωδιανὸς βαρύνει αὐτό, λέγων ὅτι οὐκ ἐκ τοῦ πατάσσω γίνεται, ὀξύνετο γὰρ ἂν ὡς τὸ ἀλαλαγή, ἀλλ᾽ ἀπὸ τοῦ πάταγος, οὗ τὸ θηλυκόν φησιν ἡ πατάγη : πέγη (?) : πλαταγή, *noise, din* ; πλατάγη, *a rattle*, but it is not unfrequently oxytone in the latter sense, e. g. Arist. Polit. 8. 6. 2 ; Plut. 2. 714 E ; Arc. 105. 9, καὶ τὸ πλαταγή δέ τινες βαρύνουσιν· Schol. Apollon. Rhod. 2. 1056, ὁ μὲν οὖν Ἡρωδιανὸς τὴν πλαταγὴν ὀξύνεσθαί φησιν ἐν τῇ Καθόλου· βέλτιον δὲ ἴσως τὴν μὲν πλαταγήν, τὸν ἦχον, ὀξύνειν, τὴν δὲ πλατάγην, τὸ κρόταλον, παροξύνειν, cf. Lob. Rhem. 266 : πρασόργη, Hesych. : σάγη, Arc. 104. 25, τὸ μέντοι σαγή τὸ πλῆθος τινὲς μὲν ὀξύνουσι, τινὲς δὲ βαρύνουσι, cf. Schol. Eurip. Rhes. 207 ; E. M. 707. 23 : ῥόγα, Suid. : σαλάγη, Hesych. : better σαλαγή, *H. D.* : σαυρίγγη, Hesych. : σμώγη, Hesych. : σπατάγγη, Athen. 91 C : it seems doubtful whether this is the proper form for the nominative, though it is that given in H. D. Should it not be σπατάγγης? στάγη (?) Hesych. : στέγη, Arc. 104. 24 : τάγγη, Alex. Aphrod. Prob. 2. 70, ed. Sylb. ; but ταγγή is also found, cf. H. D. s. v. and Lob. Par. 341 : τέγη, Arc. 104. 24 : τραγῆ = τραγέη δορά, Eust. 374. 37, 276. 11 : τρύγη, Arc. 104. 24 : ὑργη (?) Lob. Par. 34, note 36 : ὗσγη, Suid. : φυσίγγη (?) Lob. Par. 145 : ὠλίγγη, A. G. 318. 10.

73. Proper names in γα or γη are paroxytone, as Βάγα, Βέλγη, Βέργη, Γάγαι, Θίγγη, Κραύγη, Λαλάγη, Πέργη, Σέλγη, Σίγη, Ῥώγη ; except Αἰγαί and Ταγαί.

. **74.** Note.—Αἰγά, in Achaia, Strab. 387 (also Αἰγαί) : Αἶγα, St. Byz. : Αἰγᾶ (?) or Αἰγά, in Mysia; Strab. 615 : Αἰγή, in Macedonia, Herod. 7. 123 : Αἰγαί, Strab. 385. 386 ; St. Byz. s. v. ; E. M. 27. 57, 28. 24 : Ἀπῆγα, Polyh. 13. 7 : Αὐγαί, in Cilicia, H. *D.* : Βάγαι, in Lydia, Hierocles, p. 671 ; H. *D.* : Βαγαί, in Sogdiana, Arrian Anab. 4. 17. 4 : Βώλιγγα, St. Byz. : Γυγᾶ, Ἀθηνᾶ ἐγχώριος, Hesych. : Λαταγή, in India, Ælian H. A. 16. 10 : Ηαγαί = Πηγαί, Strab. 380. : Πελαργή, daughter of Potneus, Pausan. 9. 25. 7 : Σίγη, a town in the Troad, St. Byz. : Σιγή, a woman's name, Athen. 583 E : Ταγαί, Polyb. 10. 29. 3.

-ΔΑ.

75. Words in δα, whether proper or common, are paroxytone, as ἄρδα, ἐπίβδα, Ἀνδρομέδα, Ἴδα, Ἰλέρδα, Λάβδα, Λήδα, Ὀσικέρδα ; except δᾶ for γῆ, and σποδά for σπουδή.

76. Note.—The following rare words are exceptional : ἄαδα, Hesych. : ἀώκυδα (?) : κνῶδα (?) = *caput papaveris,* H. *D.* : λεδδά, Hesych.

Proper Names. Ἀδᾶ, Joseph. B. J. 1. 18. 4 : Ἄδα, daughter of Hecatomnus, Strab. 657 : ἡ Ἀλάβανδα (?) Strab. 660 ; cf. H. D. s. v. ; generally τὰ Ἀλάβανδα : Ἄλυδδα, Ptol. 5. 2. 14 ; according to Fix ap. H. D. the cod. Par. reads Ἀλυδδά : Ἀμιδα, St. Byz. : Ἀροῦνδα, Ptol. 2. 4. 15 : Ἀρύκανδα, St. Byz. : Ἀττάλυδα, St. Byz. : Βούρσαδα (?) Ptol. 2. 6. 58 : Γάλαδα, St. Byz. : Δάραδα, Strab. 771 : see above, § 70 : Ἔβουδα, Ptol. 2. 2. 11 : Ζάβιδα (?) St. Byz. : Θαμουδᾶ (?) St. Byz. : Θέρμιδα (?) Ptol. 2. 6. 57 : Θρύανδα (?) St. Byz. : Ἰδουβέδα, Strab. 161, 162, is proparoxytone in Ptol. 2. 6. 21 : Ἴλερδα, St. Byz., is rightly Ἰλέρδα in Strab. 161 : Κάλυνδα, Strab. 651 ; St. Byz. : Καρύανδα, St. Byz. ; Strab. 658 : Κέσαδα or Καίσαδα, Ptol. 2. 6. 58 : Κηδαί, an Attic deme ; Pape quotes Demosth. adv. Euerg. § 5, which proves nothing : the accent is doubtful : Κύαρδα (?) St. Byz. : Λῆδα, Eust. 1687. 16, ἰστέον δὲ ὅτι τὸ Λήδη, Λῆδα λέγεται κατὰ Ἡρωδιανὸν δωρικῶς. δώρια δέ φησι, καὶ ὁ Φιλομήλα καὶ ἡ Ἀνδρομέδα, τροπῇ τοῦ Η εἰς Α πεποιημένα. καὶ λέγει ἐκεῖνος καί τινα αἰτίαν εἰς τοῦτο, προπερισπῶν τὸ Λῆδα κατὰ τὸ μοῦσα. ἴσως δὲ Δώριον καὶ ἡ τόλμα, ὃ ἀναλογώτερον τοῦ τόλμη φησὶν Ἡρωδιανός. Pape quotes Λύδη as a woman's name from Athen. 598 C, where it does not occur : Λυδή however is. found in that author 597 A, and elsewhere, as a proper name. The former is certainly the better way of writing it. Μάλλαδα is cited by Pape from St. Byz., where however Μαλλάδα is printed in Westermann's edition. Μασανώραδα (?) St. Byz. : Μονάοιδα (?) Ptol. 2. 2. 12 : Νάαρδα (?) St. Byz. : Ὀρτόσπεδα (?) Ptol. 2. 6. 21 : Οὐάραδα, Ptol. 2. 6. 57 : Οὐάσαδα, Ptol. 5. 4. 10 : Ῥοδαί, St. Byz. : Σέβεδα (?) St. Byz. : Σέτιδα (?) Ptol. 2. 4. 12 : Σπονδή as a proper name is wrong ; it should be Σπόνδη : Φοῦνδα, St. Byz. : Ψίμαδα (?) St. Byz.

-ΔΗ.

77. Common substantives in δη are oxytone, proper names paroxytone, as ἀνακομιδή, ἀοιδή, αὐδή, ἐδωδή, κομιδή, σπονδή, σπουδή, φραδή, χλιδή, χορδή ; Ἀγαμήδη, Ἴδη, Λάδη, Λύδη, Μένδη, Νέδη, Ῥόδη, Σίδη, Χόνδη ; except ἴδη, κνίδη, κράδη, πέδη, σίδη, σχέδη, σχίδη, and the contracted words ἀδελφιδῆ, ἀνεψιαδῆ, θυγατριδῆ, ῥοδῆ, υἱδῆ.

78. NOTE.—Ἀδελφιδῆ, Pollux 3. 22: ἅλδη, in Arc. 105. 18, is doubtful; *H. D.* consider it to be a proper name: ἀνεψιαδῆ, A. G. 15. 18: αὐδῆ, in Herod. ap. Herm. de emend. rat. Gr. gr. p. 304, is a strange form, probably corrupt: ἔδη = δεσμός, E. M. 465. 56; Dindorf ingeniously conjectures πέδη: εἴδη = ἴδη, Hesych.: θυγατριδῆ, Plut. 2. 608 B: ἴγδη, Lob. Phryn. 164: ἴδη, E. M. 465. 52: ἰκτιδῆ = ἰκτιδέα, *sc.* δορά: κνήδη, a false form for κνίδη: κνίδη, Arc. 105. 25; E. M. 465. 55: κράδη, E. M. 465. 56: μελέδη (?) a false form for μελέτη: ὄβδη = ὄψις seems only to occur in the accusative as an adverb: πέδη, Arc. 105. 25: πλάδη, Suid. s. v. πλαδαρόν: ῥοδῆ = ῥοδέα, Eust. 1963. 48: Ῥόδη is a proper name: σάγδη, a barbarous word, sometimes σάγδας or ψάγδας, Athen. 691 C: σίβδη = σίδη: σίδη, Arc. 105. 25: σφίδη (?) Hesych.: σχέδη: σχίδη or σχίδα (?) Hesych.; Lob. Par. 83: υἱδῆ or υἱϊδῆ are contracted, Pollux 3. 17. Göttling quotes Μενδαί from St. Byz., where I do not find it.

-EA.

79. Substantives in εα, both proper and common, are paroxytone, as ἀλέα, θέα, *sight,* ἰδέα, ἰτέα, κοκκυγέα, λεοντέα, λευκέα, μηλέα, μορέα, πτελέα, συκέα, Ἀλέα, Θυρέα, Ἰτέα, Κεδρέαι, Μαλέα, Μαντινέα, Μενέα, Νεμέα, Πτελέα, Τεγέα, Χοιρέαι, Ὠχαλέα; except ἀδελφεά, γενεά, δωρεά, ζεά, θεά, *a goddess,* Ἀρνεαί, Ὀρνεαί, and Φεαί.

80. NOTE 1.—Ἀδελφεά = ἀδελφή, and ἀδελφεή: αἱμαλεά, E. M. 35. 5, would be better αἱμαλέα: ἀλέα = ἡ θερμασία; ἀλεά = ὁ τόπος ὁ ὑπὸ τοῦ ἡλίου θερμαινόμενος, E. M. 58. 23. The latter word was also a name of Athene, cf. Herodian ap. St. Byz. s. v., though Strab. 388 has Ἀλέα Ἀθηνᾶ: γενεά, Theog. Can. 102. 30; δεά, Dor. = θεά, must be distinguished from δέα, a Tyrrhenian word = ῥέα, mentioned by Hesych.: δωρεά, Theog. Can. 102. 30; this of course retains its accent in composition as ἀντιδωρεά: ἐρεά, which Lob. Par. 338 mentions, seems to be an error on his part; the word is rightly paroxytone in Athen. 197 B; Strab. 196, and elsewhere: θεά, *goddess,* Arc. 98. 11: θέα, *sight,* is regular: ἱέρεα is a Doric form of ἱέρεια (like the Ionic ὑπώρεα for ὑπώρεια); also ἱερέα: καίτρεα, Hesych.: κοιλώτεα, Hesych., is a false form for κολουτέα, H. D.: κόλεα, Hesych., should be κολέα: κωλέα (falsely κωλεά in Hesych.) is often contracted κωλῆ, Aristoph. Nub. 976; Herod. π. μ. λ. 6. 26: κώπεα and κῶπα (?) Suid.: νεά (*sc.* γῆ), also νέα, Lob. Par. 355; this was contracted into νῆ by Aristophanes, Herod. π. μ. λ. 7. 10: ὀχεά, Theog. Can. 102. 30; also χεά and χειά: σχελεαί should be σχελέαι, Pollux 7. 59: στελεά or στελεή = στειλειά: στερεά (*sc.* γῆ), Lob. Par. 350: τά-λεαι (??): ὑπώρεα Ionic = ὑπώρεια: φορβεά (Gottling Accent. p. 128), a false form for φορβειά: φωλεά, Tzetzes ad Hesiod. Op. 373; H. D.

81. NOTE 2.—According to Göttling Accent. p. 130 plural names of towns in εαι are oxytone when there is a parallel form in ειαι, as Κεγχρεαί = Κεγχρειαί, but Κεδρέαι, Χοιρέαι, as there are no corresponding forms in ειαι. This rule, however, does not seem to hold good; Lentz would apparently make all plural names of places oxytone, a very convenient mode of accenting if there were any authority for it. The following exceptions to our rule are met with:—Ἄρδεα, St. Byz., a very questionable accent: Ἀρνεαί, St. Byz.: Ἄττεα (?) Strab. 607: Βρεά, St. Byz. is rightly Βρέα, Theog. Can. 102. 20: Γενεά, St. Byz.: Δέρεα (?) St. Byz.: Pape quotes Εὐρυτεαί from Paus. 7. 18. 1, where however Εὐρυτειαί stands:

Ζεά, St. Byz. s. v. Ζαιά: Κεγχρέαι, St. Byz.; but Strab. 369 and 380 has Κεγχρεαί, the name to whichever city it belongs fluctuates between these two accents: Κελεαί, Paus. 2. 12. 4: Κόρσεαι, St. Byz.: Μελαινεαί, Paus. 8. 3. 3; Eust. 271. 1, and 286. 32, distinguishes the Bœotian Μίδεα from the Argive Μιδέα: 'Ορνεαί, St. Byz. s. v. 'Αρνεαί and 'Ορνειαί: some wrote Πτελεά, but Herodian made it paroxytone, Schol. Ven. Φ. 242: Τεγέα is sometimes, e. g. in St. Byz., incorrectly written Τέγεα, for the α is long, cf. Eust. 271. 1: Φεαί, Strab. 350, and Φεά, Φιά, or Φειά, cf. H. D. s. v.: Πάνθεα, a name given to Drusilla, is quoted by H. D. from Dio Cass. 59. 11, but it must be an error for Πανθέα.

82. NOTE 3.—Many of these nouns are liable to contraction; they then by rule become perispomena, though later writers not unfrequently make them oxytone, Lob. Par. 336. A list of them is subjoined. For further information reference must be made to the several terminations which they assume after contraction: ἀδελφιδῆ, αἰγῆ, ἀκτῆ, ἀλωπεκῆ, ἀμυγδαλῆ, ἀνεψιαδῆ, ἀνθρωπῆ, ἀρκτῆ, αὐδῆ (?), αὐξῆ (?), αὐλῆ (?), βοῆ, γαλῆ, γῆ, ἐχινῆ, θυγατριδῆ, ἰκτιδῆ, ἰξαλῆ, κερδαλῆ, κυνῆ, κωλῆ, λεοντῆ, λυκῆ, μοσχῆ, μυογαλῆ, νεβρῆ, νῆ, ὀσχῆ (?), παγῆ, παρδαλῆ, ῥῆ, ῥοδῆ, σησαμῆ, συκῆ, ταυρῆ, τραγῆ, υἱδῆ, φακῆ, φοινικῆ.

-ZA.

83. Words ending in ζα have the last syllable short, and the accent, both in proper and common nouns, is retracted: those in ζη are paroxytone, as ἄζη, ἀργυρόπεζα, γάζα, γλυκύριζα, κνύζα, ὄζη, ὄρυζα, ῥίζα, σχίζα, τράπεζα, φύζα, χάλαζα, Βάδιζα, Βαρύγαζα, Βόρυζα, Γάζα, Δούριζα, Τίριζα, Τυρόδιζα.

84. NOTE.—Arc. 96. 9. The quantity of the doubtful vowels before double consonants is most perplexing: see especially Lob. Par. 412. The determination of this point is of course necessary before it is possible to affix the proper accent to such words as μαζα, βυζα, κνυζα, and others. According to Herodian π. μ. λ. 31. 29, μαζα is the only word of this termination which has a long dichronous vowel in the penultimate syllable, and accordingly he accents it μᾶζα. The same thing is asserted by Draco 72. 3; 95. 2; 100. 1; and by Schol. Aristoph. Pac. 1. According to the Lex. Gr. ap. Herm. de emend. rat. Gr. gr. p. 328, the penultimate is short, whilst Mœris, p. 258, apparently reconciles these conflicting statements by asserting that μᾶζα is the Attic, μάζα the un-Attic and common form. Supposing this to be true, it will explain why μάζα is most commonly met with in our editions, the scribe having written the word not as it was anciently pronounced, but as he was accustomed to use it. If Herodian be right, βῦζα and κνύζα for βύζα (Lob. Par. 408.) and κνύζα are wrong, though they are sometimes so written. 'Αρπέζα for ἅρπεζα is incorrect. Καρζά = καρδία in E. M. 407. 21, is said to be Æolic, if so it must surely be κάρζα. Θελαμοῦζα in St. Byz. is probably erroneous.

-HA and -HH.

85. The following seem to be nearly all the words in ηα or ηη: 'Αναξίκληα, *H. D.*, which Pape makes properispomenon; βιζῆαι(?), κοῖται, στιβάδες, Hesych.; δηαί = κριθαί, a Cretan word, E. M. 264. 12; μεταδήα, Hesych. is corrupt; παρηή = παρειά: an Æolic(?) form παρηά is mentioned by E. M. 653. 33, but the accent is false.

-ΘΑ and -ΘΗ.

86. Substantives in θα and θη retract the accent, the final α being short, except in the names of women, as ἄανθα, ἄκανθα, κολόκυνθα, μίνθα, Ἔρθα, Κύναιθα, Κύπαιθα, Λύκαιθα, Σάκανθα, Σάρκανθα, Σύμαιθα, but Ἀγάθα, Σιμαίθα, Aristoph. Ach. 534 ; Theocr. 2. 101, 2. 114 ; λήθη, μάλθη, πόσθη, σάθη, σπάθη, Ἀγάθη, Αἴθη, Βρένθη, Ξάνθη, Ὄρθη· Σίθη, Σκίθαι, Σμίνθη, except κριθή and ποθή, oxytone.

87. NOTE 1.—Arc. 96. 14 : Ἐδωγαθή in Hesych. is corrupt : ἰθή (?) Hesych. : κριθή, Arc. 106. 3 ; Theog. Can. 109. 18 : γυμνοκριθή, quoted by H. D. from Myrepsus de Antidotis, c. 449, is probably an error ; I have not been able to verify the reference : πειθή (?) Hesych. : ποθή, Arc. 106. 4 ; E. M. 678. 36 ; Eust. 94. 28 ; this was the accent of Aristarchus and of Herodian : τήθη is the more usual form, though τηθή (and ἐπιτηθή, E. M. 366. 11, or ἐπιτήθη, Pollux 3. 18) is also met with, Eust. 565. 30, 971. 24 ; προτήθη is paroxytone in Pollux 3. 18 : τῐθή, if not altogether false, is at least paroxytone, Arc. 106. 2 : the accent of τίτθη is variable ; the word is oxytone in Pollux 3. 50, 2. 163 ; Plut. 2. 673 A ; Eust. 650. 21 ; paroxytone in Plut. 2. 69 C, 3 C, D, 754 D ; Arist. H. A. 7. 10. 10, Rhet. 3. 4. 3 (codd. τιτθαῖς and τίθαις) ; Plat. Rep. 343 A (codd. τιτθή, τίτθη, τίθη, and τήθη), 460 D, where Bekk. and Stallb. read τιτθή ; Aristoph. Eq. 713, Thesm. 609, Lys. 958 ; Demosth. 1155. 1312, etc ; the balance of authority makes it paroxytone : ψιθή (?) Hesych. : κακιθή (? κακηθή), Theog. Can. 109. 24.

88. NOTE 2.—Ἀμαθαί, St. Byz., though the singular is Ἀμάθη ; the accent is suspicious : Γαββαθᾶ, N. T. John 19. 13 : Γαβάθη is sometimes written Γαβαθή or θά : Γολγοθᾶ, N. T. Matth. 27. 33, is barbarous : Θεβηθά (?) St. Byz. : Κυμαίθα and Κιναίθα, Theocr. 4. 46 : Κυναίθα, Theocr. 5. 102 ; but Κύναιθα, the name of a city, Strab. 388 : Μαλόθα, Strab. 782.

-ΑΙΑ.

89. Dissyllables in αια are properispomena, the rest paroxytone, as ἀγλαία, αἶα, ἀλμαία, γαῖα, γραῖα, μαῖα, ῥαῖα, Αἶα, Ἀχαία, Γραῖα, Ζαῖα, Μαῖα, Φαῖα, Χαλδαία, except πυρκαιά, oxytone, and names of towns in the singular number, which are proparoxytone, as Ἀστυπάλαια, Ἱστίαια· Κάρθαια, Λίλαια, Νίκαια, Πλάταια (but Πλαταιαί oxytone in the plural), Ποτίδαια, Φώκαια.

90. NOTE 1.—According to Theog. Can. 103. 2 plural names of towns in αιαι are oxytone. Eust. 269. 1 says that Πλάταια and Θέσπια are oxytone in the plural, but he does not there assert that all similar nouns are so. Eust. 1419. 39 mentions a hill called Ἀνόπαια, and also a path so called.

91. NOTE 2.—Ἀδραιά, Maced. = αἰθρία, Hesych. : ἀνοπαῖα, Schol. Hom. Odyss. 1. 320, ὁ μὲν Ἀρίσταρχος ἀνόπαια προπαροξυτόνως ἀναγινώσκει ὄνομα ὄρνιθος λέγων, ὁ δὲ Ἡρωδιανὸς ἀνοπαῖα ἀντὶ τοῦ ἀοράτως, ἵν᾽ ᾖ οὐδέτερον πληθυντικόν, ὡς τὸ ‘πυκνὰ μάλα στενάχων·’ διὸ καὶ προπερισπαστέον φησίν : ἀραιά, which is really an adjective used substantively, is ἀραία in Rufus Eph., Lob. Par. 307 : γραῖα and γραία (?) Lob. Par. 347 : ἐραῖα, Suid. : λαιαί, Arist. de Gen. An. 1. 4. 16, and

5. 7. 18; also λαῖαι, λεῖαι, and λέα in E. M. 558. 57; λεά, Hesych.: λαία = λεία, Pind. Ol. 11. 46.; *H. D.*: πυρκαϊά or πυρκαιά (falsely πυρκαϊά in Arc. 194. 7) is so accented διὰ τὸ περιεκτικὸν εἶναι: φορβαιά and φορβαῖα are both corrupt forms of φορβειά.

92. NOTE 3.—The following names of towns deviate from rule in the places referred to: Αἰγαῖαι = Αἰγαί, Herodot. 1. 149; Strab. 676: Αἰγαιαί = Αὐγειαί, Strab. 364: Αἰθαία, St. Byz.: Ἀλύκαια, *Pape*, Ἀλυκαία, *H. D.*, both quoting Paus. 8. 27. 3, where Dindorf reads Λυκαία: Ἀμφαναία, St. Byz. s. v. Ἀμφαναί: Ἀναία St. Byz. : elsewhere this is τὰ Ἄναια: Ἀνακαία, A. G. 348. 23; St. Byz.: Ἀρταία (?) St. Byz.: Ἀστραία, St. Byz.: Ἀταία, St. Byz.: Ἀχαιαί (sc. πέτραι), Strab. 347: (Ἀχαιά = Demeter, E. M. 180. 34): Βαῖαι = Baiæ, Strab. 243, is wrongly accented Βαιαί in E. M. 192. 45: Δρυμαία, Paus. 10. 33. 11.: Δυμαῖαι, E. M. 291. 13: Ἐλαία, St. Byz.: Εὐταία, Paus. 8. 27. 3: Ἐφυραία, Paus. 2. 1. 1: Ζαιά and Ζεά, St. Byz.: Ἡραία, Strab. 357: it is strictly an adjective, Ἡ. πόλις or ἄκρα: Ἰασαία, Paus. 8. 27. 3: Καθαία (?) and Καρταία, Strab. 486: the former word is proparoxytone in Strab. 699: Κάρθαια is prescribed as the proper accent by St. Byz. s. v. Ἀναία, and Theog. Can. 102. 33: Κασθαναία and Καστανaία, Strab. 443: Κυρταία (?), in St. Byz. it is Κυρταῖα like Βαρκαῖα: Κυταία, or better Κύταια, St. Byz. and E. M. 548. 57: Λιμναία, Thucyd. 2. 80: Λυκαία, see above: Μελιταία, St. Byz.: Νισαία, St. Byz., Thucyd., etc.: Νυμφαία, St. Byz.: Ὀρδαία, St. Byz.: the island Παγχαία, Diod. Sic. 5. 42, is proparoxytone in Diod. Sic. 6. frag. 1: Ἡεραία, St. Byz.: Πλάταια is oxytone in the plural, Eust. 269. 1: Πυραία, St. Byz.: Πυρηναία, St. Byz., perhaps Πυρηνία would be better: Πυρωναία, St. Byz.: Ῥαία (?) St. Byz.: Ῥήναια is variable, it is proparoxytone in Strab. 486; Theoc. 17. 70; properispomenon in Hom. Hym. ad Apoll. 44; but the former is alone right: Ῥοξονοκαία, St. Byz. (*H. D.* print Ῥοξονυκαία): Τιθοραία (?) St. Byz., should be Τιθορέα, Paus. 9. 17. 4; 10. 32. 8: Τραγαία, St. Byz.: Τριταία, St. Byz.: Ὑαία, St. Byz.: Φαλανναία, St. Byz. as the name of a city probably wrong; cf. *H. D.* s. v. Φάλαννα: Φασταία, St. Byz., wants correcting: Φηγαία, a deme, St. Byz., probably Φηγαιά: Φηραία (?) Strab. 357, where Meineke reads Ἡραία: Χαλκαία, St. Byz. should be Χάλκεια.

93. NOTE 4.—Contrary to analogy, Pape has the female names Ἐτυμοκλήδαια and Σκαία, which last is oxytone in Paus. 7. 1. 6: Νίκαια, however, as the name of a woman, occurs in Phot. Bibl. 233. 40; Strab. 565.

94. NOTE 5.—Names of countries or districts are paroxytone; they are really feminine adjectives, as Ἐρυθραία (sc. γῆ), Χαλδαία, Ἀχαία, Περαία: Ἰδυμαῖα in Chœrob. E. 151. 12 seems to be an error.

-ΙΑ.

95. Common substantives in ια retract the accent, as ἀθανασία, ἀμαθία, ἀνδραγαθία, ἀνία, ἀνορεξία, ἁρμονία, γωνία, διδασκαλία, ἑστία, εὐτυχία, εὐχαριστία, ζημία, ἡγεμονία, ἴα, κακία, κονία, μαθήτριᾰ (§ 64. 4), μανία, μοναρχία, μορφώτριᾰ (§ 64. 4), ξενία, οἰκία, πενία, ποιήτριᾰ (§ 64. 4), προεδρία, σοφία, ὑπερηφανία, φιλία, χορηγία, except oxytone, αἱμασιά, ἀλαοσκοπιά (ιή), ἀνεψιά, ἀνθρακιά, ἀπομαγδαλιά, ἁρμαλιά, ἀχυρμιά, ἐσχατιά, θριά, ἰά, *a voice*, ἱμονιά, ἰωνιά, καλιά, κρινωνιά, λαλιά, λοφιά, νεοσσιά, νεοττιά, ὁρμιά, παιδιά, πατριά, πρασιά, σκιά, σκοπιά, σπογγιά, σποδιά, ·στρατιά, σχοινιά, ταρσιά (τερσιά τρασιά), φλιά, φυταλιά. The word πότνια also, though not belonging in strictness to the present rule, may be noticed. Μόρρια, in Paus. 8. 18. 5, if a feminine singular, ought to be corrected.

96. NOTE.—Αἱμασιά, Arc. 99. 9; Eust. 748. 18; E. M. 461. 34: ἀλαοσκοπιά or ιή is incorrectly paroxytone in Hom. Il. 22. 515: ἁλιά, a salt cellar, is paroxytone in Hesych. and E. M. 63. 38: ἁλιά = ἁλιαία (?) E. M. 427. 31: ἁματροχιά = ἡ τῶν τρόχων σύγκρουσις: ὁ τύπος τοῦ τρόχου, is to be distinguished from ἁματροχία = ἡ εἰς ταὐτὸ συνδρομὴ τῶν ἁρμάτων, E. M. 79. 31; S. V. Ψ. 422, ἔστι δὲ ἁματροχιὰ τὸ ἅμα τρέχειν καὶ μὴ ἀπολείπεσθαι, ... ἁρματροχία (sic) δὲ τῶν τροχῶν τὸ ἴχνος: ἀμία, L. S., is ἄμια in Eust. 868. 5; E. M. 83. 37 (?); Arist. de Part. Animal. 4. 2. 1, where one MS. reads ἀμιά, and ἄμια in Hesych. Arist. H. A. I. 1. 24, where two MSS. have ἀμίαι; see H. D. s. v.: ἀμία = φυλακία in Hesych., seems to be corrupt: ἀνεψιά, Lucian Dial. Meret. 2. 2. etc.: ἐξανέψιαι (sic), Pollux 3. 29: ἀνθρακιά, Arc. 100. 9; E. M. 801. 21: ἀπομαγδαλιά, Arc. 99. 20; Aristoph. Eq. 413; also ἱά, Plut. 1. 46: ἀρμαλιά, Theocr. 16. 35: ἁρμονία, Schol. Hom. Odyss. 5. 248, ἁρμονίῃσιν· προπερισπωμένως· ἔστι γὰρ Ἰώνων ὁ καταβιβασμός: according to A. G. 7. 31, some wrote αὐτοχειριᾷ for αὐτοχειρίᾳ: ἀχιά (?): ἀχυρμιά, Eust. 748. 18: γυμνοπαιδία is also found oxytone: δεξιά (sc. χείρ) is an adjective used substantively, Theog. Can. 105. 26: ἐσχατιά, Eust. 1183. 60; Diod. Sic. 2. 49, etc.: ἑρμακιά, Gloss. Herod. 1. p. 345, Schweig.; H. D.: ἑψία or ἐψία is found also written ἐψιά and ἔψεια; see H. D. s. v.: θαλαμιά = ἡ θαλαμία ὀπή (Schol. Aristoph. Ran. 1105 = 1071) is oxytone in Aristoph. Pac. 1198, and Schol. ad loc., paroxytone in Herodot. 5. 33: θημωνιά, or θημωνία, Eust. 1539. 18; E. M. 451. 8, occurs in Hesych. under the forms of θημονιά and θειμωνειά: θριά (falsely θρίαι in Phot. Lex. and in E. M. 455. 34); also θριαί, and as a proper name, Θριαί, Arc. 98. 15: θωϊή = θωή, E. M. 26. 24: ἰα, or ἰη, voice, or cry, is stated to be paroxytone by Joh. Philop., and it is so written in Eust. 794. 54; Etym. Gud. 268. 46, and Suid.; but it is oxytone in Etym. Gud. 269. 47, and in Herodot. 1. 85: Æschyl. Pers. 937; Eurip. Rhes. 553; quoted by H. D.: ἰμαλιά (?) Hesych.: ἰμονιά, this was the Attic accent, Arc. 99. 15: ἰωνιά, a bed of violets, Arc. 99. 14, is to be distinguished from the P. N. Ἰωνία: καλιά (ιή), E. M. 485. 51; Schol. Ven. B. 532: κοπρία ought to be oxytone from its meaning, but is not, Arc. 100. 6: κρινωνιά, Suid.: κωλιά (?) see H. D.: λαλιά, Chœrob. E. 130. 34; E. M. 657. 54: (ἀλαλιά, καταλαλιά, μογιλαλιά (?), προλαλιά, προσλαλιά, διαλαλιά, E. M. 818. 28); yet πολυλαλία and φιλολαλία are quoted by H. D., but are probably mere errors: λαχανιά or ιά, Suid. s. v. πρασιαί: λοφιά is sometimes written λοφία; its compounds however are paroxytone in the books, as ἀκρολοφία, γεωλοφία, παραλοφία (and ιά), τριλοφία: λοχιά, Hesych.: μαγδαλιά, Schol. Aristoph. Eq. 412, is paroxytone in Eust. 462. 37: μαλιή, Hesych.: μονία, remaining, is distinguished by L. S. from μονιά, celibacy; H. D. make them both paroxytone: μυρμηκιά, an ant-hill, Eust. 748. 19: μυρμηκία, a kind of tumour, Galen Def. Med. 401: Μυρμηκιά, a town, St. Byz. Μυρμήκιον: νεοσσιά, νεοττιά, or νοσσιά, Chœrob. E. 166. 3, is sometimes paroxytone: οἰκοδομία was oxytoned by the Attics; Suid.; Schol. Thucyd. 1. 93; Lob. Phryn. 487: ὁρμιά (ἡ) Theog. Can. 105. 27: ὀρυγιά, H. D.: παιδιά, Arc. 98. 23; it was paroxytone in Attic, according to E. M. 657. 51; Schol. Aristoph. Plut. 1056; Athen. 323 C, σηπίας ... ὡς αἰτίας ἡ παραλήγουσα παροξύνεται, ὡς Φιλήμων ἱστορεῖ, ὁμοίως καὶ ταῦτα, παιδία, ταινία, οἰκία: πολιά (sc. θρίξ), Arc. 100. 3: πρασιά, Arc. 99; Eust. 1574. 27; 1967. 29; E. M. 461. 34: προσεψία is oxytone in Hesych.: προστασία is, according to Arc. 99. 9, oxytone, but in our editions it is always paroxytone: πυρκαιά, Chœrob. E. 130. 34: ῥοδωνιά, Arc. 99. 13; Theog. Can. 105. 26; ῥο-

δωνία, Draco 14. 4; E. M. 705. 3; Lob. Par. 317: σιά, Dor. = θεά: σκαφιά is probably false: σκοπιά, Arc. 100. 2; Eust. 1183. 60: σπογγιά in Attic; Suid.; Greg. Cor. p. 148. ed. Schäf.: σποδιά, Arc. 100. 2; Eust. 1547. 45: (θερμο-σποδιά, ? Lob. Phryn. 603): στραγγαλιά, Hesych.; in Chœrob. E. 180. 14, it occurs both as oxytone and paroxytone; the former is probably alone correct: στρατιά, Chœrob. E. 131. 1, and στρατιή (Στρατία and ίη are proper names; cf. Philem. Lex. p. 63. § 169): σφηκιά, this is no doubt the proper accent, but the word occurs as a paroxytone in Plut. 2. 461 A, and elsewhere: ταρσιά (Ταρσία, P. N.), τερσιά, τρασιά, E. M. 764. 25: τροχιά, Arc. 100. 3 (ἀματροχιά, ἡ, ἀμαξοτροχιά, ἀρματοτροχιά), is paroxytone in Photius: τρυμαλιά and ιή, Hesych.: φλιά, Arc. 98. 15: φλογιά, ιή, Lob. Par. 318; Nicaud. Alex. 393: φορβιά is a false form of φορβειά: φυταλιά, Arc. 99. 21: χιά (?): χλιά, Diod. Sic. 34-5, frag. 37. Bkk.: χροτιή (?), Anth. Pal. 15. 35; ψιά, Hesych. and ψία, also ψειά: ὠλιγγιά, Hesych., ία *L. S.*, which seems better.

The grammarians hold that many of the above nouns are oxytone, because they are collectives; E. M. 555. 42, τὰ σημαίνοντα ἄθροισιν ἢ περιεκτικὰ τινῶν προσηγορικῶν ὀξύνεται: Chœrob. E. 131. 4; Eust. 1574. 28.

97. Proper names in ια are paroxytone, as Ἀρμενία, Ἀσία, Βοιωτία, Ἰταλία, Ἰτουρία, Καππαδοκία, Κιλικία, Κορασσίαι, Λυκία, Ὀλυμπία, Πανδοσία, Παφλαγονία, Σικελία, Τισία, Φημίαι, Φθία, except Ἐρέτρια, Πολύμνια; the demes Κηφισιά, Λουσιά, Χελιδονιά, Στειριά; and the nymphs Θριαί.

98. NOTE.—If correct, the following deviate from the rule: Αἰθαλία = Ilva, Strab. 123; 223 (also Αἰθάλεια), is falsely written Αἰθάλια in St. Byz. s. v. Αἰθάλη: Αἰθαλιά in Hesych. is a deme-name: Αἴλια, St. Byz.: Αἱμονιαί, Paus. 8. 3. 3, is elsewhere Αἱμονία: Ἀζηνία, a deme, A. G. 348. 23; St. Byz., should probably be oxytone: Ἀκμόνια, St. Byz.: Ἀκριαί, Paus. 3. 21. 7: Ἀκυτάνια (?) St. Byz.: Ἀλλάδια, St. Byz.: Ἀλλάρια, St. Byz.: Ἀλτέρνια (?) Ptol. 2. 6. 57: Ἄντια and Ἄδρια in St. Byz. s. v. Ἄγκαρα are strange, and most likely wrong: Ἀριάνια (?) St. Byz.: Βισάλτια, St. Byz.: Βρασιαί, St. Byz.: Βρυσιαί = Βρυσειαί(?): Γυμνήσιαι (sc. νῆσοι), Diod. Sic. 5. 17, is an adjective: Δῖα, Diod. Sic. 4. 69, Δία, ἡ νῆσος, Draco 40. 6: both are really feminines from δῖος: Ἐρέτρια, Strab. 446, etc.: Θέσπια is oxytone in the plural Θεσπιαί, St. Byz.; Arc. 98. 2; Eust. 265. 41, 266. 1; Schol. Ven. B. 498, ἐν μέντοι τῷ ια' τῆς καθολικῆς προσῳδίας ἐν τοῖς προπαροξυτόνοις καὶ ἔχουσι πρὸ τέλους τὴν ΕΙ δίφθογγον αὐτὸ καταριθμεῖ [sc. ὁ Ἡρωδιανὸς] καὶ τοῦτο αὐτὸ τὸ Ὁμηρικὸν παρατίθησι, καὶ ἀλλαχοῦ λέγει τὴν ΕΙ ἔχειν αὐτὸ φανερῶς, καὶ ἐπιφέρει ὅτι καὶ Θεσπιὰ ὀξυτόνως λέγεται: E. M. 305. 34, ἐπὶ τῶν εἰς Α βραχυκαταληκτούντων εἰώθασιν οἱ Ἴωνες βαρύνειν τὰς λέξεις, ὡς καὶ ἡμεῖς· οἷον, ἄγυια, ὄργυια· Πλάτεια, Θέσπεια, ὅταν δὲ γένηται ἡ τελευταία συλλάβη μακρά, Ἰωνικῷ ἔθει καταβιβάζεται ὁ τόνος· οἷον, ἀγυιά, ὀργυιά, Θεσπειά: Θρῖα (or Θρεῖα?), a deme, Phot. Lex. Θριά and Θριαί, Hesych., is falsely Θρίαι in E. M. 455. 34-49: Ἰάμνια, Eust. 265. 43; St. Byz.; Ἰαμνία, H. *D.*: Καλαυρία, Strab. 369, or Καλαύρια, Eust. 287. 29; St. Byz. has Καλαύ-ρεια, which accent and spelling are expressly prescribed in A. G. Paris. 3. 137. 4: Κηφισιά, deme, Arc. 99. 11; yet Ἐπικηφισία or ησία, St. Byz. is paroxytone: Κορσιά, Paus. 9. 24. 5; Κορσιαί, Demosth. de Fals. Leg. p. 385, is Κορσίαι in Harpocr.: Κωπιαί, Strab. 263: Λακιά (?), a deme; there seems more authority for Λακία; though *many* deme-names were oxytone, *all* were not so, St. Byz. v. Αἰξωνία: Λάμια, the monster, Eust. 265. 43; E. M. 555. 50; Theog. Can. 98. 31: Λαμία, a city in Thessaly, E. M. 555. 50: Λουσιά, a deme, is oxytone, according to

Arc. 99, though St. Byz. s. v. et s. v. 'Αζηνία has both it and Λουσία, a daughter of Hyacinthus, paroxytone: 'Ολμιαί, Strab. 380: Ὄμπνια, Arc. 95. 17; Draco 20. 21; Theog. Can. 98. 31: Πειρεσιαί, Apollon. Rhod. 1. 584, though the singular is Πειρεσία, Schol. Apollon. Rhod. 1. 37, or Πειρασία, St. Byz.; H. *D.*: Πλωθιά, a deme, is given by Pape, but his authorities do not justify such an accent; the word is Πλωθία in St. Byz. s. v. 'Αζηνία, and also Πλώθεια, St. Byz.; Harpocration has Πλωθειά: Πολύμνιά, Draco 20. 21; Diod. Sic. 4. 7; Theog. Can. 98. 31, is falsely paroxytone in Apollod. 1. 3. 1: Πότνια, Arc. 95. 16; Theog. Can. 98. 31: Πότνιαι in Boeotia is commonly proparoxytone, e. g. St. Byz.; Strab. 409,; but Ποτνιαί in Paus. 9. 8. 2, Dindorf thinks this the right accent, but gives no reasons for his opinion: Πρασιαί, in Argolis, Strab. 368; cf. Arc. 99. 9; Eust. 1967. 29: Πρασίαι, a deme, St. Byz., is Πρασιά in Strab. 399, rightly: another form of the same name, Βρασιαί, occurs in Paus. 3. 21. 7: Σκιά, St. Byz. v. Σκιάς, better Σκία: Στειριά (Στηριά, Στεριά), a deme, Arc. 99; Strab. 399; is Στείρια in St. Byz.: Ὑσίαι, in Argolis, Strab. 376; is Ὑσιαί in Paus. 2. 24. 7: Ὑσιαί, in Boeotia, Strab. 404; Paus. 9. 1. 6; as the name of a deme it is oxytone, Arc. 99. 11: Φλιαί (?) Pape quotes this from Diod. Sic. 14. 41; one of his many false references: Χελιδονιά, deme, Arc. 99. 15: 'Αβιά (Hebr.), in Zonar. 5, and N. T., is barbarous and indeclinable.

-EIA.

99. Common substantives in εια are proparoxytone, except dissyllables, and derivatives from verbs in εύω [1], which are paroxytone, as ἀκρίβεια, ἀλαζονεία, ἀλήθεια, ἀσφάλεια, βασίλεια, a queen, βασιλεία, a kingdom, βοήθεια, δεία, ἐνέργεια, ἐντερόνεια, εὐγένεια, εὐπατέρεια, εὐσέβεια, θάλεια, θεία, θεραπεία, ἰατρεία, ἱέρεια, priestess, ἱερεία, priesthood, λεία, μνεία, νηστεία, παιδεία, χρεία, ὠφέλεια. Compounds of these words retain their accent according to the general rule, as χρεία, ἀχρεία, λεία, ἀγελεία, μισεταιρεία, δεία, σιτοδεία, yet we find ἔκδεια, ἔνδεια, ὀλιγόδεια, as if from ἐκδεής, ἐνδεής, ὀλιγοδεής. The following are oxytone, ἀρειά (ειή), ζειά, παρειά, στειλειά, φορβειά, χειά; while ἀνδρεία, αἰσυμνητεία, νωθεία, πενεστεία (?), are paroxytone.

Words in ειη are paroxytone, except such as correspond with the oxytones in εια; they are oxytone, as στειλειά, στειλειή, χειά, χειή.

100. Note 1.—*Paroxytones in* εια: Αἰκεία is an error for αἴκεια; see H. D. s. v.: αἰσυμνητεία is always thus written, though there does not appear to be any verb in εύω: ἀλαβαρχεία (for ἀλαβαρχείη) seems not to occur, H. D. make it proparoxytone according to rule: ἀλεία (ἄλη), Hesych.: ἀλεία for ἀλιεία (compare ὑγεία for ὑγίεια) is found in one MS. of Arist. Œcon. 2. 4. 2: it is however almost certainly like ὑγεία, a late and incorrect form: ἀλειτεία (?) = ἀλητεία (εύω): ἀλκεία (?) L. S.: ἀλφιτεία (?), it is doubtful whether ἀλφιτεύω exists; see H. D.

---

[1] It is sometimes said that all verbal derivatives in εια are paroxytone, a statement contrary to the declarations of the grammarians (cf. E. M. 558. 1; Chœrob. A. G. Oxon. 2. 237. 1, etc.), as well as contrary to fact.

8. v. ἀλφηστεύω: ἀναγνεία retains the accent of ἀγνεία (εύω): ἀνδρεία (ἀναν-δρεία), according to Chœrob. E. 91. 31, nouns in εια from properispomenon adjectives are paroxytone, hence ἀνδρεῖος, ἀνδρεία; and this is probably the best account of the matter, ἀνδρεία being a feminine adjective used substantively, while ἀνδρία is a genuine substantive; see Lob. Par. 360. Compare also ἐλεγεία, which is strictly the feminine of ἐλεγεῖος, sub. ποίησις or ᾠδή: ἀντλεία (?) Hesych., should be ἀντλία: ἀπολλεία (?) probably false for ἀπώλεια: ἀριστοκρατεία (?) as κράτεια is proparoxytone (Chœrob. A. G. Oxon. 2. 237. 1), there can be little doubt that this and similar forms are clerical errors: ἀσκεία (?): ἀσπανιστεία (?): ἀφητορεία: ἀχρεία, Lob. Phryn. 106: βαθρεία (?) Æschyl. Supp. 859, the only place quoted, proves nothing as to the accent; if not altogether corrupt, it should by analogy be βάθρεια: βαμβακεία (?) Hesych.: δεία, Arc. 98. 18, (ἔκδεια, ἔνδεια are formed from ἐκδεής and ἐνδεής; Philem. Lex. p. 20; ἄδεια, A. G. Paris. 3. 136. 31;) ὀλιγοδεία, Suid., ὀψοδεία, Suid.; on these words in δεία, see Lob. Path. 1. 243; σιτοδεία, want of food, A. G. 1418; Chœrob. E. 92. 1; Diod. Sic. 2. 16; Lobeck Phryn. 493, writes σιτόδεια wrongly, that word meaning, according to H. D., congiarium: δημοκρατεία, if this exists at all, it should be proparoxytone: δικαστεία (?): the forms διοσημία and θεοσημία seem to be better attested than διοσημεία and θεοσημεία: εὐρυόδεια, L. S., is said to be paroxytone by E. M. 396. 24; but according to Zonar. 911 some made it proparoxytone: ἐγχεία = ἐγχείη, E. M. 313. 15: ἐλεγεία, E. M. 461. 51; vide supra: ἐντερονεία is wrong; cf. Schol. Arist. Eq. 1181, and Dind. ad loc.: θεία, Chœrob. E. 91. 35: θεομαντεία: θεοπτεία should be θεοπτία: θύεια is in Attic θυεία, Philem. Lex. p. 20; Lob. Phryn. 165: ἰδρεία = ἰδρείη, Hesych.: ἱππωνεία, Xenoph. Hipp. 1. 12; De re eq. 1. 1; 3. 1; H. D.; there is another form, ἱππωνία: καθημερεία (?): καρπιστεία (?) and ια: καστανεία = καστανέα (?) Lob. Par. 337: κερατεία (?) = κερατία, Strab. 822; H. D.: κητεία (κῆτος), Athen. and κητία, Ælian: κνιπεία and ία: κορεία and είη: κράνεια, cornel, Schol. Ambros. Odyss. 10. 242: κράνεια and κρανεία (?) a cornel spear, Lob. Par. 339: κροκοδειλεία is doubtful both in spelling and accent: Κυκλωπεία (sc. διήγησις, or the like): although this is the accentuation given by H. D., yet L. Dindorf (Thes. vol. 3. p. 2438 A) makes Εὐρώπεια, Δευκαλιώνεια, Ὀδύσσεια, Πατρόκλεια, Δολώνεια, which are exactly parallel with it, proparoxytone, and as substantives that is no doubt the best way of accenting them: thus also Λυκούργεια, Ὀρέστεια, Οἰδιπόδεια: in A. G. Oxon. 2. 189. 7, Ὀδύσσεια, Δολώνεια and Γιγάντεια are expressly made proparoxytone; cf. A. G. Oxon. 3. 278. 13; Lob. Ajax 97; A. G. Paris. 3. 76. 30: κυρεία or ία, though Dindorf condemns the latter form: κυρτεία (? εύω): λαφυροπωλεία should be λαφυροπωλία: λεία, Arc. 98. 17.: λιθεία, if not an adjective, should be λιθία or λιθέα: λυκεία (sc. δορά), Polyh. 6. 22. 3; H. D.: μνεία, Arc. 98. 16, the α is said to be short by Theog. Can. 103. 26: what does he mean? νεανεία seems to be a doubtful form for νεανεία: νεοεία (?) = νεοίη: νηλεία is a false lection in Theoph. H. P. for which μηλέα is now read: see H. D. s. v.: νουθετεία (?) Pollux 9. 139: νωθεία, Philem. Lex. p. 20; cf. E. M. 462. 9: ὀψεία is false for ὀψία: πανδόκεια, Arc. 194. 27: πανσκαφεία (?) the passage quoted from Geopon. 5. 9. p. 341 (where some read ία) proves nothing: πελατεία (?): Πενεστεία (?) Arist. Pol. 2. 5. 22, 2. 9. 2: πηλαμυδεία (?) Strab. 549, (where ία is also read,) proves nothing: προκοιτεία is probably a false form for προκοιτία: σημεία, corrupt for σημαία: σκοτεία should be σκοτία: στασιωτεία, Plat. Legg. 715 B: τανεία (?) Theoph. H. P. 4. 1. 2.; H. D.; τανία seems preferable: τελωνεία is false for τελωνία: τωθεία (??): ὑγεία, a late and incorrect form, Herodian ap. Herm. de emend. rat. Gr. gr. p. 307. 16; Chœrob. E. 92. 3; compare however E. M. 774. 36; Porson ad Eurip. Orest. 229: χημεία, Suid., or χημαία: χυμεία (? εύω). Excluding those forms which are obviously corrupt, or doubtful, it will be seen that there are really few exceptions to the rule laid down above.

101. NOTE 2.—Among the adjectives which are used substantively, the following may be noticed: Ἀργεῖαι, Hesych.; E. M. 462. 3 : βοεία (sc. δορά), so also κυνεία, λυκεία, λεοντεία, ταυρεία, ὀνεία, Lob. Par. 336. 353 : γλυκεῖα (sc. ῥίζα) and εὐθυγλυκεῖα: πλατεῖα (ὁδός and other words understood): θαλεία (?) Lob. Par. 354, note : ἡρακλεία (sc. λίθος): καδμεία, Lob. Par. 331 : χειμερεία (sc. ὥρα), also θερεία, for which θέρεια, E. M. 466. 57, is not so good; ' codices Polybii θερείαν vel θερίαν scribunt : v. Schweigh. ad 1. 25. 7; in quo l. θέρειαν est ap. Suid. s. v.' H. D.

102. NOTE 3.—*Oxytones in* εια: Ἀδελφειή = ἀδελφή, Quint. Smyrn. 1. 30 : ἀρειά (ἀρειή), Arc. 98. 25 ; Herodian ap. E. M. 139. 29 ; Draco 25. 15 : ζειά, Arc. 98. 15 ; Chœrob. E. 131. 1 ; E. M. 410. 17 ; and ζέα, E. M. 914. 24 : νευρειή = νευρά, Lob. Par. 354 : παρειά, Schol. Ven. Γ. 35 ; Arc. 98 ; Chœrob. E. 131. 1 ; E. M. 139. 33 στελεά (?) or στειλειά (στειλειή), E. M. 726. 52 : φειά (?) Chœrob. E. 131. 1 φορβειά (φορβειά, φορβιά,) Arc. 98 ; Herodian ap. Schol. Aristoph. Av. 862 ; E. M. 139 ; Chœrob. E. 131 ; Lob. Par. 354 : φορειά = βόρβορος, Arc. 98 : χειά (χειή), Chœrob. E. 131 ; E. M. 410. 17 : a later form, χέεια, occurs in Nicand. Ther. 79 if we admit the conjecture of Bentley, the MSS. have χελείαις; cf. Lob. Rhem. 188, note 11 : ψειά = ψιά or ψία, Heysch.; cf. Theog. Can. 105. 28.

103. NOTE 4.—The grammarians teach that concretes in εια are oxytone, abstracts proparoxytone ; E. M. 410. 15, etc. The older Attics made the final a in derivatives from adjectives in ης (and substantives in εύς?) long, as ἀληθείᾱ, ἀναιδείᾱ, ὑγιείᾱ, ἱερεία (?) (on which see E. M. 313. 22 ; Herod. ap. Lob. Phryn. 456); Chœrob. ap. A. G. 1314, πολλάκις οἱ Ἀθηναῖοι ἐπὶ τῶν διὰ τοῦ ΕΙΑ προπαροξυτόνων μακρὸν ποιοῦσι τὸ Α, καὶ καταβιβάζουσι τὸν τόνον. καὶ φυλάττουσι τὴν ΕΙ δίφθογγον, οἷον ἀλήθεια κοινῶς καὶ ἀληθεία Ἀττικῶς, ἱέρεια κοινῶς καὶ ἱερεία Ἀττικῶς, εὔκλεια κοινῶς καὶ εὐκλεία Ἀττικῶς : Arc. 194. 26 ; διὸ Ἀττικοὶ ἱερέως λέγοντες ἱερεία ἐκτεταμένως λέγουσιν· ἀλλ' οὐκέτι πανδόκεια βασίλεια, Eust. 1579. 28 ; E. M. 774. 33 ; Matthiä Gr. gr. § 68. vol. 1. p. 118; Göttling Accent. p. 133; Spitzner Gr. Pros. § 17. 2, d.

104. Proper names in εια have the a short, and retract the accent, as Ἀλεξάνδρεια, Ἀμάλθεια, Δεκέλεια, Θάλεια, Θεσσαλονίκεια, Ἰφιγένεια, Καισάρεια, Μάλεια, Μαντίνεια, Μήδεια, Σαμάρεια, Φιγάλεια, Χαιρώνεια, except plural names of cities, which are oxytone, as Αὐγειαί, Βρυσειαί, Ἐχειαί, Κεγχρειαί, Ὀρνειαί, so Θεσπειαί, but Θέσπεια.

105. NOTE 1.—*Names of Places.* Eust. 291. 10; Schol. Ven. B. 532, 813 ; Arc. 98. 2 ; Schol. Ven. Φ. 493 : Αἰξωνεία, E. M. 37. 2, should be Αἰξώνεια: Ἀνάγνειαι in Polyb. is false for Ἀναγνίαι : Βάτεια, as it is rightly written in St. Byz. s. vv. Ἀρίσβη, Δάρδανος, is quoted by Lob. Par. 29, from Diod. Sic. 4. 77 (should be 75), and Apollod. 3. 12. 1, as paroxytone; but in both places it is Βάτεια : Ἐρχεία, a deme, Harpoc. is Ἐρχία in St. Byz. : Ζειά, a harbour in Peiræeus, is thus spelled by Phot. Lex. s. v. Μουνυχία; but Ζέα is found in A. G. 311. 17 : Ἡλεία = Ἦλις, Strab. 351, etc., an adjective sub. γῆ : Καδμεία, St. Byz., also an adjective substantively used : Κεγχρειά (or Κεγχρέα), Thucyd. 8. 10. 20, and Wass. ad l. : Κερδεῖαι (?) ' Xenoph. Hell. 2. 1. 15 : πόλει... ὄνομα Κεδρείαις· cui Κεδρέαις restituendum puto,' W. Dindorf, rightly ; St. Byz. has Κεδρέαι : Κογχεία (?) a river, Lycoph. 869 ; H. D. : Κρωπειά, Thucyd. 2. 19 : Κυχρεία, St. Byz. (and Κύχρεια, Strab. 393) is an adjective : Λατωρεία, Athen. 31 D, or better, Λατορεία, Eust. 871. 25 : Λυγκεία, Paus. 2. 25. 5, probably an error ; H. D. have Λύγκεια :

Λυκωρεία, E. M. 571. 46, is false for Λυκώρεια: 'Οφιτεία (?) Paus. 10. 23. 10; one MS. has 'Οφιτία: Περσεία (sc. κρήνη), Paus. 2. 16. 6: Πολιτεία, St. Byz.: Ταριχεία, Strab. 834, etc., a significant name: Τενεῖαι (sc. πηγαί), Paus. 8. 13. 5: Ὑδρεία, St. Byz.: Φειά, Schol. Ven. H. 135; Theog. Can. 103. 25: Φλυεία, deme, E. M. 795. 39; false for Φλυέα; cf. H. D. s. v. Φλυεῖς. The names Αἰπεῖα, a city in Cyprus, E. M. 721. 47, and Βαθεῖα, Plut. 2. 196, are really adjectives used elliptically; the former name however occurs as a substantive Αἴπεια in St. Byz. and elsewhere; e. g. Eust. 743. 23; thus also 'Ορεῖαι, St. Byz.: Πλατεῖα, St. Byz.: Τραχεῖα, St. Byz.; Strab. 634: Χαλκεῖα, St. Byz.　On Αἰολεῖαι, Plut. 2. 299 E, where Wyttenbach reads αἱ ὀλεῖαι, see H. D. s. v.

106. Note 2.—*Names of Women.* 'Αργεία, Paus. 4. 3. 4: 'Ελευχεία (?) Apollod. 2. 7. 8, which is quoted for this accent, proves nothing, as the name is in the genitive case; Heyne and Bekker read 'Ελαχείας: Ἡδεῖα, H. D., but the passage quoted (Plut. 2. 1129 B) proves nothing as to the accent: Θεία, Hes. Th. 135; Θεῖα, Hes. Th. 371: Ἰοξεῖα (?) Tzetz.: Νικεία (?) Theocr. 13. 45: Ῥεία (?) Hes. Th. 135; Ῥείη, Hes. Th. 453; on the several forms of this word, see H. D. s. v. Ῥέα ('Αχιλλεία, Θρασεῖα, 'Ωκεῖα, as names of ships, are of course only adjectives): Νηστεία, a festival mentioned by Ælian V. H. 5. 20, is formed from νηστεύω· The name 'Ιφιγένεια has a long final syllable in Æschyl. Agam. 1526 ed. Didot, and is therefore made paroxytone.

-OIA and -OIH.

107. All substantives, both proper and common, in οια, where οι is a diphthong, are paroxytone as dissyllables, and proparoxytone as hyperdissyllables; those in οιη are paroxytone, as ἄγνοια, ἀνάπνοια, ἀνάρροια, ἀντίπλοια, διάνοια, δύσχροιᾰ, εὐθύπλοια, ζοία, μνοία, πρόνοια, 'Αλίνδοια, Βέροια, Εὔβοια, Κοία, Οἴη, Οἴα, Περίβοια, Τροία; except δοιή, πνοιή, ποιά, ῥοιά, *a pomegranate.* Words like ὀξυηκοία, φιληκοία, where οι is not a diphthong, are paroxytone.

108. Note 1.—*Common Substantives.* Γλοία (or γλοῖα) in Hesych. = γλία; δοιή, E. M. 289. 24: νεοία, Theog. Can. 103. 12: πνοιή (á): ποιά, E. M. 705. 2, 612. 42; 677. 56; Phot. Lex.; Hesych., or ποία, E. M. 770. 9; Arc. 100. 16; the Ionic form ποίη is barytone in Eust. 1851. 50; Hesych.; Suid.; but oxytone in E. M. 677. 55; see Lob. Phryn. 496: on the various forms πτοία, πτοιά, πτοῖα, see Lob. Phryn. 495: ῥοιά, *a pomegranate,* Eust. 94. 4; E. M. 705. 2; Arc. 100. 14: ῥοία, *a horse-pond* (?) Hesych.: στοιά, Phot. Lex., and στοία (?); cf. Arc.100. 18; Lob. Phryn. 495: Στοῖαι, a city mentioned by St. Byz., is barytone: φλοιά, 'φλοιάν sic Musurus; codex Φλοία apud Hesych. τὴν Κόρην· τὴν θεὸν οὕτω καλοῦσι Λάκωνες,' H. D.: χροιά (Attic χροία or χρόα, E. M. 679. 39; χροιή), see Lob. Phryn. 496; Arc. 100. 18; Eust. 94. 2; E. M. 705. 2: ψοιά, 'apud Aristot. H. A. 3. 3, Schneiderus pro ψοιάς bis emendat ψύας (codd. Bekkeri plerique ψοιάς, pauci ψύας vel ψυάς) enimvero Polybi est vox, Aristoteles νεφρούς vocat,' H. D.

109. Note 2.—*Proper Names.* 'Αβροιά, a female name, Lucian Asin. 4: Βοία, Strab. 364, is Βοιαί, Paus. 1. 27. 5; 3. 21. 7, and elsewhere: Οἰή (?) a deme, usually Ὄα or Ὄη: 'Οτροία, a town, Strab. 566.

110. Note 3.—According to Ælius Dionysius, the old Attics regarded the final α in all these words as long, e. g. ἀγνοία, προνοία, Eust. 1579. 28.　Traces of this are still found in the dramatists, see Matthiä Gr. gr. § 68, 3 b, and the authorities there quoted.

-ϒΙΑ.

111. Substantives in υια, both proper and common, where υι is a diphthong, have the final α short, and the accent is thrown as far back as possible, as ἄγυια, αἴθυια, ἄρπυια, κυνάμυια, μυῖα, νέκυια, ὄργυια, χαλκόμυια, Εἰλείθυια, Θυῖα; except μητρυιά and the plurals ἀγυιαί, ὀργυιαί, which are oxytone, and θυία paroxytone. When υι is not a diphthong, these words are paroxytone, as ὀρθοφυΐα, συμφυΐα, εὐφυΐα. The forms in υιη follow so far as they can those in υιᾰ. In the genitive and dative singular and plural ἄγυια and ὄργυια are circumflexed, as ἀγυιᾶς, ἀγυιᾷ, ἀγυιαῖς, ἀγυιῶν.

112. NOTE 1.—*Common Substantives.* Chœrob. C. 405. 27: ἐπὶ τῶν εἰς Α βραχυκαταλήκτων εἰώθασιν οἱ Ἴωνες βαρυτονεῖν τὰς λέξεις ὡς καὶ ἡμεῖς, οἷον ἄγυια, ἄρπυια, Πλάταια· ὅταν δὲ γένηται ἡ τελευταία συλλαβὴ μακρὰ Ἰωνικῷ ἔθει καταβιβάζεται ὁ τόνος, οἷον ὀργυιᾶς, ἀγυιᾶς, Θεσπιᾶς, Πλαταιᾶς. This was the practice of Aristarchus, Eust. 652. 53 ; cf. also Schol. Ven. Z. 422 ; S. V. E. 502 ; Arc. 98. 3. It is observed by Eust. (1631. 29, and 1653. 3) that ὄργυια and ἄγυια were so accented only in old Attic. According to Zonar. 24, some wrote ἀγυιᾶ, while E. M. 14. 21 declares for ἀγυιά and ὀργυιά, and such appears to be their common accent in our editions.

Εὐρυάγυια, A. G. Oxon. 2. 323. 14 : θυία (?) *citrus* : θυῖα, *a mortar* (Sext. Emp. adv. Gramm. I. 10. p. 265), according to Lob. Phryn. 165, is also found under the form θυία ; Arcadius (97. 23) mentions θυῖα, but he may refer to the proper name ; cf. Theog. Can. 102. 27 : for λυσιγυῖα, Hippocrates, De locis in hom. p. 415. 37, H. D., Lobeck Par. 333, would read λυσίγυια, Schneider proposes λυσιγυιά : μητρυιά (ματρυιά), Arc. 98. 4 ; E. M. 14. 24 : νέκυια (cf. Lob. Phryn. 494) is probably the best accentuation, though νεκυία is common, while it occurs under the strange form of νεκυῖα in Schol. Ambros. in Odyss. Ω. 1, where however Dindorf alters it to νεκυία : σικυῖα, Galen, cf. H. D. s. v. σικύα.

113. NOTE 2.—*Proper Names.* The mythical names Ἰδυῖα, Hes. Theog. 352, Εἰδυῖα, Hes. Theog. 960, or Ἴδυια, A. G. Oxon. 2. 442. 4, and Παντειδυῖα, are accented as though they were feminine participles : Νηκουία, St. Byz. : Συία (? Συία) St. Byz.

-ΚΑ and -ΚΗ.

114. Common substantives in κη (and κᾱ) are paroxytone, as ἀνάγκη, δίκη, ἐρείκη, εὐλάκα, θήκη, κάκη, λεύκη, μυρίκη, νάρκη, νίκη, παιδίσκη, πεύκη, σαμβύκη, φενάκη, φοινίκη, φρίκη; except oxytone, 1. words of more than two syllables in ικη and ωκη, as γραμματική, λεοντική, μηδική, μουσική, παρθενική, πρωτερική, πταρμική, σινωπική, χαλκιδική (yet ἑλίκη, πελίκη, and χοινίκη are paroxytone), ἀκωκή, ἰωκή (but φώκη is paroxytone); 2. ἀϊκή, ἀκή, *a point,* and *silence,* ἀλκή, *strength,* βοσκή, δοκή, προδοκή, ὁλκή, παλλακή, πλοκή, ὑλακή, φυλακή ; 3. the contracted forms ἀλωπεκῆ, λυκῆ, συκῆ, φακῆ, φοινικῆ, which are perispomena.

115. NOTE 1.—On words in ωκη see E. M. 55. 27; Arc. 107. 20; Theog. A. G. Oxon. 2. 110. 13.

The hyperdissyllables in ἴκη are nearly all feminine adjectives used substantively, as λακωνικαί, (βλαῦται`, βασιλική, (στέγη), περσικαί, τροπική, etc. ; see Lob. Par. 331 : Πηνική is possibly a mere clerical error for πηνήκη, the interchange of η, ι, and υ in MSS. and early printed books being constant and notorious. The accent of μηδική varies : 'Μηδικὴ χόρτος, Medica, sic ut χόρτος sit interpretatio. Τρίφυλλον interpr. etiam Hesychius et λωτὸν κτήνεσιν ἁρμόζοντα. Ceterum accentum μηδίκη præcipit Arcad. p. 107. 10 ; Eust. Od. p. 1967. 27 : Μηδίκη μὲν χόρτος, ὃ καὶ σημείωσαι· Μηδικὴ δὲ ἡ Περσική. Atque sic scriptum ap. Diod. 3. 43 : Ἄγρωστιν καὶ μηδίκην ἔτι δὲ λωτόν. Μηδική rursus etiam ap. Theophrastum cujus ll. v. ap. Schneider ;' H. D., and the same is the case with several words of like termination.

116. NOTE 2.—Ἀγκή, E. M. 9. 54 : αἰακή (αἰάζω), Arc. 107. 2, where Schmidt reads ἀϊκή : ἀϊκή, Schol.Ven. O. 709 ; Eust. 1039. 15 : ἀκή, *a point, silence*, Arc. 106. 19 (ἤκη is paroxytone in E. M. 424. 18) : ἄκη and ἀκή, *a cure*, see H. D. s. v. : ἁλιακὴ (ἀντὶ τοῦ ἁλιευτική, A. G. 376. 3), an adjective used substantively, cf. E. M. 63. 40 : ἀλκή, *strength*, Arc. 106. 26 : the heteroclite dative ἀλκί follows the laws of the Third Declension : ἄλκη, *an elk*, Paus. 5. 12. 1 ; 9. 21. 3 : ἀλωπεκή (sc. δορά), Eust. Opusc. 177. 48 ; *H. D.* : αὐκά, Cretan = ἀλκή, Hesych. : βατιακή, Arist. Mirab. Ausc. 49, is paroxytone in Athen. 484 E, according to the precept of Arc. 106. 28 : βῆκα (?) and βήκη, see H. D. s. v. : βοσκή, Schäfer ad Schol. Apollon. Rhod. 3. 1085 thinks that βόσκη would be more in accordance with analogy, but it is doubtful whether it would : on γλαυκή or Γλαύκη see Lob. Par. 350 ; Arc. 106. 11 : γλυκή, Hesych. : δοκή = ἡ ὑπόνοια, Arc. 106. 16 : ἠκή, Ion. = ἀκή, ἀκωκή, E. M. 47. 23 ; 49. 15 : Ἰακή (sc. διάλεκτος), and in Hesych. ἰακή = βοή : καρδαμαντική, Diosc. 1. 138 ; *H. D.* : κηκή (?) = ἀκή : λεύκη, Schol. Ven. E. 292 : λυκή (sc. δορά), Eust. 374. 40 : μυκή, *roaring*, Arc. 106. 12, and *L. S.* s. v. : μύκη, *a case, receptacle*, see H. D. s. v. : ὁλκή, Arc. 106. 25 : παλλακή, Schol. Ven. O. 709 : πλοκή, Arc. 106. 16 : ποκή, Arc. 106. 16, is πόκη (πόκαι) in Suid., cf. Lob. Par. 107 : προδοκή, such compounds as αὐλοδόκη, ἀχυροδόκη, ἱστοδόκη, καπνοδόκη, are paroxytone according to the general rule given above, § 28 ; cf. Eust. 992 : συκή, Herod. π. μ. λ. 6. 21 ; Eust. 1963. 48 ; according to Lob. Par. 379 χαμαισύκη is found as well as χαμαισυκή ; it has been before observed that late writers when all nouns in ῆ = έα oxytone ; hence they would have written συκή, and then χαμαισύκη follows from the general rule of composition ; but as there is no reason to suppose that authors of the best age ever made such forms oxytone, it seems as certain as anything of the kind can be that χαμαισυκῆ is the proper mode of accenting the word : τριβακή (sc. χλαμύς), Lob. Prol. 314 : ὑλακή, Schol. Ven. O. 709 : φακῆ, Arc. 106. 20 ; Herod. π. μ. λ. 6. 22 ; Eust. 1572. 51 ; the compounds of this word (βολβοφακῆ, πολφοφακῆ, τευτλοφακῆ) are, like those of συκῆ, found paroxytone, see Lob. Par. 379 : φυλακή, Arc. 107. 2 ; Schol. Ven. O. 335 : φοινικῆ = έα : φοινίκη, Schol. Ven. O. 709.

On the words ἀβίλτακα, ἄφακα, if indeed they belong here, which seems extremely doubtful, see H. D.

117. Proper names in κα and κη are paroxytone, as Ἄκη, Βεβρύκη, Βερενίκη, Γλαύκη, Ἑλίκη, Ἐώκη, Ἰθάκη, Καλύκη, Κίρκη, Λύκη, Ὄγκα, Σκυλάκη, Φοινίκη, Χάλκη ; except the cities Ἀνδριακή, Strab. 319 : Ἀρμοζική, Strab. 501 : Ἐλμαντική or Σαλμαντική,

St. Byz. : 'Ινδική, St. Byz. : the island Κυρακτική (Κυρικτική or Κηρυκτική), Strab. 315 : Παλῖκή, St. Byz., ' Παλίκη ap. Diod. 11. 88 et 90 cui oxytonum restituit L. Dindorf,' *H. D.*: Φωτική, Ψιττακή, St. Byz. : Κορακαί, Λευκή (or Λευκὴ νῆσος), Strab. 125, is an adjective : Λεῦκαι is however barytone, Strab. 646 : and in the singular Λεύκη, Diod. Sic. 15. 18, Σεγεστική, Strab. 313 : Συκαί, St. Byz. : Συκῆ, Strab. 319. The deme 'Αλωπεκή is oxytone.

118. NOTE 1.—The names of countries and districts in ίκη, which are really adjectives, are very frequently oxytone : the chief of them are 'Ακτική, 'Αμφιλοχική, 'Αργολική, 'Αττική, Βαιτική (according to Arc. 107. 10 this is paroxytone), Βελγική, Κελτική, Μαγιστρική, Μαρμαρική, Μασσαβατική, Μεσαβατική, Μηδική (paroxytone according to Arc. 107. 10), 'Οδομαντική, 'Ομβρική, Πακτυική, Πρετ- τανική, Σαπαϊκή, Σινδική, Χαλκιδική (but Χαλκιδίκη, *a city*, Philop.), Λιμυρική, Τρωγλοδυτική, Βυλλιακή, Αἰζική. The accents of such words are greatly confused in the books ; editors would commit no grammatical sin if they made every one of them oxytone : see Lob. Prol. 326.

119. NOTE 2.—The city 'Ακη in Phœnicia is sometimes found oxytone, though this is contrary to the express declaration of St. Byz. and Arc. 106. 19 ; cf. E. M. 47. 25 ; Schol. Ven. O. 709.

'Αλωπεκή, Arc. 107. 5 : this is sometimes falsely written 'Αλωπέκη and 'Αλω- πεκῆ : 'Αριακή, H. *D.* : 'Ασκᾶ (?) Strab. 782 : Γάζακα (?) St. Byz. : 'Ιτάλικα, Strab. 141 : 'Ιταλική, Appian Hisp. c. 38 : 'Ιταλίκη, St. Byz.: Κόρσικα, Diod. Sic. 5. 13 ; Ptol. 3. 2. 1 : but Κορσική, St. Byz. : Λοῦκα, Ptol. 3. 1. 47, etc. : Μάλακα, Ptol. 2. 4. 7 ; Strab. 156 ; but Μαλάκη, St. Byz. ; Αὐτομάλακα (?) St. Byz. : 'Ολυκα (?) St. Byz. : Πετρόσακα (?) St. Byz. is written Πετροσάκα Paus. 8. 12. 4, and that is the correct accent : Σάλμυκα, St. Byz. : Σάρακα (?) St. Byz. ; Ptol. 6. 7. 41 ; 6. 2. 10 : Συκῆ, Thuc. 6. 98 ; also Συκή, Τυκή, and Τυκῆ, cf. Ahrens de dial. Gr. ling. 2. p. 64 : Συκαί, St. Byz. : Ταύακα, St. Byz. : Ψιττακή *πόλις παρὰ τῷ Τίγριδι ἐν ᾗ τὸ φυτὸν τῶν ψιττακίων*, Athen. 14. 649 C ; gravandum sine dubio [?] exemplo aliorum ejus- dem generis, Lob. Prol. 312.

Συκῆ, Athen. 78 B, and Φακῆ, Athen. 158 C, though female names, are not dis- tinguished by their accent from the corresponding common nouns.

-ΛΑ.

120. Substantives in λα, both proper and common, have the a short, and the accent is thrown back as far as possible, as ἄελλα, ἄμιλλα, ἀνάπαυλα, ἄσιλλα, βδέλλα, δίκελλα, θύελλα, παῦλα, ψύλλα ; 'Άκριλλα, 'Άνθυλλα, Βάλα, Βῶλα, Γέλα, 'Ίππολα, Νίκυλλα, Νῶλα, Πέλλα, Σίβυλλα, Σκύλλα, Τελέσιλλα ; except the Doric forms in λᾱ, which follow the accentuation of the corresponding forms in λη, as ἀλαλά=ἀλαλή, Φιλομήλα, σκανδάλα, ἀμβολά=ἀναβολή.

121. NOTE 1.—*Common Substantives.* Arc. 96. 14 : ἀβόλλα, *a cloak*, and 'Αβόλλα, a city of Sicily, St. Byz., are paroxytone, though the latter word is pro- paroxytone in Zonar. 8 : ἀκερσίλα, a Sicilian word=ἡ μυρσίνη, Hesych. : ἀλαλά, Herod. π. μ. λ. 39. 5 : ἀποκαλά, A. G. 315. 9 : ἀττύλλα, in Hesych. can hardly be

right : βωλά, Cretan = βουλή ; in Æolic βόλλα : γαβαλά = κεφαλή, Hesych. : δι-
σκέλλα is false, it should be δίσκελλα : εἶλα, Hesych., better εἴλη, H. *D.* : ἑλλά (?)
= ἕδρα, Hesych. : ζεῦγλα, Chœrob. C. 325. 23 ; also ζεύγλα and σδεύγλα ; on Θέκλα
see Chœrob. C. 324. 25 ; A. G. 1201 : θερμόπλα = η, Hesych. : ἰζέλα, Maced. = ἡ
ἀγαθὴ τύχη, Hesych. : on ἰσσέλα (?) Hesych., see H. D. s. v. ἰξαλῆ : the compounds of κόλλα seem to vary, but are generally paroxytone, as σαρκοκόλλα, πε-
τροκόλλα, ξηροκόλλα, Hesych., and ξηρόκολλα, λιθοκόλλα, ταυροκόλλα (?), ξυλο-
κόλλα, χρυσοκόλλα and η ; but χρυσόκολλα also occurs, e. g. Strab. 764, as well
as ἰχθυόκολλα, see Lob. Par. 369 ; ' χρυσοκόλλα, hoc accentu ap. Galen. vol. 13.
p. 130. 272. 738 (ubi etiam σαρκοκόλλα et ἰχθυοκόλλα), 754 ; genit. χρυσοκόλλης
Galen. p. 272, accus. χρυσοκόλλην, sed χρυσοκόλλαν, p. 287 ; recta scriptura,
Galeno aliisque medicis et Theophr. De lap. § 26. 40, restituenda est χρυσόκολλα,
χρυσοκόλλης, χρυσοκόλλῃ, χρυσόκολλαν, pariterque in aliis hujusmodi cum κόλλα
compositis,' W. *Dindorf* ap. H. D. tom. 8. p. 1736 D : ὀπισθοτίλα, see H. D. s. v. :
σκανδάλα = η, not σκανδαλά, as it is sometimes printed : Φιλομήλα, Chœrob. C.
324. 14, both as a proper name, and that of a fish.

122. NOTE 2.—*Proper Names.* Ἀγύλλα, St. Byz. s. v. Ἀβόλλα, is more correctly
written Ἄγυλλα in Strab. 220 and elsewhere, for the last syllable is short, Lycoph.
1355 : Ἀέρλαι, H. D. : Ἀθηλᾶ, cf. Lob. Aglaoph. 1. 548 ; H. D. : Ἀκίλα (?) Strab.
769 : Ἀμύκλα and Ἀμύκλαι, St. Byz. ; Paus. 3. 19. 6 : Ἀτέλλα, St. Byz. ; Ptol. 3.
1. 68 : Βαβίλα (?) Ptol. 5. 13. 17 : Βοῖλλαι (?) St. Byz. : Βουκεφάλα, St. Byz. :
(Εὐάσπλα (?) Arrian Anab. 4. 24. 1, is indeclinable) : Ἐχέτλα, St. Byz. is Ἔχετλα
in Diod. Sic. 20. 32 : Ἴλιπα (?) Ptol. 2. 4. 13, but Ἴλιπα, Strab. 141 : Καταγέλα,
Aristoph. Ach. 581 : Μεσόλα, St. Byz. : Προπάλαι, St. Byz. : Ῥεσάλα, St. Byz.
The following names of women are paroxytone, at least in the places indicated :
Ἀρχεβούλα : Κλεόλα, Schol. Eurip. Orest. 5 : Κριτύλλα, Aristoph. Thesm. 898 :
Λαινίλλα, Ælian H. A. 7. 15 : Suid. has Λαίνιλλα, without however explaining its
meaning ; H. D. understand it to be the name of an island spelled Λαίνιλα else-
where : Μυρτίλα, Zenob. 2. 84 ; cf. Lob. Prol. 120, who mentions besides these,
Αἰθίλλα, Μυρίλλα, Χρυσίλλα, Μαξιμίλλα, Πρισκίλλα ; probably all are wrong.

-ΛΗ.

123. Common substantives in λη with a diphthong in the
penultimate are oxytone, as ἀπειλή, αὐλή, βουλή, εὐλή, ὠφειλή ;
except paroxytone, δείλη, δούλη, εἴλη, ἐξούλη in the phrase
ἐξούλης δίκη, ζεύγλη, and οὐλή, *a scar.*

124. NOTE.—On these nouns see Chœrob. E. 16. 7 ; Eust. 1169. 34 ; E. M. 392.
50 ; Philem. Lex. p. 133. § 320 ; Schol. Ven. T. 26 : ἀείλη in Hesych. is seemingly corrupt : δείλη, Philem. § 320 ; Schol. Ven. T. 26 ; Theog. Can. 110. 32 :
δούλη, Chœrob. E. 16. 11 : εἴλη, E. M. 21. 39 ; εἴλη, Arc. 108. 18 ; cf. Theog. *l. l.* :
ζεύγλη, for this accent there seems to be no express authority ; but in the books it
is paroxytone : κοίλη is an adjective used substantively, Lob. Par. 333 : the
grammarians seem somewhat uncertain as to the accentuation of οὐλή ; οὐλή, *a
scar,* is unanimously said to be oxytone, Chœrob. E. 16. 10 ; Eust. 1169. 39 ; 133.
20 ; 1869. 23 ; Philem. Lex. p. 133. § 320 ; Arc. 108. 14 ; E. M. 640. 57 : οὐλή, as
applied to barley, is barytone according to Chœrob. E. 16. 10 ; Schol. Ven. T. 26 ;
E. M. 641. 36 ; oxytone according to Eust. 1169. 39 ; 133. 20 ; this variation
arises from a difference of opinion as to the origin of the word, see L. S. s. v. :
παστείλη, *the last day of the year,* E. M. 655. 48, is regular, if really a compound :
ταύλη or ταῦλα is the Byzantine mode of spelling τάβλα = *tabula.*

125. Words in ωλη and ολη are oxytone, as ἁμαρτωλή, γαμφωλή, εὐχωλή, θεραπωλή, μεμφωλή, παυσωλή, τερπωλή, χαριτωλή, ἀνα-στολή, ἀνατολή, βολή, ἐμπολή, προμολή, στολή, σχολή, χολή; except ἀπαιόλη, ἀσβόλη, ἐριώλη, and the contracted word κωλῆ.

126. NOTE.—See Arc. 109. 20 : ἐριωλή, *a hurricane*, is paroxytone in Arc. 109. 22 ; E. M. 375. 11 ; Eust. 918. 17 ; Theog. Can. 111. 28, *et alibi*, and such seems to be its proper accent, though others make it oxytone; see *L. S.* s. v.: κωλῆ = κωλέα, Athen. 368 D ; Herod. π. μ. λ. 6. 26 : ὀνοκώλη, a name of Empusa, is a feminine adjective from ὀνόκωλος : ἀβιόλη, Hesych. : ἀβόλη (?) Theog. Can. 111. 19 : ἀπαιόλη, Schol. Aristoph. Nub. 1314,'Aριστοφάνης [sc. Byzantius] δὲ ὀξύ-νεσθαί φησι τὴν ἐσχάτην, 'Απαιόλη : ἀσβόλη, Arc. 109. 13 : θερσόλη, Arc. 109. 13, its meaning is not known : τριβόλη, Theog. Can. 111. 10.

127. The remaining substantives in λη are paroxytone, as ἀγέλη, αἰθάλη, ἄλη, ἀνθήλη, ἀρβύλη, βασίλη, ζάλη, θυμέλη, κήλη, κίχλη, κοτύλη, μαρίλη, μύλη, μυστίλη, πάλη, *wrestling*, πύλη, σάλη, στήλη, στρέβλη, τρίγλη, τρώγλη, τύλη, φιάλη; except ἀλαλή, γαμφηλή, θηλή, θυηλή, κεφαλή, ὁμοκλή, ὁπλή, πιμελή, παλή, *meal*, σμειλή or σμιλή, σταφυλή, *a bunch of grapes*, φυλή, χηλή, which are oxytone, and the contracted words, ἀμυγδαλῆ, *an almond tree*, γαλῆ, (μυογαλῆ, μυγαλῆ), ἰξαλῆ, παρδαλῆ, perispomena.

128. NOTE.—'Αλάλη = ὁ θόρυβος, Arc. 108. 23 ; E. M. 55. 47 : ἀλαλή, Herod. π. μ. λ. 39. 5 ; Eust. 994. 57, and usage is in favour of this accent : ἀμυγδαλῆ, *an almond tree*, Herod. π. μ. λ. 6. 23 ; Arc. 108. 24 : ἀμυγδάλη, *an almond*, Ammon. p. 12 ; Athen. 52 F, ὅτι περὶ τῆς προφορᾶς τοῦ τόνου τῆς ἀμυγδάλης Πάμφιλος μὲν ἀξιοῖ ἐπὶ τοῦ καρποῦ βαρύνειν ὁμοίως τῷ ἀμυγδάλῳ· τὸ μέντοι δένδρον θέλει περισπᾶν ...'Αρίσταρχος δὲ καὶ τὸν καρπὸν καὶ τὸ δένδρον ὁμοίως προφέρεται κατ' ὀξεῖαν τάσιν. Φιλόξενος δ' ἀμφότερον περισπᾷ ... ἄλλοι δὲ ἀμυγδαλὰς ὡς καλάς, Τρύφων δὲ ἐν 'Αττικῇ προσῳδίᾳ ἀμυγδάλην μὲν τὸν καρπὸν βαρέως, ὃν ἡμεῖς οὐδετέρως ἀμύγδαλον λέγομεν, ἀμυγδαλῆ δὲ τὰ δένδρα κτητικοῦ παρὰ τὸν καρπὸν ὄντος τοῦ χαρακτῆρος καὶ διὰ τοῦτο περισπωμένου : ἁπλαῖ, an adjective used substantively, Lob. Par. 333 : αὐλῆ (?) Herod. ap. Herm. de emend. rat. Gr. gr. p. 304 : γαλῆ, and μυογαλῆ, Herod. π. μ. λ. 6. 23 ; Eust. 374. 41 ; Arc. 108. 6 : μυγαλῆ is also found under the forms μυγάλη, μυγαλή, Lob. Par. 378 : γαμφηλή, Schol. Ven. I. 220 ; Arc. 109. 5 : διπλῆ, an adjective used as a substantive : ἐπιβλή (?) Hesych. : ἐπιπλή, Ælian H. A. 14. 16, where Schneider reads ἐρίπνας for ἐπιπλάς : θηλή, Arc. 108. 11 ; Eust. 872. 17 : θυηλή, Arc. 109. 6 ; Schol. Ven. I. 220 ; Eust. 872. 17 : ἰξαλῆ, Eust. 450. 25 ; also ἰξάλη in Hippocr. and Galen : ἰσθλή (?) Hesych., a corrupt form of the same word : κερδαλῆ = ἔα, *a fox*, Lob. Par. 339 ; sometimes erroneously κερδάλη : κεφαλή, Herod. π. μ. λ. 39. 1 ; Arc. 108. 23 ; the various dialectic forms of this word are also oxytone, γαβαλά, Hesych. ; κεβαλή, κεβλή, Arc. 107. 26 ; but we find κέβλη in E. M. 498. 41 ; perhaps for κελή in Theog. Can. 110. 17 κεβλή should be read : κονθηλή (?) Hesych. : κορυδαλλή (?) *L. S.* : κυλλή (?) *L. S.* : κωλῆ, Theog. Can. 110. 25 : μαρίλη, E. M. 574. 29 ; Arc. 109. 8 ; μαριλή in A. G. Oxon. 2. 259 is a mere MS. or typographical error; cf. A. G. Oxon. 2. 111. 11 : ξυλή (?) Jo. Damasc. vol. 1. p. 57 D ; *H. D.* : ὁμοκλή, Arc. 107. 25 ; A. G. Oxon. 1. 328. 6 : ὁπλή, Arc. 107. 25 : παλή, *meal*, Schol. Ven. K. 7, yet it always seems to be paroxytone in our books, the distinction between it and πάλη, *wrestling*, Arc. 108. 4, is probably an invention of the grammarians : παρδαλῆ = έη (sc. δορά),

Eust. 450: πιμελή, Arc. 109. 2 ; St. Byz. s. v. Ἀγγελή, E. M.672. 21: σμειλή, Arc. 108. 19, or σμιλή, Theog. Can. 110. 33, is always paroxytone in MSS. and our editions: σταφυλή, *a bunch of grapes*; Ptolemæus Ascalonites and Heraclides condemned this, the common accent, Eust. 341. 35 : ἀγριοσταφύλη is a false accent for ἀγριοστα-φυλή : σταφύλη, *a plummet*, Ammon. p. 124 ; Arc. 109. 17 ; Schol. Ven. B. 765: τυφλή, H. *D.* : φυλή, Herod. π. μ. λ. 39. 12 : χηλή, Arc. 108. 10; Eust. 872. 17 ; in Theog. Can. 110. 21 it is written as a proper name : χιλή (?) Suid. ; A. G. Oxon. 2. 276. 23 : ψωλή, Aristoph. Av. 560 etc. is the corresponding feminine to ψωλός, used substantively.

129. Proper names in λη are paroxytone, as Ἀγχιάλη, Ἀμύκλαι, Ἕλλη, Ζάγκλη, Θερμοπύλαι, Θούλη, Καβύλη, Μυκάλη, Ῥακώλη, Σεμέλη, Σταφύλη, Στρογγύλη, Ὕβλη ; except the demes Ἀγγελή, Ἀγρυλή, or Ἀγραυλή, Ἀγκυλή, Ἁλή, Κεφαλή, Πεντελή, Φυλή, and Αὐλαί, Ἐπιπολαί, Καλαί, Κεφαλαί, Φιλαί.

130. Note.—Ἀβιλή, Joseph. Ant. J. 4. 8. 1 ; H. *D.* : Ἀγγελή, St. Byz. ; Arc. 109. 3, is falsely Ἀγγέλη in A. G. 335. 20 : Ἀγκυλή, Arc. 109. 19; wrongly Ἀγ-κύλη in A. G. 338. 12 : Ἀγραυλή, St. Byz. : Ἀγρυλή, Arc. 106. 19; in A. G. 332. 30 it is wrongly paroxytone : Ἁλή, Arc. 108. 5, and Ἁλαί, names of demes, St. Byz., sometimes wrongly written Ἀλαί or Ἄλαι : Ἀλαί in Bœotia and Ἀλή, St. Byz. : Ἀπαιόλη, according to Aristophanes Byz. ap. Schol. Aristoph. Nub. 1134, should be Ἀπαιολή : Αὐλαί, St. Byz. : Ἐπιπολαί, Thucyd. 6. 91 ; St. Byz. : Κα-λαί, Apion and Herodorus ap. Eust. 267. 2 : Κεφαλή, Herod. π.μ.λ.39.5 ; St. Byz. s. v. Ἀγγελή: Κεφαλαί, Ptol. 4. 3. 13 : Κονθύλη, a deme, Schol. Aristoph. Vesp. 233 : Μυλαί, St. Byz. is also paroxytone, e. g. Strab. 266 ; ʽΜύλας, ap. Strab. 6. p. 266. ut ap. Theophr. H. Pl. 8. 2. 8 ; Μυλαῖς, 272, Thuc. 3. 90, rursus Μύλας, Diod. 14.87 ; 19. 65 ; Exc. p. 499. 2 ;ʼ H. *D.* : Παλή is quoted by *H. D.* from Schol. Thucyd. 1. 27, where in Didot's edition Πάλη is rightly printed : Πεντελή, St. Byz. s. v. Ἀγγελή, Arc. 109. 3 : the deme Σφενδαλή is falsely written Σφενδάλη in St. Byz. ; Hesych. : Φιλαί, Strab. 818, is generally paroxytone ; in Ptol. 4. 5. 74 we have Φιλαί (ἡ Φίλαι): Φυλή, Strab. 404, etc. : Χηλαί is also written Χῆλαι.

-MA and -MH.

131. Common substantives in μη are oxytone, as αἰχμή, ἀκμή, ἀνατομή, ἀϋτμή, γραμμή, διαδρομή, δρομή, δυσμή, ἐφετμή, νομή, ὀδμή, ὁρμή, πυγμή, στιγμή, τιμή ; except paroxytone, 1. those in ημη, ῡμη, ωμη, as ἐπιστήμη, κνήμη, μνήμη, φήμη, ζύμη, λύμη, ῥύμη, τρύμη, γνώμη· κώμη, ῥώμη ; 2. those in ἀμη, as ἄμη, θαλάμη, παλάμη, πυράμη, yet σπιθαμή is oxytone ; 3. ἅλμη, βρίμη, δέσμη (?), εἰσίθμη, θέρμη, κόμη, λόχμη, μάμμη (and α), οἴμη, πάρμη, πλή-σμη, (πλήμμη), στάθμη, τόλμη (and α), τόρμη (and α), χάρμη, χάσμη, χραίσμη, ψάμμη ; 4. the contracted word σησαμῆ, which is perispomenon.

Οἰκοδομή and διοικοδομή are oxytone.

132. Note 1.—Ἅλμη (ὀξάλμη), Arc. 110. 1 ; Lob. Par. 396 quotes ἀλμή from Lucian Gall. c. 23, where however Jacobitz reads ἄλμη : ἀνέμη, Soph. Gloss. s. v. :

ἄρμη, or ἅρμη, ἀρμή, or ἄρμα; see L. S. s. vv. and Lob. Par. 396: βάθμη, H. *D.*: βλίμη, Hesych.: βρίμη, E. M. 214. 12: δεσμή, Arc. 109. 25, according to Lob. Par. 396, this word is more frequently paroxytone; ἀναδέσμη is never oxytone, Arc. 103. 3; στηθοδέσμη, E. M. 749. 44: δοχμή, Aristarchus, δόχμη, Trypho, Eust. 1291. 43: δακτυλοδόχμη, Pollux 2. 157: δυθμή (or δύθμη?) Lob. Par. 395: εἰσίθμη, Schol. Ambros. Odyss. Z. 264, and εἰσίσθμη: ἐπιλήσμη, Schol. Aristoph. Nub. 780: ἐρίμη or ἑρμή (?) see H. D. s. v.: θέρμη and θέρμα, Lob. Phryn. 331; Theog. Can. 112. 5: ἰάσμη, *L. S.*: ἴθμη, Lob. Par. 395: ἵκμη, Theoph. H. P. 4. 11; H. *D.*: ἴσμη, Lob. Par. 395: ἐξίσμη, Hesych.; κοίμη (?) Theog. Can. 112. 13: κόμη, Arc. 110. 11: λόκμη or λόκη (?) see H. D. s. v.: λόχμη, Eust. 896. 60; Theog. Can. 112. 4: μεσόδμη, as a compound, is regular: for ξυσμή, ξύσμη also occurs, but is probably a mistake: οἰκοδομή, Lob. Phryn. 490: οἴμη, Theog. Can. 112. 15: πάλμη=*palma*, Hesych.: πλήσμη, Hesiod. Frag. 25; *L. S.*; also πλήμη or πλήμμη: σησαμή, Arc. 110. 7; Herod. π. μ. λ. 7. 1; this is not uncommonly found paroxytone, though, according to Photius, Aristarchus made it perispomenon: σίμη, Hesych. s. v. Ἀπεσίμωσε, is probably wrong: σκάλμη, Arc. 110. 2, is oxytone in the text of Pollux 10. 165: σπιθαμή, Arc. 110. 7: στάθμη, Schol. Ambros. Odyss. Z. 264, and κρεοστάθμη: τόλμη (and τόλμα), Arc. 110. 2; A. G. Oxon. 2. 417. 19: τόρμη, Hesych.: χάρμη, Arc. 110. 2: χάσμη, Arc. 109. 26: χραίσμη, Nicaud. Ther. 583: χρόμη (?) Hesych.: ψάμμη (and ψάμμα), Æschyl. Prom. 573.

133. NOTE 2.—According to Pape (Etymolog. Wörterb. d. Gr. Spr. p. 34) μάμμα and τόλμα are the only words in μα belonging to the First Declension, all others so called are neuters of the Third; but this seems hardly to be in accordance with the facts.

A distinction is drawn between θαλαμαί=τὸ τῶν Διοσκούρων ἱερόν, and θαλάμαι=αἱ καταδύσεις, Trypho ap. Ammon. p. 68; Eust. 1541. 47; and Ælius Dionysius ap. Eust. 906. 50.

134. Proper names in μα and μη are paroxytone, as Ἀριστοδάμα, Ἀρτακάμα, Αὐτοκόμα, Διοτίμα, Σεγεσάμα, Γράμμη, Εὐρυνόμη, Θαλάμαι, Θέρμαι, Ἰθώμη, Καλάμαι, Κύμη, Οἰσύμη, Σάμη, Σύμη· Τίμη, Διδύμη, one of the Liparean isles, St. Byz.; but Διδυμή, a village in Cilicia, is oxytone, as is expressly stated by St. Byz.

NOTE.—Ἱεραμαί, St. Byz.: Σίδυμα (?) St. Byz.

-NA.

135. Substantives in να have that syllable short, and retract the accent, as ἄμυνα, γέννα, δέσποινα, εὔθυνα, θέαινα, θεράπαινα, λέαινα, λύκαινα, μάραγνα, μέριμνα, μύραινα, πεῖνα, τρίαινα, χλαῖνα; except Doric forms in ᾱ=η, as δυσελένα, διθυραμβοχῶνα, μυρρίνα (?), γαλάνα, σελάνα, and ἡμίνα.

136. NOTE.—Ἀγρεῖφνα, Analect. Brunck 2. p. 53; Zonar. 29, should probably be written ἄγρειφνα: ἀθερίνᾱ=η: ἀμάνα (?) Hesych.: δολάνᾱ (?) Hesych.: ἐρίπνα=η: εὐθυκαίνα (?) Hesych.: on κατακόνα see L. S. s. v.: κυδάνα (?) Hesych.: μαγγάνα, Suid.: according to Schol. Eurip. Rhes. 817, Herodian made μάραγνα paroxytone, it is however proparoxytone in Eurip. *l. l.* and elsewhere ; Hesych. has σμαράγνα : μεμβράνα (?) N. T. : μνᾶ, Arc. 96. 24 : ὀθόννα or ὀθύννα, see H. D. s. v. : ὀξίνα, Hesych. : πῆνα, Hesych. : πισάκνα = πιθάκνη, H. *D.* : σκανά, Dor. = σκηνή : σπαρτίνα or σπαρτίνη is an adjective used substantively, Eust. 191. 33 : σωωδίνα, an epithet of Athene, see L. S. s. v. : ὑρτάνα (?) Hesych. ; Lob. Prol. 175 ; for χαύνα, a kind of fish, χάννα or χάννη is now read : ὡράνα is corrupt in Hesych., ὦ 'ράννα is suggested.

137. Proper names in *να* follow the same rule as common nouns, e. g. Ἄρνα, Ἔρινα, Ἔρκυννα, Κέρκιννα, Κίκυννα, Κόριννα, Λοῦνα, Μέθανα ; except Latin names in *ῖνα*, which are properispomena, as Ἰουστῖνα, Κωνσταντῖνα, Σαβῖνα, Φαυστῖνα, together with Ἀκυλῖνα, St. Byz., a city in Illyria, and Τερῖνα, a city, Strab. 256.

Ἀθηνᾶ is contracted from Ἀθηνάα, like Δανᾶ for Δανάη in Hecatæus ap. Herod. π. μ. λ. 8. 1.

138. NOTE 1.—Ἀθηνᾶ, Arc. 96. 24 : Αἰνιάνα (?) Strab. 508 ; Ἀνθάνα, St. Byz. : Ἀρδουέννα, Strab. 194 : Ἀρήνα, St. Byz. : Ἅρπινα is expressly said to be proparoxytone, Theog. Can. 100. 32, yet it is written Ἀρπίνα in Chœroboscus ap. A. G. Oxon. 2. 171. 10, and Ἀρπῖνα (*sic*), A. G. Oxon. 2. 298. 7 ; cf. Lob. Prol. 222 : Ἀτάρνα, St. Byz. : Ἄφιδνα is according to St. Byz. Ἀφίδναι in the plural : Ἀχάρνα, Herodian ap. St. Byz. ; the derivatives imply an oxytone, as Ἀχαρνῆθεν, etc., Göttling suggests Ἀχάρνη : Ἀχραδινά, St. Byz., is doubtful both as to quantity and to accent : Ἀχραδίνη is preferred by Lob. Prol. 218 : Βαρβασάνα (?) or Καρβασάνα (?) Ptol. 6. 17. 6 : Βαρβοράνα (?) Ptol. 7. 1. 43 : Βέλβινα expressly said to be proparoxytone, Theog. Can. 100. 32, is also found paroxytone : Γοργόνα, Lucian Mer. Dial. 1. 1 : Ἑλένα = Ἑλένη, Theog. Can. 99. 20 : Ἐλευθέρνα, St. Byz. : Ζαρίνα (?) Diod. Sic. 2. 34 : Ἱεράνα, Schol. Apollon. Rhod. 1. 471 : Ἰστριανά, St. Byz. : Καισήνα, Strab. 217, is Καίσανα in Ptol. 3. 1. 46 : Καλύμνα, Eust. 319. 28, is Κάλυμνα in Strab. 489, and St. Byz. : Καπίννα (Καπίνναι ?) St. Byz. : Καπουτάνα (?) Ptol. 6. 17. 6 : Κρώμνα, E. M. 541. 34, should be Κρῶμνα : Μολυβδάνα, ανη, St. Byz. : Μυρίννα (?) E. M. 595. 24, false for Μύρινα or Μυρίνη ; Theog. Can. 101. 1 : Οἴνα (?) St. Byz. : in Arist. Ausc. Mirab. 94 it is Οἰναρέα : Ῥέσινα, St. Byz. : Σήνα or Σήνη, Strab. 285 ; Arc. 111. 12 : Σινά is barbarous and indeclinable, Chœrob. E. 153. 27 : Σκοτινά, St. Byz. : Ταρρακινά (?) St. Byz. : Τερῖνα is proparoxytone in St. Byz. : Φαέννᾱ, a woman's name, Paus. 3. 18. 6 ; 9. 35. 1.

139. NOTE 2.—Many of these names are misaccented in Pape's Lexicon, e. g. Ἐρκύνα for Ἔρκυνα, Paus. 9. 39. 2 : Ἰντεράμνα for Ἰντέραμνα, Strab. 227 : Καλασάρνα for Καλάσαρνα, Strab. 254 : Κοτίννα for Κότιννα : Λικύμνα for Λίκυμνα, Strab. 373 : Μυρίνα for Μύρινα, Strab. 550. 573 ; St. Byz. ; Theog. Can. 101. 1 ; Lob. Prol. 280 : Χαροπείνα for Χαρόπεινα : Χριστίνα for Χριστῖνα ; the last mentioned name occurs, it is true, as a paroxytone in Chœrob. E. 139. 31, but that is the only one instance out of many of a practice common enough ; the scribes frequently substitute the acute for the circumflex : for Περπερήνα, which Göttling mentions, Περπερήνη, or ηνή, is now read in Strab. 607.

-NH.

140. Common substantives in νη are paroxytone, as αἰσχύνη, ἀνεμώνη· ἀπήνη, ἀράχνη, ἀρτάνη, βοτάνη, γαλήνη, δαπάνη, δάφνη, δικαιοσύνη, δίνη, δουλοσύνη, εἰρήνη, ζώνη, ἡρωΐνη, θοίνη, κλίνη, κορώνη, κρήνη, λεκάνη, μνημοσύνη, ὀδύνη, πλάνη, ῥαστώνη, τέχνη, τιθήνη, φήνη, ὠλένη; except oxytone, 1. abstract words in ονη, as γονή (which is also oxytone as a concrete), ἡδονή, καλλονή, μονή, πεισμονή, πημονή, πλησμονή, φονή (εὐφρόνη however and σωφρόνη are barytone); examples of concrete substantives are, ἀκόνη, ἁρπεδόνη, ἡγεμόνη, ὀθόνη, περόνη, σφενδόνη; and 2. γυνή, δεξαμενή, εἰαμενή, εὐνή, μενοινή, μηχανή, ποινή, σκηνή, στρωμνή, φανή, φερνή, φωνή, ὠνή.

141. NOTE 1.—*Words in* ονη. Philem. Lex. p. 17. § 46; E. M. 194. 47; Theog. Can. 115. 5; A. G. Oxon. 2. 385. 7: αὐονή (αὐονά Dor.) is paroxytone in E. M. 170. 45; 171. 52: ἀγχονή=ἄγξις is distinguished by the grammarians from ἀγχόνη, a rope, Philem. Lex. p. 17. § 46; E. M. 194. 50; Zonar. 28; Schol. Aristoph. Acharn. 125; the distinction however is not generally observed in MSS, see Fix ap. H. D. s. v.; the compounds of γονή or γονός are irregular, ἀπογονή and ἐπιγονή are oxytone, ἐγγόνη, δισεγγόνη, τριτεγγόνη, and προγόνη paroxytone; at least such seems to be their accentuation in our editions; the difference of meaning probably determines this variation: εὐφρόνη, Arc. 102. 6: δυσφρόνη (?) see H. D. s. v.: σωφρόνη, Arc. 102. 6; E. M. 87. 38, seems only to occur as a proper name, e. g. Aristænet. Ep. 1. 6. p. 20.

142. NOTE 2.—'Αμνή is once or twice paroxytone; MS. authority is for the former accent: ἄνη, Arc. 110. 26: βακτριανή (sc. camel), Lob. Par. 331: βαρακινή, Hesych.: βουκανή, ἀνεμώνη τὸ ἄνθος· Κύπριοι, Hesych.: βωληνή, βολωνή, or βωλινή, *a kind of vine*, Geopon. 5. 17. 5; H. D.: γανή=γυνή, see H. D. s. v.: the Doric (or Sicilian) γάνα is paroxytone in Greg. Cor. p. 345, as is the Bœotian βάννα, Hesych. or βάνα in Herod. π. μ. λ. 18. 25; though it might perhaps be inferred that Herodian considered it to be oxytone, as it is written in Apoll. de Pron. 65. 2: γενή=γενεά, E. M. 225. 23: γεντιανή is an adjective; if not one it ought to be paroxytone by Herodian's rule in π. μ. λ. 18. 18: γυνή, Arc. 112. 16; for the accentuation of the oblique cases γυναικός, γυναικί, etc. see the rules for the Third Declension: δεξαμενή, Arc. 111. 9: E. M. 328. 13: εἰαμενή, Arc. E. M. *l. l.*; in Hesych. it is wrongly ἰαμενή: εὐνή, Arc. 111. 4: ἐχινή=ἐχινέα, Arc. 112. 3; Theog. Can. 114. 3: θανή (?) Theod. Prodr. p. 221; H. D.; cf. Lob. Rhem. 259: κεστιανή (sc. βάλανος); Aetii Serm. 8. 73; H. D.: κυνή=κυνέη: ληνή or ληναί for Λῆναι is probably, or even certainly wrong, see H. D. s. v.: μαξινή (?) Hesych.: μενοινή, Theogn. Can. 114. 17: μηχανή, Herod. π. μ. λ. 18. 18; Arc. 111. 2: μυσάχνη, Eust. 575. 32, Suid., is the feminine of μυσαχνός, and is oxytone in Hesych.: νή=νέα, Aristoph. ap. Herod. π. μ. λ. 7. 9: παιδνή, Anth. Pal. 2. 410: Göttling, Accent. p. 156, quotes Schol. Ven. Ω. 315 to prove that πόρνη is oxytone; the passage does not prove it, and the word is undoubtedly paroxytone; cf. Herod. π. μ. λ. 33. 29: περγαμηνή (sc. χάρτα), Suid. etc.: ποινή, Arc. 112. 7; Theog. Can. 114. 8: προχανή is false for προχάνη, Lob. Rhem. 265: ῥινή, *a file*, Arc. 111. 24; Theog. Can. 113. 8; Chœrob. ap. A. G. Oxon. 2. 255. 6: ῥίνη, *a shark*, Arc. *l. l.*: but this distinction is not observed in our editions; in both senses the word is paroxytone: σκηνή, Herod.

π. μ. λ. 16. 30; Arc. III. 13 : στενή (sc. ὁδός), Thucyd. 2. 99, quoted by Lob. Par. 361 : στρωμνή, Theog. Can. 115. 9; A. G. Oxon. 1. 48. 12 : ὑννή, *a ploughshare,* Hesych., but ὕννη is better : φανή, Herod. π. μ. λ. 18. 22, not unfrequently found paroxytone, but wrongly : φερνή, Herod. π. μ. λ. 33. 29; Arc. 113. 23 = προίξ, Suid. ; E. M. 790. 45 ; others have this paroxytone, Zonar. 1802 ; ‘Apud Suidam Φερνή, προίξ· et Φέρνη, ἀμοιβή : sed codex Leid. utrobique Φέρνη, qui accentus etiam in locis scriptorum passim invenitur,’ H. D. : φωνή, Arc. 112. 21 ; Chœrob. E. 100. 2 : ὠνή, Arc. 112. 21 ; Chœrob. E. 100. 2.

143. Proper names in νη are paroxytone, as Αἴτνη. Ἀλκυόνη, Ἀντιγόνη, Βύνη, Δωδώνη· Ἑλένη, Ἑρμιόνη, Ἡλώνη, Ἰσμήνη, Ἰτώνη, Καρίνη, Κλυμένη, Κυρήνη, Λέρνη, Μιτυλήνη, Πελλήνη, Πέρνη, Πριήνη, Ῥήνη, Σάνη, Σήνη, Φρύνη. Names of countries or nations in ᾱνη and ηνη, and plural names of towns and places are for the most part oxytone, as Ἀκεσαμεναί, Ἀλκομεναί, Θεναί (cf. Schmidt ad Arc. 111), Κελαιναί, Κλεωναί, Arc. 112. 26 (but Κλεώνη, cf. Eust. 291. 4), Κλαζομεναί, Κολωναί, Μολωναί ; Ἀραξηνή, Ἀραρηνή, Ἀρζανηνή, Γαβιανή, Γαβιηνή, Κασπιανή, Μαργιανή, Ματιανή, Σαιδηνή, Σουσιανή ; but there are many exceptions to this rule.

144. NOTE 1.—*Plural Names of Towns which are baryfone.* Ἀθῆναι, *passim* : Ἄκκαναι, St. Byz. : Ἀκόναι, St. Byz. : Ἄντεμναι (?) ‘ap. Strab. 230 Ἄντεμναι certe scribendum pro Ἀντέμναι,’ H. D. : Ἀφάνναι (?) St. Byz. : Ἀφίδναι, St. Byz. : Ἀχαρναί is oxytone, though Ἀχάρνα is paroxytone in St. Byz., where Göttling conjectures Ἀχάρνη : Ἄχναι, St. Byz. : Ἀχραδινή, St. Byz. : Βάτναι, St. Byz. : Ἐχῖναι, St. Byz. : Θεράπναι, Strab. 409 : Ἰσχναί (?) A. G. Oxon. 1. 48. 13 : Ἴχναι in Thessaly, Strab. 435 ; and in Macedonia, St. Byz. : Καλύδναι, Eust. 319. 28 ; E. M. 486. 28 : Κάναι, Strab. 446 ; 615 : Κανή and Καναί τῆς Αἰολίδος ἄκρα, St. Byz. : Κάνναι = *Cannœ*, Strab. 285 ; Κασμέναι, Thucyd. 6. 5 : Κορβρῆναι, Polyh. 5. 44. 7 : Κολωναί, Xenoph. Hell. 3. 1. 13, is Κολῶναι in Paus. 10. 14. 1 : Κρῆναι, Thucyd. 3. 106, etc. : Λίμναι, Strab. 363 : the Arcadian Μέλαιναι (Μελαινεαί, Paus. 8. 3. 3), is distinguished by St. Byz. from the Lycian Μελαιναί : Μελαιναί in the Troad is oxytone in Strab. 603 : Μιντούρναι, Strab. 233 : Μυκῆναι, *passim* : Πότναι, Eust. 269. 34 : Σῖναι, St. Byz., or Σῖναι, Ptol. 7. 3. 6 : Ταμύναι or Ταμύνη, Arc. 194. 2 : Τελλῆναι, Strab. 231 : Τυρακῖναι, St. Byz. : Φάναι, Strab. 645, is oxytone in Aristoph. Av. 1692, and in some copies of Thucyd. 8. 24 ; H. D. : Φιδῆναι, Strab. 230.

145. NOTE 2.—The names of countries and nations in ανη and ηνη are strictly adjectives, and as such they generally retain the adjectival accent, yet the following are exceptions to the rule, Ἀδιαβήνη, Suid. : Αἰαμήνη (?) St. Byz. : Μεσσήνη, Theog. Can. 113. 13 : Χωρήνη, Strab. 514, for which H. D. have Χωρηνή. Cities of this termination are regular, as Ἀνθήνη, elsewhere Ἀνθηνή, Lob. Prol. 195, Ἀρήνη, Ἀρμήνη, Ἀτρήνη, Καρήνη, Κισθήνη, Κυδρήνη, Κυλλήνη (mountain and town), Κυρήνη, Κοδρομήνη (Κοδρομηνή in Theog. Can. 113. 21), Μαλήνη, Μεσσήνη, Μιτυλήνη or Μυτιλήνη, Μυκήνη and Μυκῆναι, Παλλήνη, Πειρήνη, Πελλήνη, Πριήνη, Πυλήνη, Πυρήνη, Συήνη, Τελλήνη, Φιδήνη, etc. The following are irregular, Ἀθμονή, a deme, for which St. Byz. has Ἀθμόνη : Αἰανή, St. Byz. : Αἰξωνή, a deme, St. Byz. s. v. ; Arc. 112. 26: Ἀκραιβατηνή, besides being variable in its accent, is written nine or ten different ways, see Fix ap. H. D. s. v. : Ἀρσηνή, a lake, Strab. 529 : Ἀχριανή, St. Byz. : Γερμηνή, Arc. III. 17, τὸ δὲ Γερμηνή ἡ συνήθεια ὀξύνει: Εἰδομένη, Thucyd. 2. 100, is falsely oxytone in St. Byz: Κυανή (sc. πηγή), Diod. Sic. 5. 4, is Κυανῇ in Ælian V. H. 2. 33: Κυανῇ (sc. λίμνη), Strab. 529: Κυνή, a city, St. Byz.: Μαντιανή, a lake, Strab. 529; Μελητηνή (?) a city, Theog. Can. 113. 21 is Μελιτηνή in St. Byz.: Ὀλανή, Strab. 529: Παταληνή, Eust. ad Dion. Per. 1093, πόλις ἀξιόλογος τὰ Πάταλα, ἀφ' ὧν ἡ νῆσος Παταληνὴ ὀξυτόνως, ὡς οἱ ἀκριβεῖς λέγουσι· τινὲς δὲ καὶ βαρυτόνως Παταλήνην ὡς Πριήνην ἀναγινώσκουσιν: Σιβερηνή, St. Byz.: Συρβανή, an island, St. Byz.; cf. Lob. Prol. 195 sqq., who, after enumerating a large number of irregular accents, at last says, 'ceterum in hoc universo genere librariorum inconstantia tanta est ut sæpe idem nomen diversos habeat accentus.'

Σιπυληνή, as an epithet of Demeter, is oxytone, Theog. Can. 113. 22, though Διδυμήνη is paroxytone, Arc. 111. 21.

146. NOTE 3.—*Female Names.* The following irregular female names are quoted by Pape, Ἀζωνή (Arc. 112. 26), Δαμιανή, Εἰδομενή, Ἐλλαμενή, Ἑρμιανή (?), Κελαινή, Ælian V.H. 3.42: Κυανή, which he cites from Ælian V. H. 2. 33, is there Κυανῇ, and is the name of a fountain; the woman's name Κυάνη is expressly declared to be paroxytone by Arc. 110. 26, though it is Κυανή in Plat. Theag. 125 E; but there cod. Clark. reads Κυάνη, which has been adopted by Stallbaum; Ποθεινή, Athen. 576 F: Ῥαδινή (?) is paroxytone in Strab. 347; Paus. 7. 5. 13: Φοιβιανή: Φωτεινή, E. M. 276. 53. Probably some, if not all of these, should be barytone, though Theog. Can. 153. 6 seems to assert that all in μενη are oxytone, and so some wrote Δεξαμενή, to distinguish it from the feminine participle δεξαμένη, but properly it is paroxytone, S. V. Σ. 44.

-ΞΑ and -ΞΗ.

147. Those in ξα have the final α short and retract the accent, those in ξη are paroxytone, as ἅμαξα, δόξα, μύξα, αὔξη, ἐπαύξη (Plat. de Legg. 815 E), Ἅμαξα, Ἄραξα, Λίξα, Φρίξα.

148. NOTE.—Αὐτοδόξα, Arist. Top. 8. 11. 14, not αὐτόδοξα: it may be doubted whether a Greek grammarian would consider it a synthetic compound. It seems to have been a question whether αὔξη should be paroxytone or perispomenon, Herodian ap. Herm. de emend. rat. Gr. gr. p. 304 decides for the former accent; Theognostus ap. A. G. 1347, on the contrary, says that Herodian made it *oxytone*, cf. Arc. 96; 113; Theog. Can. 116. 5: ἐρπυξή, Diosc. 3. 73; H. D.

-ΟΑ and -ΟΗ.

149. All words in οα and οη are paroxytone, except those in οα = οη, which follow the accent of the latter form; as ἀλόη, ζόη, ὄα, πόα, πόη, πτόα, ῥόα, *a pomegranate*, χλόη, χνόη, χρόα, Ἀρσινόη, Βερόη, Γενόα, Θεισόα, Paus. 8. 27. 4, Θόη, Λυκόα, Paus. 8. 3. 4, Μερόη, Μεσόα, Οἰνόη, Χωλόη; except oxytone, στοά, ἀκοή, βοή, πνοή (and πνοά?), ῥοή, ῥοά, χοή.

150. NOTE 1.—*Exceptions in* οα. See E. M. 705. 1; Arc. 100. 11: ἐπχροά (?) Athen. 42.E; Lob. Phryn. 495; but ἐπίχροια is quoted from Clem. Alex. Strom. 6. p. 792: ῥοά=ῥοή, *stream*: ῥόα=ῥοιά, Eust. 94. 4, *pomegranate*, is oxytone according to Arc. 100. 14; but he is doubtless mistaken, or the epitomator has not copied Herodian correctly: στοά, Arc. 100. 13, also στοιά.

Exceptions in οη. 'Ἀκοή, Arc. 103. 21 : βοή, Arc. 103. 19 ; E. M. 202. 35 ; Choerob. E. 113. 1, but βοῆ = βοέα, Theog. Can. 108. 9 : κοροή in Hesych. is probably corrupt : πνοή, Arc. 103. 20 ; E. M. 202. 35 ; ῥοή, Eust. 94. 30 ; χοή, Arc. 103. 18 ; E. M. 202. 35.

The dialectic form βούόα = βουσόα (cf. μᾶά = μοῦσα) in E. M. 391. 19 is curious.

151. Note 2.—The compounds of these words follow the general rule, e. g. ἱστοβόη, ἀναπνοή, παλιμπνόη (H. D. are mistaken in saying that this should be oxytone), ἀπορροή, διαρροή, διαρροά, ὑδρορρόη (Arc. 102. 21, τὸ ὑδρορρόη οἱ παλαιοὶ ἐβάρυναν, οἱ δὲ μεταγενέστεροι ὀξύνουσιν οὐχ ὑγιῶς), καλλιρρόη, θερμορρόη : yet it is expressly stated by Eust. 992. 57 (and perhaps by Arc. 103. 2, though the MSS. there read either ἀναρρώη and ἀναρώη), that ἀναρρόη is barytone contrary to rule : Göttling (Accent. p. 148) is quite mistaken when he says that the same thing is asserted by S. V. Ξ. 372, the passage runs as follows, βαρυντέον τὸ παναίθησι· τὰ γὰρ εἰς Η λήγοντα θηλυκὰ δισύλλαβα ὀξυνόμενα ἐν τῇ συνθέσει μὴ γινόμενα κύρια, τότε μὲν φυλάσσει τὸν τόνον ὅταν μετὰ προθέσεως συντίθηται, ὡς τὸ ἀνατολή· εἰ δὲ μετὰ ἄλλου τινός, ἀναβιβάζει τὸν τόνον, ἱστοδόκη, καπνοδόκη, ὥστε καὶ τὸ ὑδρορρόη παρὰ Ἀττικοῖς ἀναλόγως βαρύνεται, τὸ δὲ ἀναρροή ὀξύνεται : ὁμορροή is altogether false, see H. D. s. v.: δακρυρροή, quoted by H. D. from Epiph. t. 2. p. 197 A. is certainly an error, and εὐροή, Aret. p. 100, H. D. is very doubtful : ἀναχοή οἰνοχόη, τυμβοχόη (Schol. Ven. Φ. 323), πλημοχόη, ὑδροχόη are conformable to the rule : τυμβοχόη is sometimes falsely oxytone, Lob. Phryn. 498, and a distinction is occasionally drawn between προχοή, *outlet, mouth of a river*, E. M. 692. 52 ; Suid. ; and προχόη, *a pitcher*, Anth. Pal. 6. 292. 6 ; but they are frequently confounded in MSS.

152. Note 3.—*Exceptional Proper Names.* Ἀγχόη, as the name of a place, occurs in Strab. 406, but the plural is Ἀγχοαί in Hesych.: Μεσσόα (or Μεσόα), Strab. 364, is wrongly Μέσσοα in St. Byz.

-ΠΑ and -ΠΗ.

153. Words in πα and πη are paroxytone, as ἀγάπη, ἅρπη, κάπη, λύπη, πόρπη, σκέπη ; except those in οπη and ωπη, which are oxytone (but κερκώπη, κώπη, λώπη), as ἀστεροπή, ἐνωπή, ἐσωπή, κλοπή, κοπή, ὀπή, ὀπωπή, περιωπή, ῥοπή, σιωπή, σκοπή, τροπή, together with ἀστραπή, ἐνιπή· καμπή = κάμψις (but κάμπη, *a worm*, is paroxytone), μολπή, πομπή, ῥιπή, τυπή.

154. Note.—Ἀζαπᾶ· πτισάνη, Hesych.: αἰγιλώπη (?) or αἰγυλώπη, H. D.: ἀλωπά (?) Hesych.: ἀστραπή, Arc. 113. 15: βορβορόπη, Lob. Par. 466, as a compound of βόρβορος and ὀπή is regular ; another form of the same word is βορβορόκη, Arc. 107. 6 : γύπη is probably better than γυπή, Theog. Can. 116. 24 : διόπη, *an ear-ring*, is regular, the syllable δι not being the preposition διά : ἐνιπή, Arc. 113. 16 : ἐνοπή = φωνή, Arc. 113. 15 ; but Ἐνοπή, a town, Theog. Can. 116. 16, or Ἐνόπη and ἐνόπη, *an ear-ring*, Eust. 743. 16 : κάμπη = τὸ ὄρος καὶ σκώληξ, Arc. 113. 8 ; E. M. 488. 33 ; in Aristoph. Pac. 870, some books have κάμπαις for καμπαῖς, but the latter is right : κώπη, Theog. Can. 116. 31 : λαμπή (?) or λάμπη, Lob. Rhem. 271 : λίσπη, Apollonius oxytoned this word, Schol. Aristoph. Ran. 849 : λώπη, Theog. Can. 116. 31 : μολπή, Arc. 113. 9 : ὀμπή is oxytone in A. G. 287. 21, but better paroxytone in Photius : ὀνόπη, Hesych.: πομπή, Arc. 113. 9 :

προσώπη, Hesych. should be προσωπή: ῥηπή (?) cf. H. D. s. v.: ῥιπή, Eust. 301. 28; Philem. Lex. p. 63. § 169; Theog. Can. 116. 33: σηπή or σήπη, Lob. Rhem. 258, note 11: τυπή, Arc. 113. 4; Schol. Ven. E. 887; τύπη in Hesych. is false: λατύπη, χαμαιτύπη, μοιχοτύπη, are not compounds of this word, though they are regular even if they were so; according to Theog. Can. 116. 25, λατύπη and χαμαιτύπη are oxytone: ψοθόκη, ἡ ἀκαθαρσία, Arc. 107. 6; cf. Lob. Prol. 330.

155. Proper names in πα or πη are paroxytone, as Ἀερόπη, Ἀντιγόνη, Εὐρώπη, Καλλιόπη, Κάλπη, Κάπαι, Λάμπη, Μερόπη, Μετώπη, Ὄλπη, Ὄλπαι, Πηνελόπη, Πόμπη, Ῥίπη, Σινώπη, Στερόπη, Στίλπαι.

156. Note.—The Attic deme Ἀμφιτροπή is oxytone in Hesych., but paroxytone in St. Byz., though he gives the adverbial forms Ἀμφιτροπῆνδε and Ἀμφιτροπῆσι: Ἀρυπή, Theog. Can. 116. 25, is Ἀρύπη in St. Byz.: Ἐπωπή, an old name of Ἀκροκόρινθος, St. Byz. is paroxytone in Eust. 290. 25, and that is the better accent: Ζαριάσπα (?) Strab. 514, or properly Ζαριάσπη, is proparoxytone in St. Byz., but he and others have it as a neuter plural: Μολπή, a female name, Schol. Apollon. Rhod. 4. 892, should be paroxytone: Σιωπή, ἡ ὁδὸς Σιωπῆς, Paus. 6. 23. 8, can hardly be considered an exception: Στεροπή, Diod. Sic. 3. 60, yet it is expressly made paroxytone by Theog. Can. 116. 16, and Arc. 113. 13.

-PA.

157. Dissyllables in αρα, ευρα, ουρα, and all words in ορα, are oxytone, as ἀρά (but κατάρα), χαρά, εὐρά, νευρά, πλευρά, οὐρά, κουρά, φρουρά, ἀγορά, βορά, δορά, σπορά, φθορά, φορά.

158. Note.—Ἀμόρα, Hesych.: βάρα (?) Hesych., where in one sense it seems to be a neuter plural, though, as νόσημά τι καρηβαρικόν, it may be a singular μορά, E. M. 589. 23; Zonar. 1369, is μόρα in Pollux 1. 129; *L. S.*; *H. D.*; in E. M. 590. 33, both forms are found; but the express declaration of E. M. and Zonar. *ll. ll.*, that it is oxytone, ought to outweigh all other considerations; cf. Lob. Rhem. 267. The compound ἐπαρά is oxytone, but κατάρα always paroxytone, contrary to rule. Κόρα and κούρη = κόρη is paroxytone.

159. Hyperdissyllables in ηρα, ῦρα, and ουρα are proparoxytone, as μέρμηρα, μελίκηρα, ἄγκυρα, γέφυρα, ὄλυρα, ἄρουρα; except ἀθήρα and κολλύρα paroxytone.

160. Note.—Ἀθήρα (?) = ἀθήρη, ἀθέρα, ἀθάρη, Chœrob. A. G. 1173, or ἀθάρα; ἀθηρά is altogether false: ἀλματύραι (?) Hesych.: ἀμβολογήρα, Paus. 3. 18. 1; Lob. Phryn. 538: δασπλῆρα (?) Theog. Can. 107. 19: διφοῦρα (?) Hesych.; λειξούρα (?) Hesych. is λειξούρα in Suidas s. v. λεῖξα, both = *luxuria*, and are probably misaccented: μαμηρά, or μαμιρά, is a barbarous word, see H. D.: μενδῆρα (?) Theog. Can. 107. 19: μενθήρα (?) E. M. 580. 6: μερμήρα (?) Theog. Can. 107. 19, or μέρμηρα, as in A. G. 28. 4; see H. D.: ὁμοῦρα (?) = ἀμόρα, Hesych., where Schmidt reads ὅμουρα: ὀτρήρα (?) Theog. Can. 107. 19, 'qui fortasse vulgari forma dixit Amazonem quæ ap. Apoll. Rh. 2. 387, Tzetz. Posth. 8. 57. 127, Schol. Ven. Hom. Il. 3. 189, Ὀτρηρή vel Ὀτρήρη, itemque in Lycophronis libris plerisque 997, nonnullis tantum edd. ad Ὀτρηροῦ* ab n. Ὀτρηρώ aberrantibus, dicitur, nisi quis substantivum ὀτρήρα exstitisse putet;' *L. Dindorf,* ap. H. D.: πανδοῦρα (?) Pollux 4. 60, also occurs as a paroxytone πανδούρα. The rare word γέργυρα = γοργύρη is of doubtful quantity; but the penultimate is probably long, and the word proparoxytone, like γέφῦρα, ἄγκῦρα, ὅλῦρα, πλήμμῦρα; and it is actually so written in the text of E. M. 224. 56: ταυρουρά, H. D., is almost certainly false: on κολλύρα, see Arc. 194. 16.

161. Words in ιρα have the α short, and retract the accent, as αἷρα, εἷρα, μαῖρα, μάχαιρα, μοῖρα, πεῖρα, χίμαιρα; except ἑταίρα, paroxytone, and ζειρά or ζιρά, σερά, στειρά (and στεῖρα), oxytone.

162. NOTE.—Δειρά, E. M. 256. 57; and expressly Theog. Can. 107. 6 is δείρα in Hesych. and H. D.; in Attic it is δέρη: εἰρά, so expressly Theog. Can. 101. 24, yet it is always paroxytone; perhaps we should read ἱρά, cf. Arc. 97. 1: ἑταίρα, though used as a substantive, is only the feminine of ἑταῖρος: ζειρά (?), in Theog. Can. 101. 22, the ultimate is said to be short, and the word is accented ζεῖρα; ζιρά is another and less correct form of the same word: κατείρα (?) Hesych.: εἰρα = ἐκκλησία etc., Eust. 1160. 35; according to Arc. 97. 1 this is oxytone (in the MSS. of Arc. it is spelled ἠρά), and also in Theogn. Can. 101. 24, where it is written εἰρά; in E. M. 692. 38 it is ἵρα or εἶρα; cf. also E. M. 303. 39: μαῖρα, Lob. Rhem. 256: νεῖρα and πεῖρα (πειρά, *edge,* only in Æschyl. Choeph. 847 = 860. ed. Didot, where Ahrens reads πεῖραι) sometimes have the α long; see L. S. s. vv.: σειρά, Arc. 97. 1; Theog. Can. 101. 24; 107. 6: σέρα, Eust. 914. 24; a Doric form σηρά is mentioned by Etym. Gud. 497. 45: στεῖρα, *the keel of a ship,* A. G. Oxon. 3. 396. 32, mentions a form στείρη: στεῖρα (sc. βοῦς), see Lob. Par. 347: σχειρά, Theog. Can. 101. 24, the meaning is unknown: χοίρα, in Herod. π. μ. λ. 8. 12 is the proper name of a woman.

163. The rest are paroxytone, as ἄγρα, αἰώρα, ἀμάρα, αὔρα, διόπτρα, διφθέρα, ἕδρα, ἑσπέρα, ἐσχάρα, ἡμέρα, θήρα, θύρα, κιθάρα, κολυμβήθρα, λύρα, μύρρα, ὀπώρα, παλαίστρα, πήρα, πληθώρα, πορφύρα, σαύρα, σισύρα, φαρέτρα, φιλύρα, φράτρα, χαράδρα, χώρα, ὥρα; except the oxytones ἀριστερά (χείρ), ἑκυρά, ἐλπωρά, θαλπωρά, θερμαυστρά, περιστερά, πενθερά, πυρά; the properispomenon σφῦρα and the proparoxytones Δήμητρα, σκολόπενδρα, and τάναγρα.

164. NOTE.—Αἴθρα, in Lycoph. 699. 822, quoted by H. D. s. v., it is wrongly properispomenon: ἄκερα (?) Hesych.: ἀλεώρα or ἀλεωρά is variable both in termination and accent; it is *paroxytone* in Arist. H. A. 9. 8. 1 (where three MSS. read ἀλεωρή); De Part. Animal. 4. 10. 23 (one MS. has ἀλεωρά) and elsewhere; *oxytone* in Arist. De Part. Animal. 4. 5. 23 (codd. ἀλεώρα and ἀλεωρή), and in one MS. of H. A. 1. 1. 31; Diod. Sic. 3. 34, etc.: ἀλεωρή seems to be almost always oxytone; according to the rules laid down by Arc. 101. 19; 113. 18, both words ought to be paroxytone: ἡ ἀπομάκτρα is sometimes confounded with τὰ ἀπόμακτρα; see L. S. s. v. and the passage of Aristoph. there quoted: αὖρα (for αὔρα), in E. M. 557. 45, is an error: γεραρά, Demosth. 1371, is an adjective used as a substantive; cf. Æschyl. Suppl. 666: γλυκερά, Theog. Can. 106. 31: ἐγκατηρά, Alex. Trall. 1. 12; H. *D.*: ἐκυρά, the feminine of ἑκυρός, Arc. 72. 8: ἐλπωρά, Arc. 101. 22, only occurs as ἐλπωρή: εὔστρα, Hesych. is sometimes incorrectly εὖστρα: ἔψανδρα is an error, it should be ἐψάνδρα, Lob. Par. 213: θαλπωρά, Arc. 101. 22, generally θαλπωρή: θερμαῦστρά, or θερμαυστρά in Callimach. H. in

Del. 144, should probably be paroxytone, and also θέρμαστρα, another form of the same word; by rule the final a would be long, and I can find no authority for making it short: ἴαρα in Hesych. is corrupt: κασαύρα (?) cf. Lob. Par. 80: κιρρά, *a kind of fish*, Hesych. is perhaps an adjective: κράερα (?) = κραῖρα, Hesych.: κραῦρα and κραυρά, Lob. Par. 347: λαῦρα in E. M. 557. 45 is wrong: νάερρα (?) Hesych.: ξηρά (sc. γῆ); H. D. quote ξήρα, *dryness*, from Schol. Aristid. p. 326. ed. Frommel: πέλεκρα (?) Hesych.: πενθερά, Theog. Can. 106. 32: συμπενθέρα, Anna Comn. p. 54, H. *D.* is a strange accent; whoever so wrote the word regarded it as the feminine of συμπένθερος: περιστερά, Arc. 101. 7: πρῶρα, Arc. 101. 17, or better πρῷρα, has the a short in Attic, though it is not uncommonly written πρώρα (?); see Spitzner Gr. Pros. § 16. 12 b: πυρά, Herod. π. μ. λ. 17. 29, and Dindorf. in præf. p. xiii; Arc. 97. 1: σαλαμάνδρα, Arist. H. A. 5. 19. 25, is sometimes written σαλάμανδρα, Geopon. 15. 1; see Lob. Par. 212, who rightly condemns this form: σάνιτρα (?) Hesych.: σκολόπενδρα, Arc. 97. 5; 101. 27; 194. 19; σκολοπένδρα, though found in some editions, is almost certainly wrong; cf. Lob. Par. 212, note 6: σταθερά (sc. γῆ), Lob. Par. 350: σφῦρα, Herod. π. μ. λ. 17. 28; Arc. 96. 27, is not unfrequently oxytone: τάναγρα, Arc. 101. 27; 194. 19: τραφερά (sc. γῆ), Lob. Par. 350: ὑγρά is also used substantively: φωρά, *theft*, is oxytone, and φώρα, *search*, paroxytone in Hesych., though this last is oxytone in Pollux 8. 69, and elsewhere; H. *D.*: χολέρα is the accentuation in all the passages quoted by H. D., and the word is expressly said to be paroxytone in Theog. Can. 101. 16; but χολερά is also said to occur; see Lob. Par. 355.

165. ACCENT OF COMPOUNDS. Compounds retain the quantity of the words from which they are derived, as λαύρᾱ σποδησιλαύρᾱ, πήρᾱ σακκοπήρᾱ, αὔρᾱ μαψαύρᾳ, πεῖρᾰ ἀνάπειρα πρόπειρᾱ, ἄγρᾱ ποδάγρα τραγῳδοποδάγρα; the last syllable of κυνόσουρα however is short, though the a in οὐρά is long (Herod. π. μ. λ. 13. 26; Eust. 706. 1; Arc. 97. 10), σεισοῦρα (?) and λαμπουρά are both doubtful: τάναγρα, whether as a proper or common name, has a short ultimate (Arc. 101. 27; 194. 19). In accentuation, compounds conform to the general rule, except κατάρα. Χλωρο-σαῦρα, in Schol. Theocr. 2. 58, can hardly be right, though it occurs again, Schol. Theocr. 7. 22, together with σαῦρα (?).

166. Proper names in ρα throw back the accent, as Ἀντίφρα, Δάειρα, Δαῖρα, Δηϊάνειρα, Εἶρα, Ἐφύρα, Ἥρα, Θήρα, Κασσάνδρα, Κέρκυρα, Κίρρα, Κλυταιμνήστρα, Κοισύρα, Κόρα, Λιπάρα, Πάλμυρα, Πανδώρα, Πολυδώρα, Φαίδρα.

167. NOTE.—Numerous exceptions to this rule are met with, but it is to be suspected that many of them are errors, while some are certainly so. Ἄγκαρα (?) Strab. 216; St. Byz.: Ἄγκυρα, E. M. 10. 30; 220. 8; Paus. 1. 4. 5: Ἀγκύρα in Illyricum, Polyb. 28. 8. 11, where Bekker reads Ὕσκανα: Ἀγκύραι in Sicily, Diod. Sic. 14. 48; there can be little doubt that this name ought to follow the general rule; see Fix ap. H. D. s. v.: Ἀγορά, St. Byz. or Ἀγορή, Herodot. 7. 58: Αἰμηρά, Eust. 287. 36: Αἰραί, St. Byz.: Ἀμβολογήρα (?); the passage in Paus. 3. 18. 1 proves nothing as to the accent; Lob. Phryn. 538 note, is confident that it is paroxytone, but he gives no reasons for his opinion: Ἀμφείρα, so Pape, who quotes Lycoph. 1163, which proves nothing; H. D. have Ἄμφειρα, which is probably better : 'Αντικύρα, Strab. 416 (where Kramer reads 'Αντίκυρα), St. Byz. ; Herodot. uses 'Αντικύρη ; if therefore a is long (which does not seem certain), 'Αντικύρα will be the best mode of writing the word : 'Αντίκιρρα, Eust. 273. 30 : 'Αντίκυρα, Paus. 10. 36. 5, and often elsewhere : 'Αντίκῦρα, as a female name, occurs in Athen. 587 E, where Meineke writes 'Αντίκιρρα : 'Αντίσαρα, St. Byz. can hardly be right, since 'Αντισάρη is quoted from Herodian by the same author ; cf. A. G. Oxon. 4. 412. 9 : Ἄπτερα, St. Byz. ; cf. Strab. 479 : Ἀραί, St. Byz. : 'Αργυρᾶ, Paus. 7. 18. 6 : Ἄργυρα (?) another city, St. Byz. : 'Αριστεραί, Paus. 2. 34. 8 Ἀχέρραι, St. Byz. : Βαίταρρα (?) St. Byz. s. v. Βαιταρροῦς : Βοῦρα, St. Byz. s. v. Παναιούρα, Strab. 59, is Βούρα in Ptol. 3. 16. 15, but wrongly, for a is short ; Callimach. H. in Del. 102 ; Βουρά therefore is a mistake in Philo Jud. T. 2. p. 514. 28 ; *H. D.* : Γέρμαρα (?) St. Byz. : Γίνδαρα (?) St. Byz.: Γλαφυρά is, according to Arc. 101. 14, oxytone as the name of a city : Γλαφύραι, Hom. Il. 2. 712, on which passage Eust. 327. 34 observes that the ' more exact critics ' (οἱ ἀκριβέστεροι) barytoned the word to distinguish it from the adjective, but it is oxytone in most editions ; Pape quotes Γλαφύρα as a woman's name ; in Appian, Civ. 5. 7, it is in the MSS. oxytone, though Bekker has it paroxytone : Γλυκερά is oxytone according to Arc. 101. 6, though Γλυκέρα appears in Strab. 410 ; Athen. 584 A ; Suid. and elsewhere : Γόμορρα or Γόμορα, Suid. ; the genitive is usually Γομόρρας, but the accusative Γόμορρα, and perhaps Γόμορραν : Γόβορα (?) Suid. : Γυραί (sc. πέτραι), Hom. Odyss. 4. 500 : Δαρά, St. Byz. : Δαρραί, St. Byz. : Δήμητρᾰ, Paus. 1. 37. 2, etc. : Δηρά, St. Byz. : Δισοραί, St. Byz. : Ἔβορα, St. Byz. ; the Codex Vrat. has Ἔβηρα, and Ptol. 2. 5. 8 has it under the form Ἔβουρα ; if Ἔβορα be the correct orthography, the word ought to be paroxytone : Ἐλευθεραί, Diod. Sic. 4. 3 ; Strab. 375 ; Arc. 101. 8 : Ἔνυδρα (?) Strab. 753 ; Ἐραί, Thucyd. 8. 19 ; but Ἔραι, Strab. 644 : Ἐρυθρά, and Ἐρυθραί, Apion and Herodorus : others distinguished Ἐρύθραι in Boeotia from Ἐρυθραί in Ionia, Eust. 267. 6 ; cf. Chœrob. E. 27. 10 : Θερμυδραί, Apollod. 2. 5. 11 ; W. Dindorf thinks this corrupt ; the ordinary form of the word is τὰ Θέρμυδρα : Θοραί, a deme, St. Byz. : Θορά, Theog. Can. 107. 22 : Ἴνδαρα (?) St. Byz. : Ἱερά, Diod. Sic. 5. 7, etc. : Ἱρά, St. Byz. : Ἱρή, Aristarchus ; Ἵρη others, Schol. Ven. I. 150 ; Herodian also made it oxytone, Schol. Ven. I. 292, though the contrary is stated, A. G. 11. 3 ; see Lob. Par. 343 : Λαμπτραί, a deme, Phot. Lex. v. Λαμπτρεῖς : Λυκόσουρα is, like the other compounds from οὐρά, proparoxytone, Paus. 8. 2. 1 ; those not derived from that word are for the most part regular, as Κόσσουρα, Strab. 123 : Μάκκαραι, St. Byz. : Μανδαραί, St. Byz. : Μίσκερα, St. Byz. : Νόσορα, St. Byz. : Ξηρά, St. Byz. : Ὀλόβαργα (?) St. Byz. : Παναιούρα (?) St. Byz. : Πειραί, Paus. 7. 18. 1 ; Theog. Can. 101. 12 : Σαύρα (?) St. Byz. : Σιρρά, St. Byz. : Στουρά, Arrian Ind. 21. 1 ; *Pape*: Φάρα, Strab. 388, another city in Africa, is oxytone, Strab. 831 : Φαλάκραι, St. Byz. : Φαραί, St. Byz., etc. ; sometimes falsely Φάραι : Φερά, female name, Eust. 327. 12 ; Theog. Can. 101. 13 : Φεραί, St. Byz. : Φηρά, Herod. π. μ. λ. 38. 12 ; Eust. 580. 44, or Φηραί, St. Byz. : Χάραδρα (?) St. Byz. : Χείμερα (?) St. Byz.

168. The Ionic words in ρη = ρα are oxytone when the common forms are so, paroxytone in other cases, as ἀγορή (ἀγορά), ἀθάρη, ἀλεωρή (ἀλεωρά), ἀναδορή (ἀναδορά), ἀποκουρή (ἀποκουρά), ἀποφορή (ἀποφορά), ἀρή (ἀρά), βορή (βορά), δεξιτερή, δέρη, though δειρή is oxytone, ἐκυρή, ἐλπωρή, θαλπωρή, κόρη, νευρή, ξηρή (γῆ), οὐρή, πυρή, 'Αγορή, Ἄγρη, 'Αντισάρη, Ἄσχρη, Δείρη, 'Εφύρη, Κάτρη, Κύρη, 'Ολύκρη, Τερψιχόρη, Φηρή ; the following are oxytone, δειρή, θορή, καρή.

169. NOTE 1.—See Chœrob. C. 515. 1 : Δειρή is in Æolic δέῤῥα, Chœrob. ap. A. G. Oxon. 2. 194. 11 : δέρη is paroxytone, E. M. 94. 4 : δορπωρή, Zonar. 562, not δορπορή, Suid. : καρή, Arc. 113; Theog. Can. 78. 30; Eust. 1257. 52 ; A. G. 1173 ; κάρη is neuter, though there are instances of its being used as feminine ; cf. H. D. s. v. On φωρή, *theft*, see L. S. s. v.; they have also ἱερή = ἱέρεια.

170. NOTE 2.—Ἀγορή, Herodot. 7. 58 : Αἴσχρη is oxytone in Plut. 2. 474 C : Δείρη, E. M. 262. 52 ; it is oxytone in St. Byz. ; Strab. 769 ; 773 ; in Ptol. 1. 15. 11 ; 4. 7. 9; 8. 16. 12 we have either Δήρη or Δείρη : Δουσαρή, St. Byz. : Ἰρή, Aristarchus made it oxytone, others paroxytone, Schol. Ven. I. 150 ; Herodian also made it oxytone, Schol. Ven. I. 292, though the contrary is stated, A. G. 1173 ; see Lob. Par. 343 : Καιρή, St. Byz. ; in Strab. 220 it is Καιρέα : Λειμηρή, Eust. 287. 35, a name of Epidaurus, is an adjective : Νηρή(?) : Περιστερή, St. Byz. : Φηρή. E. M. 791. 46 : Ῥῆ = Ῥέα, Pherecydes ap. Herod. π. μ. λ. 7. 5.

171. NOTE 3.—The contracted words νεβρῆ, Orph. Arg. 447, ταυρῆ, τραγῆ, Eust. 374, are perispomena.

-ΣΑ.

172. Words in σα have the final α short, and the accent is retracted, as αἶσα, ἄνασσα, βασίλισσα, βῆσσα, γλῶσσα, ἔμπουσα, ἡρώϊσσα (or ἡρῷσσα), θάλασσα, λύσσα, μέλισσα, μοῦσα, νύσσα, πεῖσα, πίσσα, σάρισα, φυλάκισσα, Ἀρέθουσα, Δοῦσα, Ἔδεσσα, Ἑρμώνασσα, Ἰφιάνασσα, Κρῖσα, Κόσσα, Λάγουσα, Λάρισα, Λίβυσσα, Νῖσα, Νῦσα, Συράκουσαι, Τίρσαι, Φαῖσα ; except words in ησσα = ήεσσα, ουσσα = όεσσα, and ωσσα, which are properispomena, as τεχνῆσσα, τιμῆσσα, χερνῆσσα, Πιτυοῦσσα, Ῥοδοῦσσα, Μελιττοῦσσα, Ἰοφῶσσα : Συράκουσσα is however proparoxytone, and ἡρῷσσα properispomenon.

173. NOTE 1.—Arc. 97. 16 ; Herod. π. μ. λ. 12. 25 : βασά, Hesych. ; cf. H. D. s. v. : βηνῶσα = ἡ φωνὴ τῶν προβάτων, Hesych. : βήσασα or βησασᾶ, Diosc. 3. 53 ; βησασά, Paul. Æg. p. 277. 45, quoted by H. D. s. v., a barbarous (Syriac) word: βλήσσα (?) Hesych. : ἐπιοῦσα (sc. ἡμέρα) : ἡρῷσσα, Schol. Apollon. Rhod. 4. 1309, ἡρῷσσαι προπερισπωμένως Ἡρωδιανὸς ἐν δεκάτῳ φησίν, ἐκ συναλοιφῆς τοῦ ἡρώϊσσαι· τοῦ ἥρως δὲ τὸ θηλυκὸν γίνεται ἡρῷσσα : κατακάσα or κατακάσσα in Hesych.; Suid. ; and E. M. 494. 38, is doubtful ; ' Glossa ex versu Callimachi sumta, quem servavit Etym. M. p. 819. 4, Σκύλλα γυνὴ κατακάσα καὶ οὐ ψύθος οὔνομ' ἔχουσα. Ex quo apparet κατακάσα esse scribendum, et sic duo codd. Suidæ nisi quis κατάκασσα præferat : nam κάσσα per πόρνη explicatur a grammaticis.' *H. D.*

174. NOTE 2.—*Exceptional Proper Names.* The books present a large number of proper names accented in such a manner as to violate the rule laid down above, but the explicit statements of the older grammarians leave little doubt that the majority of these apparent exceptions are really mistakes. The following rules are given by Arcadius for the accentuation of these words—96. 3, τὰ εἰς ΣΑ ὑπερδισύλλαβα παρεσχηματισμένα προπαροξύνεται, εἰ μὴ κατὰ συναλοιφὴν εἴη ἀπὸ ὀξυτόνων εἰς ΗΣ· δαφνήεσσα φωνήεσσα· τὸ δὲ τεχνῆσσα ἀπὸ τοῦ τεχνήεσσα· καὶ τὰ ἀπὸ ὀξυτόνων εἰς ΗΣ· χερνῆς χερνῆσσα, ἀργῆς ἀργῆσσα, Κρὴς Κρητὸς Κρῆσσα, θὴς θῆσσα : Arc. 97. 12, τὰ εἰς ΣΣΑ ὑπερδισύλλαβα ἀπαρασχημάτιστα[1] προπαροξύνεται, εἰ μὴ

---

[1] ' ἀπαρασχημάτιστα dicit propter ἡρῷσσα, ut patet ex Herodian ap. Schol. Apoll. Rhod. 4. 1309 ;' *Schmidt.*

E

παραλήγοι ΟΥ· θάλασσα Ἰφιάνασσα θέρμασσα (ἡ κάμινος). τὰ δὲ παραλήγοντα τῇ ΟΥ, εἰ μὲν ἔχοιεν ἐν Σ, προπαροξύνεται· Φαέθουσα Ἀρέθουσα Αἴθουσα· εἰ δὲ δύο ἔχοιεν, προπερισπῶνται· Πιτυοῦσσα Ῥοδοῦσσα (ὀνόματα νήσων) πλὴν τοῦ Ἔμπουσσα καὶ Συράκουσσα: Arc. 97. 19, τὰ εἰς ΣΑ δισύλλαβα βαρύνεται· αἶσα μοῦσα πεῖσα (ἡ πειθώ) μεθ' ὧν γλῶσσα πίσσα νύσσα. A list of such deviations from the rule as have been noted is appended.

175. NOTE 3.—Αἰγείρουσα, St. Byz. : Αἰγοῦσα, Ptol. 3. 4. 17 : Αἴγουσα, St. Byz. : Ἀκέσα, Philostrat. Heroic. p. 703, quoted by H. D. : Ἀκέσαι, St. Byz. : Ἁλιοῦσα is better Ἁλιοῦσσα, Paus. 2. 34. 8 ; I cannot find any authority for Ἀλφειῶσα or Ἀλφειοῦσα, which are given both by Pape and by H. D. : the passages to which they refer prove nothing : Ἀνεμῶσα, Paus. 8. 35. 9 : Ἀνήτουσσα, St. Byz., or better Ἀνητοῦσσα; H. D. : Ἀνθοῦσα, St. Byz. s. v. Συκαί, is very doubtful ; Ἄνθουσα, Phot. Bib. 340. 14, is the better form, unless we regard it as a significant noun ; the name Ἀργινοῦσσα is spelled and accented in various ways, e. g. Ἀργίνουσα, Schol. Aristoph. Ran. 697 = 710 ; Ἀργίνουσαι, Thucyd. 8. 101 ; Xenoph. Hell. 1. 6. 27 (Schneider prints Ἀργινοῦσαι in his index); Diod. Sic. 13. 98 ; Ἀργινοῦσαι, Harpocr. ; E. M. 137. 15, 720. 28, on the former of which passages Sylburg observes, ' Rectius Ἀργεννοῦσαι, nempe ab ἀργεννός, 135. 39 : ut docet etiam Stephanus Byz. Posteriorem scripturam Ἀργινοῦσαι per ι, sequitur Androtion in Atticis, ut testatur idem Stephanus : vel per systolen scilicet ex ἀργεινός, vel per μεταβολὴν ex ἄργιλος;' Ἀργινοῦσσα, Strab. 615. 617 ; Ἀργίννουσα, Suid.; Zonar. 296 (where some MSS. have Ἀργένουσα and Ἀργέννουσα) ; Ἀργεννοῦσα, St. Byz. νῆσος πρὸς τῇ ἠπείρῳ τῆς Τρωάδος παρὰ τὸ Ἀργεννὸν ἀκρωτήριον, ἀφ' οὗ Ἀργεννόεις, καὶ κατὰ συναίρεσιν Ἀργεννοῦς καὶ Ἀργεννοῦσα. τὸ ἐθνικὸν Ἀργεννούσιος. Ἀνδροτίων ἐν τῷ τετάρτῳ τῆς Ἀτθίδος διὰ τοῦ ι : Ἀριστοφῶσα, woman's name, *Pape* : Ἀσαί, St. Byz. : Βαργόσα (?) Strab. 720, quoted by Pape, though it proves nothing as to the accent : Βάρουσσαι, H. *D.*, is Βαροῦσαι in Ptol. 7. 2. 28, on which L. Dindorf says, ' Præstat fortasse Βαροῦσσαι scribi :' Γήθουσσα, St. Byz., or Γήθουσα, Zonar.: Γοννοῦσα in St. Byz. is rightly, Γονοῦσσα, in pa_{us}. 2. 4. 4, 5. 18. 7; another false form of the same word, Γονοῦσα, occurs in Eust. 291. 42 : Δελφοῦσα, St. Byz. s. v. Δελφοί: Ἐλοῦσα, St. Byz. : Ἔμπουσσα, Arc. 97. 18 ; the usual form is Ἔμπουσα : Ἐρεικοῦσα, Schol. Aristoph. Plut. 586, is properly written Ἐρεικοῦσσα in Strab. 276 and St. Byz. : Θηγανοῦσα (?) is correctly Θηγανοῦσσα in Paus. 4. 34. 12 : Ἰχνοῦσα is found in three MSS. of Arist. Mirab. Ausc. 100. 2 ; the proper form is Ἰχνοῦσσα, Paus. 10. 17. 1, and this Bekker has rightly adopted in the passage of Aristot. just cited : Καββαλοῦσα, Lucian Ver. Hist. 2. 46 : Κάρουσσα (?) Arrian Peripl. *Pape* : Κηλοῦσα, Xen. Hell. 4. 7. 7, where some books read Κοίλωσσα (?) : Κισσοῦσσα, Plut. 1. 449, this is the only correct form, as Κισσόεσσα occurs in Plut. 2. 772 B : Κισσοῦσα is certainly false : Κολοσσαί or Κολασσαί is oxytone : Κοτινοῦσα, Schol. Aristoph. Plut. 586 ; Eust. ad Dion. Per. 456 : Λαπέρσα, St. Byz., a mountain in Laconia, may as a Doric form be correct : Μαισά, *Pape*, is false for Μαῖσα, Herodian 5. 3. 2, etc. : Μαράθουσσα, St. Byz. : Μελίτουσσα, St. Byz. : Μήλουσσα, St. Byz. : Μύρτουσσα, St. Byz. : Ὀφιοῦσα, Scylax p. 29 : Ὀφιοῦσσα, Strab. 306. 167 : Ἡαγασαί, Strab. 436 : Πιτυοῦσα, Schol. Aristoph. Plut. 586; Diod. Sic. 5. 16; for Πιτνοῦσσα, Strab. 394, etc., is unquestionably wrong ; cf. Arc. 97. 17 : Πιτνοῦσαι or Πιτύουσαι, St. Byz. : Πολεμοῦσα, an Amazon, Quint. Smyr. 1. 42 ; H. *D.* : Πύργησσα, St. Byz. : Ῥόδουσσα, St. Byz. for Ῥοδοῦσσα is false : Σίδουσσα, St. Byz. : Σκότουσσα, St. Byz. : Σχίνουσσα, St. Byz. should be Σχινοῦσσα : Arcadius, 97. 18, excepts Συράκουσσα from the rule, but that form does not seem to occur elsewhere ; the ordinary forms are regular, as Συράκουσαι, Συράκοσαι, Συρήκουσαι; cf. Theog. Can. 56. 28 ; Συρακοῦσαι in St. Byz. is clearly a mistake : Ταφιοῦσα s. Ταφιοῦσσα, H. *D.* quoting Pliny, N. H. 36. 21. 151 ; the latter form is correct : Τελφοῦσα (see below Τιλφοῦσσα, etc.) :

Τέλφουσα or Τελφοῦσσα, Polyb. 4. 77. 5 : Τέλφουσσα, St. Byz. : Τεύγλουσσα (?) :
Τεύτλουσσα, St. Byz. ; Thuc. 8. 42 : Τιλφοῦσα, Paus. 9. 33. 1 : Τιλφοῦσσα or
Τίλφουσσα, St. Byz. : Τιλφῶσσα, Strab. 411 : Τίλφωσσα, Herodian ap. St. Byz. ;
Τιμῶσα, a woman, Athen. 609 A : Τραγασαί (?) H. *D.* is Τραγάσαι in Pollux 6.
63, and Τράγασαι in St. Byz. : Ὑδροῦσα᾽ a name of Ceos, Hesych. : Φάκουσσα,
St. Byz. : Φασήλουσσαι, St. Byz. should be οὖσσαι.

176. NOTE 1.—*The Female Names* (also used as names of ships) Ἐπιπηδῶσα,
Ἰοῦσα, Κρατοῦσα, Ναυκρατοῦσα, Στεφανοῦσα, Τιμῶσα, Τρυφῶσα, retain their participial accent.

-ΣΗ.

177. Words in ση are paroxytone, as ἄση, ἔρση, ἐέρση, κόρση,
Γενέση, Μέσση, Τεμέση, Χρύση, except the deme-names Βησσή
and Περγασή.

178. NOTE.—The following exceptions occur :—βουσή (?) Hesych. : ῥυσή (or
ῥυσά, νόσος), Lob. Par. 333.

Proper Names.—Ἀσαί, St. Byz. : Βησσή, Arc. 113. 24 ; Theog. Can. 117. 10 ;
Βῆσσα, the Locrian city, is always properispomenon in our books : Δροσή, woman's
name, Lucian Dial. Meret. c. 10, where Jacobitz and Meineke read Δροσί, from
Δροσίς : Παγάση, E. M. 646. 39, is generally oxytone as a plural, Παγασαί : Περγασή, a deme, Arc. 113. 24 ; St. Byz. s. vv. Ἀγγελή and Περγασή.

-ΤΑ.

179. Words in τα have the final α short : the accent is retracted, as δίαιτα,‾ θῆττα, Ἔγεστα, Λάδεστα, except contracted
words in ουττα, which are properispomena, as μελιττοῦττα, οἰ-
νοῦττα, προσωποῦττα ; and Doric forms in τᾱ=τη, which retain
the accent of the latter form, as στήτα (στήτη), ἀλακάτα (ἠλακάτη) ;
the proper name Αὐγούστᾱ is paroxytone.

180. NOTE 1.—*Exceptional Common Substantives.*   Arc. 96. 16 ; Eust. 1735.
52 : αὐάτα = ἀϝάτᾱ, cf. L. S. s. v. : βαῖτα (?) is more generally found paroxytone,
and in Doric βαῖτα is certainly right ; βαίτη, Arc. 114. 18, is also not uncommon :
καινίτα = ἀδελφή, Hesych. : κήτα (?) Hesych. : μορτά, Hesych.; Pollux 7. 151,
etc., is μόρτη in Eust. 1854. 31, as Dindorf thinks, wrongly : πελλύτα (??) Hesych. :
τατᾶ, Anth. Pal. 11. 67. 4.

181. NOTE 2.—*Exceptional Proper Names.*   Several Doric names are inserted
which are not strictly exceptions to the rule :—Ἀέται (?) Hesych. : Αἴγεστα,
Strab. 254 : Αἰγέστα, Pape ; Polyb. 1. 24. 2 : Ἀράτα=τη, Dor., *Pape :* Ἀρετά,
woman's name, Anth. App. 53 : Ἀρτέμιτα, St. Byz., or Ἀρτεμίτα, Strab. 744,
also one of the Echinadæ, Strab. 59 : Ἀσβύστα, St. Byz. : Ἀσταί, St. Byz. :
Αὐγούστα, Chœroboscus, C. 326. 9, wastes nearly a page over the name Αὐγούστα,
and yet leaves the accent of the word doubtful ; as a proper name he says that thé
α is long, but that ἐπὶ τῆς βασιλίδος it is short, because it is an Italian word :
Καισαραυγούστα, Strab. 161, where Meineke alters it to Καισαραυγοῦστα : Παξαυ-
γούστα, Strab. 151, where Kramer has Παξαύγουστα, and Meineke Παξαγοῦστα :
Αὐδάτα, woman, Athen. 557 C : Γαβρῆτα, Strab. 292 : Ἔγεστα, St. Byz. is

rightly Ἔγεστα, Diod. Sic. 12. 83; 14. 48: Ἐόρτα, Strab. 318; also an Indian city, Ptol. 7. 2. 13: Ἐταζέτα, woman, so *Pape*, quoting Phot. Bib. 228. 9, which proves nothing: Ἰεταί, St. Byz.: Κερεαταί, which is quoted by *Pape* from Strab. 238, is there Κερεᾶτε or Κερεάτε: ' Κιλλουτά insula maris Indici ap. Arrian. Exp. 6. 19, nomen suspectum,' H. D.: Κοτύρτα, Thucyd. 4. 56: Κότυρτα, St. Byz.: Κουῖντα = *Quinta*, Anth. App. 375: Κρατίστα = η, woman, *Pape*: Κυρίτα, woman, Lycoph. 1392: Λαυαγήτα (?) woman: Παραπίτα, woman, Xenoph. Hell. 4. 1. 39; *H. D.*: Πικταί, Strab. 237: Πλαγκταὶ πέτραι, Hom. etc.: Προλύτα, woman, Plut. 1. 606: Σαβάτα, Strab. 226: Σπαῦτα, Strab. 523: Τεῦτα, woman, *Pape*: H. D. have Τεύτα, and quote Polyh. 2. 4: Τρήτα, Strab. 683: Φουρνίτα, St. Byz.

-TH.

182. Common substantives in τη are paroxytone, as ἀπάτη, ἄτη, βλαύτη, δαίτη, δροίτη, ἐλάτη, ἠλακάτη, κασιγνήτη, κίστη, κοίτη, πλάτη, ὠμοπλάτη; except those in ετη, οτη, κτη, and ορτη, which are oxytone, as ἀρετή, τελετή, γενετή (but μελέτη, ἐρέτη' and ἀτρυγέτη, sc. θάλασσα), βιοτή, μοτή, ποτή (but ἀβρότη, sc. νύξ and ἀμβρότη), ἀκτή, εἰρκτή, πηκτή, στακτή: ἀορτή, ἑορτή, μορτή, and the following, ἀστή, ἀϋτή, βροντή, λιτή, παλαιστή, πινυτή, τελευτή, φυστή. Those in στη involving a numerical idea are feminine adjectives, and consequently oxytone, as εἰκοστή, πεντηκοστή. Ἀκτῆ, ἀρκτῆ, and λεοντῆ are contracted.

183. NOTE I.—Arc. 113. 25-115. 3; the apparent exceptions to this rule, which are numerous, are for the most part adjectives used substantively. Probably nothing more rational than popular caprice has determined the retention of the adjectival accent in some cases, and the adoption of a substantival one in others. Ἀβαρταί = πτηναί: Κύπριοι, Hesych.: ἀβρότη (sc. νύξ): αἰζυκτή = γῆ, Hesych.: ἀκοστή, an adjective according to Buttm. Lexilog. p. 76: ἀκτή, Arc. 114. 23: ἀλεστή (?) the only passage (Joseph. A. J. 3. 10. 5) quoted by H. D. proves nothing as to the accent, the nominative might be ἀλεστής: ἀλοιτή, though found, is false for ἀλοίτη: ἀπαντή, Sept. 2 Reg. 10. 5, etc.: ἀρετή, Arc. 114. 3: ἀστή, feminine of ἀστός: ἀστραγαλωτή (ἀστραγαλωτός) Lob. Par. 352: ἀτρυγέτη (sc. θάλασσα) Auth. App. 234: αὐαντή (sc. νόσος), Hippocr. p. 484. 24.; H. D.: ἀϋτή, Arc. 114. 10: βαλλωτή, Diosc. 3. 117; H. D.; cf. Lob. Prol. 393: βλαστή, Arc. 114. 23, though he says that some barytoned it, and βλάστη is given as the proper accent by Herodian ap. Herm. de emend. rat. Gr. gr. p. 304; it seems to be always paroxytone in our books: παραβλάστη, 'apud Theophr. H. P. 1. 2. 6, codex Urbinas παραβλάστας duplici accentu,' W. Dindorf ap. H. D.: βροντή, Arc. 114. 22: βρυτταί, Hesych.: γοιταί, Hesych.: γοσταί αἱ κριθαί, Theog. Can. 13. 27: γριτή, ' Lib. Ep. 1594,' H. D.: δεκτή, Hesych.: δετή (sc. λαμπάς) Hom., etc.; δηΐταί, Hesych.: δωτή (?) Hesych.: ἐγγυητή (sc. γυνή) Lob. Par. 350: ἐγκαυτή, H. D.: ἐγκλειστή, H. D.: ἐμβατή, Schol. Aristoph. Eq. 1055 = 1057, Suid. s. v. πύελος' is probably false for ἐμβάτη, Pollux 4. 115; 7. 91: ἐρέτη, E. M. 94. 51; Lob. Par. 475: ἐρκατή (?) Hesych.: ζυγητή (?) ἡ κλεΐς, Hesych.: ζωστή, H. D.: θεμιστή, Hesych., probably false for θέμιστι: θουρητή (?) Hesych.: θρεπτή, Lob. Par. 350, really an adjective: καθέτη, if it exists, is a feminine adjective used substantively: καλαμωτή, Eust. 1533. 51: καμηλωτή, i. e. *a camel's hair coat*, Lob. Par. 332: καρατή

(?) in Hesych. is corrupt : καταρρακτή (sc. θύρα) or καταρράκτη (?) Lob. Par. 332 : κερωτή, A. G. Oxon. 2. 327. 30; Arc. 114. 14, where Schmidt reads κηρωτή : κηρωτή, strictly a feminine adjective used as a substantive, Arc. 114. 14, so also κοκκωτή (?): κομιστή, an adjective, Lob. Par. 351 : ' κοπτή edulium, κόπτη porrum sectile dici, non temere sumi videtur, v. Schweighæuser ad. Athen. T. 7. 575 ;' Lob. Par. 351 : κόρτη or κάρτη, Hesych. : κοστή and κόστη, Hesych. : κρυπτή (sc. ἀρχή) Lob. Par. 333 ; in the sense of *cellar* or *underground passage* it is sometimes oxytone, e. g. Athen. 205 A, where however Dindorf reads κρύπτη, and that is the better accent: κωλωτή (or κωλώτη) Arist. H. A. 9. 1. 23, for which Sylburg has κωλώτης in his index : λειτή (?) Hesych.=λιτή : λεπαστή, Arc. 115. 3, or λεπάστη, as some accented, Athen. 484 F: οἱ μὲν ὀξύνουσι τὴν τελευταίαν, ὡς καλή, οἱ δὲ παροξύνουσιν, ὡς μεγάλη : λιτή, Theog. Can. 117. 15 ; Arc. 114. 8 ; λοιτή is erroneous ; the word is regular Theog. Can. 117. 28 : μαλλωτή (sc. διφθέρα): μελέτη, Arc. 114. 4 ; E. M. 94. 51 : μέτη (?) Hesych. : μηλωτή (sc. δορά) A. G. Oxon. 2. 327. 29 ; Arc. 114. 14 ; Lob. Par. 332 : μισητή = ἡ ἀξία μίσους· μισήτη = ἡ καταφερὴς πρὸς συνουσίαν, Trypho ap. Ammon, p. 94 ; Valck. ; this distinction was also retained in Doric and Ionic, cf. Eust. 1650. 64, but it is often neglected : μνηστή (sc. ἄλοχος), Apollon. Rhod. 1. 780: μορτή, Lob. Par. 349 : νεάτη, when used as a substantive=νεάτη χορδή is paroxytone ; so also ὑπάτη, but νεατὴ (sc. γῆ) : οἰσπωτή, Arc. 114. 15, is οἰσπώτη in E. M. 619. 10, and Aristoph. Lys. 575, quoted by L. S. : παλαιστή, or better παλαστή, Arc. 115. 3 : παλυντή (?) : πελλαστή, Lob. Par. 349 ; πηκτή, Arist. H. A. 9. 8. 8 : πινυτή, some made it paroxytone, Aristarchus however wrote it oxytone, Schol. Ven. H. 289; I. 150; Πινύτη is a proper name Arc. 114. 10 : πλεκτή (sc. σειρά) Pollux 10. 142 ; it is also used with the ellipse of other nouns : πλέκτη, in A. G. Oxon. 3. 351. 22, may be from the masculine πλέκτης, Lob. Par. 352 : πλωτή (sc. ἔγχελυς) Pollux 6. 63 : πτερωτή, A. G. Oxon. 2. 327. 30, is also an adjective used substantively : ῥυτή, Nicand. Ther. 523 ; H. *D.* : σεβαστή =Augusta : σηπτή, adjective, Lob. Par. 352 : σκεπαστή, Eust. 1165. 52 : στακτή (sc. κονία) Lob. Par. 352 : συναπτή, H. *D.* : σχισταί (sc. βλαῦται) Lob. Par. 352; Pollux 7. 85 : τελετή, Arc. 114. 3 : τελευτή, Arc. 114. 19 ; Chœrob. E. 38. 7 : τρυπτή, Lob. Par. 351 : ὑπαντή, also ὑπάντη : φώκτη, Lob. Par. 351 : φυστὴ (sc. μᾶζα) Herodian ap. Schol. Aristoph. Vesp. 608 ; this word is occasionally, though incorrectly, paroxytone ; Mœris, p. 384, strangely enough has φυστῆ : ψυκτά (sc. μᾶζα) Lob. Par. 351.

184. NOTE 2.—The following are usually contracted :—ἀκτή =ἀκτέα is often written ἀκτή, e. g. Diosc. 4. 174 ; Theoph. H. P. 3. 13. 4 ; sometimes even ἄκτη, Galen de Simp. Med. Fac. 6. 21 =Tom. 13. 153 A : the compound χαμαιακτή is falsely written χαμαιάκτη Diosc. 4. 175 ; Galen de Simp. Med. Fac. 6. 21 : ἀρκτῆ (sc. δορά) Pollux 5. 16 : λεοντῆ (sc. δορά) Eust. 450. 25 ; Herod. π. μ. λ. 6. 21.

185. Proper names in τη are paroxytone, as Ἀμφιτρίτη, Ἀρήτη, Ἀταλάντη, Ἀφροδίτη, Ἀφύτη, Δημαρέτη, Δίκτη, Ἑκάτη, Θεοδότη, Ἰοκάστη, Κρήτη, Μελίτη, Ναπάται, Οἴτη, Προχύτη, Σπάρτη, Ταϋγέτη, except oxytone, the deme Βατή, and Λιταί, Σεβαστή, with a few others.

186. NOTE.—Ἀβρωτή (?) Lob. Prol. 393 : Ἀδρησταί, H. *D.* for which they quote Diod. Sic. 17. 91, a passage which proves nothing as to the accent : Ἀκτή, an old name of Attica, and of other places, St. Byz.; the compound Καλάκτη = Καλὴ ἀκτή, is regular : Ἀφέτη, Eust. 1967. 21 ; this is the common accent, but the word is also found as oxytone, see Lob. Par. 475 ; the plural also varies, but here there seems more authority for making it oxytone, Arc. 114. 2 ; St. Byz ; Diod. Sic. 11. 12 : **Βατή**, the deme, Arc. 113. 28 ; St. Byz. : in Herod. π. μ. λ. 42. 24 we find Βάτη (*sic*) δῆμος Ἀττικοῖς· ἀδιάφορα γὰρ τὰ τοῦ τόνου: according to E. M. 192. 13, βάτη was a Messenian word = γῇ : **Εἰρκτή** and **Εἰρκταί**, *inclosure*, also a place in Sicily, Polyb. 1. 56. 3, ' Cognominem Argorum locum dicere videtur Xen. H. Gr. 4. 7. 7,' *L. Dindorf* ap. H. D. : **Ἱμερτή**, name of Lesbos, Eust. 741. 32 : **Κλειτή**, E. M. 518. 3 ; Apollod. 2. 1. 5, is sometimes paroxytone; but according to Etym. Gud. 325. 43 most made it oxytone : **Κορσωτή**, Xen. Anab. 1. 5. 4 : **Κρεμαστή**, Xen. Hell. 4. 8. 37 : **Κριθωτή**, St. Byz.; according to Arc. 114. 13 this is paroxytone, and such is the reading of most books in Demosthenes and elsewhere, e. g. Strab. 459 : **Λεοντή**, a woman, Phot. Bib. 149. 32 : **Λητή** in St. Byz. and elsewhere is wrong; the word is expressly made paroxytone by Theog. Can. 117. 15 : **Λιταί**, Hom., etc. naturally keeps the accent of the common noun : **Λυταί**, St. Byz.; Lob. Par. 475 : **Περκωτή**, Theog. Can. 117. 33, is expressly said to be barytone, A. G. Oxon. 2. 390. 26 : the proper name **Πινύτη**, Arc. 114. 10, is oxytone according to the Schol. Ven. I. 150, and a sufficiently absurd reason is given for its being so : **Πλαγκταί** (sc. πέται) : **Πρωτή**, an island, St. Byz., but Πρώτη as the name of a woman is paroxytone : **Σεβαστή**, St. Byz., etc. : **Σητή**, St. Byz. s. v. Σητία : **Τρητή**, Ptol. 6. 7. 45 : **Φιλωτή** (?) a woman, *Pape*.

-ΥΑ and -ΥΗ.

187. Substantives, both proper and common, in υα and υη are paroxytone, as γύα, καρύα, μύα, οἰσύα, ὀξύα, σικύα, Δατύα, Κρύα, Μαρσύα, Μιλύαι, Μινύα, ἀφύη, ἐγγύη, σμινύη, χλεύη, Λιβύη, Φύη ; except **Μάντυα**, which is proparoxytone, and the oxytones ἀκουή (ἀκουά, Dor.), σκευή, and φυή (φυά, Dor.).

188. NOTE 1.—*Exceptional Common Substantives in* υα. **Αὖα** or αὔα as Æolic seems to be an error, see Ahrens de Gr. ling. dialect. 1. p. 36, note 11 : βοῦά (⅋) Hesych. : διεγγύα (?), in Schol. Thucyd. 3. 70 it is rightly διεγγύα; ἐγγυή and παρεγγυή are found in some books, though they are unquestionably wrong, see Lob. Phryn. 302 ; Arc. 103. 27 : concerning ἰγνύα, Theog. Can. 106. 21 makes the following observation, ἰγνύα· ὀριὰ Ἀρίσταρχος συστέλλει τὸ Α καὶ ἐκτείνει τὸ Τ καὶ προπαροξύνει, ἐναλλαγὴν τόνου καὶ χρόνου πεποιηκώς, ὥς φησιν Ἡρωδιανός: this explains the passage in Schol. Ven. N. 212, ἰγνύην· Ἰωνικῶς μετέβαλε τὸν τόνον, ἐπεὶ τὸ ἀκόλουθον ἰγνυά ἐστιν, ὡς Ἡρωδιανὸς ἐν τῷ ια' τῆς καθόλου: I have not however been able to find any place where ἴγνυα occurs, though ἰγνύα and ἰγνύη are common enough, see Lob. Phryn. 302.; cf. Schol. Ven. Φ. 242 : σίκυα and νέκυα (?) occur in Eust. 291. 38 ; cf. Theog. Can. 106. 20 : φυά = φυή.

189. NOTE 2.—*Exceptional Proper Names in* υα. **Αἴγουα**, Strab. 141 : Ἀτέγουα, Strab. 141 : **Γένουα**, Strab. 201. 202 ; Ptol. 3. 1. 3, is Γενόα in St. Byz. : Ἐλευθέρυα (?) St. Byz. : **Κάπυα**, St. Byz. : **Μάντυα**, St. Byz., or **Μάντουα**, Strab. 213, etc.: **Οὐιδούα** (indeclinable ?), Ptol. 2. 2. 1 : **Τράμπυα**, St. Byz. ; **Φλυά** (?) = Φλυή is said to occur also as a paroxytone, see § 191.

190. NOTE 3.—*Exceptional Common Substantives in* υη. **Ἀκουή**, Ion. = ἀκοή : σκευή, Arc. 103. 12 ; Philem. Lex. p. 68. § 186 : the compounds of this word are regular, as ἀποσκευή, κατασκευή, παρασκευή, ἐπισκευή ; the Byzantine form οἰκοσκευή, which is irregular, has been expunged by Schmidt from the text of Arcadius ; Lob. Par. 369 makes it paroxytone : φυή, Arc. 103. 25 ; A. G. Oxon. 1. 427. 26 ; so διαφυή, etc. : ἐμπύη is in some lexicons made oxytone, but apparently without authority.

191. NOTE 4.—*Exceptional Proper Names in* υή. Ἀγαυή, Schol. Ven. I. 150; the passage in Arc. 103. 10 (ἀγαυὴ ὀξύνεται ἐπιθετικὸν ὄν) seems to imply that the proper name is paroxytone, as Ἀγαύη, the daughter of Danaus, sometimes is; but even her name is frequently oxytone, e. g. Apollod. 2. 1. 3, etc.; see *Fix* ap. H. D. s. v.: Κανή, Xen. Hell. 4. 1. 20: Ναυῆ, Suid. is barbarous: Φλυή, a deme, Arc. 103. 26.

-ΦΑ and -ΦΗ.

192. Common substantives in φη are oxytone, as ἀλοιφή, ἀφή, βαφή, γλυφή, γραφή, περικαλυφή, κορυφή, ὀμφή, ὀροφή, ῥαφή, στροφή, ταφή, τροφή; except paroxytone, those in ιφη, ηφη, λφη (yet ἀδελφή is oxytone), and ρφη (yet μορφή is oxytone), as ἀγρίφη, σκίφη, ἀκαλήφη, μίλφη, σίλφη, κάρφη, νάρφη, τάρφη, σύρφη, together with λαίφη, νύμφη, σκάφη, *a canoe*, λόφη, and τύφη.

193. NOTE.—Arc. 115. 4-18; Theog. Can. 118. 4; A. G. Oxon. 1. 291. 8: ἀγρίφη τὸ σκάφιον, Arc. 115. 13; Theog. Can. 118. 7: ἀδελφή is oxytone as the feminine of ἀδελφός: cf. ἀστή, ἀστός, and the like: the compounds of this word are very irregular; ἀνδραδελφή, which occurs several times, is better ἀνδραδέλφη, in Eust. 392. 2; Zonar. 419: αὐταδελφή, Schol. Eur. Hec. 944, H. *D.*, is αὐταδέλφη in other places: γυναικαδελφή, Lob. Phryn. 306, or γυναικαδέλφη: δισεξαδέλφη, H. *D.*: ἐξαδελφή, Anna Comn. p. 44 A, quoted by H. D., who condemn the accent, which nevertheless is retained by Lob. Phryn. 306, and by L. S., and is agreeable to analogy: μητραδέλφη: πατραδέλφη: on the whole it seems best to accent these compounds according to the general rule, since analogy and some considerable authority support that view of the case: ἀκαλήφη, Arc. 115. 14: ἀλειφή seems to be an orthographical blunder for ἀλοιφή, see H. D. s. v.: ἀράφη (?) Arc. 115. 17: ἀσύφη, H. *D.*: κάρφη, A. G. Oxon. 1. 291. 14: κελύφη is a more than doubtful form for κέλυφος: κιδάφη (and κινδάφη, = *the sly*, i.e. *fox*, is an adjective, *L. S.*; Arc. 115. 17 has σκιδάφη: λαίφη = λαῖφος, E. M. 274. 2: λόφη, Diod. Sic. 17. 90, seems doubtful; some propose to read λοφία: μίλφη, *falling of the eyebrows*: νάρφη, Hesych.: νύμφη, A. G. Oxon. 1. 291. 11: ῥιφή, Lycoph. 235. 1326: σίλφη and τίλφη, Lob. Phryn. 300; A. G. Oxon. 1. 291. 14: σκαφή = τὸ σκάμμα: σκάφη = τὸ πλοῖον, Arc. 115. 6: σκίφη, Diog. Laert. 4. 27: σκύφη, H. *D.*: τάρφη, A. G. Oxon. 1. 291. 14: τίφη, Athen. 115 F, is oxytone in Arist. H. A. 8. 21. 5: τύφη, Theophr. H. P. 1. 5. 3; 1. 8. 1, etc.; H. *D.*

194. Proper names in φη are paroxytone, as Ἀνάφη, Ἐρίφη, Κάρφη, Σάμφη, Σίφη, Σκίρφαι, Τηλέφη, Τράφη, Τύμφη.

195. NOTE 1.—Pape quotes Οἰστροφή, the name of an Amazon, from Tzetzes, P. H. 180, and Κορυφή, a daughter of Oceanus, E. M. 474. 32, and also the name of a mountain, Paus. 7. 5. 9: Μορφή, Lob. Rhem. 319, note 2.

196. NOTE 2.—The Doric nouns in φᾶ seem to follow the accentuation of the common forms in φη, as ὀμφά = ὀμφή; yet ὄμφα is also found. The following rare words are somewhat irregular—ἄπφα or ἀπφά, Suid.: βάφᾱ, Dor. = ζωμός, Hesych., where the last editor prints βαφά: καφά, Dor. = λουτήρ: κέρκαφα = ἐγγύη, Hesych.: σοῖσφα or σοῦσφα is indeclinable; Cosmas Indicop. 2. p. 133 A, and 132 D; H. *D.*: Ἀλλιφαί, a town in Samnium (not Ἄλλιφαι, as Pape has it), Strab. 238, is paroxytone in Diod. Sic. 20. 35: Καφύαι, Theoph. H. P. 4. 13. 2; St. Byz., is Καφυαί in Paus. 8. 15. 6, and Καφύη in Suidas; H. *D.*

Most words of this termination are verbals, and therefore oxytone according to that general analogy already referred to, § 62.

-ΧΑ and -ΧΗ.

197. Common substantives in χη (χᾱ) are oxytone, as ἀμυχή, ἀνακωχή, βληχή, βροχή, διδαχή, εὐχή, στοναχή, ψυχή ; except paroxytone, those in ιχη, as μαστίχη, μειλίχη, μυρρίχη ; those with a consonant before χη, as ἀργυράγχη, βάκχη, βράγχη, κάλχη, κόγχη, λέσχη, λόγχη, ὄσχη (yet ἀρχή is oxytone) ; and καύχη, λάχη (?), μαλάχη, μάχη, τύχη.

198. Note.—Arc. 115. 19-28 : ἄγχη, only occurs in the compounds συνάγ-χη, ἀργυράγχη, ὑάγχη, etc. : ἀρχή, Arc. 115. 24 : ἀστράρχη, quoted by L. S. from Orph. Hym. 9. 10, is an adjective, and were it not so, would still be regular : αὐλάχα = εὐλάκα, Hesych., or εὔλαχα, Suid. ; Zonar. 908 ; cf. Thucyd. 5. 16 ibiq. schol. : αὐχή, Hesych., but αὔχη, Pind. Nem. 11. 29, a doubtful accent : the compounds κριοδόχη, κυσοδόχη are regular : καύχη, Pind. Nem. 9. 15 ; this accent seems very questionable ; cf. Lob. Rhem. 269 : λάχη is quoted by L. S. from Æschyl. S. c. T. 914 ; in Dindorf's text it is λαχαί, yet in H. D. s. v. he condemns this accent, and makes the word in both its senses paroxytone, as it is in Hesych. ; λαχή would be much more in accordance with analogy, and with the rule laid down by Arc. 115. 19 : λυμάχη, Hesych., is regular as a compound : μαλάχη, Arc. 115. 16, μαλάχη κοινόν· μολόχη Ἀττικόν, Lex. Gr. ap. Herm. de emend. rat. Gr. gr. p. 323, which is a mistake, as μαλάχη is the Attic form ; Athen. 58 D : μάχη, Arc. 115. 21 : μοσχή = ἑα (sc. δορά) Pollux 5. 16 : on ὄσχη and ὤσχη see H. D. s. v. Ὄσχος : παλάχη is the proper accent according to the rule of Arc. 115 ; but παλαχή occurs in Nicand. Ther. 449. ; H. D. : σανδαράχη or σανδαράκη : τάρχη, see H. D. s. v. Τάρχος : τύχη, Theog. Can. 118. 12 ; Arc. 115. 21 : ὑάγχη as a compound ὗς, ἄγχη is regular, like ἀργυράγχη : ὕρχα and η, Aristoph. Vest. 676, is ὑρχή in Hesych. ; φυσέχη, Plat. Cratyl. 400 B : ὤσχη (?) see above.

199. Proper names in χη are paroxytone, as Βάκχη, Δολίχη (Δολιχή, St. Byz.), Ὄχη, but Λογχή is oxytone according to Arc. 115. 24, though it occurs as paroxytone in Xenoph. Cyn. 7. 5 ; Ἀσωχή, Suid. s. v. Ἀσωχαῖος ; Σάριχα (?) St. Byz. and Χωχή, St. Byz. are also exceptions to the rule.

-ΨΑ and -ΨΗ.

200. The few words in ψα have α short, and retract the accent, as κάμψα or κάψα, δίψα, Βαίσαμψα, Σκέμψα, Στρέψα, Arc. 96. 12.

-ΩΑ and -ΩΗ.

201. All words in ωα are paroxytone, as μνῴα, ὑπερῴα, ῷα, Μινῴα : ἀλωά, if the nominative occurs in that form, is oxytone, like ἀλωή.

202. NOTE.—Κάλωα, ἡ διδασκαλία (??) E. M. 486. 14: Κριῶα, St. Byz. is false; it should be Κριώα, Arc. 100. 23 : μῶά or μῶα = μοῦσα, Aristoph. Lys. 1249. 1298 ; cf. Ahrens de Dialect. ling. Gr. 2. p. 76 and 78 ; ʻApud Pausan. 8. 10. 4, ἐοικότα λέγουσι Καρῶν οἱ Μύλασα ἔχοντες ἐς τοῦ θεοῦ τὸ ἱερόν, ὃν φωνῇ τῇ ἐπιχωρίᾳ καλοῦσιν ʼΟγώα, ubi liber unus ʼΟγῶνα, ceteris nonnisi in accentu dissentientibus, non dubium quin ʼΟσογώ sit scribendum, deleto quod sequens ʼΑθηναίοις peperit a,ʼ L. *Dindorf* ap. H. D.: ῥωά, a bad form for ῥοιά : σωά (?) Dor. = ζωή : φῶα (?) E. M. 819. 41, would be better ψώα.

203. Words in ωη are oxytone, as δμωή, ἐρωή, ζωή (and Ζωή the proper name), θωή, ἰωή : the proper name Οἰνώη is paroxytone.

204. NOTE.—Arc. 103. 29. The compound αὐτοζωή deviates from the general rule, as does εὐζωά = εὐζωή, Pind. Pyth. 4. 233 : ζωή = τὸ ἐπάνω τοῦ μέλιτος ἐφιστάμενον καὶ τοῦ γάλακτος, Eust. 906. 52, is distinguished by its accent from ζωή, *life*; ζόη is paroxytone: ποδορρώη, Callimach. Dian. 215, is corrupt for ποδορρώρη : Τρωαί = *Trojan women* ; cf. Lob. Prol. 29 sq.

ACCENTUATION OF OBLIQUE CASES.

205. The general rule is followed, but the genitive plural, being always contracted in the Attic and Common dialects, is perispomenon, as μοῦσᾰ, μούσης, μούσῃ· μοῦσᾰν; μούσᾱ, μούσαιν; μοῦσαι, (μουσάων) μουσῶν, μούσαις· μούσᾱς·

206. The Genitive and Dative of all numbers from oxytone Nominatives are perispomena, as ψυχή, ψυχῆς, ψυχῇ ; ψυχαῖν; ψυχῶν, ψυχαῖς; μαχητής, μαχητοῦ, μαχητῇ ; μαχηταῖν; μαχητῶν, μαχηταῖς.

207. Words which are perispomena in the Nominative singular retain the same accent in all cases, as long as they remain unresolved, as ʼΑθηνᾶ, ʼΑθηνᾶς, ʼΑθηνᾷ, ʼΑθηνᾶν. On the doubtful word ζελᾶς, τοῦ ζελά, see § 33.

208. The Ionic genitive in εω follows the general rule, εω being considered as one syllable, as Πηληϊάδεω, ʼΑτρείδεω, ʼΟρέστεω, Αἰνείεω ; words like Βορῆς, Ἑρμῆς, Πυθῆς therefore become Βορέω, Ἑρμέω, Πυθέω ; the genitive of Θαλῆς however seems to be always Θάλεω, as if it came from the nominative Θάλης.

209. Genitives in ιω, ειω, or ια are paroxytone, as ἐϋμμελίω, Ἑρμείω, ἐϋμμελία: those in αο are proparoxytone if from barytone common genitives; properispomena if from circumflexed genitives, as ʼΑτρείδου ʼΑτρείδαο, ʼΟρέστου ʼΟρέσταο, ʼΑργέστου ʼΑργέσταο, but ἀργεστοῦ (from ἀργεστής) makes ἀργεστᾶο.

210. NOTE I.—*Genitive Singular*. Chœrob. C. 413. 11 : αἱ διὰ τοῦ ΕΩ γενικαὶ ʼΙωνικαί, εἰ μὲν ἀπὸ βαρυτόνων κοινῶν γενικῶν ὦσι, προπαροξύνονται, οἷον ʼΑτρείδου

Ἀτρείδεω Ὀρέστου Ὀρέστεω Αἰνείου Αἰνείεω, ἀπαθεῖς δηλονότι οὖσαι. Ἐὰν γὰρ πάθωσι, πρὸ μιᾶς τοῦ τέλους ἔχουσι τὴν εὐθεῖαν, οἷον Ἑρμείου Ἑρμειέω καὶ κατὰ συγκοπὴν τοῦ Ε Ἑρμείω παροξυτόνως,

Ἥρης Ἑρμείω τε [Il. 15. 214].

Εἰ δὲ ἀπὸ περισπωμένων κοινῶν γενικῶν ὦσι, παροξύνονται, οἷον αὐλητοῦ αὐλητέω, Κασῆς Κασοῦ (ἔστι δὲ ὄνομα κύριον) τοῦ Κασέω : according to this Θαλῆς Θαλοῦ would make Θαλέω, yet both in the Attic of Plato (Rep. 600 A), and in the Ionic of Herodotus (1. 170), and in Callimachus (Auth. Pal. 6. 150), it is uniformly proparoxytone ; E. M. 153. 51 : αἱ διὰ τοῦ ΕΩ Ἰωνικαὶ γενικαί, εἰ μὲν ἀπὸ βαρυτόνων κοινῶν γενικῶν ὦσι, προπαροξύνονται· οἷον Ὀρέστου Ὀρέστεω, Ἀτρείδου Ἀτρείδεω· οὕτως οὖν καὶ Ἀσίεω, χωρὶς εἰ μὴ κατὰ πάθος ὦσι· διὰ τὸ Ἑρμείεω, καὶ κατὰ συγκοπὴν Ἑρμείω· Καὶ ἡ χρῆσις,

Ἥρης Ἑρμείω τε καὶ Ἡφαίστου.

Βορέου, Βορέεω, καὶ συγκοπῇ Βορέω,

Βορέω ὑπ᾽ ἰωγῇ

ἡ χρῆσις. Καί ἐϋμμελίεω,

Ἐϋμμελίω Πριάμοιο.

Οὕτως οὖν Ἀσίας, Ἀσίου, Ἀσίεω Ἰωνικῶς, καὶ συγκοπῇ Ἀσίω. Καὶ ὁμοίως οὐ προπαροξύνεται· ἐπειδὴ κατὰ πάθος ἐστίν, ἤγουν κατὰ συγκοπήν.

Genitives in ιω *or* ειω. Chœrob. C. 413. 20: αἱ διὰ τοῦ ΑΟ Βοιωτικαὶ γενικαί, εἰ μὲν ἀπὸ βαρυτόνων κοινῶν γενικῶν ὦσι προπαροξύνονται, οἷον Ἀτρείδου Ἀτρείδαο, Ὀρέστου Ὀρέσταο, εἰ δὲ ἀπὸ περισπωμένων κοινῶν γενικῶν ὦσι, προπερισπῶνται, οἷον ἀργεστὴς ἀργεστοῦ ἀργεστᾶο, ἀργεστᾶο νότοιο (τοῦ λευκοῦ ἢ τοῦ ταχυτάτου): Schol. Ven. P. 9, ἐϋμμελία· καὶ ἐπὶ τούτου πρὸ τέλους ἡ ὀξεῖα : cf. Eust. 845. 60 ; Schol. Ven. Λ. 306.

211. Note 2.—According to the grammarians the Ionic differed from the other dialects in its accentuation of barytone words in a with a short final syllable in the nominative singular, for, when in the course of inflexion that syllable becomes long, they are accustomed to throw the accent on to it, as ἴᾰ, ἰᾶς, ἰᾷ ; μίᾰ, μιᾶς, μιᾷ ; ἄγυια, ἀγυιᾶς, ἀγυιᾷ, etc. Chœrob. C. 405. 19 : ἰστέον δὲ ὅτι τὸ ἰᾶς καὶ μιᾶς οὐκ ἐφύλαξαν ἐπὶ τῆς αὐτῆς συλλαβῆς τὸν τόνον ἐφ᾽ ἧς ἔχει καὶ ἡ εὐθεῖα· ἡ γὰρ εὐθειά ἐστιν ἴα καὶ μία παροξυτόνως, καὶ ὤφειλεν ἡ γενικὴ παροξύνεσθαι οἷον ἴας καὶ μίας, ἵνα φυλάξῃ ἐπὶ τῆς αὐτῆς συλλαβῆς τὸν τόνον ἐφ᾽ ἧς ἔχει καὶ ἡ εὐθεῖα· οὐκ ἐγένετο δὲ οὕτως, ἀλλ᾽ ἰᾶς καὶ μιᾶς περισπωμένως. Καὶ λέγει ὁ τεχνικὸς ὅτι ταῦτα Ἰωνικὴν ἔχουσι τάσιν, καὶ οὐκ ἐσαφήνισεν ἡμῖν τὸ λεγόμενον. Ἔστι δὲ τὸ λεγόμενον τοιαύτην ἔχον τὴν ἐξήγησιν· ἐπὶ τῶν εἰς Α βραχυκαταλήκτων εἰώθασιν οἱ Ἴωνες βαρυτονεῖν τὰς λέξεις ὡς καὶ ἡμεῖς, οἷον ἄγυια, ἄρπυια, Πλάταια· ὅταν δὲ γένηται ἡ τελευταία συλλαβὴ μακρά, Ἰωνικῷ ἔθει καταβιβάζεται ὁ τόνος, οἷον ὀργυιᾶς, ἀγυιᾶς, Θεσπιᾶς, Πλαταιᾶς· ἰδοὺ ταῦτα ἐν τῇ τελευταίᾳ συλλαβῇ ἐπιδέχονται τὸν τόνον. Ἐπειδὴ οὖν τὸ ἴα καὶ μία ἐν τῇ γενικῇ καὶ δοτικῇ μακροκαταληκτοῦσι, τούτου χάριν Ἰωνικῷ ἔθει κατεβίβασαν τὸν τόνον καὶ περιεσπάσθησαν, οἷον ἰᾶς καὶ μιᾶς, ἰᾷ καὶ μιᾷ : thus also E. M. 305. 35 ; Schol. Ven. Π. 173 ; Arc. 128. 8. Except in the words mentioned in the above extract, this practice does not seem to prevail, at least in our editions.

212. Note 3.—*Vocative Singular.* The vocative of δεσπότης is proparoxytone, δέσποτα ; Chœrob. C. 431. 5 ; E. M. 258. 12 ; Lob. Prol. 372, note 1, ' accentus vocativorum ὦ Ἀβραδάτα et Ἀσιαδάτα ; Cyr. 6. 3. 12 ὦ Εὐφράτα ; Apollon. Epist. 8. 388, et similium librariis imputandus videtur qui sæpissime peccarunt in latinis ἀλβάτοι καὶ ρουσσάτοι J. Lyd. de Mens. 4. 25. p. 72 etc.'

On the forms ἀκάκητα, εὐρύοπα, etc., which are sometimes called vocatives, see above, § 57 sq.

213. Note 4.—*Genitive and Dative Dual.* According to Suidas, s. v. 'Ατρείδης, the sticklers for analogy (οἱ ἀναλογικοί) circumflexed the genitive dual of those words which had a circumflexed genitive plural and barytoned the dative dual, so that according to them μουσαῖν was the genitive, μούσαιν the dative dual, see Chœrob. C. 444. 1. This theory however has not at all affected practice.

214. Note 5.—*Nominative Plural.* Epic and Ionic forms in η = ᾰ, like ἱέρση = Attic ἱέρσᾰ, ἕρση or ἕρσα, become proparoxytone in the nominative plural, as ἕρσαι, not ἱέρσαι, as Ptolemæus Ascalonites wished to write, Schol. Ven. Ξ. 351; Apion and Herodorus ap. Eust. 991. 24.

The late Attics (οἱ νεώτεροι, οἱ μεταγενέστεροι τῶν Ἀττικῶν) retracted the accent in the nominative plural of ἡμέρα and of words in ία; the following instances are given of this practice, which has had no effect on accentuation as we know it; viz. ἥμεραι, εὐπράξιαι, τιμώριαι, αἴτιαι, τραγῳδίαι, ὁμίλιαι, κωμῳδιαι, Chœrob. C. 449. 16; Arc. 133. 9; Schol. Ven. B. 339, οὕτως συνθεσίαι τε ὡς θυσίαι τε· ὅσοι δὲ προπαροξύνουσι, πταίουσι· τῆς γὰρ μεταγενεστέρας Ἀτθίδος ἡ τοιάδε ἀνάγνωσις: Schol. Ven. E. 54.

215. Note 6.—*Genitive Plural.* The genitive plural is perispomenon when contracted (as in Attic it always is), paroxytone when resolved, as τοξοτῶν, Ἀτρειδῶν, μουσῶν, ἀελλῶν, κλινῶν, μελισσῶν, κριτῶν, but μουσάων, μελισσάων, κριτέων; Chœrob. C. 129. 35; Arc. 134. 26: scribes and editors are not in all cases quite sure whether contraction has taken place or not; see Kühner G. G. 1. 298; from this rule four words are excepted, viz. Ἐτησίαι, *the Etesian winds;* χλούνης, *a wild boar;* χρήστης, *a usurer;* and ἀφύη, *an anchovy;* which make Ἐτησίων, χλούνων, χρήστων, and ἀφύων Arc. 134. 30, 135. 3; Joh. Alex. 17. 2; Chœrob. C. 455. 29, 456. 11; E. M. 386. 56; this refinement we probably owe to the pedantry of the native grammarians, who by means of it distinguish between χρήστων (from χρήστης) and χρηστῶν (from χρηστός); ἀφύων (ἀφύη) and ἀφυῶν (ἀφυῆς); χλούνων (χλούνης) and χλουνῶν (χλουνός).

216. Note 7.—Feminine adjectives and participles following the first declension (which in the oblique cases of the singular, and in all cases of the plural, are subject to the rules laid down for oblique cases in the first declension) present some peculiarities. The rule is thus given by Chœroboscus C. 456. 13: εἰ δέ εἰσι παρεσχηματισμέναι ἀρσενικοῖς [i. e. feminine adjectives and participles in αι nom. plural], ἐὰν μὲν ὁμοφωνῶσι τῇ γενικῇ τῶν πληθυντικῶν τοῦ ἰδίου ἀρσενικοῦ καί, ὁμοτονοῦσιν αὐτῇ, οἷον οἱ Ῥόδιοι τῶν Ῥοδίων καὶ αἱ Ῥόδιαι τῶν Ῥοδίων· μία φωνὴ καὶ εἷς ὁ τόνος· οἱ Βυζάντιοι τῶν Βυζαντίων καὶ αἱ Βυζάντιαι τῶν Βυζαντίων, οἱ ἅγιοι τῶν ἁγίων καὶ αἱ ἅγιαι τῶν ἁγίων, οἱ δίκαιοι τῶν δικαίων καὶ αἱ δίκαιαι τῶν δικαίων, οἱ φίλοι τῶν φίλων καὶ αἱ φίλαι τῶν φίλων, οἱ δοῦλοι τῶν δούλων καὶ αἱ δοῦλαι τῶν δούλων, οἱ καλοὶ τῶν καλῶν καὶ αἱ καλαὶ τῶν καλῶν, οἱ σοφοὶ τῶν σοφῶν καὶ αἱ σοφαὶ τῶν σοφῶν, οἱ Λύκιοι τῶν Λυκίων καὶ αἱ Λύκιαι τῶν Λυκίων· (περὶ δὲ τῆς χώρας αἱ Λυκίαι τῶν Λυκιῶν περισπωμένως· μονογενὲς γάρ) οἱ ὕπατοι καὶ αἱ ὕπαται τῶν ὑπάτων,

> κοῦραι πετράων ἔρριπον ἐξ ὑπάτων,

ἐπὶ δὲ τῆς χορδῆς ἡ ὑπάτη τῆς ὑπάτης καὶ αἱ ὑπάται τῶν ὑπατῶν περισπωμένως· μονογενὲς γάρ· Ἐὰν δὲ παραλλάξωσι κατὰ τὴν φωνὴν πρὸς τὴν γενικὴν τῶν πληθυντικῶν τοῦ ἰδίου ἀρσενικοῦ, καὶ τῷ τόνῳ παραλλάσσουσι καὶ περισπῶνται αἱ θηλυκαὶ γενικαὶ τῶν πληθυντικῶν, οἷον οἱ μέλανες τῶν μελάνων καὶ αἱ μέλαιναι τῶν μελαινῶν, οἱ μάκαρες τῶν μακάρων καὶ αἱ μάκαιραι τῶν μακαιρῶν, οἱ πάντες τῶν πάντων καὶ αἱ πᾶσαι τῶν πασῶν, οἱ γράφοντες τῶν γραφόντων καὶ αἱ γράφουσαι τῶν γραφουσῶν, οἱ χαρίεντες τῶν χαριέντων καὶ αἱ χαρίεσσαι τῶν χαριεσσῶν, οἱ ἐξεῖς τῶν ὀξέων καὶ αἱ ὀξεῖαι τῶν ὀξειῶν, οἱ ποιοῦντες τῶν ποιούντων καὶ αἱ ποιοῦσαι τῶν ποιουσῶν. So Arc. 135. 4. Put into a practical shape, this amounts to the following rule: *Feminine adjectives and participles making* αι *in the nominative plural are paroxytone in the genitive plural, when that of their corresponding masculine form, being declined after the second declension, is paroxytone; otherwise they are perispomena.* Hence the grammarians distinguish between the adjectives Σαμίων, Ῥοδίων (sc. γυναικῶν) and the substantives Σαμῶν, Ῥοδιῶν, which are the genitives plural of the proper names Σαμία and Ῥοδία, Joh. Alex. 17. 20.   It need hardly to be observed that this difference is also apparent in the nominative plural, e. g. Ῥόδιαι Σάμιαι ὅσιαι (sc. γυναῖκες), while Ῥοδίαι Σαμίαι ὅσίαι are substantives, Joh. Alex. 17. 20.   The following forms must not be confounded, πόρνων (πόρνοι), πορνῶν (πόρναι), βάκχων (βάκχοι), βακχῶν (βάκχαι) ὄχθων (ὄχθοι), ὀχθῶν (ὄχθαι), πέτρων (πέτροι), πετρῶν (πέτραι), χήρων (χῆροι), χηρῶν (χῆραι), κούρων (κοῦροι), κουρῶν (κοῦραι), παιδίσκων (παιδίσκοι), παιδισκῶν (παιδίσκαι).   Though they do not properly belong to this place, it may be here noticed that Δαναϊδῶν (οἱ Δαναΐδαι) is distinguished by its accent from Δαναΐδων (αἱ Δαναΐδες); so also Πριαμιδῶν (οἱ Πρια- μίδαι), Πριαμίδων (αἱ Πριαμίδες), Ἰλιαδῶν (οἱ Ἰλιάδαι), Ἰλιάδων (αἱ Ἰλιάδες), Chœrob. C. 458. 1 sqq.

217. NOTE 8.—The Æolic and Doric genitives in αν are circumflexed, as κυλι- χνᾶν, Τηϊᾶν, Ahrens de Gr. ling. dialect. 1. p. 12, 2. p. 31; Chœrob. C. 457. 14; Arc. 135. 15; Kühner G. G. 1. 252, 303.

218. NOTE. 9.—*Accusative Plural.* In Doric ας in the accusative plural is short, and therefore in that dialect Μοίρᾱς, τίμᾱς, σφύρᾱς become μοῖρᾰς, τῖμᾰς, σφῦρᾰς.   Ahrens (de dialect. ling. Gr. 2. 30) quotes the following instances, πᾶσας, Theocr. 1. 83, 4. 3: Ἅρπυιᾰς, Hes. Theog. 267 (not Ἁρπυίας or Ἁρπυῖας): Μοίρᾱς in Theoc. 2. 160: τρωγοίσᾰς, Theoc. 9. 11.   The two last instances, together with others, lead him to doubt the propriety of the rule laid down above, and he concludes by saying 'haud dubitamus quin ubique acutus penultimæ servandus sit, etiam in iis Doridis generibus, quæ constanter corripiunt, ita ut scribatur, πάσᾰς, τὸς τοιούτος, τιμάες, ἀείδες, ἐνεύδεν.'   But if such strange accents are correct it might have been expected that the grammarians would have mentioned them, and this they have not done; though they do say in general terms that in Doric many words were paroxytone, which in the Common dialect were properispomena, Chœrob. C. 651. 15; Kühner G. G. 1. 252.

219. NOTE 10.—*Cases in* θε *and* φι. The old casal forms in θε and φι are accented according to the following rules :—

(a) Those with a naturally short penultimate take the accent on that syllable, as Πλαταιόθεν.

(b) Those with a penultimate long, either by nature or position, retract the accent, as πρώραθεν, Θήβηθεν, Ἀθήνηθεν, except such as are derived from oxytone or circumflexed primitives, which are properispomena, as εὐνή εὐνῆφι, ἀρχή ἀρχῆθεν, ἀγορή ἀγορῆθεν, Πλαταιαί Πλαταιᾶθεν, Θεσπιαί Θεσπιᾶθεν.   These forms are con- sidered at greater length under ADVERBS, chap. 7. §§ 841-845.

CHAPTER III.

ACCENTUATION OF WORDS BELONGING TO THE SECOND DECLENSION.

220. WORDS belonging to the Second Declension are even more difficult to accentuate than those of the first, and our perplexities are considerably increased when it is considered that no sufficient criterion has been, or probably can be, given by which to discriminate substantives from adjectives. Lobeck (Par. p. 329) justly observes: 'Nullam a Grammaticis regulam traditam esse qua substantiva et adjectiva discernantur, minus peritis mirum videatur necesse est, si reputaverint id quasi solum et fundamentum esse hujus disciplinæ, sine quo sistere nequeat; accuratius qui rem cognorint, omnino talem regulam tradi posse desperabunt. Adeo facile ex epithetis fiunt appellativa, adeo indiscreta est primitivorum et derivatorum similitudo, adeo late patet metonymiæ usus, ut proprias cujusque vocabuli notas promittere prope cujusdam insolentiæ videatur.' And yet substantives and adjectives have a very distinct accentuation, at least in the Second Declension, where it is generally true that, when they have similar terminations, they have dissimilar accents, which cannot be with certainty affixed until we have determined whether a given word belongs to the one class or the other. In most cases a fair knowledge of the usages of the language will enable the student to decide this point without much difficulty, but there are also many words so doubtful that they have been entered as exceptions to the rules laid down, e. g. δήμιος, ἀλκίβιος, ἀντακαῖος, etc. Those who wish to see some of the difficulties which beset this matter stated will derive both satisfaction and information from Lobeck's learned dissertation, ' De nominibus adjectivi et substantivi generis ambiguis,' which has been reprinted in his Paralipomena, pp. 329–388.

As in the First Declension, so here, no general rule of any practical value can be given; but it will be seen that, generally speaking, substantives in *os* pure are oxytone, those in *os* impure throw the accent as far back as possible; the majority of pure adjectives, on the other hand, retract the accent, while the impure are oxytone.

The accentuation of these words is considered under the following general heads and in the following order:—1. Simple Substantives, (*a*) Masculines and Feminines, (*b*) Neuters; 2. Simple Adjectives; 3. Compound Substantives not being verbal derivatives; 4. Compound Adjectives including Substantives, the latter half of which is derived from a verb; 5. Oblique Cases. But this arrangement, though generally adhered to, has been abandoned whenever it seemed that any advantage was to be gained by doing so.

I. SIMPLE SUBSTANTIVES OF THE MASCULINE OR FEMININE GENDER.

-ΑΟΣ.

221. Common substantives in *aos* are oxytone, as λαός, ναός; except proparoxytone, ἔρραος, μάραος, and the Æolic ὑμήναος for ὑμέναιος.

222. NOTE.—Arc. 36. 33; 38. 11. **Λάος** (?) Schol. Soph. Œd. Col. 195, ἐπ' ἄκρου λάου: ἀπὸ τῆς λάος ἐστὶ παροξυνομένης εὐθείας, γενομένης ἀπὸ γενικῆς τῆς λᾶος. Ὅμηρος·

Λᾶος ὑπὸ ῥιπῆς.

Οὕτως Ἡρωδιανὸς ἐν τῷ Ε τῆς καθόλου: **μάραος**, Eust. 1657. 20: **ὑμήναος**, Sappho ap. Hephæst. p. 129.

223. Proper names in *aos* are oxytone when they are simple and proparoxytone when compound, as Δαναός, Κραναός, Ταλαός, Ναός, Κραναοί, Ἀγέλαος, Ἀμφιάραος, Οἰνόμαος, Ἀρχέλαος, Μενέλαος, except Δᾶος=Davus, Δάοι, Λᾶος.

224. NOTE I.—It would seem from Chœrob. E. 69. 6 that dissyllabic proper names are barytone, cf. Arc. 36. 23, 38. 11; some additional examples of compound names have been included in the following list: ''Άγλαος, nom. pr. viri Dionys. Cyz. Epigr. in Anthol. Pal. 7. 78. t. 1. p. 329; Christod. Ecphr. 5. 263, in Anthol. Pal. 7. 78. t. 1. p. 48; De accentu v. Jacobs. præf. p. 35; Alius Ἀγλαός, ὀξυτόνως sine var., occurrit ap. Paus. 8. 24. 13; Bekk.=7 Sieb. Vide Schol. Leid. ad Il. O. 445. p. 427. a. 39 ed. Bekk., coll. Heyn. ad h. l. t. 7. p. 74;' *Fix* ap. H. D.: 'Ἀντώναος (?) *Pape*: Βύαοι, Nic. Damasc. p. 150, ed. Orell., but the reading is doubtful:

Δᾶος, Arc. 36. 24 ; Strab. 304, where Kramer reads Δάοι : ῎Ενναος (?) Pape : ᾽Επίδαος = ᾽Επίλαος : ῾Ερύλαος, Hom. Il. 16. 411 : ᾽Ιόλαος, Apollod. 2. 4. 11, and ᾽Ιόλεως, Eurip. Heracl. 479 : Κλάδαος, Xen. Hell. 7. 4. 29, is Κλάδεος in Paus. 5. 7. 1, etc. : Λᾶος, a city and river of Lucania, Strab. 253, etc., the city is paroxytone in Herodot. 6. 21 : Μάμαος (?) Strab. 344 : Πᾶος, Paus. 8. 23. 9 : Πίταος, St. Byz. : Σάος, an island, river, and man so called, St. Byz.; Strab. 314, etc. : Ταργίταος, Herodot. 4. 5.

225. NOTE 2.—The Æolic forms in αος = αῖος are paroxytone in the grammarians, as ᾽Αλκάος = ᾽Αλκαῖος, Θηβάος = Θηβαῖος, E. M. 66. 28 ; Greg. Cor. p. 596. ed. Schäfer ; yet Ahrens, de Dialect. Ling. Gr. 1. p. 100, makes them all proparoxytone, e. g. ῾Υμήναος (or ηος), Sappho, frag. 44.

-ΒΟΣ.

226. All words in βος throw the accent as far back as possible, as ἄραβος, βόμβος, διθύραμβος, θόρυβος, ἴαμβος, ὄλβος, φλοῖσβος, ῎Αραβος, Κάνωβος, Λέσβος, Φοῖβος; except oxytone, ἀμοιβός, ἀμορβός, βολβός, λοβός, ᾽Ερεμβοί, and Περραιβοί.

227. NOTE 1.—*Common Substantives.* ᾽Αγερρακάβος, Hesych. : ἀμοιβός seems to occur only as an adjective : ἀμορβός, also an adjective : ἀττέλαβος ὅπερ οἱ ᾽Αττικοὶ παραλόγως ὀξύνουσι, Arc. 46. 8 : βολβός is falsely written βαλβός in A. G. Oxon. 2. 397. 9 : θαμβός, Enst. 906. 53 : καὶ θάμβος μὲν ἡ ἔκπληξις, θαμβὸς δὲ κατὰ ὀξεῖαν τάσιν ὁ ἐκπλαγείς : κλωβός, Anth. Pal. 6. 109 : λόβος, Arc. 46. 1.

228. NOTE 2.—*Proper Names.* ᾽Αδερβός, Suid. : ᾽Αναζαρβός, Anth. Pal. 9. 195. 2, is ᾽Ανάζαρβος in St. Byz. ; Procop. Arc. p. 56 A, etc. ; *H. D.* : Βαταβοί (?) : Βολβός, Athen. 22 C, should probably be paroxytone ; cf. A. G. Oxon. 2. 397. 10 : ᾽Ερεμβοί, Hom. Od. 4. 84 ; Strab. 784 ; this word is strictly adjectival, cf. Arc. 46. 1, and Schmidt ad loc. : Περραιβοί, Diod. Sic. 11. 3 ; Strab. 61, etc. : so also Περραιβός the son of Illyrius, Appian. Illyr. c. 2.

-ΓΟΣ.

229. Common substantives in γος‾ retract the accent, as ἀπόλογος, ἀσπάραγος, βούτραγος, λόγος, μαίνουργος, πάγος, πάταγος, πύγαργος, πύργος, σπόγγος, τράγος, φθόγγος, ψόγος; except oxytone, ἀγός, ἀγωγός, ἀμολγός, ἀμοργός, ἀρηγός, ἀρωγός, βαγός, κραταιγός, κραυγός, λαιγός, μολγός, πελαργός, ταγός, φηγός, φαγός, and σαργός, together with λαγός = λαγώς and ζυγός.

230. NOTE.—᾽Αγός is a verbal : ἀγωγός, also an adjective : ἀμολγός, Arc. 47. 16 : ἀμοργός is another form of the same word, and also *a kind of flax* (?) : ἀρηγός, Arc. 47. 16 : ἀρωγός, an adjective used substantively, A. G. Oxon. 2. 343. 7 : βαγός = Ϝαγός, is βάγος in Hesych. : βρυτιγγοί, Hesych. : δυγός, E. M. 316. 57 : ζυγός, Chœrob. E. 76. 23 : κραγός (?) Arc. 47. 3 : τὰ διὰ τοῦ ΑΓΟΣ διβράχεα ἐπιθετικὰ καὶ μὴ ἐθνικὰ ὀξύνεται· φαγός κραγός (ὁ κραυγαστικός)· τὸ δὲ κράγος βαρύνεται : the text here is somewhat corrupt, Meineke, Lobeck, and Schmidt have attempted its restoration, but without much success : κραυγός, *woodpecker* (?)

Hesych. : **λαγός**, Ionic and Common for the Attic λαγώς, Eust. 1534. 14 : **λαρυγγός**, Hesych. = *nugator*, *H. D.* : **λοιγός**, Arc. 47. 8 ; A. G. Oxon. 1. 263. 32 : **μολγός**, *a leathern sack*: **όρειπελαργός** occurs in two MSS. of Aristot. H. A. 9. 32. 3, where Bekker rightly prefers όρειπέλαργος ; see Compound Substantives : **πελαργός**, Arc. 47. 16 ; A. G. Oxon. 2. 343. 7, ' **πελαγός** poet. ellipsi pro πελαργός dicitur teste, E. M. 659. 7,' *H. D.* : **πηγός**, A. G. Oxon. 1. 263. 32 : **ρογός**, *a barn* or *granary*, Pollux 9. 45 : **σαργός**, *a kind of mullet*, Arc. 46. 18, ' qui accentus Aristoteli vel ex libris restitui poterat ; idem constanter est ap. Athen. p. 341 A. D. quum inter utrumque [i. e. *σάργος* and *σαργός*] varietur p. 135 F ; 136 C ; et ap. Plut. Mor. p. 977 E,' *H. D.* : **φαγός**, Arc. 47. 4, on this word, which may be an adjective, see Lob. Par. 135, note 30 ; he quotes **φάγος** from Epiphanius, Tom. 1. p. 143 B : **φηγός**, Arc. 47, 8.　The rule as stated above will be found its most convenient form, but, according to Arc. 46. 19, *dissyllables in γος, preceded by a consonant, are barytone, except σαργός, while dissyllables with a naturally long penultimate, and trisyllables with a penultimate long either by nature or position, are oxytone*, cf. A. G. Oxon. 2. 343. 4 ; Chœrob. E. 76. 29 ; and these two rules are true, with some few exceptions.

231. Proper names in γος throw the accent back, as **Άμολγος**, **Άργος, Γόργος, Μάγος, Όμαργος, Πύργος, Ώγυγος** ; except compounds in ουργος, which are properispomena, as **Λυκοῦργος**, **Φιλοῦργος.**　**Πελασγός** and οἱ **Πελασγοί** are oxytone.

232. Note.—**Άβασγοί**, Tzetz. Chil. 5. 586 : **Άμοργος**, Arc. 47. 17, and A. G. Oxon. 2. 243. 8, expressly make it proparoxytone, yet **Άμοργός** is the common accent in St. Byz. ; Strab. 487 : **Βουφάγος**, a river, Paus. 5. 7. 1, where some read Βουφαγός or Πουφαγός ; also the name of a man, Paus. 8. 14. 9 : **Γολγοί**, a city of Cyprus, St. Byz. : **Βρύγοι**, for which Βρυγοί also occurs : **Γόλγος**, a man, St. Byz., is **Γολγός** in Schol. Theocr. 15. 100 : **Δημιουργός** (?) Pape, who quotes Anthol. Pal. 7. 52, but it proves nothing : **Ζυγοί** Strab. 495 ; St. Byz. : **Ίάφαγος** (?) *Pape* : **Ίππημολγοί**, Hom. Il. 13. 5 (cf. οἱ κυναμολγοί, Strab. 771 ; neither of these are strictly proper names, though they are by some treated as such) : **Ίπποφάγοι**, Ptol. 6. 4. 3, the same remark applies to this and similar names, cf. **Λωτοφάγοι, Μελινοφάγοι, Φθειροφάγοι, Χελωνοφάγοι** : **Λοχαγός**, Plut. 2. 225 E ; ' Polyh. 27. 13. 14, quod Λόχαγος potins scribendum,' *L. Dindorf* : **Λάγος**, Enst. 906. 46, is false, the proper accent is **Λᾶγος**, Arc. 47. 9 ; A. G. Oxon. 1. 264. 2 : **Μάγος**, a man's name, Æschyl. Pers. 318. ed. Didot : Μάγοι, Arc. 47. 5 : **Πελασγός**, the hero, and Πελασγοί, the people : **Πραξίεργος**, Diod. Sic. 11. 54 : **Σιαγαθουργοί** (?) St. Byz. : ' Fictum ex οἱ Άγαθυρσοί, ap. Marcian. p. 100. 3, Miller,' *H. D.* : **Φιλοῦργος**, Aristoph. Lys. 266 ; ' ubi de accentu schol. *Φιλοῦργε· ἐὰν ᾖ Φιλούργε ὡς πανοῦργε, ὄνομα κύριον· ἐὰν δὲ ὀξυτόνως, ἐπίθετον.*　Quocum consentit Arcad. p. 87. 23.　Male igitur in Bekk. Anecd. p. 315. 20, *Φιλουργός· ὄνομα κύριον Άθηναίου ἱεροσύλου·* eodemque accentus vitio apud Photium et Suidam, qui hunc Philurgum ex Isocrate memorant p. 382 A, ubi vulgo Φιλεργός, codex Vat. Φιλοργός, utrumque vitiose pro Φιλοῦργος,' *W. Dindorf* ap. H. D.

-ΔΟΣ.

233. Substantives in δος, both proper and common, retract the accent, as **ἄχερδος, κάδος, κέλαδος, μόλυβδος, νάρδος, όμαδος, ῥάβδος, σμάραγδος, Άβυδος. Άοιδος, Άραδος, Βάλδος, Λέβεδος, Λίνδος,**

Μάρδοι, Ῥόδος, Σίνδος, Τένεδος ; except oxytone, ἀοιδός, ὁδός, ὀπαδός, οὐδός, ὀρυμαγδός, σποδός, ᾠδός, Ἰνδός, Λυδός.

234. NOTE I.—Arc. 47. 20-48. 20: ἀλινδός = δρόμος, Hesych., is ἄλινδος in E. M. 64. 21 : ἀοιδός, Arc. 48. 19, is also an adjective: ἑδός, *a glutton*, Lob. Par. 135; εἰδοί = *Idus*, and ἰδοί: ἐμβαδός, *area*, Heron. de mensuris, p. 314; *H. D.*: κορυδός, Attic according to Arc. 48, 'oxytonum est ap. Aristoph. Av. 302, 472, 476, 1295, paroxytonum ap. Aristotelem aliosque;' *H. D.*: λαρυδός = *clavis in aratro*, Hesych.; *H. D.*: μασδός = μαζός: μανδός (?) Arc. 48. 3, perhaps a proper name: ὁδός, Arc. 47. 23 : οὐδός, Arc. 47. 26 : ὁπαδός and ὁπηδός, συνοπαδός and συνοπηδός, A. G. Oxon. 1. 56. 27, really an adjective: ὀρυμαγδός, Arc. 48. 15, for which ὀρυγμαδός, Hesych. is another form : σπληδός, *ashes*, Nicand. Ther. 763 : σποδός, Arc. 47. 23 : στιβδός (?) Hesych.: ταρανδός, Göttling quotes this from St. Byz. s. v. Γελωνοί, where it is proparoxytone, as also in Arist. Mirab. Auscult. 30 : υἱδός (?) Hesych. : on φειδός or φιδός (?), see Lob. Par. 135 : χληδός (or χλιδός?) *a heap of stones*, should be χλῆδος, Arc. 47. 28 ; cf. H. D. s. v.: ᾠδός, Schol. Ven. Γ. 35 ; Eust. 377. 44.

235. NOTE 2.—Ἀμαρδοί, St. Byz., or Ἄμαρδοι, Strab. 508 : Βερηκοῦνδος (?) *Pape*: Δαλισανδός, Ptol. 5. 7. 7 : Ἐορδός, Herodian ap. St. Byz. ; Strab. 326; there are instances of Ἔορδος: Ἠδοί, St. Byz. : Ἠμωδὸν (ὄρος), Diod. Sic. 2. 35; Strab. 689 : Ἰνδός, both the Indus, and an Indian, St. Byz. s. v. Βάλδος :: Ἰσσηδοί, Tzetz. Hist. 7. 685; *H. D.* : Ἴσσιδοι, St. Byz. : Καρῶνδος (?) *Pape*: for Καυδός, Arc. 48. 3, W. Dindorf conjectures Γαυδός, an island near Crete, which is frequently, if not always, written Γαῦδος : Λανδοί, Strab. 292 : Λυδός, a Lydian, also a slave's name, Strab. 304 ; it is really an adjective: Λυχνιδός, St. Byz. ; Strab. 323 ; is Λυχνιτός in Arc. 82. 11, and Theog. Can. 75. 24 : Μαιδός or Μαιδοί, a Thracian people, St. Byz. ; cf. St. Byz. in Ὤδονες, 'ubi Μαῖδοι scriptum ut ap. Thuc. 2. 98, Strabon. p. 316. 318, cujus tamen alii libri acutum exhibent;' *H. D.*: Μαροβοῦεος is quoted by Pape from Strab. 290, where Meineke has Μαρόβοδος: Μιμνηδός, St. Byz. : Ναγίδος (?) St. Byz.: Ὀδός, St. Byz. : Σεκοῦνδος, Suid. : Σινδοί, St. Byz.; Herodot. 4. 28 ; Strab. 495, and elsewhere ; but the proper accent is Σίνδοι, Apollon. Rhod. 4. 322 ; Schol. ad loc. Apollon. Rhod. τὸ Σίνδοι Ἡρωδιανὸς ἐν τῷ ἕκτῳ τῆς καθόλου βαρυτονεῖν φησὶ δεῖν· τινὲς (οἱ πολλοί, Paris.) δὲ ὀξύνουσιν οὐκ εὖ : cf. Arc. 48. 9.

-ΕΟΣ.

236. Substantives in εος, both proper and common, are oxytone, as ἀδελφεός, εἰλεός, ἐρινεός, θεός, λοχεός, φωλεός, Ἀλεός, Κελεός, Λοχεός, Σωρεός, Φενεός, Ὠρεός ; except ἔλεος, *pity*, ἤϊθεος, and compound proper names, which throw back the accent, as Φιλόθεος, Τιμόθεος, Ταμισίθεος.

237. NOTE I.—Arc. 38. 1-39. 7; Schol. Ven. Ψ. 160 : ἀδελφιδεός ; there has been much difference of opinion about the accent of this and similar words, but there cannot be a doubt that it is oxytone, A. G. Oxon. 2. 315. 26 : πρόσκειται πρὸ μιᾶς τὸν τόνον ἔχοντα, διὰ τὸ ἀδελφιδεός· θυγατριδεός, ὁ ἀδελφιδοῦς καὶ ὁ θυγατριδοῦς· ταῦτα γὰρ ὀξύνεται, the same accent is necessarily implied in the remarks of Chœrob. C. 246. 5, and in the precept of Arc. 175. 9 : ὅτι ἡ ὀξεῖα καὶ ἡ βαρεῖα συνερχόμεναι εἰς συναίρεσιν περισπωμένην ἀποτελοῦσι, χωρὶς εἰ μὴ τονικὸν κωλύσῃ παράγγελμα, ὡς ἐπὶ τοῦ ἀδελφιδέος (*sic*) ἀδελφιδοῦς, καὶ θυγατριδέος (*sic*) θυγατριδοῦς·

ταῦτα γὰρ συναιρεθέντα οὐκ ὀξεῖαν, ἀλλὰ περισπωμένην ἔσχον: Joh. Alex. 6. 24: τὸ ἀδελφιδέος (sic) ἀδελφιδοῦς καὶ τὰ ὅμοια δι' ἕτερον λόγον περιεσπάσθη. τὰ γὰρ εἰς ΟΥΣ ἁπλᾶ πάντα περισπᾶται: notwithstanding the accentuation in the text, it seems clear that these two authors regarded the uncontracted form ἀδελφιδέος either as a proparoxytone or as an oxytone, for the contraction of ἀδελφιδέος into ἀδελφιδοῦς is perfectly regular, it requires no apology, nor could there be any reason for referring it to other than the ordinary rules (see § 20). That Arcadius or his original, Herodian, did not look upon this class of words as proparoxytone, seems certain, because, if he had, the words ταῦτα γὰρ συναιρεθέντα ο ὐ κ ὀ ξ ε ῖ α ν, ἀ λ λ ὰ π ε ρ ι σ π ω μ έ ν η ν ἔ σ χ ο ν would lose all their significance. It might be worth noting that ἀδελφίδεος made ἀδελφιδοῦς, just as the change of χάλκεος into χαλκοῦς, or of ἀργύρεος into ἀργυροῦς, would naturally call for a remark; but it would be absurd, even in a Greek grammarian, to tell us that such words received the circumflex, *and not the acute*. It is therefore obvious that the highest authority on the subject held all such forms as ἀδελφ.δεός, θυγατριδεός, υἱϊδεός, ἀνεψιαδεός, to be oxytone; and the thing to which he wishes to call our attention is the fact that when contracted they do not obey the general law, for by rule they should be oxytone when contracted. Another word of the same kind is τηθελαδοῦς, Lob. Phryn. 299. Göttling, Accent. p. 170, remarks that ἀνεψιαδοῦς is occasionally to be met with in MSS. with the accent ἀνεψιάδ.υς, e. g. Demosth. Macart. 57. 3; and ἀνεψιάδοι, Demosth. Leoch. 26. 6: βορθάκεοι, Lac. = μικροὶ χοῖροι, Hesych.; *H. D.*: ἔλεος, *mercy*, is probably so accented to distinguish it from ἐλεός, *dresser, tray, kitchen table*: ἐλέος (?) Arc. 38. 19 is no doubt an error: κάπνεος (or κάπνεως) *a kind of vine*, Arist. de Gen. An. 4. 4. 12: also κάπνιος, Proverb. Bodl. 533, p. 64. ed. Gaisf.; *H. D.*: κηδεός, Schol. Ven. Ψ. 160; some barytoned the word, as the genitive of κῆδος; the scholiast considers it a verbal noun from κηδεύω, as λοχεός (λοχεύω), σωρεός (σωρεύω): λοχεός, according to Schol. Ven. Ψ. 160, most considered λοχεῖο, Hesiod. Theog. 178, to be a mere bye-form of λόχος, and accordingly wrote λοχέοιο: περίνεος, Galen; Arist. is probably a compound word: πίλεος = *pileus*, Polyb. 30. 16. 3, quoted by H. D. s. v.; it retains the Latin accent: σεμνόθεο., Diog. Laert. Praef., is of course a compound: φέως, cf. Schneider ad Theophrast. tom. 5. p. 533: φλέως, Lob. Phryn. 293; Theog. Can. 49. 6: φιβάλεοι, or φιβάλεῳ, Att. (sc. ἰσχάδες); *L. S. s. v.*: φιβάλεως, the tree that bears them, Schol. Aristoph. Ach. 802, may be mentioned here, though it belongs more properly to the Attic declension.

238. NOTE 2.—Αἰγίστεος, *H. D.*: Ἄλεος, Strab. 615; or Ἄλεως, Attic, Diod. Sic. 4. 33, but Ἀλεός, E. M. 59. 42, is more in accordance with analogy: Βολεοί, Paus. 2. 36. 3: Δάρεος (?) = Δαρεῖος, Pape: Δεκαίνεος, Strab. 298; Ἐλεός, an island and a river, Theog. Can. 50. 5; Thucyd. 8. 26, where Bekker reads Λέρος: Ἔλεος = Mercy, personified, Paus. 1. 17. 1: Ἐρινεός, St. Byz.: Κέως, Ion. Κέος, Theog. Can. 49. 6: Κλάδεος, Paus. 5. 7. 1, see Κλάδαος above, § 224: Κούνεος, Strab. 137 = *cuneus*, it keeps the Latin accent, like πίλεος: vid. sup. § 237: Λέπρεος, Paus. 5. 5. 3 and 4: Λυκίδεος (?) *Pape*: Μάνθεος, Inscr.: Πανδάρεος, Hom. Od. 19. 518, and Πανδάρεως, Paus. 10. 30. 1: Παντέλεος, Anth. app 58, is thus accented as being a compound: Πηνέλαος = Πηνέλεως, Hom. Il. 2. 494, etc.: Ποσείδεος (?) *Pape*: Πύθεος (?) *Pape*: Πύλεος, Paus. 9. 37. 1: Τέος, Theog. Can. 49. 6: Τριχόλεος, Athen. 605 F: Φένεος, Hom. Il. 2. 605, is more correctly Φενεός, Eust. 301. 14; Strab. 388; Paus. 8. 14. 4: Χίλεος, Herodot. 9. 9.

-ΖΟΣ.

239. Substantives, proper and common, in ζος retract the accent, as ἄοζος, ὄζος, ῥοῖζος, τόπαζος, Ἄραζος, Βύμαζος, except μαζός oxytone.

240. NOTE.—Arc. 48. 21 : μαζός, A. G. Oxon. 1. 443. 18 ; also the name of a fish, Athen. 322 B, where Cod. B. reads μάζους paroxytone : Ἀαζοί, which Göttling, Accent. p. 218, quotes from St. Byz., seems to be a typographical error ; and for Βυζός, which he cites also from the same author, Βυσσός is read in Westermann's edition : Λαζοί, ' Luc. Tox. c. 44 ; Phot. Bib. 238. 29 ;' *Pape*; add St. Byz.: Τριζοί, St. Byz.

-ΗΟΣ.

241. Common substantives in ηος are oxytone, as αἰζηός, πηός.

NOTE.—E. M. 32. 18; Schol. Ven. B. 599. The dialectic forms in ηος = ειος seem to retain the accent of the latter termination, Ἀχηός = Ἀχαιός, E. M. 32. 6; Theog. Can. 51. 18; Ahrens de Gr. ling. dialect. 1. p. 187, note. Ὄρηος = Ὄρειος, Καλλιῆος, Ἀριστιῆος, Ἄρηος, Κολοσίμηος (?) Κλυτόνηος, Hom. Od. 8. 119; Apollon. Rhod. 1. 134. The passage in Arcadius (39. 8), which speaks of these words, is so corrupt that little can be made of it.

-ΘΟΣ.

242. Substantives in θος, both proper and common, retract the accent, as ἄκανθος, ἄμαθος, ἀσάμινθος, κέλευθος, κύαθος, λάπαθος, λήκυθος, μήρινθος, μῦθος, πίθος, πλίνθος, πόθος, σμίνθος, τερέβινθος, ὑάκινθος, Βόηθος, Ἐρύμανθος, Ζάκυνθος, Ζῆθος, Κόρινθος, Κράπαθος, Μάραθος, Ξάνθος, Ξοῦθος ; except βοηθός, βυθός, μασθός, μισθός, ὁρμαθός, στρουθός, τιτθός, which are oxytone.

243. NOTE.—Arc. 48. 24-50. 2 ; Schol. Ven. B. 676 : βοηθός (adj.), Schol. Ven. B. 311 ; E. M. 730. 35 ; Arc. 49. 25 ; Eust. 228. 33 ; Chœrob. E. 120. 2 : βυθός, Arc. 49. 10 ; Theog. Can. 54. 19 : γύργαθος is always thus accented in our books (see H. D. s. v.), though Arc. 49. 19 expressly makes it oxytone : κακιθός or κάκιθος, Suid., or κακῖθος, A. G. Oxon. 2. 229. 22, is a corrupt form for κακηθός, Arc. 49. 25 : κάνθος, *the corner of the eye*, and *the tire of a wheel*, is false (?) for κανθός, Eust. 598. 10 ; Arist. H. A. 1. 9. 2 : ὁρμαθός, Arc. 49. 18 : πέλεθος, the Attic for σπέλεθος, is sometimes falsely written πελεθός, and σπελεθός is so accented in one MS. of Aristoph. Eccles. 595 : σκινθός, Theophrast. H. P. 4. 6. 9, is paroxytone in Theog. Can. 16. 20 : στρουθός, Schol. Ven. B. 311 ; Eust. 228. 33 ; Arc. 49. 2 ; Chœrob. E. 120. 2 ; E. M. 730. 33 ; Herod. π. μ. λ. 42. 4. According to Chares (Chæris ap. Schol. Ven.) and Trypho ap. Herodian. (Schol. Aristoph. Av. 877), the Attics wrote στρουθός : τεῦθος, *a kind of cuttle-fish*, is wrongly oxytone in Arist. H. A. 9. 2. 1, where however one MS. has τεῦθοι : τιτθός (an adjective); Lob. Par. 346 : τιτθός, Pollux 2. 163, etc.: the proper name Δαμαιθός, St. Byz. s. v. Σύρνα, is irregular : Μαραθοί (?) Athen. 575 A, is doubtful both in form and accent.

-ΙΟΣ.

244. Common substantives in ιος are oxytone, as αἰγυπιός, • ἀνεψιός, βιός, *a bow*, βομβυλιός, ἐρωδιός, κριός, μητρυιός, πατρυιός,

υἱός, χαραδριός; except ἄπιος, βίος, *life*, δακτύλιος, δήμιος, δρίος, (also neuter), ἥλιος, θρίος, κάπριος, κύριος, σφονδύλιος, which retract the accent, and the paroxytones γομφίος, κωβίος, νυμφίος, σκορπίος.

245. Note 1.—Herod. π. μ. λ. 18. 3; A. G. Oxon. 1. 107. 17: ἀγάλιος, E. M. 7. 7, or ἀγάλλιος, Hesych.: ἀέλιοι, οἱ ἀδελφὰς γυναῖκας ἐσχηκότες, Hesych.; αἰγώλιος, Arist. H. A. 8. 3. 3; or better, αἰγωλιός, Arist. H. A. 9. 1. 17; 9. 17. 2: according to E. M. 380. 35, hypertrisyllabic names of birds in ιος are oxytone; cf. E. M. 995. 11; Chœrob. E. 128. 7: τὰ διὰ τοῦ ΙΟΣ ὀνόματα ἐπὶ ζώων λαμβανόμενα ὀξύνονται, οἶον, αἰγυπιός, βομβυλιός, χαραδριός, ἀδρυφιός, παρὰ Πέρσας ὁ ἀετός, ἐρωδιός: αἰτώλιος, Arist. H. A. 6. 6. 3, this word is almost certainly an adjective, substantively used: ἀκίνιος (sc. στέφανος), Athen. 680 D: ἀλκίβιος (sc. ἔχις), Schol. Nicand. Ther. 441, so called from one Alcibius: ἄπιος, *a pear-tree*, was no doubt originally an adjective: Ἀρτεμίσιος (sc. μήν): Βάκχιος, really an adjective, Soph. Ant. 154; Eurip. Cycl. 446, etc.: βίος, *life*; βιός, *bow*, Arc. 37. 34; E. M. 198. 23: βουγάϊος is a compound adjective: βουμέλιος, Theophr. H. P. 3. 11. 4; 4. 8. 2: Γεράστιος (sc. μήν), Thucyd. 4. 119: γυλιός, E. M. 244. 21, is frequently, though perhaps wrongly, made proparoxytone, cf. A. G. 228. 30: δήμιος = ὁ δημόσιος κολαστής, is an adjective: δρίος (pl. τὰ δρία), Arc. 119. 6: ἐγωλιός, Arc. 41. 5, where Schmidt conjectures αἰγωλιός: ἐδωλιός, Arc. 41. 5, is falsely written ἐδώλιος, or εἰδώλιος, in Schol. Aristoph. Av. 884: ἐλώριος, Athen. 332 E, should probably be oxytone: ἐπικρήδιος, *a Cretan dance*, Athen. 629 C: ἥλιος, E. M. 521. 13, of which the Cretan form is said to have been ἀβέλιος, Hesych. and the Pamphylian βαβέλιος, Eust. 1654. 21: θαλαμιός, Arc. 40. 13, but θαλάμιος is the general accent in MSS. according to Göttling Accent. p. 173: θάσιος (sc. οἶνος, etc.): θρίος (?) E. M. 472. 46; Θρίος is the name of a place, Arc. 37. 21; Theog. Can. 48. 23: καλίκιοι = *calcei*, Polyh. 30. 16. 3, quoted by L. S.: καλιός, Pollux 10. 160. 161 is the proper accent, not κάλιος: κάπνιος, a herb so called, Galen T. 13. 184 B: κάπριος, also an adjective: καρχήσιοι (sc. κάλοι), Galen Lex. Hippocrat.: κέρθιος, *the Certhios, a small bird*, Arist. H. A. 9. 17. 2: κύριος is an adjective used substantively: λαβρώνιος, *a kind of cup*, Theog. Can. 55. 6, is probably an adjective: λάϊος, *a kind of bird*, Anton. Lib. c. 19. p. 124, is better oxytone, as it is in Arist. H. A. 9. 19: λύκιος, *a kind of jackdaw*, Hesych.; Περίτιος, a Macedonian month, Suid.: πράμνιος (sc. οἶνος): σιός, Dor. = θεός: σείριος (sc. ἀστήρ and οἶνος), Lob. Par. 334: τύλιος (?) *a leathern purse*, A. G. 308. 4, perhaps a corrupt form for τύλιμος or τυλιμός: χαρίσιοι (sc. ἄρτοι and πλακοῦντες), Pollux 6. 72; on the compound substantive λευκερωδιός or λευκερώδιος, see below, § 422.

246. Note 2.—*Paroxytones.* Γομφίος (sc. ὀδούς), Eust. 150. 34; 870. 11; Göttling, Accent. p. 172, remarks that there is no authority in the grammarians for this accentuation; the word is very commonly *proparoxytone*, as in Pollux 2. 92; Athen. 411 B; Aristoph. Plut. 1059; Arist. de Gen. Animal. 5. 8. 1; H. A. 2. 4, where one MS. has γομφίοι; E. M. 237. 53, etc.; *H. D.*: κωβίος, Arc. 42. 3; Chœrob. E. 128. 10; yet it is generally oxytone, e.g. Arist. H. A. 6. 15. 9: νυμφίος, *a bridegroom*, Arc. 41. 33; Herod. π. μ. λ. 19. 33; E. M. 608. 40; Theog. Can. 58. 10; Chœrob. E. 131. 15; Lobeck (Par. 355) notes that νυμφίος ὕμνος in Nonnus 47. 464, for νύμφιος ὕ. is a mistake: σκορπίος, Arc. 42. 3; Chœrob. E. 128. 10.

247. Proper names in ιος throw back the accent, as Βομβύλιος, Θρίος, Κίος, Ἰαμβλιχοπορφύριος, Πῖος, Χῖος; except Ἀσκληπιός, and 'Ιλλυριός oxytone, and those consisting of three short syllables, which are paroxytone, as Βαλίος, Δολίος, Κλονίος, 'Οδίος, Σχεδίος, Τυχίος, Χρομίος: to this rule of the grammarians there are many exceptions, of which the more important are "Αλιος, "Ανιος, Κρόνιος, Ξένιος, Στρόφιος.

248. Note 1.—'Αγρίος, A. G. Oxon. 2. 284. 13, but it is constantly proparoxytone: Αἰγίμιος, Athen. 503 D; Apollod. 2. 7. 7; Strab. 427; Suid. etc., is oxytone (?) according to Göttling Accent. p. 172: "Αμφῖος, Chœrob. A. G. Oxon. 2. 168. 17, is wrongly made paroxytone in the same book, 284. 13: "Αξιος, Eust. 359. 22, etc., this is probably correct, though 'Αξιός occurs Hom. Il. 2. 849; 21. 157; Strab. 330, and elsewhere: 'Ασκληπιός, Eust. 860. 10: according to the same author, 463. 39, Demosthenes made it proparoxytone: Γεδρωσιοί (?) *Pape*; Strab. 723 has Γεδρώσιοι, and that is its proper accent: Δέξιος, Diog. Laert. 9. 2. § 18, is more usually written Δεξιός, A. G. 129. 15; Harpocr. s. v. Στρομβιχίδης: 'Ερχίος, Arc. 41. 30; Theog. Can. 58. 26; this is falsely proparoxytone in some editions of Lucian Amor. c. 49: 'Ιλλυριός, *an Illyrian*, Arc. 40. 10: 'Ιλλύριος, the son of Cadmus, in St. Byz., is oxytone in Apollod. 3. 5. 4, and Eust. ad Dion. Per. 95: 'Ιλλύριοι, St. Byz.; Herodot. 1. 196: "Ιος, an island; Strab. 484; cf. Theog. Can. 48. 25: "Ιός, in Arcadia, Xen. Hell. 6. 5. 24, where Schneider reads Οἶος and Οἰός: Κίος, a city and river, Strab. 563; Apollon. Rhod. 1. 1178; Theog. Can. 48. 28: Κῖος ὄνομα ποταμοῦ καὶ ἔθνους: Κῖος, or Κεῖος, adjective, A. G. Oxon. 2. 192. 3: Κρῖος is sometimes properispomenon, but Aristarchus oxytoned it, E. M. 539. 20; A. G. Oxon. 2. 226. 16: Κυριός (?): Μήνιος is sometimes, though wrongly, oxytone, see H. D. s. v.: Πῖος = *Pius*, though condemned by Schmidt ad. Arc. 37. 21, is constantly so accented, the penultimate is expressly said to be long by Theog. Can. 48. 22; 107. 21; A. G. Paris. 3. 307. 10; A. G. Oxon. 1. 107. 21; Πίος is quoted by H. D. from Schol. Soph. Aj. 408; cf. E. M. 539. 25: Σηίος (?) *Pape*, apparently a typographical error for Σήιος.

249. Note 2.—*Names consisting of three short syllables.* "Αλιος, Schol. Ven. B. 495: Ptolemæus read 'Αλίος paroxytone in the Odyssey, Schol. Ven. E. 39. 683: "Ανιος, Schol. Ven. E. 39; E. M. 521. 14; Diod. Sic. 5. 62: Γλύφιος, Eust. 1665. 56: Θράσιος, Apollod. 2. 5. 11: Κλυτίος, Hom. Il. 3. 147, etc.; Eust. 395. 23. ' In codd. non raro Κλύτιος est proparoxytonum, contra regulam grammaticorum ... de qua v. Lehrs De Aristarcho. p. 279,' *H. D.*: Κρόνιος, Schol. Ven. E. 39; E. M. 521. 14; Diod. Sic. 5. 55: Λάκιος (?) Athen. 297 F; St. Byz. s. v. Γέλα: Λάσιος (?) Paus. 6. 21. 10: Λύκιος, Apollod. 3. 8. 1: Μάριος = *Mărius*, Diod. Sic. 36. 1. p. 156. ed. Bekk.: Μαριός, a town, Paus. 3. 21. 7; 22. 8: Νόμιος, Alciph. 3. 23: Νυμφίος, E. M. 221. 31, is almost certainly an error: Νύχιος, Quint. Smyr. 2. 363: Ξένιος, Schol. Ven. E. 39; E. M. 521. 14: "Οριος, Alciph. 3. 29, ' scribendum videtur "Ορειος, *H. D.*: "Οσιος (?) *Pape*; Socr. H. E. 1. , Athanas. T. 1. p. 193 A; *H. D.*: Πόλιος, Ælian V. H. 12. 31; perhaps Πόλλιος is the better reading: 'Ράκιος, Schol. Apollon. Rhod. 1. 308; Paus. 7. 3. 2: 'Ροδίος, the river, Strab. 595, etc., is in some books improperly proparoxytone; Schol. Ven. M. 20; Eust. 906. 56, distinguishes it from the adjective 'Ρόδιος; in Diog. Laert. 7. 1. § 22 it occurs as the name of a man; the passage does not determine the accent, but it should probably be 'Ροδίος, not 'Ρόδιος, as Pape prints it: Σθένιος, or Σθενίος: Σκοτίος, Schol. Ven. Z. 24: Σκύριος (?) Apollod. 3. 15. 5, proves nothing: Σόφιος, Paus. 6. 3. 2: Σπέδιος (?) Inscr., *Pape*, and *H. D.*: Σπόριος = *Spurius*, Diod. Sic. 11. 1: Στίχιος, Hom. Il. 13. 195, or Στίχιος (?) Phot. Bib. 152. 36: Στόμιος, Paus. 6. 3. 2; 14. 13: Στράτιος, Paus. 9. 37. 1; Strab. 74, Kramer; or Στρατίος, Hom. Odyss. 3. 413; Eust. 1474. 30: Στρόφιος, Enst. 1030. 11: Σχεδίος was by some made proparoxytone, Eust. 1030. 11 ; Arc. 41. 27 ; Herod. π. μ. λ. 18. 5 : Τάτιος = Tătius, Plut. 1. 27 etc. : Τάφιος, Apollod. 2. 4. 5 ; Diod. Sic. 8. 20 : Ὕπιος, St. Byz.; Apollon. Rhod. 2. 797 ; Phot. Bib. 234. 34 : Φάλιος (?) Thucyd. 1. 24, where some books have Φαλιός : it would be better to make it paroxytone : Φάνιος, Suid., probably a mistake for Φανίας : Φίλιος, Anth. App. 376 : Φλόγιος, Lucian V. H. 1. 20, and elsewhere, is false for Φλογίος, Arc. 40. 8 : Φόβιος, Parthen. 14 : Φράσιος, Nonnus Dionys. 32. 234, should be Φρασίος, Arc. 40. 22 : Φύσιος, Apollod. 3. 8. 1 : Χάριος, *Pape* : Χέδιος, Quint. Smyr. 10. 87, 'ubi recte correctum est Σχέδιον quod Σχεδίον scribendum erat παροξυτόνως,' *W. Dindorf* ap. H. D.: Χθόνιος, Paus. 9. 5. 3, etc., or Χθονίος, Apollod. 2. 1. 5 : Χρόμιος frequently occurs, but is incorrect ; the proper accent is Χρομίος, Schol. Ven. B. 495 : Χρόνιος, Paus. 8. 47. 6, should be Χρονίος.

-ΑΙΟΣ.

250. Common substantives in αιος (if there be any such) are properispomena, as ἀντακαῖος, βαρκαῖος, βουκαῖος, γαῖος (?), γραψαῖος, εὐδιαῖος, σκωπαῖος, χαῖος (?) ; except ἔλαιος (ἀγριέλαιος, καλλιέλαιος), ὑμέναιος, proparoxytone.

251. Note.—Most, if not all, the so-called substantives of this termination are adjectives used elliptically ; the following list comprises all that I have noted— Ἀγριέλαιος, Eust. 1944. 8 : ἀφυταῖος, *a kind of vine*, Theophr. C. P. 3. 15. 5 is an adjective : βαρκαῖος, *a kind of fish*, Theog. Can. 52. 33 : βουκαῖος, Theocr. 10. 1 ; Nicand. Ther. 5 : γαῖος, Eust. 188. 28, is γαιός in Hesych., A. G. 229. 16, and elsewhere : γραψαῖος, Athen. 106 D : δεραιός, Hesych.: ἔλαιος, cf. Eust. 1944. 7 : ἐλαιός, *a kind of bird*, L. S.: ἑρμαῖος ὁ τετράγωνος λίθος, Suid.: ἐρυσίχαιος in Alcman. 11 may perhaps be an adj. used substantively, but Herodian took it to be an Ethnic name ; cf. St. Byz. s. v. Ἐρυσίχη, and H. D. s. v.: εὐδιαῖος, Plut. 2. 699 F, is proparoxytone in Pollux 1. 92 : καλλιέλαιος, Pseud. Arist. de Plantis 1. 6. 4 : λαιός, *a kind of bird*, Arist. H. A. 9. 19 : πανομφαῖος, Hom. Il. 8. 250, or πανόμφαιος, Schol. Aristoph. Ach. 142 : σκωπαῖος, *a dwarf*, Eust. 1523. 63 : στειλαιός = στειλειόν or στειλειά : ὑμέναιος, Theog. Can. 52. 6 : χαῖος, or χαιός, *H. D.* s. v. : ὑπερβερεταῖος, *the last month of the Macedonian year.*

252. Proper names in αιος are properispomena, as Ἀγαπαῖος, Αἰγαῖος, Ἀλκαῖος, Βαῖος, Γραῖος, Δερραῖοι, Εὐναῖος, Μαῖος, Παῖος, Πτολεμαῖος, Σκαῖος ; except Ἀθήναιος, Εὔμαιος, with some others, proparoxytone, and the oxytone Ἀχαιός (Παναχαιός). Those which are derived from verbs are generally proparoxytone, as Τίμαιος, Φίλαιος.

253. Note.—Ἀγέλαιος, E. M. 7. 42 : Ἀθήναιος, Arc. 43. 14 ; Schol. Ven. N. 791, with this, as with other names of the same termination, there was a diversity of accent according to the grammarians, in order that they might be distinguished from the corresponding adjectives : Ἀμφίβαιος, Tzetzes ad Lycoph. 749 : Ἀρίβαιος, Xen. Cyrop. 2. 1. 5 : Ἀρίνθαιος, Basil. Epist. 179, vol. 3. p. 264; *H. D.*: Ἀρράβαιος, Arist. Pol. 5. 8. 17 : Ἀρτάχαιος (?) *Pape* ; the passages which he quotes (Herodot. 7. 63 ; 8. 130) do not prove this to be the correct accent : Ἀχαιός, Arc. 43. 19 ; St. Byz. s. v. Ἀβάντις and Ἀχαία ; Theog. Can. 52. 14 : Βαρτίμαιος, N. T. Mark 10. 46 ; Βήλαιος, Liban.; *Pape*: Βίλαιος (*sic*), St. Byz. s. v. Τίος, a river, is properly written Βιλλαῖος, and expressly said to be properispomenon by Herodian ap. Schol. Apollon. Rhod. 2. 791 : Δίαιος, Paus. 7. 12. 3 : Δίκαιος (?)

Herodot. 8. 65; 'ubi pravo accentu Δικαῖος scribi notat Lehrs de Aristarch. p. 277.'
H. D.; but it is better as a properispomenon than a proparoxytone; Ἕλαιος, a
river in Bithynia, Marcian. Heracl. p. 70; *H. D.*: Ἐλαιός, in Messenia, Paus. 4.
ί. 6: Ἕλαιος (?) in Ætolia, Polyb. 4. 65. 6: Ἕρμαιος, the proper name, is distinguished from Ἑρμαῖος the adjective by Arc. 43. 8; Schol. Ven. N. 791: τὰ διὰ
τοῦ ΑΙΟΣ τρισύλλαβα, ἔχοντα τὴν πρώτην συλλαβὴν εἰς σύμφωνον καταλήγουσαν,
προπερισπᾶσθαι θέλει, χερσαῖος, ὀρφναῖος, ἐρσαῖος, ἀρχαῖος, Ἀρναῖος, Τρικκαῖος, Ἑρμαῖος·
ὅθεν τὸ Ἑρμαῖον κάρα παρὰ Σοφοκλεῖ. τὸ δὲ ὅθι θ' Ἕρμαιος λόφος ἐστίν (Od.
16. 471) ὡς εἰς ἰδιότητα: but in the passage referred to our books, as well as the
Greek scholiast on the place, read Ἑρμαῖος λόφος: Εὐαῖοι, a people of Canaan,
Exod. 3. 8. 17: Εὔαιος (?) Iamblich. V. P. c. 36: Εὔδαιος (?) Suid.; the river
so called varies between Εὐδαῖος, Εὔλαιος, and Εὐλαῖος, Diod. Sic. 19. 19; Arrian
Anab. 7. 7. 2; Εὔμαιος, Hom. Odyss.; Ἥραιος, Schol. Ven. Λ. 301; Eust.
1562. 60: Θαλέλαιος, Synes. p. 304 D, quoted by H. D. s. v.: Θερμόλαιος (?)
the name of a Cretan month: Ἵμαιος, Strab. 519, is better Ἰμαῖος, Theog. Can.
53. 7: Κλεόδαιος (?) *Pape*; *H. D.*: but the passages in Herodotus, Pausanias,
and Apollodorus, which are quoted for this accent, prove nothing; the better
form is Κλεοδαῖος, Suid.: Κωλαῖος, a man's name, Herodot. 4. 152, but Κωλαιός (?)
a place, Polyh. 2. 55. 5: Λήναιος, Lob. Par. 342; St. Byz.: according to Philop.
Ληναῖος, *Bacchus*, is properispomenon, and Λήναιος, a man so called, proparoxytone,
yet we have Ληναῖος in Auth. Pal. 7. 292. 1: Αἴλαιος, Æschyl. Pers. 308, 969;
Λύαιος, Theog. Can. 53. 23; E. M. 193. 16: Λύγαιος, Theog. Can. 53. 3: Μάταιος (?) *Pape*: Μνήσαιος, Quint. Smyr. 10. 88; Suid. s. v. Νικαγόρας: Νείκαιος
(?) *Pape*: Νίκαιος, Schol. Ven. E. 69, or Νικαῖος, cf. Theog. Can. 53. 10: Πά-
ναιος (?) a man's name, *Pape*: the Παναῖοι, a Thracian race, is regular; St. Byz.;
Thucyd. 2. 101: Παναχαιοί, E. M. 250. 33; Apoll. Synt. 328. 14: Πείραιος,
Hom. Od. 15. 540; Schol. Ven. Λ. 301: Πειραιός, a harbour in the Corinthian
territory, Thucyd. 8. 10: Περίναιος, Zenob.; *Pape*: Πήδαιος, Schol. Ven. E. 69;
E. M. 193. 16, for which Πίδαιος, Suid. is a false form: Πύλαιος, Schol. Ven. B.
842: τοῦ Πύλαιος τὴν πρώτην ὀξυτονητέον πρὸς ἀντιδιαστολὴν τοῦ τοπικοῦ· καὶ τὸν
Ἑρμῆν τὸν Πυλαῖον (sic); Lob. Par. 342; E. M. 696. 50 is Πυλαῖος in Suid.:
Σκαῖος, Arc. 37. 5: Σκαιός, a river, Strab. 590; Theog. Can. 48. 6: Σκαιοί, a
people, St. Byz.: Τίραιος, Lucian Macrob. § 16: Τίθαιος, Herod. 7. 88: Τίμαιος,
Schol. Ven. E. 69; Theog. Can. 53. 23; Arc. 43. 10: Τόλμαιος (?) *Pape*; the
passages quoted prove nothing: H. D. have Τολμαῖος: Τρυγαῖος was Herodian's
accentuation, the rest wrote Τρύγαιος, Schol. Aristoph. Pac. 62: Τύρταιος occurs,
but Τυρταῖος, Strab. 366, is the usual accent: Ὕλαιος, E. M. 193. 17; Lob. Par.
342 is better Ὑλαῖος, in Apollod. 3. 9. 2: Ὑμέναιος, Athen. 603 D, etc.: Ὑπάχαιοι
(?) the correct form is Ὑπαχαιοί, Herodot. 7. 91; Hesych. etc.; Ὑπέλαιος, a spring,
Athen. 361 D; Strab. 640; Φεναιός = Φενεύς, Callim. Del. 71, where Arnald writes
Φενειός: Φέραιος (?): Φιλαθήναιος: Φίλαιος, Schol. Ven. E. 69; Λ. 301; Φιλαῖος,
which, according to H. D., occurs in Plutarch, is an error.

The grammarians say that proper names in αιος from nouns are properispomena, from verbs proparoxytone: a useless rule, as is clear from Τρυγαῖος,
Ἀγαπαῖος, and others, which might be derived either from nouns or verbs.

‑ΕΙΟΣ.

254. The few common substantives in ειος are oxytone, as
ἀδελφειός, ἐλειός, ἀρνειός, νειός (Arc. 37. 17), συφειός, φατειός
(Arc. 44. 28), φωλειός; except θεῖος, which is properispomenon.

NOTE.—The following are adjectives substantively used—βασίλειος (?): λεῖος, *a smooth-skinned skark*, L. S.: βακχεῖος (sc. ῥυθμός, οἶνος, etc.): for ἠθεῖος or ἠθαῖος, see Adjectives.

255. Proper names in ειος are oxytone, as Ἀλφειός, Ἀρνειός, Δαρδανειός, Ἐπειός, Ἐπειοί, Ὀλμειός, Πηνειός, Σπερχειός; except Ἄρειος, Βασίλειος, Ἕλειος, Μήδειος, Ὄρειος, Ὑπερβόρειοι proparoxytone, and the properispomenon Δαρεῖος.

256. Note.—Αἰνεῖοι (?) St. Byz. s. v. Αἴνεια: Ἀκρώρειοι, St. Byz.: Ἀργεῖος, both as a proper name and as an adjective, cf. Chœrob. E. 123. 24: Ἄρειος, *Pape*: Ἀρνεῖος, Chœrob. A. G. Oxon. 2. 174. 22: ἀρνεῖος, ὁ μὴν προπερισπωμένον: Ἀστεῖος, *Pape*: Αὐσόνειος (?) *Pape*: Βακχεῖος, A. G. Oxon. 2. 173. 31; Plat. Ep. 1. 309 C; as the epithet of Bacchus the accent varies between proparoxytone and properispomenon: Βασίλεια, Strab. 306: Βασίλειος, a river, Strab. 747; a man, Suid.; Phot. Bib. 266. 10: Δαρεῖος, Chœrob. A. G. Oxon. 2. 196. 2; E. M. 248. 31; Arc. 44. 17 says that Δαρειος is oxytone, but in the same page, l. 22, that it is properispomenon; in the former place Göttling conjectures Δαρδανειός: Δεῖος (?) Plut. 2. 1132 D: Διογένειος, *Pape*: Ἐγχέλειοι (?) Strab. 326, Meineke; on the numerous forms of this name, see H. D. s. v. Ἐγχελέας: Ἕλειος, Apollod. 2. 4. 5, etc.: Ἕλειοι, St. Byz. etc.: Ἠλεῖοι, Paus. 5. 1. 8; Plut. 1. 168: Ἡράκλειος, Suid. s. v. Βασίλειος: Ἠτεῖος (?) E. M. 248. 31: Καρνεῖος, Athen. 156 E, is Κάρνειος or Καρνειός in Paus. 3. 13. 3: Κήτειος, Strab. 616; (Hom. Od. 11. 521); yet Arc. 44. 22 says, τὸ δὲ Κητειός Πηνειός ὀξύνεται ὡς κύρια: Κρεῖος, Hes. Theog. 134, etc.: Μήδειος, Arc. 44. 11; Hes. Theog. 1001: Μήδειοι, *Pape*: Μινύειος, Strab. 346: Ὄλμειος (?) a man; the river Ὀλμειός is regular, Schol. Hes. Theog. 6; Strab. 407; Arc. 44. 16: Ὄρειος, Diod. Sic. 4. 12; Paus. 3. 18. 15: Οὔρειος, Hes. Scut. 186: Σοροάδειος, an Indian deity, Athen. 27 E: Στενήρειος, Inscr.: Στρατονίκειος as a compound is regular: Τίβειος (?) *Pape*: Ὕλλειοι, Dion. Perieg. 386, is faulty for Ὕλληοι or Ὑλληοί: Ὑπερβόρειοι is correct as a compound, and also as being an adjective.

This class of words is so entirely adjectival in its character that even the Greeks themselves seem to have been in doubt whether they should give them the accent of substantives or adjectives.

-ΟΙΟΣ.

257. Common substantives in οιος are oxytone, as γλοιός, κλοιός, κολοιός, φλοιός.

Note.—The following rare words are exceptions to this rule—βοιός (?) Arc. 37. 12: γλοιός, such is the accentuation of our books, and Arc. 37. 12 states that (ὀξύνεται) γλοιὸς ἐπὶ κόπρου, Göttling (Accent. p. 182) is therefore mistaken when he says that it is properispomenon: μνοῖος, *a furnace*, Theog. Can. 49. 24: πτοῖος (?) = πτοία.

258. Proper names in οιος are properispomena, as Βοῖοι, Κοῖος, Μοῖος, except the deme Ὀλός, which is oxytone.

259. Note.—Ἄθοιος, Theog. Can. 53. 29: Ἀνόμοιος, Phot. Bib. 279. 20, perhaps so accented as a compound: Βοῖοι, Strab. 315, is also written Βοιοί, St. Byz. s. v. Βοῖον; like many other names of nations, it oscillates between an adjectival and substantival accent: Βοῖος as the name of a man is regular, Athen. 393 E; Paus. 3. 22. 11; Arc. 37. 14: Γέλοιος (?) *Pape*: Ἔνδοιος, Paus. 1. 26. 4:

Εὔβοιος, Athen. 697 F: Ζάτοιος, Theog. Can. 53. 29: Οἰός, a deme, Arc. 37. 15; Schol. Ven. Λ. 24; Theog. Can. 49. 29: Οἶος in Tegea is regular, St. Byz.: Σμοῖος (?) is oxytone in Aristoph. Eccl. 846.

For those in ῳος, see Substantives in ωος § 338.

-ΚΟΣ.

260· Common substantives in κος retract the accent, as ἄρκος, αὐτόλυκος, δημοπίθηκος, δίσκος, θύλακος, κέρκος, κόκκος, λάκκος, λύκος, μῶκος, οἶκος, ὅρκος, πίθηκος, πλόκος, σάκκος, σώρακος, τόκος, ὕσσακος; except those in ισκος, which are paroxytone, as ἀνδριαντίσκος, ἀστερίσκος, δεσποτίσκος, παιδίσκος, σατυρίσκος.; adjectives in ἵκος used substantively, which are oxytone, as γραμματικός, μουσικός, and the oxytones ἀσκός, ἀστακός, βοσκός, διψακός, δοκός, *a beam,* (δόκος=δόκησις), θριγκός, μωκός, *a mocker,* (μῶκος, *mockery*), ὁλκός, σηκός, σκιθακός, φακός, φαρμακός, χαλκός, ψιττακός; ἀγροῖκος is generally properispomenon.

261. NOTE I.—Arc. 50. 3-52. 15; Etym. Gud. 435. 12; Herod. π. μ. λ. 41. 24: ἀγελάσκος (?) Hesych.: ἄγροικος = ὁ σκαιὸς τοὺς τρόπους: ἀγροῖκος = ὁ ἐν ἀγρῷ κατοικῶν, Ammon. s. v.; cf. Eust. 1409. 52; Lex. Gr. ap. Herm. de emend. rat. Gr. gr. p. 328: L. S. observe that the word is generally properispomenon in all senses: ἄνακος, Aristarchus made it oxytone, Eust. 1365. 45: ἀσκός, Arc. 50. 15; and ἀκκόρ, Laced. Hesych.: ἀστακός (and Att. ὀστακός), Arc. 51. 8: βίτ-τακος or βιττακός=ψιττακός: βοσκός, Lob. Phryn. 22: δαρεικός (sc. στατήρ): διψακός, *a disease of the kidneys,* Galen De Loc. Affect. 6. 3, Tom. 7. p. 511 C; also a plant, Boissonade Anecd. Tom. 1. p. 396; in the latter sense the word is proparoxytone in Galen De Simp. Med. Facult. 6. 6; Tom. 13. p. 169 B, all these places are quoted by H. D. s. v.: δοκός, *a beam;* δόκος = δόκησις, E. M. 538. 48; A. G. Oxon. 1. 223. 19: Δόκος πρὸς ἀντιδιαστολὴν τοῦ δοκός ὀξυτόνου τοῦ σημαίνοντος τὴν δόκησιν καὶ παρὰ Ἀριστοφάνει ἐν Ταγηνισταῖς σημαίνει τὴν ἀγχόνην, is faulty; read τοῦ δόκος παροξυτόνου, for δόκος = δόκησις is paroxytone both by the precepts of the grammarians (E. M. 538. 48; Eust. 1967. 25, καὶ δόκος μὲν δόκησις καὶ ἀγχόνη, δοκὸς δὲ ὁ τῆς στέγης), and in practice, e. g. δόκος δ᾽ ἐπὶ πᾶσι τέτυκται, Xenophanes ap. Sext. Emp. 7. 49 *et alibi;* though τῷ γ᾽ ἐμῷ δοκῷ (*sic*) is quoted from Callimachus by Eust. 1627. 43; 1761. 34, and Hesych. has Δοκός, σκοπή, προσδοκία, which Salmasius corrects into Δόκος: ἐνθύσκος (?) Hesych.: ἐρίθακος is sometimes found oxytone; cf. Lob. Prol. 311: κικκός, Hesych.: θριγκός, Arc. 50. 10: μάλικος ὄνομα ὀρνέου βαρυτονούμενον, Theog. Can. 59. 26: μῶκος, *mockery:* μωκός, *a mocker,* Lob. Par. 345, but there does not seem to be any good ground for the distinction: ὀστακός=ἀστακός: οὐρακός, *middle part of the oar,* Pollux 1. 90; others write οὐρίαχος: παλλακός, Hesych.: πλατίστακος, Hesych., is falsely oxytone in some editions of Athen. 308 F; see H. D. s. v.: σηκός, Arc. 50. 5; Eust. 1197. 40; Philem. Lex. p. 85. § 213; Schol. Ven. T. 72: σκιδακός (?), σκιθακός (and σκιθαρκός or σκίθαρκος), *a fish so called,* Hesych.: ὑρτακός· ὄστρεον, Hesych.; ὑστριακός or ἱστριακόν, *a kind of cup,* Athen. 500 F; L. S.: φακός, Arc. 50. 20; E. M. 538. 49: φαρμακός, Philem. Lex. p. 113. § 269; Arc. 51. 9, 'Harpocrat. Δίδυμος δὲ προπερισπᾶν ἀξιοῖ τοὔνομα, ἀλλ᾽ ἡμεῖς οὐχ εὕρομεν οὕτω που τὴν χρῆσιν. Ubi mirum et incredibile est Didy-

mum φαρμᾶκος scripsisse dici, quæ scriptura ne in Hipponactis quidem versibus
.... in quibus media syllaba producitur, probabilis est, nedum in scriptoribus
Atticis, quos syllabam illam constanter corripuisse constat. Quamobrem vereor
ne προπερισπᾶν male scriptum sit pro προπαροξύνειν, quem accentum Ionibus tribuit
Eust. 1935. 15: nam quæ Sylburg. in annot. ad Etym. M. p. 788. 5, proposuit,
non possunt probari nitunturque errore librarii, qui in verbis Harpocrationis illio
appositis περισπᾶν scripsit pro προπερισπᾶν. Alii grammatici significationis discrimen statuisse videntur inter φάρμακος et φαρμακός, ut colligi potest ex verbis
Arcadii p. 51. 9, qui de nominibus in κος agens sic scribit : Φυλακὸς ὁ φύλαξ,
Φύλακος δὲ τὸ κύριον· φαρμακὸς ὁ ἐπὶ καθαρμῷ τῆς πόλεως τελευτῶν, φαρμακεὺς δὲ
ὁ γόης. Ubi quum absurdum sit nomen in ΕΥΣ terminatum immisceri, manifesto
scribendum φάρμακυς, eodemque modo apud Ammonium leguntur p. 142 : Φαρ-
μακεύς· φαρμακὸς δὲ ὀξυτόνως, ὁ ἐπὶ καθάρσει τῆς πόλεως ῥιπτόμενος sic sunt corrigenda et supplenda Φάρμακος προπαροξυτόνως ὁ γόης φαρμακὸς δὲ .... ῥιπτόμενος,
non quod Valcken. volebat, Φάρμακος προπαροξυτόνως ὄνομα κύριον, φαρμακὸς δὲ κτλ.,
illata illa quam supra notavi de nomine proprio opinione de qua nihil compertum
habuisse videtur Herodianus cujus verba exhibet Arcadius et partem Schol. Π. Ω.
566 ;' *H. D.* : φυλακός, so Aristarchus Eust. 1365. 45; Arc. 51· 8; but φύλακος,
Philem. Lex. p. 113. § 269; Schol. Apollon. Rhod. 1. 132; Schol. Theocr. 8. 3,
and this seems best, at least in Ionic : χαλκός, Arc. 50. 10 : ψιττακός, Arc. 51.
8; Diod. Sic. 2. 53; but ψίττακος is also found.

262. NOTE 2.—According to Arc. 51. 6 all hyperdissylables in ακος, whether
substantives or adjectives, are oxytone, except θύλακος, ὕσσακος, αἴσακος, and
proper names; but this rule is quite contrary to facts, e. g. ἀμάρακος, σώρακος,
ἀβύρτακος, βάβακος, ἐρίθακος, ἄρακος, ἀσίρακος, etc. Aristarchus oxytoned φυλακός,
φαρμακός, and ἀνακός as being really adjectives, Schol. Ven. Ω. 566; E. M. 802.
3; see below, § 273.

263. Proper names in κος are so irregular that it is hardly
possible to reduce them to any order whatever; the following
rules may however be of some service.

264. (*a*) Those in ισκος are paroxytone, as Κορίσκος, Τρι-
ποδίσκος, Τριποδίσκοι, Κονίσκοι, Φαλίσκοι, Arc. 52. 13; E. M.
807. 9; except Ἀρτισκός, Herod. 4. 92; or Ἀρτησκός, Arc. 51. 19;
52. 15, and this name is almost certainly to be read for Ἀργησκός,
Theog. Can. 60. 62.

265. (*b*) Those in ουσκοι are mostly properispomena, as
Ἐτροῦσκοι, Τοῦσκοι, Strab. 219; Χηροῦσκοι, Strab. 291.

266. (*c*) A considerable number of those in ικος are oxytone
in our books, even where they are obviously adjectival, as Ἀν-
δρικός, Ἀττικός, Αἰνικός, and Ἀπογονικός, names of Cyprian
months; Γραμματικός, Γραφικός, Ἐπικός, Ἐπικουρικός, Ἐρατικός,
Θορικός, St. Byz. : Ἱερατικός, Ἰκός (ῐ?), Strab. 436 : Κελε-
στικός, Suid. : Κλασσικός, Γερμανικός, Strab. 291 : Ξανθικός,
Tzetzes, Antehom. 80 : Σοφιστικός, Τυχικός, Ὑλλικός, Paus. 2.
32. 7 : Φαρσαλικός, Δροπικοί, Herodot. 1. 125 : Ὀμβρικοί, Strab.

228, or Ὄμβρικοι, St. Byz. : Καυλικοί, St. Byz. : Μεδιοματρικοί, Strab. 194: Ὀπικοί, Strab. 242 : Ὠρικός, St. Byz. : Οὐϊνδολικοί, Strab. 292 : Νωρικοί, Strab. 206 : Ἀρκαδικός, Strab. 344 : Ἀτουατικοί. On the other hand, and without any apparent reason for the difference, we have, Δήνικος (ῐ?), Θουμέλικος, Strab. 292 : Κύζικος, Strab. 575·; Apollod. 1. 9. 18 : Μόνικος, Νήρικος, Hom. Odyss. 24. 377 : Ὄρικος, Herodot. 4. 78 : Ποσίδικος, Σίσικος (?), Σύνδικος, St. Byz. : Εἰσάδικοι, Strab. 506 : Ἔρνικοι, Strab. 228 : Βέσβικος (ῐ?), St. Byz. : Ξένικος (ῐ?), Eust. 890. 16 : Σώρικος, Ἔρικος, Τέμικος, Λυκάνικος, Theog. Can. 60. 7 : Θορικός (not Θόρυκος, E. M. 453. 22, which is a mere·clerical error, υ and ι being to the later Greeks signs of one ·and the same sound) is often, though incorrectly, proparoxytone; see Theog. Can. 60. 9.

267. (*d*) Those in ῑκος retract the accent, as Κάϊκος, Γράνικος (Γρανικός (*sic*) Plut. 1. 672), Κῖκος, Φίλικος, Ἑλλάνικος ; except Καμικός and Παλικός.

268. Note.—See Eust. 890. 12 ; Arc. 51. 25 ; Theog. Can. 60. 1 : Καμικός, Theog. Can. 60. 2 ; Arc. 52. 2 : Κάμικος, though found, e. g. Arist. Pol. 2. 10. 4, is an error: Παλικός, Arc. Theog. *ll. ll.*: Αἰνικός, the name of a poet, as it is printed in Theog. Can. 59. 33, contradicts his own rule, and is probably corrupt. Arcadius in the relative place (51. 24) has Ἄνικος, which may be right, though some have emended it. See Schmidt's note ad loc., and Lob. Prol. 324.

269. (*e*) Those in ιᾰκος are oxytone, as Ἀρκαδιακός, Κλονιακός, Κωνιακοί, Κυριακός, Ὀλυνθιακός, Σεραπιακός ; except Πίακος (ᾰ ?), St. Byz., which, according to Lob. Prol. 309, ought to be Πιακός.

270. (*f*) Trisyllables in ᾰκος are proparoxytone, as Αἴσακος, Apollod. 3. 12. 5 : Ἄνακος, Athen. 629 A : Ἄρακος, Paus. 10. 9. 9 : Ἀράνδακος, Plut. 1. 1160 D ; *H. D.* : Ἄστακος, St. Byz. ; Thuc. 2. 30, or Ἀστακός, Herodot. 5. 67 : Βάτακος (?) : Βύττακος, Polyh. 5. 79. 3 : Βώρακος : Δρίμακος, Athen. 266 B, Dindorf, where others read Δριμακός : Θάψακος, Strab. 741 : Θύλακος, Paus. 5. 23. 5 : Ἴδακος, Thucyd. 8. 104 : Ἴθακος, Arc. 51. 4 : E. M. 470. 6 : Λάβδακος, Arc. 51. 3 : Λάμψακος, Schol. Ven. N. 759 : Μάλακος, Diod. Sic. 7. 9. p. 511. 19. ed. Bekker.: Μάρμακος, Diog. Laert. 8. 1 : Μύννακος (not Μυννακός, as in Athen. 351 A ; see H. D. s. v.): Νάννακος, Suid. (H. D. remark that this name is Ἀννακός (*sic*) in St. Byz. s.v. Ἰκόνιον): Νώρακος, St. Byz. : Ὄπλακος, Plut. 1. 393 : Πάλακος, Strab. 306 : Πύρρακος : Ῥύνδακος, Apion and Herodorus ap. Eust. 959. 32 ; Schol. Ven. N. 759; and such is no doubt its proper accent, though it is oxytone in Schol. Apollon. Rhod. 1. 1165: Σάνδακος, Apollod. 3. 14. 3: Σίτακος, Arrian Ind.: Σπάρτακος, St. Byz.: Στρόφακος, Thucyd. 4. 78: Τίτακος, St. Byz. (Τιτακός in Herod. 9. 73): Ὕρτακος, Apollod. 3. 12. 5; Schol. Ven. N. 759; the city of that name is oxytone in St. Byz.: Φύλακος, Arc. 51. 9: Ὤτακος, or Ὠτακός (?) Hesych. Yet the following oxytones occur: Αἰακός, Schol. Apollon. Rhod. 1. 1165: Ἀλακός, Ἀρτακοί, St. Byz.: Ἀσακός, Διψακός, Schol. Apollon. Rhod. 2. 653; *H. D.*: Θαυμακοί, Strab. 389: Θημακός (οἱ), St. Byz.: Ἱππακός, Auth. Palat. 7. 521; *H. D.*: Μαρακοί (ᾰ ?) Xen. Hell. 6. 1. 7: Ὀλθακός, Plut. 1. 501: Πιττακός, Plut. 1. 85, etc.: Συρακοί, Xenob. Cf. Lob. Prol. 307 sqq.

271. (*g*) All others in κος retract the accent, as Φάκος, Γλαῦκος, Κώρυκος, Δημόδοκος, Σέλευκος, Δράβησκος (Δραβῆσκος, St. Byz.), Πάταικος, Ἀσσάρακος, Ἀστράβακος, Σεσίθακος, Εὐφάντακος, Ὄσκοι; except Κεραμεικός, Theog. Can. 59. 9: Ἰωλκός, Theog. Can. 59. 29 (Ἰαωλκός), Δαμασκός, the city (but Δάμασκος, a man's name, see H. D. s.v., though even that is oxytone in St. Byz.). Γραικοί (Γραῖκος is a man's name), Γαλλογραικοί, Σολκοί, Λεκκοί, Hesych.: Καλλαϊκοί, Strab. 162: Μυκοί, St. Byz.: Τροκμοί, Strab. 567: Πατυκός, St. Byz.: Γαραντεικός (?) *Pape*: Ὀξυκανός, Arrian Anab. 6. 16. 1: Ἀσκός, St. Byz. s.v. Δαμασκός: Καδοῦρκοι, Strab. 190 and Καοῦλκοι, Strab. 291, are properispomena.

272. NOTE 1.—Γραικοί, Olympiodorus in Meteora Aristot. f. 27 a: τοῦτο τὸ ὄνομα οἱ μὲν Ῥωμαῖοι παροξύνουσι Γραίκοι λέγοντες, ἡ δὲ κοινὴ διάλεκτος ὀξύνει· καθόλου δὲ οἱ Ῥωμαῖοι πᾶν ὄνομα παροξύνουσι διὰ τὸν κόμπον, ὅθεν ὑπερηνορέοντες ἐκλήθησαν ὑπὸ τῶν ποιητῶν: Σολκοί, a city in Sardinia, St. Byz., but he also calls it Σύλκοι (*sic*): Πιττάλακος, Æschin. p. 8. 24; in Demosth. 417. 21 some MSS. have Πιτταλακοῦ, others Πιτταλάκου (*sic*): Ἀρουάκοι, in Strab. 162, seems an error: Βελλοάκοι, Pape, who quotes Strab. 196, which proves nothing as to the accent; it is oxytone in Ptol. 2. 9. 8: Δάκοι, St. Byz. varies; it is Δακοί in Strab. 313, and sometimes Δᾶκοι: Ἴννκος, Herodot. 6. 24, is oxytone in Plat. Hipp. Maj. 282 E: Τασκοί, . . . Dionys. Per. 1069, ubi Eust. annotat βαρυτόνως παρὰ πολλοῖς ἀναγινώσκεσθαι;' *H. D.*: Φάκος, a place in Macedonia, Diod. Sic. 30. 14, Bekk. is oxytone in Polyh. 31. 25. 2; A. G. Oxon. 1. 223. 16, σεσημείωται τὸ φακὸς ὀξυνόμενον· ἔστι δὲ καὶ βαρυτόνως ὄνομα ὄρους, Ἑκαταῖος·

πρὸς μὲν νῶτον (*sic*) Παῦλος καὶ Φάκος·

εἰ ἔτι ὀξυτονήθη πρὸς ἀντιδιαστολὴν ἑτέρου σημαινομένου.

273. NOTE 2.—The grammarians give the following rule for the accentuation of trisyllables in ακος: τὰ εἰς ΚΟΣ (i. e. ἄκος) τρισύλλαβα τὴν πρώτην συλλαβὴν ἔχοντα λήγουσαν εἰς ἀμετάβολον προπαροξύνονται, Λάμψακος, Ὕρτακος, Ῥύνδακος, Eust. 959. 52; cf. Schol. Ven. N. 759.

-ΛΟΣ

274. (*a*) Dissyllables in λος preceded by λ, a long vowel or a diphthong, are oxytone, as αὐλός (βόαυλος, μέσαυλος), βηλός, γαυλός, *a milk pail*, θαλλός, μαλλός, πηλός, φαλλός, φελλός, χιλός; except βῶλος, γρύλλος (γρῦλος), δοῦλος, ζῆλος, ἦλος, θρύλλος (θρῦλος), μύλλος, *a kind of fish*, μῶλος, ναῦλος, οὖλος, πῖλος, πῶλος, σίλλος, στῦλος, ψύλλος, which retract the accent.

275. NOTE.— See Schol. Ven. O. 338; Arc. 52-53 : ἄθλος = ἄεθλος : βδέλλος.: βίλλος (?) Arc. 53. 21, who says that παρὰ Ἐφεσίοις βαρύνεται : βῶλος, Theog. Can. 62. 17 : γάλλος, Hesych.: γρύλλος is a common but incorrect form for γρῦλος, Arc. 52. 24 : γαῦλος, *a ressel*, Eust. 1625. 3 : γαυλός, *milk-pail*, a distinction frequently neglected in MSS; the island Γαῦλος is properispomenon, Diod. Sic. 5. 12 : δοῦλος, Arc. 53. 12 ; Eust. 794. 26 : ἐρῖλος : ζῆλος (Dor. δᾶλος), Arc. 53. 4; Eust. 1018. 61 ; Schol. O. 338 : ἦλος, Arc. 53. 4 ; Eust. 1018. 61 ; Schol. Ven. O. 338 : θρύλλος is a less correct form for θρῦλος : ἴλλος, *an eye*, but ἰλλός,. *squinting*, Eust. 907. 8 : κίλλος, Pollux 7. 56, is better oxytone, as Hesych. has it s. v. though he varies : κόλλος (?) A. G. Oxon. 1. 338. 24 : κτῖλος in Theog. Can. 61. 2 seems corrupt : κῶλος, Theog. Can. 62. 18 ; cf. Athen. 200 F, for which Strab.. 312 has κόλος : μυλλός, *pudenda muliebria*, or *a kind of cakes*, Athen. 647 A : Μύλλος, a proper name and μυλλός, *squinting*, Eust. 1885, 20 ; Arc. 53. 15 ; but μύλλος or μύλος, *a fish*, Galen Tom. 6. p. 402 A : μῶλος, Theog. Can. 62. 18: ναῦλος, Arc. 53. 8 : οὖλος, Arc. 53. 12: πῆλος, ὁ οἶνος, A. G. Paris. 4. 188. 10: πῖλος, Arc. 52. 23 ; Theog. Can. 61. 2 : πῶλος, Arc. 60. 8 : σίλλος, Arc. 53. 20; σιλλός also occurs, see Tittmann ad Zonar. 1648 : σκύλλος, Hesych. is σκύλος in E. M. 720. 19 : σκῶλος, *a stake, stumbling-block*, Hom. Il. 13. 564 : σμίλος (?) Hesych.: σπῖλος, is better σπίλος, Reg. Pros. 10. p. 423 : στῦλος, Arc. 52. 24, is written στύλος in the text of Eust. 731. 37, and elsewhere: τῖλος (?) Pollux 5. 91; is sometimes τίλος : ὕλλος, Georg. Pisid. Cosm. 951 ; *H. D.* : ψύλλος, Lob. Phryn. 332 ; Theog. Can. 61. 25 : ὧλος (or ὠλλός), Hesych.

276. (*b*) Those in ἴλος and ὕλος are paroxytone, as ναυτίλος, κτίλος, κρωβύλος ; except δάκτυλος, κόνδυλος, πίτυλος, σφόνδυλος, and several others of dactylic measure mentioned below.

277. NOTE.—A. G. Oxon. 1. 51. 17 : αἴγιλος, Arc. 55. 21 : it is also spelled αἴγιλλος and αἴγυλλος : ἄκυλος, A. G. 373. 25 : ἄμυλος is in fact an adjective : βάκχυλος, Athen. 111 D ; βήθυλος, E. M. 196. 54 ; or βηθύλος, Suid., also βηθύλλος and δηθύλλος : βράβυλος, Hesych. : γόγγυλος, E. M. 245. 39 ; Arc. 56. 25 : δάκτυλος, Arc. 56. 24 : ἔκυλος, Suid. : κάνδυλος, Pollux 6. 69 : κηρύλος, Theog. Can. 61. 20 ; Aristoph. Av. 300 is wrongly proparoxytone in Arist. H. A. 8. 3. 14, where one MS. has κηρύλλος : κόνδυλος, Arc. 56. 24 : κότυλος, Athen. 478 B; *H. D* : κρωβύλος is wrongly proparoxytone in Eust. 851. 46, and elsewhere: ὀπτίλλος, Arc. 54. 15, is better ὀπτίλος ; see H. D. s. v. : πίτυλος, A. G. Oxon. 1. 51. 25 : σφόνδυλος (and σπόνδυλος), Arc. 56. 24, is sometimes σφονδύλος : τροχίλος, 'Schol. Aristoph. Av. 79, ἔστι δὲ ὄρνεον τροχίλος, καὶ λέγεται εἶναι δριμύ· ἀξιοῦσι δέ τινες τὴν μέσην ὀξύνειν : ut alii circumflexisse videantur qui frequens est in libris accentus. V. Jacobs ad Ælian. N. A. 3. 11 ;' H. D. : φάγιλος, Plut. 2. 294 C.

278. (*c*) The rest in λος throw the accent back, as ἄγγελος,

αἰγίθαλλος, ἄμπελος, βύβλος, ἴουλος, κάπηλος, κροκόδειλος, κρύστ-
αλλος,. κύκλος, ὅμιλος, ὄχλος, πάλος, σάλος, σίαλος, σκόπελος,
στόλος, στρόβιλος, τράχηλος, τύλος, φάλος ; except αἰγιαλός, θολός,
mud (but θόλος, *dome*), κορυδαλλός, μοχλός, μυελός, ὀβελός, ὀβολός,
ὀμφαλός, which are oxytone.

279. NOTE.—ἀελλός, Hesych., is an adjective used substantively (?) see H. D. ;
on αἴολος or αἰόλος see below, § 282.: ἀσφόδελος, *the plant*: ἀσφοδελός (λειμών),
an adjective, Eust. 906. 58; Lob. Par. 341 ; E. M. 161. 12: δειλός τὸ δειλινόν,
Arc. 55. 4 : δαρχελοί, Hesych.: θόλος, *vault*; θολός,. *mud*, Enst. 794. 30; 907. 4 : ἱλός
= κατάδυσις τοῦ θηρίου, Theog. Can. 61. 1 ; A. G. Paris. 4. 181. 32, εἱλός, ὀξυτόνως ἡ
κατάδυσις τοῦ θηρίου· οὕτω καὶ Ἡρωδιανὸς ἐν τῷ περὶ Ἀττικῶν τόνολιος [τόνων μονοβι-
βλίῳ conj. Cramer], καὶ μέμφεται τοῖς τὸ ι κατατάττουσι τὴν λέξιν: Hesych. explains
it by ἰλύς, βόρβορος; γλοιός: κορυδαλλός, Arc. 54. 11 : κραπαταλός, Arc. 54. 10 ;
this is the correct spelling and accent; κραπάταλος is found in Athen. and Pollux,
and κραπάταλλος or ός in Hesych. and the above place in Arcadius ; see H. D. s. v.:
μοχλός (also μοκλός), Eust. 794. 29 ; E. M. 640. 55 ; Schol. Ven. K. 134 : μυελός,
Arc. 55. 5 ; in late Greek also μυαλός, cf. Lob. Phryn. 309 : μυχλός, Hesych., appears to be an adjective : ὀβελός, Arc. 55. 5 : ὀβολός, Arc. 56. 7 : ὀδελός = ὀβελός,.
Aristoph. Ach. 796 : ὁλός = θολός, Schol. Anth. Pal. 15. 25. 1 ; H. D.: ὀμφαλός,.
Arc. 54. 19; Chœrob. E. 68. 20 ; E. M. 553. 30 : προβαλλός, *a shield*, Arc. 54. 6 ;
in Phot. Lex. and Hesych. it is incorrectly proparoxytone ; the comic word εἱμα-
τανωπερίβαλλος (Athen. 162 A, quoted by L. S.) is regular, being a decompound :
σίαλος, *a fat hog* ; σιαλός (Ion. σιελός) = σίαλον,. Suid., but the latter word is
always proparoxytone in our editions : στρόβιλος, εἶδος ὀρχήσεως, στροβιλός δὲ ἡ
συστροφὴ τοῦ ἐχίνου, Arc. 55. 27 : σφαλός (or σφαλλός), Hesych.: φυσίκιλλος
ἄρτος, Athen. 139 A.

280. Proper names in λος retract the accent, as Αἴολος,
Ἄλος, Ἄξυλος, Ἄσβολος, Ἄστυλος, Βῆλος, Γαῦλος, Δαίδαλος,
Δῆλος, Ἧλος, Θράσυλλος, Κέφαλος, Κρεόφυλος, Κύψελος, Μᾶλος,
Μάταλλος, Μαύσωλος, Μόλος, Νεῖλος, Πάμμιλος, Πύλος, Πῶλος,
Σίγηλος, Στύμφαλος, Τάνταλος, Ὕλλος, Φάρσαλος, Φόλος, Χῶλος ;
except trisyllables in ιλος and υλος, which are paroxytone, as
Αἰσχύλος, Ῥωμύλος, Ζωίλος, Τρωίλος, Πενθίλος ; but to both these
rules there are numerous exceptions.

281. NOTE I.—*Exceptions in* ιλος *and* υλος;. Those compounded with φιλος
throw the accent as far back as possible, as Ἀγνόφιλος, Δημόφιλος, Ἐργόφιλος,
Πάμφιλος, Σώφιλος : Ἄγκυλος, Arc. 57. 7 : Αἴγιλος (?) H. D. ; the passage in
Lycoph. 108 proves nothing : Αἴτυλος, Arc. 56. 12 : Ἄκτυλος, Phot. Bib. 536. 22.
ed. Bekker : Ἄξυλος, Hom. Il. 6. 12 ; Arc. 56. 25 : Ἄργιλος, Herodot. 7. 115 :
Αὐαλός, Hesych.: Βαίτυλος, E. M. 192. 56, ought to be paroxytone : Βάσιλος,
Parthen. Erot. 1. 4 ; H. D.: Βράγιλος, H. D.: Γαίσυλος, Plut. 1. 980 : Γογγύ-
λος, is proparoxytone in Thucyd. 1. 128 ; 7. 2 ; both of which passages are quoted
by H. D. s. v., and perhaps that is its proper accent ; see E. M. 245. 39 : Δάκτυ-
λοι Ἰδαῖοι : Δάκτυλος, Schol. Apollon. Rhod. 1. 1126–1131 : Δάσκυλος, Apollon.
Rhod. 2. 805 : Δεσιλοί (?) St. Byz.: Εὐρύπυλος, S. V. Ξ. 255 : Εὐστάφυλος,
Alciph. Ep. 3. 22, quoted by H. D. as a compound, is regular : Ἴτυλος, Arc. 57. 3 ;
Hom. Od. 19. 522 : Κόρδυλος, St. Byz.: Κορπιλοί, St. Byz.: Κότυλος, Strab. 602 :

Κρώβυλος is very commonly found, but it should perhaps be paroxytone; H. D. observe (tom. 4. p. 2023 A) on κρωβύλος, 'eadem accentus inconstantia in nomine-proprio scribendo animadvertitur, cujus scripturam παροξύτονον recte defendit Boisson. ad Aristæn. p. 441:' Μικύλος, or Μικκύλος, 'Simplici κ et per diphthongum Μείκυλος cod. Pal. in epigr. Callimachi Auth. 7. 460. 3, sed in lemmate a prima manu μικ-, ab secunda μεικ-. Accentum correxit Jacobsius;' H. D.: Μόσχιλος (?), *Pape*: Μυρσίλος, Herodot. 1. 7, is in some editions wrongly printed. Μυρσίλος; see Theog. Can. 62. 8, who has Μυρτίλος: Νικάσυλος, for this *L. Dindorf* ap. H. D. quotes Paus. 6. 14. 1; but on turning to his own edition of that author I find that he prints Νικασύλος: Οἴτυλος, St. Byz.; Schol. Ven B. 585: Ὄκυλος (?): Ὀνήσυλος, or Ὀνήσυλος, Herodot. 5. 104; Theog. Can. 61. 23: Ὄξυλος, Arc. 56. 25; 'Ὀξύλος tameu scriptum in scholl. Nicand. Th. 289, ubi scriptor quidam, et Pind. Ol. 3. 19. 22, ubi Ætolus memoratur, utrobique fortasse contra libros,' *L. Dindorf* ap. H. D. s. v.: Σίπυλος, Diod. Sic. 3. 55; St. Byz.; A. G. Oxon. 1. 51. 24: Σόφιλος or Σώφιλος is regular as a compound: Σπέργιλος, St. Byz.: Στάφυλος, Arc. 57. 5; Strab. 475, *etc.*: Σώσιλος (?) Polyh. 3. 20. 5. with the variants Σώσυλος and Σωσύλος; Lob. Prol. 139: Τίτυλος, Arc. 57. 3; Theog. Can. 61. 22: Ταξίλος, Paus. 1. 20. 6, *etc.*, is generally proparoxytone, cf. Lob. Prol. 115: Τράγιλος, St Byz.: Τρίπυλος, Plut. 1. 1046: Τρίσιλος (?) *Pape*: Τρόχιλος is quoted by Göttling (Accent. p. 184) from Paus. 1. 14. 2, where Dindorf prints Τροχίλος: Τρώγιλος, Thucyd. 7. 2, or Τραγίλος or Τραγιλός, Thucyd. 6. 99: Ὑρώκυλος (?) *Pape*: Ὠγυλος, St. Byz.

282. NOTE 2.—Γαιτοῦλο:, St. Byz.; in Strab. 826 Meineke prints Γαιτούλοι, and rightly, Eust. Dion. Per. 215: ὅτι Γαιτοῦλοι ἔθνος μέγιστον Λιβυκόν. Τούτους Ἀρτεμίδωρος Γαιτουλίους λέγει· Ἡρωδιανὸς δὲ προπαροξύνει, λέγων ὅτι τὰ εἰς ΛΟΣ παραληγόμενα διφθόγγῳ τῇ διὰ τοῦ ΟΥ προπαροξύνεται: Ἰαμβοῦλος, Diod. Sic. 2. 60; Ἰάμβουλος is quoted by H. D. from Lucian V. H. 1. 3: Tzetz. Hist. 7. 644. 724: Pape has Ἰκτομοῦλοι from Strab. 218, but the place does not justify that accentuation: Καδμῖλος, Arc. 56. 2, occurs under the form Κάσμιλος, Schol. Apollon. Rhod. 1. 917: Καμβῦλος (?) Polyh. 8. 17. 4: Κυδρῆλος, Strab. 633, a very questionable accent.

The proper name Αἰολος is very variable in its accentuation: according to Eust. 631. 32; 1681. 3, it is said to be proparoxytone, and so Philoponus accented it; Arcadius 56. 6 makes it paroxytone, and that accent is common in our books, e.g. Diod. Sic. 4. 67; Strab. 20. 23; even in Eustathius himself, contrary to his own rule, 1644. 12. On the whole it seems better to write Αἴολος for the proper name, αἰόλος for the adjective. The common substantive, αιολος, *a kind of fish*, is equally uncertain; it is an adjective used elliptically, and vacillates, like others of the same kind, between an adjectival (αἰόλος) and substantival accent (αἴολος); see Lob. Par. 344, and H. D. s. v.

283. NOTE 3.—*Oxytones in* λος. Ἀγχιαλός, a city, Enst. 1681. 3; yet elsewhere (1396. 25) he says that it is proparoxytone; E. M. 14. 36 however remarks, ἡ μὲν πόλις ὀξύνεται· ὁ δὲ παραθαλάσσιος τόπος, προπαροξύνεται: as the name of a man is regular, Ἀγχίαλος, Hom. Od. 1. 180, *etc.*: Αἰγηλοί (and Αἰγλοί), St. Byz.: Αἰγιαλός, Schol. Ven. B. 592: Αἰτωλός, Chœrob. E. 23. 14, τὰ γὰρ εἰς ωλος ἀρσενικὰ πρὸ τοῦ ω τὸ τ ἔχοντα ὀξύνεται, St. Byz. s. v. Αἰτωλία: Παναίτωλος, Polyh. 10. 49. 11: Ἀρτωλός (?) Chœrob. E. 23. 9: Αὐαλός, Hesych.: Βαστουλοί, Lob. Prol. 132: Γάλλος is paroxytone in all senses, Schol. Ven. Π. 234; Arc. 53. 15: Ἑλλός, Schol. Ven. Π. 234, and Ἑλλοί: Θάλλος, Plut. 1. 747; I do not know why Pape says that Θαλλός would be more correct: Θετταλός, or Θεσσαλός, Arc. 54. 20; Hom. Il. 2. 679; Diod. Sic. 5. 54, *etc.*; 'In codd. interdum προπαροξυτόνως scribitur,' H. D. s. v.: Ἰταλός, Chœrob. E. 68. 21; Arc. 54. 24; E. M. 553. 30: Καστωλός,

St. Byz. s. v. Αἰτωλία; Arc. 57. 15: Κερμαλός (?) Plut. 1. 19: Κορυδαλλός, a deme, Arc. 54. 11; this is sometimes found falsely accented, e.g. St. Byz.: in Diod. Sic. 4: 59 Κορυδαλλῷ is now read for the incorrect Κορυδάλλῳ; it is also oxytone as the name of a man, e. g. Herodot. 7. 214: Μαγδωλός, St. Byz.: Μαλλός, a city, Arc. 53. 17; so called, according to St. Byz., from Μάλλος, its founder: Μαλλοί, an Indian people, St. Byz.: Strab. 701: Μανταλός, the founder of the Phrygian city Μάνταλος, St. Byz.: Μαυσωλός, a river, and Μαυσωλοί are oxytone in St. Byz.: Ὀμφαλός, Diod. Sic. 5. 70: Πακτωλός, Chœrob. E. 23. 9; St. Byz. s. v. Αἰτωλία: Πενθηλός in Suidas is an error for Πενθίλος: Σελλοί is oxytone, like Ἕλλός: Σίγηλος, Eust. 1967. 36; hence Σιγηλός, Strab. 404, is faulty: Σικελός, Diod. Sic. 5. 50; Arc. 55. 10, is sometimes Σίκελος: Σικελοί, St. Byz.: Σπαρτωλός, St. Byz.: Τριβαλλός, Strab. 301, etc.; Arc. 54. 5, though it is occasionally proparoxytone: Φελλός, a city of Pamphylia, St. Byz.; Strab. 666, but Ἀντίφελλος Strab. 666: Φέλλος, a man, Herod. π. μ. λ. 11. 23.

-ΜΟΣ.

284. Common substantives in μος with a long penultimate are oxytone, the rest retract the accent, as θῡμός, *anger*, but θῠμος, *thyme*, ἀγερμός, ἁγιασμός, ἄνεμος, ἀριθμός, βαθμός, βωμός, γάμος, γίγγλυμος, δεσμός, δημός, *fat*, δρόμος, ἑσμός, θάλαμος, θεσμός, κάλαμος, κομμός, κύαμος, κυδοιμός, λαιμός, λιμός, μερισμός, νόμος, *law*, ὀφθαλμός, πόλεμος, πορθμός, ῥυθμός, τόμος, φιμός, φορμός, χρησμός, χυμός, ψαλμός, ψωμός; except 1. oxytone νομός, *pasture*, οὐλαμός, ποταμός, φωραμός, φωριαμός, χηραμός; 2. ἄμμος, βλάστημος, δῆμος, *people*, ἔρημος, θέρμος, κόσμος, κῶμος, μῖμος, μῶμος, ὄγμος, οἶμος, ὅλμος, ὅρμος, πότμος, τόρμος, σῖμος, ψάμμος, which retract the accent.

285. NOTE.—Αἱμος, according to H. D. s. v. the right form is αἱμός; Chœrob. E. 28. 1 expressly makes it barytone, but he may possibly refer to the proper name, cf. E. M. 568. 38: ἁλιμός (?) Hesych.: ἄμμος, Arc. 59. 8: ἀφλοισμός was by Tyrannion incorrectly made proparoxytone, Schol. Ven. O. 607: βλάστημος, Æschyl. Suppl. 317; S. c. T. 12; this is directly opposed to Herod. π. μ. λ. 33. 4, yet accords with Arc. 61. 5; see Lob. Par. 397: βόρμος = βρόμος, E. M. 205. 3: βρῖμος, Theog. Can. 63. 9: βρῶμος, Theog. Can. 63. 21; Arc. 60. 8: βῶμος, Æolic for βωμός, Greg. Cor. 617, ed. Schäfer: γίγγλυμος is in some places falsely oxytone: γολαμός = οὐλαμός, Hesych.: γροῦμος, Hesych.: δῆμος, *people*, Aristarchus ap. Schol. Ven. Θ. 240; Herodian ap. Schol. Ven. M. 213; E. M. 265. 3: δημός, *fat*, Arc. 59. 16: ἐπίκορμος, Eust. 1692. 62, is a compound of κορμός: ἔρημος (sc. γῆ), Lob. Par. 361: ἡδύοσμος, *mint*, Strab. 344; *L. S.*, is an adjective used as a substantive: θεμός = θεσμός, Hesych.: θέρμος, *lupine*, Lob. Par. 341 (cf. Lob. Par. 360) quotes θερμός in this sense from Galen: θύμος, *thyme*: θῡμός, *anger*: Θῦμος, a proper name, Arc. 59. 28; Theog. Can. 63. 14: κῆμος, *a plant so called* (?) Theog. Can. 63. 5: κημός, *the cover of the voting urn*, is regular: κινδαμός (?) Arc. 60. 24: κομμός, *lamentation*, is paroxytone in Arist. Poet. c. 12. 3; and in Nicol. Damasc. Excerpt. p. 457 (59 Orell.) quoted by H. D.: κόμμοι in a different signification occurs in Hesych.; A. G. Oxon. 1. 338. 24: τὸ κόμμος οὐ δὲ σύνηθες [βαρύνεται]: κόσμος, Arc. 58. 27: κρῆθμος (the ordinary form is τὸ κρῆθμον and κρηθμόν; it is also spelled κρίθμος or ον, Arc. 58. 14). This word furnishes one example among many others of the strange tricks played by the old Greek grammarians; ὀξύνεται δὲ ὁ σταθμός, says Eustathius, 582. 17, κανόνι τοιούτῳ. τὰ εἰς ΜΟΣ λήγοντα, ἔχοντα πρὸ τοῦ Μ τὸ Θ, ὀξύνεται, μηνιθμός, πορθμός, σκαρθμός, ἰσθμός. οὕτω καὶ σταθμός. τὸ κρῆθμος οἱ μὲν τοῦ Ὁμήρου ὑπομνηματισταὶ βαρύνεσθαί φασιν εἰς ἰδιό-τητα, ἐν δὲ τοῖς ἀντιγράφοις τοῦ Λυκόφρονος [238] καὶ αὐτὸ ὀξύνεται : this passage shows also the corruption and the cure of the place in Philem. Lex. p. 72. § 198; the word should doubtless be oxytone, and it is so found in Dioscorides, Hesychius, and others ; see H. D. s. v. : κῶμος (and the barbarism κῶμο), Arc. 60. 6 ; Theog. Can. 63. 26 : λεμός (?) Hesych. : λίημος, Hesych. : μάμμος, Hesych. : μῖμος, Joh. Alex. 3. 7 ; Theog. Can. 63. 9 : μύρμος, Hesych. ; Lycoph. 176 : μῶμος, Arc. 60. 7 ; ʻ Μωμός, quod ponit Theog. [Can. 63. 20] scribendum βωμός ;ʼ H. D. : νάθμος (?) Hesych. : νόμος, *law* ; νομός, *pasture*, Schol. Ven. T. 249 : νούμμος=*numus*, Zonar. 1405, or νοῦμος, A. G. 109. 24 : ὄγμος, Schol. Ven. Λ. 68 ; Arc. 58. 6 ; Eust. 831. 57 : οἶμος, Arc. 60. 11 ; Chœrob. E. 28. 1 ; Schol. Ven. Λ. 24 ; E. M. 568. 38 ; Lob. Rhem. 282, note 20 : ὄλμος, Chœrob. E. 1. 28 ; Eust. 831. 57 ; E. M. 817. 29 : ὅρμος, *har-bour*, and this is perhaps the best accent for the word in all senses, though Eust. 1788. 46 says : ὀξύνεται δὲ παρά τισι τῶν ἐσύστερον ὁ τοιοῦτος ὅρμος (i. e. *necklace*) καθὰ καὶ ἀλλαχοῦ ἐρρέθη πρὸς διαστολὴν τοῦ κατὰ τὸν λιμένα : ὄρχαμος : dactyls in αμος are oxytone (Arc. 60. 17) if the first syllable is long by nature ; proparoxytone if it be long only by position, Eust. 1347. 12 ; E. M. 804. 17 ; this word is written ἄρχαμος in Eust. 1094. 54 : οὐλαμός, Schol. Ven. Ω. 228 : ὄχμος=πύργος s. ὀχυρὸς τόπος, Lycoph. 443, quoted by H. D., or ὀχμός (?) Eust. 1528. 23, quoted by H. D. : πλεῦμος, Galen Lex. Hippocr. Tom. 2. p. 99 F : ποταμός, Arc. 60. 15 ; Eust. 1347. 12 ; Schol. Ven. Ω. 228 : πότμος, Arc. 58. 19 : ῥῆμος (?) *a peel*, in Athen. 113 C, the only place quoted for the word, κεράμῳ is now read : σῖμος [σῖμος], *a fish*, *tunny*, Eust. 906. 56 ; Artemid. 2. 14, was wrongly oxytone in Athen. 312 A : σκινδαλαμός or σκινδαλμός, Schol. Aristoph. Nubb. 130 : ἰδίως σκινδαλμοὺς καλοῦμεν τὰ λεπτό-τατα τῶν ξύλων καὶ τὰ τῶν καλάμων ξύσματα. τοῦτο μὲν ἐπὶ τῆς εὐθείας ὀξύνεται, ἐπὶ δὲ τῶν πλαγίων παροξύνεται, Arc. 59. 2 ; 60. 24 : τῖμος, Æschyl. Choeph. 916 ; Eust. 1148. 37 ; τόμος=ὁ τετμημένος : τομός=ὁ τέμνων, Arc. 59. 24 ; A. G. Oxon. 1. 371. 1 : τόρμος, Diod. Sic. 2. 8, etc., and this is the constant accent in our books, yet it is expressly made oxytone by A. G. Oxon. 1. 285. 13 : τυλιμός (?) E. M. 773. 5 : φῖμός is sometimes falsely φῖμος, e. g. Sept. Eccles. 20. 29, and there is one instance of φῖμος : φλῶμος is false for φλόμος : φωραμός, Schol. Ven. Ω. 228 ; E. M. 804. 19 ; A. G. Oxon. 1. 430. 14 ; φωριαμός, Arc. 60. 20 ; E. M. 688. 18 : φωρίαμος is Attic, according to Herodian : χαμός, Lob. Par. 346 : χηραμός, E. M. 688. 18 : χλαμός (?) =χλαῖνα, Hesych. : χῶμος (?) =χῶμα, Hesych. : χωριαμός, Hesych. ; Lob. Prol. 155 : ψάμμος, Arc. 59. 9 : ψόμμος, Hesych. : ὧμος, *shoulder* : ὠμός, *raw*, Schol. Ven. Γ. 35 ; Eust. 377. 44 ; Theog. Can. 63. 27.

286. Proper names in μος throw back the accent, as Αἶμος, Ἄλμος, Ἔλυμος, Θέρμος, Θῦμος, Ἰάλεμος, Κάδμος, Κῶμος, Λάτμος, Μῶμος, Νικόδημος, Πάτμος, Πέργαμος, Πρίαμος, Πύραμος, Ῥῆμος, Σάμος; but there is a considerable number of exceptions, which are mentioned in the following note.

287. NOTE.—Ἀγαμός, St. Byz. : Ἀγχεσμός, Paus. 1. 32. 2 : Ἀκιαμός (?) St. Byz. s. v. Ἀσκάλων : Βρυσμός, E. M. 249. 15 : Βωμοί, certain hills in Ætolia so called, St. Byz. ; the word does not acquire the distinctive accent of a proper name, because it seems to have retained the greater part of its ordinary significa-tion : Δραγμός, St. Byz. : Δρυμός, vacillates between the accent which it should have if it retains its significance, and that of a proper name ; it is oxytone accord-ing to Arc. 60. 1, and in Strab. 445 ; but Δρύμος (? Δρῦμος) in Herodot. 8. 33;

Harpoc. and Eust. 638. 57 ; all these passages are quoted by H. D. : Θυμός, the name of a dog, Xen. de Ven. 7. 5, quoted by H. D. ; as the name of a man it is properispomenon, Arc. 59. 28 : Ἰσθμός, *passim*, is always oxytone : Καταβαθμός or Καταβασμός, Strab. 791, etc. : Κυδοιμός, Hom. Il. 18. 535 : Λιμός, *Famine* personified, Hes. Theog. 227, quoted by Göttling ; also a place, Λιμοῦ πεδίον, A. G. 278. 4 : Ὀλμός, a man's name, St. Byz. s. v. Ὄλμωνες, is Ὄλμος in Paus. 9. 24. 3, or as he elsewhere (9. 34. 10) calls him, Ἄλμος : Πορθμός =*fretum Siculum*, Polyb. 1. 7. 1, and of others, Polyh. 16. 29. 8 : also the name of a city in Euboea, Demosth. de Coron. p. 248. 15, etc. ; H. *D.* : Ποταμός (or Ποταμοί) an Attic deme, Strab. 398 : Ῥωγμοί, St. Byz. : Σημός, Harpocrat. s. v. Ἑκάτης νῆσος, is rightly Σῆμος in Athen. 38 A ; 614 A ; Suid. ; Schol. Apollon. Rhod. 1. 1304 ; Schol. Pind. Ol. 11. 73 : Τρωκμός, Arc. 58. 17 ; in Strab. 187 ; Ptol. 5. 4. 9, and elsewhere, it occurs under the form Τρόκμοι (*sic*), but in the former author, 561, it is correctly accented Τροκμοί : Τρωγμοί, Phot. Bib. 228. 3 : Φυλαμός, Lycoph. 593, is rightly Φύλαμος St. Byz. s. v. Αὔσων : Φωριαμοί, St. Byz. That many of these exceptions are nothing but mistakes seems probable both from the uncertainty of the books in some cases, and from the absence of any reason why they in particular should vary from the analogy of hosts of proper names having the same termination.

-ΝΟΣ.

288. Polysyllables in ωνος, are oxytone, as κολωνός, οἰωνός, κοινωνός, κορωνός, μελεδωνός.

Note.—Arc. 66. 6 ; Chœrob. C. 411. 13 : Ἄγωνος, Æol. = ἀγών, Hesych. L. S. have κερκόρωνος from Ælian H. A. 15. 14, where Schneider would read with Gesner κερκίωνας for κερκορώνους.

289. All in ῑνος are properispomena, as γελασῖνος, γῖνος (and γίννος), ἐχῖνος, ἰκτῖνος, κεστρῖνος, σταφυλῖνος, φοξῖνος ; except κάμινος, κυκλάμινος, συκάμινος proparoxytone, and χαλινός oxytone.

290. Note.—E. M. 488. 4 : τὰ διὰ τοῦ ΙΝΟΣ πρὸ μιᾶς τὸν τόνον ἔχοντα ἐκτείνουσι τὸ Ι, πλὴν τοῦ ἐχίνος, καρκίνος· πρὸ δύο δὲ τὸν τόνον ἔχοντα, συστέλλει, πλὴν τοῦ κάμινος, E. M. 793. 45 : γάκινος, E. M. 219. 41, is a compound : γρῖνος, Eust. 1926. 55, is falsely accented γρίνος in Hesych. : γύρινος, Arc. 65. 16 ; E. M. 243. 49, is occasionally to be found properispomenon ; St. Byz. s. v. Βιθυνία spells the word γέρυνος ; Göttling thinks γυρῖνος the correct accent when the ι is long, and he is probably right : ἴρινος, a plant, Nicand. Ther. 647, and schol. ad l. : ἐρινός = ἐρινεός, Arc. 65. 18 : ἐρυθρῖνος, Arist. H.A. 8. 13. 3, two MSS. read ἐρυθρινός, a wrong accent, as is ἐρύθρινος found elsewhere ; cf. Lob. Prol. 207 ; who shows by many examples how very irregular the books, both manuscript and printed, are in accenting this termination : ἰκτῖνος, Herodian ap. Eust. 1825. 12, is proparoxytone according to Theog. Can. 67. 17 ; E. M. 470. 35, ' Utroque modo in codd. Aristophanis, Æliani, aliorumque scriptorum scribitur ;' H. *D.* : κάμινος, Theog. Can. 67. 17 ; E. M. 488. 6 : κυκλάμινος, Theog. *l. l.* : κύμινος (?) Theog. *l. l.* : μέλινος (?) = μελίνη : μύρινος, Arist. H. A. 8. 19. 5, where one MS. has μαρῖνος : ὅρμινος, Athen. 478. D, for which Pollux 6. 61 has ὄρμενος, and Hesych. the right (?) form ὁρμῖνος : συκάμινος, Theoph. H.P. 1. 1. 7 ; χαλινός, Arc. 65. 18 ; Chœrob. E. 139. 10 ; E. M. 805. 16 ; in Æolic it was χάλλινος.

291. The rest retract the accent, as ἄγνος, βόθυνος, θάμνος, θύννος, θύσανος, κίνδυνος, κοίρανος, κότινος, κροῦνος, κύκνος, κῶνος, λύχνος, νάννος, οἶνος, ὄκνος, πόνος, πρῖνος, ῥάμνος, ῥάφανος, στέφανος, τόνος, τύραννος, ὕμνος, ὕπνος, ὦνος; except oxytone, ἀμνός, ἀρνός βαυνός (βαῦνος, *Attic*), βουνός, γουνός, ἑανός, ἐλλεδανός, ἱπνός, καπνός, κεραυνός, κρημνός, κρουνός, ληνός, λιχανός, οὐρανός, παιδνός, πλυνός, ῥινός, ὠκεανός, and the paroxytones καρκίνος and παρθένος.

292. Note.—Ἀκεανός, *a kind of pulse*, Suid, is proparoxytone in Eust. 1528.44, but is expressly said to be oxytone in Theog. Can. 67. 2 : ἀμνός, Arc. 62. 17 ; Eust. 541. 44 : ἀραχνός, Æschyl. Supp. 886, quoted by L. S., but Ahrens reads ἄραχνος : βαυνός, ὅπερ κοινῶς μὲν ὀξύνεται, Ἀττικῶς δὲ βαρύνεται, Schol. in Dionys. Thrac. A. G. 654. 33, thus also Arc. 64. 7 : βρενός, Hesych. : γονός = ὁ γεννητικός, E. M. 239. 11 ; but the word does not seem to be oxytone in this signification, at least in the printed books ; γονός, where it does occur, appears either to be an adjective or another form of γουνός : γουνός, E. M. 12. 36 : γρυνός (or γρουνός), Arc. 63. 25 : δεκανοί (sc. θεοί), Stob. Ecl. vol. 1. p. 468, ed. Heeren : δελκανός, Athen. 118 B : ἑανός (sc. πέπλος) : ἕλïνος, Nicaud. Alex. 181, is oxytone in E. M. 330. 39, perhaps a mistake ; both these passages are quoted by H. D. : ἐλλεδανός, Arc. 64. 17 : ἐχῖνος, Chœrob. ap. A. G. Oxon. 2. 170. 30 ; Theog. Can. 67. 22 ; E. M. 488. 5, is possibly a proper name, for ἐχῖνος, *a hedgehog*, is regular : ἱπνός is sometimes paroxytone, e. g. Arist. de Part. An. 1. 5. 6. : καπνός, Arc. 62. 14 : καυνός (?) Arc. 64. 6, καῦνος = κλῆρος, is barytone in E. M. 267. 18, and elsewhere : κεραυνός, Arc. 64. 8 : κρουνός, Arc. 64. 7 : καρκίνος [ï], Theog. Can. 67. 22 ; A. G. Oxon. 2. 236. 14 : Herod. π. μ. λ. 20. 8, 'καρκῖνος sæpissime in codd. scriptum et inter properispomena memoratum ab Arcad. p. 65. 16, si sana lectio : de qua dubitat L. Dindorfius, vol. 2. p. 833 D. Sed poetarum versus ubique καρκίνος scribendum esse arguunt. Et ι breve esse annotavit Etym. M. p. 488. 5 ;' H. D. : λαμνός (?) H. D : ληνός, Arc. 63. 20 : ὁ λιχανός (δάκτυλος) seems to be always oxytone, but ἡ λίχανος (sc. χορδή) varies ; it is proparoxytone in Diod. Sic. 3. 59 ; oxytone in Plut. 2. 1029 A (quoted by H. D.), Arist. Prob. 19. 20. 1 ; 'Adjectivum λιχανός, Hipp. Mul. 1. 703. T. 2, Lucian. Tim. § 54, Athen. 1. 15 D, ubi substantive dicitur ἡ λίχανος, accentum ad principium rejicit,' Lob. Par. 355 : μέδιμνος, Thom. Mag. p. 602, asserts that the Attics made this word paroxytone ; in printed books however it seems to be always proparoxytone : 'μερμνός, ὁ, *Accipiter*, Ælian N. A. 12. 4 ; H. D. : μόρφνος varies between an adjectival and substantival accent ; 'Accentu gravi Lycophr. 838 : Τὸν χρυσόπατρον μόρφνον ἁρπάσας γνάθοις. Et μόρφνος ut ὕπνος scriptum τὴν ἀνάγνωσιν ferre tradit schol. ad l. Hom. [Schol. Ven. Ω. 316] testaturque Etym. M. p. 591. 25, in quo μορφνοῖο scriptum in l. Hesiodi, p. 796. 2, Atque etiam Arc. p. 62. 8 : Τὸ δὲ μόρφνος, ὁ μέγας (μέλας Passov.) ἔχει τὸ ορ aperte hunc probat accentum, quum antea dixisset : Τὰ εἰς νος ἁπλᾶ ἔχοντα πρὸ τοῦ η ἕν τι τῶν ἀντιστοίχων ὀξύνεται, ἐπιθετικὰ ὄντα καὶ μὴ ἔχοντα πρὸ τοῦ τέλους ορ, componatque cum μόρφνος barytonum ὄκνος. Gl. : Ὁ μορφνός, ἀγρικὸν ὄρνεον, Emussulus, Gl.,' H. D. ; see also Lob. Par. 344 : νωτιδανός, cf. H. D. T. 3. p. 1717 C ; ξηνός, Suid. : ὀκορνός, Hesych. : οὐρανός (also ὠρανός and ὀρανός, ὄρανος, Æolic), Herod. π. μ. λ. 7. 18 ; Arc. 64. 13 ; cf. Eust. 128. 41 : παιδνός, Hom. is an adjective : πανός, a Messapian word = ἄρτος, *panis* : πάνος = ὁ δίφρος, Arc. 63. 10 : παρθένος, Herod. π. μ. λ. 8. 26 : ἀειπάρθενος is properly proparoxytone, but in Dio Cass. is paroxytone, the reason being, as *Fix* ap. H. D. s. v. suggests, that the ancients wrote such words as two, ἀεὶ παρθένος : πελανός, Arc. 64. 13, but the word is always proparoxytone in the books.; 'πελανός oxytonum ap. Arcad. 64. 13, quod ex πεδανός corruptum videri posset, quod in loco simili memorat Herodian Π. μον. λ. p. 7. 24, nisi Eustathii verba p. 1601. 4, dubitationem injicerent ; Θυσιῶν ἀ πελάνους τινές φασιν, ἢ καὶ ὀξυτόνως πελανούς,' W. *Dindorf* ap. H. D. : **περκνός**, in Hom. Il. 24. 316, was by Ptolemæus Ascalonites taken as an adjective, and rightly; Aristarchus however barytoned it as a substantive, Schol. Ven. ad l., and Lob. Par. 344 : **πλυνός**, Arc. 63. 26 : σκέπανος (Lob. Par. 344), or σκεπανός, also occurs under the form σκεπινός, Athen. 322 E ; σκύμνος, Arc. 62. 21 ; according to an idle distinction of the grammarians σκύμνος is applied to lions' whelps, σκυμνός, to the young of other animals, or of man, E. M. 720. 22 ; so Ptolemæus Ascalonites ap. Schol. Ven. Σ. 319 ; Eust. 1653. 29 : σπίνος, Herod. π. μ. λ. 40. 1, σт σπῖνος (?) Theophr. de lapid. fr. 2 ; *H. D.*: τιθηνός, Nicaud. Alex. 31, etc. : φασιανός (sc. ὄρνις) : φανός, Arc. 63. 12 : φοινός = φόνος, Nicaud. Alex. 187 ; Lob. Par. 341 : φρῦνος (?) ' In libris interdum φρύνος scriptum. Sed ῡ produci poetarum loci docent et annotarunt Herodian Περὶ μον. λέξ. p. 33. 14. et Περὶ διχρόνων, p. 287. 1, apud quem φρυνός oxytonum est inter alia in ῡνος oxytona positum. Φρῦνος ap. Arc. p. 193. 17 [where Schmidt rightly has φρυνός] ;' *H. D.*; ψανός = ψηνός : ψευδυνοὶ σπόνδυλοι, Suid.: ὠκεανός, Theog. Can. 67. 1.

293. Proper names in *νος* are extremely irregular; in general however they retract the accent, as Ἄλαινος, Δάρδανος, Ἕλενος, Ἐπίδαμνος, Εὔθοινος, Θῶνος, Κύδνος, Κύκνος, Κύρνος, Λῆμνος, Μύκονος, Μύρσινος, Νῖνος, Οὔννοι, Τῆνος, Ὤλενος; except the following classes of words, when consisting of more than two syllables: 1. Those in *ᾱνος, ηνος, ῡνος,* and *ωνος,* which are oxytone, as Ἀβασηνοί, Ἀφρικανός, Βιθυνός, Γαληνός, Γελωνός, Ἡρωδιανός, Ἰσμηνός, Κολωνός, Λουκιανός, Μηδαβηνοί, Σειληνός; 2. Those in *ῖνος,* which are properispomena, as Ἐρυθῖνοι, Ἱππαρῖνος, Λατῖνος, Μαρκελλῖνος, Ψευδαντωνῖνος; 3. Participial forms in *μενος,* which are oxytone, as Ἀκουμενός, Ὀρχομενός, Στησαμενός, Σωζομενός. These rules are however subject to a multitude of exceptions.

294. NOTE 1.—Ἀμνός, Athen. 173 A : Ἀπιδανός, Arc. 64. 18 ; Herodot. 7. 129 ; and Ἠπιδανός : Ἀργεννός, *H. D.*: Βασιννοί, St. Byz. : Γληνός, Apollod. 2. 7. 8, is elsewhere properispomenon, e. g. Paus. 4. 30. 1 : Ἐδούοι, Zonar. 612, is Ἔδουοι in Suid. : Ἐχῖνος [ῑ], Theog. Can. 67. 22 ; E. M. 488. 4 : Ἠριδανός, Strab. 215 ; Θαμβοφάνος, Alciph. 3. 56 ; *Pape*: Θυνός, Θυνοί, Strab. 295 : Θῦνος, 'ap. Hippocr. p. 1238 D : Τῷ τοῦ Θύνου· si scriptura sana;' W. *Dindorf* ap. H. D. : Ἴτανος, Herodot. 4. 151, is also written Ἰτανός, St. Byz. : Καινοί, St. Byz. ; Strab. 624 : Κάλανος, Strab. 686 ; 716 : Arrian Anab. 7. 2. 4, is made oxytone by Plut. 1. 668. 701 : Καμοῦνοι, Strab. 206 : Κανός, Plut. 2. 786 C : Καταννοί, St. Byz. : Καῦνος, Eust. Dion. Per. 533 : ἡ Καῦνος, ἣν Ἡρωδιανὸς ἐν τῇ καθόλου προσῳδίᾳ ὀξύνει : Κελαινός, Strab. 579, or Κέλαινος, Paus. 4. 1. 5 : Κιανός, Galen Tom. 2. p. 363 C : Κοινός, a Macedonian king, E. M. 523. 38, should be Κοῖνος, Eust. 906. 44 : Κρημνοί, Herodot. 4. 20 : Λαπιθανός, Anth. Pal. 6. 307 : Λιβυρνοί, St. Byz. : Λοθρόνος (?) Plut. 1. 177 : Οὐλτοῦρνος, Strab. 238 : Οὐρανός retains the accent of the corresponding appellative : Πέλιγνοι, Strab. 219 ; Pape has Πελιγνοί : Πλυνός, Strab. 838 ; Herodot. 4. 168 ; Tzetz. ad Lycoph. 149, is Πλύνοι in Scylax p. 485 ; *H. D.*: Ῥαδινός (?) *Pape*: Ῥοδανός, Diod. Sic. 5. 25 ; Strab. 208 ; Arist. Meteor. 1. 13. 28 : Σικανός, Arc. 64. 14 ; τόπος [ποταμός?] Ἰβηρίας, Chœrob. E. 79. 11 ; a son of Briareus, Schol. Theocr. 1. 65, Σίκανος, a king of Sicily, is quoted by H. D. from Joh. Malal. p. 114. 21 ; Σικανοί, Strab. 270; it does not appear that the

Greek poets ever lengthened the penultimate : Σκύμνος, Ptolemæus Ascalonites oxytoned this to distinguish it from the appellative σκύμνος, Schol. Ven. Σ. 319, but he does not seem to have found any to follow his practice; as a proper name it is always barytone : Τωυγενοί, Strab. 183 ; yet Τωύγενοι, Strab. 293 ; the latter form is probably the right one : Φάνος, Arc. 63. 10 (or Φᾶνος, Demosth. 851. 21), is falsely Φανός, Aristoph. Eq. 1253 ; cf. Lob. Par. 342 ; Φᾶνος is better than either: Φρυνοι (?) Strab. 516 : Ὠγενός, Lycoph. 231, is better Ὠγενος, St. Byz., for which the false form Ὠγῆνος occurs in Clem. Alex. Strom. 6. p. 741 ; *H.D.* : Ὠκεανός is, as Οὐρανός, accented like the common substantive.

295. NOTE 2.—*Exceptions in* ανος. Ἄδανος [? ᾱ], St. Byz. s. v. Ἄδανα : Ἄδρανος (?) : Ἀδρανός [? ᾱ] Plut. 1. 241 : Ἀρβάζανοι in Pape seems to be a misprint ; St. Byz. has the word oxytone : Ἀρτάβανος, Herodot. 7. 46, etc. : Βαγίστανος, Diod. Sic. 2. 13, it is oxytone in St. Byz. : Βρετaννoί (Βρετανοί, Dion. Per. 284) : Κάντανος, St. Byz. : Κάρανος : Κοριολάνος (*sic*), Plut. 1. 218 : Μαρκόμᾱνοι (?) appears under the form Μαρκόμαννοι in Strab. 290 : Μεγάπανος, Herodot. 7. 62 : Σεγοσιανοί, Strab. 186 ; for which Pape has Σεγοσίανοι : even compounds in ανος remain oxytone, as Ἀνδρονικιανός ; on this termination see Lob. Prol. 181. Lucian always has Λουκιᾱνός.

296. NOTE 3.—*Exceptions in* ηνος. St. Byz. s. v. Ἀβασηνοί ; Lob. Prol. 192 sqq. : Γαλῆνος is unquestionably false, the name is oxytone, as is expressly stated by Theog. Can. 67. 12 : Γέρηνος (?) Theog. Can. 68. 5 : Γοργῆνος (?) *Pape* : Εὔηνος, 'In accentu variatur inter Εὔηνος et Εὐηνός ; priorem exhibent libri plerique vel omnes ap. Hesiod. Soph. Arist. Eth. Nic. 7. 11. Apollod. geographos, Pausan. Max. Tyr. diss. 38. p. 225, et lexicographos, alterum omnes ut videtur ap. Hom. unus ap. Aristot., consentiente Theognosto in Crameri Anecd. vol. 2. p. 67. 34, ubi inter oxytona in ηνος ponitur Εὐηνός ; ex quo depravatum videtur Ἐηνός, ὄνομα ποταμοῦ in Lex. de spirit. p. 215,' L. Dindorf ap. H. D. : Εὐσάγηνος (?) Alciph. : Κάρηνος, Herodot. 7. 173 : Κύλληνος (?) Theog. Can. 68. 7 : Λάηνος (?) *Pape*, should probably be Λαηνός : Μίσηνος (?) *Pape* is written Μισηνός in Strab. 245 : Μύκηνος (?) Theog. Can. 68. 7 : Σάκχηνοι in St. Byz. has been corrected into Σακχηνοί : Σέρηνος, Suid. : Σίκηνος seems to be an incorrect mode of spelling Σίκινος : Τροίζηνος, Hom. Il. 2. 847 ; Eust. 359. 10 ; Theog. Can. 68. 6 : Ὕπηνος, Paus. 5. 8. 6.

297. NOTE 4.—*Exceptions in* ινος. For Ἀργυρῖνοι, Suid., there also occurs the false form Ἀργύρινοι, St. Byz. ; Lycoph. 1017 (?) : Βουδινοί, St. Byz., is less correct than Βουδῖνοι, in Herodot. 4. 21, 108, 109 ; H. D. : Βουλινοί, St. Byz. ; according to H. D. the codex Vratisl. reads Βουλῖνοι and Βουλῖνος : Βύξινος (ῐ ?) Zenob. : Γεμινός, Artemid. 2. 44 ; *Pape* : Ἕλινοι, St. Byz. : Καϊκινός (?), 'Καικῖνον ex libris optimis restitutus Thucyd. 3. 103 ; ubi alii Καικηνόν, vulgo Καϊκινόν,' H. D. : Καμαρῖνοι, Suid. : Κάσινος, Strab. 237 Kramer, where Meineke properly reads Κασῖνος : Κλουσινοί, Plut. 1. 68, Λαρινός, Λάρινος, and Λάρεινος, Lob. Prol. 212 : Μορινοί, Strab. 194 Kramer, where Meineke reads Μορῖνοι : Μύρκινος, St. Byz., etc. : Παρθινοί (?) : Ποίνινος (?) *Pape* : Σίκινος, Strab. 484 ; St. Byz. : Ταυρῖνοι, Strab. 204, where Kramer reads Ταυρινοί, a form which occurs elsewhere, e. g. Polyb. 3. 60, though it is condemned by Dindorf : Τικῖνος, Strab. 209, where Kramer reads Τίκινος, which occurs in St. Byz. ; Polyb. 3. 64 : Χάλινος (?) *Pape*; cf. Lob. Prol. 202 sqq.

298. NOTE 5.—The following names in εῖνος should probably be spelled ῖνος ; Pape is the authority for most of them.

Ἀντωνεῖνος : Αὐγουρεῖνος (?) : Ἐραξεῖνος : Ἐρασεῖνος = Ἐρασῖνος, which is falsely Ἐρασινός in the Chron. Pasch. p. 61. 20 ; H. D. : Καπιτωλεῖνος : Κλινατεῖνος: Παυλεῖνος (?): Ποθεινός, Luc. Rhet. Præc. c. 24; Athen. 19 E: 'Ρη-γεῖνος: Σευηρεῖνος (?): Τυρτυλλεῖνος: Φαεινός, Schol. Aristoph. Eq. 959: Φιλεῖνος = Φιλῖνος: Φροντεῖνος = Φροντῖνος: Χαρεῖνος = Χαρῖνος.

299. NOTE 6.—*Exceptions in* ῦνος. Βόθυνος, A. G. 173. 26: Γρύνοι (?) St. Byz.: Δέρκυνος, Apollod. 2. 5. 10: Εὔθυνος, Athen. 120 A; Schol. Lucian Tim. 30; Μαιδοβίθυνοι, St. Byz. s. v. Μαιδοί, is more correctly Μαιδοβιθυνοί in Strab. 295: Μάκυνος (?) Auth. Pal. 9. 518: Μαριάνδυνοι (?) St. Byz., who says that they were so called from one Μαριανδυνός (*sic*): Μαριανδυνοί, Strab. 345, and so expressly Arc. 66. 3: Μόσυνος, Nic. Dam. p. 148 ed. Orell.; H. *D.*: Πάχυνος, Strab. 106, etc.; Arc. 66. 3 (the υ is sometimes short): 'Ρόσκυνος, Athen. 332 A; Theog. Can. 68. 10: Σίγυνοι, or Σίγυννοι, Apollon. Rhod. 4. 320; also Σίγιννοι, Strab. 520; Τόλυνος, E. M. 761. 47; but the name is suspected: Χάμυνος, Paus. 6. 21. 1; cf. Lob. Prol. 227.

300. NOTE 7.—*Exceptions in* ωνος. Ἄγωνος, Eust. 1335. 59: 'Αλίζωνοι, Strab. 549: 'Αλπωνος, St. Byz.; Strab. 60: Ἄνωνος. in the passage of Paus. (3. 20. 7), cited by Pape, Dindorf reads Ἄννονος: Γίγωνος, a city, Herodot. 7. 123: Ἴτωνος, Paus. 5. 1. 4: Καννωνός, Theog. Can. 68. 19, is perhaps falsely written Κάννωνος in Xen. Hell. 1. 7. 20; Aristoph. Eccles. 1089; for which Κάνωνος is another form: Κορωνός, Theog. Can. 68. 19, or Κόρωνος, Hom. Il. 2. 746; Diod. Sic. 4. 37, according to the precept of Arc. 66. 9: Ὄζωνος (?) Suid.; Dindorf thinks, and with reason, that this is a genitive case: 'Οθρωνός, Lycoph. 1027; 1034; Suid.; Theog. Can. 68. 19; is falsely Ὄθρωνος in St. Byz., and 'Οθρῶνος in Hesych.: 'Ονόχωνος, Schol. Apollon. Rhod. 4. 132; Herodot. 7. 129, 196; cf. Lob. Prol. 230.

Compounds (which are rather uncommon) throw back the accent, as Τρικό-λωνος, Paus. 8. 3, 4.

301. NOTE 8.—*Irregular Participal Forms.* 'Αγαπώμενος, Auth. Palat. Append. 375: Ἄρμενος, Strab. 503: Ἄσμενος (?) *Pape*: Δαμάρμενος, Paus. 5. 13. 5: Δέγμενος, Paus. 5. 4. 2: Δεξάμενος, St. Byz.: Δημάρμεμος, Herodot. 5. 41; 6. 65: Διαδούμενος, Plut. 2. 1058 F: Εὐκτίμενος (?) Inscr.: Θεοκλύμενος, Hom. Od. 15. 256; Eurip. Hel. 1184: 'Ιάλμενος, Herod. π. μ. λ. 8. 31; Arc. 64. 27: Καύμενος (?) *Pape*: Κλύμενος, E. M. 521. 4.; Arc. 64. 28: Ὄρμενος, Arc. 64. 28; Herod. π. μ. λ. 8. 31: Φιλήμενος, Polyh. 8. 26.

302. NOTE 9.—The rule for the accentuation of these words is thus stated by Arcadius, 64. 23: τὰ διὰ τοῦ ΜΕΝΟΣ μετοχικὰ ὀξύνονται, εἰ μὴ πάθος τι γένηται παρὰ τὴν φωνήν, τότε γὰρ προπαροξύνεται. τὰ δὲ ὀξύτονα ταῦτα· Τισαμενός, 'Ακεσα-μενός, Φαμενός, 'Ιαμενός, Σωζομενός, τὸ 'Ιάλμενος προπαροξύνεται ὡς πάθον, ὥσπερ καὶ τὸ Ὄρμενος, Κλύμενος, ἴκμενος: according to this it would seem that any participal form in μενος is proparoxytone when it is not absolutely identical with the participle whence it is derived: e. g. ἰάλλομαι makes ἰαλλόμενος, or ἰηλάμενος, but in no case ἰάλμενος: as therefore there is no fear that the latter word should be confounded with any actual participle of ἰάλλω, it does not require the help of a special accent to distinguish it from one: in like manner κλύμενος is at least an irregular participle of κλύω; it has lost or never had a connective vowel: but why proper names which are exactly identical with participles do not receive a dis-tinguishing accent, the grammarians do not explain; cf. Eust. 501. 8; 1228, 26; Philemon Lex. p. 6. § 16: 'Ακεσσαμενός ὡς κύριον ὀξύνεται, πρὸς διαστολὴν τῆς μετοχῆς, ὥσπερ καὶ τὸ Σωζομενός καὶ Τισσαμενός. Upon this principle 'Αγαπώμενος at least ought to be oxytone; cf. Schol. Ven. Φ. 142.

-ΞΟΣ.

303. Substantives in ξος, both proper and common, retract their accent, as πύξος, τάξος, Ἄξος, Λίπαξος, Νάξος, Ῥοῖξος; except ἰξός and μυοξός oxytone.

304. NOTE 1.—*Common Substantives.* Ἀπαξός (?), Hesych. probably an adjective : ἀραξός, E. M. 134. 40 : ἰξός, Arc. 66. 13 : κριξός, Doric for κρισσός or κιρσός, *L. S.* : μυοξός, μύοξος, or μυωξός, Lob. Par. 405, note.

305. NOTE 2.—*Proper Names.* Ἄξος, St. Byz., is wrongly Ἀξός in Herodot. 4. 154 : Δαοξός (?) Theog. Can. 69. 10 : Κοραξός ; for [ὀξύνεται].. καὶ τὸ Καραξὸς ὡς ἐθνικόν, Arc. 66. 14 ; Lobeck (Par. 404, note) proposes to read καὶ τὸ Καραξὸς ὡς ἐπίθετον ὀξύνεται, βαρύνεται δὲ ὡς ἐθνικόν, and adds, 'etsi gentis nomen sæpius oxytonum est Scylac. § 76. p. 31, quam proparoxytonum, adjectivum autem non legi nisi Plutarch. Flum. 18. 8, ubi Maussacus κόρακος correxit sicut Corais Xenocr. 1. 19. 5, piscis nomen scripsit pro κόραξος (non κοραξός). Salmasius vero ad Tertull. de Pall. p. 215, non solum illic retinet κοραξός, quod parum apte cum φριξός confert, sed et aliis locis restituere conatur ;' Κόραξος occurs also in St. Byz., and Κοραξοί, or, as one MS. reads, Κορεξοί, in Aristot. Meteor. 1. 13. 27 : Λιξός (?), Theog. 69. 10, should probably be Λίξος, as in St. Byz. s. v. Λίγξ : Ὀαξός, Scylax, should be Ὄαξος, St. Byz. : Ηαξοί, Polyb. 2. 10. 1, is better Πάξοι in Dio Cass. 50. 12 : Σιξός (?) Theog. 69. 10, seems false for Σίξος, St. Byz. : Φριξός, Theog. *l. l.* ; but the proper name is always Φρῖξος (or less correctly Φρίξος) in the books.

-ΟΟΣ and -ΟΥΣ.

306. All substantives, both proper and common, in οος, retract the accent, as αἴμοος, ἀνάπλοος, ἐπέκπλοος, θρόος, πλόος, ῥόος, Πείροος, Πειρίθοος, Πρόθοος, Σόος, Τιμόνοος. All *simple* words in ους of the Second Declension are perispomena, whatever may have been the accent of the forms from which they come ; as νόος νοῦς, βόος βοῦς, ἀδελφιδέος ἀδελφιδοῦς (cf. § 237), θυγατριδέος θυγατριδοῦς ; Θαμοῦς, Plat. Phædr. 274 D, Ἀμοῦς. The name Ἰησοῦς is perispomenon, according to this general analogy. All *compound* words in ους, on the other hand, are paroxytone, as ἀκλίνους, εὔπλους, εὔχρους.

307. NOTE.—On these words see Arc. 38. 1 ; 42. 4 ; 93. 6 ; 126. 4 ; Chœrob. C. 245. 21 ; A. G. 708 : Δεξόος, as a proper name in Plut. 1. 393, seems to violate all analogy, and should be corrected.

Almost all these words are liable to contraction ; and when that takes place they conform to the general rule laid down above, § 20, at least in the nominative singular, for the oblique cases (which are considered below) are somewhat anomalous. Hence θρόος, ῥόος, πλόος, ἐπέκπλοος, Πειρίθοος, become θροῦς, ῥοῦς, πλοῦς, ἐπέκπλους, Πειρίθους ; γόος however is never contracted, Chœrob. C. 244. 24. The national name Χοῖ, St. Byz., is probably to be referred hither.

308. Substantives in πος, both proper and common, throw back the accent, as ἄνθρωπος, δόρπος, ἵππος, κῆπος, κόλπος, κόμπος, *din,* κόπος, πάππος, πρόπαππος, ῥύπος, ῥῶπος, τόπος, τρόπος, *mode,* τύπος, ὕσσωπος, Αἴσωπος, Ἄτροπος, Εὔριπος, Κάμπος, Κάρπος, Κρῶπος, Λάμπος, Μελάνωπος, Μέλαμπος, Ὄλυμπος, Φίλιππος ; except oxytone, ἀτραπός, καρπός, κλοπός, μαστροπός, ὀπός, πομπός, σκοπός, στενωπός, τροπός, *a thong,* and Ἀριμασποί, Ἀσωπός, Ἰνωπός, Ὠρωπός, oxytone.

309. NOTE 1.—*Common Substantives.* Ἀταρπός or ἀτραπός, Arc. 67. 15 : γρῖπος or γρῖπος, E. M. 241. 28 is written γριπός, Anth. Pal. 6. 23. 5 : ἵπος, Arc. 66. 18, is oxytone in A. G. 44. 19 and Hesych. : καρπός, Arc. 66. 23 ; Eust. 907. 8 ; Chœrob. E. 46. 20 : κλοπός, 'Hom. H. in Merc. 276, Βοῶν κλοπὸν ὑμετεράων ; Oppian. Cyn. 1. 517 ; Ἐρίφων κλοπός (vulgo κλόπος),' H. D. : κομπός, *a boaster,* is really an adjective, and therefore oxytone : λόπος, Theog. Can. 68. 31, is occasionally oxytone in the books : μαστροπός (wrongly μαστρωπός), is accented thus by a false analogy : μολπός, Hesych. : ὀπός, Theog. Can. 68. 32 : πολύπος, is a doubtful form ; πούλυπος is expressly said to be proparoxytone by Eust. 768. 48 : πομπός (really an adj.), Arc. 67. 4 : σκοπός, Arc. 67. 4 : στενωπός (really an adjective), Lob. Par. 332 ; Arc. 67. 22 ; 87. 1 : ταρπός (?) Pollux 7. 174 : τρόπος ὁ τρέπων : τροπός ὁ τετραμμένος [*the thong for fastening the oar to the thole*], Arc. 67. 2.

310. NOTE 2.—*Proper Names.* Ἀριμασποί, St. Byz. : Ἀσωπός, Arc. 67. 18 : Βοπός, Phot. Bib. 447. 15 : Εὐρωπός, Theog. Can. 69. 19 ; St. Byz. ; 'In accentu variatur inter Εὔρωπος et Εὐρωπός. Sed viri quidem nomen gravari, ut Εὐρώπη, testatur Eust. ad Dionys. v. 270 ; conf. id. ib. 175 ; Schol. Lycophr. 1283,' *L. Dindorf* ap. H. D. : Ἰνωπός, Theog. Can. 69. 19 ; Ἰνώποιο in Hom. Hym. ad Apoll. 18 is false for Ἰνωποῖο : Κνωπός, a king of Erythræ, Athen. 259 E, is Κνῶπος in St. Byz. s. v. Ἐρυθρά, and this is probably the correct accentuation ; so also Κνῶπος a river and city in Bœotia, Schol. Nicand. Ther. 889 : Οἰνωπός (?), for this name, which occurs in the MSS. of Arc. 67. 18, Schmidt reads Ἰνωπός : Ὠρωπός, Arc. 67. 19.

311. Common nouns in ρος throw back the accent, as ἄγγαρος, αἴγειρος, αἴλουρος, ἄργυρος, βόθρος, βόρβορος, δίφρος, οἱ ἔνεροι, κάπρος, κέγχρος, κόμαρος, λάρος, λῆρος, μάγειρος, οἶστρος, ὄνειρος, πάγρος, πάπυρος, πέτρος, σίδηρος, σπόρος, ταῦρος, φθόρος, φόρος, ὦχρος ; except oxytone, ἀγρός, ἀφρός, ἀχυρός, γαμβρός, δαιτρός, δορός, ἐκυρός, θαιρός, θεωρός, θησαυρός, θορός = θορή, ἰατρός, καιρός (but καῖρος = *licium*), κηρός, μηρός, νεβρός, νεκρός, νεφρός, ξυρός, ὀρός, *serum lactis,* οὐρός, *trench,* πενθερός, πυρός, σορός, σταυρός, σωρός, ταρρός, τυρός, χορός, and ἑταῖρος properispomenon.

312. NOTE.—Ἀγορατρός (?) : ἀγρός, Arc. 73. 19 : ἀγχοῦρος, *the dawn,* Arc. 73. 10 : ἀκαρός, E. M. 26. 29 ; 45. 13 : ἀλιτρός is an adjective, though it is used substantively : ἀφρός, Eust. 907. 3 : ἀχυρός, *Attic*, Arc. 75. 5 ; Ælius Dionysius ap. Eust. 1698. 31 : it was also proparoxytone, A. G. 7. 24 : βαλαρός, a Corsican word meaning *an exile*, Paus. 10. 17. 9 : βαλλιρός (?) Arist. H. A. 8. 20. 2 ; some MSS. have it barytone, which is more agreeable to analogy, unless indeed the word be adjectival : βδαροί, Hesych. : βορός ὁ πολλὰ ἐσθίων, Arc. 68. 24, is an adjective : δαιτρός, Arc. 74. 15 : δαρός ὁ δεδαρμένος, Arc. 69. 3, probably an adjective : δειρός, Hesych. : δορός, Hom. Odyss. 2. 354 : ἐκυρός, Arc. 72. 8 : ἑταῖρος, Arc. 72. 18 ; Herod. π. μ. λ. 21. 4 ; but ἔταρος : θαιρός, Chœrob. E. 47. 3 : θεωρός, Arc. 72. 13 : θησαυρός, Arc. 72. 23 : θορός = *semen genitale* : θόρος = ἀφροδισιασ-τής, Hesych. : ἰατρός, E. M. 250. 29 : ἰδρός, Poet = ἰδρώς : ἰωρός, Arc. 72. 14 : καιρός, *opportunity* : καῖρος = τὸ διάπλεγμα, ὃ οὐκ ἐᾷ τοὺς .στήμονας συγκέεσθαι, Eust. 1571. 56 ; on the accent see Eust. 907. 12 ; Theog. Can. 70. 20 ; Chœrob. E. 46. 35 ; 47. 2 ; Arc. 69. 17 : κέρκουρος, Arc. 73. 12, sometimes wrongly κερκοῦρος : κηρός, Arc. 68. 5 : λικροί, Hesych., is probably false ; he has λέκροι (?) in the same signification, i. e. *the buds* or *knots on stags' horns* : λῆρος, Arc. 68. 10, the accent ληρός = *some unknown feminine ornament*, is doubtful, as the MSS. vary : L. S. have μαστρός ; it is barytone in Hesych., and Arist. ap. Harpocr. s. v. μαστῆ-ρες ; H. D. also write μάστρος : μηρός, cf. Arc. 68. 5 : μολοβρός is an adjective, Arc. 74. 22 : μόρμυρος, Arist. H. A. 6. 17. 7 ; Athen. 313 E ; 136 C ; E. M. 591. 3, is paroxytone in Auth. Palat. 6. 304. 4 ; Artemid. 2. 14. p. 168 ; Eust. 1150. 33 ; 1230. 44 ; all these passages are quoted by H. D. : μυλωθρός, Athen. 168 A ; Suid. : μῶρος or μωρός is an adjective : ναιθροί, Hesych. : νεβρός, Arc. 73. 14 : νεκρός, Arc. 73. 14, really an adjective : νεφρός, 73. 15 : ξυρός, Arc. 69. 8 ; on the quantity of the penultimate, see H. D. s. v. : ὀρός (and ὀρρός, Arc. 68. 23) = ὑδατῶ-δες τοῦ γάλακτος, A. G. 743. 11 ; Eust. 906. 59 ; but ὄρος, *a mountain*, and ὅρος, *a boundary* : οὐρός, *a trench* ; but οὖρος, *a fair wind*, Aristarchus ap. Schol. Ven. B. 153 ; Eust. 906. 48 ; Arc. 70. 2, ' Cum ὁλκοί conjungit Pollux 10. 148 ap. quem οὖρος scriptum ib. 134 contra præceptum Arcadii ;' H. D. : περιστερός, Theog. Can. 70. 23 : πόρος, A. G. Oxon. 1. 370. 30 : πρὸς διάφορον σημασίαν διάφορον ἔχει καὶ τὸν τόνον· καὶ γὰρ πόρος μὲν παροξυτόνως, τὸ πλατούμενον, πορὸς δὲ ὀξυτόνως τὸ πλατοῦν : πυρός, Arc. 69. 7 : σινδρύς, an adjective sometimes used elliptically : σιρός (also σιρρός and σειρός), Arc. 68. 14 ; Ammonius ap. E. M. 714. 17 ; Theog. Can. 69. 33 : σορός, Arc. 69. 1 : σταυρός, Arc. 69. 22 : στελεφοῦρος (?) Theophrast. H. P. 7. 11. 2 ; H. D. : σχερός, Hesych. : σωρός, Arc. 69. 11 ; E. M. 742. 20 : ταρρός, Attic = ταρσός : τηρός (?) Æschyl. Supp. 248 : ' τιμωρός, *cicuta*, Diosc. Notha. p. 468 (4. 79), *Boissonade* ap. H. D. : τυρός, Arc. 19. 1 ; Eust. 907. 10 : φηρός, Arc. 68. 6 ; Theog. Can. 69. 30 ; τὸ φῆρον is barytone : φιτρός, Arc. 74. 16 ; falsely φίτρος in Hesych. : φορός, *a favourable wind*, Arc. 68. 21, is really an adjective, as is φρουρός, Arc. 70. 3 : χονδρός, Arc. 73. 23, but in the books it is always paroxytone : χορός, Arc. 68. 24 : on χλῶρος or χλωρός, see Lob. Par. 341.

313. Proper names in ρος retract the accent, as Γλάφυρος, Γύαρος, Δῶρος, Ἐπίδαυρος, Ἐπίκουρος, Ἶρος, Ἰσόδωρος, Κέρβερος, Κίμβροι, Κόδρος, Κύπρος, Κῦρος, Λάρος, Μαίανδρος, Μέταυρος, Ὅμηρος, Πάνδαρος, Πάρος, Πέτρος, Πίνδαρος, Σάτυρος, Σκάμανδρος, Στάγειρος, Σῦρος, Σφαῖρος, Τάρταρος, Τύρος, Φαῖδρος, Φάληρος, Φάρος ; except Λοκροί, Νευροί, Οἰνωτρός, Τελεσφορός, Τευκροί, oxytone (but Τεῦκρος, *Teucer*), and Ἀγχοῦρος, Ἀρκτοῦρος, pro-perispomena.

314. NOTE.—Cf. E. M. 660. 50 : Ἀγχοῦρος (?) Arc. 73. 10 : Ἀμφοτερός, Schol. Ven. Π. 415 : εἰς διαστολὴν τὸ κύριον ὀξυτόνως ἀνέγνω ὁ Ἀρίσταρχος, ὡς δεξιτερόν·

καὶ, he complacently adds, ἐπείσθησαν οἱ Γραμματικοί : Ἀρκτοῦρος, Arc. 73. 10 : Ἀρός, *a river*, St. Byz. s. v. Δρῦς : Βάλακρος, Diod. Sic. 17. 27 is oxytone in St. Byz. s. v. Βέροια : Βρομερός, Thucyd. 4. 83 : Βωσφόρος is paroxytone according to the analogy of compound adjectives and substantives, the last factor of which is derived from a verb : Διζηρός, St. Byz. : Ἑκατερός (?) Plut. 2. 177 F : Ἔρυθρος, Arc. 74. 28 ; it is incorrectly oxytone in Eust. 267 and elsewhere : Ἑωσφόρος, Hes. Theog. 381 : Καιρός, Paus. 8. 25. 9, and Eust. Opusc. p. 339, quoted by H. D. : Καλαβροί, St. Byz. s. v. Κανταβρία : Κανταβροί, St. Byz., is proparoxytone in Strab. 153 ; Appian Iberic. 80 : Καρτερός, Galen Tom. 13. p. 547 D : Κρατερός, *Pape*, but Arrian, e. g. Anab. 7. 12. 3, has Κράτερος : Λοκρός, Hesiod ap. Strab. 322 : Λοκροί, *passim* : Μηρός, Diod. Sic. 2. 38 : Νευροί, Arc. 69. 26, is falsely Νεῦροι in St. Byz. : Οἰνωτρός, Arc. 75. 1 ; St. Byz. s. v. Οἰνωτρία, 'unde corrigenda prosodia apud Pausaniam et Dionys. A. R. 1. 11–13, ubi gentis (ut ap. Steph. B. in Ἀριάνθη, Ἀρίνθη, Νίναια, Σέστιον) ducisque nomen est proparoxytonum ;' H. D. : Παλαιρός, *Pape*) is Πάλαιρος in Strab. 450. 459 : Σεβῆρος, Herodian ; Suid., etc. ; Σεβρός, Paus. 3. 15. 1 ; Σμικρός et Μικρός vitioso accentu nonnulli ap. Demosth. et Isæum, ut Μικρός scribitur ap. Diog. L. 5. 73,' L. Dindorf ap. H. D. ; Lob. Par. 342 ; Σμῖκρος is the proper accentuation : Στεφηφόρος (?) : Σῦρος, *the island Syrus*, but Σύροι, *the Syrians*, Arc. 69. 5 : Τελεσφόρος, Athen. 616 C, has the accent of a verbal adjective : Τευκροί and Τευκρός, the ethnic noun, Arc. 74. 5, though it is occasionally properispomenon, e. g. Eust. 713. 26 ; but Τεῦκρος, the hero, Arc. *l. l.* : Χόμαροι, Ptol. 6. 11. 6 : Χυτροί, St. Byz. : Ψενηρός, St. Byz., but Meineke reads Ψένηρος, which seems preferable.

-ΣΟΣ.

315. Common substantives in σος throw back their accent, as βύσσος, *byssus*, δρόσος, θίασος, θύρσος, κάβαισος, κυπάρισσος, νῆσος, νόσος, παράδεισος, χέρσος ; except βυσσός, *bottom*, κερασός, κισσός, κολοσσός, κρωσσός, μολοσσός, νεοσσός, πεσσός, πυρσός, ταρσός, χρυσός, which are oxytone.

316. Note.—Ἀρσός (?) Arc. 76. 5 : ἡ βύσσος, St. Byz. s. v. Βυσσός ; cf. Schol. Ven. Ω. 80 ; but ὁ βυσσός : γαῖσος, Arc. 75. 19 ; Theog. Can. 72. 25 ; in several passages however this word is oxytone, doubtless an erroneous accentuation : καμασός (?) Hesych. : κεισός, Hesych. : κερασός, Arc. 76. 22 : κηνσός, *a plant*, Hesych, κῆνσος, *census*, Arc. 75. 11 : κιρσός, *a varicose vein*, Arc. 76. 4 ; also, κρισσός and Dor. κριξός : κισσός, Arc. 76. 13 ; Schol. Ven. Ω. 80 : κολοσσός, Theog. Can. 73. 21 : κροσσός or κροσός, Hesych. : κρωσσός, Arc. 75. 7 : κυπάρισσος, Arc. 77. 11 : κυρσός, Suid. : κυσός (and κυσσός ?), Hesych., is κύσος in Eust. 746. 18, while it is expressly made properispomenon by Theog. Can. 72. 17 : μολοσσός, Theog. Can. 73. 21 ; Arc. 77. 21 ; this is, strictly speaking, an adjective ; but it is constantly used substantively : νάρκισσος, Arc. 77. 11 : νεοσσός, Theog. Can. 73. 21 ; Arc. 77. 20 : νῆσος, Herod. π. μ. λ. 11. 15 ; Arc. 75 : νοσσός=νεοσσός, A. G. Oxon. 1. 338. 24 : οἶσος, Eust. 1533. 57, or οἰσός, Theoph. H. Pl. 6. 2. 2, both places quoted by H. D. : ὀρσός, Hesych. : πάσσος (sc. οἶνος), Eust. 1843. 31 ; Polyb. 6. 2. 3 = *vinum passum* : πεσσός, Schol. Ven. Ω. 80 : πεσός=πεσσός in the sense of *pessory*, cf. Eust. 1397. 6 : πίσος, Arc. 75. 4, is oxytone elsewhere : πυρσός, Arc. 76. 4 : ὑρισός (?) Athen. 372 C ; ὑρισσός, Hesych. : ὑσσός, Theog. Can. 24. 8 : χρυσός, Arc. 75. 13 ; Herod. π. μ. λ. 38. 30 ; according to Eust. 1340. 38 words in σος are oxytone : as a fact however there are more barytones than oxytones.

317. Proper names in σος are hardly reducible to rule[1]; with the exceptions given below, however, it may be said that they draw back the accent, except those in σσος, which are oxytone, as Βλαῖσος, Διόννσος, Ἔρεσος, Ἔφεσος, Θάσος, Κροῖσος, Μόλσος, Μύρσος, Νῖσος, Πελοπόννησος, Πήγασος, but Ἐρεσσός, Ἁλικαρνασσός, Κολοσσός, Παρνασσός, Βεσσός.

318. Note 1.—Lob. Prol. 408 : Ἀγορησός, St. Byz. : Ἀμισός, Theog. Can. 73. 17 ; Strab. 519 : Ἀμνησός, Suid., or Ἀμνισός, A. G. Oxon. 2. 172. 14, is Ἀμνισσός, in Eust. 1861. 39 : Ἀμφρυσός and Ἀμφρυσσός are false for Ἄμφρυσος, Strab. 433 ; St. Byz. ; this was Herodian's accentuation ; Schol. Apollon. Rhod. 1. 54 : Ἀνδρασός, Suid. s. v. Μέδουσα : Ἀπαισός, Hom. Il. 2. 828 ; Ἄπαισος seems to be expressly made barytone in Theog. Can. 73. 31 : Ἀσσησός, St. Byz. : Βηρωσός, or more properly Βηρωσσός, is also written Βήρωσσος, Theog. Can. 74. 3 ; on the various forms of this name, see H. D. : Βολογεσός (?) St. Byz. s. v. Βολογεσιάς : Βραισοί, St. Byz. : Βριλησός, E. M. 214. 9 is Βριλησσός, Strab. 399 ; Thucyd. 2. 23, yet we find in Theog. Can. 73. 2 : τὸ Κήσος, Βρίλησος δι' ἑνὸς Σ γραφόμενα βαρύνονται : Βρυσός (?), Herod. π. μ. λ. 38 : Γαισος, Hesych. : Γαλαῖσος, Polyb. 8. 35. 8 : Γάλαισος, a man's name : Γέδρωσοί, Dion. Per. 1086 : Γεδρωσός, Arrian Ind. : Δοιδαλσός, Strab. 563, or Δυδαλσός, Phot. Bib. 228. 15 : Ἐβυσός, St. Byz. s. v. Βυσσοί is another form of the latter name : Ἔβυσσος, in Strab. 159, is the island Ebusus (*Iviza*) : Ἐδεβησός, St. Byz. ; H. D. quote it as Ἐδεβησσός, which is doubtless the correct form : 'Ἰάλυσος s. Ἰάλυσσος, urbs Rhodi, Scythiæ, Adriæ ... St. Byz. ubi scriptum Ἰάλυσσος ... Ἰαλυσός ap. Strab. 14. p. 655 : Ἰήλυσον ap. Diodor. 4. 58 : sed oxytonum Ἰηλυσόν, 13. 75, et Ἰηλυσοῦ Thucyd. 8. 44, ubi v. Wass : Ἰηλυσσός est ap. Hom. Il. B. 656, ubi libri plures Ἰηλυσός, vitiose, quantum ex adjectivo Ἰηλύσιος colligi potest ap. Dionys. Perieg. 505 : Ἰηλυσίων πέδον ἀνδρῶν, et ex nomine Ialysi, quod tertia syllaba correpta dixit Pindarus,' H. D. : Ἰλισός, Arc. 77. 16, an incorrect form for Ἰλισσός : Καρδησός, St. Byz. : Καρησός, Schol.

[1] Perhaps others may be more fortunate than I have been in bringing these troublesome words to something like order, and to assist them in that thankless task the following abstract of the rules given by Arcadius (75. 3–78. 5) is appended.

Dissyllables.—1. Those consisting of two short syllables are barytone, as Θάσος, Κάσος.   2. Those with η in the penultimate are barytone, as Βῆσος, Μνῆσος, Ῥῆσος.   3. Feminine nouns with ω in the penultimate are oxytone, as Κνωσός. 4. Masculines with a long dichronous vowel in the penultimate are barytone, as Ἶσος, Κῖσος, Κρῖσος, Πῖσος, except Λισός, and Μυσός.   5. Names of cities with a diphthong in the penultimate are oxytone, as Παισός, Λουσός, Πραισός.   6. Those with a liquid before the termination are barytone, except some with ι or α in the penultimate ; hyperdissyllables with α in the penultimate are proparoxytone, as Βάργασος, Μέγαρσος, Ἀγάθυρσος.   7. Those in σσος are oxytone, as Βεσσός, Θυσσός, Ἀσσός, but Νέσσος the Centaur.   *Hyperdissyllables.*—1. Those in ἄσος are proparoxytone, as Ἅρπασος, Δάμασος.   2. Those in εσος are proparoxytone, as Ἔφεσος, Ἔρεσος.   3. Those in ησος are oxytone, except *paronyma* and compounds, as Ταρτησσός, Λυρηνσσός, Λυκαβησσός, except, according to some, Κάρησσος, and Μάρπησσος from Μάρπησσα : Μυόνννησος, Χερρόνησος, etc., are compounds.   4. Those in ισσος are proparoxytone, as Μέλισσος, except Τελμισσός.   5. Those in ἴσος are oxytone, except those derived from feminine nouns, as Κηφισός, Ἰλισός, Κερδισός, but Ἄρκισος from Ἄρκισα, Λάρισος from Λάρισα.   6. Those in οσσος are oxytone, as Μολοσσός.   7. The rule for those in υσος is wanting.   8. Those in ωσσος are oxytone, as Κερωσσός. Göttling's rules are even more complicated still, but, as they do not avoid a host of exceptions, it is unnecessary to quote them.

Ven. M. 20 : Τυραννίων ὀξύνει τὸ Κάρησος ὡς Παρνασσός· οὕτως γὰρ ὑπὸ Κυζικηνῶν ὀνομάζεσθαι τὸν ποταμόν. ὁ δὲ Ἀρίσταρχος βαρύνει ὡς Κάνωβος. εἴπομεν δὲ ἐν ἑτέροις ὅτι οὐ πάντως ἐπιρακτεῖ ἡ ἀπὸ τῶν ἐθνῶν χρῆσις καὶ ἐπὶ τὴν Ὁμηρικὴν ἀνάγνωσιν, ὁπότε περὶ τοῦ Γλισᾶντα (Il. 2. 504) διελάβομεν, εἴγε Διονύσιος ἱστορεῖ τοὺς ἐγχωρίους συστέλλειν τὸ Ι καὶ μὴ περισπᾶν. τό τε Λύκαστος ὁ αὐτὸς ἱστορεῖ ὀξύνεσθαι, ἡμῶν ἀναγινωσκόντων βαρυτόνως (Il. 2. 647) ; Arc. 77. 4, τὸ μέντοι Κάρησσος (sic) τινὲς βαρύνουσι ; the city Κάρησος is barytone, Demetrius ap. Strab. 603 : Καρκασός (?), Xen. Anab. 7. 8. 18 : Καρμυλησός (?), or Καρμυλησσός, Strab. 665 : Κερδισός, Arc. 77. 17 ; Suid.: Κερωσός is false ; the correct form is Κερωσσός, Arc. 78. 4 ; Apollon. Rhod. 4. 573 : Κηφισός (Καφισός *Dor.* Pind. Pyth. 4. 81), Chœrob. A. G. Oxon. 2. 228. 25 ; Arc. 77. 16 ; 'In codd. non raro Κηφισσός duplici σ scriptum ;' *H. D.*: Κνωσός, Diod. Sic. 5. 78 ; Arc. 75. 7 ; Theog. Can. 72. 10, who observes that Trypho wrote Κνωσσός, 'Κνωσός et Κνώσιος in libris modo simplici modo duplici σ scripta reperiuntur : simplex ut in aliis hujusmodi nominibus, commendatur numorum inscriptionumque auctoritate ;' *H. D.* : 'Κριμισός, ὁ, Crimisus, fluvius Siciliæ, ap. Lycoph. 961, ubi codd. nonnulli κρημισσός vel κριμησός, plerique κριμισσός, quod in Κριμισός recte mutavit Bachmannus, analogiam similium nominum secutus, de quibus v. Arcad. p. 77. 14 : Κρίμησος scribitur apud Plut. V. Timol. c. 25. 27, 28 : Κριμισσός ap. Diodor. 19. 2 ; Ælian. V. H. 2. 33, aliosque, libris plerumque nonnihil discrepantibus, etiam ap. scriptores Latinos : v. Staver. ad Cornel. Nep. Timol. c. 2, et Heyn. ad Virg. Æn. 5. 38 : Κριμισός est ap. Dionys. A. R. 1. 52, et Suidam (cujus codex Par. A. κριμνισός, Leid. κριμνησός) et in Etym. Gud. p. 347. 40 ;' *H. D.* The passage in Arc. referred to runs as follows, τὰ εἰς ΣΟΣ ὑπερδισύλλαβα ἔχοντα τὴν πρὸ τέλους συλλαβὴν εἰς Ι ἐκτεταμένον λήγουσαν ὀξύνεται· εἰ δέ τι βεβαρυτόνηται, τοῦτο παρώνυμον ὤφθη ἀπὸ θηλυκοῦ· Κηφισύς, Ἰλισός, Κερδισός· τὸ δὲ Ἄρκισος Ἄρκισα, Λάρισος, Λάρισα ἀπὸ θηλυκῶν. Now as the feminine Κρίμισσα exists, and as Lycophron himself uses it (v. 913), it may be doubted whether Bachmann has 'followed the analogy of similar nouns.' It is expressly said to be barytone by Theog. Can. 73. 16 ; cf. Lob. Prol. 414 : Λουσός, Arc. 75. 16 : Λουσοί, St. Byz. : Λυρνησός is found in some books for Λυρνησσός, St. Byz. ; Strab. 584 ; Arc. 77. 4 : Μαγαρσός, Arrian Anab. 2. 5. 9 : Μαυσός, St. Byz. : Μοισοί (?) Strab. 295 ; see H. D. s. v. Μυσία : Μυκαλησός (?) is properly Μυκαλησσός in St. Byz., Hom., etc. : Μυσοί, Arc. 75. 12 ; Theog. Can. 72. 18 : Μυσός, a man's name, Herodot. 1. 171 : Ναϊσός, St. Byz. : 'Inter utramque scripturam per simplex, et quod frequentius, duplex σ, variatur etiam ap. Byzantinos qui sæpe urbem memorant ;' *L. Dindorf* ap. *H. D.* : Παγασός is quoted by H. D. from Paus. 10. 5. 8, where Πάγασος is rightly read in Dindorf's own edition : Παισός, Arc. 75. 16 ; Theog. Can. 72. 23 : Πανισός (?) *Pape :* Παμισός, Strab. 316, is expressly said to be Πάμισος in Theog. Can. 73. 16 : Παραισός, Theog. Can. 73. 33, where it is wrongly printed as a common substantive. St. Byz. is rather amusing, Πάραισος (sic) περὶ ἧς Ἡρωδιανὸς ἐν ὀγδόῳ· τὸ μέντοι Πάραισος (sic) ὀξύνεται. ἐγένετο δὲ ὁ Πάραισος Μίνῳ συγγενής, ἀφ᾽ οὗ ἡ πόλις ἡ Πάραισος ὁμοτόνως τῷ οἰκιστῇ. This is one out of a host of accentual blunders in the same author. Are the scribes or the modern editors to blame ? According to some, Παραισός is only another form for Πραισός : Παρακαρησός (?), Suid. : Παρμισός, Schol. Apollon. Rhod. 4. 132 : Παρνασός, the older and perhaps better form of Παρνασσός, Arc. 76. 24 : Περμησός occurs in some MSS. for Πέρμησσός, Strab. 407 : Πιγνισός or Πιτνίσος (?) are read in some books of Strab. 568 for Πίτνησσός : Πραισός, Theog. Can. 72. 23 ; Arc. 75. 16 : Πρυμνησός, Lob. Prol. 411 : Ῥωσός, Theog. Can. 72. 11 ; see below, § 319 : Σαλμυδησός for Σαλμυδησσός is not uncommon : Ταμασός or Τάμασος, and Ταμασσός ; on these various forms, concerning which there is much diversity of authority and opinion, see H. D. s. v. ; in St. Byz. it is absurdly printed Ταμάσος : Ταρσός, St. Byz. ; also called Θαρσός, Arc. 76. 3 ; A. G. Paris. 4. 192. 3 : Τάρσος· ἡ πόλις παροξυτόνως :

Ταρσοί, Xen. Anab. 1·. 2. 23 : Τευμησός, or Τευμησσός, cf. Lob. Prol. 410 : Τραυσοί (not Τραῦσοι, as Hesych. has it), Herodot. 5. 3 : Τυμνησός, St. Byz. s. v. Ἀγορησός : he elsewhere (s. v.) calls it Τυμνισσός; while H. D. quote him as reading Τυμνησσός : Χρυσός (?) ; cf. Herod. π. μ. λ. 38. 30 : Χρύσος (sic), Nicetas Chon. Hist. p. 314 C ; 328 C ; 344 C ; 345 C ; *H. D.*

319. Note 2.—*Exceptions in* σος. Ἀδόπισσος is quoted by H. D. and Pape from Ptol. 5. 9. 16, but there it is regular Ἀδοπισσός : Ἀκάρασσος, *Pape*, is rightly Ἀκαρασσός in St. Byz. : Ἀκρόλισσος, Strab. 316 : Ἄλυσσος, Paus. 8. 19. 3, is strictly an adjective, and therefore regular : Ἄντασσος (?), *Pape*, is Ἄντασος in Paus. 2. 4. 4 : Ἀράϊσσος (?) *Pape* : Ἀρχέμισσος, Theog. Can. 73. 8 : Ἄσσος, St. Byz. ; Strab. 606 : according to Arc. 76. 12 it is oxytone : Βάλισσος, Plut. 1. 557 : Βαρβάλισσος (?) St. Byz., is Βαρβαρισσός· (?) Ptol. 5. 15. 17 : Βάσσος, Lucian adv. Indoct. c. 23 : Βεσσός, Arc. 76. 12, 'In libris non raro Βέσσοι scriptum,' H. D. : there can be no doubt, however, that the word is oxytone ; it is also spelled Βησσοί, Herodot. 7. 111, and, with a false accent, Βῆσσοι, Eust. 277. 35 : Βῆσος, the name of a man, Arc. 75, note, is written Βῆσσος in Arrian Anab. 3. 8. 3, etc., or Βησσός, Strab. 724, though elsewhere he has Βῆσσος, e. g. 513 ; 518 : Βόσσος, Phot. Bib. 30. 20 : Βούβασσος, St. Byz. s. v. Ὑγασσος, perhaps only another form of Βύβασσος, St. Byz. ; the codex Vratisl. has Βυβασσός : Δόρυσσος, Herodot. 7. 204 ; Paus. 3. 2. 4, both places quoted by H. D. : Ἔλασσος, 'Paus. 10. 26. 4 . . . ubi est var. Ἔλεσσον vel Ἔλεσσος et scrib. videtur Ἔλασος quum nihili sit Ἔλασσος,' L. Dindorf ap. H. D. : Ἔρβησος (?) is mentioned by Göttling Accent. p. 213, but it is oxytone in St. Byz. ; Ptol. 3. 4. 13 ; 'Accentus verus videtur Ἐρβησσός,' L. Dindorf ap. H. D. : Εὐήνισσος, Alciph. 3. 52, Pape : Ἤλισσος, Anthol. Palat. 12. 22 : Θάλασσος, Alciph. 1. 7, Pape : Θυσσός, Arc. 76.12, is Θύσσος in Herodot. 8. 22 ; Thucyd. 4. 109, quoted by Göttling : Ἰάλυσσος or Ἰήλυσσος, see above, § 318 : Καρύασσος, cf. Göttling Accent. p. 213 : Κίβισσος, Diog. Laert. 1. 26 : Κίσσος, a man, Strab. 481 ; Plut. 1. 689, is paroxytone ; but Κισσός, a city, Strab. 330 ; 'Montis nomen Κισσός est ap. Nicandr. Ther. 804 . . . et Lycoph. 1237 . . . ubi var. lect. Κίσσου et Κισοῦ,' H. D. : Κράσσος, Strab. 747 : Κρύασσος, St. Byz. s. v. Ὑγασσος, yet he has Κρυασσός, s. v. from Κρύασσος (Κρύασος Cod. Vratisl.), the founder : Κύβασσος is quoted by Göttling Accent. p. 213 from St. Byz., but he has it rightly oxytone : Κυπάρισσος, St. Byz. : Κύρμισσος, Theog. Can. 73. 8 : Λάρισσος is false for Λάρισος, Arc. 77. 17 ; cf. H. D. s. v. : Λίσσος, a city of Dalmatia, Strab. 316 ; Diod. Sic. 15. 13, but Λισσός, a town of Crete, Herod. π. μ. λ. 38. 26 ; Arc. 75. 12 (?) : also as the name of a man, Suid. s. v. Ἰδαῖος : Μάρπησος, Arc. 77. 5 ; for which Μαρπησσός also occurs : Μέλισσος, Theog. Can. 73. 8 : Arc., etc. : Μούκισσος, St. Byz., or Μωκισσός, on which see H. D. s. v. : Νάρκασσος, St. Byz. : Νάρκισσος, Arc. 77. 11 : Νέσσος, Arc. 76.14 ; Eust. 1340. 39 : Νίσσος (?), *Pape*, but his reference seems incorrect : Νόσσος (?) : Παροπάμισσος, St. Byz. : Πρίνασσος, St. Byz. : Πόλισσος, Theog. Can. 73. 8 : Ῥυτίασσος, St. Byz. s. v. Ῥύτιον : Ῥωσσός, or Ῥῶσσος, is Ῥῶσος in St. Byz. ; according to Herod. π. μ. λ. 38. 27, Ῥωσός is the proper accent : Σάρδησσος, St. Byz. ; according to H. D. it should be oxytone : they quote no authorities : Σύασσος, St. Byz. : Τέρτησσος, *Pape*, is false ; the word is expressly made oxytone by Arc. 77. 3 ; Theog. Can. 72. 32 : Τίασσος, Ptol. 3. 8. 9, or Τίασος, as some MSS. read ; for Τνύσσος in St. Byz. Meineke reads Τνυσσός : Τριπόλισσοι, St. Byz. : Ὑγασσος, St. Byz. : Ὑδισσος[1] is read by Salmasius for Ὑδις, as the

---

[1] Supposing the emendation of Salmasius to be right, still there may be doubts as to the correctness of the accent ; for, according to Herodian, the names of cities or nations and of their founders or eponymous ancestors have the same accent ; St. Byz. s. v. Αἱμονία : Ἡρωδιανὸς δέ φησιν, ὅτι τοῖς συνοικισταῖς συνεχῶς ὁμοφωνεῖ τὰ

name of the founder of Ὑδισσός in St. Byz.: Ὕσσος, Arc. 76. 13; Arrian Peripl. Pont. Eux. p. 6: Φάσσος, Apollod. 3. 8. 1: Ψησσοί, St. Byz.

-ΤΟΣ.

320. Common substantives in ετος are oxytone, as ἀετός, βροχετός, βρυχετός, νιφετός, πυρετός, τοκετός, συρφετός, ὑετός; except proparoxytone, ἔμετος, *vomit,* κάπετος, ῥυάχετος.

321. NOTE.—Αἴβετος, Hesych.: ἀλετός, Eust. 1885. 10 *et alibi* is proparoxytone in Plut. 2. 289 F: ἀφυσγετός, such was the accentuation of Aristarchus, but Tyrannion wrote ἀφύσγετος, Schol. Ven. Λ. 495; Arc. 81. 19; E. M. 347. 22: βρούχετος (?) Hesych.: βρυχετός is proparoxytone in E. M. 216. 26: 'ἔμετος, ἡ τῶν περιττωμάτων κένωσις. Ἐμετὸς δὲ αὐτὸ τὸ κενωθέν, Suid. Quod discrimen observatum ap. Theodot. Jesaiæ 28. 13: Δεισαλία εἰς δεισαλίαν, ἐμετὸς εἰς ἐμετόν, ... Arcad. novit nonnisi unum ἔμετος p. 81. 12;' *H. D.*: ἔργετος, Hesych.: κάθετος (sc. γραμμή, etc.); καίπετος (?) Hesych.: κάπετος, cf. Arc. 81. 13: λαιλάπετος (?) Hesych.; it is expressly made oxytone by Schol. Ven. Λ. 495: πάγετος, ὅπερ ὀξύνει ἡ συνήθεια, Arc. 81. 14, 'Distinguit Eranius Philo p. 172, Πάγετος μὲν τὸ κρύος, παγετὸς δὲ ὁ χειμών;' *H. D.*: ῥυάχετος, Aristoph. Lys. 170: σκάπετος, Hesych.; most of these words are verbal derivatives; and it will be seen that several of the exceptions in the succeeding sections belong to the same category.

322. Dissyllables in στος are oxytone, as ἀστός, βλαστός, ἱστός, κεστός, μαστός, ξυστός, παστός; except κίστος, κόστος, and νόστος, which are paroxytone.

NOTE.—Arc. 79. 16; Chœrob. E. 74. 32: κίστος, *a plant. so called,* see H. D. s. v.: κόστος, Arc. 79. 21; in Hesych. it is falsely oxytone: νόστος, Arc. 79. 21: σχιστὸς (sc. χιτών, etc.), Lob. Par. 332.

323. The rest in τος throw back the accent, as ἄρκτος, ἄρτος. ἄσφαλτος, βάτος, βάρβιτος, βίοτος, δέλτος, θάνατος, κάκτος, κοῖτος, κρότος, μίλτος, μίτος, νότος, οἶτος, πάτος, πλατάνιστος, πλοῦτος, σῖτος, σκότος, φόρτος; except ἀγοστός, ἀλαλητός, ἀμαξιτός, ἀτραπιτός, βουλυτός, γλουτός, γωρυτός, δειπνηστός, δορπηστός, ἐνιαυτός, κιβωτός, κολοσυρτός, κονιορτός, κοντός, κροκωτός, κωκυτός, λεπιδωτός, λιβανωτός, λωτός, μοτός, ξυστός, ὀϊστός, πρωκτός, σκηπτός, στρατός, στρεπτός, φορυτός, and φρυκτός, which are oxytone.

324. NOTE.—Ἀβρυτοί, Hesych.: ἀγοστός, Arc. 83. 20: αἰητός and ἀητός = αἰετός: ἀλαλητός, Arc. 82. 1; and the Dor. form, ἀλαλατός: ἀλοητός, *threshing time,* 'non videtur autem distingui accentu, duplex hujus nominis signif., ut fit in ἄροτος, ἄμητος, et ἀροτός, ἀμητύς. De accentu vid Reiz. De acc. incl. 112,' *Schäfer* ap. H. D.: ἀλοιτός (=ἀλοίτης), really an adjective: ἀμαξιτὸς (sc. ὁδός),

ἐθνικά, δηλονότι καὶ γραφῇ καὶ τόνῳ. τὸ Τεῦκρος [?] ὡς τριγενὲς ὠξύνθη. εὑρίσκεται καὶ πόλεσιν ὁμοφωνοῦντα τὰ τῶν κτιστῶν ὀνόματα, Κάμικος καὶ ὁ κτιστὴς [?] καὶ ἡ νῆσος. ὁμοίως Τροιζήν, Κολοφάν, Κόρινθος, Κῶς, Σικυών, Κύρνος, Λέσβος: St. Byz. s. vv. Ἀβαντίς, Αἰνία, Τροία. At the same time it is true that, in our editions at least, several exceptions to Herodian's rule are to be found.

Theog. Can. 75. 24; Arc. 82. 11 : ἄμητος, ὁ καιρὸς τοῦ θέρους· ἀμητός, ὁ θερισμός, Theog. Can. 75. 13; Schol. Ven. T. 223; Arc. 81. 27; E. M. 83. 7; this is reversed by Ammon. p. 15; Hesych. contradicts himself, and the books vary : ἄροτος, τὸ τοῦ ἀροτριᾶν ἔργον . . . καὶ τὸν ἐνιαυτὸν παρὰ Σοφοκλεῖ, προπαροξυνόμενον ἀναλόγως τῷ ἄμητος; Eust. 811. 27; but ἀροτός (?) *seed-time* : ἀτραπιτός, Arc. 82. 11 : βουλυτός, (sc. καιρός), Hom. Il. 16. 779; Arc. 82 : βρητός, Heysch. : βρότος, ὁ μολυσμός, τὸ αἷμα : βροτός, ὁ φθαρτός, Arc. 78. 22; Eust. 636. 62 ; 907. 9; E. M. 214. 50; 656. 19; Schol. Ven. Z. 202 : γακτός, Hesych. = ϝακτός : γλουτός, Arc. 78. 11 : γωρυτός, cf. Arc. 82 : δειπνηστός (sc. καιρός) ; Eust. 1814. 36 : δοκεῖ δὲ κρεῖττον εἶναι δειπνητὸς γράφειν ὁμοίως τῷ ἀμητός· ἔστι δὲ δειπνηστὸς ἢ δείπνηστος, ὁ τοῦ δείπνου καιρός, ἄλλως δὲ σαφέστερον εἰπεῖν, δειπνητὸς ὀξυτόνως, αὐτό φασι τὸ δεῖπνον, βαρυτόνως δέ, ἡ ὥρα τοῦ δείπνου ὁ δὴ καὶ ἐπὶ τοῦ ἀμητὸς καὶ ἄμητος παρατετήρηται : δορπηστός (sc. καιρός) : δρυφακτός, Arc. 83. 15, ' Ubique scribi-tur δρύφακτος ut ξυλόφρακτος, etsi contrarium jubet Arcadius . . . qui fortasse illud, quia substantivi intellectum habet, alio atque adjectiva accentu notandum putavit,' Lob. Par. 15, note 15 : ἐνιαυτός, Arc. 84. 11 : ἑψητοί, Eust. 867. 49; Athen. 301 C : καρυωτός (sc. φοῖνιξ), Diod. Sic. 2. 53 : κιβωτός, cf. Arc. 82, note : κολοσυρτός, Arc. 83. 8 : κονιορτός, Arc. 83. 8 : κοντός, Arc. 79. 13 : κροκωτός (sc. χιτών), Lob. Par. 332 : κωκυτός, Arc. 82 : λεπιδωτός (sc. ἰχθύς ?), Lob. Par. 344 : λοπητός, Theoph. H. P. 5. 1. 1 ; 5. 1. 2 : λυρτός, Athen. 500 B : λωτός, Arc. 78. 15 : μορτός or μόρτος Theog. Can. 64. 2, really an adjective : μοτός, and also μότος (?), see H. D. s. v. : μυττός, Hesych. : μυωτός, εἶδος χιτῶνος, Arc. 82, note, is an ad-jective : μυττωτός (and μυσωτός ?), Pollux 6. 70, etc. : νοττός (?) = νοσσός : οἶστός, Arc. 83. 20, and οἰστός : πλατάνιστος, Arc. 80. 20, some wrongly made it paroxytone, E. M. 807. 9 : πότος, τὸ συμπόσιον· ποτός, τὸ πινόμενον, Arc. 78. 24; E. M. 685. 4; Ammon. p. 118; the former is however sometimes oxytone : ῥυτός (?) : σκαφητός, cf. Reiz. de Inclin. Accent. p. 111 : σκηπτός is a verbal adjective : στατός (sc. ἵππος, χιτών, etc.), Lob. Par. 332 : στρατός, Arc. 78. 25 ; Schol. Ven. Z. 202 ; Στράτος is the name of a city : στρεπτός (sc. πλακοῦς, etc.) : τρύγητος ὁ καιρὸς μονογενῶς, τρυγητὸς δὲ τὸ τρυγώμενον, Arc. 81. 25; but Ammon. p. 15, ὀξυτόνως . . . ὁ τρυγητός, ὁ καιρὸς τοῦ τρυγᾶν ; Theog. Can. 75. 13, agrees with Ar-cadius ; the books vary ; see H. D. s. v. ; but the distinction in the case of this and similar nouns is probably an idle invention of the grammarians ; and some readers may be disposed to agree with Moschopulus (ad Hesiod. Op. 386), when he says, αἰτία δὲ οὐ φαίνεται δι' ἣν ἕκαστον τούτων ἐπὶ τοῦδε μὲν τοῦ σημαινομένου ὀξυτονη-θήσεται, ἐπὶ δὲ τοῦδε προπαροξυνθήσεται : φορυτός, Arc. 82. 20 : χειριδωτός (sc. χιτών) : χυτός, *a kind of fish*, Arist. H. A. 5. 9. 4 : χωρυτός = γωρυτός, Hesych. : ὠτός, Arist. H. A. 8. 12. 11, is better ὦτος, E. M. 826. 20 ; Eust. 1522. 56, etc.

The Attic forms in ττος = σσος follow the accent of the latter form, as κιττός = κισσός, Arc. 80. 14.

325. Proper names in τος retract the accent, as Αἴγυπτος, Αἴπυτος, Ἁλίαρτος, Ἄνυτος, Ἄρατος, Βάττος, Βύτος, Ἥφαιστος, Θεαίτητος, Κλῆτος, Μάκιστος, Μέλητος, Μίλητος, Μυτίστρατοι, Νάστος, Νέστος, Νήριτος, Πλεῖστος, Πλοῦτος, Πρῶτος, Στράτος, Σχέτος, Τρῖτος ; except those in υτος ; which are oxytone, as Καρδυτός, Κωκυτός, Βηρυτός, and Ἀραχωτοί, Ἀριζαντοί, Βοιωτός, Γαργηττός, Γεραιστός, Ἐνετοί, Θεσπρωτοί, Ἰαπετός, Κελτοί, Κολ-λυτός, Λυκαβηττός, Μολοττοί, Ῥαιτοί, Σηστός, Σπαρτοί, Σφηττός, Ὑμηττός, Φαιστός (the city), but Φαῖστος (the hero), Χριστός.

326. NOTE.—'Αγαπητός, Suid.: 'Αετός, the old name of the Nile, Diod. Sic.
1. 19: 'Αζωτός, Strab. 759, seems to be commonly "Αζωτος, St. Byz.; Ptol. 5. 16. 2:
Αἰνετός, Apollod. 1. 9. 4: 'Ακύτος (?) St. Byz.: 'Αλτός, St. Byz.: 'Αμαξιτός,
St. Byz.; Thucyd. 8. 101, etc., is sometimes paroxytone: 'Αμάραντος, Arc. 83. 5:
'Αμάραντος τὸ κύριον, τὸ δὲ ἐθνικὸν ὀξύνεται: cf. E. M. 77. 52; Schol. Apollon. Rhod.
2. 401: 'Αποδωτοί, St. Byz., is 'Απόδωτοι in Thucyd. 3. 94: 'Αραχωτοί, Strab. 513,
etc.; there are several forms of this name: see Muller on Dionys. Pers. 1096:
'Αρδηττός, a place, Plut. 1. 13; but "Αρδηττος, a man's name: 'Αριζαντοί, Herodot.
1. 101: 'Αρμάτος (?) Suid., the name of a man: Βενεβεντός, St. Byz., appears as
Βενεβεντόν in Strab. 249, and Βενέβεντον or Βενεουεντόν in Plut. 1. 399: Βηρυτός,
Arc. 82: Βοιωτός, both as the name of a man and of the people, Arc. 82: Βουθρωτός
and Βουτρωτός, St. Byz.: Βουτός, Arc. 78. 11, and Βουτοί, Hesych., is Βοῦτος in
Strab. 802: Βροτός, E. M. 215. 37: Γαργηττός, St. Byz.: Γεραιστός, a town and
promontory of Euboea, St. Byz.; E. M. 227. 46; H. D. quote Γέραιστος from
Dicæarch. Stat. Gr. 22. 34: Γέραιστος, a son of Zeus, is thus accented by St. Byz.
s. v.: he also mentions Γεραιστός (sic), a son of Mygdon s. v. Παρθενόπολις: H. D.
also mention Γέραιστος, a Cyclops, Apollod. 3. 15. 8: Γλυτός, Galen Tom. 13.
p. 858 C; *H. D.*: Δαλμάτος (?) *H. D.*: Δεβελτός, or Δηβελτός, Suid.: Ἐνετοί
[Ἐνετοί] and Ἐνετός [Ἐνετός], St. Byz., etc., 'More Rom. retracto accentu
Οὐενέτους dicit Polyb.' H. D.: Θεσπρωτός, Apollod. 3. 8. 1: Θεσπρωτοί, Strab. 6,
etc.: Ἰαπετός, Schol. Ven. Λ. 495; E. M. 347. 25: Ἰστοί, a harbour in Icaria,
Strab. 639: Ἰστός, an island, St. Byz.: Καρδυτός, Arc. 82 (p. 94. 20; Schmidt):
Κελτοί, Strab. 10, etc.: Κητοί, Harpoc.; Κηττοί (?) Suid.; Κηττός, Phot. H. D.
Κιβωτός, Strab. 569: Κλειτός, Schol. Ven. O. 445; Arc. 78. 10, yet in the face
of these express declarations, Κλεῖτος stands in Hom. Il. 15. 445, Od. 15. 249,
and in Eust. 1025. 6; Arrian Anab. 1. 5. 1; 15. 8; Diod. Sic. 17. 20, etc.: the
name is however oxytone in Apollod. 2. 1. 5, quoted by H. D.: Κολλυτός, on the
various forms of this name, see H. D.: Κοπτός, Strab. 781: Κορνοῦτος, Suid.:
Κραστός, St. Byz.: Λατός (?) *Pape:* Λαυρεντός, Arc. 83. 6: Λεωνάτος (?) Phot.
Bib. 64. 41: Λομεντός (?) Arc. 83. 6: Λυκαβηττός, St. Byz. s. v. Γαργηττός:
Λυκαστός, Eust. 313. 12: Λύκαστος δὲ ἀπὸ Λυκάστου, φασίν, αὐτόχθονος, ἢ παιδὸς
τοῦ Μίνωος. ἔστι δὲ καὶ Ποντικὴ Λύκαστος κατὰ τὸν γραφέα τῶν ἐθνικῶν, ὃς λέγει
καὶ ὅτι τὴν Κρητικὴν Λύκαστον ὀξύνουσιν οἱ ἐγχώριοι· οὐκ ἐπικρατεῖ δέ φησιν, ἡ ἐθνικὴ
παράδοσις, τουτέστι παρὰ τοῖς ἄλλοις οὐκ ὀξύνεται: Λύκτος, St. Byz., 'Hom. Il. B.
647, ubi alii male Λυκτόν, ut annotat schol., alii Λύττον,' *H. D.*: Λυχνιτός, Theog.
Can. 75. 24; Arc. 82. 11, or Λυχνιδύς, St. Byz.: Λωμεντός, St. Byz., he holds
that all in εντος are oxytone; yet even he has 'Ράρεντος, as Göttling observes:
add also Πόλλεντος, Σώρεντος: Μάδυτος, 'vitiosum esse accentum ap. Steph. Byz.
in ultima positum constare videtur ex Theognosto Can. p. 75. 33, Μάδυτος ponente
inter barytona, non inter oxytona,' *H. D.*: Μισητός, St. Byz.: Μολοττοί, *Attic*;
Arc. 77. 21, and Μολοτός, Theog. Can. 75. 29; on which see H. D. Νωμεντός,
St. Byz.: 'Ογχηστός, Strab. 410; Paus. 9. 26. 5; Ὄγχηστος, the founder of it,
St. Byz. (also the place itself, Hom. Il. 2. 506), is oxytone in Paus. 9. 26. 5, and
Eust. 270. 13; and that would be correct according to Herodian's rule referred to
above, p. 93, note: Ὀνωρᾶτος, Suid.: Παιτοί, Arc. 78. 12, is written Παῖτοι in
Herodot. 7. 110; Theog. Can. 74. 11: Πιλᾶτος occurs Chœrob. A. G. Oxon. 2.
400. 16; E. M. 671. 53, *et alibi:* 'Πιλάτος correptis duabus syllabis primis dixit
Nonn. Jo. c. 18, 140, 156, 174, 180,' H. D.: and thus it is printed in many
editions of the Testament; Πίλατος, however, seems the more correct accent:
Πιστός, Phot. Bib. 532. 40, 'Joseph. in Vita c. 9 et seqq., p. 907. 28; 913. 2;
921. 23; 942. 10, ed. Huds., ubi accentu inconstanti modo Πιστός modo Πίστος
scriptum: recte Πίστου ap. Phot. Bibl. p. 6. 38,' *H. D.*: Πλατανιστός, Strab. 669
Kramer, where Meineke reads Πλατανιστῆς: Πλειστός, Paus. 10. 8. 8, etc.; 'In

libris plerumque Πλεῖστος scriptum, de quo accentu Etym. M. p. 676. 5 : Ἀπολλώνιος
(Arg. 2. 711), Πολλὰ δὲ Κωρύκιαι νύμφαι Πλειστοῖο θύγατρες, τινὲς ἀναγινώσκουσι
προπερισπωμένως, ἐπειδὴ καὶ ὑπὸ τῶν ἐγχωρίων λέγεται Πλειστός ὀξυτόνως· ἔστι δὲ
ποταμὸς ἐν Δελφοῖς. Ἡρωδιανὸς δὲ ἐν τῇ καθόλου Πλεῖστος βαρύνει,' H. D. :
Πλεύρατος, or Πλευρᾶτος (?) Polyb. 2. 2. 4 ; 10. 41. 3 : Ηοτῖτος, Plut. 1. 131 : Πυρετός, Herodot. 4. 48 : Ῥαιτοί, Strab. 292 : Ῥειτός, a river near Eleusis, so Orus :
Herodian wrote Ῥῖτος, E. M. 703. 15 ; Chœrob. A. G. Oxon. 2. 256. 15 ; in Thucyd.
4. 42 it is Ῥεῖτος : Σεβαστός = *Augustus*, Paus. 3. 11. 4 : Σεβέννυτος, St. Byz. :
Σεγιμοῦντος, Strab. 291, or Σεμιγοῦντος : Σηστός, Arc. 79 (p. 91. 6, Schmidt) :
Σητοί, St. Byz. : Σιντοί, St. Byz. s. v. Σιντία, or Σίντοι, Thucyd. 2. 98 : Σπαρτοί
(sc. ἄνδρες) : Στράτος, Arc. 78. 25, is falsely Στρατός, St. Byz. *et alibi* : Συνετός,
Diod. Sic. 11. 2, is better written Σύνετος in Auth. Pal. 14. 123 : Συπαληττός,
St. Byz. : Σφηττός, a deme, St. Byz. : Σφῆττος, a son of Trœzen, St. Byz. :
Τιαραντός, Herodot. 4. 48 : Τουρκουάτος (*sic*) Plut. 1. 179 : Τυφησστός, St. Byz. :
Ὑηττός, St. Byz. : Ὑηττος, its founder, St. Byz. ; ' Vici pariter atque viri nomen
Ὑηττος proparoxytonum est ap. Pausan. 9. 24. 3, et 36. 6 seqq.,' H. D. : Ὑμηττός,
St. Byz. s. v. Γαργηττός, 'proparoxytonum ap. Theoph. De sign. 1. 20 et 2. 6 . . . ut
notavit Lob. Path. p. 411,' H. D. : Φαῖστος, the hero, but Φαιστός, a city of Crete,
Schol. Ven. B. 648 ; E. 43 ; Eust. 313. 18 : Χρηστος is also written Χρηστός :
Χριστός is of course an adjective.

-ΥΟΣ.

327. Common substantives in νος are oxytone, as εἰλυός, ἐννυός,
νυός, σικυός (or σίκυος), σμιννός ; except ἔγγυος proparoxytone.

NOTE.—Ἔγγυος is an adjective used substantively : ἐννυός, Pollux 3. 32 is
doubtful : on ἴδυος (?) see H. D. s. v. ἰδυῖα : μόλτυος (?) Hesych. : ναὖος, *Æol.* =
ναός, cf. Schol. Ven. M. 137 : ὄνευος, a kind of crane, Schol. Thucyd. 7. 25, where
some read ὄνος : πυός, such was Herodian's accentuation, Schol. Aristoph. Pac.
1116 = 1150, though it is sometimes πύος, which must be wrong, since the υ is
long, cf. Draco, p. 77. 16, who has πῦος : there seems to have been some confusion
between τὸ πύος (or πῦος) and ὁ πυός ; Eust. 291. 38 : σικυοὶ οὓς οἱ παλαιοὶ καὶ
σικύους παροξυτόνως ἔγραψαν ; Arc. 42 (p. 46. 22. Schmidt) προπαροξύνεται σίκυος :
ψαῦος, Æol. (? is it a proper name), Schol. Ven. M. 137, *et alibi*.

328. Proper names in νος (ανος, ενος, ονος) retract the accent,
as Ἀλάσυος, Ἄρενος, Αὖος, Βεῦος, Δρῦος, Κάνδυος, Κόλουοι, Πέρνος,
Τίμανος, Τραῦος ; except oxytone, Ἀγαυός and Τιτυός.

NOTE.—Theog. Can. 51. 22 ; Schol. Ven. M. 137 : Ἀγαυός, Arc. 45. 15 :
Βατανοί = *Batavi*, Ptol. 2. 9. 4 : Ἐδούοι = *Ædui*, Strab. 186, and Αἰδούοι :
Ἐλουοί, Strab. 190 : Τιτυός, Arc. 42 (p. 46. 23 Schmidt) : Φλυός (?) or better
Φλῦος, Paus. 4. 1. 5.

-ΦΟΣ.

329. All in φος retract the accent, as γόμφος, ζόφος, κέρφος,
κνάφος, κόλαφος, κόρυφος, κόσσυφος, κρόταφος, λόφος, ὄροφος,
ὄρφος, σέρφος, σκάριφος, τάφος, τῦφος, ψῆφος, ψόφος, Γόμφος,
Ἔπαφος, Κίτυφος, Πάφος, Σέριφος, Σίσυφος, Σόφος ; except
oxytone, ἀδελφός, ἀλφός, κρυφός, συφός, τροφός, and Δελφός,
Δελφοί.

330. NOTE.—Ἀδελφός, Arc. 84. 25; the Attic vocative is ἄδελφε, Ammon. p. 117, though this precept appears to be neglected in our books, e. g. ἀδελφὲ καὶ φίλε, Philostr. 84 Boiss., quoted by H. D.: ἀλφός, Arc. 84. 18, an adjective used substantively: κρυφός, Arc. 84. 17; Göttling, Accent. p. 227, notes that this accent ought to be restored to Pind. Olymp. 2. 107: μόμφος, A. G. 107. 19, is oxytone in Eust. 1761. 39: πολφός, Arc. 84. 19; not πόλφος, as in some of the passages quoted by H. D.: πομφός, Galen Lex. Hipp. p. 548; *H. D.*: συφός = συφεός, Arc. 84. 17, τροφός is oxytone like many other verbals: τυφός = τυφώς (?) *L. S.*: Δελφός, Paus. 10. 6. 3: Δελφοί, Paus. 10. 6. 5, etc.

-ΧΟΣ.

331. All in χος retract the accent, as ἄρριχος, βάτραχος, βόστρυχος, βρόχος, ἔλεγχος, ἦχος, κόγχος, μόσχος, ὀλοίτροχος, στίχος, στόμαχος, τάριχος, τοῖχος; Ἀμφίλοχος, Ἰάμβλιχος, Ἴναχος, Κόλχος, Μόσχος; except those in ουχος, which are properispomena, as ῥαβδοῦχος, ἀρχιραβδοῦχος, εὐνοῦχος, ἀρχιευνοῦχος, Δαοῦχος, Δημοῦχος, Καρδοῦχοι, Τιμοῦχος, Φανοῦχος, and ἀρχός, μοιχός, μοναχός, μυχός, πτωχός, ῥηχός, τροχός, a *hoop*, oxytone.

332. NOTE 1.—Ἀμαξοτροχός (?) *H. D.*, an accent contrary to all analogy: ἀρχός, Arc. 85. 3, is more an adjective than substantive: δόλιχος, τὸ ὄσπριον, καὶ τὸ ὄνομα τοῦ δρόμου, προπαροξυτόνως· δολιχός, δὲ τὸ ἐπίθετον ὁ μακρός, Suid.; Schol. Ven. K. 52; Eust. 1678. 43; Arc. 85. 6; in this sense the word is sometimes, though wrongly, oxytone, cf. Lob. Par. 341: δοχός, Hesych.: θριγχός and τριγχός = θριγκός, see H. D. s. v.: λοχός (?) ἡ λοχεύουσα; H. D. quote Dioscor. 3. 4, and Mœris p. 247, where the MS. reading is λόχος, and that would seem to be correct: λόχος, *ambush*, etc., is regular: μοιχός, Arc. 85. 3: μοναχός is an adjective used as a substantive: μυχός, Arc. 85. 2: οὐραχός = οὐραγός, cf. H. D. s. v.; Lob. Prol. 333: πτωχός, Arc. 85. 3, an adjective used substantively: ῥηχός, Hesych.; Herodot. 7. 142, also occurs as ῥῆχος: σικχός, Hesych., is strictly an adjective: τρόχος, ὁ τόπος ἐν ᾧ τρέχουσι: τροχός, ὁ κύκλος, Arc. 85. 1; so E. M. 686. 10, except that τροχός is said to be ὁ τρέχων; Ammon. p. 137: Τροχοὶ ὀξυτόνως, καὶ Τρόχοι βαρυτόνως διαφέρουσι παρὰ τοῖς Ἀττικοῖς. φησὶ Τρύφων ἐν δευτέρᾳ περὶ Ἀττικῆς προσῳδίας. τοὺς μὲν γὰρ περιφερεῖς Τροχοὺς ὁμοίως ἡμῖν προφέρονται ὀξυτονοῦντες· Τρόχους δὲ βαρυτόνως λέγουσι τοὺς δρόμους.

333. NOTE 2.—Ἀρρηχοί, Strab. 495: Δόλιχος, 'ap. Hom. H. Cer. 155 ubi codex pravo accentu Δολιχοῦ;' H. D.: Ἔρωχος, Paus. 10. 3. 2, in Herodot. 8. 33, is sometimes found oxytone: Μυχός, Strab. 409, where it is hardly a proper name: Πετραχός, (?) *Pape*, is Πέτραχος in Paus. 9. 41. 6: Σουλχοί, H. D. quote Strab. 225, where Meineke has Σοῦλχοι: Σκοροδομάχοι, Lucian V. H. 1. 13; the name of this imaginary race is of course a compound adjective, and paroxytone in accordance with the general rule.

334. NOTE 3.—According to Theog. Can. 76. 25 all hyperdissyllables in ιχος are proparoxytone, and such is unquestionably their proper accent; Schol. Theocr. 4. 20: Πύρριχος· ἀπὸ τοῦ πυρρὸς πύρριχος κατὰ παραγωγήν. τινὲς παροξυτόνως λέγουσι πυρρίχος, ἔστιν οὖν ὑποκοριστικὸν Αἰολικῶς: this accentuation however is in the books only found in ὀσσίχον, Theocr. 4. 55, where Ahrens reads ὀσσιχόν; cf. Arc. 85. 6.

-ΨΟΣ.

335. Dissyllables in ψος retract the accent, hyperdissyllables are oxytone, as γύψος, θάψος, κινδαψός, χορδαψός, Θάψος, Λάμψος, Μόψος, Σκινδαψός, Τρανιψοί.

336. NOTE I.—Ἰψός, *ivy*, Hesych.: a tree called ἴψος (*sic*) is mentioned by Theophrastus, H. P. 3. 4. 2: καλυψός (?) Arc. 85. 12; E. M. 219. 47: κινδαψός, Arc. 85. 12: λυκαψός, Paul. Æg. 7. 3. p. 228. 49, is λύκαψος in Nicand. Ther. 840, where, however, Otto Schneider prints λυκαψός; both passages are quoted by H. D. who also mention λύκοψος (?) but quote no place; cf. Lob. Par. 333: σκινδαψός, St. Byz. s. v. Γαληψός; 'sæpe in libris est proparoxytonon contra præceptum, Etym. M. p. 219. 49,' H. D.: χεραψός, E. M. 219. 47, and as a proper name, St. Byz.: χορδαψός, Arc. 85. 12.

337. NOTE 2.—Αἴδηψος, St. Byz., is false and contrary to his own rule, s. v. Γαληψός; it is rightly Αἰδηψός in Strab. 425: Γαληψός, St. Byz.; 'Γαληψός et Γαλήψου scripta sunt ap. Harpocr.,' H. D.; the latter is unquestionably wrong; E. M. 219. 47: Λαδεψοί, St Byz.; Λάδεψοι codex Rehdig. H. D: Λυκαψός, St. Byz. s. v. Γαληψός; yet under the name he has Λύκαψος: Σκινδαψός, St. Byz. s. v. Γαληψός: Τάκομψος, St. Byz.: Τρανιψοί, St. Byz. s. v. Λαδεψοί; (codex Rhedig. has Τράνιψοι, H. D.)

-ΩΟΣ and -ΩΙΟΣ.

338. All substantives in ωος and φος are properispomena, as δμῶος (?), Ἀχελῷος, Λῷος, Πιτῷος, Γελῷος; except λαγωός, κλῳός, κολῳός, πατρωός, oxytone.

339. NOTE.—δμῶος, Chœrob. C. 92. 9; in E. M. 770. 35 it is written δμωός: for the false form ἔρρωος or ἐρρωός, ἔρραος is now read in Lycoph. 1316: κλῳός, Att. = κλοιός, E. M. 26. 36: κολῳός, Chœrob. E. 118. 21; E. M. 26. 20: λαγωός, E. M. 26. 20: λῷος, Arc. 38. 8, and λῶος: πατρωός, E. M. 26. 23; Arc. 42. 26, is falsely πατρῶος in Artemid. 3. 26 and elsewhere: Ἀκράθωοι, St. Byz.: Ἀχελῷος, Arc. 42. 24, is sometimes oxytone, though wrongly: Ἄωος, Strab. 316, is better Ἀῶος in E. M. 117. 33: Δρῶοι, Thucyd. 2. 101: Τρῳός, *Trojan*, Eust. 541. 21, or Τρῶος, Chœrob. C. 92. 9; the latter is most consonant with analogy, if the word be used substantively.

SUBSTANTIVES OF THE NEUTER GENDER.

340. Neuters when strictly substantives are regular, and, with few exceptions, they retract their accent; but such is the freedom of the Greek language, that adjectives in the neuter gender are very commonly used as substantives, and their accentuation is not so regular. In general, however, when such adjectives, by the ordinary usage of the language, require a substantive to be understood with which they agree, and without which they would not be easily intelligible; or when the neuter of an adjective or participle is used to mark in a general manner locality or time, or is equivalent to a collective noun, or to a substantive denoting quality or state[1], they still continue to all intents and purposes adjectives, and as such they naturally retain their adjectival accent. Examples of the first class are— τὸ Ἀβδηριτικόν (sc. πάθος), τὸ ἀγνευτικόν (sc. θῦμα), τὸ βλητόν (sc. ζῶον), τὸ ἐλαφόβοσκον (sc. φυτόν), τὸ ἐπιμανδαλωτόν (sc. φίλημα), τὸ λαγωβόλον (sc. ξύλον), τὸ Μελιταῖον (sc. κυνίδιον, ὀθόνιον, etc.): of the second—τὸ καθῆκον, τὸ εἰκός, τὰ παραθαλάσσια, τὰ παράλια, τὰ καρτερά, τὸ ἔσχατον, ἐξ ἑωθινοῦ, τὸ Ἑλληνικόν, τὸ ναυτικόν, τὸ ὑγρόν, τὸ ἀγαθόν, τὰ ἀγαθά. Such instances, it is clear, are adjectives, and nothing else, though it may not be necessary to supply any particular substantive in order to render them intelligible. But there are many words of somewhat doubtful grammatical character, partly adjectives, partly substantives, which, by form and descent, belong to the one class, and by accent to the other. Unfortunately it is impossible to lay down any rule which will determine with certainty whether a given word belongs to the one category or the other. The rules which follow, together with the lists of words appended to them, will, it is hoped, leave no doubtful word at least in ordinary Greek.

1. *Common Substantives.*

341. *General Rule.*—Common neuter substantives retract the accent, as ἔργον, ξύλον, ὅπλον, βάλσαμον, κάρδαμον, δικαστήριον, κοιμητήριον, ἀκρωτήριον, ἀνθρώπιον, ὀρνίθιον, πινάκιον, λαμπάδιον, ὅριον, ἀρχίδιον, γηΐδιον, ἐλάδιον, κρεάδιον, βασιλείδιον, λεξείδιον, ξιφίδιον, οἰκίδιον, ἱματίδιον, ἀνδράριον, γυναικάριον, κοράσιον, ἐλκύδριον, τειχύδριον, εἰδύλλιον, ξενύλλιον, ξυλήφιον, πολίχνιον, πτολίεθρον, σπαθάλιον, βιβλαρίδιον, βοϊδάριον, πινακίσκιον, ῥηματίσκιον, ἁμάρτιον, γυμνάσιον, ἐρείπιον, ναυάγιον, εὐαγγέλιον, ἀκρομφάλιον, ἡμίμναιον, ἔλαιον, γύναιον, ἐπικεφάλαιον, σπήλαιον, προβόλαιον, προπύλαια, κᾶλον, ναῦλον, πέταλον, ῥόπαλον, κύπελλον, εἴδωλον, κειμήλιον, πέδιλον, δρέπανον, τήγανον, λείψανον, τέκνον, δίδακτρον, ἄροτρον, ἄρθρον, κλεῖθρον, στέργηθρον, ἄλευρον, δῶρον, βλέφαρον, ἔντερον, ἄλφιτον; except—

342. 1. *Oxytone.*—(a) Those which have a corresponding mas-

---

[1] Donaldson, Greek Grammar, p. 388.

culine form in ός: δαιτρόν (δαιτρός), δεσμά (δεσμός), ἐανόν (ἐανός), ἐλεόν (ἐλεός), ἐρετμόν (ἐρετμός), ἐρινεόν or ἐρινόν (ἐρινεός), ζυγόν (ζυγός), κολεόν and κουλεόν (κολεός), μυελόν (μυελός), ξυρόν (ξυρός), πηδόν (πηδός?), πρυμνόν (πρυμνός adj.), πυρσά (πυρσός,) ῥινόν (ῥινός), στελεόν or στελειόν (στελεός?), τροφόν (τροφός); and

(b) Verbal adjectives in τον (τός), as, βοτόν, δοτόν, ἑρπετόν, λεκτόν, ξυστόν, ποτόν, φυτόν.

(c) ἱερόν (really an adjective), λουτρόν, πλευρόν, πτερόν, τὰ πυρά, σφυρόν, χρεών (which, like εἰκός, is participial), and ᾠόν.

343. 2. *Paroxytone.*—Diminutives of dactylic measure in ιον, whether the first syllable be long by nature or position, as καρφίον, κλειδίον, κρουνίον, παιδίον, τιτθίον, τυμβίον, φανίον, ψιχίον, ψωμίον. From these diminutives must be distinguished—

(a) Neuters from adjectives in ιος, as ὅρκιον (ὅρκιος), αὔλιον (αὔλιος), αἴτιον (αἴτιος), δέσμιον (δέσμιος), ἴσθμιον (ἴσθμιος), φύξιον (φύξιος), and—

(b) Those which appear as dactyls only in consequence of contraction, as βώδιον=βοίδιον, γήδιον=γηίδιον, ζώδιον, κώδιον, νοίδιον, ῥοίδιον, στώδιον. These and all other trisyllabic diminutives are proparoxytone, as θρόνιον, θύριον, λίθιον, πτύχιον, but πεδίον and τεκνίον are paroxytone.

(c) ὀστέον, which is singular in its accent, see § 346.

There are many exceptions to this rule, on which see §§ 347–352.

344. 3. *Properispomenon.*—Those in ειον, ωον, and ῳον, as λυχνεῖον, πορθμεῖον, στοιχεῖον, ἀγγεῖον, γραφεῖον, ᾠδεῖον, σημεῖον, θωρακεῖον, πανδοκεῖον, διδασκαλεῖον, βαλανεῖον, ἐλεγεῖον, τὰ Ἀλῶα, ζῷον, μητρῷον, ἡρῷον; except προάστειον, γένειον, γήρειον, δάνειον, κηλώνειον, κηρύκειον, κόπειον, κώνειον, σκιάδειον, σκιράφειον, περίστωον (but προστῷον); αἰδοῖον keeps the accent of the adjective of which it is the neuter; a considerable number in αιον also are properispomena: see § 355.

345. *Compound Substantives* retract the accent, as ζυγόν, βούζυγον, περίζυγον (and περιζυγόν), φυτόν, ζωόφυτον, σύμφυτον, βούνευρον, βούσταθμον, δαφνέλαιον, γήπεδον, οἰκόπεδον; except those in ειον, the greater part of which are properispomena, as, ἀργυροπωλεῖον, γλωσσοκομεῖον, γραμματοφυλακεῖον, δαφνηφορεῖον, ἑρμογλυφεῖον: αὐτοζῷον seems to be always properispomenon.

346. NOTE I.—The following list of words comprises all the exceptions to the rule above given that I have noted, and it will be seen that the greater number of them are adjectives used elliptically : Ἀβδηριτικόν (sc. πάθος or the like), Cic. ad Att. 7. 7 : ἀγαρικόν, Galen de Simpl. Med. Fac. 6. 5, etc. : ἀγκυλητόν : ἀγνευτικόν (sc. θῦμα), Philo Jud. Tom. 2. p. 206. ; H. *D.* : ἀγρηνόν, *a net* and *a kind of dress*, Pollux 4. 116 : ἀδριανόν, Athen. 2. 68 E, Dindorf, where the common text had ἀδριανὸν σίναπυ : ἀερικόν, a tax imposed by Justinian, cf. Ducange Gloss. : ἀηνά, δένδρα μικρὰ ἄκαρπα, Hesych. : αἰδοῖον (sc. μόριον): αἰηνά, Hesych. : αἱμαγωγόν, this, like several others to be mentioned, is nothing but the neuter of an adjective, and accented according to the rules laid down for compound verbal adjectives ἀκιδωτόν, Diosc. 3. 17 : ἀκοντικόν, Hesych. : ἀκρατοφόρον : ἀλειπτόν, Suid. ; is ἄλειπτον, E. M. 61. 3 : ἁλιακόν, ἀκάτιον ἁλιευτικόν, E. M. 63. 40, the feminine ἁλιακή has been mentioned above, §. 116 : ἀλητόν, Hesych. or ἄλητον 'sic semper scribitur apud Hippocratem v. Foes. Oec. et Eustach. ad Erotian. p. 64, quo mirabilius est ἄλιτον in Aretaei libris identidem repetitum [it is hardly to be marvelled at since by many scribes η, ι, and υ are used indiscriminately] ; Cur. Acut. 1. 10. 237 ; 2. 2. 250. c. 5. 272 ; Diut. 2. 4. 534. c. 12. 340, ubi semel ἄλφιτον praebet : Ἀλητόν tamen est oxytonum ap. Hesychium ut ἀρπαστόν Athen. 1. 14 F ; Artemid. 1. 55 ; in Athen. 7. 297 F, ἡ ἄλφιτα ἢ ἄλητα (codd. ἄλιτα) alterutrum delent Critici immemores Homerici ἄλφιτα τεύχουσαι καὶ ἀλείατα Odyss. 20. 108, ἄλφιτον καὶ ἄλητον Hipp. de Nat. Mul. p. 544. T. 2, ἄλητον κἀλφίτων Athen. 11. 500 F, prius accentu eodem quo ἄητον ;' Lob. Par. 353, note 58 : ἀλμενιχιακόν (sc. βιβλίον), Euseb. P. E. 3. 92 C : τὰ Ἀλῶα, Eust. 772. 25 : ἄμεργον (?) a Cretan word = ἡ εἱμαρμένη, Hesych. : Ἀμμωνιακόν, Diosc. 3. 98 : ἀνακτορόν, such is the accent presented by Arc. 123. 3, but the passage is corrupt, the correct form is ἀνάκτορον, cf. Theog. Can. 131. 6 : ἀνδρομητόν (?) and ἀνδρομηρόν (?) Hesych. ; *L. S.* : ἀπελλόν, Hesych. : ἀρακτόν, Diosc. 5. 114 ; H. D. : ἀρπαστόν, see Lob. Par. 353, note 58 : ἀρρενικόν or ἀρσενικόν, Diosc. Theophr. etc. : ἀστρολαβικόν (sc. μηχάνημα or the like) : ἀστρολάβον (sc. μηχάνημα) : αὐαρά (κάρυα), Hesych. : βαθρικόν (?) *a small staircase* : βαρυοῦλκον is an error for βαρυουλκόν, neuter of a verbal adjective : τὰ βασιλικά and τὸ βασιλικόν : βαστά (sc. ὑποδήματα), Hesych. : βατραχιοῦν, the name of one of the law-courts of Athens, Paus. 1. 28. 8 : βεκός, Hesych., βέκος, Hipponax ap. Strab. 340 ; in Herodot. 2. 2 the MSS. vary between βεκός, βεκκός, and βέκκος : τὰ βηλά (?) *sandals* : βλητόν (sc. ζῷον), Schol. Nicand. Ther. 760. 764 ; τὰ βλητά in another sense, Pollux 1. 133 : βοιόν (?) = τῶν πεντήκοντα ἐτῶν ἀριθμός, Theog. Can. 130. 9 : βορσόν, Hesych. : βοτόν, Arc. 123. 17 : βουαγετόν, Hesych. : βρεκτόν, H. D. : βυθόν (?) Hesych. : γαβαθόν (?) = τρύβλιον, Hesych. : γλοιόν (?) Theog. Can. 130. 9 : γωλεόν, Nicand. Ther. 125 : δαιτρόν, Hom. etc. : for δακετόν the better form seems to be δάκετον : δεκανικόν, H. D. : δελτωτόν, Arat. Phænom. 235 : δερματικόν (sc. ἀργύριον) : τὰ δεσμά (δεσμός) ; on the accentuation of heterogenea like this, see Schol. Ven. A. 133 ; E. M. 585. 33 ; Arc. 122. 18 : διαλειπτόν, Hippocr. p. 635. 17 ; H. D. : δοτόν, Chrysost. T. 5. p. 57. 2 ; H. D. : δρεπτόν (sc. φίλημα), Arc. 123. 20 ; E. M. 287. 27 : ἐανόν, see L. S. s. v. : ἐλαφόβοσκον, Galen T. 13. p. 136 ; ἐλαφοβόσκον is quite wrong : ἐλεόν, ἡ μαγειρικὴ τράπεζα, Arc. 118. 26 ; cf. Theog. Can. 121. 5 : ἐμβαδόν, *area*, Casii Problem. p. 331. 10. ed. Sylb. ; cf. above. § 234 : ἐνδυτόν, Eurip. Bacch. 138, etc. : ἐπιμανδαλωτόν (sc. φίλημα), Aristoph. Ach. 1201 : ἐρετμόν, Hom. etc. : ἑρπετόν, Arc. 123. 26, for which the Æclic form is ὄρπετον: ἐφολκόν, a verbal adjective: ζυγόν, Arc. 122. 19: βούζυγον, Lactant. Inst. Div. 1. 21. 36: περιζυγόν, Xen. Cyr. 6. 2. 32, where some MSS. have the better form περίζυγον: ἡμιδαρεικόν (?) Xenoph. Anab. 1. 3. 21: ἡμιεκτέον (sc. μέτρον), Aristoph. Nub. 645: θεωρικόν (sc. ἀργύριον) and θεωρικά (sc. χρήματα): θηλυφόνον (sc. φυτόν), aconite, Hesych.: Θηραϊκόν (sc. ἱμάτιον): θοιόν (?) Theog. Can. 20. 20. Hesych. has θοιά, ζεῦγος ἡμιόνων: θορικά (sc. μόρια), Arist. de Gen. Animal. 3. 5. 3: ἵδρωα, Galen T. 9. p. 116 B, is ἱδρῶα in Pollux 4. 202: Ἰσθμιακόν, a *kind of chaplet,* Athen. 677 B: καθῆκον, a participle used substantively: καπητόν (?) Hesych.: καταζωστικόν, H. *D.*: καρωτόν, Athen. 371 E: κηλωστά, *lupanaria,* Lycoph. 1387, for which some books have κηλωτά: Κιμβερικόν (sc. ἔνδυμα): κολεόν, Ion. κουλεόν, Theog. Can. 121. 4: κολχικόν (φυτόν), Diosc. 4. 84: κοπτόν (sc. φάρμακον), Galen, but κόπτον, a *kind of unguent,* is paroxytone in Alex. Trall. 7. p. 117; H. *D.*: κροκωτόν (sc. ἔνδυμα): κυμινοδόκον = κυμινοθήκη, Pollux 10. 23. 93: κυνοκτόνον, aconite, Diosc. 4. 78: λαγωβόλον (sc. ξύλον): λαπαρόν, H. *D.*: λεκτόν and λεκτά, Sext. Emp. Inst. 2. 104; Plut. 2. 1119: λεοντοφόνον, Arist. Mirab. Ausc. c. 146: λεπυρόν, Suid.: λεπτόν (sc. νόμισμα, ἔντερον, etc.): τὰ λευκά and τὸ λευκόν, see L. S. s. v.: λιβανωτόν, H. *D.*: λιγυστικόν, H. *D.*: λογχωτόν, Diosc. 5. 114: λοετρόν, Herod. π. μ. λ. 37. 15: λοῦτρον and λουτρόν, 'De accentu utriusque formæ acuto v. Herodian. π. μ. λέξ. p. 37. 15. 21; Arcad. p. 123. 10; 133. 17; Schol. Ven. Hom. Il. O. 676. Significationis pro accentu barytono et oxytono discrimen faciunt schol. Lycoph. 1103: Λουτρόν, τὸ θερμόν, λοῦτρον, τὸ βαλανικόν· Eust. Il. p. 1037. 40: Τὰ εἰς ΤΡΟΝ λήγοντα μονογενῆ οὐδέτερα βαρύνεται· σεσημείωται τὸ λουτρὸν πρὸς διάφορον σημασίαν. Ἔστι γὰρ καὶ λοῦτρον Ἀττικῶς παρὰ τῷ κωμικῷ τὸ ἀπόλουμα, οἷον Κἄκ τοῦ βαλανείου πίεται τὸ λοῦτρον [Aristoph. Eq. 1401, where λούτριον is now read]......Od. p. 1560. 32: Λοῦτρον μοναχῶς τὸ ἀπόλουμα βαρυτόνως. Minus etiam considerate Etym. M. p. 568. 47: Λοῦτρον βαρύνεται· ἐπειδὴ πᾶν εἰς ΤΡΟΝ λῆγον ἀπαρασχημάτιστον βαρύνεται, κέντρον, δένδρον, σεῖστρον· τὸ δὲ λουτρὸν πρὸς διαφορὰν σημαινομένου· ἐπὶ μὲν γὰρ τοῦ τόπου βαρύνεται, ἐπὶ δὲ τοῦ ὕδατος ᾧ λουόμεθα ὀξύνεται. Idem. ib. 54: Λουτρόν....δεῖ δὲ βαρύνεσθαι ὥστε παραλόγως ὀξύνεται,' H. *D.*: λυκοκτόνον, aconite, Galen T. 13. p. 158 D: λυκοπερσικόν (?) a *kind of plant,* is λυκοπέρσιον in Galen T. 13. p. 106 A: λυχνικόν, *the time of lamp-lighting:* λωτρόν (?) Hesych.: μαρυπτόν, Athen. 663 A: μεσαυλικόν (sc. κροῦμα): μεσόλαβον (?) Vitruv. 9. 3; if not corrupt, should probably be μεσόλαβον: μοτόν, lint, is better paroxytone, as in Hesych.: μοιόν, Arc. 121. 24; Theog. Can. 130. 9: μυελόν (?) = μυελός: μυοκτόνον and μυοφόνον, aconite, are both adjectives: μυττωτόν, Hesych., etc.: ξυρόν, Herod. π. μ. λ. 38. 33; Arc. 122. 22; Theog. Can. 130. 30: ξυστόν, the compound παράξυστον, Schol. Aristoph. Av. 1150, is regular: ὀρθόπτωτόν, *L. S.*: ὄρπετον, Æol. = ἑρπετόν, Theocr. 29. 13; Sappho, etc.: ὀστέον, Herod. π. μ. λ. 37. 30; Arc. 119. 2: Theog. Can. 121. 8: some wrote ὄστεον, Schol. Ven. Ω. 793: the Attic form is ὀστοῦν; Doric, ὄστιον; Ionic, ὀστεῦν: it is probable that ὀστέον, if it be a correct form at all, results from the resolution of ὀστοῦν, and that the latter could arise from ὄστεον is clear from such words as ἀργύρεος, ἀργυροῦς, χάλκεον, χαλκοῦν, etc.: ὀστά = ὀστέα is quoted by H. D. from Oppian. Cyn. 1. 268, a very odd form: τὰ παιδικά: παλτόν, Xenoph. Hell. 3. 4. 14, etc.: παρειόν, Schol. Ven. Γ. 35: παστόν, Eust. 1278. 54, and πάστον, Hesych.: πεζόν (sc. στράτευμα): πεσσόν (πεττόν), Pollux 9. 97: πετεηνά, πετεινά, and πτηνά (sc. ζῶα): πηδόν, Schol. Apollon. Rhod. 4. 200: πινικόν or πιννικόν, a *pearl,* Salmas. ad Plin. p. 1124, 1173, quoted by H. D.: πομφολυγηρόν, Paul. Ægin. 7. 17; *H. D.*: πλευρόν, Schol. Ven. Γ. 35: ποτητά = πετεινά: ποτόν, Hom.: προηγμένα, a participle used substantively: πρυμνόν, Hom.: πτερόν, Arc. 137. 13, the compound ἀκρόπτερον is regular: πυρόν, Theog. Can. 130. 30, or τὰ πυρά, Schol. Ven. Γ. 35: πυρσά, Eurip. Rhes. 97, heteroclite plural of πυρσός: ῥινόν, Soph. fr. 122: ῥυπόν = ὑποστάθμη γάλακτος,

Phot. 349. 9, H. *D.* seems to be an error, as the word is, at least in its ordinary sense, paroxytone : ῥυτόν, Arc. 123. 16 : ῥυτά=πήγανα, Phot. 493. 3 ; *H. D.*: ῥυτρόν (?) the proper form is ῥύτρον· σαμῆον, Dor. =σημεῖον : σειρόν, Stob. Ecl. vol. 2. p. 449 ; H. *D.* : σιδωτόν (?) : σκελετόν (sc. σῶμα) : σκιορόν in Arc. 123. 4 is probably corrupt : σκολιόν (sc. μέλος), our books vary between this and σκόλιον, Eust. 1574. 11 : στελεόν or στελειόν, Theog. Can. 121. 3 : στυρόν (?) Theog. Can. 130. 30 : σκυρόν (?) the proper form is σκύρον :' συρτόν, *a led horse*, *H. D.* : σφυρόν, Arc. 122. 22 ; Herod. π. μ. λ. 38. 33 : ταβάλα or ταβῆλα, Hesych. is a Persian word : τιλτόν, Pollux 6. 9. 49, etc., also τίλτον, Athen. 113 F : τραγανόν (sc. μόριον), this also seems to be used substantively with the accent τράγανον : τριβακόν (sc. ἱμάντιον), though τρίβακον is not uncommon, cf. Lob. Prol. 314 : τροφόν, Plat. Polit. 289 A : τρωκτά, Suid., etc. : ὑποταμνόν (?) Hom. H. in Cer. 288 ; the accent is quite contrary to analogy : φαλλικόν (sc. ᾆσμα, ὄρχημα, etc.) : φαρικόν (or φαριακόν ?), Nicand. Alex. 398 ; Hesych. has φάρικον : φορβόν, Orph. Arg. 1111, for which φόρβον (φόρβα) occurs in Hesych. : φυτόν, Arc. 123. 16 ; the compounds ζωόφυτον, σύμφυτον are regular : χρεών (Ion. χρεόν), Arc. 182. 22 hardly belongs to this declension, but is put here for want of a better place : τὰ ψευδοπανικά, Polyæn. 3. 9. 32 : ᾠόν, Arc. 122. 2, yet its other forms, ὤεον, ὤϊον, are regular, Eust. 1686. 48 ; Theog. Can. 130. 19 ; E. M. 822. 45 ; Schol. Ven. A. 464 : τὰ γὰρ εἰς ΟΣ λήγοντα μεταπλασσόμενα εἰς οὐδέτερον γένος τὸ εἰς ΟΝ λῆγον, τὸν αὐτὸν τόνον φυλάσσει· ὁ ζυγός τὸ ζυγόν—τὰ ζυγά, δίφρος δίφραν δίφρα. ὅθεν εἰ καὶ μηρός, καὶ μηρόν καὶ μηρά.

347. Note 2.—*Tribrach Diminutives.* A considerable number of diminutives consisting of three short syllables are found in the books paroxytone, though such an accentuation must be regarded as erroneous, since it is contrary to the express precepts of the grammarians (cf. Schol. Ven. B. 648; I. 147; N. 71 ; E. M. 451. 16; 520. 15). Some of these false forms have been noted, and a list of them is appended. The word πεδίον, *plain*, is excepted by all authorities. Βρακίον, *H.D.* : βρεφίον, H. *D.* : δοκίον, *H. D.* ; but the places quoted do not warrant this accent : θρονίον, Vita Nili jun. p. 33. 2, Hase ap. H. D., is false for θρόνιον : ' Eustath. ad Il. B. p. 268. 8, observari jubet τὸ κώμιον ὑποκοριστικῶς λεχθὲν καὶ προπαροξυτόνως, ὡς καὶ λύρα, λύριον· θύρα, θύριον. Paulo clarius rem totam enucleat Etymologicum Bibliothecæ Lugd. Bat. MS. in Λῆδος : ubi docet, si ὑποκοριστικαὶ παραγωγαί sint δακτυλικαί, πρὸ μιᾶς ἔχειν τὸν τόνον, ut ψωμίον, ὠτίον, κλειδίον, παι ίον, κηρίον, δᾳδίον· εἰ δὲ ἐν τρισὶ βράχεσιν ὦσι, προπαροξύνονται, θρόνος, θρόνιον· πτύχος, πτύχιον· φλέβιον, τόπιον, ὄριον, μόριον, κόριον, λόγιον,' Hemsterhuis. ad Schol. Aristoph. Plut. 1098; cf. A. G. 794. 22 : θυρίον, Alciph. 3. 30, should be θύριον, Eust. 268. 8 ; 1854. 55 ; Hemster. *supra* : κλᾰδίον (?) : κλᾰνίον, Heysch. : κρῐκίον, *L. S.*, H. *D.*, but the passage quoted does not justify it : κτενίον, is expressly stated to be κτένιον, by Arc. 119. 9 ; Theog. Can. 122. 6 : λαβίον, Strab. 540 : λαγίον is false for λάγιον, Schol. Ven. N. 71 ; E. M. 451. 16 : λιθίον is quoted by H. D. from Paus. 2. 25. 8, where however Dindorf properly reads λίθιον : κοφίον, Schol. Aristoph. Ach. 1109 ; a mistake for λόφιον, Suid. ; Pollux 7. 157 ; Hesych. ; A. G. 794. 33 : μαζίον, Schol. Thucyd. 2. 13, may perhaps be right, though μάζιον occurs in Athen. 646 C : νεφίον, *L. S.* : ξιφίον, Diosc. 4. 20 ; Theoph. H. P. 7. 13. 2 : πεδίον, *a plain* (the compound words γεοπέδιον, ὁροπέδιον are regular) : πέδιον is, according to E. M. 658. 23, the diminutive of πέδη ; so also Theog. Can. 122. 6 ; 121. 31 ; A. G. Oxon. 1. 335. 21 : πλᾰτίον (?) : ποδίον (?) Eust. 1196. 15 : πυρίον, Eust. 729. 65, a false form for πυρεῖον : πτῠχίον ; there does not appear to be the slightest authority for this, πτύχιον being undoubtedly the right accent, Arc. 119. 9 ; Theog. Can. 122. 6 : ῥᾰκίον (?) is mentioned in the lexicons, but is false for ῥάκιον, Theog. Can. 122. 7 ; Schol. Ven. N. 71 ; E. M. 375. 28 : ῥαφίον (??) : σακίον, Pollux 10. 152 : σινίον, Hesych. : σκᾰφίον ; this is the common accent, though σκάφιον is found : σκᾰφίον, Hesych., etc. : σπῖνίον, Athen. 65 E : στολίον (?) is better στόλιον, E. M. 58. 14 : σφῦρίον, N. T. Acts 3. 7 : τεκνίον, A. G. Oxon. 2. 322. 8 : φορίον is a false form for φορεῖον : χόλιον, Marc. Anton. 6. 57 : χόριον, Arist. H. A. 6. 22. 17 ; 3. 14, and elsewhere ; for which the false form χορίον occurs in Hippocrat. De nat. pueri, p. 238, *H. D.*, and in many other places ; the word is also written χωρίον : ψᾰλίον is false for ψάλιον ; and ψελίον is also said to occur.   All of these, with the exception of πεδίον and τεκνίον, are unquestionably either false in accent or spelling, or both.

348. NOTE 3.—*Dactylic Diminutives.*   The rule for the accentuation of dactylic diminutives in ιον, stated above, is that which is given by the best authorities, ancient and modern ; but the application of it is beset with difficulties, because it is hard to say what constitutes a diminutive of the class in question. It is not the mere external form of the word, for αὔλιον, δέσμιον, ὅρκιον stand to αὐλή, δεσμός, ὅρκος in the same apparent relation that βυβλίον, τειχίον, χρυσίον do to βύβλος, τεῖχος, and χρυσός, and yet they are not diminutives : nor is it signification alone ; ἄρκιον is a *little bear* (Theog. Can. 122. 14), but it is not paroxytone. In short, there are words diminutive in form and signification which are not paroxytone, while there are others diminutive in form and accent, though not in meaning. The following lists will, it is hoped, facilitate the application of the rule.

349. NOTE 4.—*Diminutives in Form and Accent, but not in Signification.* Αἴμνιον, Suid. ; Theog. Can. 5. 33, or αἰμνίον, A. G. Oxon. 1. 81. 24, a variant of ἀμνίον, Arc. 119. 29 ; A. G. 794. 6 ; for which Manuel Moschopul. Gramm. p. 33 ed. Titze has ἄμνιον : ἀμφίον, which sometimes occurs, is false for ἄμφιον, A. G. 794. 32 : ἀντίον, τὸ τοῦ ἱστοῦ, Theog. Can. 123. 28 : ἀντλίον, in Eust. 1728. 59, is better proparoxytone, A. G. 411. 19 : ἀπτρίον (?) A. G. 794. 12 : ἀψίον = τὸ πρόσωπον, Hesych. : βιβλίον, *a book*, Theog. Can. 122. 16 : τὸ Ῥήγιον, β ί β λ ί ο ν, κρώσιον, ἐπὶ δυσὶ τόνοις δύο σημασίας ἐπήνεγκαν ; I do not know what is the meaning of βίβλιον : βροχίον τὸ συνεχῶς βρεχόμενον, E. M. 211. 15 : βυβλίον, Arc. 119. 20 ; Chœrob. E. 143. 23 is only another form of the word βιβλίον : γαγγλίον, *H. D.* : γλαυκίον, Athen. 395 C, is quoted by H. D. from Galen t. 13. p. 166, as proparoxytone : γογγρίον, *H. D.* : εἴριον became in later times εἰρίον, Eust. 912. 52 ; but he denies that it is a diminutive, Eust. 743. 2 ; ἐρκίον, Eust. 233. 44 ; Schol. Ven. N. 71 ; Chœrob. E. 143. 23 ; E. M. 631. 25 : Schol. Dion. Thrac. 856. 4 : ἠνίον, Hom. : ἠρίον, A. G. 794. 9 ; E. M. 437. 12 : θηρίον, Arc. 119. 19 ; Theog. Can. 122. 11 : ἰκρίον, Hesych. ; see below, § 352 ; ἰνίον, Schol. Ven. I. 147 : ἰστίον, Arc. 120. 8 ; Eust. 233. 44 : ἰσχίον, Arc. 120. 8 ; Eust. 233. 44 ; E. M. 631. 25 : ἰτρίον, Aristoph. Ach. 1092, and elsewhere, is expressly made proparoxytone by Arc. 119. 18, and such is its proper accent : ἰχνίον, Eust. 233. 44, is more correctly written ἴχνιον, E. M. 375. 28 ; 451. 16 : καυλίον, Arist. H. A. 8. 2. 29 : κεντρίον, Theod. Prodr. p. 77, *H. D.*, cf. E. M. 503. 39 ; is also κέντριον : κεσκίον (?) Hesych. : κηρίον, A. G. 794. 9 : κισσίον, A. G. 794. 11, κίσσιον, in another sense, Diosc. 3. 106 : κλανίον (?) Hesych. ; κοινίον, Hesych., is false for κοινεῖον ; cf. Arc. 121. 5 : κουρίον (?) κουρεῖον : κραμβίον, A. G. 793. 36, in Hesych. κραμβίον = τὸ κώνειον, where H. D. thinks κραμβεῖον the right reading, but the passage just quoted from A. G. is clear both as to spelling and to accent : κρανίον, Hom. etc. : κρωσίον, Theog. Can. 122. 16, quoted above, says that it is paroxytone in one signification, and proparoxytone in another ; but it does not seem to have two meanings : μηρίον, Theog. Can. 122. 11 : μνασίον = μέτρον τι διμέδιμνον, Hesych. ; but μνάσιον, a plant, Theoph. H. P. 4. 9. 8. 2 ; *H. D.* : ξεστίον, *H. D.* : ξηρίον (sc. φάρμακον), Theog. Can. 122. 11 : this is a strange accent, as the word is nothing but the neuter of ξήριος : ὀγκίον (or ὄγκιον), Eust. 1898. 63 ; Theog. Can. 123. 28 : οἰκίον, perhaps also a diminutive in meaning: πηνίον, Hom.: πυξίον, A. G. 794. 7; perhaps hardly a fair instance: ῥηγίον (?) and ῥήγιον; cf. Theog. Can. 122. 16: σαγίον, A. G. 793. 36: σαννίον, Hesych., is false for σάννιον, τὸ αἰδοῖον, Theog. Can. 123. 11; it is not a diminutive: σαυνίον, *a javelin*, Strab. 717; for which σαύνιον᾽ Arrian Ind. c. 16. 10, is a better form; the word seems to be the same as σάννιον, mentioned above, Pollux 10. 143: σευτλίον; see below, τευτλίον: σινίον, Hesych.: σιτίον, A. G. 794. 11; Theog. Can. 122. 13: σκαμνίον, A. G. 794. 5: σκαρφίον, Constantin. de Adm. Imp. c. 9. p. 19; *H. D.*: σμηνίον, Hesych.: σμηρίον (?): σμυρνίον (?) and σμύρνιον; for which σμυρνεῖον also occurs: σπαρτίον, A. G. 794. 12; for which the corrupt form σπερτίον occurs in Theog. Can. 122. 12: σπληνίον, Pollux 2. 220: σπονδίον (?): σταθμίον, Pollux 4. 173; but στάθμιον, Suid.: σταμνίον, A. G. 794. 6; perhaps this is diminutive in signification; the same remark applies to σταυρίον, Chœrob. E. 143. 23; Theog. Can. 122. 12: στερνίον: στηθίον, Arist. Physiog. 6. 11: στρουθίον, Theog. Can. 122. 12: συκίον (?) σύκιον is the better form: σφηκίον, Arc. 119. 14, perhaps diminutive in meaning: σφηρίον (?) Theog. Can. 122. 11: σφιγγίον, Lucian pro Merc. Cond. 1: σχοινίον, Arc. 120. 4; Theog. Can. 122. 12: τειχίον, Chœrob. E. 143. 23; E. M. 375. 28; Schol. Ven. I. 147; μεσοτείχιον is regular as a compound: τεκνίον: τευτλίον or σευτλίον, Athen. 621 E; but τεύτλιον also occurs: τυβίον (?) A. G. 793. 36; its meaning is unknown: φερνίον, Pollux 6. 94, etc., should be φέρνιον, Arc. 119. 28: φορτίον, Theog. Can. 122. 11; E. M. 451. 16: φρουρίον, Arc. 120. 3: φυκίον, E. M. 451. 16: φωλίον, Paus. 4. 18. 4: χαλκίον, Eust. 1680. 27: χαρτίον, Arc. 119. 14; Theog. Can. 122. 11: χρυσίον, Schol. Ven. N. 71; Eust. 1680. 27; Theog. Can. 122. 11 is incorrectly χρύσιον in Aristoph. Lys. 930: χωρίον, A. G. 794. 8; Theog. Can. 122. 13: ὠτίον, E. M. 375. 28; in the case of several of the above words, it is hard to tell whether they are diminutive in meaning or not; e. g. θηρίον may be applied either to an elephant or a bee; χρυσίον may mean a little bit of gold, or merely a gold piece, without any necessary implication of smallness.

Compounds of these diminutives seem generally to follow the general rule and retract the accent, as μεσοκήπιον, μεσοτείχιον, ἡμιτύμβιον; though H. D. quote παλαιοχωρίον from Anna Comn. p. 442.

350. NOTE 5.—*Diminutives in Form and Signification but not in Accent.* Αἴγιον (?) Theog. Can. 123. 14, perhaps only occurs as a proper name: ἄρκιον, Theog. Can. 122. 14: ἄσκιον, *L. S.*, or ἀσκίον, A. G. 794. 5: βώλιον is quoted by H. D. from Aristoph. Vesp. 203, where Bergk writes βωλίον: γάμβριον = τρυβλίον, Hesych.: γάνδιον = κιβώτιον, Hesych.: γάριον, Arrian Diss. Epict. 2. 20. 29: γείσιον or γίσιον, Hesych., etc.: δένδριον (?) is better δενδρίον, as in Athen. 649 F: δέρριον, Hesych.: ζώνιον, Ammon. 65: ἡμισφαίριον, Euseb. P. E. 3. 92 D: ἡμιτύμβιον, Suid.: ἡμιφόρμιον, Pollux 10. 169: κάδδιον, A. G. 794. 16; yet καδίον, Sept. 1 Kings 17. 40: κάλπιον, Athen. 475 C: κέρνιον, Theog. Can. 123. 11: κλίσιον, in Homer ι is short and the word is proparoxytone, but in Attic it is κλισίον (or κλεισίον), E. M. 520. 15: κώμιον, Eust. 268. 8: κώνιον, Eust. 1196. 15, is κωνίον in Auth. Pal. 5. 13: κώριον, Dor. = κόριον, Aristoph. Ach. 731: λῄδιον, Eust. 193. 35; Didymus and Philemon wrote λῃδίον, Eust. 1146. 60: λήμιον (?) is better λημίον, Hippocr. p. 943 D; *H. D.*: λύχνιον, Eust. 1854. 55; for which λυχνίον is preferred by Lob. Phryn. 314: μείλιον is not a diminutive according to Eust. 743. 2; Trypho was in doubt whether to make it paroxytone, Schol. Ven. I. 147: νήττιον, Athen. 65 D: ὄβριον (?) Theog. Can. 122. 24: ἐποίκιον καὶ ἐνοίκιον [sc. προπαροξύνεται] ὧν τὰ πρωτότυπα ἄχρηστα, A. G. 794. 22: ὄρφιον (?) or ὀρφίον, Alex. Trall. 7. p. 362; *H. D.*: ὄσπριον, Theog. Can. 122. 24, can hardly be considered diminutive in signification: πάρδιον, Arist. H. A. 2. 1. 20, is probably not a diminutive: πλαίσιον, Theog. Can. 123. 14, perhaps not a fair instance: πλέθριον (?) Paus. 6. 23. 2: πόσθιον, Suid.: πρέμνιον, Hesych.: ῥάβδιον (?) is certainly better as a

paroxytone: ῥάκτριον (?) Theog. Can. 122. 23: ῥάμφιον, A.G. 794. 33: ῥάπιον (?):
ῥάριον, E. M. 702. 37: ῥήγιον (?) cf. Theog. Can. 122. 16: ῥίζιον frequently occurs
in MSS. for ῥιζίον: ῥύμβιον (?) H. D. have only ῥυμβίον: ῥώπιον, Dio Cass. 63.
28, a questionable instance: σάκκιον (?) is better σακκίον: σάννιον, τὸ αἰδοῖον,
Theog. Can. 123. 11, perhaps not a diminutive: σεύτλιον, see above, § 349:
προσκήνιον, περισκήνιον, Theog. Can. 125. 21, are regular as compounds: σφόγ-
γιον (?) H. D. have only σφογγίον: τέχνιον, Arc. 119. 24, for which τεχνίον occurs,
e. g. Athen. 55 E; Schol. Aristoph. Nub. 508: τρύβλιον, Arc. 119. 19, is not a
diminutive in signification, though τρυβλίον occurs in Aristoph. Plut. 1108: φάριον,
Pollux 10. 66, does not seem to be a diminutive: φάττιον, Aristoph. Plut. 1011:
φόρμιον, Hesych., is better φορμίον Diog. Laert. 4. 3: φύσκιον (?) should be paroxytone: χηλίον, Schol. Arati 173 = χηλή: χημίον, Oribas. T. 1. p. 119. 3; 239. 4,
is χήμιον in Xenocr. de aquatil. p. 190 ed. Cor., *H. D.*: χλαίνιον, Auth. Pal. 12. 40,
seems false for χλαινίον: ψέλλιον (?) = ψέλιον: ψώθιον, Hesych., etc. : ὤμιον, Anth.
Pal. 11. 157: ὤπιον (?) Hesych. : ὤριον (?).

351. NOTE 6.—The following are the principal words which are dactyls only
from contraction: βώδιον, βοΐδιον, or βοίδιον, Theog. Can. 121. 24: γήδιον,
Apoll. de Adv. 566. 12: γράδιον = γραΐδιον, Lob. Phryn. 88: ζώδιον = ζωΐδιον
Theog. *l. l.*: κώδιον, Theog. Can. 124. 3: μύδιον = μυΐδιον, Theog. Can. 121. 25;
Arc. 120. 13: νοΐδιον = νοΐδιον, Suid.; Aristoph. Eq. 100: ῥοΐδιον or ῥούδιον =
ῥοίδιον, A. G. 794. 17: σκοίδιον (?) σκιάδιον, Hesych. : στῴδιον = στωΐδιον, E. M.
550. 6.

352. NOTE 7.—Such words as αἴθριον = *atrium*: ἄκτιον, Ælian N. H. 13. 28:
δέμνιον Theog. Can. 123. 10; Eust. 1037. 31: δέσμιον, Anth. Pal. 9. 479: ἔδριον,
Hesych. : εἴριον, Eust. 743. 2: θέρμιον: θίνιον, Herodian ap. Theog. Can. 125. 11:
ἴκριον, Theog. Can. 122. 23; Eust. 1037. 81; Schol. Ven. O. 676: ἴχνιον, Theog.
l. l.: Eust. 233. 44; Schol. Ven. N. 71: κήθιον or κήτιον, Athen. 477 D: κοίνιον:
κόρσιον, κρώπιον, κρώβιον, or κρόπιον, Hesych. : κώδιον, Arc. 120, or κῴδιον: λείριον,
Theog. *l. l.*; Eust. 743. 2: λίντιον or λέντιον: λίστριον: παίγνιον, E. M. 480. 49;
Schol. Ven. N. 71; Theog. Can. 123. 10: ποίμνιον, Theog. *l. l.*; Arc. 119. 27;
Eust. 743. 2: φέρνιον, Theog. *l. l.*; φρούριον, Theog. Can. 122. 23: φρύγιον: φρύ-
νιον: φύλλιον: χέννιον, Hesych. : ψύλλιον : ὤνιον, Theog. *l. l.*, are not diminutives
at all, and they accordingly follow the general rule.

353. NOTE 8.—According to Arcadius (121. 1–19) neuters in ειον are accented
according to the following rules :—*Trisyllables*: 1. Proper names are proparoxytone, as Βούδειον, Χλούνειον, Σίγειον. 2. Those in νειον[1] preceded by a single

---

[1] This part of the text in Arcadius is clearly corrupt; the words are: τὰ διὰ τοῦ
ΕΙΟΝ τρισύλλαβα προπαροξύνονται, εἰ ἡ πρὸ τέλους συλλαβὴ εἰς φωνῆεν λήγοι·
Ὄνειον, κόνειον, γένειον, δάνειον, τὸ δὲ κοινεῖον προπερισπᾶται καὶ λυχνεῖον καὶ πορνεῖον οὐ μόνον ἔχοντα τὸ Ν. Nor is the relative passage in
Theognostus (Can. 128. 4) altogether better sound: τὰ διὰ ΕΙΟΝ τρισύλλαβα καθαρεύοντα τοῦ Ν προπαροξύνονται μονογενῆ, ἀπὸ ἑνὸς φωνήεντος ἀρχόμενα, διὰ τῆς ει
διφθόγγου γράφονται· ὄνειον, φάνειον, κράνειον, κώνειον, δάνειον, γένειον, κάνειον δ
καὶ κάνεον, ξάνειον, κτένειον δ φοροῦσιν γυναῖκες ἐπὶ τοῦ ἀναδήματος. It seems
obvious that νειον must be read for ειον in both places, and if the words ἡ πρὸ
τέλους συλλαβή in Arcadius can mean ' the syllable before the end*ing*,' the inser-
tion of ἕν before φωνῆεν, and of καθαρεύοντα after τρισύλλαβα, will make the passage somewhat more consistent with the examples, for it will then run : ' Trisyllables in νειον pure are proparoxytone if the syllable before that termination
ends in a single vowel.' Such a rule would exclude κοινεῖον, because νειον is preceded by more than a single vowel, and λυχνεῖον and πορνεῖον as not being in
νειον pure. But it seems highly probable that there is a deeper corruption yet in
both authors.

vowel are proparoxytone, as Ὄνειον, κόνειον, γένειον, δάνειον, but κοινεῖον is properispomenon because ν is preceded by a diphthong, and λυχνεῖον, πορνεῖον, because it is preceded by a consonant. 3. All other trisyllables of this ending are properispomena, as πορθμεῖον, στοιχεῖον, ἀγγεῖον, γραφεῖον, ᾠδεῖον, σημεῖον. *Hypertrisyllables*: Simple and parasynthetic words are properispomena, as θωρακεῖον, πανδοκεῖον, διδασκαλεῖον, βαλανεῖον, ἐλεγεῖον; except proper names, names of months, and synthetic compounds, all of which are proparoxytone, together with κηρύκειον. Neuter adjectives retain the accent of their masculines, as Ἡράκλειον, Αἰάκειον, Διοσκούρειον; except Ἡφαιστεῖον and Κορυβαντεῖον.

354. NOTE 9.—*Exceptions in* ειον. Ἀκάτειον (?) false for ἀκάτιον: ἀκρόλειον, Suid., is a compound: ἄλειον, a Rhodian festival of the sun, Eust. 1562. 54: ἀλκιβιάδειον, Galen T. 13. p. 479 F: ἀλκυόνειον (and ἀλκυόνιον), Diosc. 5. 136, etc.: ἄνθειον (?): ἄρκτειον, Diosc. 4. 106; H. *D*.: αὔλειον, strictly a neuter adjective: βασίλειον (sc. δῶμα, etc.): βήτειον, Theog. Can. 128. 13: βήχειον, Theog. Can. 128. 13; βλάστειον (?) is written βλαστεῖον in Nicand. Alex. 609: βρένθειον, *an unguent*, Chœrob. A. G. Oxon. 2. 233. 14; cf. Athen. 690 E: γάνειον is regular according to the rule of Arcadius above mentioned: γένειον, Theog. Can. 128. 7: γήρειον, *old age*, Theog. Can. 128. 7: γήτειον, E. M. 411. 44: γωλειόν (?) Nicand. Ther. 351; H. *D*.: δάνειον, Theog. Can. 128. 7: διαύλειον, Suid., is better written διαύλιον, Hesych.: ἐγχέλειον, Eust. 1231. 36, is really an adjective: ἐλένειον, A. G. Oxon. 2. 279. 31: ἐμβρύειον (sc. κρέας), Athen. 372 C: ἐναύλειον, H. *D*., probably a wrong accent; the place which they quote, Eurip. Hel. 1107, proves nothing: ἐπίγειον, H. *D*.: ἐπιγόνειον (sc. ὄργανον), Pollux 9. 59, etc.: ἐπίνειον (πόλισμα or the like): ἐπίσειον (or ἐπίσιον), Pollux 2. 170: ἐχίειον = ἔχιον, *a plant so called*, Nicand. Ther. 65: ζήτρειον according to Orus, but also ζητρεῖον, Eust. 837. 45; the latter is Chœroboscus' accent, E. M. 411. 44: ζώτειον, Theog. Can. 128. 12; E. M. 412. 40: also ζώστειον, ζώντειον, and ζωντειον (?): ἡμιπήχειον, Sext. Emp. Hist. 7. 105, is quoted for this, but it proves nothing as to the accent: ἠριγένειον, Hesych.: θέειον = θεῖον, Hom., etc.: θώρειον (?) Theog. Can. 128. 12: κάνειον (or κάνεον), Theog. 128. 12: κάρειον = κάρη (?) Athen. 684 A, where some read καρήνοις for καρείοις: καστάνεια (sc. κάρυα), E. M. 493. 25: καστόρειον (sc. μέλος?): καταμάγειον (?) Artemid. 1. 64; H. *D*.: κελέβειον: κενταύρειον (sc. φυτόν), Diosc. 3. 6: κηλώνειον, Pollux 7. 143: κηρυκεῖον τὸ μονογενὲς καὶ προσηγορικόν, ὅπερ ἐπίσταται καὶ ἡ συνήθεια, τὸ γὰρ ἐπιθετικὸν προπαροξύνεται, Theog. Can. 128. 31; Arc. 121. 14: κήτειον (?) Theog. Can. 128. 14: κλιμάκειον (?) for which κλιμάκιον seems a better form: κόνειον (?) perhaps false for κώνειον: κούρειον (or κούριον), Attic; κουρεῖον, Common; Theog. Can. 128. 22; but it is usually κουρεῖον in Attic writers, at least in our editions: κόψειον, Hesych.: κρομμνογήτειον, Theoph. H. P. 4. 6. 2; H. *D*.: κτένειον, Theog. Can. 128. 7: κυάθειον, Nicand. Ther. 591: κυκλώπειον (δῶρον, ξένιον, etc.): κώνειον, Theog. Can. 128. 7: λεξίδειον, Theog. Can. 421. 23, for which λεξείδιον or λεξίδιον are better forms: μαλάκεια = μαλάκια or μαλάχεια, Oppian Hal. Γ. 638; H. *D*.: μονογένειον, H. *D*.: μορμολυκεῖον, Theog. Can. 129. 1; E. M. 590. 52, is in several places wrongly written as a paroxytone: νάπειον (?) Nicaud. Alex. 430: ξάνειον, Theog. A. G. Oxon. 2. 128. 7: ὄνειον, Theog. A. G. Oxon. 2. 128. 7, perhaps a proper name: ὄστρειον, Theog. Can. 121. 8; Theodos. Gramm. 73. 27: παράσειον, Lucian Navig. c. 5: παρασίτειον, Athen. 235 D (or παρασίτιον?): πατάνειον is false for πατάνιον: πετάλειον, Nicand. Ther. 629: πόδειον in Phot. 436. 1 and elsewhere is false for ποδεῖον, Theog. Can. 128. 26: πράσειον, A. G. Oxon. 2. 279. 31: προάστειον (?) or προαστεῖον, Lob. Par. 253: προβαλάνειον (?): τὰ προτέλεια is strictly an adjective: σκιάδειον (?): ὑμένειον (?) or ὑμένιον, H. *D*.: φάνειον, Theog. Can. 128. 6: φοινίκειον, Theodos. Gramm. 71. 4: φυσίδειον, Theog. Can. 121. 23: φυτώρειον (?): χαράδρειον, Nicand. Ther. 389: χείλειον and χείλιον, Theog. Can. 128. 13 : χέλειον, Nicand. Alex. 561 : χελύνειον, a bad form for χελύνιον : χελώνειον (?) = χελώνιον : χοιροτροφεῖον, χοιροσφαγεῖον, and χοιροφορβεῖον, are all more or less doubtful : ψύλλειον (?) A. G. Oxon. 2. 279. 31 : ὤρειον (?).

355. NOTE 10.—*Exceptions in* αιον. See Arc. 120. 20-28 ; Theog. Can. 127. 3-24 : ἀγναῖον (?) : ἀρχαῖον, Arc. 120. 23 : ἐξαμηναῖον, H. *D.* : εὐναῖον, Xenoph. Cyn. 5. 7, really an adjective : ἡμίμναιον, Pollux 9. 55, is sometimes written ἡμιμναῖον : ἠτραῖον, H. *D.* : καναστραῖον, Suid. : κλαιόν (?) Hesych. : κορυφαῖον, *part of a net*, Pollux 5. 31 : κοταῖον (?) : κραταῖον (?) : κραταιόν (sc. οὖδας) : κρηπιδαῖον, Pollux 5. 120 ; 'κρηπίδαιον proparoxytonum in cod. Jungerm,' H. *D.* : λαριναῖον, Hesych. : μελιταῖον (sc. κυνίδιον, ὀθόνιον, etc.) : μουσαῖον, H. *D.* : νυμφαῖον also occurs in the form νύμφαιον : ὁλκαῖον, Pollux 6. 99 : ὀπαῖον, Plut. 1. 159 : οὐραῖον seems in all its senses to retain the adjectival accent, though it is made proparoxytone by Theog. Can. 127. 7 : σεληναῖον, H. *D.* : τριχαῖον (?) : τροπαῖον, ' Arc. p. 120. 22 : Τρόπαιον, καὶ τροπαῖον Ἀττικῶς ; Mire Schol. Dionys. Bekk. An. p. 678. 20 : Ἡμεῖς μὲν ἀναλόγως τρόπαιον λέγομεν ὡς σπήλαιον, σύλαιον, ὁ δὲ Θουκυδίδης τροπαῖον Ἀττικῶς ; Schol. Thucyd. 1. 30 : Τροπαῖον ἡ παλαιὰ Ἀτθίς, ἧς ἐστιν Εὔπολις, Κρατῖνος, Ἀριστοφάνης, Θουκυδίδης, τρόπαιον ἡ νέα Ἀτθίς, ἧς ἐστι Μένανδρος καὶ οἱ ἄλλοι : Schol. Aristoph. Thesm. 697 : Τροπαῖον προπερισπωμένως ἀναγνωστέον παρὰ Ἀριστοφάνει καὶ παρὰ Θουκυδίδῃ, τρόπαιον δὲ προπαροξυτόνως παρὰ τοῖς νεωτέροις ποιηταῖς : cf. Elmsl. ad Heracl. 403,' *L. Dindorf* ap. H. D ; to the references add E. M. 769. 14 : χαλαστραῖον (sc. νίτρον), Arc. 120. 27.

356. NOTE 11.—*Exceptions in* φον. Περίστφον, E. M. 665. 7 ; Arc. 122. 10 ; yet it is written περιστφον in E. M. 413. 29, and is expressly said to be accented like ὑπερφον and στφον in A. G. Oxon. 2. 371. 26 ; προστφον on the other hand is properispomenon, E. M. 665. 7 ; Arc. 122. 10 ; though Suidas has πρόστφον.

2. *Proper Names.*

357. In general, neuter proper names retract the accent, as Περγάντιον, Αἰάντιον, Βυζάντιον, Ἄμηρον, Ῥήγιον, Ἴσθμιον, Ἴλιον, Δῖον, Θρόνιον, Σούνιον, Ἄκτιον, Ὁρμένιον, Ἀρτεμίσιον, Βουπράσιον, Λιλύβαιον, Δίρκαιον, Κίρκαιον, Πήδαιον, Λήναιον, Πάγγαιον, Πείραιον, τὰ Ἀθήναια, Λήναια, Ἑστίαια, Λύκαια (sc. ἱερά), Βούδειον, Σίγειον, Χλούνειον, Λαύρειον, Γορδίειον, Δορίειον, Βόρειαν, Λύρκειον ; except

1. The names of temples and precincts (*temenica*) in ειον, which are for the most part properispomena, as Ἀνουβεῖον, Ἡφαιστεῖον, Ἰακχεῖον, Καπιτωλιεῖον, Κορυβαντεῖον, Νεμεσεῖον, Φορβαντεῖον.

2. Those in φον, which are always properispomena, as Λητφον, Μητρφον, Νυκτφον, Πτφον (Arc. 122. 2).

But every part of this rule, except the last, is liable to numerous exceptions, lists of which are given in the following sections.

358. Names of festivals in ια, αια' and εια, though adjectives, conform to the general rule, and are proparoxytone, as Ἀθήναια (sc. ἱερά), Ἀπατούρια, Διάσια, Διόμεια, Ἑκατόμβαια, Ἕρμαια, Ἥραια, Λήναια, Νέμεια, Πανάκεια.

NOTE 1.—On these words, see Theodos. Gr. 69. 16.   Ἀδριανεῖα' (?) H. D.: in Paus. 5. 16. 2 we have Ἡραῖα for Ἥραια, Eust. 1560. 62 : Θησεῖα, Hesych.: Ἰθωμαῖα, Paus. 4. 33. 2 : Καλλιστεῖα (?): Καπετωλεῖα, St. Byz. : Πάνεια is also found properispomenon: Χάλκεια, according to Herodian ap. E. M. 805. 47, this was generally properispomenon, and such is its usual accent in our books.

359. NOTE 2.—*Exceptional Proper Names.* Ἀβακαῖνον (sic), πόλις Σικελίας οὐδετέρως καὶ παροξυτόνως, St. Byz., where we should read Ἀβάκαινον (cf. Zonar. 9) and προπαροξυτόνως: Ἀβεντῖνον = *mons Aventinus,* is strictly an adjective : Ἀδρανόν, Diod. Sic. 16. 68 : Αἰγαλέον (?) a mountain so called, Strab. 359 : Αἰπιόν, Polyh. 4. 77. 9 : Ἀλπίον (?) Paus. 3. 18. 2, where Dindorf reads Ἀλπεῖον : Ἀμανόν (ὄρος) varies in the books between oxytone and proparoxytone ; Lobeck Prol. 181 prefers the former accent : Ἀπεννῖνον (ὄρος), yet Ἀπέννινον is most common, e. g. Strab. 201–2 ; 211 ; Ἀπεννινός as in Dionys. A. R. 1. 9. 14 = p. 8. 5 Sylb. is quite wrong: Ἀργυροῦν (ὄρος), Arist. Meteor. 1. 13. 20, is of course an adjective, as is Ἀσπορδηνόν, Strab. and Ἀσσωρόν, St. Byz.: τὰ Βατά, Strab. 496–7 : Βοιόν, Arc. 121. 23 ; cf. Thucyd. 1. 107, for which the false forms Βοῖον and Βύϊον are found : Βουθρωτόν, Strab. 324 ; also Βουθρωτός: Ἑλληνικόν, St. Byz. : Ἐρυθρόν, Ptol. 4. 4. 5 : Ἱερόν (sc. πόλισμα), Demosth. 468. 10, etc. : Καβυλλῖνον, Strab. 192 : Καινόν, Aristoph. Vesp. 120 : Καλεόν, Theog. Can. 121. 3 ; Arc. 118. 26 : Καμαρῖνον, Strab. 227 : Καρικόν, St. Byz. : τὰ Κασιανά, Strab. 752 : Κασινάτον (?) Plut. 1. 177 : Κασῖνον and Κασλῖνον, Strab. 237 : Κιλβανόν, Eust. Dion. Per. 830 : Κροιόν (? Κλοιόν, cf. Schol. Ven. Ξ. 284), Theog. Can. 130. 9 ; Λαβικόν, Strab. 237 : Λεκτόν, Schol. Ven. Ξ. 284 : τὰ Λευκά, Strab. 281 ; also Λευκόν, Callim. Dian. 41 ; like τὰ λευκὰ ὄρη, Ptol. 3. 17 ; λευκὸν τεῖχος, Thucyd. 1. 104, or λευκὸν πεδίον, Paus. 4. 35. 11, are all adjectives : ʻInter Λουγδοῦνον et Λουγδουνόν variant libri Herodiani 3. 7. 5,ʼ H. D.; the commonest form seems to be Λούγδουνον : Λυπερόν (ὄρος), Phot. Bib. 228. 28 : Μακεδνόν, St. Byz. : Μεγαρικόν, St. Byz. : Μισηνόν, Strab. 60 : ʻΝίκιον, Athen. 157 A. C. ubi Νίκιον scriptum,ʼ H. D.: Νωρικόν, the country so called, Ptol. 2. 14 ; but Νώρικον, a city, Eust. Dion. Per. 521 : Ὀλόκρον (ὄρος), Plut. 1. 266: Πεδίον, Paus. 8. 25. 12 : Πελασγικόν (or Πελαργικόν), Thucyd. 2. 7: Πελτινὸν πεδίον, Strab. 629: ʻquod Πελτηνόν scribendum,ʼ H. D.: like Ταβηνὸν πεδίον: Πορθμίον, St. Byz.: Πτελεόν, Schol. Ven. Ξ. 283–4, for which Πτελέον, St. Byz., is probably an error : τὰ Πτερά, St. Byz.: Ῥουσπῖνον, Strab. 831 : Ῥύτιον, Tyrannion made this paroxytone, Schol. Ven. B. 648 : Σαμικόν, St. Byz., etc. : Σεντῖνον, Strab. 227 : Σιτικόν, St. Byz. : Ταλετόν (?) Paus. 3. 20. 4 : Τεανόν, St. Byz. : Τειχίον, Thucyd. 3. 96, where Τείχιον also is read ; Τηνερικὸν πεδίον, and τὸ Τρητὸν ὄρος, are adjectives : Φαλακρόν (ἄκρον) Ptol. 3. 4, is probably an error for Φάλακρον, St. Byz.: Φαλίσκον, Strab. 226 : Φίρμον Πικηνόν, Strab. 241 : Φωκικόν, Paus. 10. 5. 1 : Χυτόν and Χωλόν τεῖχος, St. Byz. : Ὠρικόν, Strab. 316.

360. NOTE 3.—*Exceptions in* αιον. Ἀθήναιον, τὸ τέμενος, Arc. 120. 25, is sometimes falsely accented Ἀθηναῖον: Ἀμυκλαῖον and Ἀραχναῖον, St. Byz.: Ἀριγαῖον, Arrian Anab. 4. 24. 6: Ἕρμαιον, Herodian ap. Herm. de emend. rat. Gr. gr. p. 308. 20 ; yet we have Ἑρμαῖον in Polyh. 4. 43. 2, there is much uncertainty as to its accent, but it seems best to make it proparoxytone when decidedly a substantive, and properispomenon as an adjective ; cf. Arc. 43. 8 ; Theog. Can. 127. 9: Ἐρυθραῖον (ἄκρον) Ptol. 3. 17. 4: Ἑστιαῖον, *temple of Vesta,*

Dio Cass.: Ἥραιον, Arc. 120. 21, but it is very commonly Ἡραῖον, e.g. Thucyd. 3. 75: Θυραῖον, St. Byz.: Ἱμεραῖον (?) but Ἱμέραιον also occurs: Καναστραῖον, St. Byz. s. v. Ἀραχναῖον, but Κανάστραιον is found: Κηναῖον (?) or Κήναιον, Soph. Tr. 753, etc.: Κιρκαῖον, Strab., is better written Κίρκαιον, Arc. 120. 22; the books vary: Κορυφαῖον, St. Byz.: Λιλύβαιον, Arc. 120. 6, is frequently misaccented Λιλυβαῖον: Νειλοπτολεμαῖον (?) *H. D.*: Νησαῖον, St. Byz.: Νισαῖον πεδίον, also Νίσαιον: Παγγαῖον ὄρος, Æschyl. Pers. 494, also Πάγγαιον, Suid., etc.: Πισσαῖον, St. Byz.: Πτολεμαῖον is a false form for Πτολεμαεῖον: Σηταῖον (?) St. Byz.: Συρμαῖον (πεδίον), St. Byz.: Τυριαῖον or Τυραῖον, Xen. Anab. 1. 2. 14: Τύπαιον, St. Byz., or Τυπαῖον, Paus. 5. 6. 7: Τυχαῖον (ὄρος) St. Byz.: Χαλαστραῖον, St. Byz. s. v. Ἀραχναῖον.

It is very probable that many of the foregoing words are mere mistakes of scribes and editors; the rules given by the old grammarians are tolerably clear and precise, Herodian ap. Herm. de emend. rat. Gr. gr. p. 308. 20: τὰ μέντοι [τοπικῶς σχηματιζόμενα] διὰ τῆς αι διφθόγγου ἐκφερόμενα οὐκέτι περισπᾶται, ἀλλ᾽ ἀναβιβάζεται μόνον [ἤ τόνον], Ἕρμαιον, Νύμφαιον. St. Byz. s. v. Ἀγάθη implies that adjectives in αιος are properispomena, substantives in αιον, proparoxytone, but s. v. Ἀραχναῖον, he says, προπερισπαστέον δέ· τὰ γὰρ διὰ τοῦ αιον ἁπλᾶ ὑπὲρ τρεῖς συλλαβὰς ἔχοντα τὴν τετάρτην ἀπὸ τέλους διὰ τοῦ α καὶ τὴν ἑξῆς διὰ τοῦ α ἢ διὰ τοῦ υ, προπερισπᾶται· Χαλαστραῖον, Καναστραῖον, Ἀμυκλαῖον; to which may be added from Arc. 120. 27, and Theog. Can. 127. 22, Στεφαναῖον and Ἡλακαταῖον.

361. NOTE 4.—*Exceptions in* ειον. Ἀμαλθεῖον, Cic. Att. 1. 16: Γαμβρεῖον, St. Byz., is Γάμβριον in Xenoph. Hell. 3. 1. 6; see Lob. Par. 26: Δασκυλεῖον (?) *Pape*; the passages which he quotes do not prove this: τὰ Ἐμπορεῖα and τὸ Ἐμπορεῖον, if correct, are hardly proper names: Ἐμπόριον, in Strab. 159, is perhaps a better form: Ἡμεροσκοπεῖον, St. Byz.: Θυτεῖον, Æschin. 3. 122, *Pape*: Ἰσεῖον, St. Byz. πόλις Αἰγύπτου, ἀπὸ Ἴσιδος … προπερισπᾶται δέ, ὡς Ἡρεῖον καὶ Νεμεσεῖον καὶ τῶν ὅσα μὴ τῆς γενικῆς τὸ δ ἐφύλαξαν τεμενικῶν· τοιοῦτος γὰρ ὁ τύπος: Λύκειον, Attic; Theog. Can. 127. 28, also Λυκεῖον: τὰ Μελαγγεῖα, Paus. 8. 6. 4: Μούσειον, a place near Olympus; St. Byz.: Ὀγκεῖον, χωρίον Ἀρκαδίας, St. Byz.: τὰ Πορθμεῖα (?) St. Byz. has Πορθμία and Πορθμίον (sic): Σχεδιεῖον (sc. μνῆμα), Strab. 425, where some books read Σχεδίειον.

It is by no means unlikely that a more minute examination of MSS. would considerably diminish these exceptions, nearly all of which ought to be proparoxytone according to the rules given by Herodian. See Theog. Can. 127, 25; 129. 5; Arc. 121, 1-11; E. M. 533. 29.

362. NOTE 5.—The accentuation of the *temenica*, as they are called, is exceedingly capricious; as they are really nothing more than the neuters of adjectives in ειος with ἱερόν, or some such word, understood, they ought properly to be proparoxytone, but for some reason or other they are generally properispomena. In accordance with one of the leading principles of the Greek grammarians, namely, that of marking difference of meaning by difference of accent, they were perhaps distinguished from the neuter of their adjective in order to show their quasi-substantival character. For convenience sake, it has been assumed that they are properispomena, and a list of the exceptions to this rule is appended. In order, however, that the reader may form his own judgment on the matter, the following passages from Herodian and others are quoted. Theog. Can. 129. 15: Τὰ ἐπὶ τεμενῶν διὰ τοῦ ΕΙΟΝ οὐδέτερα μονογενῆ ὑπὲρ τρεῖς συλλαβὰς προπαροξύτονά τε καὶ προπερισπώμενα διὰ τῆς ΕΙ διφθόγγου γράφονται· τούτων δὲ αὐτῶν ὅσα ἀπὸ τῶν εἰς ΙΣ παράγονται τῆς γενικῆς καθαρᾶς οὔσης, μὴ φυλαττούσης τὸ σύμφωνον τῆς γενικῆς· τὰ γοῦν προπερισπώμενά εἰσι τοιαῦτα, οἷον πρυτανεῖον, Νεμεσεῖον, Σεραπεῖον· οὐ γὰρ ἐφύλαξε τὸ δ τῆς γενικῆς τοῦ Σεράπιδος· τοιοῦτο καὶ τὸ Ὀσιρεῖον, Ἀνουβεῖον, Τεκοσεῖον, Βενδίδειον δὲ προπαροξύτονον· ἐφύλαξε γὰρ τὸ δ τῆς Βενδῖδος γενικῆς· ὁμοίως καὶ τὸ Θετίδειον. προπερισπῶνται δ' ὁμοίως διὰ τῆς ΕΙ διφθόγγου γραφόμενα καὶ ὅσα ἀπὸ τῶν εἰς ΟΣ καθαρῶν, τῷ Ι παραληγομένων, κύρια καὶ κτητικά, καὶ ὅσα τῇ ΕΙ διφθόγγῳ παραλήγεται, οἷον Ἀσκληπιεῖον (Ἀσκληπιὸς γάρ), Ὀλύμπιος, Ὀλυμπιεῖον, Καπιτώλειον, Ἀμμωνιεῖον (τὸ γὰρ κτητικὸν διὰ τοῦ ῑ). οὕτω δὴ καὶ τὸ προπαροξύτονα, Πλουτώνειον, Ἡράκλειον, Ποσειδώνειον, Χαρώνειον, Αἰάκειον, Διοσκόρειον, Ἑλένειον, Κλεοπάτρειον, Τιμώνειον, Μαυσώλειον, Καισάρειον. οἷς ὅμοια καὶ ἐπὶ ἑορτῶν Μούσειον, Σεράπειον, Ἡράκλειον, Ὁμήρειον. In this passage some obvious corrections have been made. Herodian ap. Herm. de emend rat. Gr. gr. 19. p. 307: ἔτι ἁμαρτάνουσιν οἱ λέγοντες Σεραπεῖον ὡς Ἀσκληπεῖον· οὐ γάρ ἐστιν ὅμοια· ὅθεν Ἀσκληπεῖον μὲν ἐροῦμεν, Σεραπεῖον δὲ οὔ, ἀλλὰ Σεραπίδιον λόγῳ τοιούτῳ· ὅσα ἐπὶ τῆς γενικῆς διὰ τοῦ δος κλίνονται, ταῦτα καὶ ἐπὶ τοῦ κατηχητικα[1] (sic) σχήματος τὸ δ φυλάξει. ἔστιν οὖν Σέραπις, Σεράπιδος, διὰ τοῦτο καὶ Σεραπίδιον ἐροῦμεν· καὶ Ἶσις Ἴσιδος· Ἰσίδιον οὖν ἐροῦμεν, ὡς καὶ Εὐριπίδης ἀπὸ τῆς Θέτιδος Θετίδιον εἶπε·

Θετίδιον αὔδα.

Herodian ap. Herm. de emend rat. Gr. gr. 19. p. 308: ὁμοίως ἁμαρτανοῦσιν οἱ λέγοντες Διονυσεῖον, ὡς Ἀσκληπεῖον. ὅσα ἐπὶ τῆς γενικῆς ὀνόματα περισπᾶται, ταῦτα καὶ τοπικῶς σχηματιζόμενα περισπᾶται. ἐπεὶ οὖν Ἀσκληπιὸς Ἀσκληπιοῦ, Διόνυσος δὲ Διονύσου καὶ Θησεύς Θησέως, ἐπεὶ οὐ περισπᾶται, διὰ τοῦτο οὐκ ἐροῦμεν Θησεῖον οὐδὲ Διονυσεῖον, ἀλλὰ Διονύσιον καὶ Θήσειον. τὰ μέντοι διὰ τῆς αι διφθόγγου ἐκφερόμενα οὐκέτι περισπᾶται, ἀλλὰ ἀναβιβάζεται μόνον [leg. τόνον] Ἕρμαιον, Νύμφαιον. E. M. 451. 45: τὰ ἀπὸ τῶν εἰς ευς διὰ τοῦ ειον γινόμενα μονογενῆ, προπερισπᾶται, βαλανεῖον, βαφεῖον, πλὴν τοῦ Θησεύς Θήσειον. The books however are not accented in such a manner as to be consistent with any of these passages. The following exceptions to our rule occur.

363. NOTE 6.—*Temenica in* ειον. Ἀγρίππειον, Joseph. B. J. 1. 21. 1; H. D.: Ἀδριανεῖον (?) or Ἀδριάνειον, Epiphan. Panar. p. 136 B; H. D.: Αἰάκειον, Arc. 121. 17; Theog. ap. A. G. 1343; Lob. Phryn. 369: Αἰάντειον (sc. σῆμα): Ἀκαδήμειον, Suid.; Lob. Phryn. 367: Ἀμαζόνειον (ἱερόν), Harpocr.; Suid.: Ἀμμωνίειον ?) or Ἀμμωνιεῖον, Theog. Can. 129. 28: Ἀμφεῖον or Ἄμφειον,, Xenoph. Hell. 5. 4. 8; perhaps hardly a fair instance: Ἀμφιάρειον (?) or Ἀμφιαράειον, Strab. 399 ⁚ Ἀνάκειον, Schol. Lucian Conviv. c. 24; Andocid. p. 7. 10, is Ἀνακεῖον in Eust. 1119. 10; Lucian Pisc. c. 42, and elsewhere: Ἀνακτόρειον, A. G. Oxon. 2. 332. 27⁚ Ἀπολλώνειον, Eust. 270. 19: Ἀράτειον, Plut. 1. 1051: Ἀσκλήπειον or Ἀσκληπεῖον, Herodian ap. Herm. de emend. rat. Gr. gr. p. 307. 19, or Ἀσκληπιεῖον, Theog. Can. 129. 27: Ἀστάρτειον, for which Ἀσταρτεῖον also occurs: Ἀχίλλειον (?): Βενδίδειον, Lucian Icaromenipp. 24: Βερενίκειον, H. D. quote Athen. 202 D, which place does not prove this to be the correct accent: Διονύσειον is un-Attic, Διονύσιον being the proper form, Herodian ap. Herm. de emend. rat. Gr. gr. p. 308; Lob. Phryn. 368: Διοσκούρειον (or Διοσκόρειον), A. G. 1343; Arc. 121. 18: Ἑκάτειον, (sc. θῦμα, ἄγαλμα), Suid.; Aristoph. Lys. 64: Ἑλένειον, Theog. Can. 129. 31: Ἐρέχθειον, Paus. 1. 26. 5; Plut. 2. 843 F: Ἡράκλειον, Eust. 270. 19; Arc. 121. 17; Lob. Phryn. 369: Ἡρώδειον, Suid.: Ἡρώειον (sc. μνῆμα), Hesych.: Ἡφαίστειον (?) is quoted, but Ἡφαιστεῖον, Arc. 121. 18, is the better form: Θετίδειον, Theog. Can. 129. 24: Θήσειον, E. M. 451. 45; Herodian ap. A. G. Oxon. 3. 252. 16; or Θησεῖον, Chœrob. A. G. Oxon. 2. 219. 13; and such is the accent in our editions: Ἰολάειον, H. D.: Ἱπποθοώντειον, Hesych.: Ἱππολύτειον, Schol. Ambros. Odyss. Λ. 321: Ἴσειον, Plut. 2. 353 A, or Ἰσεῖον, Eust. 270. 19: Καισάρειον, Strab. 794:

---

[1] Hermann conjectures κατοχητικοῦ, which is improbable, there being no such word in the language. There can be little doubt that the true reading is κτητικοῦ; Cf. Theog. Can. 129. 26.

Καπετώλειον, Chœrob. A. G. Oxon. 2. 233. 25: Καπετώλειον, ΕΙ δίφθογγος καὶ προπαροξύνεται: Κλεοπάτρειον, Theog. Can. 129. 31: Λαμπέτειον (σῆμα), St. Byz.: Λύκειον, Theog. Can. 127. 28, is perhaps not to be considered a *temenicon*: Μαυσώλειον, Theog. Can. 129. 31: Μενελάειον, H. *D.*: Μελανίππειον, Suid.: Ὀλυμπεῖον, Theog. Can. 129. 27; St. Byz. s. v. Καπετώλιον; the books vary between Ὀλυμπίειον, Ὀλυμπιεῖον, Ὀλυμπεῖον, and Ὀλύμπιον: Ὁμήρειον, Theog. Can. 129. 33: Ὀρέστειον, Eurip. Or. 1647, etc.: Πάνθειον (or Πάνθιον, Schol. Pind. Ol. 3. 60; 8. 12): Πανδρόσειον (?): Πανεῖον, temple of Pan, and an artificial hill at Alexandria, Strab. 398: Πλουτώνειον, A. G. 1343: Ποσείδειον and Ποσειδεῖον, Eust. 270. 19, are both false for Ποσίδειον, Strab. 343, etc.: Ποσειδώνειον, A. G. 1343: Πρωτεσιλάειον, H. *D.*: Σεραπεῖον (or better Σαραπεῖον), Zonar. 1631; and this form is common enough, though condemned by A. G. Oxon. 3. 252. On Σεραπεῖον, cf. Lob. Phryn. 372: Τιμώνειον, Strab. 794.; Theog. Can. 129. 31. It is doubtful whether all the above names are really *temenica*, though every one of them has been considered to be so by some authority or other.

II. SIMPLE ADJECTIVES.

As the Greek grammarians generally mix the accentuation of substantives and adjectives together, additional authorities for any of the following sections may be supplied, if required, from the general references given in §§ 221–339.

-ΑΟΣ.

364. Adjectives in αος are oxytone, as ἀγλαός, ἀλαός, γεραός, κεραός; except ἵλαος, πρᾶος, and σάος, which retract the accent.

NOTE.—Ἀλαός is oxytone, though a compound, Arc. 38. 14: ἵλαος, Att. ἵλεως: πρᾶος or πρῷος, for πρᾷος, Arc. 36. 25; E. M. 553. 18: πρᾷος makes πραεῖα and πρᾷον in the feminine and neuter, and consequently the nominative plural is πρᾷοι or πραεῖς, πραεῖαι, πραέα: σάος (σῶς), Arc. 37. 24.

-ΒΟΣ.

365. Adjectives in βος are oxytone, as κολοβός, ῥαιβός, ῥεμβός, στραβός, στιλβός, ὑβός; except κράμβος and φοῖβος, which retract the accent.

NOTE—See Arc. 46. 2–11: Ἅβος, Doric = ἧβος or ἡβός, Theocr. 5. 109: αἶβος, Hesych.: κράμβος, Aristoph. Eq. 539; Hesych.: κύβηβος, Phot. Lex.: στόμβος, Galen Lex. Hippocr., may perhaps be a substantive: φοῖβος = καθαρός, Apollon. Lex. Hom.; Schol. Ven. T. 72.

-ΓΟΣ.

366. Adjectives in γος are oxytone, as ἀγωγός, ἀμοργός, ἀργός, γοργός; except λήθαργος, Μάγος, μάργος, and ὀλίγος paroxytone.

NOTE—Δαῦγος, Hesych.: λαίμαργος is considered by the grammarians to be a compound of λαι and μάργος: λίταργος, Suid., but it is oxytone in Chœrob. A. G.

Oxon. 2. 236. 25: **Μάγος**, see above, § 232 : **μάργος**, Arc. 46. 24; the Greek grammarians consider it to be a compound : **ὀλίγος**; the Tarentine form of this word was **ὀλίος**, Herod. π. μ. λ., 19. 23.

-ΔΟΣ.

367. Adjectives in δος are oxytone, as ἀοιδός, λορδός, μυνδός ; except μύδος=ἄφωνος, Hesych., and φροῦδος=πρόοδος, which is regular as a compound, Arc. 47. 26.

-ΕΟΣ.

368. Adjectives in εος retract the accent, as αἰθάλεος, ἀνάπλεως, ἀργύρεος, δαιδάλεος, Ἑκτόρεος, θέλεος, κήλεος, μέλεος, νέος, Νηστόρεος, πλέος, τέλεος, χρύσεος, except—

1. Hypertrisyllables in λεος (both simple and *compound*) where λ does not belong to the root of the word; all such are paroxytone, as ἀζα-λέος, ἀρπα-λέος, θαρσαλέος, κραται-λέος, καταλευγαλέος, σμερδαλέος, but αἰθάλεος (αἰθάλ-η), δαιδάλεος (δαίδαλ-ος), θέλεος ·(θέλ-ω), because in them λ belongs to the word from which they are formed.

2. Verbals in τεος, which are paroxytone, as ἀσκητέος, γραπτέος, διαλεκτέος, λεκτέος, πειρατέος, πρακτέος, συνεκποτέος, Arc. 38. 21.

3. Ionic forms in εος=ος, which take the accent of the corresponding form in ος, as ἀλεός (ἀλός), δαφοινεός (δαφοινός), ἠλεός (ἠλός), χήνεος (χήνειος), but ἀργύφεος (ἄργυφος).

4. The possessive pronouns ἐός, τεός, Dor.=σός, oxytone.

Adjectives in εος contract into οῦς, as ἀργύρεος ἀργυροῦς, μολύβεος μολυβοῦς, χάλκεος χαλκοῦς.

369. Note 1.—*Words in* λέος. Herod. π. μ. λ. 4. 7; Theog. A. G. Oxon. 51. 8; Arc. 38. 24: τὰ διὰ τοῦ ΑΛΕΟΣ παράγωγα ὑπὲρ τρεῖς συλλαβάς ἐστι καὶ παροξύνεται, χωρὶς εἰ μὴ ἔνδειαν ἔχῃ τοῦ Ι ἀπὸ κτητικοῦ ὀνόματος, οἷον· νηφαλέος αὐαλέος σμερδαλέος θαρσαλέος. πρόσκειται εἰ μὴ ἔχῃ ἔνδειαν τοῦ Ι ἀπὸ κτητικοῦ ὀνόματος διὰ τὸ δαιδάλειος δαιδάλεος, κονισάλειος κονισάλεος: αἰθαλέος, Philem. Lex. p. 22. § 54: αἰθάλεος. τοῦτο διαφέρει· πρὸ μιᾶς γὰρ ἔχει τὸν τόνον, καὶ πρὸ δύο. πρὸ μιᾶς γὰρ ὑπάρχει ἀπὸ τοῦ αἴθω, ὡς νήφω, νηφαλέος. ἡνίκα δὲ πρὸ δύο ἔχει τὸν τόνον, ἀπὸ τοῦ αἰθάλειος γέγονε, κατὰ ἀποβολὴν τοῦ ῑ. ὡς παρὰ ᾿Απολλωνίῳ [Apollon. Rhod. 4. 777], αἰθάλεοι πρηστῆρες; cf. E. M. 261. 50; Chœrob. A. G. Oxon. 2. 195. 18: ἐρευθαλέος is sometimes erroneously ἐρευθάλεος (ἐρευθ-ος); thus also ἠθάλεος for ἠθαλέος: ὑαλέος is also a mistake for ὑάλεος, of which ὑέλεος is a later form.

370. Note 2.—*Ionic forms in* εος=ος. ᾿Αλεός (ἀλός), Herod. π. μ. λ. 4. 19, is ἄλεος in E. M. 59. 45: ἀφνεός (ἀφνός, ἀφνειός), Eust. 1769. 52: **δαφοινεός**

(δαφοινός), Eust. 1160. 52; Schol. Ven. Σ. 538: ἐνεός (ἐνός), Theog. Can. 50. 13, for which ἐννεός also occurs: ἐτεός (ἐτός), Theog. Can. 50. 31; Arc. 38. 22; Joh. Alex. 29. 5: ἠλεός (ἠλός): κανεός (?) Theog. Can. 50. 13: κενεός (κενός), Theog. Can. 51. 6: κηδεός, cf. Schol. Ven. Ψ. 169: κηλεός, Schol. Ven. Θ. 217, but commonly proparoxytone, Arc. 44. 8: στερεός: φηγίνεος = φήγινος, *fagineus*, Anth. Pal. 6. 33: φλεγεός, a false form for φλόγεος: χήνεος, Ion.=χήνειος, Herodot. 2. 37; on the redundance of the ε in these forms, see Eust. 223. 43; 247. 32; 1160. 52; 1443. 62; Schol. Ven. Σ. 538.

371. NOTE 3.—Ἀγωρέος (?) Hesych., certainly a false accent: ἰός, Arc. 179. 25; cf. Arc. 38. 4: καρχαρέος, E. M. 493. 1, is certainly false for καρχάρεος or καρχαλέος: κύδεος (?) probably false for κήδεος: παλεός = παλαιός: σεός (?) and τεός, Dor. = σός: ταραβέος, if it occurs, is probably false for ταρβάρεος or ταρβαλέος: ψωδαρέος, Hesych., 'ex ψωραλέον corruptum esse conjecit Ruhnken.' H. *D.*

-ΖΟΣ.

372. Adjectives in ζος are oxytone, as πεζός, πρωϊζός, χθιζός.

NOTE.—Ὄβρυζος, Schol. Thucyd. 2. 13. 5: ὄλιζος, Eust. 1643. 1: ἔτι ἰστέον καὶ ὅτι τὸ ὀλίγον ὄλιζον καθ' Ἡρακλείδην Ἴωνες φασὶ οἱ νεώτεροι: Eust. 1160. 16: ἐν δὲ ῥητορικῷ λεξικῷ Αἰλίου Διονυσίου φέρεται καὶ ὄλιον τὸ ὀλίγον. φησὶ γάρ· ὀλίγον. τὸ δὲ ὄλιον ἢ βάρβαρον ἢ Ἰακόν. τοῦ δὲ ὀλίζου ἡ χρῆσις καὶ παρὰ Λυκόφρονι· δοκεῖ δὲ ἡ λέξις Αἰολέων εἶναι. διὸ καὶ προπαροξύνεται τὸ ὄλιζον οὐ τονούμενον κατὰ τὸ ὀλίγον; but it is the neuter of ὀλίζων, H. *D.*: πρωϊζός (πρῶζος) is false for πρωϊζός, Arc. 48. 23; both these words are made oxytone by Eust. 225. 42; Göttling Accent. p. 306 remarks that πρωΐζ' ὅτ' ἐς Αὐλίδα in Hom. Il. 2. 203 is false for πρωΐζ' ὅτε, and that πρώιζον and πρῷζον are found in E. M. 691; A. G. 295. 27; though there can be no question that such accents are utterly erroneous.

-ΗΟΣ.

373. Adjectives in ηος are oxytóne, as αἰζηός, Ἀχηός, εὐνηός, παληός.

NOTE.—Αἰζηός is oxytone, though αἴζήιος is proparoxytone, Herodian ap. Theog. Can. 57. 15: Παληός and Ἀχηός (or Ἀχηός, Theog. Can. 51. 18) are Bœotian forms; E. M. 32. 6: κοιρανῆος, Stob. Flor. 7. 13, is contracted from κοιρανήιος.

-ΘΟΣ.

374. Adjectives in θος are oxytone, as ἀγαθός, αἰθός, βοηθός, ἐφθός, ξανθός, ὀλισθός, ὀρθός, τιτθός, τυτθός; except ἀκόλουθος proparoxytone, νόθος paroxytone, and the properispomenon λοῖσθος.

NOTE.—Schol. Ven. B. 311: Ἀκόλουθος, probably a compound: κόμαιθος, Lycoph. 924, is a compound: λοῖσθος is merely a shorter form of λοίσθιος, Arc. 49. 14: νόθος, Arc. 49. 9, where it is obvious that παροξύνεται should be read for ὀξύνεται: παναιθός was the common accent, but Euphranor wrote πάναιθος, Schol. Ven. Ξ. 372: ψαίνυθος may be implied by the adverb ψαίνυθα used by Lycoph. 1420.

-ΙΟΣ.

375. Adjectives in ιος retract the accent, as ἅγιος, ἄγριος, ἀγώνιος, ἀίδιος, αἰζήϊος, αἰφνίδιος, ἅλιος, ἄξιος, δῖος, ἴδιος, ἰήϊος; ἴος, νήπιος, Κιλίκιος, Ῥόδιος, Σαλαμίνιος, Χῖος ; except βαλιός, δεξιός, λαλιός, μονιός, πελιός, πολιός, σκολιός, oxytone, and ἀντίος, μυρίοι, *countless numbers,* πλησίος, paroxytone ; ἀντίος retains its accent in composition, as ἐναντίος, ὑπεναντίος, but the compounds of πλησίος are regular, as παραπλήσιος.

On the accentuation of these words, see Arc. 39. 15–41. 27.

376. NOTE I.—*Oxytones.* Βαλιός, Theog. Can. 57. 32 ; Eust. 1190. 12 : καὶ ὅρα ὅτι τὰ μὲν ἐπίθετα ξανθὸς καὶ βαλιὸς ὀξυτόνως, τὰ δὲ οἷον κύρια βαρύνεται πρὸς διαστολήν ; the adjective is, however, frequently barytone in the later writers : δεξιός, Theog. Can. 58. 4 : ἐψιός, A. G. Oxon. 2. 322. 25 ; Arc. 41. 15 : Ἰλλυριός, see above, § 248 : λαλιός, Theog. Can. 57. 32 ; Arc. 41. 3 : μνιός, ὁ ἀπαλός, E. M. 472. 46 ; perhaps a substantive : μονιός = μόνος, Eust. 772. 59 ; Theog. Can. 55. 19, 'scribitur vero μονιός oxytonωs ap. Hesychium, Photium, Suid. et Eust. Od. p. 1409. 61, item ap. Lucian. et in Fabulis Æsopi et præcipitur a Moschop. Π. σχεδ. p. 215 fin. : μόνιος autem proparoxytonωs apud Callim. ubi accentum mutavit Ernest. et ejus schol.,' H. *D.* ; but μούνιος seems to be regular : πελιός, Eust. 869. 62 ; Theog. Can. 57. 32 ; Arc. 41. 3 : πολιός, Theog. Can. 57. 32 ; the neuter of this is used substantively in E. M. 680. 40, but is proparoxytone to distinguish it from the adjective ; cf. Nicand. Ther. 64, where the scholiast says, τονοῦται δὲ καὶ πόλιον καὶ πολιόν· ἄμεινον δὲ τὸ πόλιον, ἵνα μὴ ᾖ ὡς ἐπίθετον : σκολιός, Theog. Can. 57. 32 ; σποδιός (?) Athen. 394 A, where formerly σποδίος was read ; σπόδιος is probably a better accent ; cf. Theog. Can. 54. 20 : τιός, Bœot. = τεός, Apoll. de Pron. 135 A : τροχιός, Anth. Pal. 6. 258 : φαλιός, Theog. Can. 57. 32 ; Arc. 41. 4, is very commonly proparoxytone.

377. NOTE 2.—*Paroxytones.* Ἀντίος, Theog. Can. 58. 20 ; Apoll. de Adv. 596. 16 : παρὰ τὸ ἀγχοῦ δύναται γεγενῆσθαι τὸ ἀγχός, προσλαβὸν τὴν ἐν πρόθεσιν κατὰ παρολκήν, ὡς ἔχει τὸ ἐναλίγκιος, ἐναντίος, ἐνέπειν· αἱ δὴ τοιαῦται τῶν προθέσεων παρελκόμεναι, καθάπερ πλεονάσματα οὖσαι, οὔτε τάσιν οὔτε ἄλλο τι τῶν παρεπομένων ἐναλλάσσουσι. καὶ γὰρ τὸ ἐναντίος οὐκ ἀνεβίβαζε τὸν τόνον, ὀφεῖλον. εἴπερ οὖν σύνθετον, τί οὐ συμμεταβάλλει τὸ γένος ; ὅπερ ἴδιον συνθέσεως : the compounds (or decompounds) κατεναντίος, ὑπεναντίος, are also paroxytone : ὀλίος, Tarent. = ὀλίγος, Herod. π. μ. λ. 19. 25 ; E. M. 621. 51 : μύριος, Ammon. p. 96 : Μύριοι, ἐπὶ ἀριθμοῦ· Μυρίοι δέ, οἱ πολλοί : Arc. 41. 21 : μύριος ὁ ὡρισμένος ἀριθμός· μυρίος ὁ ἀόριστος : Theog. Can. 58. 9 : Μύριος ἡ τῶν δέκα χιλιάδων ἀπαρίθμησις· ἐπὶ γὰρ τοῦ ἀορίστου παροξύνεται ὁμοίως καὶ τὸ νυμφίος καὶ νύμφιος, Herod. π. μ. λ. 19. 33 : πλησίος, Arc. 41. 14, is erroneously πλήσιος in E. M. 156. 21 : παραπλήσιος, E. M. 531. 50.

-ΑΙΟΣ.

378. Dissyllabic adjectives in αιος are oxytone ; those of more than two syllables properispomena, as Ἀθηναῖος, Αἰγαῖος, ἀμοιβαῖος, ἀναγκαῖος, ἀρουραῖος, ἀρχαῖος, βαιός, Γαζαῖος, γενναῖος, Ἑρμαῖος, ἡσυχαῖος, Ἡραῖος, Ἱμεραῖος, κνεφαῖος, κορυφαῖος, λαιός, Μουσαῖος, πηγαῖος, πυγμαῖος, πυλαῖος, Ῥωμαῖος, σκαιός, σπουδαῖος, φαιός, Χαλδαῖος, ὡραῖος ; except 1. oxytone, ἀραιός, *thin,* Ἀχαιός, γεραιός, γηραιός, δηναιός, ἠβαιός, κραταιός, παλαιός ; 2. proparoxytone, βέβαιος, βίαιος, γύναιος, δείλαιος, δίκαιος, μάταιος; and 3. properispomenon, γραῖος for γεραιός.

379. Note 1.—*Oxytones.* Cf. Arc. 37. 4; 42. 28-44. 5 : 'Ακμάος, Æolic for ἀκμαῖος, is so written in Grammat. Meermann p. 661, ed. Schäfer : ἁλαιός (?) = ἀλαός : ἁλαιός = παλαιός, Æschyl. Frag. 425 ed. Didot, should probably be ἀλεός : ἁραιός = ὁ μὴ πυκνός, Arc. 44. 5, but ἀραῖος from ἀρά is regular : 'Αχαιός, Arc. 43. 19 : βαλαιός, Hesych. : γεραιός, Theog. Can. 52. 17 : γηραιός, Arc. 44. 4, but the compound καταγήραιος, if indeed a genuine form, seems to be proparoxytone : δηναιός, E. M. 417. 29 : ἠβαιός, E. M. 417. 29 : 'Ηραῖος, Schol. Ven. Λ. 301 : κραταιός, Arc. 44. 5; Theog. Can. 52. 17 : παλαιός (παλαιόρ or παλεόρ, Doric, Aristoph. Lys. 988); Arc. 43. 27 ; Herod. π. μ. λ. 4. 19.

380. Note 2.—*Proparoxytones.* 'Αγέλαιος, *common* : ἀγελαῖος, *belonging to the herd*, Eust. 1752. 61 : ἀγελαῖος μέν, ὁ ἐξ ἀγέλης· ἀγέλαιος δὲ κατὰ τοὺς παλαιοὺς προπαροξυτόνως ὁ ἀμαθής, thus also Suid. and others ; this distinction is to be found in many of the grammarians, but probably it has little or no foundation in fact; ἀγελαῖος is best in both significations. An equally vain distinction between ἀγόραιος ὁ πονηρὸς καὶ ἐν ἀγορᾷ τεθραμμένος and ἀγοραῖος ὁ ἐν ἀγορᾷ τιμώμενος is also drawn by some authors : ἀγόραιος, *in foro educatus* : ἀγοραῖος, *forensis*, Philop. According to Ammon. : ἀγόραιος, ἐὰν προπαροξυτόνως, σημαίνει τὸν πονηρὸν τὸν ἐν ἀγορᾷ τεθραμμένον· ἐὰν δὲ προπερισπωμένως σημαίνει τὸν ἐν ἀγορᾷ τιμώμενον· According to Zonar. 19 : ἀγοραῖος προπερισπώμενος, οἱ ἐν ἀγορᾷ ἀναστρεφόμενοι ἄνθρωποι : ἀγόραιος δὲ προπαροξυτόνως, ἡ ἡμέρα ἐν ᾗ ἡ ἀγορὰ τελεῖται : ἀγοραῖος in both meanings is the best and most usual accent : 'Αιγαῖος, for this Αἴγαιος is said to be found, though very rarely ; see Lob. Ajax 219 : 'Αμφίβαιος, a name of Neptune, is of course a compound : βέβαιος, Arc. 44. 3 ; Theog. Can. 53. 24 : βίβλαιος (?) Chœrob. E. 136. 2 : βίαιος, Theog. Can. 53. 9 ; Chœrob. E. 60. 3 : γύναιος, Hom. : δείλαιος, Arc. 43. 14 ; Theog. Can. 52. 25 : δίκαιος, Chœrob. E. 60 3 ; E. M. 198. 54 : κεφάλαιος is given in the lexicons as proparoxytone, but it seems somewhat doubtful whether it occurs as an adjective : ληθαῖος, this is proparoxytone in Orph. Lith. 195, *H. D.*, but probably is an error : Λυαῖος, Theog. Can. 53. 3 ; λύαια (*sic*) παύσιμα, Theog. Can. 22. 2 : μάταιος, Arc. 44. 2 ; Theog. Can. 53. 24 : μέσαιος is doubtful for μεσαῖος, cf. Athen. 95 A. ibiq. Schweigh. : ῥούσαιος, Georg. Cedren. p. 19, H. *D.*; probably false for ῥούσιος : τύχαιος (?) τυχαῖος is a better accent : χάϊος is regular as a proparoxytone, since αι does not form a diphthong.

-ΕΙΟΣ.

381. Adjectives in ειος retract the accent, as Αἰάντειος, 'Αλεξάνδρειος, βασίλειος, βρότειος, γέγειος,, δεσπότειος, δούλειος, ἔτειος, ἡμετέρειος, θεῖος, θήρειος, 'Ιππάρχειος, Κεῖος, Κρήτειος, λεῖος, λύκειος, 'Ομήρειος, πλεῖος, Τεῖος, τέλειος, χήνειος, χρεῖος, χρύσειος; except 1. properispomenon, ἀγρεῖος, ἀνδρεῖος, ἀστεῖος, 'Αργεῖος, ἀχρεῖος, *Homeric*, ἄχρειος, *Attic* Βακχεῖος, γυναικεῖος, ἐλεγεῖος, ἑταιρεῖος, ἠθεῖος, 'Ηλεῖος, θεμιστεῖος (and θεμίστειος), Καδμεῖος, λοχεῖος, μαντεῖος, μουσεῖος, νυμφεῖος, ὀθνεῖος, οἰκεῖος ; 2. oxytone, ἀφνειός, φατειός, with θαμειός and ταρφειός.

382. Note 1.—*Properispomena.* Cf. Arc. 37. 16; Lob. Ajax 93. sqq. : ἀγρεῖος, E. M. 13. 24 : ἀγχεῖος, Zonar. 21 : Αἰάντειος, Chœrob. A. G. Oxon. 2. 174. 2 is a clerical error for Αἰάντειος, Arc. 45. 2 : αἰγεῖος, Chœrob. A. G. Oxon. 2. 174. 2 seems to be always αἴγειος : ἀκατεῖος (?) Arc. 45. 6 ; Fix ap. H. D. suggests Ἑκατεῖος : ἀλεῖος, *crammed* ; also Dor. = Ἠλεῖος : ἀνδρεῖος, Eust. 217. 40 ; A. G. Oxon. 2. 196. 1 ; Chœrob. E. 123. 25 : ἀνθρωπεῖος, Chœrob. A. G. Oxon. 2. 174. 2, yet it is always proparoxytone : Ἀργεῖος, Eust. 217. 40 ; Theodos. Gramm. 73. 11 ; Schol. Ven. B. 269 ; A. G. Oxon. 2. 288. 20 : ἀρχεῖος (?) *L. S.* : ἀστεῖος, Theodos. Gramm. 73. 11 ; Chœrob. E. 123. 24 : ἀχρεῖος, Homeric ; ἄχρειος, old Attic ; Eust. 217. 40 ; Schol. Ven. B. 269 ; A. G. Oxon. 2. 284. 19 ; Arc. 87. 6 : ἄχρειος τὸ κοινόν, ἀχρεῖος δὲ τὸ Ἀττικόν : Chœrob. E. 123. 25 merely mentions ἀχρεῖος : Βακχεῖος, Chœrob. E. 123. 25 ; Theodos. Gram. 73. 11 : γιγαντεῖος (?) H. D. have γιγάντειος : γοργεῖος (?) H. D. have γόργειος only : γυναικεῖος, Arc. 45. 6 : δειρεῖος (?) Hesych. : Δηλεῖος, A. G. Oxon. 2. 288. 21 : δηρεῖος, E. M. 248. 31 : ἑρκεῖος, also ἕρκειος (which is the usual accent), Eust. 1930. 28 ; Schol. Ven. Φ. 471 : ἑταιρεῖος, Arc. 45. 6 ; Eust. 1930. 28 ; Chœrob. A. G. Oxon. 2. 198. 24, though some wrote ἑταίρειος : ἠθεῖος, Arc. 44. 8 ; E. M. 422. 21 ; so Aristarchus, Schol. Ven. Z. 518 : Ἦλεῖος, Arc. 44. 8 ; St. Byz. s. v. Ἦλις : Ἡρακλεῖος, Philop. : θεμιστεῖος, Schol. Pind. Olymp. 1. 18 ; Herodian wrote θεμίστειος, but usage made it properispomenon : θυννεῖος seems false for θύννειος, cf. Athen. 116 E ; Aristoph. Eq. 354 : ἰαμβεῖος only occurs as a neuter, ἰαμβεῖον, which is sometimes falsely written ἰάμβειον : ἰκνεῖος, an adjective (?), Hesych. : Καδμεῖος, Chœrob. A. G. Oxon. 2. 173. 31 ; Theodos. Gramm. 73. 12 : Καρνεῖος, Callim. in Apoll. 71, or Κάρνειος, Schol. Theocr. 5. 83 ; Thucyd. 5. 75, etc., is Καρνειός in MS. of Hesych. : κυνεῖος, Chœrob. A. G. Oxon. 2. 174. 2, yet it seems to be always written κύνειος in the books ; it appears to be expressly made proparoxytone in A. G. Oxon. 1. 373. 15 : Λελεγεῖος (?) *Pape* : λοχεῖος, probably a false accent ; none of the passages quoted in the lexicons prove that the word is properispomenon : μαντεῖος, E. M. 248. 31 : μεγαλεῖος, Arc. 45. 6 : Μεναν- δρεῖος (?) the word is Μενάνδρειος in Lucian Amor. c. 43 : μουσεῖος (?) Anth. Pal. 9. 372. 6, which is quoted by H. D. for this accent proves nothing ; the word is proparoxytone in Eurip. Bacch. 410 : νομαδεῖος (?) and νομάδειος : νυμφεῖος, Anth. Pal. 7. 188. 7, but the word is proparoxytone, Auth. Pal. 7. 507. 3 : οἰκεῖος, Schol. Ven. Z. 518 : ὀξεῖος (?) : ὀχεῖος (?) : παιδεῖος, Arc. 44. 18, is proparoxytone in Plat. Legg. 747 B and elsewhere : Πανεῖος (?) H. D. have only Πάνειος, which is no doubt correct : παρθενεῖος, Schol. Aristoph. Av. 918, but almost everywhere else it is παρθένειος : Ἡρσεῖος (?) H. D. quote Eurip. Hel. 1480, which proves nothing ; the word is doubtless regular : Πηλεῖος (?) : πληγεῖος = παλαιός (?) Hesych. : πρα- σεῖος (?) Pollux 10. 42 : πρυτανεῖος, Arc. 45. 6 : σπονδεῖος, but Σπονδειός, a proper name, Arc. 44. 17 : δισπόνδειος, Hermog. de Ideis, p. 231 = Tom. 2. p. 296. 8. ed. Spengel, is written δισπονδεῖος in Aristid. Quint. p. 48 ; H. D. : σπερμεῖος, H. D., almost certainly a mistake : Ταρπεῖος (?) *H. D.* : τυμβεῖος (?) *L. S.*, but H. D. have only τύμβειος : φυλλεῖος (?) seemingly occurs only as τὸ φυλλεῖον : χορεῖος is quoted by H. D. from Ælian N. A. 2. 11 ; but there it is rightly proparoxytone, though it is χόρειος in Athen. 618 C.

383. NOTE 2.—*Oxytones.* Ἀλειός = πένης, Hesych. : ἀμβλειός is an altogether erroneous form, destitute of any authority : ἀφνειός, Chœrob. A. G. Oxon. 2. 174. 34 : θαμειός, Aristarchus ; θαμεῖος, Pamphilus ; S. V. A. 52 : ὀλειός = ὀλοιός occurs in E. M. 622. 25 : ταμειός (?) : ταρφειός, Aristarchus ; ταρφεῖος, Pamphilus. ; S. V. A. 52 ; Dionys. Thrax derived θαμεῖαι and ταρφεῖαι from θαμύς and ταρφύς, but the accentuation of Aristarchus has been generally adopted, cf. Schol. Ven. Λ. 69 ; M. 158 ; T. 357 : φατειός, Arc. 44. 28.

-ΟΙΟΣ.

384. Dissyllables in οιος are oxytone, as γλοιός, δοιός, κροιός, σμοιός, σκοιός ; except the interrogative pronominals, as ποῖος (κοῖος), which, together with τοῖος, οἶος, οἷος, and polysyllables, are properispomena, as ἀλλοῖος, αἰδοῖος, παντοῖος, ἑτεροῖος ; except ὀλοιός oxytone, and ὁμοῖος, γελοῖος, which are proparoxytone in the later Attic.

385. Note—Arc. 37. 11 ; 45. 8 ; Schol. in Dionys. Thrac. 678. 16 ; E. M. 224. 40 : οἶος, Arc. 37. 11 : ποιός, *of some kind*, is oxytone, ποῖος, *of what kind ?* properispomenon : ἄμοιος (?) Sicilian = κακός, Hesych. : γελοῖος : ' De accentu autem v. γελοῖος vel γέλοιος magna est veterum magistrorum dissensio. Apollon. De pronou. p. 323 : οὐκ ἐξωμάλισται τὰ τῶν διαλέκτων, μάλιστα δὲ τὰ τῶν Ἀττικῶν. Ὅμοιος καὶ γέλοιος προπαροξύνοντές φασιν, ἀλλ' οὐκέτι τὰ τούτοις παραπλήσια. Contra ap. Arcad. p. 45. 10, γελοῖος simpliciter inter properispomena enumeratur. Mœris, p. 109 : Γέλοιον, βαρυτόνως, Ἀττικῶς· γελοῖον, προπερισπωμένως, Ἑλληνικῶς. Quocum consentit Schol. Aristoph. Ran. 6 addito, ἡ δὲ σημασία ἡ αὐτή. Contra Etym. M. p. 224. 39, postquam ostendit adjectiva trisyllaba in οιος properispomena esse, οἱ δὲ μεταγενέστεροι τῶν Ἀττικῶν, inquit, τὸ γελοῖος καὶ ὁμοῖος προπαροξύνουσιν, οὐκ εὖ· γέλοιος λέγεται ὁ γέλωτος ἄξιος, γελοῖος δὲ ὁ γελωτοποιός. Idem discrimen statuit Ammon. p. 36 et a plerisque statui tradit Eustath. p. 205 extr. ex Ælio Dionysio, qui tamen addiderat videri omnino veteres Atticos hujusmodi adjectiva ὁμοῖον ἑτοῖμον γελοῖον pronunciasse. In Etym. autem MS. Trajectino praeceptum illud sic invertitur : Γέλοιος προπαροξυτόνως μὲν λέγεται ὁ γελωποιός (sic), προπερισπωμένως δὲ ὁ γέλωτος ἄξιος, quam lectionem sequitur Thom. M. p. 185 nisi quod de neutro genere sic praecipit : Γελοῖον δὲ οὐδετέρως μόνον τὸ γέλωτος ἄξιον. Non minor in codd. scripturæ discrepantia est, modo γέλοιος modo γελοῖος exhibentibus : vid. Schneid. ad Plat. de Rep. vol. 2. p. 14. Ad haec accedit tertia τόνωσις γελοιὸς cujus memoriam Eustath. servavit p. 906. 51 (ex Philopono) et p. 1967. 24 : Γελοῖος μὲν ὁ καταγέλαστος προπερισπωμένως, γελοιὸς δὲ ὀξυτόνως ὁ γελωτυποιός, et iisdem verbis Grammat. ap. Montef. in Bibl. Coisl. p. 470 ; qui quum pleraque omnia cum Suida communia habeat, non omittendum ap. Suidam non ὀξυτόνως legi sed προπαροξυτόνως, omninoque vereor ne oxytonum istud γελοιός recentiorum errore sit grammaticorum, qui negligenter ad ultimum vocabuli syllabam retulissent quod antiquior aliquis dixerat primum ὀξύνεσθαι : quomodo Eustathius ipse loquitur p. 205 extr.,' L. Dindorf ap. H. D. : ὀλοιός, but ὀλοΐος and ὀλώϊος are regular : ὁμοῖος, old Attic : ὅμοιος, late Attic, Eust. 341. 17 ; 1817. 15 ; Theog. Can. 54. 3. In A. G. 678. 18 the latter is merely called Attic, as contrasted with the Homeric accent. According to Schweighæuser the best MSS. of Herodotus have ὁμοῖος : πάροιος, Hesych. : τραπέζοιος, a Bœotian form, Theog. Can. 53. 30 : ψοθοιός, ὁ ἀκάθαρτος, Theog. Can. 53. 28.

-ΥΙΟΣ.

386. Those in υιος retract the accent, as πήχυιος, τριπήχυιος ; except the oxytone γυιός.

Note.—Ἰδυῖος (?) an old word = *witness*, Eust. 1154. 35 ; 1158. 20 ; 1570. 40, may perhaps be regarded as an adjective.

-ΚΟΣ.

387. Adjectives in κος are oxytone, as βοεικός, γλαυκός, Γραικός, γραμματικός, δαφνιακός, Δηλιακός, ἰαμβικός, Ἰλιακός, Κορινθιακός, κτητικός, κωμικός, λευκός, Λιβυκός, λογικός, Λυδιακός,

Πυθαγορικός, ῥοικός, φιλικός, φυσικός, χρονικός, ψυχικός; except
1. pronominals in ικος, which are paroxytone, as ἡλίκος, πηλίκος,
τηλίκος, ὁπηλίκος (Arc. 52. 6): 2. ἄγροικος, ἄρεσκος, σόλοικος,
which are proparoxytone: and 3. θρῆσκος, σῶκος properispomena.

388. NOTE.—Ἄγροικος in all significations is proparoxytone in Attic according
to Thomas Magister (quoted below); the Common dialect distinguished ἀγροῖκος
from ἄγροικος, but the evidence is so conflicting that it is impossible to say what
exact meaning it assigned to each. 'De accentu lites sunt inter Grammaticos
. . . . Zonar.: 'Αγροῖκος· ὁ ἀμαθής, 'Άγροικος· ὁ ἐν τῷ ἀγρῷ αὐλιζόμενος. Ammon.:
'Αγροῖκος καὶ ἄγροικος διαφέρει, προπερισπωμένως μὲν ὁ ἐν ἀγρῷ κατοικῶν, προπαροξυτόνως δὲ ὁ σκαιὸς τοὺς τρόπους. "Ptol. Ascal. s. potius, qui antiquum nomen
mentitur, recentioris ævi magistellus, ab Ammonio diversus abit § 7; "Αγροικος
βαρύτονον, ὁ ἐν ἀγροῖς διατρίβων· ἀγροῖκος δὲ προπερισπώμενον, ὁ μὴ ἥμερος. Secundum communem Gr. sermonis dialectum distinxit Noster, uti e Thoma M. licet
æstimare: ('Αγροῖκος, ὁ ἐν τῷ ἀγρῷ οἰκῶν, παρὰ τοῖς Ἕλλησιν ἁπλῶς· ἄγροικος δέ,
ὁ ἰδιώτης καὶ ἀπαίδευτος· οἱ 'Αττικοὶ δὲ ἐπὶ τοῦ ἐν τῷ ἀγρῷ οἰκοῦντος, καὶ ἐπὶ τοῦ
ἰδιώτου, καὶ ἀπαιδεύτου καὶ ἀναισθήτου, προπαροξυτόνως ἄγροικος λέγουσιν. 'Αριστο-
φάνης ἐν Πλούτῳ· 705: Λέγεις ἄγροικον ἄρα σύ γ᾽ εἶναι τὸν θεόν· ἤγουν ἀναίσθητον.
Καὶ πάλιν ἐν Νεφέλαις· 46: Ἔπειτ᾽ ἔγημα Μεγακλέους τοῦ Μεγακλέους 'Αδελφιδῆν,
ἀγροῖκος [?] ὤν, ἐξ ἄστεος· ἤγουν ἐν τῷ ἀγρῷ οἰκῶν). Judicium Jungermanni ad
Poll. 9. 12, p. 982, certi quid de accentu vix proferri posse existimantis considerari
inprimis meretur." Valck. Eran. Philo: 'Αγροικος βαρυτόνως, καὶ ἀγροῖκος, προπερισπωμένως διαφέρει. Άγροικος μὲν γάρ, ὁ γνώσεως ἄμοιρος, ἢ ὁ ἐν τῷ ἀγρῷ οἰκῶν·
ἀγροῖκος δὲ προπερισπωμένως, ὁ μὴ ἥμερος, ἴσος τῷ ἄγριος. Lex. ap. Hermann, Gr.
Gramm. 328: Άγροικος· ὁ ἐν ἀγροῖς διατρίβων, ἀγροῖκος δὲ ὁ ἀπαίδευτος. Lex.
Rhetor. post Phot. p. 664, Porson: 'Αγροικος, ὁ ἀμαθής· ἀγροῖκος, ὁ ἐν ἀγρῷ
αὐλιζόμενος· Πλάτων δὲ τὸ ἐναντίον τούτου. Etym. Gudian.: Άγροικος καὶ
ἀγροῖκος, διαφορά (1. διάφορα)· Άγροικος μὲν ὁ ἀμαθὴς καὶ ἀπαίδευτος· ἀγροῖκος δὲ ὁ
μὴ ἥμερος, ἀλλ᾽ ἴσως (malim ἴσος τῷ e Philon.) ἄγριος ἢ ἐν ἀγρῷ διαιτώμενος. Cfr.
Eran. Philon. h. v.; Steph. Byz. s. v. 'Αγρός—Καὶ συνθέτως ἄγροικος καὶ ἀγροῖκος.
Alia vid. ap. Kulenk. ad Ammon. p. 5 ed Lips;' *Fix* ap. H. D.; the books are as
inconsistent as the grammarians: δαῦκος, Hesych.: θρῆσκος (?) cf. Theog. Can.
14. 31: πέρκος is a doubtful form for περκνός; in Arist. H. A. 9. 36. 1, quoted
by L. S., it is a substantive, or at least is used as one: μαίμαρκος (?) Arc. 51. 12:
σόλοικος, Arc. 51. 20: σῶκος, Philem. Lex. p. 85. § 213; Tyrannion oxytoned it
to distinguish it from the proper name Σῶκος, Eust. 1197. 40; Arc. 50. 4 seems
to imply that the adjective is oxytone, and yet in l. 23 he says that adjectives in
ωκος are not oxytone: according to Schol. Ven. T. 72 σῶκος is the proper accent.

-ΛΟΣ.

389. Adjectives in λος are oxytone, as Αἰτωλός, ἁμαρτηλός,
ἁπαλός, ἀπατηλός, δειλός, ἐσθλός, Θεσσαλός, 'Ιταλός, καλός, ὀλός,
ὁμαλός, πολλός, σιγηλός, στρεβλός, τραυλός, τυφλός, ὑψηλός,
φειδωλός, χθαμαλός, χωλός, ψωλός; except 1. ἀείδελος, ἄλλος,
ἀσύφηλος, ἀτάσθαλος, βέβηλος, δαίδαλος, δείελος, δῆλος, δοῦλος,
εἴκελος, (θέσκελος), ἔκηλος, ἔκπαγλος, ἐρύγμηλος, ἔωλος, ἴζαλος,
κάπηλος, κίβδηλος, κόβαλος, κοῖλος, κόλος, λάλος, μάχλος, ὅλος,

οὖλος, πέτηλος, σαῦλος, and φαῦλος, which retract the accent: 2. paroxytone, αἰόλος with those in ἴλος and ὕλος, as αἱμύλος, γογγύλος, κωτίλος, ποικίλος, στρογγύλος, φίλος, but ἀήσυλος αἴσυλος, are proparoxytone, and παχυλός oxytone.

390. Note 1.—'Αείδελος, Arc. 55. 7: ἀίδηλος is a compound adjective, and therefore proparoxytone: αἴθαλος, Nicand. Ther. 659: αἴκολος (?) Hesych.: ἀκαλός, E. M. 44. 29, is sometimes ἄκαλος, but wrongly: ἄλλος, Schol. Ven. Π. 234; A. G. Oxon. 1. 70. 11: ἀμάνδαλος, Æolic, Alcæus 97; L. S.: ἄρδαλος (?), L. S.; according to Arc. 54. 17 those in αλος with a long antepenultimate are proparoxytone, except Θεσσαλός, and the rule is generally true: βέβηλος, Theog. Can. 62. 2; Schol. Ven. Σ. 580: γάγγαλος (?) Hesych.: γοιδοῦλος and γοδοῦλος (?) Hesych.: δαίδαλος, Arc. 54. 19; E. M. 33. 33: δείελος; this is the usual accent, but according to Arc. 55. 4, τὸ δειελός, τὸ δειλινὸν ὀξύνεται: δαῦλος, Eust. 274. 24: δῆλος, Theog. Can. 61. 7; according to Schol. Ven. Κ. 466 it is a contraction of δέελος: δοῦλος, Arc. 53. 12: δύσκολος, a compound word: εἴκελος and ἴκελος, Arc. 55. 8: ἔκηλος; the grammarians say that those in ηλος with only two terminations are barytone, and they frequently are so: ἔκπαγλος is strictly a compound, and therefore regular; the same is the case with ἐξίτηλος and ἐρύγμηλος, which last Tyrannion made oxytone, but wrongly, Schol. Ven. Σ. 580; cf. E. M. 379. 20: εὔκηλος, Arc. 55. 13: ἔωλος, Arc. 57. 21; Chœrob. E. 23. 15: ἤκαλος, E. M. 44. 32: ἠπίαλος (?) this is perhaps not an adjective: Θεσσαλός, St. Byz.: τὸ Θετταλή δρᾶμα Μενάνδρου βαρύνεται παρὰ 'Αττικοῖς εἰς ἰδιότητα τεθέν: ἴξαλος, Arc. 54. 19: ἴτηλος, Hesych.: καλός was paroxytone in Æolic, Eust. 1534. 20; and so is the barbarism καλάνι: κάπηλος, E. M. 379. 30; Arc. 55. 14: κίβδηλος, A. G. Oxon. 2. 291. 26; Schol. Ven. Σ. 580; Chœrob. E. 116. 20: κόβαλος, generally used as a substantive, but in Aristophanes sometimes as an adjective: κοῖλος (Æolic κόϊλος), Joh. Alex. 6. 23; Schol. Ven. Κ. 134: κόλος, cf. Arc. 52. 16: λάκος, Arc. 52. 18: νενίηλος is probably a compound: νύσταλος (?): ξύσιλος, E. M. 737. 3: ὅλος, Arc. 52. 18, who holds that all dissyllables with a short penultimate are paroxytone, except ὁλός ὁ ὀλέθριος: οὖλος, Schol. Ven. Κ. 134; Arc. 53. 12: παίπαλος (?): πέμπελος ὁ παλαιός, Arc. 55. 8: πέταλος is perhaps rather a substantive than an adjective, though πετάλη may be regarded as its feminine: πέτηλος (?) Aratus 271; H. D.: πίαλος, Arc. 54. 24: πολύς, πολλή, πολύ keep the accent throughout on the last syllable: ῥάκελος (?) σκληρός, Hesych.: σαῦλος, cf. Arc. 53. 10: στράβαλος or στραβάλος, Hesych., where the last editor has rightly printed στραβαλός: φαῦλος, Arc. 53. 10.

391. Note 2.—*Paroxytones.* Αἰόλος, Arc. 56. 6: τὸ δὲ αἰόλος, εἴτε κύριον, εἴτε ἐπίθετον παροξύνεται; see above, § 282; the imaginary singular μεγάλος is also paroxytone, E. M. 553. 30; Chœrob. E. 68. 24; Arc. 54. 19.

392. Note 3.—*Exceptions in* ἴλος *and* ὕλος. A. G. Oxon. 1. 51. 17: Μύτιλος (μυτιλλός (?) Herod. π. μ. λ. 21. 2) is apparently another and perhaps false form for μίτυλος: ἀίδυλος, Hesych., αἴδυλος, Suid., and αἰδύλος, Zonar.: αἴσυλος, Arc. 56. 12; this author strangely considers the word to be a compound of ἀ and σῦλῶ; ἀήσυλος is another form of the same: βαίκυλος (?) Hesych.: βέκυλος (?): ἴτυλος, Schol. Theocr. 3. 7, quoted by H. D.: κόϊλος, see above, § 390: μίτυλος, a Lacedæmonian word = ἔσχατος, Arc. 55. 23, is written μιτυλός in Hesych.: παχυλός, this strange accent is amply supported by the books, but I find no distinct statement about it in the grammarians.

-ΜΟΣ.

393. Adjectives in μος throw back the accent, as ἀγώγιμος, αἰρέσιμος, ἄλκιμος, ἀλώσιμος, βρώσιμος, γνώριμος, δίδυμος, ἕβδομος, ἐτήτυμος, νόμιμος, χρήσιμος, ὠφέλιμος ; except ἀμός, θερμός, ἰταμός, μηδαμός, νεοχμός, ὁμός, οὐδαμός, σιμός, τομός, ὑμός oxytone, and ἐρῆμος, ἑτοῖμος, which are properispomena in old Attic, though they are regular, ἔρημος, ἕτοιμος, in later Attic.

394. NOTE—Ἀμός, Dor. = ἡμέτερος, Arc. 59. 19 ; Apoll. de Pron. 144 A : ἐθελημός, Hesych. has ἐθελήμως, which implies ἐθέλημος, but the oxytone form is decidedly the best : ἐπήτριμος, for which Ptolemæus Ascalonites wrote ἐπητριμός, Schol. Ven. Σ. 211 : ἐρῆμος, old Attic, ἔρημος, new Attic, Eust. 341. 12 ; 217. 45 ; 531, etc. ; E. M. 374. 14 ; Arc. 61. 6 ; Herod. π. μ. λ. 33. 1 : ἑτοῖμος, old Attic, ἕτοιμος, new Attic, Eust. 206. 1 ; 341. 12 ; 822. 5, etc. ; Herod. π. μ. λ. 33. 10 : θελεμός, or θελημός, E. M. 103. 48 ; Chœrob. E. 57. 8 ; Arc. 61. 3 : θερμός, Philop., see above, § 285 : ἰταμός, Arc. 60. 15 : λαιμός (?) Hesych. : μηδαμός and οὐδαμός, cf. Arc. 59. 19 : νεοχμός, cf. Arc. 58. 12 : ὁμός, cf. Arc. 59. 21 : σαυχμός = σαχνός, Hesych. : τομός, Arc. 59. 25, see above, § 285 : ὑμός = ὑμέτερος, Apoll. de Pron. 144 A : φαρυμός (?) τολμηρός, θρασύς, Hesych.

-ΝΟΣ.

395. (a) Adjectives in υνος and ινος retract the accent, except such as are derived from adverbs, or involve the idea of time, which are oxytone, as ἀκάνθινος, ἀμπέλινος, ἀνθρώπινος, βύβλινος, γηθόσυνος, δεσπόσυνος, δουλόσυνος, ἐλεφάντινος, πέτρινος, ῥόδινος, ὑπέρινος ; but πυκινός from πύκα, ἀδινός (ἅδην), ταχινός (τάχα), θαμινός (θαμά), μηδαμινός, οὐδαμινός, χθεσινός, ἐαρινός, τητινός, ἑσπερινός, ἡμερινός, θερινός, ὀπωρινός, περυσινός, χειμερινός, ὀψινός, all involving the notion of time : the following are also oxytone, ἀληθινός, δροσινός, πεδινός, ῥαδινός, φυζακινός.

396. NOTE—Cf. Theog. Can. 67. 23 ; E. M. 58. 53 ; Eust. 709. 52 ; Arc. 65. 9 ; Schol. Ven. N. 29 : ἀβρινός (?) Hesych. : ἀλευρινός (?) H. D. : ἀληθινός, Chœrob. A. G. Oxon. 2. 180. 4 ; E. M. 58. 53 ; Theog. Can. 67. 23 : ἀνθινός seems to be more frequently oxytone than proparoxytone, but that may be the work of editors ; cf. Lob. Prol. 189 : δροσινός, Hesych. ; in Anth. Pal. 9. 570 the MS. has no accent : ἐλάϊνος, sometimes falsely oxytone : κάλινος is sometimes found oxytone : λεπτακινός, μηδαμινός, and οὐδαμινός, Theog. Can. 67. 23 : ποθινός is but another form of ποθεινός, with the penultimate shortened for metrical reasons, Anth. Pal. 7. 403 : ῥαδινός, Chœrob. A. G. Oxon. 2. 180. 4 : σκυλάκινος is sometimes falsely oxytone : τητινός, A. G. 66. 17, is sometimes proparoxytone, but such an accentuation is false, as being contrary to analogy and express precept : φυζακινός, Theog. Can. 67. 23 ; Schol. Ven. N. 102 : φυζινός, Chœrob. A. G. Oxon. 2. 180. 4 : χήλινος ; 'Vitiosum accentum χηλινόν notavit Lobeck. Pathol. Prol. p. 201, rectum χήλινον qui nunc Polluci [7. 172] restitutus est, servavit Hesych. in gl. Κεχήλωμαι,' H. D. : ψυχινός is false for ψυχεινός ; Ἐλωρινὴ ὁδός in Thucyd. 6. 70 should probably be Ἐλωρίνη.

397. (*b*) Those in ῑνος are properispomena, as ἀγρωστῖνος, ἀγχιστῖνος, Λατῖνος, προμνηστῖνος; except λαρινός oxytone.

NOTE.—Arc. 65. 19; on λαρινός, which was Herodian's accent, though others seem to have written λάρινος, see Schol. Aristoph. Pac. 924; on ἀγρωστῖνος, St. Byz. s. v. Ἀγρός: Ἀλεξανδρῖνος, St. Byz., elsewhere Ἀλεξανδρινός, cf. Diog. Laert. 7. 18.

398. (*c*) The remaining adjectives in νος are oxytone, as ἀγανός, ἀϊδνός, Ἀσιανός, ἐλεεινός, ἐραννός, ἐρυμνός, εὐδιανός, ἠπεδανός, ἱκανός, καινός, κεδνός, κοινός, κραιπνός, οὐτιδανός, πελιδνός, πετεινός, ποθεινός, πρυμνός, πυκνός, ῥιγεδανός, ῥικνός, ῥοδανός, σεμνός, σκοτεινός, στενός, στρυφνός, συχνός, ταπεινός, τερπνός, τιθηνός, Χριστιανός, ψεδνός, ψυχεινός; except βάσκανος, γόεδνος, δύστηνος, ἔνος, ἵκμενος, κάγκανος, κάρβανος, κλύμενος, λάγνος, λίχνος, μόνος, ξένος, πλάνος, which retract the accent, and the properispomna, ἐκεῖνος (κεῖνος and κῆνος), χαῦνος.

399. NOTE.—Ἀγανός, Schol. Ven. Ξ. 172: ἀϊδνός, though oxytone, is in fact a compound word: ἀκμηνός, E. M. 49. 42: ὁ δὲ Ἀρίσταρχος λέγει τὴν ἄκμηνον προπαροξυτόνως παρὰ τὴν ἀκμήν· Θέων δὲ ὀξύνεσθαι ἀξιοῖ, ὡς ἀγαθός· ἔνιοι δὲ προπερισπῶσιν: Eust. 1944. 38: ἀκμηνὸς δὲ νῦν [i. e. Hom. Od. 23. 191] ὀξύνεται· φασὶ γὰρ ὅτι Ἀρίσταρχος ἐνταῦθα μὲν ἐπὶ τοῦ θάμνος ἀκμηνός, ὅ ἐστιν ἀκμὴν ἔχων τοῦ νεάζειν, ὠξυτόνησεν, ἐν δὲ Ἰλιάδι ἐπὶ τοῦ δηλοῦντος τὸν νῆστιν ἐβαρυτόνησεν. ἕτεροι δέ φασι, καὶ τὰ δύο προπαροξυτόνησαν: βλάνος, Hesych.: γόεδνος seems to be the accent of the books, but by analogy it ought to be oxytone: γρῶος (?) Lycoph. 631; 1280: δύστηνος, Theog. Can. 68. 1; Arc. 65. 8, is probably a compound: ἐκεῖνος, κεῖνος, and κῆνος, Arc. 179. 13: ἔνος, cf. Arc. 111. 4: ἵκμενος, Arc. 64. 28: κλύμενος, Arc. 64. 28: λάγνος, Schol. Ven. Ξ. 351; Arc. 62. 2: λίτανος (?) is read by Seidler in Æschyl. S. c. T. 102, ed. Didot: λίχνος, Schol. Ven. Ξ. 351; Arc. 62. 7: Μαριάνδυνος, such was the Æolic accent, but the common one Μαριανδυνός, Eust. Dion. Per. 787; cf. Arc. 66. 3, and above, § 299: μορφνός=σκοτεινός, Suid.: as a substantive it varies, see above, § 292: νώδυνος is regular as a compound: ὀλίσθανος (?) Galen.: ξένος (Ion. ξεῖνος, Æol. ξέννος), Arc. 63. 15: πέπανος occurs as well as πεπανός, but the latter seems the more correct accent: cf. Arc. 64. 10; Lob. Prol. 183: πλάνος, Arc. 63. 12: σκύδμαινος (?)=σκυθρωπός, Hesych.: τῆνος, Doric for ἐκεῖνος: τοσσῆνος, Doric for τοσοῦτος, Theocr. 1. 54: χαῦνος, Arc. 64. 8; for βάσκανος, κάγκανος, κάρβανος, μόνος, the books seem to be the only authorities.

-ΞΟΣ.

400. Adjectives in ξος are oxytone, as διξός, λοξός, τετραξός, τριξός, φοξός, φριξός, Arc. 66. 14.

-ΟΟΣ.

401. Those in οος retract the accent, as ὄγδοος, σόος; except θοός, ὀλοός, oxytone: ἀθρόος and the multiplicatives in πλοος are paroxytone, as ἁπλόος, διπλόος, δεκαπλόος. When syncopated they become oxytone, as ἁπλός, διπλός.

402. NOTE.—Schol. Ven. M. 26. The numerals in πλοος remain paroxytone even when compounded, as πενταπλόος; but this does not seem to be the case with the compounds of such forms as ἁπλός, διπλός: e. g. we have διάδιπλος, cf. Eust. 890. 51 ; Arc. 42. 10 : ἀγνοός (?) Hesych.: ἀθρόος, ὁ συνηθροισμένος is distinguished by its accent from ἄθροος, ὁ ἀθόρυβος, Eust. 1387. 11 ; 1788. 36 ; Arc. 42. 13 ; Aristarchus aspirated the word, Eust. 966. 10 ; Schol. Ven. B. 439 ; contrary to rule, it is contracted into ἄθρους, not ἀθροῦς, Eust. 1447. 52, though Ptolemæus Ascalonites wished to write ἀθροῦς, in the accusative plural: ἀκοός, E. M. 51. 24 : ζοός, though most wrote ζόος, in which case Ptolemæus Ascalonites would have been justified in making ζώς perispomenon ; ζῶς is however condemned by Schol. Ven. E. 887 ; Herod. π. μ. λ. 41. 31 : διὸ καὶ τὸ ζόος παρ' Ἐπιχάρμῳ οἱ πλείους ἐβάρυναν, cf. E. M. 413. 30 : θοός, Herod. π. μ. λ. 41. 29 : ὄγδοος, E. M. 615. 30 : ὀλοός, and οὐλοός, Arc. 42. 21 : σόος, or σῶς, Schol. Ven. Σ. 887 ; E. M. 413. 30.

-ΠΟΣ.

403. Adjectives in πος are oxytone, as αἰπός, γρυπός, λοιπός, χαλεπός, ποδαπός ; except λίσπος.

NOTE.—It is doubtful whether the words ποδαπός, ἀλλοδαπός, ἐχθροδοπός, ἡμεδαπός, τηλεδαπός, ἐχθοδοπός, παντοδαπός, ὁποδαπός, are compounds are not. See L. S. s. v. ποδαπός: they are all oxytone, Arc. 67. 7 ; A. G. Oxon. 1. 369. 29 : λίσπος, Apollonius appears to have written λισπός, Schol. Aristoph. Ran. 848. cf. § 154, Ἀρτίπος, ἀελλόπος, Eust. 768. 48, ἀλιτρόπος, μικρόπος, τετράπος, ὠκύπος, are paroxytone, even when declined after the Second Declension, Schol. Ven. I. 105.

-ΡΟΣ.

404. Adjectives in ρος are oxytone, as ἀκιρός, ἁβρός, ἀγαυρός, αἰσχρός, ἀφαυρός, βδελυρός, δροσερός, ἐχθρός, ἐχυρός, θαλερός, ἱερός, ἱλαρός, ἰσχυρός, θολερός, κρυερός, λαιψηρός, λιπαρός, λυπηρός, μιαρός, νεαρός, νωθρός, ξηρός, ξυηρός, ὀτρηρός, πενιχρός, πικρός, πνιγηρός, πυῤῥός, σκληρός, σοβαρός, τορός, τρυφερός, φοβερός, ψυχρός ; except 1. comparatives and comparative forms, possessive pronouns, and numerals, definite or indefinite, in τερος, which are proparoxytone, as ἀβέλτερος, ἀμφότερος, ἁρπαγίστερος, βέλτερος, δασύτερος, δεύτερος, δημότερος, ἑκάτερος, ἐξέτερος, ἕτερος, μετεξέτεροι, μηδέτερος, πρότερος, φέρτερος, ὕστερος ; 2. the following, which retract the accent, ἄκρος, βάρβαρος, γαῦρος, γλίσχρος, ἐλεύθερος, ἕταρος, ἥμερος, θοῦρος, κάρχαρος, κραῦρος, λάβρος, λάληθρος, λοίδορος, μαῦρος, μέρμερος, μῶρος, *Attic*, νύκτερος, ὀλίγωρος, παῦρος, πέπειρος, σινάμωρος, ταλαίπωρος, ὑλακόμωρος, φλαῦρος, φλύαρος, χῆρος : in Attic πόνηρος and μόχθηρος are proparoxytone when they signify *wretched* ; 3. properispomenon ἑταῖρος. Ἀείσυρος and ἀήσυρος are regular if compounds.

405. NOTE.—Ἀβληχρός, Heracleides Milesius barytoned it as a compound; Eust. 705; Schol. Ven. Θ. 178: ἀγαυρός is oxytone, though, according to the Greek grammarians, a compound of γαῦρος, Eust. 1444. 10: ἄγλαυρος (?) Nicaud. Ther. 441: ἄιδρος, Hesych. is a compound: ἄκρος, Arc. 74. 6; but φαλακρός is oxytone, on which see below: ἀμαυρός, Eust. 1444. 11: ἀμυδρός, according to Eust. 463. 41 it ought to be ἄμυδρος, but it is always and rightly oxytone: ἀμφότερος, Arc. 71: ἀφαυρός, Eust. 1444. 11: βάρβαρος, Arc. 70. 12: βδέλυρος, *Attic*, Eust. 341. 15, but it is always oxytone in the books: παμβδελυρός: Aristoph. Lys. 969, is strange: γαῦρος, A. G. Oxon. 2. 355. 1; cf. Arc. 69. 19: τὰ εἰς ΡΟΣ δισύλλαβα τῇ ΑΥ διφθόγγῳ παραληγόμενα ἐπὶ ἐμψύχων τιθέμενα βαρύνεται, φλαῦρος, σαῦρος, καῦρος ὁ κακός: γλίσχρος, Arc. 74. 2, is often oxytone in MSS: δαῖρος or δαιρός, *burning, caustic*; the ancients themselves were in doubt which was the proper accent, Arc. 69. 17; Theog. Can. 70. 20: δεξιτερός, Arc. 71: δεύτερος, Arc. 70. 22: δημότερος, a comparative from δῆμος used adjectively, St. Byz. s. v. Δῆμος: δίκρος is only another form of the compound adjective δίκροος or δίκρους: ἑάρτερος, Nicand. Ther. 380: ἕλλερος, Eust. 635. 5; Arc. 123. 1: ἕτερος, Arc. 70. 27: ἑταῖρος, Theog. Can. 71. 4; Arc. 72. 18: ἡμέτερος, Arc. 179. 24: θοῦρος, Arc. 70. 4: ἵμερος: κάρχαρος, A. G. Oxon. 1. 55. 19: καῦρος, Arc. 69. 21: κοῦρος, Arc. 70. 4; Schol. Ven. B. 153: λάβρος, or, as it is incorrectly written by late authors, λαῦρος: λῆρος, Schol. Ven. B. 599; Arc. 68. 10; see § 312: λοίδορος, also a substantive: μαυρος = ἀμαυρός, Arc. 69. 22; μέτερρος, Æolic = μέτριος: μόχθηρος, Attic, Eust. 341. 12; Arc. 71. 16; but except in that dialect and in Æolic, if it has the word, it is oxytone; in the books it seems to be commonly oxytone in all senses; Ammon. p. 95: μοχθηρὸς μὲν γὰρ ὀξυτόνως, ὁ τὰ ἤθη πονηρός. λέγουσι δὲ ἁπλῶς τὰ φαῦλα καὶ μοχθηρά...μόχθηρος δὲ ὁ ἐπίπονος; Arc. 71. 16: ἱστέον δέ, ὅτι τὸ πόνηρος καὶ μόχθηρος [ἀεὶ] οἱ Ἀττικοὶ ἀντὶ τοῦ ὀξύνειν προπαροξύνουσιν, ὅταν τὸν ἐπίμονον [? ἐπίπονον] καὶ ἐπίμοχθον σημαίνῃ: according to Trypho ap. Ammon. 116, the word was proparoxytone in Attic, because that dialect has a tendency to throw the accent back; Eust. 341. 14: πᾶν γὰρ εἰς ΡΟΣ λῆγον παρώνυμον, παρεσχηματισμένον τοῖς γένεσιν, ὀξύτονόν ἐστι καθ' Ἡρωδιανόν. διό, φησιν, εἰ καὶ πόνηρος μὲν καὶ μόχθηρος βαρυτόνως ἐπὶ τῶν ἐπιπόνων καὶ ὑπομενετικῶν, πονηρὸς δὲ καὶ μοχθηρὸς ἐπὶ τῶν κατὰ ψυχὴν φαύλων, ἀλλὰ τοῦτο οὐκ εὖ. εἰ γὰρ πόνος καὶ μόχθος τὰ πρωτότυπα, εὐλόγως πονηρὸς καὶ μοχθηρὸς τὰ τούτοις παρακείμενα, κᾶν διαφόρων ἔχηται σημασιῶν, ἵνα ᾖ ἀνάλογα τῷ κάματος καματηρός, ὄλισθος ὀλισθηρός, βλάβη βλαβερός, κράτος κρατερός: μῶρος, afterwards μωρός, Eust. 1749. 37; Arc. 69. 13: μωρὸς καὶ μῶρος Ἀττικῶς, Schol. Plat. Lach. 197 A; cf. Theog. Can. 79. 9; some assigned a different meaning to each accent: 'Accentum adjectivi qui in libris modo in priori modo in altera, grammatici Atticos in illa ponere consentiunt, ut Suidas: Μῶρος παρὰ Ἀττικοῖς προπερισπᾶται: Arc. 69. 13: Μωρὸς καὶ μῶρος Ἀττικῶς: Eust. Il. 245. 37: Μήορος μῶρος παρ' Ἀττικοῖς, ὁ παρὰ τοῖς ὕστερον ὀξυτόνως μωρός: Od. 1447. 56: Τὸ δὲ μωρὸς πάλαι ποτὲ ὀρθῶς εἶχε προπερισπᾶσθαι (quibus addit exx. hujus accentus) ... ὕστερον δὲ συνεξέδραμε τῷ πυλωρὸς θυρωρός καὶ τοῖς ὁμοίοις, quæ repetit 1749. 39; Μωρὸς vero scriptum in Etym. M. p. 593. 12; Photius: Μωρός· ἔνιοι τὴν πρόσκαιρον εὐήθειαν προπερισπωμένως, τὴν δὲ κακίαν ὀξυτόνως· οἱ δὲ ἁπλῶς προπερισπῶσι· σύγκειται δὲ κατὰ στέρησιν τῆς ὥρας.' H. D.: νέωρος, Arc. 72. 14: νωῖτερος, Arc. 179. 23: ὀλίγωρος, Arc. 72. 15, belongs to the compound adjectives: ὅμηρος, said to mean *blind* in the Cumæan dialect; cf. Schol. Lycoph. 422: πέπειρος, Arc. 71. 21, fem. πέπειρᾶ, Draco p. 79. 20: πέρπερος, Arc. 70. 13; perhaps a compound: πηρός, Schol. Ven. B. 599: πηρὸν ὡς χρηστὸν κατ' ὀξεῖαν τάσιν παρὰ τῷ Ποιητῇ· παρὰ δὲ τοῖς Ἀττικοῖς πῆρον ὡς λῆρον: according to Hesychius: πηρόν, ἐστερημένον τῆς φωνῆς. ἐνεὸν δέ, πεπηρωμένον καὶ βεβλαμμένον αὐτοῦ τὴν διάνοιαν τὸν ἐνεὸν καὶ ἄφωνον, προπερισπωμένως δὲ τὸν τυφλόν: πονηρός, Arc. 71. 16: ἱστέον δέ, ὅτι τὸ πόνηρος καὶ μόχθηρος ἀεὶ οἱ

'Αττικοὶ ἀντὶ τοῦ ὀξύνειν προπαροξύνουσιν, ὅταν τὸν ἐπίμονον [leg. ἐπίπονον] καὶ ἐπίμοχθον σημαίνη : Ammon. p. 116 : Πόνηρον βαρυτονούμενον ὡς σόλοικον, καὶ Πονηρὸν ὀξυτονούμενον ὡς κυδοιμόν, φασὶ διαφέρειν παρὰ τοῖς 'Αττικοῖς· ὁμοίως μόχθηρον
καὶ μοχθηρόν. Πονηρὸς γάρ ἐστιν ὀξυτόνως ὁ κακοήθης· Πόνηρος δὲ ὁ ἐπίπονος :
Trypho ap. cund. condemns the distinction as absurd, though, no doubt, πονηρός
was proparoxytone in Attic, cf. Eust. 341. 12 ; A. G. Oxon. 1. 372. 29 : ὁ κατὰ ψυχὴν
ὀξυτόνως, ὁ δὲ κατὰ σῶμα προπαροξυτόνως· καὶ παρ' Εὐπόλιδι τὸ θηλυκὸν πονήρα·

καὶ μὴ πονηρούς, ὦ πονήρα, προξένει·

τὸ μὲν πρότερον ὀξύνοντες· τὸ δὲ ἐπὶ τῆς προμνηστρίας τὸ δεύτερον βαρυτονοῦντες :
ῥάρος, Suid. seems to make this Æolic word an adjective = ἰσχυρός, as well as a
substantive, cf. Hesych. s. v. and Arc. 200. 22 : σινάμωρος, probably a compound :
σκόλυθρος, Suid.: στεῖρος, Manetho 1. 125 ; H. D. ; but the feminine στεῖρα (sc.
βοῦς) is the only common form of the word : συνάμωρος is false for σινάμωρος :
σφαῖρος, Empedocles ap. Simplic. in Arist. Phys. 425 b. 2 ed. Berolin. : σφέτερος,
Schol. Ven. A. 280 ; Arc. 179. 24 : ταλαίπωρος, perhaps a compound : for τιμάο-
ρος and τιμωρός see Compound Adjectives : ὑλακόμωρος, perhaps a compound :
ὑμέτερος, Arc. 179. 24 : ὕστερος, Arc. 70. 22 : φαλακρός, Arc. 74. 21 ; some consider this to be a compound, like δείλακρος, but Lobeck, Par. 42, thinks it a simple
word, and the accent confirms his view : φλαῦρος (for which φαῦρος, Hesych.,
seems to be a false form), Arc. 69. 21 : φλύαρος, Arc. 70. 18 ; cf. Draco 95. 26 ;
this is rather a substantive than an adjective, and sometimes is wrongly oxytone ;
thus also φλυαρῶς for φλυάρως : χείμαρρος : 'De accentu formæ trisyllabæ in
casibus in os, ον, vel οι exeuntibus dissenserunt grammatici, quorum opiniones
Eustath. p. 496, præeunte partim schol. vet. ad Il. Δ. 452, exposuit : ἰστέον δὲ
ὅτι γενικὸν μὲν ὄνομα τὸ ποταμοί, εἰδικὸν δὲ τὸ χείμαρροι, καὶ ὅτι τὸ χείμαρροι, ὡς ἐν
τοῖς 'Απίωνος καὶ 'Ηρωδώρου φαίνεται, Πτολεμαῖος μὲν ὁ 'Ασκαλονίτης, παροξύνει ὡς
ἀπὸ τοῦ χειμάρρους, ἵνα φέρῃ τὸν τόνον τῆς ἑνικῆς εὐθείας. Νικίας δὲ προπαροξύνει
πιθανώτερον ἐκ τοῦ χειμάρροος, ἵνα ἔχῃ συγκοπὴν ἐκ τοῦ χειμάρροοι . . . ὁ δὲ 'Ηρωδιανὸς ἑτεροῖόν τι λέγει ἐν οἷς φησὶν ὅτι χειμάρρους ῥητέον σὺν τῷ ν, ἀλλ' οὐχ ὥς
τινες χείμαρρος· τὸ γὰρ εἰς ους ἁπλᾶ κατὰ τὴν σύνθεσιν φυλάσσει τὸ ν, οἷον νοῦς σύν-
νους . . . οὕτω γοῦν καὶ ῥοῦς χειμάρρους. Ὅμηρος χειμάρρους κατ' ὄρεσφι καὶ
πάλιν χειμάρροοι, ἀλλ' οὐ χείμαρροι ὡς οἱ πολλοί φασιν. Ὡς γὰρ ἀπὸ τοῦ ἀλκίνους
ἀλκίνοοι, οὕτω καὶ ἀπὸ τοῦ χειμόρρους· χειμάρροοι : quibuscum comparandæ aliæ
annotationes Eustathii, p. 525. 31 ; 858. 38 ; 925. 10 ;' H. D. : χείμερος (?) Arat.
1084, or ῥός, Hesych.: χέρρος or χέρσος ; on the latter word, see Arc. 76. 3 ·
χῆρος, Arc. 135. 20.

-ΣΟΣ.

406. Adjectives in σος are oxytone, as βλαισός, δισσός, λισσός,
περισσός, σός, τιθασός, τρισσός, ῥυσός ; except βάναυσος, μέθυσος
proparoxytone ; ἴσος, μέσος, the interrogative πόσος and its
correlatives, are paroxytone.

NOTE.—'Αγασός, Dor. = ἀγαθός : βάναυσος, Arc. 76. 21, usually considered to
be a compound : γαυσός = κυρτός, it was not known whether this word used by
Hippocrates was oxytone or properispomenon, Galen vol. 18. pars. 2ᵃ. p. 519,
ed. Kühn. : ἴσος, Attic, Arc. 75. 4 : or Epic ἶσος ; the later Epic poets use both
forms, but prefer the Attic : μέθυσος (μέθυσσος in Arc. 78. 2 is an error) : μέσος
and μέσσος, Arc. 75. 4 : πόσος and correlatives, Arc. 75. 4 : ὁπόσος : ὅσος (ὅσσος),
Arc. 75. 5 : τόσος (τόσσος), Arc. 75. 5 : χέρσος, Arc. 76. 3.

·ΤΟΣ.

407. Adjectives in τος are oxytone, as ἀγητός, αἰσθητός, ἀριθμητός, βασιλευτός, Βοιωτός, γελαστός, διδακτός, δυνατός, ἐθιστός, ἑλετός, ἑλικτός, κινητός, κλειτός, λεκτός, λιτός, λυτός, μισθωτός, ὁρατός, ὀρεκτός, πεπτός, ῥητός, τριπτός, χρηστός, χυτός, χωριστός, φθιτός; except 1. ordinal numerals, superlatives and superlative forms, which retract the accent, as πρῶτος, τρίτος, πέμπτος, ἕκτος, δέκατος; ἄριστος, ἔσχατος, λῶστος, μέσατος, νέατος and νῆτος, ὀλίγιστος, πλεῖστος, πύματος, ῥᾶστος, ὠκύτατος; numerals in στος, even though ordinals, are regular, as ὀλιγοστός, πολλοστός, εἰκοστός, τριακοστός, πεντηκοστός; 2. those in κοτος, as ἀλλόκοτος, νεόκοτος, παλίγκοτος, ὑπέρκοτος, together with the following, also draw back the accent, ἔκατος, ἕκαστος, ἠλέματος, ἠλίβατος, κασίγνητος, λήϊτος and λῆτος, πάχετος, τηλύγετος; 3. the pronominal οὗτος and its compounds are properispomena, as τηλικοῦτος, τοιοῦτος, τοσοῦτος; πόστος and ὁπόστος are paroxytone.

408. NOTE.—Cf. Arc. 78. 6-84. 12; Eust. 971. 57; Chœrob. E. 2. 12; 110. 22; 133. 4: Ἀλλόκοτος, etc., together with αἶητος, Schol. Ven. Σ. 410, and ἄητος, Arc. 82. 6, ἠλίβατος, τηλύγετος, are compounds, and therefore regular; they are merely mentioned here for convenience: δύστος ὁ δύστηνος, Arc. 80. 3 : κασίγνητος was made oxytone by some when used as an adjective, Schol. Ven. I. 563 : κονδῖτος (?) =*conditus*, like λαῖτος, *lætus*, Hesych., cf. Arc. 78. 10, have a Latin accent : νέατος, *uttermost*, is proparoxytone as an irregular superlative form, but νεατός, *fallowed*, is oxytone: πάχετος, Hom. Od. 8. 187 : πέρατος is false for περατός, Arc. 81. 7 : on οὗτος, Arc. 84. 7 : ἔκαστος, Arc. 83. 27 : πόστος ἐκ τοῦ πόσατος, Arc. 80. 3.

-ΥΟΣ.

409. Adjectives is νος (ανος, ονος) are oxytone, as ἀγανός, ἀκουός; except αὖος properispomenon, and κρήγυος proparoxytone.

NOTE.—Arc. 45. 15: Αἴγνος, St. Byz.: αὖος, this was the accentuation of Ptolemæus and Herodian: Nicias made it oxytone, Schol. Ven. M. 137; Arc. 37. 8 is corrupt.

-ΦΟΣ.

410. Those in φος are oxytone, as κυφός, κωφός, σκνιφός, σομφός, σοφός; except ἄργυφος, κοῦφος, στέριφος, φλήναφος, which retract the accent.

NOTE.—Ἄργυφος, Arc. 84. 24: κίδαφος (?) Hesych.: κοῦφος, Arc. 84. 21: λέμφος, Eust. 1761; Ammon. 87; Phot. Lex., is oxytone in Hesych.; but perhaps it ought not to be considered an adjective: στόμφος and στόμβος are substantives in accent, and perhaps in sense: φλήναφος; cf. Arc. 84. 22.

-ΧΟΣ.

411. Adjectives in χος are oxytone, as δολιχός, μοναχός, πτωχός; except ἀγέρωχος, ἀδόλεσχος, ἥσυχος, κύμβαχος, μείλιχος, νηπίαχος, τάριχος, which retract the accent.

Note.—Arc. 84. 28: ἀγέρωχος and ἀδόλεσχος are really compounds and regular: ἠπίαχος (?): Ἴακχος (?) Eurip. Cycl. 69: μείλιχος, Theog. Can. 76. 25: ὄσσιχος is ὀσσίχος in Theocr. 4. 55, and in Hesych.: see above, § 334: πύρριχος, Theocr. 4. 20; see H. D. s. v.: τάριχος, Theog. Can. 76. 25, is both a neuter substantive of the Third Declension, a masculine of the Second, and perhaps an adjective.

-ΨΟΣ.

412. Adjectives in ψος are oxytone, as γαμψός, κομψός.

Note.—Arc. 85. 10: Αἴαψος ὁ ποικίλος, Suid.

-ΩΟΣ and -ΩΙΟΣ.

413. Those in ῳος and ωος are properispomena, as ἀθῷος, αἰδῷος, τὰ Ἀλῷα, ἀνδρῷος, ἀρκτῷος, ἠῷος, κερδῷος, μητρῷος, Μινῷος, ὀρεσκῷος, σῷος; except ζωός, παρωός, and Τρωός oxytone.

414. Note.—See Arc. 38. 7; 87. 12; E. M. 26. 20; 29. 25; Chœrob. E. 118. 20: ἀθῷος, Eust. 218. 3: Ζεὺς Ἄθῳος προπαροξυτόνως ὁ ἐν τῷ Ἄθῳ τιμώμενος μετὰ προσγραφῆς τοῦ ῑ πρὸς διαστολὴν τοῦ ἀθῶος ὁ ἀζήμιος: Eust. 358. 41; St. Byz. s. v. Ἄθως· τὸ τοπικὸν Ἄθωος χωρὶς τοῦ ῑ, καὶ Ἀθώους, τοὺς ἐνοικοῦντας, τὸ δὲ δηλοῦν τὸ ἀζήμιον προπερισπᾶται καὶ διὰ τοῦ ῑ, ἐκ τῆς θωῆς: cf. E. M. 26. 20: not an unfair specimen of the contradictions which are scattered broadcast over the pages of Greek grammarians; the different accent of the two words is probably their invention; as to the ι subscriptum, there can be little doubt that it ought to be written, for ἀθῷος = ἀθώιος; according to Eust. 953. 45, this was by some written ἄθωος (*sic*): ζωός, Arc. 38. 9: παρωός also occurs in the forms πάρωος and παρῶος: it is difficult to say which is right: Τρωός, see above, § 339.

-ΟΥΣ.

415. Simple adjectives in ους are perispomena, as ἀλουργοῦς, ἀργυροῦς, ἐρεοῦς, χρυσοῦς.

Note.—Arc. 93. 6; 126. 4. The accent of those in ους = οος or εος is irregular, e. g. ἀργύρεος ought to form ἀργύρους, but does not; cf. Chœrob. C. 160. 35; Philem. Lex. p. 30. § 79.

III. Compound Substantives.

416. In determining the accent of compound words, the Greek grammarians lay considerable stress on the distinctions which they draw between Synthesis, Parasynthesis, and Parathesis. Retraction of the accent was held to be characteristic of Synthesis, and the retention of it a distinctive mark of

Parasynthesis and Parathesis. It cannot be denied that these distinctions have a foundation in fact, but the plan of the present work compels us to neglect them, for they involve a whole theory of Greek etymology, and require that we should be able to determine correctly the pedigree of every compound word, which is a feat considerably less easy than it appears to be. Moreover they introduce needless difficulties into the subject. A modern will find it hard, and perhaps impossible, to say why νεάοιδος is a synthetic and λυραοιδός a parasynthetic compound : not indeed that any one should be branded as a grammatical sceptic who altogether doubts the fact, though in so doing he flies in the face of Apollonius the Crabbed. Who can explain why κέρτομος is proparoxytone and καρατόμος or λατόμος paroxytone ? In determining the accent of such words as these Synthesis and Parasynthesis will be of little avail. They can never teach us the accent when it is doubtful, though they may account for it when known, or rather they may reveal to us the opinions formed by Greek philologists a thousand years ago concerning the genealogy of this or that word ; whatever may be the interest which their opinions on such matters ought to excite, it must be confessed that they are often wrong, and hardly ever of the slightest use. For these, as well as for other reasons which need not be stated, the accentuation of compounds, like that of other words hitherto discussed, has been made to rest on merely empirical rules, which, objectionable as they are from the scientific point of view, may still be tolerated on the score of utility. Precepts based upon considerations of what ought to be have no doubt much to recommend them, only the misfortune is, that in grammar, as elsewhere, people have resolved to sanction what ought not to be.

417. Note.—Apoll. de Synt. p. 330. 4 : πᾶν μέρος λόγου συντεθὲν καὶ εἰς ἕτερον σχῆμα μεταπεσὸν ἔχει τὸ μεταπεπτωκὸς οὐκέτι σύνθετον, παρασύνθετον δέ. ἔνθεν οὖν καὶ αἱ τάσεις τῶν τε ἁπλῶν καὶ τῶν δοκούντων συνθέτων εἶναι τὸν αὐτὸν ἐπέχουσι τόνον [τόπον?], ἐπεὶ τὰ ἁπλᾶ καὶ παρασύνθετα μιᾶς ἔχεται ἀναλογίας, ὡς δείκνυται ἐν τῷ Περὶ Σχημάτων. σύνθετον γοῦν φαμὲν τὸ ἐξ ὀξυτόνου εἰς βαρεῖαν τάσιν μετεληλυθός, ἐπὶ τῶν εἰς ος πάνσοφος, νεάοιδος. παρασύνθετον δὲ τὸ μὴ ἀναβιβάσαν τὸν τόνον καθ᾽ οὐδὲ συνετέθειτο, συνθέτῳ δὲ ῥήματι παρέκειτο, τῷ ἐπακούῳ τὸ ἀγορῆς ἐπακουὸν ἐόντα, τῷ λυραοιδῶ λυραοιδός, μεσῳδῶ μεσῳδός : Apoll. de Syut. p. 324. 23 : ἰδοὺ γὰρ ἔχει τὸ ἰδίωμα τῆς παραθέσεως τὸ συντηρεῖν τοὺς τόνους : Apoll. de Syut. p. 328. 15 : τό γε μὴν ἀναβιβάζειν τὸν τόνον ἴδιόν ἐστι συνθέσεως : Chœrob. C. 477. 21 : παρασύνθετον δὲ τὸ ἀπὸ συνθέτου γιγνόμενον, ὡς ἀπὸ τοῦ Ἀντίγονος συνθέτου γίνεται τὸ ἀντιγονίζω παρασύνθετον : cf. Schol. Ven. K. 109 ; O. 309 ; Chœrob. E. 78 ; E. M. 37. 11 ; 694. 43 ; 131. 32 : 269. 3 ; Arc. 85. 21 ;

86. 16, etc.   He who is interested in this subject will do well to read with care Lobeck's dissertation, De Parathesi et Scriptura hyphen, reprinted in Lob. Path. 1. 543–632.

418. Compound substantives throw the accent as far back as possible, as ἡμίθεος (θεός), θεόταυρος (ταῦρος), ἱερόδουλος (δοῦλος), σύνδουλος ; ἱππίατρος, κτηνίατρος, λογίατρος (ἰατρός) ; ἱπποπόταμος (ποταμός) ; λαγώπυρος, λευκόπυρος ; λακκόπλουτος, λευκόνοτος, λογέμπορος ; μαλακόκισσος, ὀρθόκισσος, ῥοδόκισσος, χαμαίκισσος ; μελαναίετος, ὑψαίετος, χρυσαίετος ; μέσσαυλος, μεσσέγγυος, μεσόνεοι, μετακόνδυλοι, μητροπάρθενος ; μικρόνησος, χερσόνησος ; ξυλόλωτος, ξυλόσπογγος, ὁμόγαμβροι, ὄναγρος, ὀρείχαλκος, παρανύμφιος, περίνεος, περίναιος, πρόβλαστος, πρόπυργος, πρόραχος, ῥιγοπύρετος, ὕφορμος, πεζέταιροι, σύαγρος, βούτραγος, ἀνάρρους, ἔκπλοος, μέθοδος, Μενέλαος, ἀλίτυρος, θέοινος, πλαγίαυλος, Ἑλλήσποντος, Προκόννησος, ἡμιόβολος, λεόπαδρος ; except 1. oxytones with a long penultimate in μος, which remain oxytone, as τιναγμός, ἀνατιναγμός, αὐτοαριθμός, ἐπισυρμός, ἐπισπασμός, διορκισμός, μετασφαιρισμός ; though compounds in δεσμος and σταθμος follow the general rule, as κατάδεσμος, κυνόδεσμος, βούσταθμος, ἐπίσταθμος ; 2. those in ισκος which remain paroxytone, as φιλοσοφομειρακίσκος ; 3. those the last factor of which is one of the verbal terminations enumerated below under Verbal Adjectives, as ἀγορανόμος, ἀρχιεννοῦχος, ἀσπιδοποιός, βουκόλος, γεωμόρος, γεωργός, δημιουργός, ἐργολάβος, ζωγράφος, ἡμεροδρόμος, κηπουρός, κυνηγός, μυρεψός, νεωκόρος, οἰνοχόος, σκυτοτόμος, σοροπηγός, στρατηγός, συφορβός, τραγῳδός, τυμβωρύχος.   To avoid useless repetition, all such substantives are included amongst the Verbal Adjectives.   Ἀρτοπόπος and οἰσοφάγος are both paroxytone, and somewhat remarkable.

419. NOTE 1.—*Compounds in* μος. The following are the chief compounds ending in δεσμος and σταθμος : Ἀνάδεσμος, cf. Arc. 103 (p. 117. 15 Schmidt) ; but ἀναδεσμός also occurs, though the authority for it is not great; ἀπόδεσμος, Pollux 7. 66: γονατόδεσμος, διάδεσμος, ἔνδεσμος, Diosc. 3. 97, ἐπίδεσμος, ἐρωτόδεσμος : ζυγόδεσμος, Themist. Orat. 2. p. 30 B; this is generally neuter ζυγόδεσμον; καρπόδεσμος, κροκόδεσμος, κατάδεσμος, Plat. Rep. 364 C: κεφαλόδεσμος, Schol. Æschyl. Supp. 115: κυνόδεσμος, μαστόδεσμος, περίδεσμος, προεπίδεσμος, Lob. Phryn. 293: σκελόδεσμος, στηθόδεσμος, Pollux 7. 66: στρωματόδεσμος, A. G. 113. 26, this is falsely oxytone A. G. 303. 12; Lob. Phryn. 401: σύνδεσμος, Arc. 59. 1 ; Arist. Eth. Nic. 8. 12. 7; see H. D. s. vv.: σχηματόδεσμος, ὑπόδεσμος, χειρόδεσμος, χονδροσύνδεσμος, ὠρόδεσμος, Lob. Par. 377. Ἄδεσμος, βαρύδεσμος, ἐννεάδεσμος, λυγόδεσμος, λινόδεσμος, σιδηρόδεσμος, πολύδεσμος, are adjectives. Βούσταθμος, ἐπίσταθμος, ζυγόσταθμος, ἰσόσταθμος, κολόσταθμος, ναύσταθμος, are substantives and proparoxytone : the words ἀντισταθμος, βαρύσταθμος, παράσταθμος, σύσταθμος, and εὔσταθμος, are adjectives; cf. Lob. Par. 377, who observes Par. 385: 'Male ἀπόδασμος scribitur Eustath. 1366. 52 ut in codd. nonnullis Platonis, Civ. 8. 366 A;' both it and ἀναδασμός should be oxytone: βούλιμος seems to be thus accented in the books, though there is some authority for βουλιμός, 'de accentu singulare est grammatici præceptum in Osanni append. ad Philem. p. 297: Βουλιμός· ὁ μέγας λιμός, ὡς ἀσπασμός, οὐ βούλιμος,' W. *Dindorf* ap. H. D., but the grammarian is probably right: πούλιμος, Wyttenbach's conjecture in Plut. 2. 694 A for πολύλιμος, is correct, because the word is expressly said to be Æolic; compounds from barytones in μος are regular, as πρωτόκοσμος: ἀνδρόβασμος· στενὴ ὁδός, Hesych. is possibly a false accent: ἀρχιμῖμος (*sic*), Plut. 1. 474, is monstrous.

420. NOTE 2.—*Compounds in* ισκος. These are of very rare occurrence; I have only noted three: ἀκροχηνίσκος, Pollux 1. 146: τοιχοπυργίσκος, E. M. 147. 6: and φιλοσοφομειρακίσκος, Athen. 572 B; for διαυλίσκος is no longer read in Polyb. 10. 46. 1, Scaliger's emendation δύο αὐλίσκους being approved by H. D., and χείρ, καλαθίσκος has been substituted in Pollux 4. 105 for the old χειροκαλαθίσκος.

421. NOTE 3.—'Ὀρειπέλαργος, Arist. H. Animal. 9. 32. p. 618. 34 [=9. 32. 3] in codd. nonnullis acuitur;' Lob. Par. 378, but Bekker writes it proparoxytone, as it should undoubtedly be: Μαντομάγος, Eudocia p. 287, is contrary to all analogy: for συνοπαδός see § 234: τετραπιαζός (?) a surgical instrument so called, H. D.

422. NOTE 4.—There seems to have been some disposition on the part of the grammarians to retain the accent in compounds from oxytones in εος and ιος, but it is questionable whether their practice is correct: πατραδελφεός, Pind. Isth. 8. 144: μητραδελφεός, Pind. Pyth. 8. 36; λευκερινεός, Eust. 1205. 5: λευκερωδιός is the reading of several MSS. in Arist. H. A. 8. 3. 12, and Bekker has retained it, though one MS. has λευκορώδιος and two others λευκορόδιος: ἐξανέψιος is not unfrequently oxytone, but in Attic at least it was barytone, Trypho ap. Ammon. p. 54: αὐτανεψιός, Plat. Euthyd. 275 B, is written αὐτανέψιος, Pollux 3. 28: παρανυμφίος, Eust. 652. 42, is so written in one MS. of Pollux 3. 40, but Bekker reads παρανύμφος: μελλονύμφιος, Pollux 3. 45, seems to be proparoxytone without variation: συγκορυφαῖος (?) H. D.; on the compounds of πλόος see Schol. Ven. M. 26; Eust. 890. 51.

423. NOTE 5.—Ou ἄψορρος see Lob. Par. 330: for ἐπιθυμιατρός, *L. S.*, there does not seem to be any authority; Chœrob. E. 78. 5 appears to assert that compounds of ἰατρός remain oxytone, and mentions ἀρχιατρός, cf. E. M. 250. 29; while Arcadius 86. 18 says: τὸ δὲ ἰατρὸς φιλίατρος ἀναβιβάζει, καὶ ἐν τῷ ἀρχιατρὸς καὶ ἱππιατρὸς φυλάττει; in MSS. both ἱππίατρος and ἱππιατρός are found, yet κτηνίατρος and λογίατρος seem to occur without variation; it is just possible that these words were made oxytone from an idea that they were in some way or other verbals with an active meaning; I have somewhere seen κέρκουρος and τράχουρος made properispomena, but have lost the reference, and cannot at the moment recover it: ἀρχιεταῖρος also occurs, but is contrary to analogy, and probably wrong, cf. πεζέταιρος, παραβαλέταιρος, etc; for σύαγρος and those in ουρος and ωρος see below, §§ 432, 456.

424. NOTE 6.—Ὑπαιετός stands in some MSS. of Arist. H. A. 9. 32. 3 for ὑπαίετος or ὑπάετος: Lob. Par. 378: 'pro μελαναιετός et ὑπαιετός Bekkerus proparoxytona substituit, ut ἁλιαίετος scribitur Eur. Polyid. 1; Arist. H. A. 8. 3. p. 583. 23 [=9. 32. 4; cf. 9. 34. 6], Mirab. 60, etsi in hoc quoque libri variant, et ὑψιαίετος Anton. Lib. c. 20, βυρσαίετος et γρυπαίετος apud Aristophanem sine ullo discrepantis scripturæ indicio;' to these may be added χρυσαίετος, γυπαίετος, νυκταιἔτος, ἱππάετος: there is no valid ground for making any of these compounds oxytone: Συοβοιωτοί, Hesych., may perhaps be defended as a name applied to a nation, E. M. 215. 1: τὰ γὰρ εἰς ΟΣ ὀνόματα δισύλλαβα, ὀξύτονα, ἐν τῇ συνθέσει ἀναβιβάζει τὸν τόνον ... χωρὶς τῶν ἐπὶ ἐθνικῶν λαμβανομένων· οἷον Ἀχαιός, φιλαχαιός· Βοιωτὸς φιλοβοιωτός; 'Ελαιοτρυγητός, *vindemia olearum,* Schneid. sine test.' H. D.: this is indefensible on any grounds.

425. NOTE 7.—Göttling (Accent. p. 228) says that ἀδελφός appears to retain its accent in composition when the compound is a substantive, but there is no authority for such an accentuation beyond an isolated instance or two, which are probably mistakes; ἀνδράδελφος is made oxytone by L. S., and γυναικάδελφος is written γυναικαδελφός in Chron. Pasch. p. 303 C; Constant. Cærem. p. 384 B; *H. D.*; the rest seem to be regular, ἐξάδελφος, μητράδελφος, αὐτάδελφος, ψευδάδελφος, συνάδελφος, δισεξάδελφος, πατράδελφος, ἀντάδελφος, πρωτεξάδελφος, ἀνδροεξάδελφος, τεκνάδελφος: ὀλοοίτροχος or ὀλοίτροχος, Schol. Ven. N. 137: Δημήτριος ὁ γονύπεσος δασύνει, ἵν' ᾖ ὅλος τροχοειδὴς καὶ κατὰ πᾶν μέρος ἀστήρικτος, τῷ δὲ τόνῳ ὡς κακότροποι· ὄντως δὲ καὶ Ἑρμαπίας καὶ Νικίας καὶ Ἀριστέας καὶ Ἀριστόνικος. Κωμανὸς δὲ καὶ Πτολεμαῖος ὁ Ἀσκαλωνίτης ψιλοῦσι καὶ παροξύνουσιν, ἀκούοντες τὸν ἐπὶ τὸ τρέχειν ὀλοὸν καὶ δεινόν.

IV. COMPOUND ADJECTIVES.

426. Compound Adjectives fall into two main classes, for either 1. the latter half is derived directly or indirectly from a verb, or 2. from a noun. The former may for convenience be called *Verbal*, the latter *Nominal* derivatives.

Verbal Derivatives.

General rule.—Verbal derivatives retract the accent, except

Oxytone.—1. All in τος with three terminations;

       2. Those with a *long* penultimate and active meaning.

Paroxytone.—Those with a *short* penultimate and active meaning when the part preceding the verbal ending is a substantive, an adjective, or their equivalents.

These distinctions are purely arbitrary as far as accentuation is concerned; a Verbal derivative merely means here that a word is accented in a particular way, and in practice this general rule is subject to so many modifications and exceptions, that we shall consider in detail (*a*) verbal adjectives (so called) with a long penultimate, (*b*) those with a short penultimate, (*c*) those in τος, which we exclude entirely from the two preceding classes.

427. NOTE—That *all* verbal adjectives are not accented in accordance with the rules so positively laid down by writers, both ancient and modern, is clear from the following words, taken at random: ἐρίμυκος, μεγαλόμυκος, ἱερόσυλος, γυμνα-σίαρχος[1], ὠκύμολος, αὐτόμολος, μεγαλόβρομος, μεγαλόβρυχος, μεγαλόηχος, μεγάμυκος, νεκρόταγος, δευτερόγαμος, ὀψίγαμος, μεγαλόκομπος, ἱππόδαμος (Schol. Ven. Λ. 270), σακέσπαλος (the Codex Ven. of Homer, Il. E. 126, has σακεσπάλος, cf. Dindorf Præf. Hom. Il. Oxon. 8vo. 1856. p. 11), χειρότονος, πορνόφιλος, βριήπυος, Schol. Ven. N. 521, διφθεράλοιφος, πυρίβρομος, πολύκροτος, κωδωνόκροτος, πυρίτροχος, πύρπνοος (not πυρπνόος), ταυρόθροος, ὀξύγοος, ὀξυήκοος, ὀρείοικος (cf. L. S. s. v.), ἀερίοικος, πολύ-θουρος, ἀποινόδορπος, πτολίπορθος (E. M. 694. 43), γαστρίμαργος, αἰσόσυλος, ἐπήορος, etc.; as far as form and meaning go, these words, and a multitude of others, are verbals in exactly the same sense as those to which the rule applies, but they are not accented as such; and this treatment is usually justified by saying that they are derived from nouns and not from verbs, which is in fact to say that the rule is by no means universal, and that it is arbitrary and capricious. Lobeck (Ajax 188 sqq.) has collected numerous instances of irregular accents; it is clear that the scribes had not the least notion how to write many of these verbal adjectives, and editors of printed books are equally at a loss.

428. *It is to be noted that a large number of these verbal adjectives are used elliptically as substantives,* e. g. βουκόλος, βου-φορβός, δορυξόος, ἱστοριογράφος, οἰωνοσκόπος, τραγῳδός, χοιρο-βοσκός, etc.

(a) Verbal Derivatives with a Long Penultimate.

429. When the penultimate is long, those with an active meaning are oxytone, the rest proparoxytone. Decompounds, or words consisting of more than two factors, are generally proparoxytone, whether their meaning be active or passive, as στρατηγός, ἀρχιστράτηγος, συναγωγός, ἀρχισυνάγωγος. Although the rule is stated thus broadly by writers on the subject, it is only applicable to the following terminations, and a reference to the sections which follow will show that the books present many irregularities: αγος (and ηγος), αγρος, αγωγος, ακονος, αλγος (?), αμοιβος, ῳδος, αρωγος, ασκος, βοηθος, βοσκος, εργος (ουργος and ωργος), but κακοῦργος and πανοῦργος are properi-spomena; εψος, κουρος, λοιγος, λοιχος, μολγος, οιγος, ολκος (ουλκος and ωλκος), οπαδος, ουρος (and ωρος), πηγος, ποιος, words of this ending remain oxytone however compounded; πομπος, φορβος. For examples of each reference may be made to the sections which follow.

---

[1] On these it is observed by Arc. 90. 17: τὰ ἀπὸ δισυλλάβου ῥήματος, οὗ ἡ ἄρχουσα μακρά, συντεθειμένα προπαροξύνεται, μυκῶ, ἐρίμυκος, συλῶ, ἱερόσυλος, ἄρχω, γυμνασίαρχος; he seems to have forgotten the existence of such words as βροτο-λοιχός from λείχω, ὑλοκουρός from κείρω, and the like; in short, his rule is absurd; though it may be accepted as evidence concerning the accent of those in μυκος, συλος, and αρχος.

430. -αγος and -ηγος (ἄγω ἡγέομαι).—Arc. 88. 1, as ἀληγός, ἁρματηγός, ἀρχαγός, ἀρχηγός, θαλαμηγός, ἱππηγός, νεκυηγός, κυνηγός, ξεναγός, ξυληγός, ὁδαγός, ὁδηγός, οὐραγός, ὀχετηγός, ποδηγός, προαγός, σιτηγός, στρατηγός, ταριχηγός, ὑδρηγός, χορηγός, etc.

Decompounds.—Ἀρχικύνηγος, but ἀρχικυνηγός is quoted by H. D. from Manetho 5. 289; συγκύνηγος is oxytone in Plut. 2. 749 E; in Eurip. Iph. T. 709 we have συγκυναγός, but in Bacch. 1135 ξυγκύναγος: φιλοκύνηγος: καθοδηγός is quoted by H. D. from Orph. Hymn. 7. 8; Clem. Alex. p. 102 ed. Pott.; Schol. Hom. Il. B. 494, and προοδηγός from Maccab. 2. 12. 36; Orac. Sibyll. 8. p. 778, but they are both contrary to analogy: ἀστράτηγος, ἀντιχόρηγος, ἀντιστράτηγος, ἀρχιστράτηγος, ἀξιοστράτηγος, ἀποστράτηγος, μονοστράτηγος, πρωτοστράτηγος, ὑποστράτηγος are all regular, but συστράτηγος or ξυστράτηγος is often oxytone in MSS. e. g. Xenoph. Anab. 2. 6. 29: ὑπολόχαγος is also oxytone in Xenoph. Anab. 5. 2. 13; both passages are quoted by H. D., who also have ἐπιχορηγός from Epiphan. t. 1. p. 946 D.

431. -αγος (ἄγνυμι).—Ναυαγός and νανηγός are by usage oxytone, though passive in signification, Arc. 90. 3.

432. -αγρος (ἀγρέω?).—Ποδαγρός, *suffering from the gout,* Lucian Tragœdop. and elsewhere, is irregular in every respect, yet it seems well established, and is supported by the somewhat doubtful χειραγρός. All other compounds with this termination are proparoxytone, as σύαγρος, πολύαγρος, μύαγρος, etc.

433. -αγωγος (ἄγω). *With an Active meaning.*—Ἀγκαλιδαγωγός, αἱμαγωγός, ἀναγωγός, ἐπανάγωγος, ἀπαγωγός, δημαγωγός, γεροντραγωγός, γλευκαγωγός, ἐπαγωγός, ἐλεφανταγωγός, ἱππαγωγός, ἰακχαγωγός, κοπραγωγός, κυφαγωγός (?) this is the accent given by L. S. and H. D., but it seems doubtful; κυναγωγός, λοχαγωγός, μυριαγωγός, μυσταγωγός, νωταγωγός, νυμφαγωγός, A. G. Oxon. 2. 393. 26, ξεναγωγός, ὀδονταγωγός, οἰναγωγός, ὁπλιταγωγός, ὀχλαγωγός, παιδαγωγός, φορταγωγός, παραγωγός, *leading alongside* or *together* (παράγωγος, *derived, superfluous,* H. D. quote this as oxytone from Schol. Hom. Il. Π. 635 [?] but that accent is probably a mistake, though it is a mistake which recurs, e. g. Schol. Ven. A. 496), εὐπαράγωγος is also used in a passive sense; περιαγωγός; the decompound συμπεριαγωγός, Plat. Rep. 533 D, is irregular; προαγωγός, A. G. Oxon. 2. 393. 27; προσαγωγός, συναγωγός (ἀσυνάγωγος, ἀρχισυνάγωγος, ἀποσυνάγωγος), σιταγωγός, σκευαγωγός, ὑπαγωγός, ὑδραγωγός, ὑλαγωγός, φωταγωγός, χειραγωγός, χολαγωγός, χρεαγωγός, ψυχαγωγός.

With a Passive meaning.—Ἀδιάγωγος, ἀνάγωγος=ἀκόλαστος καὶ ἀπαίδευτος, δυσανάγωγος, δυσδιάγωγος, δυσπαράγωγος, δυσπεριάγωγος, εὐανάγωγος (not εὐαναγωγός), εὐδιάγωγος, παράγωγος, εὐπεριάγωγος, εὐσυνάγωγος, ἀπαράγωγος, εὐάγωγος (this is oxytone in Isocr. p. 224 A), ἀπαιδάγωγος, etc.

434. -ακουος.—Ὑπακουός, ἐπακουός, Arc. 45. 15; 90. 12; Apoll. Synt. p. 330, quoted above, § 317; E. M. 51. 23.

435. -αλγος (ἀλγέω?).—Κεφαλαλγός in Plut. 2. 133 C is very suspicious, though it receives some slight confirmation from ποδαλγός, Greg. Naz. Ep. 57, and χειραλγός, Georg. Al. Vita Chrys. Tom. 8. p. 255. 17, quoted by H. D.; γλώσσαλγος is proparoxytone in Pollux 6. 119.

436. -αμοιβος (ἀμείβω).—Ἀργυραμοιβός, ἀλφιταμοιβός, ἀντημοιβός, ἀνταμοιβός, ἀντιαμοιβός, ἐξημοιβός, though this appears to be rather passive than active, ἐπαμοιβός, ἐπημοιβός, χρυσαμοιβός: ἱεράμοιβος in Hesych. is doubtful.

437. -αοιδος and -ῳδος (ἀείδω).—Arc. 86. 24: τὰ παρὰ τὸ ᾄδω γινόμενα, εἰ μὲν τῇ ΟΙ διφθόγγῳ παραλήγονται, ὀξύνεται· τραγῳδός, κωμῳδός, μελῳδός· εἰ δὲ τῇ

Οἱ διφθόγγῳ, εἰ μὲν ὑπὲρ τρεῖς συλλαβὰς ὦσι, προπαροξύνεται· λιγυάοιδος ὑπεράοιδος· εἰ δὲ τρεῖς ὁμοίως· ὑμνάοιδος ἐπάοιδος λυράοιδος. τὰ δὲ ἐξ αὐτῶν ὀξύνεται· ὑμνῳδός, ἐπῳδός, λυρῳδός. According to this, compounds in αοιδος are proparoxytone, yet ἐπάοιδος is oxytone in the Septuagint and in Philo Jud. 401 A; H. *D.*; so θεσπιαοιδός, ἱεραοιδός, Hesych., ἱμαοιδός, Pollux 4. 53 : κιθαραοιδός, H. *D.*, is probably with more correctness made proparoxytone by L. S. : λυράοιδος, Arc. 86. 24 ; this, according to Apoll. de Syut. 330. 20, as a parasynthetic word, is oxytone, and it seems to be so accented in the books : νεάοιδος, Apoll. de Syut. 330, this is also oxytone : περιάοιδος, Hesych., is oxytone in Suid. : στιχαοιδός, Auth. Plan. 4. 316, quoted by H. D. : φιλαοιδός, Theocr. 28. 23.

Those in ῳδος are regular : ἀντῳδός, ἀπῳδός, ἀρνῳδός, αὐλῳδός, βαρβιτῳδός, ἐνῳδός, ἐπῳδός, θεσπιῳδός, θρηνῳδός, ἱλαρῳδός, κιθαρῳδός, κωμῳδός, λυρῳδός, λυσιῳδός, μαγῳδός, μελῳδός, μεσῳδός, μονῳδός, νομῳδός, παρῳδός, ποικιλῳδός, προσῳδός, ῥαβδῳδός, ῥαψῳδός (ψευδοραψῳδός, Hesych., is irregular), στιχῳδός, συνῳδός, τραγῳδός, (ἀτράγῳδος, παρατράγῳδος), τρυγῳδός, ὑμνῳδός, χρησμῳδός, ψαλμῳδός, ψαλτῳδός, yet, in the face of all this, we have ἄνῳδος in Arist. H. A. 1. 1. 29, and πρόσῳδος, E. M. 691. 48.

438. -αρωγος (ἀρήγω).—Ἐπαρωγός, συναρωγός, A. G. Oxon. 2. 343. 4.

439. -ασκος (ἀσκέω), as φωνασκός, which seems to be the only word thus compounded, Arc. 88. 3.

440. -αυγος (?)—Φωταυγός is quoted by H. D. from Nicet. Dav. Paraph. Greg. Naz. p. 69. 22 ; Dronk. and φώταυγος from Zonar. 1836, and elsewhere : the former accent cannot be right : cf. περίαυγος, ὕπαυγος.

441. -βοηθος.—Συμβοηθός is irregular, though apparently well established : ἀβόηθος is passive in meaning.

442. -βοσκος (βόσκω), Arc. 87. 25.—Αἰγοβοσκός, ἀνθοβοσκός, Soph. Frag. 110. ed. Didot : βοοβοσκός, γηροβοσκός (γηρωβοσκός?) : ἐλαφόβοσκος, *fed on by deer*, hence τὸ ἐλαφόβοσκον, *a plant so called* : κραιπαλόβοσκος δίψα seems to be passive in meaning : λωτοβοσκός or λωτόβοσκος, according as it is active or passive : ὀρνιθοβοσκός (?) παιδοβοσκός, πολυβοσκός, πορνοβοσκός, Arc. 87. 25 : προβοσκός, Herodot. 1. 113; some MSS. read πρόβοσκος (προβόσκων) : προβατοβοσκός, ὑοβοσκός, Arc. 87. 25 : χειροβοσκός, in the sense of *one who supports himself by his hands*, may be right : χοιροβοσκός, χηνοβοσκός, Arc. 87. 25 : χιονόβοσκος, *snow-fed*, Æschyl. Supp. 560, should probably not be oxytone : ἱερακοβοσκός, Ælian H. A. 7. 9 : καμηλοβοσκός, Strab. 768.

443. -δεψος (δέφω).—Σκυλαδέψος and σκυτοδεψός in L. S. are somewhat doubtful : σκυλάδεψος occurs in Eust. 710. 18 : σκυλόδεψος, Demosth. 781. 18 : σκυτόδεψος, Plat. Gorg. 517 E, where Stallbaum has σκυτοδεψός ; and βυρσόδεψος in Suid., H. D.

444. -εργος, -ουργος, -ωργος (ἔργω, ἐργάζομαι).

-εργος, *with Active meaning*, as ἀεργός and ἀργός, αἰσυλοεργός, συνεργός, Arc, 88. 17 : (ἀσύνεργος), ἀγαθοεργός, ὀλβιοεργός, δημιοεργός, παντοεργός, ἐτωσιεργός. κακοεργός, ὀλοεργός, ὀβριμοεργός, λυροεργός, φυτοεργός, ἁλιεργός, ἀμπελοεργός, ἀνυσιεργός, ὑποεργός, ταχυεργός (not ταχύεργος, though that is quoted by H. D. from Appian. Pun. c. 47), ἀγλαοεργός.

With Passive meaning : ἡμίεργος, ἀμφίεργος, κάτεργος, ἄνεργος, καλλίεργος, πάρεργος, πρόσεργος.

NOTE—Many words of this termination are irregular in their accent, e. g. ταλαεργός, *bearing work* ; one does not see upon what principle this can be oxytone, and yet it always is : ἄπεργος, *not working, idle,* is proparoxytone, but ἀμβολιεργός, *putting off work, lazy,* oxytone : ἀξιοεργός, *capable of work;* χαριεργός : φύγεργος, *shunning work, L. S.,* is oxytone in E. M. 199. 1, as is φιλεργός in Strab. 378, and elsewhere ; the adverb however is φιλέργως in Ælian, but φιλεργῶς in Pollux 3. 121 : the latter form is approved of by H. D. s. v., and yet under the word φιλοεργός (which they quote from Anth. Pal. 6. 48 ; 7. 423 ; Const. Manass. Chron. etc.) they say, ' scribendum φιλόεργον et φιλοέργους secundum regulam Arcadii, p. 87. 18 :' μίσεργος, Pollux 6. 172 : ἠλιτοεργός, *missing the work,* Anth. Pal. 7. 210, quoted by H. D., and ἔπεργος, in an active sense, are not astonishing amidst so much inconsistency : πολύεργος, Arc. 87. 21 ; Schol. Nicand. Ther. 7, is oxytone in Theocr. 25. 27 : ἐκάεργος, though active in sense, is always proparoxytone, Arc. 87. 21.

The active and passive meanings of περίεργος (ἀπερίεργος is regular as a decompound) and δύσεργος do not appear to be distinguished accentually : ἐνεργός remains oxytone even when passive, while in εὔεργος or εὐεργός (cf. E. M. 394. 46) both meaning and accent are confused ; Arcadius, 89. 13, makes it oxytone.

445. -ουργος (= οεργος).—These are oxytone, as ἐλεφαντουργός, αὐτουργός, πρωτουργός, δημιουργός, ὑπουργός, ψευδουργός, αἰσχρουργός, ἀθεμιτουργός, βαναυσουργός, παντουργός, φαυλουργός, ἀνοσιουργός, ῥᾳδιουργός, ἐθελουργός, συνιερουργός, except κακοῦργος and πανοῦργος, Arc. 87. 20 ; A. G. Oxon. 1. 305. 28.

Note.—There is no lack of irregularities here, e. g. ἀλουργός is oxytone, though it is not active in meaning. The following decompounds deviate from the rule : συνδημιουργός, Plat. Legg. 671 D : βαυκοπανοῦργος, Arist. Eth. Nic. 4. 7. 15 : τριπανοῦργος, Auth. Pal. 12. 57 : L. S. have τριπάνουργος, which is perhaps better, and ἀπάνουργος : παγκάκουργος is παγκακοῦργος in Hesych., Schmidt however prints it proparoxytone, φιλοκακοῦργος, Sept. : συλλειτουργός is quoted by H. D. from Epiphanius and other late writers : φλαυρουγός, in Soph. Phil. 35, is in some books φλαυρούγου, and therefore φλαυροῦγος : λαθροκακοῦργος, H. D.

446. -οργος, -ωργος (ἔργω).—In Hesych. we have ὠμοργός and ὑποοργός, λαοργός, which are regular. On the proper name Φιλοργός (?) see above § 232.

Those in ωργος are regular, as γεωργός, λεωργός, λειωργός, συγγέωργος, φιλογέωργος, πανγέωργος, συγγέωργος, Schol. Aristoph. Plut. 223 : ξυγγέωργυς βαρυτόνως· σύνθετον γάρ, ὡς πάγκαλος, πάνσοφος. τὰ γὰρ εἰς ΟΣ ὀξύτονα συντιθέμενα βαρύνεται : yet it is falsely oxytone in Pollux 6. 158 : φιλογέωργος, Schol. Apollon. Rhod. 1. 188, is oxytone in Diod. Sic. 1. 15, and elsewhere.

Note.—The rules given by Arcadius for the accentuation of these words are on a par with the accentuation itself. He says (17. 18) : τὰ εἰς ΟΣ συντιθειμένα παρὰ τὸ ἔργον μὴ ὄντα κύρια ὀξύνεται· ἐλεφαντουργός αὐτουργός· τὸ μέντοι κακοῦργος καὶ πανοῦργος βαρύνεται, ὁμοίως καὶ τὸ ἐκάεργος περίεργος πολύεργος πάρεργος : and again, 88. 12, ὅσα πρόθεσιν ἔχει ἐν τῇ ἀρχῇ προπαροξύνεται· περίβολος Ὑπέρβολος . . . χωρὶς τῶν ἀπὸ κλειτός καὶ κλυτός . . . καὶ τὰ παρὰ τὸ ἔργον ὑπουργός συνεργός.

447. -εψος (ἔψω).—These are regular, as μυρεψός, χυτρεψός.

448. -κουρος (κείρω).—Arc. 73. 2, has ὑλοκουρός, ὁ τὴν ὕλην τέμνων ; and according to analogy σιτόκουρος ought to be oxytone ; but it is not so in our books : πρωτόκουρος, περίκουρος, ἀμφίκουρος, τρίκουρος, ἄκουρος, are regular, having a passive sense.

449. -λοιγος (— ?) oxytone, as ἀθηρηλοιγός, βροτολοιγός, E. M. 25. 24 ; 250. 29.

450. -λοιχος (λείχω), oxytone, as αἱματολοιχός, αἰσχρολοιχός, βροτολοιχύς (Eust. 518. 41), κνισσολοιχός (Eust. 1817. 38), ματτυολοιχός, ματιολοιχός (Herodian ap. Schol. Aristoph. Nub. 450): τραπεζολοιχός; κνισσολοιχός (or κνισολοιχός) is written κνισολοῖχος in Athen. 125 B.

451. -μολγος (ἀμέλγω), Arc. 87. 27. These are regular, as βουμολγός, ἱππημολγός, (ἱππομολγός).

452. -οιγος (οἴγνυμι). Θυροιγός occurs in Hesych., and seems to be the only word of this termination.

453. -ολκος, -ουλκος, -ωλκος (ἕλκω), Arc. 87. 27. They are regular, as ἀνθολκός, ἰχθυολκός, ἐφολκός, βελουλκός, λιθουλκός (also used substantively), ψυχουλκός, νεωλκός, κυνουλκός. Πάρολκος, *a tow rope*, is thus accented in Schol. Thucyd. 4. 25: ἀφολκός, *a lighter*, H. D.: διολκός is oxytone in Strab. 355; Hesych: paroxytone in Strab. 369, 380: both words should be oxytone. Δίολκος, as a proper name, is regular, Ptol. 4. 5. 10: ψυχουλκός, *a plant*, is falsely written ψυχοῦλκος in Hesych.: σύνολκος, *drawn together*, is regular: ἐνδίολκος, H. D.

454. -οπαδος (ὀπάζω?). Συνοπαδός is regular.

455. -ουρος, -ωρος, as κηπουρός, θυρωρός, ἀρκυωρός; these are commonly said to come from οὖρος, *custos*, but their accentuation, as well as the authority of the ancient grammarians, shew that their termination is of a strictly verbal character. They are regular as οἰκουρός (συνοίκουρος), συκουρός,·συκωρός, πυλουρός, πυλωρός, A. G. Oxon. 2. 254. 10, πυλαωρός, Dor. πυλαρός, ἀρκυωρός, θυρωρός, ἀκτωρός, σκευωρός, Theog. Can. 72. 4, σκοπιωρός. It is more than doubtful whether the oxytone θεωρός, Doric θεαρός, belongs to this head, and the same remark applies to several other words mentioned here: ἀρχιθέωρος, E. M. 151. 32, is oxytone in Arist. Eth. Nic. 4. 2. 2, and elsewhere: πανθέωρος, συνθέωρος, (wrongly oxytone, Pollux 2. 55), φιλοθέωρος; cf. Lob. Ajax. 335, note 2; τιμωρός (L. S. derive this from τιμή, ἀείρω, αἴρω), but its uncontracted form is τιμήορος, μυλωρός, Theog. Can. 72. 4. Δύσουρος, εὔωρος, πανάωρος are passive in meaning, but ἐπίουρος (only used substantively), Schol. Ven. N. 450, ὀλίγωρος are proparoxytone. H. D. quote ἑρκοῦρος for ἑρκουρός from Anth. Palat. 12. 257. 2, where however ὀρκούρος stands in the text: οἰκουρός, Arc. 70. 5; 73. 5; 86. 11, was by some written οἰκοῦρος, Eust. 1423. 7: ὁδουρός is improperly ὅδουρος in Eust. 1445. 19, and ὁδοῦρος in Hesych.: μύχουρος in Lycoph. 373 can hardly be correct: οἰκόθουρος, ὁ οἰκουρὸς κύων, Hesych., is doubtful both as to derivation and accent: Lycoph. 345 has φρύκτωρος for φρυκτωρός: Apollon. Rhod. 1. 1227, ὑλήωρος for ὑληωρός: Hesych. τεμένωρος for τεμενωρός: Etym. Gud. 30. 17, ἀκταίωρος for ἀκταιωρός. The word ἀγχοῦρος, Arc. 73. 10, = φωσφόρος has a strange accent, but it may be compared with Ἀρκτοῦρος, Arc. 73. 10, νυκτοῦρος, Plut. 2.941 C, and κλαγγοῦρος ὁ κρακτικός, Arc. 73. 10: τηλουρός is accented like a verbal, and according to Göttling, Accent. 209, really is one (cf. Arc. 73. 6), though he does not mention the verb from which he supposes it to be derived: αὐλίκουροι, Suid., appears to be corrupt; cf. Lob. Prol. 147, note; 272: τετράορος (ἄρω), τέτρωρος is proparoxytone. Those in ωρος from ὥρα are necessarily proparoxytone, as ὑπέρωρος, ἔξωρος.

-οχος, -ουχος (ἔχω). See Verbal Adjectives with a short penultimate, § 495.

456. -πηγος (πήγνυμι), Arc. 88. 1. All of these, both compounds and *decompounds*, with active meaning, are oxytone, as ἀμαξοπηγός, σοροπηγός, ἁρματοπηγός, τορνευτολυρασπιδοπηγός. Παλίμπηγος, Pollux 6. 164, is passive in meaning.

457. -ποιος (ποιέω), Arc. 88. 2. All, decompounds as well as compounds, are oxytone, as σιτοποιός, ἀρχισιτοποιός, ἀσπιδοποιός, διθυραμβοποιός, τραγῳδοποιός, παιδοποιός; αὐτόποιος, Soph. Œd. Col. 698, is the one solitary exception, and therefore probably a false accent.

458. -πομπος (πέμπω). *Active*—᾿Αναπομπός, εὐθυπομπός, νεκροπομπός, παραπομπός, προπομπός, ψυχοπομπός.

Passive, etc.—εὔπομπος, ναυσίπομπος, τηλέπομπος.

NOTE.—Ναυσίπομπος, *ship-wafting*, Eurip. Phœn. 1727, ought, from its meaning, to be oxytone: ὠκύπομπος is thus accented in Eurip. Iph. T. 1138, but it is oxytone in the same play, 1428: ταχύπομπος in Æschyl. Supp. 1046, ed. Didot., might perhaps be considered passive in sense.

459. -φορβος (φέρβω), Arc. 88. 3. *Active.*—Βουφορβός (Arc. 46. 11), ἱπποφορβός (Arc. 88. 3), ὀνοφορβός, συφορβός, συοφορβός, ὑλοφορβός, ὑοφορβός, ὑφορβός.

Passive.—Εὔφορβος, and the same accent seems to occur when the word is active.

NOTE.—Μονόφορβος, Hesych., μυόφορβος, πάμφορβος, and πολύφορβος are all of them probably errors, but there is authority for αὐτόφορβος, Arc. 88. 4: τὸ δὲ αὐτόφορβος οἱ πλείους βαρύνουσι.

(b) Verbal Derivatives with a Short Penultimate.

460. Verbal derivatives with a short penultimate and active meaning are paroxytone, unless they are compounded with a preposition, or with a *privativum*, εὖ, δυς-, ἀεὶ, ἄγαν, ἀρι-, ἄρτι, ἐρι-, ὁμοῦ, πάλιν, or ἡμι-, in which case they are proparoxytone. Those which are passive in signification retract the accent. Hence δισκοβόλος, *throwing the discus*, ἐλαφηβόλος, *deer-hitting*, ἐπεσβόλος, *word-throwing*, τηλεβόλος, *far-throwing*, λιθοβόλος, *stone-throwing*, but λιθόβολος, *hit with stones, stoned*, διάβολος, though transitive in meaning, is proparoxytone, because compounded with a preposition, and the same is the case with ἐπίβολος, περίβολος, σύμβολος, παλίμβολος. Διόβολος, δροσόβολος, νιφόβολος, χιονόβολος are passive in meaning, and therefore proparoxytone.

The following are the terminations to which this rule applies: βαφος, βολος, βορος, γλυφος, γονος, γραφος, δοκος, δομος, δονος, δορος, δοχος, δρομος, δροπος, ηγορος, θοος (only βοηθόος), θορος, κλοπος, κολος, κομος, κοος, κοπος, κορος, κροκος (?), κτονος, λαβος, λαλος, λογος, λοχος, μαχος, μορος, νομος, ξοος, πλαθος, πλοκος, ποκος, πολος, πονος, πορος, προπος, ραφος, ροφος, σκαφος, σκοπος, σοος, σπορος, στολος, στροφος, σφαγος, τοκος, τομος, τορος, τραγος, τροφος, τυπος (κτυπος), φαγος, φθορος, φοβος, φονος, φορος, χοος, ὡρυχος; for examples of each reference may be made to the following sections.

461. Note—E. M. 775. 47 : ὥσπερ γὰρ τὸ ὑδροφόρος, παροξυτόνως μὲν σημαίνει ἐνέργειαν· προπαροξυτόνως δὲ πάθος· τὸ μὲν γάρ ἐστιν ὁ φέρων τὸ ὕδωρ· τὸ δὲ τὸ ἀπὸ ὕδατος φερόμενον. ἆρα καὶ ἐν πᾶσι τοῖς ἀπὸ ῥημάτων συντιθεμένοις ταὐτὸν εἶναι εὑρίσκομεν; φασὶν ὅτι ἐπίπαν. ὅτι δὲ ἔνια μόρια παραβαίνοντα τὸν λόγον, ὡς αἱ προθέσεις καὶ τὰ ἐπιτακτικά. οἷον ἐπίσκοπος καὶ ζάχρυσος, ἐνέργειαν σημαίνει, οὐ πάθος καὶ προπαροξύνεται καὶ τὰ ὅμοια· ὥσπερ τὸ ναύβατος παροξυτόνως [?] μὲν παθητικός· προπαροξυτόνως δὲ ἐνεργητικός· τὸ μὲν γὰρ δηλοῖ τὸν ἐπιβαίνοντα ἐπὶ τὴν ναῦν· τὸ δὲ τὸν ὑπὸ τῆς νηὸς βαινόμενον. ἆρα καὶ τὰ λοιπὰ τὸν αὐτὸν λόγον φυλάττει; λέγεται πάλιν ὡς ἐπίπαν· ἰδοὺ ἀτερπὴς μῦθος, ὁ μὴ τέρπων ὀξύνεται ἐνεργητικός, καὶ ἀνηλεής ὁ μὴ ἐλεῶν· καὶ φιλομηδής (sic) ἡ φιλοῦσα τὸν γέλωτα, καὶ ἀνεμοσκεπὴς χλαῖνα ἡ ἐκ τοῦ ἀνέμου σκέπουσα· καὶ δυσαής, ὁ δεινῶς πνέων· τοὐναντίον δὲ τριήρης ναῦς, ἡ ὑπὸ τριῶν ἐρεσσομένη· ἐν γὰρ τοῖς παροξυτόνοις ἐστὶ παθητικὸν ὁμοίως καὶ ἀλίηρης καὶ πανώλης καὶ ἐξώλης τὸ ἀπόλλυσθαι παθητικῶς ἐγκείμενον : on the accentuation of these adjectives see Arc. 85. 21–91. 6; Schol. Ven. Γ. 354; E. M. 215. 1; 394. 46; 408. 23; 453. 2; 475. 1; 686. 10; 694. 43; Eust. 423. 20; 578. 40; 642. 42; 769. 26; 843. 55; 907. 5; 924. 28; 992. 55; 1091. 58; A. G. Oxon. 1. 8. 10; 32. 6; 139. 16; 286. 6; 312. 14; 354. 16.

462. Note.—It is sometimes stated that all verbal adjectives with a short penultimate are proparoxytone when compounded with an adverb; but this is not the case, witness λαθροβόλος, λαθροφάγος, μαψιλόγος, μαψιτόκος, μογιλάλος, and a hundred besides: nor is there any more truth in the assertion that those compounded with πολύ retract the accent, e. g. πολυβόλος, πολυγράφος, πολυηγόρος, πολυκτόνος, πολυλόγος, πολυπόρος, πολυτόκος, πολυφάγος, πολυφόρος, etc., are all pretty well attested; however, we find E. M. 681. 30 saying, ὅσα τὰ ΠΟΛΥ' ἔχει ἐν τῇ συνθέσει κατὰ τὴν ἀρχήν, ὀνόματος ἐπιφερομένου ἢ ῥήματος ἐν τέλει προπαροξύνεται, πολύκαρπος, πολύϊδος, τὸ δὲ πολυφάγος παροξύνεται, καὶ τὰ παρὰ τὸ φαγεῖν συντιθέμενα κατὰ τὸ τέλος παροξύνονται, ποηφάγος ὁ ποιμήν· παμφάγος, ὠμοφάγος : Arcadius (89. 7) also holds or seems to hold the same opinion : ὅσα ἐν τῇ ἀρχῇ συντίθεται ἐκ τοῦ πολύ, προπαροξύνεται, πολύστροφος, πολύκαρπος, πολύφιλος : the former passage is probably corrupt, the latter certainly so ; but even as they stand it is by no means clear that Herodian ever meant to assert that verbals with an active meaning were proparoxytone when compounded with πολύ : at any rate, practice is against him if he did ; see especially Lob. Path. 1. 568 sqq.

463. -βαφος (βάπτω). *Active.*—Ἀνθοβάφος, πορφυροβάφος, πτιλοβάφος.

Passive, etc.—Ἄβαφος, δίβαφος, χολόβαφος or χολοίβαφος.

464. -βολος, βαλος (βάλλω), Arc. 88. 18. *Active.*—Δισκοβόλος, ἑκατηβόλος, δευτεροβόλος, πρωτοβόλος, ἑκηβόλος, ἑκασβόλος, τηλεβόλος, ἐλαφηβόλος, ἀκροβόλος, one that throws from afar : ἀκρόβολος, struck from afar : ἰθυβόλος, εὐθυβόλος, πολυβόλος, πλειστοβόλος, δεξιοβόλος, ἰσοβόλος, κερασβόλος, ὠκυβόλος.

Passive, etc.—Πρόβαλος, ἐπίβολος and ἐπήβολος, δίβολος, δύσβολος, τρίβολος, παλίμβολος, ὀρθόβολος, εὔβολος.

Note.—E. M. 355. 4: Σκέρβολος, Schol. Aristoph. Equit. 821, forms an exception : κραταιβόλος, in L. S., *hurled with violence*, is a typographical error for κραταίβολος : on ἀμφώβολος or ἀμφώβολον, see H. D. s. v. : πυρεκβόλος, which is quoted by H. D., can hardly be correct.

465. -βορος (βρώσκω). *Active.*—Ἀνδροβόρος, δημοβόρος, δωροβόρος, θυμοβόρος, παιδοβόρος, ὠμοβόρος, νεοβόρος, σκοτοιβόρος.

Passive, etc.—Διάβορος, θηρόβορος, νεόβορος : πολύβορος and πάμβορος are irregular and perhaps mistakes.

Note.—Διάβορος occurs in both a passive and an active sense; of the latter Soph. Trach. 1084 is an instance, οὐδ' ἀγύμναστόν μ' ἐᾶν ἔοικεν ἡ τάλαινα διάβορός νόσος: 'quod,' says W. Dindorf in H. D., 'διαβόρος potius scribendum.' This is seemingly a slip of the pen, for διαβόρος would violate all analogy; such adjectives as these are not paroxytone when compounded with a preposition, even though they are transitive in meaning: πάμβορος is quoted by H. D. from Ælian, N. A. I. 27, but the passage proves nothing: λιχνόβορος, Anth. Pal. 9. 86. 1, in an active sense is a false accent.

466. -γλυφος (γλύφω). *Active.*—'Ανδριαντογλύφος, ἑρμογλύφος, ζωογλύφος, λιθογλύφος, πτερνογλύφος, τυρογλύφος, τοκογλύφος, ἀγαλματογλύφος.

Passive, etc.—Τρίγλυφος.

Note.—The Aristophanic decompound κυμινοπριστοκαρδαμογλύφος remains paroxytone: ὀδοντόγλυφον, *a tooth-pick*, takes the accent of a substantive.

467. -γονος (γίγνομαι). *Active.*—'Ανδρογόνος, δακρυογόνος, διγόνος, παιδογόνος, πυριγόνος, τεκνογόνος, τριγόνος, ἀρρενογόνος, τελειογόνος, ἀριστογόνος, πρωτογόνος, καρπογόνος, ζωογόνος, θηλυγόνος, δακρυογόνος, ταχυγόνος.

Passive, etc.—'Αγονος, ἀπόγονος, δίγονος, ἔγγονος, ἔκγονος, ἐπίγονος, θεόγονος, νεόγονος, ὁμόγενος, πυρίγονος, πρόγονος, τρίγονος, τηλέγονος, τελειόγονος, ἀρτίγονος, κεβλήγονος, παλαίγονος, πηλόγονος, πρωτόγονος, ὀψίγονος, ὀρνιθόγονος, ἑτερόγονος, χρυσόγονος, θεόγονος, εὔγονος, σιτήγονος, αὐτόγονος.

Note.—Πολύγονος is almost always proparoxytone, but it ought to be paroxytone: ὀλιγόγονος is also proparoxytone: 'Αρχέγονος, τελεσσίγονος, ἀρχαιόγονος, φιλόγονος, are hardly to be considered verbals; it is remarkable that νεογνός is oxytone, though the longer form νεόγονος is regular.

468. -γραφος (γράφω): Arc. 90. 23; A. G. Oxon. 2. 397. 32. *Active.*—Δελτογράφος, ἐπιγραμματογράφος, ζωγράφος, ἰαμβειογράφος, λογογράφος, μυθογράφος, νομογράφος, πεζογράφος, πολυγράφος, σημειογράφος, ὡρογράφος, ἐπιστολιαγράφος, ὀρθογράφος, καλλιγράφος (E. M. 694. 43), τραγῳδιογράφος, βιβλιογράφος, παροιμιογράφος, ἱστοριογράφος, λεξικογράφος, σιλλογράφος, ὑπομνηματογράφος, ταχυγράφος, γεωγράφος, etc.: 'Αρχιζωγράφος, *H. D.*, is a doubtful accent.

Passive, etc.—'Αγραφος, ἀντίγραφος, ἀπόγραφος, αὐτόγραφος, ἔγγραφος, ἀνεπίγραφος, ἰδιόγραφος, κατάγραφος, ὁμόγραφος, περίγραφος, πρόσγραφος, ἱερόγραφος, λεπτόγραφος, μεσόγραφος, ἀγιόγραφος, εὐπερίγραφος, ψευδεπίγραφος.

469. -δοκος (δέχομαι). *Active.*—'Ακοντοδόκος, δωροδόκος, ἀνθοδόκος, γρυτοδόκος, ἱεροδόκος, ἰοδόκος (yet some wrote ἰόδοκον, Schol. Ven. O. 444), ξεινοδόκος (Eust. 1024. 61; Schol. Ven. Γ. 354; Arc. 88. 7), ὁδοιδόκος, πρεσβυτοδόκος, πυληδόκος, σιτοδόκος, σμηνοδόκος, μελανδόκος.

Passive, etc.—'Ενδοκος, used substantively: μητρόδοκος.

Note.—Eust. 1898. 34: Πάνδοκος seems to be an exception, cf. H. D. s. v. ἀδωροδόκος, *one who does not receive gifts*, is, if correct, irregular: the passages quoted by H. D. prove nothing.

470. -δομος (δέμω). *Active.*—Λιθοδόμος, οἰκοδόμος, πηλοδόμος, τειχοδόμος.

Passive, etc.—Λεπτόδομος, ὀπισθόδομος (sub.), πρόδομος, ἀρτίδομος, ψευδισόδομος, πηλόδομος, ἰσόδομος.

Note.—Μετοικοδόμος in L. S. is suspicious: φιλοικοδόμος occurs in Arist. Eth. Nic. 10. 5. 2, but it is contrary to analogy, as is φρουροδόμος, quoted by H. D. from Anth. Pal. 9. 245: indeed the latter is monstrous and should be altered.

471. -δονος (δονέω). *Active.*—Ἐτνοδόνος.

Passive, etc.—Ἁλίδονος, οἰστρόδονος, πολύδονος.

472. -δορος (δείρω). *Active.*—Βουδόρος (Lob. Ajax 189), προβατοδόρος.

Passive, etc.—Ἄδορος, ἀμφίδορος, νεόδορος, ἀρτίδορος, αὐτόδορος.

473. -δοχος (δέχομαι). *Active.*—Χοληδόχος, οὐρηδόχος, οὐροδόχος, ἐμβρυο-δόχος, etc.

Passive, etc.—Ἀνάδοχος, διάδοχος, ἀδιάδοχος : πάνδοχος is irregular.

474. -δρομος (δραμεῖν). *Active.*—Βοαδρόμος, βοηδρόμος, ὀρειδρόμος, ὀριδρόμος, οὐριοδρόμος, ἑλικοδρόμος (not ἑλικόδρομος), οὐρανοδρόμος, ὑδροδρόμος, αἰθεροδρόμος, γυροδρόμος, νυκτιδρόμος, ἡμεροδρόμος, παταγοδρόμος, λαιψηροδρόμος, μακροδρόμος, δολιχοδρόχος, σταδιοδρόμος, διαυλοδρόμος, σταφυλοδρόμος, ὁπλιτοδρόμος, ἱπποδρόμος, *one who races on horseback*, ἁρματοδρόμος, σκολιοδρόμος, σκοπελοδρόμος, σκυλακο-δρόμος (?), ὠκυδρόμος.

Passive, etc.—Διάδρομος, παράδρομος, κατάδρομος, μετάδρομος, ἐπίδρομος, περί-δρομος, ἀμφίδρομος, ἔκδρομος, σύνδρομος, ἀπόδρομος, πρόδρομος, εὔδρομος, ὁμόδρομος, παλίνδρομος, ἀμμόδρομος (used as a substantive), ἱππόδρομος, *race-course*.

NOTE.—The irregularities of this termination are numerous, but most of them ought to be corrected, unless the best MSS. support them, as they violate a very constant analogy : e. g. the following with an active meaning occur as propar-oxytones, ἁλίδρομος, πολύδρομος, τανύδρομος (??), ναυσίδρομος, ὁμόδρομος, πυρίδρομος, ἀνεμόδρομος, ἀλάδρομος, ὀρθόδρομος, ἰσόδρομος, δωδεκάδρομος, ὑψίδρομος, αὐτόδρομος : εὐθύδρομος, 'Strab. 25 eodemque accentu Pollux I. 194, de equo ; Suidas in Ἀκαμ-πίας : sed analogia compositorum cum δρόμος, quæ non sunt a præpositionibus formata, poscit εὐθυδρόμος,' *Hase* ap. H. D., yet they print ἰθύδρομος, Anth. Pal. 6. 103, without one word of comment, as also βραχύδρομος, whilst ταχυδρόμος is given as the correct form (L. S. have ταχύδρομος) : ἀελλόδρομος, ἑπτάδρομος, ἰσό-δρομος are all active in meaning, as in ὀξύδρομος, Schol. Pind. Ol. 13. 51 : 'sed scribendum potius ὀξυδρόμος ut ταχυδρόμος,' H. D. : πυργόδρομος (?) ὠκυδρόμος (?) : ἀκαμπιόδρομος may be defended as a decompound, cf. ἀνισόδρομος : κυματόδρομος should be κυματοδρόμος : φιλόδρομος, *fond of running*, is no exception, nor is τελεόδρομος : αἰθεροπτηνοδρόμος, Psell. in Cantic. Cant. p. 280, Meurs., H. D., is probably a mistake.

475. -δροπος (δρέπω). *Active.*—Βατοδρόπος, χειροδρόπος, E. M. 191. 53.

Passive, etc.—Νεόδροπος, ὠμόδροπος.

NOTE.—Χειροδρόπος also occurs under the form of χεδροπός (κεδροπός, Ionic), on which Dindorf in H. D. says : 'Oxytonum χεδροπός, idque per o scriptum, ut μαστροπός et ἐχθοδοπός memorat Herodian Epim. p. 208 : in locis Theophrasti (H. Pl. 1. 6. 5 ; 8. 2. 1 ; 8. 2. 2 ; 8. 9. 1 ; C. Pl. 4. c. 6, 7, 8, 9, et 10), Schneiderus χέδροπα et χεδρόπων scripsit suo ipsius arbitrio : nam codex Urbinas, ut plus uno in loco diserte annotatum est, oxytonum habet : idem accentus χεδροπά et χεδροπῶν est ap. Aristot. De gen. anim. 3. 1. p. 750. 24. et 2. p. 752. 21 (cùm var. lect. χεδρωπά et χεδρωπῶν) : unde De partt. anim. 2. 7. p. 653. 24, pariter scribendum erat χεδροπῶν pro χεδρόπων, et H. A. 8. 5. p. 594. 17, τοὺς καρποὺς τοὺς χεδροπούς ex pluribus codicibus, non τοὺς χέδροπας, quod est in aliis, ut χεδροπῶν ap. Hesych., qui per ὀσπρίων exp., et ap. Plutarch. Mor. p. 378 B, C, male χεδρόπων p. 273 C : qui accentus pariter corrigendus ap. Polluc. 6. 60, τὰ ὄσπρια ἃ καὶ χέδροπα ὠνόμαζον, et ap. Maxim. Περὶ κατ. 511 : Ἄλλα χέδροπα.'

476. -ηγορος, -αγορος (ἀγορέω), Arc. 89. 5. *Active.*—Δημηγόρος, ἐτυμηγόρος, θεηγόρος, βουληγόρος, δηθαγόρος, δικηγόρος, κακηγόρος (not κακήγορος, though that accent is common, e. g. Athen. 220 A, nor κακάγορος), πυλαγόρος, κυλικηγόρος, χρησμηγόρος, ψευδηγόρος, μεγαληγόρος, σεμνηγόρος, ὑψηγόρος (H. D. would, without the slightest reason, read ὑψήγορος), πολυηγόρος. Μακρήγορος (?), χρυσήγορος (?), are both almost certainly mistakes.

Passive, etc.—Εὐήγορος, κατήγορος, παρήγορος, προσήγορος, ἀπροσήγορος, δυσπροσήγορος, εὐπροσήγορος, φιλοπροσήγορος, συνήγορος.

477. -θοος (θέω).—Βοηθόος is paroxytone, though βοηθός is oxytone; the rest are, for some reason or other, proparoxytone, ἀρηΐθοος, ἱππόθοος, ὠκύθοος.

478. -θορος (θρώσκω).—Βουθόρος is quoted from Æschyl. Supp. 301 ed. Didot, yet the passage does not prove this to be the proper accent; but ἱπποθόρος, though so accented in E. M. 145. 45, seems to be more generally proparoxytone.

479. -κλοπος (κλέπτω). *Active.*—Γαμοκλόπος, κυνοκλόπος, βοοκλόπος, πολυκλόπος.

Passive, etc.—Ἄκλοπος, ἐπίκλοπος.

480. -κολος (κολέω). *Active.*—Βουκόλος, θεοκόλος: the decompounds ἐπιβουκόλος, Schol. Ven. E. 178; ἱπποβουκόλος, οἰοβουκόλος, Æschyl. Supp. 304, and ἀρχιβουκόλος, Schol. Ven. A. 39, are irregular; E. M. 113. 32; Arc. 86. 5: δύσκολος is from κόλον.

481. -κομος (κομέω), A. G. Oxon. 1. 153. 15; Schol. Ven. N. 132. *Active.*— Ἀνθοκόμος, ἀλσοκόμος, γειοκόμος, γηροκόμος (Arc. 87. 10), γαλακτοκόμος, ἐλαιοκόμος, ἐρνοκόμος, εἰροκόμος, ἱπποκόμος (Arc. 87. 9), ἱεροκόμος, κηποκόμος, λεοντοκόμος, μελισσοκόμος, νοσοκόμος, νυμφοκόμος, ὀρειοκόμος, ὀρεοκόμος, ὀρεωκόμος, παιδοκόμος, σμηνοκόμος, ὑλοκόμος, *taking care of wood* (ὑλόκομος from κόμη, *thick grown with wood*), φυτηκόμος, φυτοκόμος, τριχοκόμος, τραπεζοκόμος, ὡραιοκόμος; ἡδύκομος seems to be irregular.

482. -κοος (κέω, καίω?). *Active.*—Θυοσκόος (Arc. 42. 7), θυηκόος, ὀρνιθοκόος, πυρκόος.

483. -κοπος (κόπτω). *Active.*—Ἀρτοκόπος, ἀργυροκόπος, δημοκόπος, θυροκόπος, λιθοκόπος, ξυλοκόπος, ὀχλοκόπος, χρεωκόπος, συμβολοκόπος.

Passive, etc.—Μεσόκοπος (Lob. Ajax 104), νεόκοπος, ἀπόκοπος, διάκοπος, ἀδιάκοπος, ἐπίκοπος, παράκοπος, ἀπρόσκοπος, ἄκοπος, κατάκοπος, ὑπέρκοπος, ὑπόκοπος, ὁλόκοπος, σητόκοπος, δύσκοπος.

Note.—On ἰήκοπος see Lob. Ajax 189, note. Προκοπός in Polyb. 8. 17. 6, H. D., is most likely an error: πρόκοπος, in a different signification, occurs in Aretæus, see H. D. s. v.; πολύκοπος, if correct, seems irregular.

484. -κορος (κορέω). *Active.*—Μυλοκόρος, ἱεροκόρος, νηοκόρος, νεωκόρος (συννεωκόρος), σηκηκόρος, σηκοκόρος, τραπεζοκόρος (?).

485. -κροκος (κρέκω). *Active.*—Are there any? L. S. have ἀνθοκρόκος, *worked with flowers*, but it ought to be proparoxytone.

Passive.—Λινόκροκος, ἰανόκροκος.

486. -κτονος (κτείνω), Arc. 91. 2. *Active.*—Ἀδελφοκτόνος (ἀδελφεοκτόνος), ἀνδροκτόνος, ἀνθρωποκτόνος, αὐτοκτόνος, ἀλληλοκτόνος, βροτοκτόνος, ἐλαφοκτόνος, ζωοκτόνος, θηλυκτόνος, θηροκτόνος, ἱποκτόνος, κυνοκτόνος, κυριοκτόνος, ληστοκτόνος, λιμοκτόνος, λυκοκτόνος, μητροκτόνος, μυοκτόνος, νηπιοκτόνος, ξενοκτόνος, ξιφοκτόνος, οἰωνοκτόνος, παιδοκτόνος, παρθενοκτόνος, πατροκτόνος, περσοκτόνος, πολυκτόνος, πρωτοκτόνος, πυθοκτόνος, συοκτόνος, ταυροκτόνος, τεκνοκτόνος, τιτανοκτόνος, τιτυοκτόνος, τυραννοκτόνος, φονοκτόνος, χοιροκτόνος.

Passive, etc.—Ἀνθρωπόκτονος, λῃστόκτονος, μητρόκτονος, νεόκτονος, πατρόκτονος, συόκτονος, ταυρόκτονος, τραγόκτονος, χοιρόκτονος. Ἀντικτόνος is quoted by H. D. and L. S. from Æschyl. Eum. 464; the passage proves nothing, and there can be little doubt that the accent is wrong; cf. Lob. Ajax 189.

-κτυπος, see τυπος, § 520.

487. -λαβος (λαμβάνω). *Active.*—Δεξιολάβος, ἐργολάβος, παντολάβος, σαρκολάβος, ὀξυλάβος, ἀρχολάβος, λιθολάβος.

NOTE.—Ἀστρόλαβος is mentioned by L. S. as a substantive, but from its meaning it should be paroxytone; ὀξύλαβος occurs in Schol. Ven. Σ. 477, but it should be ὀξυλάβος; συνεργολάβος, Strab. 354, H. *D.*, is irregular.

488. -λαλος. *Active.*—Μογιλάλος (Arc. 89. 9), ὀξυλάλος, ὀρθρολάλος, τριποδηλάλος, νευρολάλος, ὀξυλάλος, ἐρημολάλος, Anth. Pal. 7. 196. 2.

Passive, etc.—Εὔλαλος, ἄλαλος, κατάλαλος, ἀμφίλαλος, περίλαλος, πρόλαλος.

NOTE.—Ἀείλαλος, if correct, is irregular; also ὀλιγόλαλος, πολύλαλος, μεγαλόλαλος (?), ἡδύλαλος, ταχύλαλος, ὑψίλαλος, ἀληθινόλαλος (?).

489. -λογος (λέγω), Arc. 85. 25; 89. 18. *Active.*—Ἀθερολόγος, αἰθερολόγος, αἰσχρολόγος, αἰτιαλόγος, ἀκανθολόγος, ἀκριβολόγος, ἀκρολόγος, ἀκυρολόγος, ἀνδρολόγος, ἀνθολόγος, ἀνθρωπολόγος, ἀειλόγος, ἀπεραντολόγος, διλόγος, πολυλόγος, *much speaking*, κνιπολόγος, *a kind of woodpecker* (?), φρυνολόγος, ἐνοικιολόγος, ἐνοικολόγος, ὑπολεπτολόγος (?), πεντηκοστολόγος.

Passive, etc.—Ἀναξιόλογος, ἀντίλογος, ἀξιόλογος, ἀπρόσλογος, ἀναμφίλογος, ἀλεξίλογος, *promoting discourse*, ὁμόλογος, ἀνομόλογος, πολύλογος, *requiring many words*, παλίλλογος.

NOTE—Εὐρεσιλόγος is undoubtedly incorrect, Lob. Phryn. 770. Ἀρτιλόγος is no exception, since it is not a compound of ἄρτι. On φιλόλογος H. D. remark 'φιλολόγος, sic sæpe scriptum in codicibus Platonis aliorumque scriptorum: sed rectus accentus φιλόλογος est, quum non ut δικαιολόγος, τερατολόγος, et alia ab λέγω derivatum, sed cum λόγος compositum sit, ut monet Aread. p. 89. 20;' ἀφιλόλογος, μισοφιλόλογος are regular. Λυπησιλόγος in Suid. and elsewhere for λυπησίλογος is obviously an error; see Lob. Phryn. 769-70. ὀλιγόλογος is doubtful; ἰδιόλογος, μαψίλογος, H. *D.*, should probably be μαψίλογος; on μισολόγος they say 'ceterum μισόλογος scribendum, ut φιλόλογος, παραδοξολόγος, H. *D.*, συντομολόγος, H. *D.*, μονολόγος, on this H. D. remark that μονόλογος is the better accent, but μονολόγος is exactly parallel to μονομάχος and μονοφάγος.

490. -λοχος (λοχάω). *Active.*—Βωμολόχος, δειπνολόχος, νυκτιλόχος, φρυνολόχος.

Those from λέχος are proparoxytone, ἄλοχος, γαιάλοχος, ναύλοχος, Arc. 90.2, ναυσίλοχος, ὁμόλοχος, etc.

491. -μαχος (μάχομαι). *Active.*—Ἀελλόμαχος, αἱρεσιομάχος, ἀνδρομάχος, εὐθυμάχος, γροσφομάχος, θεημάχος, θεομάχος, θηριομάχος, θηριμάχος, θωρακομάχος, ἱππομάχος (Arc. 87. 9), κυπελλομάχος, λογομάχος, μονομάχος, Μαραθωνομάχος, ναυμάχος, *fighting with ships*, ὁπλομάχος, ὀφιομάχος, πυγμάχος, πυργομάχος, πυγμαιομάχος, πνευματομάχος, τηλεμάχος, τειχομάχος, χειρομάχος, χριστομάχος, ἑκατονταμάχος (?), ὠκυμάχος, Arc. 89. 28.

Passive, etc.—Ἄμαχος, ἀπόμαχος, ἀντίμαχος, ἀπρόσμαχος, ἐπίμαχος, εὔμαχος, δύσμαχος, ναύμαχος, *belonging to a sea-fight* (Schol. Ven. O. 389), πρόμαχος, σύμμαχος, φιλοσύμμαχος, ὑπέρμαχος, αὐτόμαχος, Arc. 90. 9.

. NOTE.—Eust. 1021. 50: ἰστέον δὲ ὅτι τῶν τοιούτων ὀνομάτων ἀρέσκει τοῖς παλαιοῖς ὅσα μὲν ἐκ τοῦ μάχη πεποίηνται, προπαροξύνειν τὸ τέλος, οἷον φιλόμαχον γένος, σύμμαχος, πρωτόμαχος, ἀντίμαχος, ἐπίμαχος . . . . . . ὅσα δ' ἐκ τοῦ μάχεσθαι σύγκειται, παροξύνεσθαι, πυγμάχος, ναυμάχος, ὁπλομάχος, τειχομάχος, πυργομάχος, μονομάχος; cf. Arc. 89. 1; Athen. 154 E. Hence λάμαχος, ἀψίμαχος, ἀξιόμαχος, ἰσόμαχος, φυγόμαχος, βουλόμαχος.

The following appear to be irregular : ἀγχέμαχος (Arc. 90. 5), or ἀγχίμαχος, ἀδικομάχος (A. G. 344. 6), ἀλκίμαχος, δορίμαχος, δορύμαχος or δουρίμαχος (there does not seem to be any good authority for this accentuation, nor for πυρίμαχος or πυρόμαχος) ; πρωτόμαχος is proparoxytone according to Athen. 154 E. Βιημάχος is occasionally proparoxytone, but without sufficient reason, see H. D. s. v. Μενέμαχος in Appian. Iber. 51 should be μενέμαχος. Παμμάχος, Aristoph. Lys. 1321 (where Bergk reads πάμμαχος) is πάμμαχος in Auth. Plan. 4. 52, quoted by H. D.

492. -μορος (μείρομαι).

The only paroxytones are γεωμόρος (γαμόρος, γημόρος, γειομόρος) : the rest are proparoxytone, as ἰσόμορος, δύσμορος : on ἐπιγεώμοροι, E. M. 395. 53 ; A. G. 257. 10, H. D. observe, 'utroque loco male scriptum ἐπιγεώμοροι,' though why it is 'male scriptum' I do not see ; ἐπιγεωμόροι is contrary to analogy.

493. -νομος (νέμω), Arc. 85. 25 ; 91. 2.　　*Active.*—Ἀστρονόμος, ἀγορανόμος, ἀγρονόμος, αἰγονόμος, ἀνθονόμος, ἀστυνόμος, κληρονόμος, οἰκονόμος, οἰονόμος, ὀπισθονόμος, πεζονόμος, ποιονόμος, *feeding on grass* ; βουνόμος, *cattle-feeding* ; νυκτινόμος, θηρονόμος, *feeding (wild) beasts* ; ἐρημονόμος, πολυνόμος.

Passive, etc.—Ἄνομος, ἐπίνομος, ποιόνομος, *with grassy fields* ; παράνομος, σύννομος, αὐτόνομος, βούνομος, *fed on by cattle* ; ἰσόνομος, λυσίνομος, κακόνομος, ὁμόνομος, ἀρχαιόνομος (these are from νομός), θηρόνομος, *fed on by beasts.*

NOTE.—The decompounds μονοκληρονόμος and συγκληρονόμος, Schol. Aristoph. Av. 1652, are irregular : μισγονόμος (γῆ) is thus accented in Hesych., but it must be an error, as also is ἀθυρονόμος, Hesych., which L. S. have correctly proparoxytone ; αἰθερόνομος in H. D. and L. S. should be paroxytone : χρυσόνομος, in Æschyl. Pers. 80, can hardly mean *feeding on gold, L. S.* ; see Schol. ad l. : νυκτινόμος is sometimes, though improperly, proparoxytone : ἰσοκληρονόμος (?) H. D., ὑψίνομος and ὁμόνομος are doubtful, as is πολύνομος ; αὐτόνομος seems to be always proparoxytone.

494. -ξοος (ξέω).　　*Active.*—Λαοξόος, κεραξόος, λιθοξόος, δορυξόος (also δορυξός), κεραοξόος.

Passive, etc.—Ἄξοος, τετράξοος, δίξοος, ἀντίξοος, ἀμφίξοος, μονόξοος, εὔξοος.

495. -οχος, -ουχος (ἔχω), Arc. 90. 14.

All in ουχος, whether compound or decompound, are properispomena, as ἀσπιδοῦχος, δᾳδοῦχος, ἑστιοῦχος, εὐνοῦχος, ἀρχιευνοῦχος, κλειδοῦχος, κληροῦχος, κυνοῦχος, λαμπαδοῦχος, λυχνοῦχος, οὐρανοῦχος, ὀφιοῦχος, πατροῦχος, πολιοῦχος, πρυμνοῦχος, ῥαβδοῦχος, σκηπτοῦχος, etc. Ἀκρηστόλουχος (?), Hesych., is very doubtful.

Those in οχος (even when active) are proparoxytone, as αἰγίοχος, ἀστύοχος, γαιήοχος, δρύοχος, ἔνοχος, ἔξοχος, ἔποχος, ἡνίοχος, κάτοχος, μέτοχος, νήοχος, σύνοχος, ὑπείροχος, ὕποχος, E. M. 432. 23. Yet Schol. Apollon. Rhod. 2. 967, distinguishes between the active and passive meanings of λιμένοχος, ἐὰν μὲν τὴν συνεχομένην, προπαροξυτόνως· ἐὰν δὲ τὴν συνέχουσαν τὸν λιμένα, παροξυτόνως.

496. -πλαθος (πλάσσω). *Active.*—Ἱπνοπλάθος, κοροπλάθος, κουροπλάθος, πηλοπλάθος, λογοπλάθος.

497. -πλανος (πλανάω). These are proparoxytone, as ἀείπλανος, ἀπόπλανος, ἀερόπλανος, νυκτίπλανος, ἀρχίπλανος, ἀλίπλανος, δύσπλανος, πολύπλανος, τηλέπλανος,

Æschyl. Prom. 577, ώκύπλανος ; yet ἐρωτοπλάνος, Anth. Pal. 7. 195. 6, and ποντοπλάνος are paroxytone ; why ἁλίπλανος should have a different accent from
ποντοπλάνος, when the meaning of both words is similar, does not appear : λαοπλάνος
is paroxytone in the places quoted by H. D.

498. -πλοκος (πλέκω). *Active.*—Γριφοπλόκος, δολοπλόκος, δικτυοπλόκος, ζωνιο-
πλόκος, ἰοπλόκος, κεκρυφαλοπλόκος, λινοπλόκος, οἰσυοπλόκος, πυτινοπλόκος, στεφανη-
πλόκος, στεφηπλόκος, στεφανοπλόκος, σχοινοπλόκος, σπαρτοπλόκος, ψιαθοπλόκος,
αἱμυλοπλόκος.

Passive, etc.—Ἅπλοκος, διάπλοκος, ὁμόπλοκος, περίπλοκος, εὔπλοκος, πολύπλοκος.

499. -ποκος (πέκω). *Active.*—Οἰοπόκος, εἰροπόκος.

Passive, etc.—Ἄποκος, ἀμφίποκος, ἐπίποκος, εὔποκος.

500. -πολος (πολέω). *Active.*—Αἰπόλος, ἀγροπόλος, ἀκροπόλος, θαλαμηπόλος,
ἀγνοπόλος, αἰγοπόλος, μουσοπόλος, βουπόλος, ἀοιδοπόλος, δικασπόλος, θεηπόλος, θεο-
πόλος, ὑμνηπόλος, θυηπόλος, θεμιστοπόλος, νυκτιπόλος, νηοπόλος, μαντιπόλος, μυστιπόλος, μητροπόλος, μυροπόλος, οἰοπόλος, οἰνωπόλος, ἱπποπόλος, ὀνειροπόλος, ταυροπόλος,
etc. ; ὑψίπολος, H. D., should probably be paroxytone.

Passive, etc.—Περίπολος, ἀμφίπολος, πρόπολος, πρόσπολος, δίπολος, τρίπολος,
ἔμπολος, ἐρανέμπολος, τετράπολος.

NOTE.—Eust. 92. 44: σκοπητέον δὲ ὡς τὸ μὲν δικασπόλος, καὶ τὰ κατ' αὐτὸ
παροξύνεται· ἀμφίπολος, δὲ καὶ πρόπολος τὰ μετὰ προθέσεων προπαροξύνονται : Eust.
578. 40: δοκεῖ δὲ παροξυτονεῖσθαι καὶ ἡ εὐθεῖα τοῦ ἀκροπόλοις καθὰ καὶ τὰ κατ' αὐτό.
τὰ γὰρ παρὰ τὸ πολῶ, εἰ μὲν προθέσει σύγκειται προηγουμένῃ, προπαροξύνονται, οἷον
ἀμφίπολος, πρόπολος, πρόσπολος· εἰ δὲ ὀνόματι, παροξύνονται, ὡς δῆλον ἐκ τοῦ ὀνειροπόλος, μαντιπόλος, οἰωνοπόλος, θυηπόλος, ὃ καὶ ἱερεὺς καὶ θυοσκόος δὲ ἐν 'Οδυσσείᾳ.
οὕτω γοῦν ἀναλόγως καὶ ἀκροπόλος. ὁμοίως δὲ καὶ μυστιπόλος καὶ αἰπόλος καὶ θαλαμηπόλος καὶ δικασπόλος ὁ καὶ θεμιστοπόλος : Eust. 642. 41 : ἴσως δὲ ἔχοι ἂν ἀπορίαν,
διά τι μὴ ὥσπερ πρωτότοκος ἐν σημασίᾳ παθητικῇ ὁ πρῶτος τεχθεὶς προπαροξυτόνως,
πρωτοτόκος δὲ ἐν παροξυτονήσει ἡ πρώτως τεκοῦσα, οὕτω κατὰ διαφορὰν σημασίας
παθητικῆς τε καὶ ἐνεργητικῆς ἀμφίπολος μὲν τάφος ὁ ἀμφιπολούμενος προπαροξύνεται
διὰ πάθος εὐλόγως εἰς ὃ ἀναλύεται, ἀμφίπολος δὲ ἡ ἀμφιπολοῦσα πρὸ μιᾶς ἔχει τὸν
τόνον διὰ τὴν ἐνέργειαν ἣν δηλοῖ. τὴν δὲ τούτων λύσιν οὐχ ὑποδύσκολόν ἐστιν εὑρεῖν :
cf. E. M. 37. 49 ; 93. 37 ; Arc. 88. 22 ; A. G. Oxon. I. 108. 11.

501. -πονος (πονέω). *Active.*—'Αριστοπόνος, ἀρουροπόνος, βιοπόνος, ἀροτροπόνος,
γεωπόνος, γηπόνος, γεηπόνος, εἰροπόνος, ἐργοπόνος, ματαιοπόνος, νυμφοπόνος, ὀψοπόνος,
σιτοπόνος, δαιτροπόνος.

Passive, etc.—Ἄπονος, αὐτόπονος, ἀντίπονος, διάπονος, δύσπονος, ἔμπονος, ἐπίπονος,
Ἡφαιστόπονος, κατάπονος, μελεόπονος, δορίπονος.

502. NOTE.—Those from πόνος are of course proparoxytone, as ἀκεσίπονος,
λαθίπονος, λυσίπονος, παυσίπονος, ῥυσίπονος, τλησίπονος, φερέπονος, ἀφερέπονος, φιλό-
πονος, ἀφιλόπονος, φυγόπονος, ἀπειρόπονος, ἐθελόπονος, θρασύπονος : πολύπονος is
rather passive than active in meaning, and is therefore properly proparoxytone,
but ὀλιγόπονος is probably wrong.

503. -ποπος (πέπτω).—'Αρτοπόπος appears to be paroxytone in all the places
quoted by H. D., though in several of the passages, if not in all, it may be a variant
of ἀρτοκόπος.

504. -πορος (πείρω). *Active.*—'Αεροπόρος, ἀεριπόρος, ἁλιπόρος, ἀκροπόρος, βρα-
δυπόρος (this is proparoxytone in all the passages quoted by H. D.), βουπόρος, θαλασ-
σοπόρος, ποταμηπόρος, πρωτοπόρος, ὀπισθοπόρος, ὑγροπόρος, μεσοπόρος, ποντοπόρος,

ὁδοιπόρος, παροδοιπόρος (?) συνοδοιπόρος (?) προοδοιπόρος (?) ναυσιπόρος, νυκτιπόρος, νυκτοπόρος, κελευθοπόρος, λινοπόρος, μετεωροπόρος, ἰθυπόρος, λαοπόρος, παντοπόρος, πολυπόρος, πεζοπόρος, γλαυκηπόρος (?) ἑλιξοπόρος, παιδοπόρος (?).

Passive, etc.—Ἄπορος, ἀντίπορος, ἀκρόπορος, βραχύπορος, δύσπορος, εὔπορος, εὐρύπορος, Arc. 89. 27, ἔμπορος, ἑλαιέμπορος, κερδέμπορος, καμηλέμπορος, λογέμπορος (such is the accent in our books, though Eust. 1447. 40 expressly states that it is the only compound of ἔμπορος that is *paroxytone*), μεγαλέμπορος, συνέμπορος, σωματέμπορος, πεζέμπορος, ταριχέμπορος, φιλέμπορος, χριστέμπορος, ψυχέμπορος, τετράπορος, ἑπτάπορος, πεντάπορος, πανήπορος, πανάπορος, στενόπορος, πολύπορος, ναυσίπορος, ἰθύπορος, δύσπορος· δίπορος, πυκνόπορος, ἀγχίπορος, ὀξύπορος, παλίμπορος.

NOTE.—Εὐθύπορος, *straight-going*, is doubtful: τηλέπορος seems to be generally proparoxytone, though it is paroxytone in Orph. H. 17. 9, quoted by H. D.: ὑψίπορος, like most others in ὑψι, is proparoxytone: ὠκύπορος is paroxytone in Hesych., yet Arcadius, 89. 28, expressly makes it proparoxytone, indeed he says that all compounded with ὠκύς are so, except ὠκυμάχος, but his rule is probably wrong, since we find ὠκυβόλος, ὠκυδρόμος, ὠκυτόκος: ταχυπόρος is falsely proparoxytone in Æschyl. Ag. 486, and Eurip. El. 451, both quoted by H. D.: ὀψίπορος should be paroxytone: παντοπόρος, *ad omnia callidus*, Soph. Ant. 369, is a strange accent for such a meaning: τηλέπορος (?) Aristoph. Nub. 967.

505. -προπος (πρέπω).—Θεοπρόπος appears to be the only word of this termination.

506. -ραφος (ῥάπτω). *Active.*—Ἱστιορράφος, δικορράφος, δολορράφος, κακορράφος, μηχανορράφος, σκηνορράφος, λινορράφος, νευρορράφος, ὑποδηματορράφος (this is falsely proparoxytone in Chœrob. C. 623. 28), παλαιορράφος.

Passive, etc.—Ἄρραφος, κατάρραφος, πολύρραφος.

507. -ροφος (ῥοφέω). *Active.*—Αἱματορρόφος.

508. -σκαφος (σκάπτω). *Active.*—Φυτοσκάφος, πυργοσκάφος.

Passive, etc.—Φυτόσκαφος.

509. -σκοπος (σκέπτομαι), Arc. 88. 25. *Active.*—Βροτοσκόπος, ἀστεροσκόπος, θυοσκόπος, μετεωροσκόπος, μηλοσκόπος, οἰωνοσκόπος, ὀρνεοσκόπος, τερατοσκόπος, τηλεσκόπος.

Passive, etc.—Ἀδιάσκοπος, ἄσκοπος, εὔσκοπος, ἐπίσκοπος, ἀρχιεπίσκοπος, κατάσκοπος, ἀπόσκοπος, τηλέσκοπος.

NOTE.—Πάνσκοπος, Anth. Pal. 7. 580, if correct, is irregular: so also πολύσκοπος, ταννύσικοπος, ὠκύσκοπος (?) Auth. Pal. 9. 525.

510. -σοος (σώζω and σεύω). *Active.*—Βιοσόος, βουσόος, βοοσόος, βροτοσόος, δορυσόος, κεμαδοσσόος, κυνοσσόος, λαοσόος, λιθοσόος, μελισσόος, μηλοσσόος, νεκυσσόος, νηοσόος, οἰνοσόος, ψυχοσόος.

Passive, etc.—Δύσσοος, εὔσοος, πυρίσοος, παλίνσοος.

NOTE.—Ἀεισόος in Nonn. p. 112. 28, quoted by H. D., is passive in sense, and should be proparoxytone: ξενόσοος, *saving strangers*, should be ξενοσόος.

511. -σπορος (σπείρω). *Active.*—Πυκνοσπόρος, πρωτοσπόρος, φυτοσπόρος, πυρισπόρος, παιδοσπόρος.

Passive, etc.—Ἄσπορος, ἀγχίσπορος, ἀπόσπορος, βαθύσπορος, δεκάσπορος, ἐπίσπορος, εὔσπορος, μηλόσπορος, μανόσπορος, ὀψίσπορος, ὁμόσπορος, πρωτόσπορος, πυκνόσπορος, πρωτόσπορος, πολύσπορος, χειμόσπορος, πυρίσπορος.

512. -στολος (στέλλω). *Active.*—Πυργοστύλος, ἐργοστόλος, γαμοστόλος, ναυστύλος.

Passive, etc.—Ἰδιόστολος, μονόστολος, αὐτόστολος, περίστολος, ὁμόστολος, ὑψίστολος, ἀπόστολος, ψευδαπόστολος.

Note.—Ἱερόστολος, Plut. 2. 351 B, seems to be irregular; it should most probably be paroxytone: ἄστολος, εὔστολος, ποικιλόστολος, etc., are derived from στολή.

513. -στροφος (στρέφω). *Active.*—Ἀσπιδηστρόφος, βουστρόφος, *boves regens,* ἑδροστρόφος.

Passive.—Ἀδιάστροφος, βούστροφος, *a bobus aratus.*

514. -σφαγος (σφάττω). *Active.*—Ταυροσφάγος, μηλοσφάγος, παρθενοσφάγος.

515. -τοκος (τίκτω), Arc. 91. 2. *Active.*—Ἀριστοτόκος, ἀλαστόκος, ἀρτιτόκος (?) ἀγχιτόκος, αὐτοτόκος, αἰνοτόκος, αἰωνοτόκος, ἀπαρτιτόκος (?) ἀπειροτόκος, ἀρρενοτόκος, ἀρρητοτόκος, βραδυτόκος, διδυμοτόκος, διτόκος, δευτεροτόκος, δισσοτόκος, καλλιτόκος, κλεψιτόκος, μονοτόκος, ὀλιγοτόκος, ὀξυτόκος, παντοτόκος, πρωτοτόκος, πολυτόκος, τελειοτόκος, ταχυτόκος, ὠμοτόκος, ὠκυτόκος.

Passive, etc.—Ἀρτίτοκος, ἄτοκος, αὐτότοκος, αἰωρότοκος, ἀπότοκος, δευτερότοκος, δύστοκος, εὔτοκος, ἐγγειότοκος, κοινότοκος, πρωτότοκος, ὠκύτοκος.

Note.—Ἀεξίτοκος, *nourishing the fruit of the womb,* is regular: μογοστόκος was so accented by Aristarchus, Schol. Ven. Λ. 270: ἑπτάτοκος (?) is doubtful: κλεψιτόκος, *partum furans,* H. D., seems to be an error.

516. -τομος (τέμνω), Arc. 91. 2. *Active.*—Βαλαντιητόμος, δρυοτόμος, καρατόμος (E. M. 215), λαιμοτόμος, λατόμος, λιθοτόμος, ξυλοτόμος, πετροτόμος, σκυτοτόμος, ὑλοτόμος, ἀρτιτόμος, καινοτόμος, etc.

Passive, etc.—Ἀμφίτομος, ἀπότομος, ἄτομος, διχότομος, ἔντομος, ἡμίτομος, καράτομος, νεότομος, λαιμότομος, περίτομος, σύντομος, ἀρτίτομος, καινότομος, etc.

Note.—Ἀμφιτόμος is so contrary to analogy that it can hardly be correct; see H. D. s. v.: the substantive βούτομος, whatever its derivation, is proparoxytone: κέρτομος is singular in its accent: the decompounds ἐπικέρτομος and φιλοκέρτομος are regular: ἑτοιμοτόμος, *ready for cutting,* is probably an error.

517. -τορος (τιτράω). *Active.*—Βουτόρος, ὀξυτόρος, ῥινοτόρος, γυιοτόρος, πολυτόρος, λαοτόρος.

Passive, etc.—Διάτορος (a distinction is sometimes made between διάτορος, *pierced,* and διατόρος, *piercing,* wrongly, as the latter form does not exist).

518. -τραγος (τρώγω). *Active.*—Κριθοτράγος, κοτινοτράγος, συκοτράγος.

519. -τροφος (τρέφω). *Active.*—Ἀλεκτρυονοτρόφος, ἀνθοτρόφος, βουτρόφος, γηροτρόφος, δονακοτρόφος, ζευγοτρόφος, ζωοτρόφος, ἱπποτρόφος, καρποτρόφος, κουροτρόφος, λαοτρόφος, λωτοτρόφος, μηλοτρόφος, παιδοτρόφος, τεθριπποτρόφος, χιονοτρόφος, παντοτρόφος, ὁμοτρόφος, πολυτρόφος, μονομαχοτρόφος.

Passive, etc.—Ἀπότροφος, ἄτροφος, δύστροφος, ἔντροφος, εὔτροφος, νεότροφος, ὀλιγότροφος (?) ὁμότροφος, ὀρεσίτροφος, σύντροφος, χιονότροφος.

Note.—Παντρόφος is quoted by H. D. from Anth. Pal. 7. 476. 9, though they condemn that accent, and πάντροφος from Orph. H. 25. 2, and Nonn. Joann. c. 9. 154.

520. -τυπος, -κτυπος (τύπτω). *Active.*—Βουτύπος, ὀρειτύπος, χαμαιτύπος, χειμωνοτύπος, χοιροτύπος, χοροκτύπος, ὀροκτύπος, ὀμβροκτύπος.

Passive, etc.—'Αντίτυπος, ἄτυπος, ἔντυπος, ἔκτυπος, ἐρίκτυπος, πρόστυπος, ἀρτίτυπος, ἀλίκτυπος.

NOTE.—'Αρματόκτυπος, Æschyl. S. c. T. 204, is from κτύπος: βαρύκτυπος (?) in an active sense: ἐπτάκτυπος (?) Pind. Pyth. 2. 70: ἐτερόκτυπος (?): ὀρίκτυπος, *H. D.*

521. -φαγος (ΦΑΓΩ), Arc. 89. 11; E. M. 681. 30.   *Active.*—'Αδηφάγος, αἰγοφάγος, ἀνδροφάγος, αὐτοφάγος, δημοφάγος, ἰαμβειοφάγος, λωτοφάγος, σαρκοφάγος, τρυγηφάγος, ἀλληλοφάγος, δριμυφάγος, παμφάγος, καρποφάγος, κλεψιφάγος, ὀλιγοφάγος, πολυφάγος, μονοφάγος, νυκτιλαθραιοφάγος (?) μονοφάγος, ὀλιγοφάγος: ἐλαιοφιλοφάγος, for this H. D. quote Athen. 64 F, a place which does not prove that accent to be correct.

Passive, etc.—Αὐτόφαγος (?): οἰσοφάγος as a substantive is well established, but the accent is difficult to account for.

522. -φθορος (φθείρω).   *Active.*—Πολυφθόρος, ὑστεροφθόρος, βροτοφθόρος (not βροτόφθορος as in H. D.), ἀνδροφθόρος, ἀλιφθόρος, αὐτοφθόρος ('Ελληνοτρωοφθόρος, Tzetz. Hist. 5. 772, *H. D.*, is irregular), θυμοφθόρος, λαοφθόρος, λινοφθόρος, μητροφθόρος, ναυφθόρος, οἰκοφθόρος, πολιτοφθόρος.

Passive, etc.—'Αδιάφθορος, ἐπίφθορος, πολύφθορος, ἀρηΐφθορος, ἄφθορος.

NOTE.—Ναύφθορος, *naufragus*, is singular, but may be correct.

523. -φοβος (φοβέομαι).   *Active.*—Αἱμοφόβος, ὑδροφόβος, ψυχροφόβος, Galen T. 10. p. 210 E; H. D.
Passive, etc.—'Αφοβος, ἔκφοβος, ἔμφοβος, ἐπίφοβος, κατάφοβος, περίφοβος, ὑπέρφοβος.

NOTE—H. D. quote θεόφοβος, *God-fearing*; it should probably be paroxytone, as also κακόφοβος.

524. -φονος (ΦΕΝΩ); Arc. 91. 2.   *Active.*—'Αλληλοφόνος, ἀνδροφόνος, αὐτοφόνος, βουφόνος, γιγαντοφόνος, γοργοφόνος, δολοφόνος, ἐλλοφόνος, θηλυφόνος, θηροφόνος, θηριοφόνος, λαγωφόνος, λαγωοφόνος, λαοφόνος, λεοντοφόνος, Μηδοφόνος, μηλοφόνος, μητροφόνος, μυοφόνος, μυσφόνος, νεβροφόνος, νηττοφόνος (a kind of eagle), ξενοφόνος, οὐλοφόνος, παιδοφόνος, πατροφόνος, πολυφόνος, ταυροφόνος, χιμαιροφόνος, φασσοφόνος, ὠκυφόνος.

Passive, etc.—'Αντίφονος, ἀπόφονος, νεόφονος.

NOTE.—The accentuation of μαιφόνος, Arc. 91. 2 (and ἰαιφόνος, Hesych.), is singular; by analogy it should be proparoxytone, but it does not seem to occur with that accent: βελοβυνθοθαμβοσεισμοφόνος, quoted by H. D., is as monstrous in accent as in composition.

525. -φορος (φέρω), Arc. 88. 9; A. G. Oxon. 1. 90. 14.   *Active.*—'Αγαλματοφόρος, ἀγγελιαφόρος, ἀγκαλιδοφόρος, ἀπειληφόρος, ἀρχιλυχνηφόρος (!) ἀσκοφόρος, ἀσπιδοφόρος, ἀφροφόρος, ἀωσφόρος, διφόρος, ἐνιαυτοφόρος, ἐπιγαμματοφόρος, ὀλιγοφόρος, πολυφόρος, ἀειφόρος, παρενιαυτοφόρος (?) παντοφόρος, φιλοκαρποφόρος (?) λεωφόρος, ὀλιγοφόρος, ὀψιφόρος.

Passive, etc.—Διάφορος, ἀδιάφορος, δύσφορος, εὔφορος (A. G. Oxon. 1. 90. 17), ἀνείσφορος, ἀνώφορος, ἀσύμφορος, ἐξάφορος.

NOTE.—Πάμφορος, though active, is proparoxytone in all the places quoted by H. D.: πτηνοτοξοπυροφόρος (?) H. D.: φιλοκαρποφόρος: all three are probably wrong.

526. -χοος (χέω), Arc. 89.—'Αργυροχόος, θυηχόος, λοετροχόος, λουτροχόος, λατροχόος, οἰνοχόος (ἀρχιοινοχόος, H. D., παροινοχόος, are both suspicious), ἀρχιοι-

νοχόος (?) σιαλοχόος, τυμβοχόος, ὑδρηχόος, ὑδροχόος,· φυλλοχόος, χρυσοχόος, ῥινο.
χόος (not ῥινόχοος).

Passive, etc.—Πρόχοος, E. M. 93. 37.

NOTE.—Ὀλιγόχοος, *yielding little*, is contrary to analogy, ὀλιγόχους is however quite correct; perhaps the former accent has arisen from a confusion of the
two forms: the same remarks apply to πολύχοος.

The compounds of χόος, χοῦς are of course proparoxytone, as ἑξάχοος, ἡμίχοος.

527. -ωρυχος (ὀρύσσω); Arc. 91. 2. *Active.*—γεωρύχος, μιλτωρύχος, ῥιζωρύχος,
τοιχωρύχος (Arc. 91. 4), τυμβωρύχος, φρεατωρύχος, φρεωρύχος.

Passive, etc.—Κατώρυχος, ὑποκατώρυχος.

NOTE.—Ὀφθαλμώρυχος should be corrected, it is of course paroxytone; and
πεδώρυχος, quoted by H. D. from Anth. Pal. 10. 101, must be an error.

528. On ὀλοοίτροχος, E. M. 622. 39 says: Πτολεμαῖος καὶ Ἀριστόνικος ψιλοῦσι
παροξύνοντες, ἀκούοντες τὸν ἐπὶ τὸ τρέχειν ὀλεόν· ἐπένθεσις δὲ τοῦ υ περιττή. οἱ δὲ
δασύνουσιν, ἵν' ᾖ ὅλος τροχοειδής, καὶ κατὰ πᾶν μέρος ἀστήρικτος; cf. Schol. Ven. N.
137. The word ὀρεσσιπάτος (*sic*) is quoted by H. D., but the passage referred to
proves nothing, and I suppose it must be regarded as a misprint, as must ὠκυρ-
ρόος in E. M. 821. 33, which cannot be right for several reasons. The following
words in H. D. may be noticed here for want of a better place. Ἀβρογόος and
ἀδρογόος are mere oversights, for all words in γοος are proparoxytone: ἀδρανέος is
a mistake for ἀδράνεος; αἰσχροπράγος (*sic*) is a thoroughly impossible accent;
ἀνθρωποφλόγος should be proparoxytone, and so should βιβλιοτάφος; εὐωδός for
εὐώδης is without a parallel, and almost certainly wrong; ὀγκοτράφος should be
ὀγκότραφος; lastly, ταυροθρόος should be proparoxytone.

(c) Verbal Derivatives in τος.

529. Verbal derivatives in τος, compounded with a *privativum*,
are proparoxytone; of the remainder, those with three terminations are generally oxytone, those with two terminations, proparoxytone. In fact, however, these words are in such a state of
confusion that no rule can be depended on, and all must be left
to observation.

530. NOTE 1.—Arc. 83. 22: Τὰ εἰς ΣΤΟΣ ἐπιθετικὰ ἁπλᾶ ῥηματικὰ ὑπὲρ δύο
συλλαβὰς ὀξύνεται, λῃστός, μεριστός, ὀνομαστός. τὰ δὲ σύνθετα προπαροξύνεται,
φραστὸς ἄφραστος, ἀλίαστος ἄλαστος: E. M. 269. 3: διαμετρητός· ἡ εὐθεῖα διαμετρητός, σχήματος παρασυνθέτου. Καὶ πόθεν διαχωρίζεται τὰ παρασύνθετα ἐκ τῶν
συνθέτων; Ἐκ τῆς διαφορᾶς τοῦ τόνου. Τὰ μὲν γὰρ σύνθετα προπαροξύνεται, τὰ δὲ
παρασύνθετα ὀξύνεται. Ταῦτα δὲ ὀξύνεται, ἐπειδὴ ἀπὸ ῥήματος ἔσχον τὴν σύνθεσιν·
οἷον ἐκλέγω, ἐκλεκτός· ἐπίλεκτος δὲ προπαροξύνεται, ὅτι ἀπὸ ὀνόματος ἔσχε τὴν σύνθεσιν, ἐκ τῆς ἐπὶ προθέσεως, καὶ τοῦ λεκτός. Οὕτως οὖν καὶ διαμετρῶ διαμετρήσω,
διαμετρητός: E. M. 347. 22: ἐξαίρετος· προπαροξύνεται, ἐπειδὴ τὰ διὰ τοῦ ΕΤΟΣ
ὑπὲρ δύο συλλαβὰς προπαροξύνεσθαι θέλουσιν, ἀριδείκετος, ἀμαιμάκετος· χωρὶς εἰ μὴ
ἁπλᾶ ὄντα πρὸ τοῦ Ε τὸ Π ἔχει, διὰ τὸ Ἰαπετός· ἢ ἀπὸ ῥήματος συντεθείη, διὰ τὸ
ἐπαινετός. Σεσημείωται τὸ ἀφυσγετός: E. M. 474. 18: ἱππόβοτον· Διατί ἀνεβίβασε
τὸν τόνον; Τὰ εἰς ΟΣ ὀξύτονα δισύλλαβα ἐν τῇ συνθέσει προπαροξύνεται· βατός
(ἄμβατος) Ἄμβατος ἔστι πόλις. φατός, ἀρητφατος. Χωρὶς εἰ μὴ παρασύνθετα

ὦσι, διὰ τὸ μετρῶ μετρήσω μετρητός· καί, διαμετρητῷ ἐνὶ χώρῳ: E. M. 569.
22: Ἀπὸ μὲν οὖν τοῦ λέγω λεκτός, καὶ ἔκλεκτός, σύνθετον ὀξύτονον· ἀπὸ δὲ τοῦ
ἐκλέγω συνθέτου παρασύνθετον, διάλεκτος βαρύνεται, Schol. Ven. Γ. 344; A. G.
Oxon. 1. 135. 29. Such are fair specimens of the rules given by the Greek grammarians for the accentuation of these words, and it is quite needless to quote more
of them. Modern writers are not more helpful. 'Verbal adjectives,' says Göttling, Accent. p. 313, 'are in general oxytone as *parasyntheta,* barytone as *syntheta.*' Lobeck, in his dissertation, 'De motione adjectivorum minus mobilium'
(printed in the Paralipomena, p. 455 sqq.), has accumulated, with preternatural
diligence, a vast number of instances in which the printed books violate, or seem
to violate, the rules of the grammarians. His researches prove that these words
have been brought into such incredible confusion that it would be quite useless to
attempt the construction of a more precise rule than that given above.

531. NOTE 2.—Lobeck, in the above-mentioned dissertation, lays down the
rule that all compound verbal adjectives in τος are oxytone when they indicate
possibility merely, and are proparoxytone when they denote a completed act; thus
διαλυτός, *capable of being dissolved, dissoluble,* is oxytone, but διάλυτος, *dissolved,*
is proparoxytone, Lob. Par. 478: Primum igitur constituimus, adjectiva, quorum
significatio latinis in *ilis* exeuntibus respondet, acuto sono finiri; quem canonem
H. Stephanus aliquoties sequitur: Διάλυτος, *dissolutus*; διαλυτός, *dissolubilis*;
μετάπειστος, *in aliam sententiam adductus*; μεταπειστός, *qui potest a sententia dimo-
veri.* Neque hæc novitia est doctrina sed a veteribus ipsis tradita. Suidas, Ἐξαί-
ρετον τὸ ἐπίλεκτον· (hoc ex Schol. Didymi ad Il. 2. 227) ἐξαιρετόν δὲ ὀξυτόνως τὸ
ἐκβαλλόμενον id est τὸ ἐκβάλλεσθαι δυνάμενον, quod uno verbo ἐξαιρέσιμον, exem-
tile dicitur.' And this rule holds of very many words, but the exceptions and
variations are countless and bewildering. Lobeck, 498, sums up his results as follows: 'Quæstio erat de accentu verbalium. Quæ quum aut syntheta sint aut
parasyntheta, veterum sententiis consultisque hæc acui statuimus, illa gravari.
Sed quod caput est rei, qua ratione decomposita a compositis discerni queant, id
neque illi perspexisse videntur, neque nobis scire contigit, neque omnino de omnibus sciri posse videtur. Si quis vero nos attendere jubeat ex duabus adjectivi par-
tibus utra quoque loco prævaleat, præpositio an adjectivum, et hinc definiri velit,
utri sit imponendus accentus, is parum reputaverit hanc rationem longe a nostra
intelligentia remotam et a Græcis ipsis neglectam esse, qui ἀπευκτός quidem dixere
sed ἀπεύχετος omniaque polysyllaba sopito præpositionis accentu pronunciare
coacti sunt. Has igitur in angustias compulsi duas illas constituimus regulas de
oxytonesi potentialium et contrario absolutorum tenore, quarum neutra per omnia
servatur, sed apparet tamen id ordinarium esse, quod secus est extra ordinem.
Idque vel hoc exemplo confirmare licet, quod in quadraginta novem, quæ collegi,
adjectivis cum præpositione ἀπό conjunctis sex nec plus reperiuntur oxytona,
ἀπευκτός, ἀποδεκτός, ἀπαρεστός, Simpl. in Ench. 5. p. 74; ἀποφαντός, Philo Legg.
All. 2. 70 B: ἀποδεικτός, Aristot. Anal. Post. 1. 10. p. 76. 33, et ἀπωστός, quod
unum a potentiali significatione maxime sejunctum est.'

532. Those ending in κλυτός or κλειτός are somewhat irregular;
when compounded with an indeclinable word of more than one
syllable they are oxytone, as ἀγακλυτός, ἐπικλυτός, παρακλυτός,
περικλυτός, τηλεκλειτός (τηλέκλειτος in Apollon. Rhod. 3. 1097 is
probably false), τηλεκλυτός; when, with a declinable word, or
with an indeclinable monosyllable, they are proparoxytone, as
δύσκλυτος, θεόκλυτος, πάγκλειτος, πάγκλυτος, πρόκλυτος, τοξόκλυ-

τος, while parathetic compounds are oxytone, as δορικλυτός, δουρικλυτός, δουρικλειτός (but δορίκλυτος occurs in Suid.), ὀνομακλυτός, Il. 22. 51 (or according to some ὀνομάκλυτος), ναυσικλειτός, Od. 6. 22 (or, as others wrote, ναυσίκλειτος), ναυσικλυτός (or ναυσίκλυτος, Od. 15. 415), and upon this principle ποσσίκλυτος might be oxytone.

533. NOTE.—E. M. 215. 20: Τὸ δὲ κλειτὸς καὶ κλυτὸς εἰ μὲν μετὰ ἀπτώτου συντεθῇ ὑπὲρ μίαν συλλαβήν, φυλάσσει τὴν ὀξεῖαν τάσιν· οἷον κλειτὸς ἀγακλειτός· εἰ δὲ μετὰ πτωτικοῦ ἢ ἀπτώτου μονοσυλλάβου προπαροξύνεται· πρόκλειτος, ὀνομάκλυτος, τὸ δὲ δουρικλυτὸς ἐν παραθέσει.

Schol. Ven. Κ. 109 : Τὸ κλυτὸς εἰ πτωτικὸν κατάρχοι ἐν συνθέσει βαρύτονόν ἐστι τοξόκλυτος, ὀνομάκλυτος· εἰ δὲ ἄπτωτον, φυλάσσει τὸν αὐτὸν τόνον, περικλυτός, ἀγακλυτός, διὸ σημειωτέον τὸ ναυσικλυτὸς ὀξυνόμενον . . . τὸ μὲν οὖν δουρὶ κλυτὸς ἐν παραθέσει ἐστίν.

S. V. Χ. 51 : Ὀνομακλυτός, Ἀρίσταρχος ὑφ' ἓν ὡς πασιμέλουσα. ἐν δὲ Ὀδυσσείᾳ ὄνομα κλυτός Αἴθων κατὰ παράθεσιν. εἰ δέ, φασίν, οὐκ ἔστιν ἐξ οὐδετέρου καὶ ἀρσενικοῦ σύνθετον, τί ἐστι τὸ Ἀστυάναξ καὶ ποιηματογράφος ; κατὰ σύνθεσιν οὖν ἐστίν, ὡς τὸ τοξόκλυτος παρὰ Πινδάρῳ καὶ περίκλυτος [?] : Schol. Ambros. in Odyss. H. 39; Eust. 1566. 64; Arc. 88. 16; 90. 6; A. G. Oxon. 1. 378. 12.

(d) Nominal Derivatives.

534. *General Rule.*—Compound adjectives, of which the second half is derived from a noun, retract the accent, as καλλίναος, παναγήραος, πολύπραος ; ἄνηβος, ἔφηβος, πάνολβος, πολύφλοισβος, χρυσεόστιλβος ; ἐγχεσίμαργος, κακόψογος, καλλίφθογγος, λήθαργος, νεόζυγος, πολύπυργος ; ἄναυδος, ἑκατόμποδος, ἔμπεδος, κενόσπουδος, ὁμόσπονδος ; ἀνάπλεως, ἄνεως, ἀνίλεως, ἀξιόχρεως ; ἀνάπλεος, κατάπλεος, παγχρύσεος ; βαθύρριζος, μονοτράπεζος ; ὠχρόξανθος ; αὐτοάγαθος (and αὐτοαγαθός), πανάγαθος, φιλάγαθος ; βαρύμοχθος, δολόμυθος, εὐθυκέλευθος, μονόλιθος, ὀλιγόμισθος, ταχύρροθος ; παραπλήσιος, πολλαπλήσιος ; δισπόνδειος (see § 382), εὐγένειος, λεπτόγειος, παλιμβάχειος, περίθειος ; δεκάβοιος, ἑπτάβοιος, παγγέλοιος, πανόμοιος, προσόμοιος ; ἄδικος, δικαιάδικος, δυσάρεσκος, ἐπίορκος (Schol. Ven. Γ. 279), θυμάγροικος, παρακρουσιχοίνικος, φιλόδικος ; ἀγχίαλος, ἀΐδηλος, ἀκόνδυλος, ἀλλοπρόσαλλος, ἄπτιλος, διάγκυλος, διάδιπλος, ἔπιλλος, εὐτράπελος, κατάδηλος, λιγουροκώτιλος, μεσάγκυλος (Ε. Μ. 113. 32), παραστρόγγυλος, προδείελος, προσείκελος, σύμπολλοι, χρυσοποίκιλος ; ὅμαιχμος, ῥάθυμος ; ἡμίονος, νήποινος, πάναγνος ; ἀλίπλοος, ἀνεμόθροος, ἀνέμπλοος, εὔνοος ; νήλωπος ; ἀβέλτερος, ἄϊρος, γλυκύπικρος, δείλακρος (see § 542), δίαιθρος, ἐπίκηρος, ζώπυρος, λειαύστηρος, λευκόπυρρος, μεγαλοπόνηρος, νώθουρος, οὐδενόσωρος (Schol. Ven. Θ. 178), ὑφέσπερος ; ἄϊσος, ἀρτιοπέρισσος; πάμπρωτος, περιέσχατος, ἰσάδελφος, σύζωος, πολύζωος; except **oxytone**, 1. ἀεργηλός, ἀϊδνός, ἀκιδνός, ἀλαός, ἀμενηνός, ἀμυσχρός, δαφοινός, ἐπηετανός, ἐπικοινωνός, εὐδεινός, εὐδιανός, καταριγηλός, νεογιλός, νεογνός, νωδός, παμβδελυρός, παμμυσαρός, ὑποχαροπός, χαροπός. 2. All in ημερινος, οπωρινος, as ἀμφημερινός, αὐθημερινός, ἐφημερινός, ἰσημερινός, καθημερινός, μεθημερινός, μετοπωρινός, φθινοπωρινός, together with δυσχειμερινός, μεσημβρινός, προπερυσινός and προχθεσινός. 3. Those in ικος, where κ does not belong to the root of the word, as ἀναθεματικός, πολεμολαμαχαϊκός, τελεσιουργικός, ὑπεραττικός, ψευδαττικός, but ἄδικ-ος. 4. Those in ωπος from ὤψ, as ἀγριωπός, αἱματωπός, δεινωπός, εἰσωπός, but μέτωπος, and πρόσωπος, with their compounds, are proparoxytone, as αἰσχροπρόσωπος, ἀμφιπρόσωπος, ἀνδροπρόσωπος; ἀντιμέτωπος, εὐρυμέτωπος. The words ἀμφίσωπος, ἔνωπος, and περίωπος, are also proparoxytone, 5. Ordinals in στος, as πεντηκαιεικοστός. **Paroxytone**, 1. Verbal adjectives in τεος and τεον, as διαλυτέος, διασαφητέος. 2. Compounds of ἀντίος, as αὐτεναντίος, ἐναντίος, προσαντίος. 3. Multiplicatives in πλοος, as διπλόος, δεκαπλόος. 4. Those in πος = πούς, as ἀρτίπος, and the word κορυθαιόλος. **Properispomena**, 1. Those in ωος, as ἀθῷος, ὀρεσκῷος, ὑπερῷος. 2. Pronominal words in ουτος, as φιλοτοιοῦτος.

Compound adjectives in αιος are somewhat irregular. The following are properispomena. 1. All expressing number, weight, or measure, as δεκαμναῖος, διμοιραῖος, ἑξαμηνιαῖος, ἡμιμναῖος, πεντηκονταμηναῖος, τετραδραχμαῖος. 2. All in ιαιος, as ἐπιπολιαῖος, ἐπωμιαῖος, κατανωτιαῖος. 3. All in δαιος, as ἐπουδαῖος, κατουδαῖος. 4. All with two consonants before the termination αιος, as ἀπευκταῖος, ἀποπομπαῖος, διανταῖος, ἐπακταῖος, Κορακοπετραῖος, παναρχαῖος. Words which fall under none of these heads are properispomena, if the removal of the first factor (or factors) of the word leaves at least four syllables; if less than four syllables, they are proparoxytone, as ἀνα-δεξιμαῖος, ἀπ-αθηναῖος (Pollux 3. 58), ἀπο-δεκαταῖος, ἐξ-ορισιμαῖος, ἐπιστολιμαῖος; ἀ-κέραιος, ἀκριβοδίκαιος, ἀκροκνέφαιος, ἀντιπέραιος, δυσόρφναιος, ἐνεύναιος, εὐέλαιος, κρουνοχυτρο-λήραιος, λεπτόγαιος, λευκόφαιος, μισο-γύναιος, παμπάλαιος, περιδέραιος, προθύραιος, προστρόπαιος, φιλορρώμαιος. Φιλαθήναιος and φιλάρχαιος are proparoxytone, and ἐμπολαῖος properispomenon.

NOTE 1.—It will be seen that the distinction between verbal and nominal derivatives is an imaginary one as far as accents are concerned. A word is not in point of fact accented in an exceptional manner because it is derived from a verb, but conversely it is called a verbal derivative because the Greek grammarians or the Greek people accented it in a particular way. No theories of derivation, certainly no Greek theories, seem to be of any use in determining the accent of a word. No two words can be more exactly parallel than ἀποπομπαῖος and ἀποτρόπαιος are, yet their accents differ.

535. NOTE 2.—Ou ἀλαός see Arc. 38. 14 : χηλαργός, Soph. Elect. 861, is simply monstrous, and H. D. are quite right in saying, 'rectus accentus videtur χήλαργος, ut πόδαργος non ποδαργός'; the adverb ἐμπεδῶς is formed from ἐμπεδής, not from ἔμπεδος, which makes ἐμπέδως according to rule; for πάναιθος, approved by Euphranor, most wrote παναιθός, Schol. Ven. Ξ. 372 ; Eust. 992. 56 : καλοκάγαθος, Pollux 4. 11, is proparoxytone according to rule; it also occurs in the form καλὸς κἀγαθός, see Lob. Path. 1. 563, note; on παραπλήσιος see E. M. 531. 50 ; Chœrob. C. 526. 13 : πανδῖος and πανδία for πάνδιος and πάνδια can hardly be defended, though Dindorf thinks πανδία the best way of writing the word; the authority however for doing so is small, and analogy is against it : εὐνηός, with some more of the same termination in E. M. 32. 9, are blunders which ought to have been corrected long ago.

536. NOTE 3.— -αιος. According to the Greek grammarians compound adjectives in αιος are proparoxytone, E. M. 113. 32 ; Arc. 86. 13 ; still more distinctly by Schol. Aristoph. Achar. 142 : Τὸ φιλαθήναιος προπαροξύνειν δεῖ, ἐπεὶ τὰ εἰς ΟΣ λήγοντα προπερισπώμενα ἁπλᾶ ἐν τῇ συνθέσει ἀναβιβάζει τὸν τόνον, οἷον δῆμος Ἀριστόδημος, πῶλος ἐχέπωλος. καὶ Ὅμηρος Θαλυσιάδην ἐχέπωλον κνεφαῖος ἀκροκνέφαιος, ὀμφαῖος πανόμφαιος, ἀρχαῖος φιλάρχαιος ; see also Philem. Lex. p. 4. § 9 : βαθυχαῖος (?) Æschyl. Supp. 865 = 859, Didot : ἐμπολαῖος seems to be properispomenon in all the places quoted : ἐνεύναιος, for which ἐνευναῖος also occurs, e. g. Pollux 6. 10 ; H. D. : ἐξαπίναιος 'vel ἐξαπιναῖος ; variant enim libri inter utrumque accentum, neque ex præceptis Arcad. p. 43. 4, satis certo colligere licet uter accentus præferendus sit ;' H. D. : ἐπιπόλαιος, Arc. 43. 2 : Τὸ μέντοι ἐπιπόλαιος οὐκ ἀπὸ τοῦ ἐπιπολῆς παρῆκται, ἀλλὰ παρὰ τὸ ἐπιπολάζω πλὴν οἱ πλείους αὐτὸ περισπῶσιν : ἐπιτροπαῖος (?) the passage cited for this, Herodot. 3. 142, proves nothing : ἐπουραῖος (?) Hesych. : εὐδίαιος, Pollux 1. 92, or εὐδιαῖος, Plut. 2. 699 F ; H. D. : ἰσάρχαιος, Chœrob. C. 526. 13 : μισορρώμαιος, Plut. 1. 941, and φιλορώμαιος, Arc. 43. 9 ; Chœrob. C. 526. 12, it is falsely properispomenon, Chœrob. C. 516. 30, and 523. 30 : παναχαιός, E. M. 250. 29 : πανόμφαιος, Schol. Aristoph. Ach. 142 ; but πανομφαῖος also is met with : φιλαθήναιος, E. M. 113. 32 ; Chœrob. C. 526. 13 : φιλάρχαιος is prescribed by the Scholiast on Aristophanes *supra*, and is common, but the accent is not certain, for we find παναρχαῖος, Pollux 5. 150 : φιλαχαιός, E. M. 215. 6 : εὐρυστιχαιός (sic) in E. M. 180. 27, is omitted by H. D. : βαθυαίδοιος, Tzetzes in Lycoph. 831 is wrongly βαθυαιδοῖος in E. M. 2. 24.

537. NOTE 4.— -ειος. Those in ειος seem to be all proparoxytone, though there is at least one trace of another accentuation, for Eustathius says (1551. 54), ἔστι δὲ παλιμβακχεῖος, ἢ προπαροξυτόνως παλιμβάκχειος.

538. NOTE 5.— -κος. Chœrob. E. 77. 34 : Τὰ εἰς ΟΣ ὀνόματα ἐν τῇ συνθέσει ἀναβιβάζουσι τὸν τόνον, κακὸς ἄκακος, σεμνὸς ἄσεμνος, τερπνὸς ἄτερπνος, Ῥωμαϊκὸς πολυρωμαϊκος (sic) ; 'In Etym. M. p. 205. 4, ubi de accentu hujusmodi compositorum agitur, est Ῥωμαϊκὸς πολυρωμαϊκός, quod φιλορωμαϊκός scribendum videbatur Sylburgio, recte, nisi quis præferat Ῥωμαῖος φιλορώμαιος,' W. Dindorf ap. H. D. : the passage from Chœroboscus seems to show that Sylburg's emendation is not required ; as a matter of practice the rule about the retraction of the accent is ·

always disregarded, except in the word ὑπερσυντελικός, which is sometimes oxytone, as in Chœrob. C. 745. 10. 15. 26 ; 746. 5, etc. : sometimes proparoxytone, as in E. M. 193. 50 ; 252. 56 ; 318. 16, etc. ; the reason given by Göttling, ad Theodos. Gramm. p. 220, for making the word proparoxytone is of no weight : it is, he says, a parasyntheton, and therefore proparoxytone : so are ἀνταποδοτικός, δυσαναφορικός, Hesych., παρεκβατικός, παρακαθεκτικός, and others, yet they are oxytone : ἀνάττικος is said to be always proparoxytone, and such appears to be the accent of ἀφύσικος : it is not improbable that they were considered to fall under the rule concerning words compounded with a privativum, cf. §. 460.

539. NOTE 6.—·λος. Νεογιλός is oxytone, Arc. 54. 15, so also ἀεργηλός, Nicand. Ther. 50 : δημεχθηλός· μισούμενος ὑπὸ τοῦ δήμου, Hesych. is an extraordinary accent on more accounts than one : ἐπικαμπύλος, Hom. Hym. ad Merc. 90, a Greek grammarian might defend this as he does ἐπιβουκόλος by saying (what is not true) that ἐπί is superfluous : καταριγηλός, Hom. Odyss. 14. 226 : κορυθαιόλος is paroxytone, Arc. 86. 4 ; Chœrob. C. 526. 15 : Τὸ κορυθαιόλος οὐκ ἔστιν ἀπὸ τοῦ αἴολος, ἀλλ' ἀπὸ τοῦ αἰολῶ, τουτέστι κινῶ : E. M. 113. 32 ; 531. 47 ; Eust. 352. 28 : Κορυθαιόλος δὲ παροξύνεται μὲν ὑπὸ τῶν παλαιῶν : Etym. Gud. 338. 49 seems (for it is not quite clear) to make it proparoxytone : the cod. Venet. varies, but has κορυθαιόλος in Il. Χ. 471, and elsewhere ; see Dind. præf. ad Hom. Il. Oxon. 8vo. 1856, p. 19 ; the rest in αιολος are regular, as παναίολος, Arc. 86. 4 : νομοαίολος.

540. NOTE 7.— -νος. Δαφοινός, E. M. 250. 29 ; Arc. 64. 3 : ἐπικοινωνός, but μετακοίνωνος and συγκοίνωνος are regular : ἐπιταπεινός is quoted by H. D. from Oribas. Coll. 4. 14, but the accent is contrary to analogy : μισοχριστιανός (?) Chron. Pasch. p. 619. 21 ; Η. D. : νεογνός : περιστεγανός (?) Hesych. : on those in ημερινος, οπωρινος, see E. M. 691. 56 ; A. G. Oxon. 2. 425. 23 : the Doric τοσσῆνος for τοσοῦτος is also to be remarked.

541. NOTE 8.— -οος, -πος. On those in οος see Schol. Ven. Μ. 26 ; E. M. 453. 2 : the multiplicatives in πλοος are regular when contracted, as ἁπλοῦς, διπλοῦς, etc. ; Tzetzes ad Lycoph. 521 : on the very doubtful accent δικρόος for δίκροος see Lob. Phryn. 233 : χείμαρροι, Hom. Il. 4. 452, is right, though in antiquity there was a doubt on the matter ; Schol. Ven. ad loc. : Πτολεμαῖος ὁ Ἀσκαλωνίτης παροξύνει, ἐπεὶ τὸ ἑνικόν ἐστι χειμάρρους. Νικίας δὲ ὡς εὔζωνοι, καὶ μήποτε πιθανώτερον : ἀμφισωπός is proparoxytone in Hesych., together with περίωπος, E. M. 91. 12 ; cf. Lob. Ajax 340 : μόνωπα, in Callimach. ap. Schol. Aristoph. Av. 873, should be corrected ' aut μονῶπα [from μονώψ] aut μονωπά scribendum ;' H. D. : on the accentuation of these words see Arc. 67. 9 ; 86. 28 ; Theog. Can. 69. 20 ; Eust. 1389. 4 ; 768. 40 : ἄνθρωπος is by the old grammarians referred to this head : ἀελλόπος, which properly belongs to the third declension, is used by Nonnus Paraph. Joh. p. 126 as an adjective of the second declension, and the accent varies in the books between ἀελλόπος and ἀελλοπός ; Fix ap. H. D. rightly thinks that when it belongs to the second declension the word ought to be written ἀέλλοπος : ὑποχαροπός is oxytone in Xen. Cyneg. c. 5. 23 and elsewhere : ἑλίκωπος, H. D., is certainly a false accent.

542. NOTE 9.— -ρος. Ἀβληχρός, Eust. 705. 59 : ἐν δὲ τοῖς Ἡροδώρου καὶ Ἀπίωνος φέρεται ὅτι Ἡρακλείδης μὲν ὁ Μιλήσιος βαρύνει τὴν λέξιν, λέγων ὡς βληχρόν ἐστι τὸ ἰσχυρόν, καὶ ἐν συνθέσει ἄβληχρον ὡς ἄκακον. ἡ δὲ παράδοσις ὀξύνει : ἀγαυρός, Schol. Ven. Θ. 178, has ἄγαυρος : ἀμυδρός, Eust. 463. 41, seems to think that strictly this should be proparoxytone, as a compound : ἀμυσχρός, though a compound, is oxytone : αὐτονοερός (?) : ἐξιατρός· ἐκθυτικός, Hesych., possibly a mistaken accent ; if the word is an adjective it should in all probability be ἐξίατρος: ἐπισμυγερός is irregular; Schol. Ven. I. 456, the preposition was held to be reduudant: ζαβρός, Hesych.; if a syncopated form of ζάβορος, is irregular, but may be compared with νεόγονος, νεογνός: κολοβούρος, Hesych., should be corrected, κολόβουρος is the proper reading; cf. κόθουρος, κόλουρος, μείουρος, etc.: φαιουρός, in Lycoph. 334, should also be emended: παμβδελυρός and παμμυσαρός, Aristoph. Lys. 969, are singular, but seem to be so accented in MSS.: παμμίαρος, Aristoph. Ran. 466: παμπόνηρος, Aristoph. Equit. 415: πάναισχρος is also regular, as is ὑπομύσαρος, yet παγγλυκερός, Aristoph. Lys. 970 seems to be well attested; it is possible that some grammarians may have regarded such words as mere parathetic compounds, or as two words rather than one; the correctness of περικρυερός may be doubted: ποδαβρός, E. M. 678. 1, Herodot. I. 55, should probably be proparoxytone like πάναβρος, Lucian Rhet. Præc. c. 11: πολυφθονερός, in Diog. Laert. 10. 8, has been corrected by Bake (ad Cleomed. p. 434) into πολυφθόρους; see H. D. s. v.: φαλακρός is considered to be a compound by the Greeks, e. g. E. M. 787. 1: φαλακρὸς ὁ τὸ ἄκρον ἔχων φαλόν, ὅ ἐστι λευκόν· παρὰ τὸ φάος· φάλιον γὰρ τὸ λευκόν: Arcadius, 74. 21, classes it with simple adjectives, and Lobeck, Par. 42, maintains that neither it nor δείλακρος is a compound at all: 'δείλακρος et φαλακρός non composita esse, ut vulgo creditur, sed simplicia significat mobilitas ἡ δειλάκρα, Arist. Plut. 973. Athen. p. 697 C: ἡ φαλακρά Lucian. pro Imagg. § 5, quæ si quis oblivione originis, ut ἀργή, σκυθρωπή, declinata esse atque ideo etiam φαλακρός acuta ultima dici contendat, tamen nullam rationem afferre poterit, cur illa compositis potius quam simplicibus adnumeranda sint.' But the existence of a feminine termination is no proof that the words are simple. The compounds of φαλακρός are regular, as ἡμιφάλακρος, ὀπισθοφάλακρος.

543. NOTE 10.— -τος. Ἀμφιβῶτος for ἀμφίβατος = ἀμφιβόητος is an error: αὐτενιαυτός (?) *L. S.*: φιλοβοιωτός, E. M. 215.

Attic Declension.

544. These words in ως and ων retain the accent of the common form, e. g. ἴλαος ἴλεως, κάλος κάλως, λαός λεώς, ναός νεώς' πλέος πλέως; ἅλως, γάλως, γάλοως; ἀνώγεως, ἀνώγεων, βαθύγεως, εὔγεως, λεπτόγεως, ὑπόγεως; ἀείζωος ἀείζως; ζωός ζώς; ἄκερως, βούκερως, δίκερως, εὔκερως, πολύκερως, χρυσόκερως. Monosyllables are perispomena, as Γλῶς, Κρῶς, Κῶς, σῶς, Τλῶς; except ζώς and δώς' oxytone: ὀρφῶς and λαγῶς are said by the grammarians to be circumflexed, though the common form of the former is ὄρφος, and of the latter λαγός.

545. NOTE—Arc. 126. 25; Joh. Alex. 7. 36; Chœrob. C. 64. 20; 253. 9; 360. 21: according to Schol. Ven. E. 887, Ptolemæus Ascalonites circumflexed ζώς. The following polysyllables are also perispomena: Ἰναρῶς, Chœrob. C. 261. 31: ἔστι γὰρ Ἰναρῶς ὄνομα βασιλέως, Παραμιζῶς ὄνομα εὐνούχου, Σαβακῶς, Μανεῶς, ταῦτα δὲ ὀνόματα εἰσὶ κύρια. Καὶ ἰστέον ὅτι τινὲς μὲν ὀξύνουσιν αὐτά, τινὲς δὲ περισπῶσι. τὸ δὲ Σαβακῶς Ῥωμανὸς βαρύνει, Σαβάκως λέγων. Ἀποβολῇ δὲ τοῦ Σ ποιοῦσι τὴν γενικήν: Arc. 94. 8: τὰ εἰς ΩΣ Περσικὰ ἢ Αἰγύπτια παροξύνεται· φάργως Ἰνάρως. Our books follow the accentuation of Arcadius. 'Herod. 3. 12: ὑπὸ Ἰνάρω (libri aliquot Ἰνάρου) τοῦ Λίβυος' 15; 7. 7; Thucyd. 1. 104. Accus. Ἴναρον ap. Strabon. 17. p. 801, ubi duo codd. Ἰνάρων, ap. Suidam lemma gl. sine explicatione positæ est Ἰνάρωνος· Ἴναρος, Ἰνάρου, Ἴναρον, ap. Ctesiam in Photii. Bibl. p. 40;' H. *D.* Göttling, Accent. p. 284, says that the MSS. of Herodot. 3. 15 read Ἰναρῶς, and Ἴναρω for the genitive, not Ἰνάρω as it is printed. Κανεῶς, A. G. 1197, in the same passage of Gaisford's edition of Chœroboscus (quoted above), is Μανεῶς, perhaps one or other is a misprint: λαγῶς, Chœrob. *l. l.*; Joh. Alex 8. 36; E. M. 635. 32: Μανεθῶς, Joh. Alex. 9. 1; on the numerous forms of the name see H. D.: ὀρθῶς, Chœrob. Joh. Alex. *ll. ll.*; Arc. 94. 3: τὰ εἰς ΩΣ Ἀττικὰ ὁμοτονοῦσιν ἐκείνοις, ἀφ' ὧν ἐσχηματίσθησαν· ναός νεώς, λαός λεώς, ἀξιόχρεος ἀξιόχρεως. τὸ δὲ λαγῶς καὶ ὀρφῶς περισπῶνται. Schol. Aristoph. Vesp. 493=491: ἐν τοῖς πλείστοις ὀρφῶς, ἔν τισι δὲ ὀρφούς. μήποτε δὲ καὶ τὸ ἑνικὸν τοῦ ἰχθύος οὕτως ἔλεγον ὀρφώς, ὡς λαγώς καὶ ταώς. Chœrob. C. 260. 17: ἰστέον ὅτι ταῦτα εἰς ΩΣ Ἀττικὰ φυλάττουσι τῆς κοινῆς εὐθείας τὸν τόνον· εἴτε γὰρ προπαροξύνεται τὸ κοινόν, εἴτε παροξύνεται, εἴτε ὀξύνεται, τὴν αὐτὴν τάσιν φυλάττει καὶ παρὰ τοῖς Ἀθηναίοις, οἷον τὸ λαὸς καὶ ναὸς ὀξυτονούμενα παρ' ἡμῖν φυλάττουσι τὴν ὀξεῖαν τάσιν καὶ παρὰ τοῖς Ἀθηναίοις λεὼς γὰρ καὶ νεὼς λέγουσιν ὀξυτόνως· καὶ πάλιν τὸ Τάλος καὶ κάλος παροξυνόμενα παρ' ἡμῖν, καὶ παρὰ τοῖς Ἀθηναίοις παροξύνονται, οἷον Τάλως καὶ κάλως· καὶ πάλιν τὸ Μενέλαος καὶ Ἰόλαος προπαροξυνόμενα παρ' ἡμῖν καὶ παρὰ τοῖς Ἀθηναίοις προπαροξύνονται Μενέλεως, Ἰόλεως· Σεσημείωται τὸ ὀρφῶς καὶ λαγῶς περισπώμενα, ταῦτα γὰρ οὐκ ἐφύλαξαν τὸν τόνον τῶν κοινῶν· τοῦ[το] μὲν γὰρ ὀρφῶς τὸ κοινὸν ὀρφος ἐστὶ βαρυτόνως, τοῦ δὲ λαγῶς ὀξυτόνως λαγός. Ἰστέον καὶ τοῦτο, ὅτι ἐπὶ πάσης πτώσεως τὰ εἰς ΩΣ Ἀττικὰ τῆς ἰδίας εὐθείας τὸν τόνον φυλάττουσιν. Chœrob. C. 261. 20: δεῖ δὲ γινώσκειν ὅτι τὰ πολλὰ εὑρίσκονται παρὰ τοῖς Ἀθηναίοις εἰς ΩΣ μὴ ἔχοντα προϋποκείμενον κοινόν, οἷον κορώνεως, φιβάλεως, δαμερίππεως, χελιδώνεως, ἱέρεως, προπαροξύνονται δὲ ὅλα ταῦτα, καὶ ἀποβολῇ τοῦ Σ ποιοῦσι τὴν γενικήν, ὁμοίως τοῖς ἄλλοις Ἀττικοῖς. Ἔστι δὲ τὸ μὲν κορώνεως καὶ φιβάλεως καὶ δαμαρίππεως καὶ χελιδώνεως εἴδη φυτῶν, τὸ δὲ ἱέρεως τὸν ἱερέα σημαίνει· ἱέρεως γὰρ παρ' αὐτοῖς ὁ ἱερεύς. Athen. 315 C: Ἀριστοφάνης Σφηξὶν

Ἦν μὲν ὠνῆταί τις ὀρφώς, μεμβράδας δὲ μὴ θέλῃ.

τὴν μέντοι ἑνικὴν εὐθεῖαν ὀξυτόνως προφέρονται Ἀττικοί· Ἄρχιππος Ἰχθύσιν ὡς πρόκειται τὴν δὲ γενικὴν Κρατῖνος Ὀδυσσεῦσι Τέμαχος ὀρφῷ χλιαρόν: Σαβακῶς, Chœrob. 261. 32: Σπαραμιζῶς, A. G. 1197; Gaisford has Παραμιζῶς: Ταλῶς, Joh. Alex. 8. 36; in Chœrob. 260. 24 it is printed Τάλως, and at 66. 17 he expressly says that in Attic it is paroxytone: ταῶς, Joh. Alex. 9. 1; Chœrob. C. 261. 7. Reg. de prosod. ap. Herm. de emend. rat. Gr. gr. p. 451: τὰ εἰς ΩΣ ὀξύνονται, ἱδρώς, λαγώς, ἀγνώς, ὁ ἀγνωστος. τὸ μέντοι ταῶς καὶ τυφῶς παρὰ τοῖς παλαιοῖς εὗρον, ἃ καὶ δικατάληκτά εἰσι. καὶ ὁ ταῶν καὶ ὁ τυφῶν. ἀλλὰ καὶ τὸ λαγῶς περισπώμενον εὗρον. σὺ δὲ κατὰ τὴν συνήθειαν ὄξυνε. I suppose the writer means the custom of the Alexandrians who said ταός (or ταώς), cf. Arc. 37. 1; Schol. Aristoph. Vesp. 493: Τυφῶς, Joh. Alex. Chœrob. etc. *ll. ll.*

546. Note 2.—There is some difference of opinion as to the accentuation of words in γηρως = γήραος, as ἀγήρως, βαθύγηρως· ἐσχατόγηρως, εὔγηρως, καλόγηρως, παντογήρως, πολύγηρως, σύγγηρως, ταχύγηρως, ὑπέργηρως. Hermann (De emend. rat. Gr. p. 24 sqq.) would make them all paroxytone; and such is also the opinion of Kühner, G. G. § 77. vol. 1. p. 249: he thinks that words of this class can be proparoxytone only when the final ω is preceded by ε in the penultimate syllable, and that it is therefore a mistake to extend such an accentuation to words in which ω is preceded by η. But Chœroboscus, 259. 13, has εὔγηρως as an example, and he probably had good warrant for it. Kühner also observes that in Æschyl. Agam. 78, all the MSS. have ὑπεργήρων. All the manuscripts are, however, only transcripts of the Medicean, and in Dindorf's edition ὑπέργηρων is printed: ἀγήρως seems to be always paroxytone, and παντογήρως is found in Soph. Ant. 606; the rest are all proparoxytone in MSS. and printed books, though here and there instances to the contrary may be found; cf. Chœrob. C. 363. 27; 365. 16; 378. 16·

547. NOTE 3.—The epenthesis of ο which occurs in the Epic forms of these words does not of necessity produce any effect on the accent, e. g. Ἄθοως = Ἄθως, genitive Ἄθοω· Eust. 980. 49 : τὸ δὲ Ἄθοω προπαροξύνουσιν οἱ παλαιοί, τὸν φυσικὸν τόνον φυλάσσοντες· γέγονε γὰρ ἐκ τοῦ Ἄθω, πλεονάσαντος τοῦ ἐν τῇ παραληγούσῃ Ο μικροῦ, ὡς καὶ ἐν τῷ φῶς φόως, καὶ Κῶς ἡ νῆσος, Κόως, οἷον Κόων εὖ ναιομένην. καὶ ἔστι πως Ἀττικὴ καὶ ἡ Ἄθοω προπαροξύτονησις. Ἀθηναῖοι γὰρ ἐν πολλοῖς ὀκνοῦσι μετατιθέναι ὑποβιβαστικῶς τὰς τῶν εὐθειῶν ὀξείας. ἐν γοῦν τῷ πόλεως ὄφεως συνήκεως οὐκ ἐταπείνωσεν ἡ μακροκαταληξία τῆς γενικῆς τὴν προπαροξυτόνησιν. So also Schol. Ven. Ξ 229. Yet Eust. 391. 44 has Ἀθόω, and in E. M. 347. 10 it is said that Herodian so accented it. Γάλως, like many other words of this termination, is inflected in several ways, for the genitive is either γάλω or γάλοως, γαλόω (?) and γάλωτος. Eust. 391. 44 has γαλόως, dative γάλῳ and γαλόῳ, but it would appear from E. M. 220. 9, who also vouches the same forms, that they would be γάλοως, γάλοω in Attic (see Schol. Ven. Γ. 122), if that dialect used them. Eust. 1281. 8 : καὶ ὅρα τὸ γαλόῳ πρὸ μιᾶς ἔχον τὸν τόνον ὡς ἐν τοῖς τοῦ Ἡροδώρου κεῖται καὶ Ἀπίωνος ; cf. Schol. Ven. X. 473. These manifold inconsistencies are perhaps to be explained from the varying quantity of the final syllable ; the termination εως is sometimes treated as a dissyllable, though more often as a monosyllable ; possibly the same was the case with οως.

V. OBLIQUE CASES.

(1) *Of the Attic Declension.*

548. The accent of the nominative singular is retained unaltered throughout all cases and numbers, as Μενέλεως, Μενέλεω, Μενέλεῳ, Μενέλεων ; κάλως, κάλω, κάλῳ, κάλων ; ζώς, ζώ, ζῴ ; Τυφῶς, Τυφῶ, Τυφῷ ; λεώς, λεώ, λεῴ, λεών ; λεώ, λεῴν ; λεῴ, λεών, λεῴς, λεώς.

549. NOTE 1.—Chœrob. C. 260. 30 : ἰστέον καὶ τοῦτο, ὅτι ἐπὶ πάσης πτώσεως τὰ εἰς ΩΣ Ἀττικὰ τῆς ἰδίας εὐθείας τὸν τόνον φυλάττουσιν. These cases are very commouly misaccented in the grammars and elsewhere ; e. g. we find λεῶ and λεῷ for λεώ and λεῴ : νεῷ for νεῴ : νεῶν for νεῴν, etc. in Matthiä Gr. Gr. § 70. The old writers are however almost unanimous in maintaining the rule given above ; cf. Reg. Prosod. ap. Herm. de emend. rat. Gr. Gr. p. 452. § 138 : καὶ τὰ Ἀττικὰ τοῦ νεώ, τοῦ λεώ. τὸν γὰρ τόνον τῆς κοινῆς εὐθείας φυλάττουσιν Ἀττικοὶ ἐν πάσαις ταῖς πτώσεσιν : Chœrob. C. 415. 24 ; 446. 5 ; 464. 24 ; 466. 29 ; Joh. Alex. 5. 10 ; 9. 26 ; 20. 11 ; Theodos. Can. 984. 31 ; A. G. 1160.

550. NOTE 2.—Ionic forms are regular in their accentuation as Τυνδάρεος, genitive Τυνδάρεου or in Ionic Τυνδάρεω ; such forms however sometimes puzzle the grammarians and scribes, who do not always feel sure whether they were dealing with a mere Ionic variety or with the real Attic declension. Eust. 1686. 23 : Τυνδάρεω, ὃν Ὅμηρος μὲν κοινῶς κλίνει, καθὰ δηλοῖ τὸ Τυνδάρεου παράκοιτιν, ὡς Πανδάρεου, καὶ τὸ ὑπὸ Τυνδαρέῳ παροξυτόνως λεχθέν. οἱ μέντοι μεθ᾽ Ὅμηρον Ἀττικοὶ Τυνδάρεων προπαροξυτόνως φασίν, ὡς Μενέλεων. οὕτω δὲ καὶ τὸν Πηνέλεων Ἀττικοὶ μὲν διὰ μακρᾶς ληγούσης προάγουσι καὶ προπαροξυτονοῦσι κατὰ πᾶσαν τὴν κλίσιν, ὁ δὲ ποιητὴς κοινότερον προφέρει, ὡς δηλοῖ καὶ τὸ Πηνελέοιο ἄνακτος ; Schol. Hom. Odyss. Λ. 299 : ἢ ῥ᾽ ὑπὸ Τυνδάρεω, παροξυτόνως τὸ Τυνδάρεω, ἀκολούθως τῷ οὐχ ὡς Τυνδάρεω κούρη κακὰ μήσατο (Od. Ω. 199), yet in the printed editions this direction is not observed. The writer of the Medicean manuscript of Æschylus (Agam. 83) does not seem to have been quite clear in his mind whether he ought to write Τυνδαρέω θύγατερ, or Τυνδάρεω or Τυνδαρέου.

551. Note 3.—Athen. 400 A : Τρύφων δέ φησι : Τὸν λαγὼν ἐπ' αἰτιατικῆς ἐν Δαναΐσιν Ἀριστοφάνης ὀξυτόνως καὶ μετὰ τοῦ Ν λέγει

Λύαας ἴσως ἂν τὸν λαγὼν ξυναρπάσειεν ὑμῶν.

Καὶ ἐν Δαιταλεῦσιν

Ἀπόλωλα· τίλλων τὸν λαγὼν ὀφθήσομαι.

Ξενοφῶν δ' ἐν Κυνηγετικῷ χωρὶς τοῦ Ν λαγῶ καὶ περισπωμένως. ἐπεὶ τὸ καθ' ἡμᾶς ἐστι λαγός. ὥσπερ δὲ ναὸν λεγόντων ἡμῶν ἐκεῖνοί φασι νεών καὶ λαὸν λεών, οὕτω λαγὸν ὀνομαζόντων ἐκεῖνοι λαγὼν ἐροῦσι. τῇ δὲ τὸν λαγὸν ἐνικῇ αἰτιατικῇ ἀκόλουθός ἐστιν ἡ παρὰ Σοφοκλεῖ ἐν Ἀμύκῳ σατυρικῷ πληθυντικὴ ὀνομαστική

Γέρανοι, χελῶναι, γλαῦκες, ἰκτῖνοι, λαγοί.

τῇ δὲ λαγὼν ἡ διὰ τοῦ Ω παραπλησίως προσαγορευομένη λαγὼ παρ' Εὐπόλιδι ἐν Κό-λαξιν Ἵνα πάρα μὲν βατίδες καὶ λαγῷ καὶ γυναῖκες εἰλίποδες. εἰσὶ δ' οἳ καὶ ταῦτ' ἀλόγως κατὰ τὴν τελευτῶσαν συλλαβὴν περισπωμένως προφέρον-ται. δεῖ δὲ ὀξυτονεῖν τὴν λέξιν, ἐπειδὴ τὰ εἰς ΟΣ λήγοντα τῶν ὀνομάτων ὁμοτόνα ἐστι, κἂν μεταληφθῇ εἰς τὸ Ω παρ' Ἀττικοῖς· ναὸς νεώς, κάλος κάλως. οὕτως δ' ἐχρή-σατο τῷ ὀνόματι καὶ Ἐπίχαρμος καὶ Ἡρόδοτος, καὶ ὁ τοὺς Εἵλωτας ποιήσας.

552. Genitives in ωο, if from oxytone Attic genitives, are properispomena, as Πετεώ· Πετεῶο, Ταλαός, Ταλαώ, Ταλαῶο; if from · barytone Attic genitives, they are proparoxytone, as Μίνω, Μίνωο; Ἀνδρόγεω, Ἀνδρογέωο.

553. Note.—Choerob. C. 413. 1 ; Eust. 1830. 59 : ἰστέον δέ, ὡς Ὅμηρος μὲν ἀναλόγως καθὰ ἥρως ἥρωος, οὕτω καὶ Μίνως Μίνωος ἔκλινεν. οἱ δὲ ὕστερον καὶ ἰσοσυλλάβως ὡς Μενέλεως Μενέλεω, οὕτω καὶ Μίνως Μίνω. ἄλλοι δὲ καὶ ἄλλως ἔφασαν καινότερον, ὅτι ὥσπερ Ἀττικῶς Πετεὼς Πετεώ καὶ πλεονασμῷ Πετεῶο ἐν Ἰλιάδι, καὶ Ἀνδρόγεως Ἀνδρόγεω καὶ Ἀνδρογέωο, οὕτω καὶ Μίνως Μίνω καὶ Μίνωο. ἦν δὲ ἄν, φασι, καὶ Ἄθως Ἄθωο, εἰ μὴ ἐκώλυε τὸ μέτρον ἐν τῷ ἐξ Ἀθόω δ' ἐπὶ πόντον ἐδύσατο κυμαίνοντα.

(2) *Of the Common Declension.*

554. The general rule holds, except that oxytone words be-come perispomena in the Genitive and Dative of all numbers, as λόγος, λόγου, λόγῳ, λόγον ; λόγω, λόγοιν ; λόγοι, λόγων, λόγοις, λόγους : ἄγγελος, ἀγγέλου, ἀγγέλῳ, ἄγγελον, ἄγγελε ; ἀγγέλω, ἀγ-γέλοιν ; ἄγγελοι, ἀγγέλων, ἀγγέλοις, ἀγγέλους : κακός, κακοῦ, κακῷ, κακοῖν, κακῶν, κακοῖς·   According to E. M. 472. 46, ἴος, *one*, makes ἴον in the gen., but ἰῷ in the dative.

555. *Cases in* θε *and* φι.—These follow the rules given above (§ 219), as Ἀργόθεν, οὐρανόθεν ; ἀριστερόφιν, δεξιόφιν, θεόφιν, Ἰλιόφι, ὀστεόφιν, στρατόφιν.

Contracted nouns present some peculiarities, which are noted below.

556. Note.—The epic gen. in οιο and the Doric in ω are regularly accented, as Καυκάσοιο, πολυφλοίσβοιο, καλοῖο, E. M. 474. 52 : so also the genitive and dative dual in οιῖν, as ἵπποιῖν, ὤμοιῖν, σταθμοῖν.

'The genitive of nouns feminine in ος is formed also by Callimachus in αων, νησάων, ψηφάων ; but τᾶν ἀοιδᾶν, *Eur. Hipp.* 738, is suspicious.' Matthiä Gk. Gr. § 69. 4. The old dative in οισι is also regular, as κακοῖσιν, οἴκοισιν.

Contracted Substantives and Adjectives.

557. The rule given above (§ 20) for the accentuation of syllables resulting from contraction is here to be applied *only to the Nominative Singular*, and not to the oblique cases. The accent of the nominative singular being determined, the word follows the rule which has just been given for the accentuation of oblique cases in the common declension, except that the nominative and accusative dual in ω are invariably oxytone ; e. g. ἔκπλοος becomes by the rule ἔκπλους, εὔνοος εὔνους, εὔξοος εὔξους, ἁπλόος ἁπλοῦς, διπλόος διπλοῦς, Πειρίθοος Πειρίθους, νόος νοῦς, ὀστέον ὀστοῦν, these are then treated exactly as if they were not contracted at all ; hence ἔκπλου, ἔκπλῳ ; εὔνου, εὔνῳ, εὔνουν, εὔνοιν, εὖνοι, εὔνων, εὔνοις, εὔνους ; εὔξου, εὔξω ; ἁπλοῦ, ἁπλῷ ; διπλοῦ, διπλῷ, διπλοῦν ; Πειρίθου, Πειρίθῳ ; νοῦ, νῷ, νοῦν ; ὀστοῦ, ὀστῷ, ὀστοῦν, ὀστᾶ, ὀστῶν, ὀστοῖν ; but ἐκπλώ, εὐνώ, εὐξώ, ἁπλώ, διπλώ, νώ, ὀστώ.

558. Note—It would, one might think, puzzle the perverse ingenuity even of a Greek grammarian to justify this strange departure from the ordinary rule of contraction ; as Πειρίθοος makes Πειρίθους, so Πειριθόου ought to make Πειριθοῦ, ἐκπλόου ἐκπλοῦ, but by some unaccountable caprice they do not ; Ptolemæus Ascalonites (Schol. Ven. K. 373) did write εὐξοῦ = εὐξόου, but he is condemned by the grammarians for doing so. On δίκροος or δικρόος (?) see Lob. Phryn. 233. Kühner, G. G., I. 137, observes that the adjective ἐπίπνους retracts the accent ; Plat. Symp. 181 C, οἱ ἐκ τούτου τοῦ ἔρωτος ἔπιπνοι, and so it stands in C. F. Hermann's edition there can be no reason why this one word should have an exceptional accent.

559. The rule of contraction is also set aside in all *simple* contracted words in ους, which are perispomena, from whatever form they are derived, e. g. ἀδελφιδοῦς, ἀργυροῦς (from ἀργύρεος), χρυσοῦς (χρύσεος), χαλκοῦς (χάλκεος). Κάνεον also makes κανοῦν. Chœrob. C. 160. 35 ; Philem. Lex. p. 30, § 79.

560. Note.—The modern grammarians do not agree with the ancients as to the accent of the nominative and accusative dual in contracted nouns and adjectives of the common declension. Apoll. de Pron. 118 A: τὰ δυϊκὰ εἰς Ω λήγοντα οὐδέποτε περισπᾶται· οὐδὲ γὰρ θέλει τὸ πτωτικὸν Ω περισπᾶσθαι ἐπὶ τέλους. Joh. Alex. 14. 32 : τὰ εἰς Ω λήγοντα δυϊκὰ ἢ ὀξύνεται ἢ βαρύνεται ἀπέστραπται δὲ τὴν περισπωμένην. ὀξύνεται μὲν ἀπὸ περισπωμένων καὶ ὀξυνομένων, χρυσοῦς χρυσώ,

καλὸς καλώ· πρὸ μιᾶς δὲ ἔχει τὸν τόνον τὰ ἀπὸ βαρυνομένων, Ὅμηρος Ὁμήρῳ, φίλος
φίλω. Arc. 179. 2 : τὸ ἐν τοῖς δυϊκοῖς Ω ἀποστρέφεται τὴν περισπωμένην. A. G.
1160 : τὸ γὰρ πτωτικὸν Ω ἀπέστραπται τὴν περισπωμένην. πτωτικὸν δὲ λέγομεν τὸ
ἐν τοῖς πτωτικοῖς ἐπὶ τέλους εὑρισκόμενον ἄνευ πάθους, οἷον πάντα τὰ εἰς Ω λήγοντα
δυϊκά ... τὰ γοῦν εἰς ΟΥΣ ἐν πάσαις ταῖς πτώσεσι περισπώμενα ἐν τῇ εὐθείᾳ τῶν
δυϊκῶν ὀξύνεται, διπλοῦς διπλοῦ, διπλῷ διπλοῦν, διπλὼ δὲ στρατηγὼ ὀξυτόνως.
Chœrob. C. 441. 14 : ἡ δὲ εἰς Ω λήγουσα καὶ εἰς Α εὐθεῖα τῶν δυϊκῶν ἐν τῇ αὐτῇ
συλλαβῇ ἔχει τὸν τόνον ἐν ᾗ καὶ ἡ γενικὴ τῶν ἑνικῶν, οἷον Ὁμήρου Ὁμήρω, ἀνθρώπου
ἀνθρώπω, Ἀριστάρχου Ἀριστάρχω, ἀέλλης ἀέλλα, τραπέζης τραπέζα, ἀμάξης ἀμάξα,
καλοῦ καλώ, αοφοῦ σοφώ. Καὶ ταῦτα μὲν ἐν τῇ αὐτῇ συλλαβῇ ἔχουσι τὸν τόνον, οὐ
τὸν αὐτὸν δὲ τόνον ἐπεδέξαντο· τὸ μὲν γὰρ καλοῦ καὶ σοφοῦ περισπᾶται, τὸ δὲ καλὼ
καὶ σοφὼ ὀξύνεται. Τὸ γὰρ Ω ἐν τοῖς δυϊκοῖς ἀποστρέφεται τὴν περισπωμένην τάσιν,
οἷον σεμνῶ, ἀγαθῶ, καλῶ, σοφῶ, πτωχῶ, δειλῶ. Ὅτι γὰρ τὸ Ω τὸ ἐν τοῖς δυϊκοῖς
ἀποστρέφεται τὴν περισπωμένην τάσιν, δῆλον, εἴγε τὸ μὲν οἱ καὶ τὸ τοὺς ὀξυνόμενα
καὶ προσλαμβάνοντα τὴν τῆς ΔΕ συλλαβῆς ἔκτασιν προπερισπῶνται, οἷον οἶδε, τοῦσδε,
τῷ κανόνι τῷ λέγοντι, ὅτι πᾶσα φύσει μακρὰ πρὸ μιᾶς συλλαβῆς βραχείας ἐφ'
ἑαυτῆς ἔχουσα τὸν τόνον περισπᾶται, ἡ δὲ εὐθεῖα τῶν δυϊκῶν γενομένη κατ' ἐπέκτασιν, οἷον τώδε οἱ ἄνθρωποι, οὐ προπερισπᾶται ἀλλὰ παροξύνεται διὰ τὸ [τὸ] Ω
τὸ ἐν τοῖς δυϊκοῖς ἀποστρέφεσθαι τὴν περισπωμένην τάσιν, οἷον καλώ, σοφώ. The
same doctrine is also implicitly contained in Eust. 153. 41. Chœrob. C. 250.
19 : ἰστέον δὲ ὅτι πᾶσαι αἱ πτώσεις συναιρεθεῖσαι περισπῶνται, οἷον πλόος πλοῦς,
πλόῳ πλῷ, χωρὶς τῆς εὐθείας τῶν δυϊκῶν, ὡσαύτως δὲ καὶ τῆς κλητικῆς τῶν δυϊκῶν·
αὗται γὰρ συναρεθεῖσαι οὐ περισπῶνται, ἀλλ' ὀξύνονται, οἷον τὼ πλόω, τὼ πλώ, ὦ
πλόω ὦ πλώ. Τὸ γὰρ Ω ἐν τοῖς δυϊκοῖς ἀπέστραπται τὴν περισπωμένην τάσιν, οἷον τὼ
καλώ, τὼ σοφώ, τὼ ἀγαθώ.

These passages seem clear enough ; the dual in ω, if accented on the last syllable
at all, is oxytone under all circumstances.   Yet our modern grammars constantly
have χρυσῶ, ἀργυρᾶ, χαλκῶ, for χρυσώ, ἀργυρώ, χαλκώ. Matthiä, § 119 a; Jelf,
§ 126 ; Arnold, § 178 ; Donaldson, § 205.

561. The feminines of adjectives belonging to this declension
follow, in the accentuation of their oblique cases, the rules laid
down for nouns of the First Declension, §§ 205–218.   The nominative singular has a long final a, and therefore is paroxytone
when the corresponding masculine is paroxytone or proparoxytone ; when the masculine is oxytone, the feminine is so
likewise, hence ἀργύρεος, ἀργυρέᾱ, ἀργυρέας, ἀργυρέᾳ, ἀργυρέαν ;
ἀργυρέᾱ, ἀργυρέαιν ; ἀργύρεαι, ἀργυρέων, ἀργυρέαις, ἀργυρέας ; or,
if contracted, ἀργυρᾶ, ἀργυρᾶς, ἀργυρᾷ, etc. : καλός, καλή, καλῆς,
καλῇ, καλήν : σοφός, σοφή, σοφῆς, σοφῇ, σοφήν.

562. Note.—It will be observed that ἀργύρεαι is proparoxytone, and as such
does not follow its nominative singular ἀργυρέα ; but it must not be forgotten that
ἀργυρέα, et similia, are only paroxytone by the accident of a long final vowel, and
as soon as that disappears the accent falls back to its proper place.   The accent
therefore of the masculine must always be remembered in determining that of the
nominative plural ; ῥᾴδιος, ῥᾳδίᾱ, ῥᾴδιαι, οὐράνιος, οὐρανίᾱ, οὐράνιαι, τέλειος, τελείᾱ,
τέλειαι ; Chœrob. C. 449. 1, see above, § 216.

CHAPTER IV.

ACCENTUATION OF WORDS BELONGING TO THE THIRD DECLENSION.

1. SUBSTANTIVES.—(a) MONOSYLLABLES.

563. NEUTER monosyllables are perispomena, as δῶ, κρῖ, οὖς, πῦρ, σταῖς, στῆρ, φᾶρ, φῶς, ὦς ; εἶ, μῦ, νῦ, ξῦ, οὖ, πῖ, ῥῶ, ταῦ, φῖ, χῖ, ψῖ, ὦ.

564. NOTE.—Arc. 124. 11 ; Theodos. Gramm. 198. 1. The neuter κάρ, which only occurs in union with prepositions, as ἐπίκᾰρ, ἀνάκᾰρ (or ἐπὶ κάρ, ἀνὰ κάρ), is necessarily oxytone as being short (see § 12) ; on the other word κάρ, if it be really another, which is found in the Homeric expression τίω δέ μιν ἐν καρὸς αἴσῃ (Il. 9. 378), see Lob. Par. 73. The same is the case with σᾰν, which is oxytone in Herodot. 1. 139 ; Athen. 453 D, etc. Both σάν and σᾶν occur in Schol. Aristoph. Nub. 23 ; Lob. Par. 77 : ' Σκώρ oxytonum est in Edd. vett. Aristoph. Rann. 146 ; Plut. 305, ubi Brunckius σκῶρ', tanquam masculinum esset, scripsit, in Anecd. Bekk. p. 1208, aliisque locis ad Phryn. p. 293, indicatis, sed circumflectendum esse, ut neutra, credimus antiquis v. Theodos. de Accent. p. 189 ; Regg. Pros. 449, exceptis qui dorice scripserunt ; etenim Joannes de Ton. p. 7, [20] : σκῶρ· τοῦτο δὲ φασὶ Δωριεῖς ὀξύνειν : quod si verum est, male nuper in Epicharmi versibus Athen. 7. 319 F, 320 C, pro oxytono e codd. successit circumflexum ; Lob. Par. 88, σταῖς . . . estque ea usitatior hujus vocabuli tonosis sive sebum significat sive farinam maceratam ; Hippocr. de Nat. Mul. p. 550, et 597, T. 2 ; Herodot. 2. 36 ; Aristot. Probl. 31. 9 ; Athen. 1. 32 B ; 12. 548 C ; 14. 645 B ; Galen. Comm. in L. de Articc. 2. 41. 469 ; T. 18. P. 1 ; Stob. Flor. 85. 21. p. 491. 11 ; rarius oxytonum Arist. Meteor. 4. 9. 459 G, p. 386. ed. Bekk. ; cujus tot libri mirabiliter conspirant, Galen. de Antid. 1. 9. 50 ; de Locc. affect. 2. 9. 111 ; T. 8 ; Oribas de Fract. 2. 82 ; Moschopul. Sched. p. 199 : et in Eupolidis versu ap. Etym. M. 422. 43 ; quem afferens Eustathius p. 1166. 38, σταῖς scribit. Sed quod Photius ait στάς ἄνευ τοῦ ῖ ὁ Ἀττικὸς λέγει, ὁ δὲ Ἰὼν σταῖς, hodie nusquam apparet præterquam in στατίτης . . . et στατίνη :' **φῶς**=φάος and φόως.

565. Monosyllables of the masculine and feminine gender are oxytone, as Ἄν, Δάν, Πάν ; Ζήν, γλήν, μήν, ῥήν, σπλήν, φρήν, χήν, ψήν ; θίν, ἴν, ῥίν ; κλών,· πρών, Ῥών, χθών, Χών ; Νάρ, Ῥάρ, Πάρ, ψάρ ; Ἥρ, θήρ, κήρ (fate), σήρ ; Σῆρες, Τρῆρες ; Γίρ, Εἴρ, σείρ, φθείρ, χείρ ; Νώρ, σώρ, φώρ ; Ζάς, κράς, Πράς, Φθάς ; Γλῆς, Ζῆς, Κρῆς, σῆς ; Δίς, λίς, ἴς, ῥίς ; θώς, Τρώς ; κλείς, κτείς, μείς ; Ζεύς,

Νεύς, Φλεύς; ἅλς, χέρς, Λέξ, πλάξ, σάρξ, στίξ, φλόξ; Πράξ, σπάξ; κρέξ; βήξ, κήξ, ῥήξ, σφήξ; θρίξ, ψίξ; νύξ, πνύξ, Στύξ, Φρύξ; δόρξ, Λίγξ, λύγξ, στράγξ, τρώξ; κνίψ, λίψ, Νίψ; κλέψ, φλέψ; γύψ, ὄψ; θώψ, σκώψ, ὤψ; δαίς; except perispomena, βοῦς (and βῶς), βῶξ, ναῦς, γραῦς (νεῦς, γρεῦς), Θρᾷξ, Θῶν, λᾶς, οἷς, παῖς, Ταῦξ, φθοῖς, and those in υς, as δρῦς, Θῦς, μῦς, σῦς.

566. NOTE 1.—Arc. 124-127; Joh. Alex. 12. 21; 7. 20; Theog. Can. 132-134; E. M. 64. 31; 770. 19: αἴξ, according to Arc. 125. 6, this was perispomenon in Attic; Joh. Alex. 7. 25 is rather more guarded: τὸ δὲ γλαῦξ καὶ αἴξ παρ' ἡμῖν [i. e. in the κοινὴ διάλεκτος] μὲν ὀξύνονται, παρὰ δὲ 'Αθηναίοις καὶ ταῦτα τινὲς περισπῶσι: of αἴξ Lobeck (Par. 99) says: 'ubicunque inveni oxytonum est;' and no doubt that is the better accent: 'βαῦς ἡ, vocabulum ignotum apud Joann. Alex. τονικ. παραγγ. p. 7. 35; eo fortasse referenda Hesychii glossa, Βαῦ· εἶδος ἄνθους,' W. Dindorf ap. H. D.; cf. Lob. Par. 91: may it not be a bye-form of βοῦς or βῶς? on the latter form see Suid. and Hesych. s. v. Schol. Ven. H. 238: Βνῶν (?) Schol. Tim. Plat. 21 E: βῶξ = βόαξ, Philop. de Creat. Mundi, p. 188 B; Theog. Can. 132. 25; Lob. Par. 109: γλαῦξ, Herod. π. μ. λ. 41. 21; Eust. 1451. 62: παρὰ τοῖς παλαιοῖς ἡ γλαῦξ περισπᾶται, οἳ καὶ ὀξύνεσθαι μὲν λέγουσι τὸ γλαῦξ πλὴν Δωρικῶς· Schol. Aristoph. Vesp. 1086 = 1081: τὸ γλαῦξ . . . 'Αττικοὶ μὲν περισπῶσιν, οἱ δὲ Δωριεῖς ὀξύνουσιν: cf. Joh. Alex. 7. 25, quoted above; E. M. 36. 51: Γνῆς, St. Byz., is expressly said to be oxytone, Choerob. C. 43. 17: δάς = δαῖς, Schol. Hes. Scut. 275; it is sometimes falsely perispomenon: on the Syracusan ὁ δεῖν = ὁ δεῖνα, see Lob. Par. 71: Δρῦς, St. Byz.: Ζάς, cf. E. M. 655. 27: θεύς = θεός, Herod. π. μ. λ. 6. 8, is perispomenon in Eust. 775. 48; 1387. 29; Arc. 130. 20; H. D.: Θρᾷξ, Arc. 125. 7; Theog. Can. 132. 29; yet according to Reg. Pros. ap. Herm. de emend. rat. Gr. gr. p. 423, it is oxytone, and Lobeck (Par. 99) says that he has found it 'modo perispomenon Xenoph. Anab. 7. 3. 26; Paus. 5. c. 12. 5; 26. 3: Appian. Civ. 4. 136; lege synæresis ἀπὸ τοῦ Θρᾷξ βαρυτόνου ὀνόματος Eustath. ad Dion. 322; Regg. Pros. N. 126. p. 449; Anecd. Cram. T. 1. 25; [add E. M. 36. 51]; modo oxytonum Polyb. 5. 65. 9; Strab. 14. 611; Appian. Civ. 1. 116; Athen. 7. 272 F; 11. 489 A; Sext. c. Gramm. 3. 288; Schol. Il. O. 741; ut Bekkerus scripsit Plat. Charm. p. 156 D; et in iisdem Regg. Pros. N. 6. 423 sancitur; v. Göttling ad Aristot. Polit. p. 406:' Θῦς, Athen. 144 F: Θῶν, Theog. Can. 132. 2; Choerob. C. 294. 24; E. M. 459. 55: κλείς, Lob. Par. 92: 'κλείς circumflexum habet in Aristot. Probl. 29. 14. p. 952. 21; et in codd. Laur. et Paris. Nicom. 5. 2. p. 1129. 30; contra Grammaticorum præceptum οὐδὲν εἰς ΕΙΣ μονοσύλλαβον περισπᾶται εἰ μὴ τὸ εἰς Anecd. Cram. 1. 171; Regg. Pros. N. 127. p. 450; Eusth. 857. 40; neque quod in diastasi κληίς dicitur (κλᾱΐς Æolicum est), extra diastasin barytonum esse potest; itaque etiam Atticum κλής scribitur:' κῦρ, a very late word for κύριε, Lob. Par. 77: λίς and κίς were oxytoned by Aristarchus; Æschrion on the contrary wrote λῖς, κῖς, but the tradition followed Aristarchus; Schol. Ven. Λ. 239; 480; Eust. 841. 21: τὸ δὲ λὶς κατὰ μὲν 'Αρίσταρχον, ὥς φασιν οἱ περὶ 'Απίωνα καὶ 'Ηρόδωρον, ὀξύνεται, συνεξομοιούμενον τῷ χαρακτῆρι τοῦ κίς κιός· ἔτι δὲ καὶ τῷ τὶς καὶ θὶς καὶ ῥίς, εἰ καὶ διαφόρως ταῦτα κλίνεται πρὸς τὸ λίς. ὁ Αἰσχρίων δέ, φασι, περισπᾷ διὰ τὸ καὶ τὴν αἰτιατικὴν περισπᾶσθαι. ὡς γὰρ μῦς μῦν, δρῦς δρῦν, οὕτω καὶ λῖς λῖν. εἰ δὲ μηδὲν τῶν εἰς ΙΣ περισπᾶται, ἀλλ' ὁ Αἰσχρίων τοῦτο ἐποίει, ἐκφεύγων θηλυκὸν ἐπίθετον ὀξύτονον τὸ λὶς πέτρη, ἐν 'Οδυσσείᾳ ῥηθέν. καὶ οὕτω μὲν ἐκεῖνος τὸ· λὶς ὁ λέων περιέσπα ἐπὶ τοῦ λέοντος πρὸς διαστολὴν τοῦ ἐπιθετικοῦ. ἀλλ' ἡ παράδοσις, φασι, τῷ 'Αριστάρχῳ πείθεται: cf. E. M. 567. 7: μείς is wrongly perispomenon in Stob. Ecl. 1. 27. p. 556; Lob. Par. 92: νηῦς, if this form is resolved it is doubtful whether it should be written νηῦς or νῆῦς: there is the same difficulty with regard to γρηῦς : Bekker, Dindorf, and Thiersch prefer γρηῦς, Buttmann and Lobeck, Path. 2. 44, are for γρῆυς and νῆυς, rightly as I venture to think : πῆς = παῖς, Theog. Can. 134. 32 : πούς, Lob. Par. 93 : 'quod Buttmannus dicit Gramm. § 41. Adn. 8. multo sæpius ποῦς legi quam πούς, adeo falsum est, ut præ decem circumflexionis exemplis centum contraria proferri possint:' Πρᾶς, Chœrob. C. 16. 15 : τοῦτο δὲ κατὰ ἀκρίβειαν ὀξύνεται καὶ διὰ τοῦ NT κλίνεται· ἰστέον ὅτι ὁ Ἡρωδιανὸς ἐν τῷ Ὀνοματικῷ λέγει αὐτὸ περισπᾶσθαι καὶ διὰ τοῦ NT κλίνεσθαι, ἐν δὲ τῇ Καθόλου ὀξύνεσθαι, ὁμοίως δὲ καὶ διὰ τοῦ NT κλίνεσθαι : it is perispomenon Reg. Pros. 57. p. 433 ; St. Byz. s. v.; but cf. E. M. 655. 27 : προίξ is perispomenon in Herod. π. μ. λ. 41. 19, but wrongly ; Arc. 125.6 ; Lob. Par. 105 : πρών is incorrectly πρῶν in Schol. Æschyl. Pers. 132, quoted by H. D.: πτώξ, Theog. Can. 132. 24 ; Göttling Accent. p. 242 : 'Nach der Stelle des Grammatikers, welche ich zu Theodos. p. 236, mitgetheilt habe, ward auch πτῶξ perispomenirt; vgl. Herodian bei Herm. de emend. p. 306:' Ταῦξ, Herod. π. μ. λ. 41. 23 ; E. M. 36. 51 : ὦλξ = αὖλαξ, Theog. Can. 132. 24, is falsely ὦλξ in Orion 120. 11 ; Lob. Par. 111 : ὤρ = ὄαρ, Lob. Par. 78 : the name of the Egyptian city Ὢν is indeclinable, though feminine : on Σῦρ, Herod. π. μ. λ. 12. 21.

567. Note 2.—The grammarians are not quite consistent in the acccount which they give of the Æolic accentuation of monosyllables ; Chœrob. C. 333 says : ἐπὶ τούτων γὰρ (sc. μονοσυλλάβων) φυλάττουσι τὴν ὀξεῖαν τάσιν, οἶον νύξ, Στύξ· πῶς γὰρ δύναται τὰ μονοσύλλαβα βαρύνεσθαι ; on the other hand Gramm. Meerm. § 27 ed. Koen. περισπῶσιν ὡς ἐπίπαν τὰ μονοσύλλαβα ὀνόματα· ῥῶξ, πτῶξ, δρῶψ, χρούς, βούς, θρούς, βούς, χνούς, νούς, χῆν, Ζεῦς ; cf. Ahrens de Græcæ ling. dialect. 1. p. 11 : he does not notice the former passage at all : probably the Æolians circumflexed those monosyllables which are naturally long, and oxytoned those which were naturally short, and if so, βλήρ, Æol. = δέλεαρ, in E. M. 200. 27, and Hesych. should be corrected βλῆρ : yet we have μείς declared to be Æolic by Eust. 1174. 19, and oxytone by Arc. 125.

Ahrens de Gr. ling. dial. 2. p. 27 : 'monosyllaba apud Dores oxytona sunt quæ apud Lesbios perispomena, vulgo vel oxytona vel perispomena . . . Exemplo sunt σκώρ pro vulgari σκῶρ . . . et γλαύξ pro Attico γλαῦξ . . . Quanquam Doricum βῶς pro βοῦς περισπᾶσθαι fertur:' I can add nothing to this, though I doubt whether the learned author is justified in his assertion by ancient authorities.

568. *Oblique Cases.*—The dissyllabic Genitive and Dative singular and Dative plural are oxytone, as θήρ, θηρός, θηρί, θηρσί ; οἶς, οἰός, οἰί, οἰσί ; πούς, ποδός, ποδί, ποσί ; the Accusative singular in ν when long, and the Vocative singular when formed by casting off s, the Genitive and Dative dual, and the Genitive plural, are perispomena, as γραῦν, δρῦν, λῖν, κλεῖν, μῦν, ναῦν, οἶν, σῦν ; βοῦ, Ζεῦ ; βοοῖν, δρυοῖν, μηνοῖν, συοῖν, φρενοῖν, φωτοῖν, χειροῖν, χθονοῖν ; γνηπῶν, θητῶν, μηνῶν, οἰῶν, Κρητῶν, σητῶν, χηνῶν ; the remaining cases are accented on the penultimate, as κλεῖδα, μῆνα, χῆνα, φῶτα, νίφα ; δρύε, μύε, σύε ; αἶγες, παῖδες, χεῖρες ; Πάν is oxytone in the Genitive and Dative singular only, Πανός, Πανί, Πᾶνα, Πᾶνες, Πάνων, Πᾶνας, Πᾶσι and Πάνεσσι ; except

1. The contracted forms ἦρος, ἦρι (for ἔαρος, ἔαρι) ; Θῶνος, Θῶνι (for Θόωνος), Θῶντος ; κῆρος κῆρι (for κέαρος, κέαρι, but

κηρός, κηρί, from κήρ, *fate*); λᾶος, λᾶϊ (for λάαος, λάαϊ); υἷος, υἷι (for υἷιος, or ὗιος, from ὗις); Θέτι (for Θέτιι), μάστι (for μάστιι), μῆτι (for μῆτιι), σπῆϊ (for σπέεϊ), together with Φθάντος Φθάντι, Ὤψ Ὤπος, and Μῆνι.

2 In the ordinary dialect the Genitive and Dative dual and the Genitive plural of the following words are paroxytone: δᾱς, δᾱδοιν, δᾱδων; δμώς· δμώοιν, δμώων; θώς· θώοιν, θώων; κρᾱς, κράτων; οὖς, ὤτοιν, ὤτων; παῖς, παίδοιν, παίδων; σής, σέων; Τρώς, Τρώων; φῶς, φώτοιν, φώτων; φώς, φωδοιν, φωδων. Λάων from λᾶας is also paroxytone, and the same is the case with δούρων from δόρυ.

It may be as well to say that these rules do not apply to dissyllabic cases of participles; βάς, or στάς, for instance, make βάντος, στάντος, βάντι, στάντι, στάντα, στάν; στάντε, στάντοιν; στάντες, στάντα, στάντων, στᾶσι, στάντας; ζῶν, ζῶντος, ζῶντι, and so on.

569. NOTE I.—*Genitive Singular.* Chœrob. C. 408. 10 sq.; Arc. 428. 13; Schol. Ven. E. 266: on κρέως, κέρως, etc., which do not come from monosyllabic nominatives, see below, § 679: on Ὤπος, see Chœrob. C. 411. 23; Hom. Od. I. 429: the genitive and dative of πρών are found falsely accented: 'πρωνός recte ὀξυτόνως scriptum ap. Chœrob. in Theodos. p. 294. 19; Etym. M. p. 692. 49; Zonar. p. 1575, et in epigr. Damostrati Auth. Pal. 9. 328: Οὐρείου πρωνός: male πρῶνος et πρῶνι in libris quibusdam Pausaniæ 2. 34. 11, et 36. 1. 2, ubi nomen collis est prope Hermionen siti,' H. D.: those who wrote πρῶν πρῶνος, regarded the word as contracted from πρεών, gen. πρεόνος; cf. Suid. s. v. Πρῶνες: Schol. Ven. M. 462: λᾶος προπερισπαστέον ὡς κλῆρος· ἀπὸ γὰρ εὐθείας δισυλλάβου κατὰ τὴν τοῦ ποιητοῦ χρῆσιν, καὶ ὤφειλε τρισυλλαβεῖν ἡ γενική, συναλοιφὴν δὲ λαβοῦσα βαρύνεται: Schol. Ven. E. 266: υἷος προπερισπαστέον· ἀπὸ γὰρ εὐθείας ἐστὶ μὴ εἰρημένης τῆς υἷις, ἧς γενικὴ ὤφειλεν εἶναι τρισύλλαβος ὡς μάντιος, αὕτη τοίνυν συναλοιφὴν παθοῦσα καὶ δισύλλαβος γενομένη βαρύνεται, ἧς ἀκόλουθος δοτική. Νηληΐῳ υἷι ἐοικώς (Il. 2. 20) καὶ αἰτιατικὴ ἀλλ᾽ υἷα Κλυτίοιο σαώσομεν (Il. 15. 427) καὶ πληθυντικὴ εὐθεῖα υἷες ὁ μὲν Κτέατον (Il. 2. 621) καὶ αἰτιατικὴ υἷάς τ᾽ ὀλλυμένους (Il. 22. 62)· ἀποδείξομεν δὲ καὶ τὸ υἷάσι δὲ Πριάμοιο (Il. 2. 463) παρὰ τοῦτο κεκλίσθαι κ. τ. λ.

570. *Dative Singular.*—υἷι, Schol. Ven. Π. 177: Θέτι, Hom. Il. 18. 407: μάστι, Il. 23. 500: Μῆνι, Herodot. 2. 99: μῆτι, Il. 23. 318: σπῆϊ, Il. 24. 83; Chœrob. C. 417: on δάϊ or δαΐ see Schol. Ven. Ξ. 387: the heteroclite κλαδί, λιτί, ἀλκί, are oxytone like other dissyllabic datives, A. G. 1226; Schol. Ven. Σ. 352.

Accusative Singular.—Schol. Ven. Λ. 480: λῖν περισπαστέον κατὰ νόμον τῶν μονοσυλλάβων αἰτιατικῶν· πᾶσα γὰρ αἰτιατικὴ μονοσύλλαβος εἰς Ν λήγουσα περισπᾶται, ἀπέστραπται δὲ τὸν ὀξὺν τόνον, μῦν, μνᾶν, σῦν ὗν· ταύτῃ καὶ ἡ κλεῖδα αἰτιατικὴ γενομένη κλεῖν περισπᾶται, τῆς εὐθείας ὀξυνομένης· ταῦτα Ἡρωδιανὸς ἐν τῷ πεντεκαιδεκάτῳ τῆς καθόλου: Arc. 130. 17; Chœrob. C. 421. 23; Schol. Ven. Θ. 441; Λ. 480; Σ. 352.

Vocative Singular.— Chœrob. C. 241. 29.

Nominative Dual.—Arc. 131. 16 has λίε, while Chœrob. C. 441. 7, writes λῖε and κῖε.

Genitive and Dative Dual.—The genitive and dative in οιν have the same accent as the genitive plural, hence ἀνδρῶν ἀνδροῖν, χειρῶν χειροῖν or χεροῖν, but παίδων παίδοιν, Arc. 132. 10; Chœrob. C. 445. 14: the Homeric ποδοῖιν is properispomenon Il. 15. 18.

571. NOTE 2.—*Nominative Plural.* In Doric this case was *paroxytone.* Ahrens de Gr. ling. dialect. 2. p. 29: 'Æque in nominativo et accusativo pluralis declinationis tertiæ apud Dorienses paroxytona fuisse traduntur, quæ vulgo sunt proparoxytona, vel properispomena, ut παῖδες, γυναῖκες, πτῶκας (Chœrob. Bekk. 1236 [= in Can. 427. 21] οἱ Δωριεῖς ὀξεῖαν παρέχουσιν ἐπὶ τῶν τοιούτων· οἷον παῖδες, αἶγες, γυναῖκες· ταῦτα γὰρ ἡμεῖς περισπῶμεν, οἱ δὲ Δωριεῖς παροξύνουσιν.—J. Gr. 243 a: τὰ εἰς ΕΣ λήγοντα θηλυκὰ ὀνόματα πληθυντικὰ ὀρθῆς πτώσεως παροξυτονοῦσι, γυναῖκες, χεῖρες, νάες, ὀρνίθες.—Scholl. Theocr. 1. 109: τοῦ δὲ πτῶκας τὸ ΑΣ μακρόν. οἱ γὰρ Δωριεῖς τῶν εἰς ΕΣ ληγόντων εὐθειῶν τῶν πληθυντικῶν ὁμοίως παροξύνουσι καὶ μακρὸν ἔχουσι τὸ Α, ὅτι τὰς παρ' ἡμῖν εἰς ΕΣ ληγούσας εὐθείας τῶν πληθυντικῶν ἐκεῖνοι διὰ τῆς ΑΙ προφέρουσιν. Grammaticulus, qui recte Dorico more πτῶκας scriptum invenit, quæ profert, inde male colligit). Quod valde mirum esset, nisi, et in Latinorum declinatione tertia nominativus et accusativus pluralis ultimas longas haberent, ut pedēs, et in Gothorum iis declinationibus, quae Græcorum et Latinorum tertiae respondent, ut a *fisks*, piscis, descendit *fiscôs* n. pl. et *fiskans* acc. pl., et apud ipsos Græcos pronomina personalia, quæ priscas formas servare amant, ut ἡμεῖς et ἡμᾶς. Inde augurari licet, antiquitus eos tertiæ declinationis casus ultimas produxisse et in Dorica dialecto accentum certe priscum hæsisse.' Kühner G. G. 1. 251 thinks all this incredible, and that the accusative has in some mysterious way been confounded by the grammarians with the nominative; a professed grammarian should have more faith.

572. NOTE 3.—*Genitive Plural* is perispomenon, as μηνῶν, χηνῶν, Κρητῶν, θητῶν, σητῶν, γνητῶν, except the paroxytones mentioned above, to which may be added Κώων, πλώων, Τλώων; Chœrob. C. 453. 15: τὰ εἰς Σ λήγοντα μονοσύλλαβα περιττοσυλλάβως κλινόμενα ταύτην ἔχουσι τὴν διαίρεσιν· τὰ μὲν ὀξύτονα, ἐὰν μὲν διὰ συμφώνου κλίνωνται, περισπῶσιτὴν γενικὴν τῶν πληθυντικῶν, οἷον σῆς σητὸς σῆτες σητῶν, Κρὴς Κρητὸς Κρῆτες Κρητῶν, θὴς θητὸς θῆτες θητῶν (σημαίνει δὲ τὸν μισθωτόν), γνὴς γνητὸς γνῆτες γνητῶν· ἐὰν δὲ διὰ καθαροῦ τοῦ ΟΣ κλιθῶσι, βαρύνονται κατὰ τὴν γενικὴν τῶν πληθυντικῶν, οἷον Τρὼς Τρωὸς Τρῶες Τρώων, δμὼς δμωὸς δμῶες δμώων, θὼς θωὸς θῶες θώων (ἔστι δὲ εἶδος θηρίου), σεὺς σέος [sic] σέες σέων (σημαίνει δὲ τοὺς σκώληκας) τούτῳ γὰρ τῷ κανόνι βαρύνονται. Τὸ δὲ τίνων καὶ κράτων πρὸς διάφορον σημασίαν διάφορον ἔχουσι καὶ τὸν τόνον· τὸ γὰρ τίνων πευστικὸν μὲν ὑπάρχον βαρύνεται, ἀνταποδοτικὸν δὲ ἤγουν ἀόριστον, περισπᾶται, οἷον τίνων ἤκουσας; τινῶν. Καὶ τὸ κράτων δὲ ἀπὸ τοῦ κρᾶτες (ὃ σημαίνει τὴν κεφαλὴν) ὑπάρχον βαρύνεται, ἀπὸ δὲ τοῦ κράτη ὑπάρχον περισπᾶται, οἷον τὰ κράτη τῶν κρατῶν. Τὸ δὲ φῴδων καὶ δᾴδων ἀπὸ τοῦ φῳδῶων καὶ δαΐδων γινόμενα κατὰ συναίρεσιν τὴν βαρεῖαν τάσιν ἐφύλαξαν. Ταῦτα μὲν περὶ τῶν ὀξυνομένων. Τὰ δὲ περισπώμενα ἐκ τοῦ ἐναντίου γίνονται· ἐὰν μὲν γὰρ διὰ καθάρου τοῦ ΟΣ κλίνωνται, περισπῶσι τὴν γενικὴν τῶν πληθυντικῶν, οἷον μῦς μυὸς μύες μυῶν, βοῦς βοὸς βόες βοῶν, σῦς συὸς σύες συῶν, δρῦς δρυὸς δρύες δρυῶν, ἐὰν δὲ διὰ συμφώνου κλίνωνται, βαρύνονται ἐν τῇ γενικῇ τῶν πληθυντικῶν, οἷον παῖς παιδὸς παῖδες παίδων, πᾶς παντὸς πάντες πάντων. Τὸ δὲ λάων ἐβαρύνθη πρὸς ἀντιδιαστολὴν τοῦ οἱ λαοὶ τῶν λαῶν· ἄλλως τε δὲ οὔτε ἔστι τοῦτο ἀπὸ μονοσυλλάβου εὐθείας τῆς λᾶς, ἀλλ' ἀπὸ δισυλλάβου τῆς λᾶας· ἀπὸ γὰρ τοῦ λᾶας γέγονεν ἡ γενικὴ λάαος καὶ κατὰ κρᾶσιν τῶν δύο ΑΑ εἰς ἐν Α δηλονότι μακρόν, λᾶος οἷον

λᾶος ὑπὸ ῥιπῆς·

καὶ λοιπὸν ἡ εὐθεῖα τῶν πληθυντικῶν λάαες λᾶες καὶ ἡ γενικὴ λαάων λάων. Yet κίς and λίς make κιός and λιός, κιῶν, λιῶν. Schol. Ven. Γ. 198 : ὁ μὲν Ἀρίσταρχος οἰῶν ὡς αἰγῶν, ὁ δὲ Ἡρωδιανὸς ὀΐων ὡς δαΐδων, λέγων ὡς οὐ κλίνει τὸ μονοσύλλαβον ὁ ποιητής, εἰ μὴ μέτρον κωλύσειεν. Cf. Joh. Alex. 18. 16; Arc. 134. 10; 132. 11; A. G. 1251; Theodos. Can. 1005. 29; Eust. 1425. 52; 318. 46; Schol. Ven. N. 103; Chœrob. E. 50. 2 sq.

The word φρέαρ should properly be barytone in all its cases, but φρητός, φρητί are oxytone, Chœrob. C. 410. 11, and the genitive plural is φρητῶν, A. G. 1265; Joh. Alex. 19. 34; E. M. 800. 15 : in like manner στέαρ, στήρ makes στέατος or στητός, στητί, Θράξ, Θρῆξ, Θρήϊκος, and Θρᾳκός or Θρηκός.

573. NOTE 4.—In Doric the genitive plural of all monosyllables was perispomenon, as παντῶν, παιδῶν, Τρῶων, Apoll. de Adv. 581. 21 : de Pron. 33 B; Ahrens de Gr. ling. dialect. 2. p. 32. The pronominal τίς was alone excepted, Apoll. de Pron. 33 B; 35 B. Pamphilus extended this to all dialects; Schol. Ven. N. 103; Eust. 922. 49.

574. NOTE 5.—*Dative Plural.* Those in εσσι, as θήρεσσι, χείρεσσι, retract the accent; σπέσσι is a syncopated form of σπέεσσι, Chœrob. C. 462. 20. This author also presumes that the dative plural of Φθάς, if it had one, would be Φθᾶσι, not Φθασί : Ὑιάσι or υἱέσι is paroxytone, Chœrob. C. 463. 19; Joh. Alex. 11. 23.

575. Compounds from monosyllables retract the accent, as αἰγίπᾱν, ἀντίχειρ, ἀντίχθων, αὐτόχθων, διάπηξ, Ἐτεόκρης, νεόμην, ὁμόδαις, Σαμόθραξ; except ὑποδμώς oxytone.

NOTE.—Chœrob. C. 176. 2 : πᾶν γὰρ ὄνομα μονοσύλλαβον ἐν τῇ συνθέσει ἀναβιβάζει τὸν τόνον, οἶον χθὼν αὐτόχθων, παῖς εὔπαις, Θρὰξ Σαμόθραξ [sic], δαὶς ὁμόδαις, κλεὶς κατάκλεις, πούς δίπους, χωρὶς τοῦ πτὼξ πολυπτώξ,

πολυπτῶκές τε Μέλαιναι.

Τὸ δὲ Μέλαιναι τόπος ἐπὶ (ἔστι) τῆς Ἀττικῆς, πολυπτῶκες δέ, οἶον αἱ ἔχουσαι πολλοὺς λαγωούς. Τοῦτο γὰρ τὴν ὀξεῖαν τάσιν ἐφύλαξε τοῦ ἀπλοῦ. Τὸ γὰρ [Od. δ' 386.]

Ποσειδάονος ὑποδμώς,

οὐκ ἀντίκειται ἡμῖν ὀξυνόμενον, ἐπειδή, ὡς ἐν τῷ περὶ προθέσεως εἰ θεῷ φίλον μαθησόμεθα, παρέλκουσαν ἔχει τὴν ὑπὸ πρόθεσιν, ὥστε μηδὲ παρέχειν ἔμφασιν ὅτι σύνθεσις γέγονεν. ἀντὶ γὰρ τοῦ Ποσειδάονος δμῶς ἐστί; cf. E. M. 358. 10; 435. 32; Arc. 20. 17. Ἀνακλείς, Pollux 7. 107, should be ἀνάκλεις, like ἀντίκλεις, Chœrob. C. 206. 28 and κατάκλεις, A. G. Oxon. 2. 342. 13; 296. 2; κατακλείς is therefore an error, though it is so accented by H. D. in all the passages which they quote except one, E. M. 495. 19; besides this the following exceptional words occur : ἀντισφήν, Philo, Belop. p. 67 C, H. D. is contrary to all rule, and almost certainly an error : αὐτοαήρ, αὐτοπῦρ, αὐτοείς are accents for which there is no authority beyond that of the scribes : ἀρχιφώρ, Diod. Sic. 1. 80, L. S., should probably be ἀρχίφωρ : διασφάξ, Arc. 18. 22; Draco 19. 9; on this and others of the same termination see Compound Adjectives, under which head ἐπιβλής is considered : ἐπιπλάξ (?) H. D. : ἡμικρής, Lycoph. 150 is a false accent : ἐτεοδμώς seems to be false for ἐτεόδμως : κατακλῶθες, Hom. Od. 7. 197, is written κατάκλωθες in E. M. 495. 24, but the former accent is correct, since the word is not derived from a monosyllabic noun, but from the verb κλώθω : περιχθών for περίχθων is probably an error, cf. Lob. Par. 382 : ὠμοκλείς, Tzetzes, Alleg. p. 107. 48, H. D. ought to be ὠμόκλεις : σαμπῖ, L. S., if such a word really exists, its accent may be defended on the ground that it is a parathetic compound. The musical writers use such words as ἡμιθῆτα, ἡμιμῦ, ἡμιφῖ; they are hardly grammatical forms, and their accents are arbitrary.

(*b*) Words of more than One Syllable.

Neuter Substantives.

576. All neuter substantives throw the accent back, as ἄστυ, αὐτόκαλλος, βέλος, γῆρας, δάκρυ, δέλεαρ, δέμας, δίκερας, ἔαρ, κέρας, κρέας, κυνόσαργες, μέθυ, ὄνειαρ, ὄνειδος, οὖας, πέλαγος, πῶϋ, σίνηπι, τεῖχος, ὕδωρ; except ἰῶτα properispomenon.

NOTE.—Arc. 118-124; Theog. Can. 131. 28: **Αὐτομῆκος** is better written as two words: βουμανές, Hesych.: ἡμεροκαλλές (?) E. M. 429. 44: ἰῶτα was thus accented by Herodian, Theog. Can. 78. 11: ὀνοχειλές, Hesych.: τριχομανές, *a plant:* the following Proper Names retain the adjectival accent; **Ἀβαρές**, Joseph. Ant. 8. 48: **Διαμπερές**, Plut. 1. 404.

Masculine and Feminine Substantives.

577. The irregularities of these words are so great that it is impossible to give any general rule which can be depended on, but it may perhaps assist the memory to mention the main result of the special rules subjoined. Speaking then in the widest terms, and neglecting the numerous exceptions which occur, it may be said that masculine and feminine substantives of this declension throw the accent as far back as possible, except those in αν, ας (gen. ᾰδος), ευς, ην, ηρ, ις (gen. ῑδος, ῐδος, and ινος), υς (gen. υδος), ως (gen. οος) and ω, which are oxytone: those in ξ and ψ always take the accent on the penultimate.

-AN.

578. Those in αν are oxytone, as Ἀγριάν, Ἀζάν, Ἀζᾶνες, Ἀλκμάν, Βραχμάν, Ἰάν, παιάν, πελεκάν, Τιτάν. Compounds are paroxytone, as Αἰγίπαν, Αἰνοτίταν, Ἑρμόπαν, Εὐήπαν, εὐπαίαν, Τιτανόπαν.

579. NOTE—Arc. 8. 4; Chœrob. C. 68. 15; 270. 23: ἰστέον δὲ καὶ τοῦτο ὅτι τὰ εἰς Ν λήγοντα ἀρσενικὰ ἢ θηλυκὰ ἢ ὀξύνονται ἢ βαρύνονται, ... οὐδέποτε δὲ περισπῶνται, χωρὶς εἰ μὴ ὦσιν εἰς ΩΝ .... οἷον Ξενοφῶν: Lob. Par. 189: **Αἰλᾶν** (?) Epiph. Panar. 618 B, H. *D.*: **Βαραβᾶν** (*sic*) and **Βαριωνᾶν** are, according to E. M. 715. 11, barbarous and indeclinable, see § 32, and Chœrob. E. 83. 9: **Δαρειάν**, Æschyl. Pers. 663, another form for Δαρεῖος: **Δυμᾶν**, St. Byz., is probably a mistake for Δυμάν or for Δυμᾶνες: **Μεγᾶν**, according to E. M. 715. 11, barbarous and indeclinable: μεγιστᾶν, Apoll. de Adv. 570. 10, but such an accent cannot be defended; the proper form is μεγιστάν; thus also for νεᾶν, Apoll. de Adv. 570, νεάν ought to be read, and for ξυνᾶν, ξυνάν: on the Doric forms Ποσειδᾶν (?) (gen. ᾶνος), Ποτιδάν, Ποτειδάν, Ποσειδάν, see Ahrens de Gr. ling. dialect. 2. p. 243 sq.; Ποσείδαν seems to be the Æolic form of the word, but there is great confusion both as to its accent and even its declension: Σοάνες, Strab. 496. 499; Göttling, Accent. p. 263, thinks Σοᾶνες better; Σόανες, St. Byz., is undoubtedly wrong: ψαγδάν or ψάγδαν is variable both in accent and declension; see L. S. s. v.: ὦ 'τᾶν or ὠτᾶν, E. M. 825. 19; Joh. Alex. 37. 32: τὸ ὦ τᾶν δύο περισπωμένας ἔχει: A. G. 940. 21; Philem. Lex. § 319. p. 133; Schol. Plat. Apolog. Soc. 25 C: οἱ δὲ Ἀττικοὶ τὴν πρωτὴν συλλαβὴν περισπῶσι, τὴν δὲ δευτέραν βαρύνουσι, καὶ βέλτιον οὕτως. ἀδύνατον γὰρ μίαν λέξιν εὑρεθῆναι δύο ἔχουσαν περισπωμένας. Δίδυμος δὲ τὸ πλῆρες εἶναί φησιν ὦ ἔταν, ἀγνοῶν ὡς ἀπὸ τοῦ ἔτης ἡ κλητική ἐστιν ἔτα, καὶ Δωρικῶς ἔταν: cf. H. D. s. v. ἔτης, and Apoll. de Adv. 570. 12: ὦ 'τάν is also found.

-HN.

580. Those in ην (gen. ενος or ηνος) are oxytone, as αὐχήν, ἐσσήν, κηφήν, λιμήν, ποιμήν, πυθμήν, σωλήν, ὑμήν, Κεβρήν, Κωφήν, Σειρήν, Τροιζήν, Ὠλήν; except εἴρην, Ἕλλην. Compounds are paroxytone, as ἀπύθμην, ἀρχιποίμην, μελείρην, φιλέλλην, Φιλοποίμην.

581. NOTE.—Arc. 8. 12-10. 4; 9. 3; Joh. Alex. 3. 11: Γέρην, *a village in Lesbos*, called after Γέρην, son of Poseidon, is mentioned by St. Byz.; and this accent is prescribed by Chœrob. C. 69. 21; 276. 21: εἴρην, Chœrob. C. 69. 21; 276. 21; Arc. 9. 18: Ἕκτην, Arc. 9. 9. is spelled Ἐγκτην in Etym. Gud. 158. 40: Ἕλλην, Arc. 9. 3: ἐπιποιμήν (?) 'Regulam migrant ἱππολειχήν, τοῦ φιτυποιμένος, Æsch. Eum. 911, in quo nullus editorum offendit, τοῦ ἀρχιποιμένος, I. Petr. 5. 4, ubi codd. quos Lachmannus sequitur, proparoxytonum præbent; ἐπιποιμήν [Hom. Od. 12. 131] excusatur pleonasmo præpositionis, propter quem illud ab Eustathio, p. 1117. 48, cum ἐπιβουκόλος, hoc autem a Schol. ad Π. E. 178, cum ἐπιμήνις comparatur adjecta regula ὅταν παρέλκῃ ἡ πρόθεσις, οὐ ποιεῖται ἐξαλλαγὴν τόνου, id quod ad ἐπιπρητὴν transferre licet, sed in συμποιμήν; Nicet. Eug. 6. 436 hæc ratio non convenit nec in πελαγολιμήν.' Lob. Par. 195; he also (Par. 379) says of ἱππολειχήν, 'Eutecn. et Schol. ad Nic. Ther. 945. quod Schneiderus in Lex. tacite gravat.' But all these words ought probably to be paroxytone; for ἐπιποιμένες in the Homeric passage ἔπι ποιμένες has been suggested: Θέρην, the name of a river, Arc. 9. 27: Ἵκην (?) *Pape*: Κέβρην (?) or Κεβρήν, St. Byz., 'Κερβήν inter oxytona ap. Arcad. p. 9. 9, corruptum ex Κεβρήν;' *H. D.*: πέρην (?) Arc. 9. 27: περπέρην (?) Arc. 9. 16: Σέβην, Chœrob. C. 69. 22; 276. 22: ὑποπυθμήν is false for ὑποπύθμην, Eust. 869. 8; Lob. Par. 195: Τροιζήν, Eust. 287. 18: σημείωσαι δὲ ὅτι τινὰ τῶν παλαιῶν ἀντιγράφων Τροίζηνα προπαροξυτόνως ἔγραψαν οἷς καὶ Ἡρωδιανὸς συνηγορεῖ, ἐν τῷ περὶ ταχυτῆτος καὶ δηϊότητος εἰπὼν ὡς ἡ Δωρὶς καὶ Αἰολὶς διάλεκτος, οὐδέποτε κατὰ γενικὴν περιττοσύλλαβον, τὸ Η μετατιθέασιν εἰς ἄλφα, εἰ μὴ βαρύνοιτο. Ἕλλην Ἕλλαν, Τροίζαν Τροίζαν. ποιμὴν δὲ καὶ λιμὴν οὐκ ἂν ἐροῦσι διὰ τοῦ ἄλφα, ἐπεὶ ὀξυτονεῖται. ἐπὶ μέντοι μονοσυλλάβων, μετατιθέασι τό, σφὴξ καὶ μήν, σφᾶς λέγοντες καὶ μάν. σεσημείωται φησὶ τὸ ἐσθάς ὀξυνόμενον. καὶ διὰ τοῦ ἄλφα λεγόμενον παρὰ Πινδάρῳ ἐν πυθιονίκαις.

-IN.

582. Those in ιν (gen. ινος) are oxytone, as δελφίν, πηρίν.

-ΥΝ.

583. Those in υν are paroxytone, as Γόρτυν, μόσσυν, πόλτυν, τέκτυν, Φόρκυν.

NOTE.—Chœrob. C. 70. 8; 283. 5: ἰστέον ὅτι πάντα τὰ εἰς ΥΝ βαρύνονται, οἷον μόσυν (sic) Φόρκυν, Γόρτυν, ἐπειδὴ τὰ πολλὰ παρὰ τοῖς Αἰολεῦσιν εὑρίσκονται. καὶ λοιπὸν ὡς δοκοῦντα εἶναι Αἰολικὰ εὐλόγως βαρύνονται : Arc. 10. 5.

-ΩΝ.

584. *Common Substantives in ων, gen. ωνος or ονος.* *General Rule.*—Collectives, or those which indicate a quantity of any object (called by the Greeks περιεκτικά); those which signify a place, names of months, and generally all that involve the idea of space or time are oxytone, without an exception, as ἀμπελών, *a vineyard,* αὐλών, *a glen,* ἀχυρών, *a chaff-heap,* βοών *a cowhouse,* ἠϊών, *a shore,* ἰστών *a weaver's room,* κευθμών *a hiding place,* λειμών *a meadow,* λουτρών, *a bath room,* πυλών, *a gateway;* δαφνών· λευκών, πλατανών, ῥοδών· σιτοβολών, συκών; Ληναιών, Ποσειδεών· Ἐλαφηβολιών, Γαμηλιών, Παχών, names of months; αἰών *ævum,* πλειών, *a full time, a year,* χειμών, *winter time:* the rest are paroxytone, except those in βων, γων, δων, εων, αιων, ειων, ζων, νων, υων, ψων, which are oxytone (but ἄμβων, τρίβων, πώγων· κλύδων, κώδων, σπάδων, ὀπέων, κύων are barytone), together with χιών, ἀγκών· εἰκών, μιμαλλών, ἡγεμών, δαιτυμών· θηλαμών· κηδεμών, τελαμών, χιτών, κατηφών, κολοφών, oxytone, and ταών perispomenon.

NOTE—Arc. 13. 6; 16. 7; 18. 8; Chœrob. E. 73. 1; C. 295. 9; Lob. Ajax. 134-144. It will be noticed that most feminines of this termination are oxytone, and the masculines (with the exception of the collectives and some others) paroxytone.

Special Rules.

585. Those in αων are paroxytone, as διδυμάων, ὀπάων, συνοπάων, τετράων; except ταῶν perispomenon, and ἀών oxytone.

NOTE.—'Ἀών, Dor.=ἠϊών: ἀών, *a kind of fish,* Athen. 321 D; 327 C: ὀπάων is made oxytone by Theog. Can. 28. 23, but falsely. On ταών or ταῶν see below, § 617.

586. Those in βων are oxytone, as ἀρραβών, βουβών· ῥυμβών; except ἄμβων, στίλβων, and τρίβων paroxytone.

NOTE.—Theog. Can. 30. 29: ἄμβων, cf. Theog. Can. 31. 5; Arc. 10. 10: στράβων, Arc. 10. 10, or στραβών (?) Pollux 2. 51: στίλβων, Mercury, is paroxytone, as being the participle of στίλβω: τρίβων, Arc. 10. 9; A. G. Oxon. 2. 423. 30.

587. Those in γων are oxytone, as ἀγών· ἀρηγών, ἀσπιδογοργών, γοργών· θιαγών, λαγγών, λογγών, σταγών· τρυγών; except καταπύγων and πώγων paroxytone.

Note.—Schol. Ven. Φ. 141 ; Theog. Can. 31. 6 ; 38. 13 : **καταπύγων**, Schol. Ven. Φ. 141 ; Eust. 1228. 16 ; Theog. Can. 31. 18 ; Arc. 10. 23 : **λύγων**, Theog. Can. 31. 7, the meaning is unknown; it is written **λήγων** in Chœrob. 74. 28 : **προάγων**, Arc. 10. 20, but the word is often oxytone in our books, cf. Lob. Par. 201 ; 545 : **πώγων**, Theog Can. 31. 7 : **στίγων** (?) Eust. 725. 31, or **στιγών**, which is quoted by H. D. from Pollux 3. 72, but it is there paroxytone in Bekker's edition : **τρίγων**, Chœrob. C. 74. 29.

588. Those in **δων** are oxytone, as **ἀηδών, ἀλγηδών, μυδών, οὐδών, πετροχελιδών, σαρδών, σινδών, χελιδών**; except **κλύδων, κώδων, σπάδων** paroxytone.

Note.—Theog. Can. 32. 11 : **ἀΐδων**, Hesych.: **ἀκόδων**, Arc. 11. 9 : **κιβδών**, Phot. 163. 9, is **κίβδων** in Mœris 239 : **κλύδων** (**εὐρυκλύδων**), Arc. 11. 5 : ' **κλυδών**, ὦνος scriptum etiam invenitur. Hunc accentum agnoscere videtur Herod. π. μ. λ. 9. 5 : sed **κλύδων** paroxytonum recte ap. Arc;' H. *D.* : **κλώδων**, a *Mænad*, Plut. I. 665 : **κτηδών** is falsely paroxytone in Hesych. : **κώδων**, Arc. 11. 4 ; Chœrob. C. 75. 12 : **πέδων**, Eust. 1542. 48, with the compounds **ὀψιπέδων**, Hesych., **τριπέδων**, Eust. 725. 31 : **πόρδων**, Epictet. Diss. 3. 22. 80 : **σμόρδων** (?) Hesych. : **σπάδων**, *spado*, Theog. Can. 31. 30, but **σπαδών** τὸ σπάσμα, Suid., Phot. Lex. : **σχαδών**, Athen. 56 E ; 104 F ; Hesych. is paroxytone in Arist. H. A. 5. 22. 12 : **τετράδων**, *L. S.* : **φείδων**, Pollux 10. 179 : **φλέδων** and **φλεδών** : 'sic hæc differre videntur ut **φλεδών**, i. e. **φυλαρία** feminini, **φλέδων** vero de homine dictum et masculini et feminini generis sit ; v. Lobeck ad Soph. Ajac. p. 169;' H. *D.* : but the books vary : **ἀκροχόρδων** is found as an oxytone in Galen, but without adequate authority : **χλίδων**, Chœrob. C. 75. 14, is generally oxytone in manuscripts : **ψίδων**, Theog. Can. 31. 29, for which **ψιδών** also occurs.

589. Those in **εων** are oxytone, as **βολεών, γαργαρεών, ἐγχελεών, ἱστεών, καστανεών, κυκεών, μυρτεών**; except **ὀπέων** Ionic = **ὀπάων**, Theog. Can. 28. 22.

590. Those in **ζων** are oxytone, as **ἀλαζών, ἀμαζών, διομεια-λαζών, πτωχαλαζών, ψευδαλαζών**, Arc. 11. 19.

591. Those in **ηων** are paroxytone, as **ξυνήων, παιήων**; except **πρηών** = **πρών**, which is oxytone, Theog. Can. 29. 6 ; Arc. 11. 21.

592. Those in **θων** are paroxytone, as **γνάθων, γρόνθων, κάνθων, κώθων, μάλθων, πύθων.**

Note.—Cf. Chœrob. C. 77. 24 ; E. M. 696. 28. **Ἀκανθών, μαραθών, ὀρνιθών, ψαμμαθών** are collectives : **κιθών**, Arc. 11. 26 ; A. G. Oxon. 2. 423. 32 : 'Ion. pro **χιτών** ; **κίθων** autem Hesychio πῶμα πίθου, operculum dolii ;' H. *D.* : **πιθών**, Arc. 11. 26 : probably he means **πιθών** = **πιθεών** : **πίθων**, Theog. Can. 33. 28, perhaps refers to the name given to Tiresias, Eust. 1665. 53, but see Chœrob. C. 77. 32, where it is said that **πίθων** is a diminutive of **πίθηκος** : **σιθών** (?) Arc. 11. 25, ought probably to be written as a proper name, cf. Chœrob. C. 287. 29 : **ψυθών** = **ψιδών** (?) Hesych.

593. Those in **ιων** are paroxytone, as **ἀκανθίων, ἀμπελίων, βραχίων, θυρσίων, καρβατίων, κίων, πρίων**; except **ἠϊών, χιών** oxytone.

NOTE.—Arc. 18. 3, ἀμπελίων is oxytone in Pollux 6. 52: ἠιών, *a shore,* but ἠίων, *a hearing, news*: σμηνιών = σμῆνος, is a collective: πρίων or πριών (?), cf. Lob. Ajax 135; the word is always paroxytone in the books: χιών, Arc. 16. 13: Ἐρειπιών, κοπριών, λακιών, τοφιών, fall under § 584: βραχίων was in late Greek wrongly made oxytone, Chœrob. C. 285. 21: βραχίων ... ὅπερ ἐν τῇ συνηθείᾳ παραλόγως ὀξύνουσι βραχιὼν λέγοντες.

594. Those in αιων and ειων are oxytone, as αἰών, ἀνδρειών, βαιών, γαιών, ἐλαιών, πλειών.

NOTE.—Παιών, the measure *pœon*, is not uncommonly paroxytone: with this exception, the words of this termination fall more properly under § 584; cf. Lob. Ajax 136.

595. Those in κων are paroxytone, as δόρκων, μήκων, μύκων, σαλάκων, φύσκων; except ἀγκών, εἰκών oxytone.

NOTE.—Ἀγκών (γαλιαγκών, γαλιάγκων is common in the books, γοννναγκών), Theog. Can. 39. 3; Arc. 12. 12: εἰκών, Arc. 12. 13: ἑλικών, *a musical instrument so called,* Aristid. Quint. 3. p. 117; *H. D.*: γυναικών, δονακών, λευκών, σφηκών, φαρμακών, φοινικών, come under § 584.

596. Those in λων are paroxytone, as αἰσάλων, ἄλων, δόλων, κήλων, κοτύλων, χείλων; except αὐλών, μιμαλλών, πυλών oxytone.

NOTE.—Αὐλών, Theog. Can. 38. 30; Arc. 12. 24; μιμαλλών, E. M. 130. 27; Arc. 13. 5; Theog. Can. 36. 7, where it is μιμαλών: μυλών, Theog. Can. 36. 2; Arc. 12. 25, ὡς τοπικόν, for which the false form μύλων occurs in Eust. Opusc. p. 275. 6, *H. D.*, and also χειρομύλων for χειρομυλών (?): πυλών, Theog. Can. 36. 2: σπαταλών, Athen. 352 B: χείλων, *labeo*: χειλῶνες, τῶν ἀλεκτρυόνων τινές (?) Hesych.: χελλών or χελών, Arist. H. A. 4. 17. 3, where two MSS. read χέλλων, but χελών seems to occur without variation in H. A. 8. 2. 26: in 5. 11. 3, two MSS. have χάλλων; in Athenæus we have κόλων, κολών, χελών: ἀμπελών, μηλών, etc., are collectives, E. M. 130. 27.

597. Those in μων are paroxytone, as ἄκμων, ἀλήμων, ἀρτέμων, γνώμων, δαίμων, ἰχνεύμων; except ἀκρεμών, δαιτυμών, ἡγεμών, θηλαμών, θημών, κευθμών (§ 584), κηδεμών, λειμών (§ 584), πανηγεμών, τελαμών, χειμών (§ 584) oxytone.

NOTE.—Ἀγρεμών is better paroxytone: ἀκρεμών, Arc. 14. 2; Suid.; Theog. Can. 35. 15; but the books often have it ἀκρέμων: γαγγαμών, E. M. 219. 18, is an altogether false form: δαιτυμών, Arc. 14. 1: ἡγεμών (καθηγεμών, ὑφηγεμών), Theog. Can. 34. 25; Chœrob. E. 154. 34; θημών (and σημών, Dor.) collective: κεραμών, Arc. 13. 19 = κεραμεών: κευθμών, Theog. Can. 39. 9: κηδεμών (φιλοκηδεμών), Arc. 14. 2; Theog. Can. 34. 25: κρεμών, Theog. Can. 35. 14; Arc. 13. 11; λειμών, Chœrob. E. 127. 1: πλαταμών, Arc. 13. 19: σταθμών (?) Hesych.: τελαμών, Arc. 13. 17: φραγμών, a collective: χειμών, Theog. Can. 39. 8; Chœrob. E. 127. 1: χελμών (?) Hesych., for which χελλών (above, § 596) has been suggested: χηραμών, Orph. Arg. 1264, *H. D.*

598. Those in νων are oxytone, as κανών, κοινών, παρθενών.

NOTE.—On μέμνονες, see Schneider ad Ælian. N. A. 5. 1.

599. Those in ξων are paroxytone, as ἄξων, μύξων, σμύξων.

NOTE.—Πρηξών ... οὕτως γὰρ τοὺς ἀγοραίους καλοῦσι Σικελοί, Theog. Can. 38. 20.

600. Those in πων are paroxytone, as γρίπων, δράπων, κάπων, σάπων, σκίμπων.

601. Those in ρων are paroxytone, as ἄκρων, γάστρων, γλίσχρων, εἴρων, κέντρων, μυοπάρων, σάρων, Σκείρων, τρήρων.

NOTE.—Οἰορῶν οὕτως δὲ ἡ χάραξις τοῦ ἀρότρου, Theog. Can. 38. 31, or οἰρῶν, Arc. 15. 9 : παρών (?) cf. Schol. Aristoph. Pac. 143 = 142, where it is rightly paroxytone : σφαιρῶν, a *kind of net*, Oppian. Hal. 3. 83 ; H. D. : σχαιρῶν (?) Arc. 15. 10 : Κοπρῶν, κηρῶν, λουτρῶν, ἀφεδρῶν, ἀχυρῶν, ἀντρῶν, ἀνδρῶν, θυρῶν, προθυρῶν, belong to § 584.

602. Those in σων are paroxytone, as βίσων, καύσων, μαίσων, φώσων.

NOTE.—Πετασών, *petaso*, Athen. 657 E : θιασών, χρυσών, belong to § 584.

603. Those in των are paroxytone, as γείτων, ἐργάτων, κύρτων, μύρτων, πάκτων, τέκτων ; except χιτών oxytone.

NOTE.—Ἀλετών, collective : κερατών, Plut. 1. 9, but κεράτων is mentioned by Chœrob. C. 79. 16 : κροτών, *a tick*, Theog. Can. 39. 3 ; Arc. 16. 24 ; yet it is generally paroxytone : πακτών for πάκτων is a mere fancy or mistake of Salmasius : χιτών, Arc. 15. 19 : κοιτών, προκοιτών, ἱστῶν, προβατῶν, § 584.

604. Those in νων (and ανων) are oxytone, as ἀλεκτρυών, ἀλκυών, ἱππαλεκτρυών, μυών, χαυών ; except κύων paroxytone, Arc. 15. 27.

605. Those in φων are paroxytone, as γνίφων, γραμματοκύφων, κύφων, ξίφων, σίφων ; except κατηφών and κολοφών oxytone.

NOTE.—Κατηφών, Arc. 16. 3 ; Schol. Ven. Ω. 253 : κολοφών, Arc. 16. 3 : κύφων is certainly paroxytone, Chœrob. C. 77. 30, though Schol. Aristoph. Plut. 606, says : κύφων ὁ ξύλινος δεσμός, ἐν ᾧ δεσμεύονται οἱ ἐν τῇ φρουρᾷ, ὃν καὶ κυφῶνα περισπωμένως λέγουσι : σκυφῶν, Galen 4. p. 144 ; H. D. : ψηφών, 'Calculator, Manethoni 5. 277, restitui voluit Riglerus, Φειδωλὸς ψηφὼν (codex ψήφων) ὁ φιλάργυρος ἠδὲ δανειστής,' H. D. : but the reading of the MS. is more in accordance with analogy.

606. Those in χων are paroxytone, as ἄρχων, Βάκχων, βλήχων, γλήχων, σπέρχων.

NOTE.—Chœrob. E. 73. 1 ; Arc. 16. 6 : τὸ δὲ γλήχων ὤφειλε βαρύνεσθαι· εἰ δὲ θηλυκὸν καὶ διὰ τοῦ Β, ὀξύνεται, but βλήχων is also barytone in the books : perhaps Arc. has confused βλήχων with ἡ βληχώ, gen. βληχοῦς, though Chœrob. C. 77. 34 says : καὶ τὸ γλήχων γλήχωνος βαρυνόμενον ἐπὶ τῆς γενικῆς φυλάσσει τό Ω, εἰ καὶ παρὰ Ἀττικοῖς ὀξύνεται καὶ θηλυκῶς λέγεται : προμαχών, Lob. Phryn. 167, also προμαχεών : μυχών and τραχών belong to § 584.

607. Those in ψων are oxytone, as ὀψών.

Note.—Πρών becomes πρώονες, Schol. Ven. Θ. 557 : πρώονες· ὡς σώφρονες. τὸ γὰρ πρῶνες πληθυντικὸν διῃρέθη, καὶ εἰς ὀξεῖαν καὶ βαρεῖαν ἡ περισπωμένη μετηνέχθη.

608. Names of men, gods, and heroes in ων (gen. *ovos* or ωνος) are paroxytone, as Ἀγαμέμνων, Ἀλκμαίων, Ἄμμων, Ἀμφιτρύων, Ἀμφίων, Δευκαλίων, Θέων, Κλέων, Μαχάων, Πανδίων, Πλάτων, Σόλων, Τρύφων, Φίλων; except Γηρυών, Κερκυών, Παιών, Σαρπηδών, Τελαμών.

609. Note.—Ἄβρων, Chœrob. C. 286. 14, is falsely oxytone, Chœrob. C. 74. 10 : Ἀβείρων is written Ἀβειρών in Suid. : Ἀβεσαλών, Suid. : Ἀγών, Phot. Lex. : Ἀδραμών· ὁ Ἕρμων παρὰ Λυδοῖς, Hesych., yet St. Byz. s. v. Ἀδραμύττειον says : τὸν Ἕρμωνα Λυδοὶ Ἀδραμυν καλοῦσι Φρυγιστί, *H. D.* : Ἀμυδών, Chœrob. C. 296. 10 : Ἀτμών, E. M. 715. 12, is barbarous : Αὐλών, Paus. 3. 12. 9 : Βραυρών (?) Theog. Can. 38. 33 : Γηρυών, Arc. 15. 17, not Γηρύων, as it sometimes is : Γιγών, Γιγῶν, Γιγγρών, Γιγρών, etc., an obscure demon, is written and accented all sorts of ways, but his name should be paroxytone : Ἐδεκών, Polyb. 10. 34 : Ἐλεών is quoted from Plut. 2. 301 A, but there it is correctly paroxytone : Ἑλικών, Tzetz. ad Hesiod. Op. p. 30. Gaisf., *H. D.*, is better paroxytone, as in Plut. 1. 966 A, and elsewhere : Ἠλεκτρύων, Arc. 15. 22 ; Chœrob. C. 71. 14 ; 284. 2 : but Ἠλεκτρυών (gen. όνος and ῶνος) is not uncommon, though no doubt faulty : Ἰσαιών (?) Suid. : Καλυδών (?) the hero from whom the city Καλυδών received its name, St. Byz. ; Chœrob. C. 296. 10 : Κερκυών, Arc. 15. 17, but Κερκύων is very frequent in the books : Λειμών (?) Paus. 8. 53. 2 : Μακεδών, the eponymous hero of the Macedonians, St. Byz. : Μαραθών, a hero so called, Paus. 2. 6. 5 : Μεδεών, son of Pylades, St. Byz. ; Schol. Ven. B. 717 : Μελετεών (?) : Μυρμιδών, Apollod. 1. 7. 3 : Ναασσών, Chœrob. E. 83. 9 : Παιών, cf. Theog. Can. 38. 3 ; A. G. Oxon. 1. 276. 13 : Πηλεγών, Eust. 1228. 13 : Πλευρών, Apollod. 1. 7. 7 : Σαρπηδών, gen. όνος or Σαρπήδων, gen. όντος, cf. Schol. Ven. M. 379 ; Φ. 141 ; Ψ. 800 ; Theog. Can. 32. 17 and 32 ; Chœrob. C. 295. 2 : Σεθών : 'Ap. Herodot. libri consentire perhibentur in accentu Σεθών, quum Σέθως vel Σέθος sit ap. Eust. et Schol. Hom. Od. Ξ. 278, Σέθω et accus. Σέθων ap. Joseph. c. Apion. p. 461, 462,' *L. Dindorf* ap. *H. D.* : Σηών, Sept., is barbarous and indeclinable : Σιγών, *Pape* : Σιδών, Chœrob. C. 296. 20 : Σικυών, Paus. 2. 6. 5 : Σιλοών, *Pape* : Τελαμών, E. M. 715. 11 : Τενθρηδών, cf. Herod. π. μ. λ. 9. 16 : Φλεών (?) a name of Dionysus : Χαιρών, Theog. Can. 38. 32, but in our books it is paroxytone : Χελιδών, Herod. π. μ. λ. 9. 6, also as the name of a woman.

610. Names of cities, places, and rivers in ων (gen. *ovos, ωνος*) are oxytone, as Ἀβυδών, Ἀγκών, Αἰγών, Ἀλαβών, Ἀργανθών, Αὐλών, Βαβυλών, Βραυρών, Δωδών, Καρχηδών, Κιθαιρών, Κολοφών, Μαραθών, Πυθών, Σιδών, Στρυμών; but to this rule there are many exceptions, of which the more important are Ἀσκάλων, Κρότων, and Λακεδαίμων.

611. Note.—*Names of Places.* E. M. 513. 28 ; Arc. 16. 17 ; St. Byz. s. v. : Αἰσών . . . ὀξύτονον τὸ Αἰσών· τὰ γὰρ εἰς ΩΝ δισύλλαβα ἐπὶ πόλεων ὀξύνεται, εἰ μὴ διαστολὴν ἔχοι σημαινομένου, ὡς τὸ Κρότων βαρύνεται· ὀξυνόμενον γὰρ δηλοῖ ζούφιον· ἢ χαρακτῆρι ὑπάγοιτο, ὡς τὸ Ἴτων, συναπενεχθὲν τῷ Τρίτων, Γείτων, Βίτων· οἶον Ἡίων, Κρόννων, Γύρτων, Νέων (sic), σεσημείωται τὸ Οἴβων, ἔστι πόλις Ἰταλίας : Ἀγκών, on which St. Byz. says, ἴσως δὲ βαρύνεται κατὰ τοὺς ἐγχωρίους ὡς Ἄντρων : Ἀδέρκων, St. Byz. : Ἀδράνων, *Pape* : Ἀκκάρων, Joseph. A. J. 5. 2. 4 ; *H. D.* : Ἀλβίων, St. Byz. : Ἄλμων, St. Byz. : Ἀντρών, Eust. 324. 34 : καὶ τὴν Ἄντρωνα δὲ τινὲς μὲν βαρύνουσιν ὡς τὴν Ἴτωνα, τινὲς δὲ Ἀντρῶνα φασὶν ὡς Πυθῶνα· Ἡρωδιανὸς δέ φησιν ὡς Πλευρῶνα, Arc. 14. 25; 15. 4: Ἀραυσίων, Strab. 185: Ἀρβῶν, St. Byz., is paroxytone in Polyb. 2. 11: Ἀσκάλων, E. M. 130. 27; Theog. Can. 39. 16; Arc. 17. 4: Ἀσσάλων, Arc. 17. 5: Ἀτμῶν, E. M. 715. 11: Αὐενίων, St. Byz., is false for Αὐενιών, Strab. 185: Βλησίνων (?) Strab. 224: Βραύρων, St. Byz., should be Βραυρών, Strab. 399: Γύρτων, St. Byz., a blunder for Γυρτών, Strab. 442: Δάσκων, St. Byz.: Δέρθων, Strab. 217, or Δέρτων, St. Byz., or Δερτών (?) Ptol.: Δευκαλίων, an island so called, Strab. 435: Εὐαίμων (?) St. Byz.: Ζαβουλών, Chœrob. E. 154. 34: Ἴτων, Arc. 16. 19; Eust. 324. 23: τὴν δὲ Ἴτωνα προπαροξύνεσθαι φασὶν οἱ παλαιοὶ ὡς Μήκωνα. τινὲς δὲ ὀξύνουσι. According to St. Byz. the natives called it Ἰτών: Κάρμων, Strab. 141: Καστάλων, St. Byz., but Κασταλάν, Polyb. 10. 38. 7; 11. 20. 5; also Κάστλων, Plut. 1. 569; cf. H. D. s. v.: Κράνων, St. Byz., false for Κραννών, Strab. 442: Κρεμμύων, St. Byz.: Κρήστων, St. Byz., false for Κρηστών: Κρομμύων, St. Byz., or Κρομυών: Κρότων, Theog. Can. 34. 13, and this is the common accent, but Κροτών also occurs, cf. Arc. 26. 24: Κύρτων, St. Byz.: Κώθων, St. Byz.: Λακεδαίμων, Theog. Can. 39. 17: Λάκμων, St. Byz.: Λήρων (?) Strab. 185: Λύσκων, St. Byz.: Μόθων, a rock so called, Paus. 4. 35. 1: Μόρων, Strab. 152: Μύλων, St. Byz.; Athen. 337 C: 'ubi libri optimi μυλῶνα vel. μυλῶν';' H. D.: Μύων, St. Byz.: Νάρβων, Strab. 181: Νέδων, St. Byz., this has also a genitive Νέδοντος, Chœrob. C. 75. 19: Νέσσων, St. Byz.: Νέων, 'accentus autem, in quo variant etiam libri Strabonis 9. p. 439, in ultima ponendus videtur, ut diserte præcipit Steph. Byz. in Αἴσων, ubi tamen male Νέων ;' L. Dindorf ap. H. D.: Ὀβούλκων, Strab. 141, or Ὀβόλκων, St. Byz.: Ὄβρων, Suid.: Ὀλιζών is oxytone, not Ὀλίζων, as Nicias wrote, Schol. Ven. B. 717; Theog. Can. 38. 26: Ὄλμωνες, St. Byz.: Ὀλοοσσών, Herodian made it paroxytone, Schol. Ven. B. 739, and Ὀλόσσων, Pape: Ὄρτων, Strab. 242: Οὐάδμων, Pape: Οὔλπων (?): Οὔρσων, Strab. 141: Πάρνων, Paus. 2. 38. 7: Παρπάρων (?) St. Byz.: Πίων, false for Πρίαν: Πομπέλων, Strab. 161: Πρίων, Polyh. 1. 85, the name is significant: Πριάμων (?) Strab. 315, or Πρόμων or Πρώμων: Πύρων (?) Pape: Πώγων, Strab. 373: Ῥίζων, St. Byz.: Ῥουσκίνων, Strab. 182: Σάλων, St. Byz. s. v. Σαλώνεια, Strab. 315: Σάνδων (?) St. Byz.: Σαπυσελάτων (? gen.), Paus. 2. 25. 10: Σάρων, St. Byz.: Σάσων also occurs under the form Σασών: Σατίων, Polyh. 5. 108. 8: Σισάπων, Strab. 142: Σκάρδων, Strab. 315: Σόρων, Paus. 8. 23. 8: Σούλμων, Arc. 16. 24: Ταράσκων, Strab. 178, or Ταρούσκων: Ταρράκων, St. Byz., also Ταρρακῶν and Ταρρακών: Τέκμων, St. Byz.: Τράρων, Schol. Lycoph. 1159: Τράχων, Suid., but Τραχών also occurs: Χαύων, St. Byz.: Χρυσονδύων, Polyb. 5. 108.

612. Note 2.—*Names of Rivers and Streams.* Ἄζων, Chœrob. C. 76. 24: Αἴσων, Plut. 1. 263; Theog. Can. 33. 14: Ἀκίδων (gen. τος and ωνος), Strab. 348: Ἁλιάκμων, Strab. 330: Ἀλίζων, Theog. Can. 33. 22; in Plut. 2. 515 D, it is Ἀλιζών; Βρύχων, Theog. Can. 33. 30: Γαίσων, Herodot. 9. 97: Διάγων, Paus. 6. 21. 4: Δρίλων, Theog. Can. 35. 29: Ἐρίγων, Theog. Can. 31. 15: in the books the accent varies between Ἐρίγων and Ἐριγών, but the latter is probably right, since the passage in Theog. is by no means conclusive: Ἴων, Strab. 327: Καύκων, St. Byz., etc.: Κνακών, Theog. Can. 38. 9; Herod. π. μ. λ. 17. 22, is falsely Κνακίαν in Plut. 1. 287, H. D.; (but Sintenis has Κνακιών) and Κνηκείων, Lycoph. 550, where W. Dindorf proposes to read Κνηκιών; another form Κνακυών occurs in Chœrob. C. 296. 29: Κύνδων, Theog. Can. 31. 28: Λάδων, Strab. 343: Chœrob. C. 75. 15: Λήθων, Athen. 71 B.; H. D.: Νάρων, Theog. Can. 36. 15; Chœrob. C. 288. 2: Νέδων, gen. ωνος and οντος: Ὄζων, Theog. Can. 32. 11: Πρίων, St. Byz.: Ῥουβίκων, Strab. 217: Σαλάγγων, Schol. Ven. Φ. 141: Σίρβων, a lake, St. Byz.: Τρίτων, an old name of the Nile, Schol. Apollon. Rhod. 4. 269.

613. All masculine proper names in αων are paroxytone, as Ἄονες, Ἰάονες, Κάων, Φάων, Χάων, Theog. Can. 30. 11 ; Arc. 17. 26 ; 18. 7.

614. National names (Ethnica) in ων (gen. ωνος, ονος) are oxytone, as Ἀλαζών, Ἀμαζών, Ἀμφικτυόνες, Αὐσόνες, Βιστών, Μακεδών (φιλομακεδών), Μυγδών, Μυρμιδόνες, Νασαμῶνες, Παφλαγών (βυρσοπαφλαγών), Πελαγόνες, Σιδών, Σιδόνες, Σιθών ; except those in αων, as Ἰάονες, Χάονες (see above, 613).

615. NOTE.—Cf. Schol. Ven. Φ 141 ; Theog. Can. 30. 15 ; Chœrob. C. 289. 13 : Ἄγωνες, Polyb. 2. 15. 8 : Αἴμων, St. Byz. s. v. Αἱμονία : Ἀργείων, Theog. Can. 30. 16 : Αὔσων, St. Byz. s. v. Αἱμονία : Βήρωνες, Strab. 162 : Βίστονες, St. Byz. s. v. Βιστονία : τὸ ἐθνικὸν Βιστών (sic), τῶν εἰς ΤΩΝ δισυλλάβων, βαρυνομένων, οἷον Πλάτων, Κρίτων, εἰ μὴ διαστολὴ γένοιτο σημαινομένου· χιτὼν γὰρ πρὸς διαστολὴν ὀξύνεται τοῦ κυρίου καὶ ποτάμου, καὶ τὸ κροτὼν τὸ ζωύφιον πρὸς ἀντιδιαστολὴν τοῦ τῆς πόλεως ὀνόματος, ἢ περιεκτικὸν διὰ τὸ κοιτών, ἱστών, ἢ ἐθνικὸν διὰ τὸ Ο κλινόμενον, ὡς τὸ Βίστονος, Herodot. 7. 110 : Ἑστίωνες, Strab. 206 : Ἠδῶνες also occurs under the forms Ἠδῶνες, Ἤδωνες, Ἠδωνες, but there is more authority for making it oxytone than paroxytone : Ἴωνες, St. Byz. : Καύκωνες, Hom. etc. ; Chœrob. C. 289. 19 : Κέλωνες, Diod. Sic. 17. 110 ; H. *D.* : Κέντρωνες, Strab. 204 : Κίκονες, Theog. Can. 30. 16 ; cf. Arc. 12. 10 ; Chœrob. C. 289. 22 : Κύδωνες, Hom. etc. ; Chœrob. C. 289. 21 : Λάκων, Theog. Can. 30. 16 : Λίγγονες, Strab. 193, also Λίγγωνες and Λόγγονες : Λούσωνες, Strab. 162 : Μαιόνες (Μηόνες Μηλόνες) : ' accentum acutum, quem præbent libri plures paucioresve Herodoti 1. 7 ; 7. 74, testatur schol. Ven. Hom. Il. Δ. 394, qui nom. pr. [i. e. of the founder of the nation] gravari dicit εἰς ἀποφυγὴν τοῦ ἐθνικοῦ, consentiente Etym. M. in Βαιών citato (sive grammat. in Cram. An. vol. 1. p. 276. 6), dissentiente Eustathio,' *L. Dindorf* ap. H. *D.* : Μακροπώγωνες, Strab. 492, may perhaps be better considered an adjective : Μάκρωνες, Arc. 14. 24 ; 15. 3 : Μέμνονες, Theog. Can. 30. 18 ; Chœrob. C. 289. 29 : Μέρονες, *Pape* : Μύνδονες (or Μύνδωνες), St. Byz. : Μύτωνες, Chœrob. C. 289. 19 : Ὀλόσσονες (?) Lycoph. 906 : Οὐάσκωνες, Strab. 155 : Οὐέννωνες, Strab. 206 : Οὐέττωνες, Strab. 162 : Παίονες, Herodot. 5. 15, is said to be oxytone, A. G. Oxon. 1. 276. 9 : Πανίωνες : Πίκτονες, Strab. 190 : Σάντωνες, St. Byz., also Σάντονες : Σάξονες, St. Byz. : Σέμνονες, Ptol., or Σέμνωνες, Strab., but Σεμνόνες also occurs ; Σέννονες, St. Byz. ; Σένονες, Σένωνες, Σέννωνες, etc. : Σήνωνες = Σένονες, Polyb. 2. 17. 7 : Σιροπαίονες, Herodot. 5. 15 : Σουεσσίωνες, Strab. 196 : Συλίονες, St. Byz. : Τεύτονες, Strab. 196 : Χαύονες, St. Byz. : Χῶνες, Strab. 253 : Ὠδονες, St. Byz. : Ὠστίωνες, St. Byz.

· According to Chœrob. C. 289. 12, national names in ων, gen. ονος, are oxytone, those in ων, gen. ωνος, paroxytone, except Κίκονες, Μέμνονες ; but this rule is no better than the one given above.

616. Names of women in ων (gen. ονος, ωνος) are oxytone, as Γοργών, Πλαγγών, Τερηδών.

617. The following words in ων (gen. ωνος) are perispomena, Ποσειδῶν, ταῶν, Τυφῶν.

NOTE.—Ποσειδῶν (Ποσειδέων), Chœrob. C. 298. 9 ; Arc. 16. 10 ; Herod. π. μ. λ. 10. 12 ; Chœrob. C. 299. 5 : οἱ μὲν γὰρ Δωριεῖς Ποτιδᾶν λέγουσιν ὀξυτόνως, οἱ δὲ Αἰολεῖς Ποτίδαν καὶ Ποσείδαν λέγουσι βαρυτόνως : so Ζηνοποσειδῶν, Athen. 337 D :

ταῶν, Arc. 16. 10 ; 94. 6 ; Chœrob. C. 300. 13, sometimes falsely ταών : Τυφῶν, Theog. Can. 29. 31 ; Arc. 16. 10 ; Chœrob. C. 300. 13 is often wrongly either Τύφων or Τυφάν : Φερῶν, Herodot. 2. 111 ; the readings vary between this and Φέρων, Φερών, and Φέρωνα : ̔Φέρων the founder of Berœa is paroxytone in St. Byz.

618. (*b*) Those in ων (gen. οντος) are paroxytone, as γέρων, δράκων, θεράπων, λέων ; Αὐτομέδων, Κρέων, Μέδων, Νέδων, Σαρπήδων, Theog. Can. 30. 7.

619. (*c*) Those in ων (gen. ωντος and ουντος) are perispomena, as ἀμνοκῶν, ἀμφιφῶν ; Ἀθηνακῶν, Εὐρυπῶν, Ἱπποθῶν, Ξενοφῶν, Σολομῶν, Χαρναβῶν.

NOTE.—Ἀμνοκῶν, Chœrob. C. 298. 13 : Σολομῶν, gen. ῶντος, is also inflected Σολόμων, gen. ωνος, Theog. Can. 29. 29 ; 37. 11 : Ἐξικρών and Ἑρμοκρών in Arc. 14. 26 ; 15. 5, have been rightly emended by Schmidt. See also Arc. 10. 12 ; 12. 6 ; 16. 2 ; E. M. 513. 28 ; Chœrob. C. 299. 32 ; Herod. π. μ. λ. 10. 1 sq.

-Ξ and -Ψ.

620. Nouns in ξ and ψ are all accented on the penultimate, they are therefore either properispomena or paroxytone,. as ἀλώπηξ (χηναλώπηξ), ἄναξ, αὖλαξ, θώραξ, Καππάδοξ, κλῖμαξ, Λέλεξ, μύρμηξ (λεοντομύρμηξ), οἶαξ, πέρδιξ ; ἀγχίλωψ, καλαῦροψ, κατῆλιψ, κίκνωψ, κώνωψ, λαῖλαψ.

621. NOTE 1.—Arc. 18. 18 ; E. M. 109. 45. The compound words in ξ, the latter half of which consists of a monosyllabic verbal root, are occasionally used in a substantive sense, e. g. ἀπορρώξ, διασφάξ, ὑποσφάξ : their accentuation is considered below, §§ 724-728.

Ἀγριοβρόξ, Hesych. : ἀεισκῶπες, Arist. H. A. 9. 28. 1, where one MS. has ἀεὶ σκῶπες, should probably be ἀείσκωπες, as in Eust. 1524. 6 ; those who made it oxytone considered it to be derived from σκώπτω : Ἀλμῶπες, Thucyd. 2. 99, is accented like an adjective : ἐρνύγας, Arist. Poet. 21. 17, cannot be right : μερτρύξ (?) Diosc. 3. 131, *H. D.* : πτέρυξ, Eust. 229. 37 : τὸ δὲ πτέρυγος λάβεν [Π. 2. 316] ἀρέσκει τοῖς παλαιοῖς κατὰ τὴν Ἀριστάρχειον ἀνάγνωσιν, ὡς δ᾽ ἄλλοι φασί, κατὰ παράδοσιν παροξύνειν, ἀπὸ εὐθείας ὀξυτόνου τῆς ἡ πτερύξ, ὃ δηλοῖ οὐ τὰ πτερὰ μόνα, τὸ μόριον δὲ μετὰ τῶν περικειμένων πτερῶν, καθὰ δηλοῖ καὶ Ἡρωδιανός, εἰπὼν ὅτι τὰ εἰς ΥΞ θηλυκά, μονοσύλλαβα μὲν ὄντα, ὀξύνεται· στύξ, νύξ, τρύξ· ὑπὲρ μίαν δὲ ὄντα συλλαβὴν βαρύνεται· κάλυξ, ἄντυξ, πομφόλυξ. τὸ πτερὺξ σεσημείωται ὑπὸ Ἀριστάρχου ὀξυνθὲν διὰ τὸ ἐννοίας περιεκτικῆς εἶναι, Eust. 1334. 26 : Chœrob. C. 81. 15 ; Etym. Gud. 485. 18 ; E. M. 694. 20 ; Schol. Ven. B. 316. This arbitrary accentuation of Aristarchus is not generally followed in our books, and with reason.

622. NOTE 2.—According to the grammarians ι and υ are never long by *nature* before ξ in hypermonosyllabic nouns, hence they prescribe κῆρυξ, φοῖνιξ, not κήρυξ or φοίνιξ, though both forms are to be met with. On the quantity of these dichronous vowels see Lob. Par. 411, who proves that the grammarians and their rules, manuscripts, and printed books are involved in a hideous mass of contradictions. Cf. also Chœrob. C. 221. 35 ; 292. 25 ; 311. 1 sqq. ; 425. 33 ; Draco, 44. 5 ; 92. 23 ; 93. 5. 8 ; 100. 3 ; E. M. 460. 55 ; Schol. Ven. K. 258 ; Etym. Gud. 207.

16; 320. 32; Reg. Pros. ap. Herm. de emend. rat. Gr. gr. p. 433, n. 63 sqq.; Priscian, p. 753, ed. Putsch.

Such forms as θῶμιγξ, ἷλιγξ, λᾶϊγξ, εὐλάϊγξ, μῆνιγξ, μῆριγξ, πῶϋγξ, σῆραγξ, σμῆριγξ, σμῶδιγξ, στῆριγξ, σῦριγξ, φαῦσιγξ, φῦσιγξ, φῶτιγξ, ψάφιγξ, ὦλιγξ, ὦριγξ, appear monstrous enough, yet they are often found thus accented; cf. Lob. Phryn. 71.

-AP.

623. Nouns in αρ retract the accent, as Αῖσαρ, Ἄραρ, δάμαρ, Ἴσαρ, Καῖσαρ, Arc. 19. 14; Chœrob. C. 83. 34.

-HP.

624. Those in ηρ (gen. ηρος and ερος) as ἀήρ, αἰθήρ, ἀνήρ, ἐλατήρ, γαστήρ, γενετήρ, πατήρ, σωτήρ, στατήρ, χαρακτήρ; except paroxytone, εἰνάτηρ, θυγάτηρ, μήτηρ, φράτηρ. Proper names and those of nations are paroxytone, as Βύζηρες, Δημήτηρ, Δόβηρες, Ἐρίηρ, Ἴβηρ, Πίηρ; except Ἐλευθήρ oxytone.

625. NOTE.—Chœrob. C. 85. 24; E. 6. 21; Arc. 19. 19, who says that τὰ εἰς ΗΡ θηλυκὰ μὴ μετατιθέμενα κατά τι ἔθος ποιητοῦ εἰς διάφορον γένος βαρύνεται ... τὸ δὲ γαστήρ ὀξύνεται: and in accordance with this rule we have εἰνάτηρ, θυγάτηρ, μήτηρ: the oblique cases of these, except the vocative, are accented as if the nominative had been oxytone: φράτηρ, Chœrob. C. 320. 13; A. G. Oxon. 1. 346.16: φράτηρ Ἀττικοὶ μὲν βαρύνουσιν, οἱ δὲ Δωριεῖς ὀξύνουσιν: the word is not unfrequently oxytone in the books, though such an accent is certainly false, cf. A. G. 992. 11: Ἀνήρ, Hesych.: Ἀστήρ, Arc. 20. 4, but in 19. 13 he makes it paroxytone, and the latter seems to be the proper accent, for in Eust. 1967. 22 we have Ἀστηρ, πόλις distinguished from ἀστήρ, ὁ κατ᾽ οὐρανόν: Δημήτηρ, Arc. 19. 26: Ἴβηρ, Chœrob. C. 320. 16: Πίηρ, Chœrob. C. 320. 16; Ἐλευθήρ, Chœrob. C. 318. 10; Arc. 20. 3.

626. Compounds in ηρ which retain η in the genitive are oxytone; while those which have ε are paroxytone, as δετήρ ἀμαλλοδετήρ, στατήρ ὀβολοστατήρ; but ἀνήρ γυναικάνηρ λιπάνηρ, δαήρ πολυδάηρ, Arc. 28. 8, πατήρ αἰνοπάτηρ, and therefore συμπατήρ, quoted by H. D. from Joannes Damascenus, is most likely a false accent.

-EIP.

627. Substantives in ειρ are paroxytone, as Ἀλάζειρ, ἀντίχειρ, Βέχειρ, Ἐλάτειρ, Λίγειρ, Σάπειρ, χρυσοέθειρ.

NOTE.—Arc. 20. 15; Chœrob. C. 86. 14: Ἀλιζίρ (gen. Ἀλιζίρος) occurs in Herodot. 4. 164: this is written Ἀλάζειρ in Theog. Can. 41. 25, and the word is probably better paroxytone.

-ΥΡ.

628. Substantives in υρ are paroxytone, as Ἄσσυρ, Ἴλλυρ, Κέρκυρ, Λίγυρ, μάρτυρ, Φίλυρ.

N

NOTE.—Arc. 19. 17 : the Egyptian month Ἀθύρ, Plut. 2. 356 C, is barbarous and indeclinable.

-ΩΡ.

629. Those in ωρ are paroxytone, as ἀφήτωρ, Ἕκτωρ, ἑστιάτωρ, ἠλέκτωρ, ἵστωρ, Κάστωρ, Μήστωρ, νεμέτωρ, Νέστωρ, οἰκήτωρ; except ἰχώρ oxytone.

NOTE.—Arc. 20. 20; Chœrob. C. 320. 32 ; E. 45. 19 : Ἀδώρ, which Pape quotes from Strab. 529, is Ἄδωρ in Kramer's edition, and Ἄδων in that of Meineke: ἄχωρ is paroxytone according to Arc. 20, but is oxytone in A. G. 6. 25 ; 475. 2 : ἰχώρ, Herod. π. μ. λ. 32. 13.

-ΑΣ.

630. (a) Those in ας (gen. άδος) are oxytone, as ἀμασυκάς, δυάς, λαμπάς, μονάς, πολυδειράς, τριάς, φυγάς, Ἀρκάς, Ἑλλάς, Παλλάς.

NOTE.—Arc. 22. 22 ; Chœrob. E. 101. 27; C. 350. 25 : τὸ μὲν ἀναδενδρὰς ὁ μὲν Ἡρωδιανὸς ὑπολαμβάνει μόνως συστέλλειν τὸ Α καὶ ὀξύνεσθαι, ὁ δὲ Λούπερκος ἐν τῇ περὶ Γενῶν πολλοῖσιν ἀποδείκνυσιν ὅτι ἐκτείνει τὸ Α καὶ περισπᾶται, καὶ ὅμως διὰ τοῦ ΔΟΣ ἔχει τὴν κλίσιν.

631. (b) Those in ας (gen. ᾱδος) are perispomena, as Βοιβᾶς, Βιττᾶς, Κυρᾶς.

These are peculiarly Ionic forms : Chœrob. C. 42. 29 ; Joh. Alex. 8. 19.

632. (c) Those in ας (gen. αντος) are paroxytone, as ἀδάμας, ἀλίβας, γίγας, ἐλέφας, κιλλίβας, λυκάβας, Αἴας, Ἀρυάς, Ἀφίας, Βίας, Βύζαντες, Γαράμαντες, Ἐλέας, Θόας, Κάλχας, Παπίας, Σατύας, Φλεγύας; except ἀνδριάς, ἱμάς oxytone.

633. NOTE.—Arc. 21. 3; Joh. Alex. 8. 22 : σεσημείωται τὸ. ἱμὰς καὶ ἀνδριὰς ὀξυνθέντα· ἱμάντος γὰρ καὶ ἀνδριάντος, ἅπερ παρ' Ἀττικοῖς περισπᾶται ; 'De nominativi accentu acuto Epim. Hom. Cram. Anecd. vol. 1. p. 217. 10 ; Herodian. ap. Chœrob. Can. p. 98. 1, et Περὶ μον. λ. p. 34. 9 ; Aread. p. 21. 3 ; 193. 14, et Draco, 12. 9 ; 41. 25, apud quem nullum nunc vestigium circumflexi ab eo, ut ab Heliodoro et Tyrannione, secundum Herodianum probati : sed dativi pluralis vitiosus accentus ἀνδριάσι pro ἀνδριᾶσι frequens in libris,' H. D. ; cf. H. D. s. v. ἱμάς and E. M. 101. 43 : ἀλλᾶς (=ἀλλάεις ?), Herodian ap. Eust. 300. 15, gen. ἀλλᾶντος, Chœrob. C. 426. 15, not ἀλλάντος, as Joh. Alex. 8. 18 : Γαιωνᾶς (gen. Γαιωνᾶτος) is very doubtful : on Γαρίμας the following observation is made by E. M. 221. 41 : Γαρίμας, ἐκ τοῦ μαρίκας· ἢ ἐκ τοῦ γαρίκας τὸ μαρίκας· βάρβαρον δὲ τὸ ὄνομα, καὶ ἡ κλίσις, καὶ ὁ τόνος. Ἡρωδιανὸς περὶ παθῶν : but it is regular if paroxytone, and that is its accent in the books : Γλισσᾶς (gen. ᾶντος, Chœrob. C. 426. 15 : άντος, Joh. Alex. 8. 17) or Γλίσσας, Γλίσσαντος, Eust. 269. 18, or Γλισσᾶς, gen. ᾶ; cf. S. V. 504 ; Schol. Ven. M. 20, and H. D. s. v. : διξᾶς (gen. ᾶντος), Pollux 9. 81 : ἐξᾶς (gen. ᾶντος), Pollux 4. 174 ; Arc. 21. 22 : ἰλᾶς (=ἰλάεις, gen. ᾶντος), Chœrob. C. 43. 5 ; Arc. 21. 26 : πελεκᾶς (gen. ᾶντος, Chœrob. C. 426. 15, or άντος, Chœrob. C. 42. 28) : of this word various forms occur, as πελεκάν, ανος : πελεκᾶς, ανος : πελεκᾶς, ᾶ : πελέκας (?) Schol. Aristoph. Av. 882 = 883 : μήποτε πελέκας προενεκτέον ὡς ἀλίβας· ὁ δὲ πελεκῖνος τῷ πελεκᾶντι προσέρριπται. πελεκὰν μέντοι πελεκᾶνος

κοινῶς, πελεκᾶς δὲ πελεκᾶντος 'Αττικῶς. πελεκᾶς πελεκᾶ Δωρικῶς : thus also Suidas :
it occurs as a proper name in Polyh. 5. 77. 9 : τετρᾶς, Arc. 22. 15 : τριᾶς (gen.
ᾶντος), Pollux 4. 175 : τριξᾶς (gen. ᾶντος), Pollux 9. 81.

(*d*) Λᾶας, gen. λάαος, is properispomenon, Chœrob. C. 27. 30.

-ΗΣ.

634. (*a*) Those in ης (gen. ητος and ηθος) are paroxytone, as
γλυκύτης, δασύτης, δριμύτης, κακότης, κοσμιότης, λέβης, λευκότης,
λογιότης, μεσότης, ποιότης, ποσότης, Δάρης, Μάγνης, Μένδης, Μί-
λης, Πάρνης ; except ἁδροτής, βραδυτής, γυμνής, δηϊοτής, ἐσθής,
Κουρῆτες, *the Curetes* (but κούρητες, *young men*, is regular), κουφοτής (?) ποτής, ταχυτής, τραχυτής, χερνής, ψιλής, which are
oxytone.

635. Note 1.—Schol. Ven. E. 9 ; Chœrob. C. 43. 10-55. 33 : ἁδροτής, Arc. 28.
8, but ἁδρότης is by no means uncommon : ἀνδροτής is oxytone in Eust. 1090. 32 ;
E. M. 103. 1, but ἀνδρότης would appear to be the correct accent, cf. Herod. π. μ. λ.
33. 22 : βραδυτής, Arc. 28. 8 ; E. M. 103. 1 : ' In codd. interdum παροξυτόνως
scribitur βραδύτης, ut βραδύτητος, apud Polyb. 10. 32. 12, βραδύτης apud Herodianum, Περὶ μον λέξ. p. 40. 7, contra ipsius Herodiani regulam ;' W. Dindorf
ap. H. D. : γυμνής is always oxytone, but I find no express declaration of its
accent in the grammarians : δανοτής, Herod. π. μ. λ. 40. 12 : δηϊοτής, Aristarchus
ap. Schol. Ven. Γ. 20 ; E. M. 103. 1 ; Eust. 669. 47 : περὶ δὲ τοῦ τόνου τῆς δηϊοτητος,
ὥσπερ καὶ τῆς ταχυτῆτος καὶ τῆς βραδυτῆτος καὶ τῶν ὁμοίων προπερισπωμένων ἀμφι-
λογεῖται· οἱ μὲν γὰρ συνηγοροῦσιν ὀξέως τονοῦσθαι τὰς αὐτῶν εὐθείας . . . πλείους δὲ
ἀντιλέγουσι γενναιότερον, βαρυτονοῦντες καὶ αὐτὰ κατὰ τὸ φιλότης φιλότητος,
κακότης κακότητος : some think that it was barytone in the nominative δηϊότης,
and properispomenon in the other cases, cf. Herod. π. μ. λ. 40. 8 : ἑρπής, Chœrob.
C. 54. 35, appears to be always paroxytone in our books : ἐσθής, Arc. 28. 9 : ἰσότης,
Mœris 202 : Ἰσότης, ὡς ἀρότης, 'Αττικῶς, ἰσοτὴς ὡς βραβευτής, 'Ελληνικῶς : Herod.
π. μ. λ. 40. 7 declares for ἰότης, ἰσότης, κακότης : Κουρής, Eust. 1179. 20 : ὅτι ἐν
δυσὶ τόποις κούρητας οἴσοντας 'Αχιλλεῖ τὰ δῶρα, ἐνταῦθα λέγει τοὺς νέους, ὅπερ
'Ηρωδιανὸς ἀναγινώσκει τῷ τόνῳ ὡς πένητας, κλίνων ὡς ἰαμβικὸν ἀπὸ τοῦ κόρος ὁ νέος,
κόρης κόρητος. τὸ μέντοι ἔθνος Κουρῆτας ὡς ἀδμῆτας : Schol. Ven. T. 193 ; this
accentuation is condemned by Schol. Ven. I. 529, but E. M. 534. 13 agrees with
Eustathius : κουφοτής, said to be Attic by Arc. 28, and Chœrob. C. 352. 11, but
Herod. π. μ. λ. 40. 7 has κουφότης : ποτής, Arc. 28. 9 ; Chœrob. C. 352. 11 : ταχυτής, Chœrob. C. 352. 11 ; E. M. 103. 1 : τραχυτής, Chœrob. C. 352. 11, in Attic
only : ψιλής, Chœrob. C. 55. 4 ; Eust. 511. 10 : χερνής, Chœrob. C. 55. 4.

636. Note 2.—The passage in Chœrob. C. 55. 3 is obscure : σεσημείωται τὸ
κουρὴς κουρήτος, δηλὴς δειλῆτος (*sic*) καὶ τὸ ψιλὴς ψιλητός, ὅτι τῶν εἰς ΗΣ ὀξυτόνων
δισυλλάβων ἐν σύμφωνον ἐχόντων ὡς ἔγνωμεν, εἰς ΟΤΣ ἐχόντων τὴν γενικήν, οἷον
σαφὴς σαφοῦς ψευδής, ψευδοῦς, ταῦτα διὰ τοῦ ΤΟΣ ἐκλίθησαν· εἰσὶ δὲ ἐθνικά, ἤγουν
ἔθνος σημαίνουσι ; for δηλὴς δειλῆτος perhaps we should read Δαρης Δαρῆτος (cf.
Eust. 511. 10), and write the rest of the passage thus, ἐν πρὸ τοῦ Η σύμφωνον
ἐχόντων, ὡς ἐ. εἰς .ΟΤΣ ἔχουσι, τὴν. γ. κ.τ.λ., and strike out the last three words
altogether.

637. (*b*) All substantives in ης (gen. εος) are, if contracted,

perispomena, if uncontracted, paroxytone, as Ἀντισθένης, Ἀριστοτέλης, Δημοσθένης, Ἡρακλέης, but Ἡρακλῆς, Περικλῆς; except πρυλής oxytone: τριήρης and other similar words are adjectives.

638. NOTE I.—E. M. 435. 4: Ἀλειπής, a fountain at Ephesus, so called from its never failing, fluctuates between an adjectival and substantival accent, it is oxytone in E. M. 60. 47, Orion 618. 11; paroxytone in Etym. Gud. 32. 57; Ἀψευδής, so Aristarchus, Schol. Ven. Σ. 39; Hom. Il. 18. 46: Εὐθαλής (?) is so accented by H. D., but should probably be paroxytone: Ἰαμενής, Suid., should perhaps be Ἰαμένης: Ἰμφής, St. Byz.: Νημερτής, Hom. Il. 18. 46; Schol. Ven. Σ. 39; Chœrob. C. 352. 18: all proper names in κλης=κλέης are perispomena. Eust. 583. 32: τὸ Πυλαιμένης κύριον βαρύνοντες οἱ παλαιοὶ λέγουσιν, ὅτι τὰ τοιαῦτα κύρια ὡς ἐπιπλεῖστον βαρύνεσθαι φιλεῖ. ἡ μέντοι συνήθεια πολλὰ παρέφθειρεν ὀξυτονοῦσα, ὡς τὸ Εὐτυχὴς καὶ τὸ Εὐμενὴς τὰ κύρια: πρυλής, Schol. Ven. Ε. 9: τὰ εἰς ΗΣ δισύλλαβα ὀξύτονα, ἐν ἔχοντα σύμφωνον, εἰς ΟΥΣ περατοῦται κατὰ τὴν γενικήν, σαφοῦς πρηνοῦς πρυλοῦς φραδοῦς. Schol. Ven. Ε. 744: πρυλέεσσ'· πεζοῖς ὁπλίταις, πρύλις, ὡς δαμάσω δάμαλις περύω πέρυλις καὶ πρύλις (sic); the grammarians were therefore not quite agreed as to the form of the nominative singular; πρυλέες in our books is always paroxytone, which implies a nominative πρυλής or πρυλίς, cf. Eust. 893. 37, who leaves the question rather undecided; Arc. 30. 19: τὸ δὲ πρύλις βαρύνεται, ἡ ἔνοπλος ὄρχησις; A. G. Oxon. 1. 342. 6.

639. NOTE 2.—Ἄρης is paroxytone, Arc. 25. 5. The following forms of the genitive occur in the grammarians or elsewhere, Ἄρητος, Ἄρεως, Ἄρου, Ἄρους, Chœrob. C. 46. 5, Ἄρεος, Ἄρηος, Ἄρηως, Ἄρεω, Ἄρενος; on its vocative see Eust. 518. 19.

-ΕΙΣ.

640. Those in εις (gen. εντος) are paroxytone, as Ὀπόεις, Σατινόεις.

-ΙΣ.

641. It may be observed that in general all those which form their accusative in ν are barytone, Arc. 36. 17.

(*a*) Those in ις (gen. ιος and εως) retract the accent, whether simple or compound, as αἴσθησις, ἅλωσις, βάδισις, δόσις, γνῶσις, ἕξις, ζήτησις, θέσις, μάθησις, μάντις, ὄφις, πόλις, πόσις, πρόπολις, Ἄβοτις, Ἀτάρβηχις, Κράμβοτις, Μέμφις, Ψέντρις. Many of these words are inflected in more than one way.

642. NOTE.—Chœrob. C. 56. 33: τὰ εἰς ΙΣ ὀνόματα Αἰγύπτια ὡς ἐπὶ τὸ πλεῖστον διὰ καθαροῦ τοῦ ΟΣ κλίνονται, οἷον Ξόϊς Ξόεως, Ἀθλίβις (sic) Ἀθλίβεως, Σόϊς Σόεως, Θμόϊς Θμόεως, Ταμίαθις Ταμιάθεως, cf. St. Byz. s. v. Κορκυρίς; Schol. Ven. Λ. 676; Ξ. 387: for χατίς, Hesych., it is better to read with Dindorf χᾶτις, as a Doric form of χῆτις: Ἀδραμύττις (?) St. Byz.; for Ἀθλίβις in Chœrob. C. 56. 33: Ἄθλιβις (or Ἄθριβις), St. Byz., is alone correct: Ἀταρβίκις, St. Byz., is no doubt an error for Ἀτάρβικις, or Ἀτάρβηχις: Θμούϊς (?) St. Byz.: Πάπρημις, Herodot. 2. 59, is falsely oxytone in St. Byz., and for Ὠφθίς in the same author Meineke reads Ὄφθις; on the accent of ἧνις see Schol. Ven. Κ. 292: Κραταιίς, Hom. Od. 12. 124; according to Hesych. it is proparoxytone, and it is so accented in Apollon. Rhod. 4. 829; cf. Schol. Ven. Λ. 676. Schol. Aristoph. Ach. 93 : τοῦ πρέσβεως προπαροξυτόνως ὡς μάντεως, ἀπὸ εὐθείας τῆς ὁ πρέσβις. οἱ δὲ παροξυτόνως ὡς χαλκέως, ἀπὸ εὐθείας τῆς ὁ πρεσβεύς. οἵτινες ἁμαρτάνουσι· οὐ γάρ ἐστιν ὁ πρεσβεύς.

643. (*b*) Those in ις (gen. ῖδος) are oxytone, as ἀψίς, βαλβίς, ἰκτίς, κνημίς, κρηπίς, ὀπισθοκρηπῖδες, σφραγίς.

NOTE.—E. M. 518. 16; Arc. 36. 14. The following Thracian names are perispomena : Ἀταγαρτῖς (Ἀταργατῖς, Arc. 36. 18), Chœrob. C. 354. 21 ; Strab. 748 : ἐν ᾗ τιμῶσι τὴν Συρίαν θεὸν τὴν Ἀταργάτιν (*sic*) : Schol. Ven. B. 461 : ἡ δὲ Δερκετὼ παρὰ Σύροις καλεῖται Ἀταργατῖς (ἀτάρκατις in the MS.) : Ἀταρτῖς, Chœrob. C. 103. 25, who also mentions Βενδῖς (but the false form Βένδις is not unknown to the books), Μενδῖς, Μολῖς, Τιτῖς (Τοτῖς, Arc. 36. 14); cf. Göttling, ad Theodos. p. 243.

On μάγαδις, or μαγαδίς, see L. S. and H. D. s. v.; and on ἀψίς, ἀψίδος, or ἄψις, ἄψιδος (?) see E. M. 184. 32; Chœrob. C. 353. 23 : ταῦτα δὲ τὰ εἰς ΙΣ ὀξύτονα εἰς Α μόνως ἔχουσι τὴν αἰτιατικήν, οἷον κρηπίδα (*sic*), ἀσπίδα, ἀψίδα, βολίδα, ῥανίδα. Παρὰ δὲ τοῖς Αἰολεῦσι γίνονται εἰς Ν κατὰ τὴν αἰτιατικὴν μετὰ βαρείας τάσεως, κνήμιν γὰρ λέγουσι καὶ σφράγιν καὶ ἄψιν, ὡς παρ' Ἡσιόδῳ [Opp. 424],

> τρισπίθαμον δ' ἄψιν τάμνειν,

ἀντὶ τοῦ ἀψίδα. Ἰστέον δὲ ὅτι τὰ εἰς ΙΣ ὀξύτονα οὐ γίνονται παρὰ τοῖς Ἴωσι κατὰ ἀποβολὴν τοῦ Δ ἐν τῇ γενικῇ, οὐδὲ γὰρ λέγουσι κνημῖδος κνημῖος, ἀσπίδος ἀσπίος, ὡς Πάριδος Πάριος, καὶ Θέτις Θέτιος.

644. (*c*) Common substantives in ις (gen. ῖδος) being feminine are oxytone, as ἀσπίς, γλυφίς, δαΐς, ἐλπίς, ἐμπίς, ἐφημερίς, κυσολαμπίς, λακίς, ξυστίς, ὀπωροβασιλίς, πατρίς, πηκτίς, πυραμίς, σκελίς, τυραννίς; except 1. ἄμπωτις*, ἄμυστις*, αὖλις, βάκκαρις*, βᾶρις*, δάπις, ἔρις, εὖνις, θέμις*, ἶβις*, ἴκτις, ἶρις, κάλπις, κάνναβις*, καρύατις, κύπρις, μῆνις*, μῆτις*, μύτις, ὄλπις, ὄπις, σίκιννις, τᾶλις, τάπις, τίγρις*, τρόπις*, φύλοπις, which retract the accent, with νεᾶνις (νεῆνις, νῆνις) properispomenon. 2. Feminines formed from, or implying, paroxytone substantives in ης, ending for the most part in αιτις, ατις, ετις, ητις, ῖτις, ῦτις, ωτις, which are accented on the penultimate, as ἀνδρωνῖτις, ἀνεμῶτις, ἀρθρῖτις, Βορεῆτις, Βρομιῶτις, γαμέτις (γαμέτης), ἱκέτις (ἱκέτης), ἱππότις, καρδιᾶτις, κασωρῖτις, κλέπτις (κλέπτης), οἰνοπότις, ὀλβιοδῶτις (ὀλβιοδώτης) and ὀλβιοδότις, ὀνῖτις, πεταλῖτις, πολῖτις (πολίτης), πρεσβῦτις, προηγέτις, προστάτις (προστάτης), συνεργάτις (συνεργάτης), σωρῖτις (σωρίτης), ὑπηρέτις, χλοῦνις (χλούνης); except ναυτίς oxytone, and those in πωλις (πώλης) and κοιτις, which are proparoxytone, as λαχανόπωλις, ἀρτόπωλις, παράκοιτις; yet βούλευτις and ὕβριστις appear to be proparoxytone. Those from oxytones in της are themselves oxy-

---

* Those marked with an asterisk have another genitive besides that in δος.

tone, as στεφανωτίς; εὑρέτις paroxytone forms an exception.
3. Those in ωπις from ὤψ, when not compounded with prepositions, are properispomena, as αὐλῶπις; otherwise they are
regular, as προμετωπίς, προσωπίς.

It must be noticed that many of those in τις have no actual
masculine form corresponding to them in use, and also that no
nouns in ις, ἴδος, are oxytone if they have an accusative in ν.

645. NOTE.—The rules given by Arcadius (28. 13–36. 18) are so confused and
defective that little use can be made of them. The following list contains all the
irregular words that I have noted, but probably it might be much enlarged. On
these words see Lob. Prol. 455 sqq.: ἄβαλις· μοχθηρὰ ἐλαία, Hesych.: ἀγλαοφῶ-
τις (!) 'ἀγλαοφωτίς scribitur ap. Phot. Bib. 215 a. 33 Bekk. Bast. Ind. Scap. Ox.
'Αγλαοφώτιδα [?] accus. Poeta de virib. herbar. in Fabric. Bibl. Gr. T. 2. p. 654 ;'
Fix ap. H. D.: ἄγρωστις (gen. ιος, ιδος), Hom. Od. 6. 90; Arc. 35. 18 ; cf. Lob.
Par. 443: ἄγρωστις is the feminine of ἀγρώστης : ἄμοργις, *wine-lees*, is said by
Arc. 29. 23 to be barytone, but in all the passages quoted by H. D. it is oxytone,
like ἀμοργίς, *fine flax*; Bergk in his edition of Aristophanes most inconsistently
writes ἀμοργίδος, Lyst. 735, and ἄμοργιν only two lines lower down : ἀμφίταπιν in
Diog. Laert. 5. 72 has been corrected in some editions into ἀμφίταπον : ἄμφωτις,
Eust. 308. 44, is elsewhere oxytone. On ἀνάπωτις, ἄμπωτις,· or ἄμπτωσις, see
Lob. Phryn. 340 : for ἄρυστις, gen. ιδος, I can find no authority ! in the passage
cited by L. S. the genitive is ιος : αὖλις, Arc. 31. 1 : αὖλις ἡ ἔπαυλις [βαρύνεται],
Αὐλὶς δὲ ἡ πόλις ὀξύνεται: βαύκαλις, Arc. 31. 10 : βολβίτις or βολβῖτις (?) Lob.
Phryn. 357 : βούβαλις (gen. ιος, ιδος), Arc. 31. 9, is oxytone in Hesych. and Arist.
H. A. 3. 6. 2 : βούπρηστις (gen. εως, but Nicand. Alex. 335, quoted by H. D. has
ιδος) is falsely βουπρῆστις in Heysch : δάϊς, *battle*, Herodian is inclined to make
this word oxytone, but whether oxytone or not, he has no doubt that the dative
δάϊ should be oxytone ; Ptolemæus Ascalonites consistently writes both nominative
and dative paroxytone ; see Schol. Ven. Ξ. 387, and such must be its accent
because the accusative is δάϊν ; Schol. Hom. Od. A. 428 : δαῒς ὀξυτόνως ἡ λαμπάς,
δάϊς δὲ βαρυτόνως ἡ μάχη : δαῖτις (?), in Galen Tom. 1. p. 88 B it is oxytone :
ἔπηλις, Arc. 31. 12 ; Eust. 1562. 38 : ἐφηλίς (gen. ιδος) also occurs as ἔφηλις (gen.
ιος), see H. D. s. v.: ἔρις, Arc. 195. 5 ; Chœrob. C. 355. 19 : εὔμαρις, Arc. 34. 4, is
oxytone in Eurip. Orest. 1370 : εὖνις (gen. ιδος and ιος), Arc. 32. 17 : ἴασπις,
L. S., H. D.: ἴβις (gen. ιος and ιδος), ' constans in libris accentus vitium est ἴβις,
quod correxi ap. Aristoph. Av. 1296. Nam ι produci apparet ex versu Timoclis
ap. Athen. 7. p. 300 A ;' W. Dindorf ap. H. D.: ἴκτις, Arc. 35. 6 : Eust. 809. 56 : εἰ
δὲ καὶ ταὐτὸν ἴκτις αὕτη βαρυτόνως (i. e. the weasel), καὶ ἰκτὶς ὀξυτόνως ἡ παρὰ τῇ
κωμικῷ [Aristoph. Ach. 845] μεμνημένῳ ἰχθυοφάγου ἰκτίδος, οὐκ ἀναγκαῖον ἄρτι
ζητεῖν : ἵππουρις, A. G. 44 ; A. G. Oxon. 1. 210. 30 ; Lob. Prol. 461 : ἱππότιγρις,
masculine and *feminine*, Dio Cass. 77. 6 ; H. D.: ἴρις or ἴρις, Chœrob. C. 355. 19 :
ἴσατις is sometimes falsely ἰσάτις : κάλπις, Arc. 33. 10 ; A. G. Oxon. 2. 342. 23,
is oxytone in Athen. 468 F, quoted by H. D.: κάνναβις (gen. εως, ιος, and ιδος),
Arc. 29. 17 : κάπαρις, Chœrob. C. 355. 29 : καπηλίς : ' Caupona ... Aristoph.
Thesm. 347, Pl. 435. 1120 ; κάπηλις proparoxytonum ap. Aread. 31. 12, et hoc accentu Phanias Eresius ap. Athen. 2. p. 84 E : κάπηλίς τις γυνή. Itemque Œnom.
ap. Euseb. Pr. Ev. p. 259 A : μὴ πλουσίαν λαβεῖν γυναῖκα ἀλλὰ χερνῆτίν τινα ἢ
κάπηλιν,' H. D.: κίθαρις (gen. ιδος? and ιος), Chœrob. C. 355. 18 : κίσηρις
(gen. ιδος and εος), Chœrob. C. 355. 26 ; E. 132. 11 : κιστίς, Arc. 35. 16, is paroxytone in Aristoph. Ach. 1103 : κύβηλις (gen. ιος and ιδος ?) Arc. 31. 12 : κύμιν-

δις (gen. εως and ιδος): **κυνοπρῆστις** (?) Hesych.: **ληῖς**, Aristarchus, but **λῆϊς**, Menecrates, Schol. Ven. Λ. 676: **λινόζωστις** (gen. ιδος and ιος) is sometimes written λινοζῶστις: **μῆλις** for μηλίς is an error, Arc. 30. 23: **μῆνις** (gen. ιος and ιδος): 'μηνίς voluisse Glauconem Tarsensem refert Schol. Hom. Il. A. 1, et oxytonum μηνίς non dicens quid sit, ponit Draco, p. 23. 25; 45. 27: quorum ll. priori ex altero τὰ γὰρ ἄλλα vel ἄλλα πάντα, utroque autem Μινωΐς corrigendum videtur pro μηνίς ex Regg. prosod. p. 447 n. 118 ult. *Mῆνις* præcipit Aread. 32. 13; 196. 5;' H. D. It may be doubted whether the emendation is wanted: Glaucon probably meant what is reported of him: **μύτις**, Arist. H. A. 4. 1. 19, is μυττίς (*sic*) in Hesych.: **νεᾶνις**, Arc. 32. 20: **ξύστις**, Schol. Aristoph. Nub. 70; Schol. Theocr. 2. 74: ξύστις Ἀττικῶς, ξυστὶς δὲ κοινῶς, but it seems to be oxytone in our editions whether of Attic writers or others: **ὄλπις**, Theocr. 18. 45: **ὄνωνις**, 'ὀνῶνις, ὀνώνιδος, scriptum ap. Chœrob. [C.] 354. 31, et in Etym. M. 626. 35;' H. D.: **οὖλις**, 'i. q. οὖλον, Alex. Trall. 8. p. 483;' H. D.: **πέρσις** (gen. ιδος, Paus. 10. 25. 5, H. D.) Arist. Poet. 18. 15; cf. Lob. Phryn. 607: Περσίς is from Πέρσης, Arc. 36. 2; Schol. Ven. Ξ. 387: **πλημμυρίς**, Eust. 1640. 55: τὸ δὲ πλημυρὶς τινὲς τῶν παλαιῶν προπαροξύνουσι, καὶ δι' ἑνὸς δὲ Μ γράφουσιν ὡς ἀπὸ τῆς πλήμης: cf. E. M. 676. 30, where πλημμύρις (*sic*) and πλημμυρίς occur; cf. A. G. Paris 3. 463. 15: **πόρπις**, Arc. 33. 10, yet πορπίς, *a brooch*, is oxytone in Hesych.: **πρῆστις** (?): προκνίς is paroxytone in Eust. 1688. 31, quoted by H. D.: **πτέρις** is sometimes oxytone: ῥαπίς, E. M. 702. 33, is paroxytone in Eust. 658. 58: **στέρις** (gen. εως and ιδος): **σίκιννις** 'accentum σικιννίς in locis Luciani [Salt. c. 22 and 26; Pollux 4. 99] refellit σίκιννιν ap. Dionys. A. R. 7. 72. med. p. 1491. 4;' *H. D*: **σίννις**, ὄρνεον ἁρπακτικόν, Zonar. 1644, σίνις is masculine: **σμύρις**, Diosc. 5. 166. H. D.: **τᾶλις**, Arc. 30. 25: **τάπις**, Xenoph. Anab. 7. 3. 18: **τῆλις** (gen. ιος, εως, and ιδος) Arc. 30. 24: **τίγρις** (gen. ιος and ιδος) is also masculine: **τράμπις**, Arc. 33. 9; E. M. 157. 21; Chœrob. E. 150. 30: **τρόπηλις**, Arc. 31. 14, also τρόπαλλις, which is oxytone in Aristoph. Ach. 778: **τρόπις** (gen. ιος, εως, and ιδος) Arc. 33: **τυρόκνηστις** (accus. τυρόκνηστιν) is falsely τυροκνῆστις in Athen. 169 B: **ὑποκιστίς** is sometimes proparoxytone: **φύλοπις**, Arc. 33. 15: **χρυσομήτρις** in Arist. H. A. 8. 3. 6 is very suspicious: **ψιλόδαπις**, Athen. 255 E, where Dindorf has ψιλόταπις: **κόνις**, *dust*, is distinguished both by its inflexion and accent from **κονίς**, *a nit*, Arc. 37. 2; Ammon. 84.

646. *Paronyma in ις from Masculines in ης.*—The following passages from the grammarians embody their general doctrine as to the accent of this class of words, which may be considered rather as adjectives than substantives, at least in very many cases: Schol. Ven. I. 571: τὰ εἰς ΙΣ παρώνυμα θηλυκά, παρακείμενα τοῖς εἰς ΗΣ ἀρσενικοῖς βαρυνομένοις προπερισπᾶται, εἰ φύσει μακρᾷ παραλήγοιτο, πρωθῆβις, πολιῆτις, ἀλεῖτις, πλανῆτις, πρεσβῦτις· οὕτως δὴ καὶ ἠεροφοῖτις. ὅσα δὲ παρὰ τὸ πωλεῖν ἀνεβίβασε τὸν τόνον, ἀρτόπωλις, ἀλφιτόπωλις· ἀλλ' οὖν καὶ ὅσα παρὰ τὸ κοῖτος παράκοιτις, ἄκοιτις. τὸ μέντοι δολόμητις οὐκ ἔστι θηλυκόν, ἀλλὰ καὶ ἀρσενικόν. καὶ ἴσως τὸ μῆτις ἔγκειται, ὡς τὸ πολύμητις, δολόμητις, καὶ ἔστι σύνθετον: Schol. Ven. P. 40: Φρόντιδι ὡς Ἥλιδι· οὕτως Τυραννίων, καὶ ἐπείσθη ἡ παράδοσις. ὁ μέντοι κανὼν ὀξυτονεῖ τὸ φρόντις· τὰ γὰρ εἰς ΤΙΣ λήγοντα θηλυκὰ δισύλλαβα, μὴ ὄντα ἐπιθετικὰ παραληγόμενα δὲ τῷ Ο, ἤτοι μόνῳ ἢ σὺν ἑτέρῳ φωνήεντι, ὀξύνεσθαι θέλει, κοιτίς Προιτίς, φροντίς, οὗτίς τὸ ζῶον παρ' Ἀλκμᾶνι. οὕτως οὖν καὶ φροντίς, εἰ μὴ ἄρα, ἐπεὶ κύριον τοῦτο, καὶ βαρυτονηθήσεται. οὐ μάχεται τὸ πόρτις· καὶ γὰρ χωρὶς τοῦ Τ, πόρι ες π ε ρ ὶ βοῦς ἀγελαίας. μὴ ὄντα ἐπιθετικὰ πρόσκειται διὰ τὸ πότις ᾧ παράκειται τὸ πότης : Chœrob. C. 356. 13: ἰστέον δὲ ὅτι πάντα ταῦτα τὰ εἰς ΙΣ θηλυκὰ τὰ γινόμενα ἀπὸ τῶν εἰς ΗΣ ἀρσενικῶν, ὑπὲρ δύο συλλαβὰς ὄντα, πρὸ μιᾶς ἔχουσι τὸν τόνον, οἷον ὁ κυνηγέτης καὶ ἡ κυνηγέτις, ὁ δεσπότης, καὶ ἡ δεσπότις, ὁ τοξότης καὶ ἡ τοξότις, ὁ πολίτης καὶ ἡ πολίτις [πολῖτις]. Σεσημείωται ἐν τῷ κανόνι τὰ παρὰ τὸ κοίτη καὶ τὰ παρὰ τὸ πωλῶ· ταῦτα γὰρ προπαροξύνονται ἐν τοῖς θηλυκοῖς, οἷον ἄκοιτις, παράκοιτις, πορφυρόπωλις, ἀρτόπωλις, λαχανόπωλις. Πρόσκειται ὑπὲρ δύο συλλαβάς, τῇ μήνιδι, τῇ ἔριδι, τῇ τοξότιδι, τὴν μήνιδα, τὴν ἔριδα, τὴν τοξότιδα, καὶ μῆνιν καὶ ἔριν καὶ τοξότιν : E. M. 595. 36 : μύστις παρὰ τὸ μύστης· τοῦτο παρὰ τὸ μύω. Οὐ μόνον δὲ ἀπὸ βαρυτόνου γίνεται εἰς I παρώνυμον, οἷον πλανήτης πλανῆτις· ἀλλὰ καὶ ἀπὸ ὀξυτόνου, οἷον ὑβριστής, ὕβριστις· αἰχμητής, αἴχμητις· βουλευτής, βούλευτις. It is possible that the scribe has affixed wrong accents to these words, unless indeed they form their accusative in ιν : Arc. 35. 24 : τὰ εἰς ΙΣ θηλυκὰ ἀπὸ τῶν εἰς ΗΣ ἀρσενικῶν γενόμενα πρὸ μιᾶς ἔχουσι τὸν τόνον· ὁ κυνηγέτης ἡ κυνηγέτις, ὁ δεσπότης ἡ δεσπότις, ὁ πολίτης ἡ πολῖτις, χωρὶς τῶν ἀπὸ τῆς κοίτης καὶ πωλῶ· ταῦτα γὰρ προπαροξύνονται· ἄκοιτις παράκοιτις, ἀρτόπωλις, λαχανόπωλις. τὸ Σκυθὶς δὲ δισυλλαβοῦν ὀξύνεται, ὡς τὸ Περσίς. It is a mistake to infer from this last passage that Σκυθὶς and Περσίς are oxytone merely because they are dissyllables ; of the former word Σκύθιν occurs beside Σκυθίδα, and therefore it would seem that Σκύθις is not to be condemned as false : Schol. in Æschinem κατὰ Κτησιφῶντος, 172 : Σκύθιν· ὡς ἀπ' εὐθείας εἴρηται τοῦτο μᾶλλον βαρυτόνου· κακῶς δέ. τὰ γὰρ τοιαῦτα ἐθνικὰ ὀξύνεσθαι θέλει, ὡς Κολχίς, Περσίς, Σκυθίς, οὐκοῦν Σκυθίδα καὶ οὐ Σκύθιν, ὡς τὸ Κολχίδα, Περσίδα. τινὰ δὲ τῶν βιβλίων ἔχει κτητικῶς Σκυθικήν. Ἄγροτις, St. Byz., is given as the feminine of ἀγρότης : ἄκοιτις is the feminine of ἀκοίτης : on αἰχμαλωτίς and αἰχμαλῶτις (?) Lob. Ajax 88 : αὐθεντίς from αὐθέντης is a singular deviation from rule, Arc. 35. 23 : βούλευτις, E. M. 595. 40 ; Lob. Phryn. 256 : ὀρυκτίς (ὀρύκτης), Anna Comnena 380 C. ; H. *D.* is a doubtful accent : λιμνῆστις is probably wrong : for λινόζωστις (gen. εως and ιδος) λινοζῶστις is also met with : μύστης makes μύστις, and πλάστης πλάστις, πλάτης πλᾶτις ; yet ναύτης forms ναυτίς : ὕβριστις from ὑβριστής is also remarkable, if correct, see Lob. Phryn. 256 : οἰφόλις and μαινόλις from οἰφόλης, μαινόλης are regular : σύμμυστις (?) Theophyl. Simoc. Hist. p. 79. 13. ed. Bonn ; H. *D.* : the passage does not prove this to be the right accent. It is not uncommon to find those in πωλις misaccented even in the best lexicons : on καρυῶτις and περονῆτις, see H. D. s. v.

647. Feminine oxytones in ις retain their accent in composition, provided they retain their gender, as αἰγίς καταιγίς, νυχίς παννυχίς, σκελίς περισκελίς.

NOTE.—Arc. 28. 19 ; E. M. 333. 21 ; Chœrob. E. 92. 35 ; Lob. Prol. 455 ; Schol. Ven. B. 175 : the substance of which passage is that oxytones in ις retain their accent as long as they remain substantives, but as adjectives they retract it, as ἐλπίς εὔελπις, ἀσπίς λεύκασπις.

648. Masculine proper names in ις (gen. ἴδος) retract the accent, as Ἀγέπολις, Ἆγις, Ἄδωνις, Ἆκις (a river in Sicily, Theocr. 1. 64), Ἄλκις, Ἄναμις, Ἆπις, Γράνις, Θέσπις. Σποράκις, Suid. is false for Σποράκης.

649. Feminine proper names and patronymics in ις (gen. ἴδος) are oxytone, as Ἀκίς, Αὐτοθαΐς, Βαυκίς, Δαυλίς, Ἐλπίς, Εὐρυλεωνίς, Εὐτυχίς, Θαΐς, Θηβαΐς, Θεσπρωτίς ; except 1. those in τις from paroxytone masculines in της, which are accented on the penultimate, as Ἀλκέτις, Βαιῶτις, Βαρκέτις, Ἑστιαιῶτις, Ζεφυρῖτις, Ζεφυριῶτις, Καρεῶτις, Καρκινῖτις, Κερκιννῖτις, Λιβανῖτις, Λιμενῶτις, Λογγᾶτις, Μύστις (Nonn. Dionys. 9. 99), Παγχενῖτις, Σαῶτις ; 2. those in ωπις, which are properispomena, as Γοργῶπις,

Ἐριῶπις, Ἐσῶπις, Ῥοδῶπις, Ὦπις ; except Εὐρωπίς, Κυκλωπίς, Προσωπίς ; 3. all in πολις (gen. πολιδος) are proparoxytone ; 4. the following retract the accent, Ἄλκηστις *, Ἄμαστρις *, Ἄρτεμις, Βριτόμαρτις. Ἔρις, Ἦλις, Θέμις *, Θέτις, Ἶρις, Ἶσις, Κύπρις, Παρύσατις, Σεμίραμις, Φᾶσις, together with some others of less importance mentioned below.

650. Note.—Cf. Schol. Ven. Λ. 677 ; E. M. 518. 16 ; Lob. Prol. 512 ; the genitive cases of some of the following words are doubtful : Ἀβαντίς, Eust. 281. 29, is falsely Ἀβάντις in St. Byz., though it is rightly oxytone in the next line : Ἄξιλις or Ἄξιρις, St. Byz. : Αἰητίς? (Αἰήτης), *Pape* : Ἄνθις, Athen. 586 B, ' scribendum Ἀνθίς ;' *L. Dindorf* ap. H. D. : Ἀνοῦτις (?) Athen. 609 A : Ἄρτεμις, Arc. 32. 3 : Ἀρχίδαμις, *Pape* : Αὐλίς is oxytone, Arc. 31. 2, though the accusative Αὖλιν occurred in Euphorion, Schol. Ven. B. 496 : Αὐλίκωμις, *Pape* : Βάρχις (?) *Pape* : Βάσιλις, St. Byz. is rightly Βασιλίς in Paus. 8. 29. 5 : Βῆγις, *Pape* : Βούλις, Paus. 10. 37. 2 : Βριτόμαρτις (gen. ιδος, E. M. 214. 23 ; also εως) : Βύβλις (?) *Pape*, as the name of a spring it is oxytone in Theocr. 7. 115 : Γίγγις or Γίγις, Suid. ; Plut. 1. 1020 : Δάμαρις, Act. Apost. 17. 34 : Δαμόκρατις (?) : Δάφνις, Paus. 10. 5. 5 : Ἔρις, personified, Hom. : Εὐῆρις, Paus. 1. 27. 4 : Εὐρύθεμις, Apollod. 1. 7. 10 : Εὐρύκωμις, Eumath. de Ismen. amor. p. 2 : Εὐφράτις secund. Etym. M. p. 157. 51, dicta Assyria s. Babylonia : quod scribendum Εὐφρατίς, ut est ap. St. Byz. ;' H. D. : Ἦλις, Arc. 31. 1 : Θάπις, Phot. Bib. 62. 22 : Θέστυλις, Theocr. 2. 69 : Θέτις, E. M. 676. 32 : Ἱλάρις (?) St. Byz. : Ἶρις, Eust. 391. 33 : A. G. Oxon. 2. 221. 9 : Ἶσις, very often falsely written Ἴσις : Ἴφις, Apollod. 2. 7. 8 : Κάνυτις (? gen.) St. Byz. : Κνῆμις, *Pape* : Κορωνίς : ' Nomen [pro]paroxytonum potius esse Κόρωνις videtur Göttlingio De accentt. p. 271, propter Hesiod. fr. ap. schol. Pind. Pyth. 3. 14 et 48, ubi accusativus est Κόρωνιν, male Κορωνίν scriptus : verum quum accusativo Κορωνίδα Pausanias utatur 2. 11. 7 et 26. 6, rectius sic statuemus, legitimam hanc esse nominis formam, ab Hesiodo solo propter metri necessitatem in Κόρωνιν mutatam,' *W. Dindorf* ap. H. D. : Κρεῦσις (gen. ιος, St. Byz. ιδος, Paus. 9. 32. 1) : Κυλάβαρις, Plut. 2. 817 : Κύπρις, E. M. 676. 32 : Λάμαξις (? gen.) : Μάκρις, Arc. 33. 18 : Μέμφις (gen. ιδος and ιος), see above, § 642 : Μένουθις (? gen.), Arc. 30. 5 : Μεσάτις (?) *Pape* : Μῆτις, Apollod. 1. 2. 1 : Μῖσις, Anth. Append. 240 : Μούζουρις, Lucian de Hist. scrib. c. 31 : Μοῦσις, Inscr. : Νέφερις (? gen.), Strab. 834 : Νίκιππις, Anth. Palat. 7. 186. 1, quoted by H. D. : Ξενέφυρις (? gen.), St. Byz. : Ξύστις (? gen. ιος), St. Byz. : Ὀδάτις (?) Athen. 575 B : Ὀνασίφορις (?) Inser. : Ὀνησικράτις : Ὀρόβατις : Οὖπις : Ηαρύσατις, Xenoph. Anab. 1. 1 is paroxytone in some editions of Plut. : Περίαπις, Apollod. 3. 13. 8 : Πλεῖστις, Inscr. : Πράκτις (?) Lycoph. 1045 : Πρήμνις, Strab. 820 : Πρόκρις, Arc. 33. 18, is falsely oxytone in Athen. 553 B : Πρόμηθις, Anth. Pal. 13. 27 : Πυῆνις, St. Byz. : Ῥοδῶπις, Herodot. 2. 134 : Σάραπις (an island), St.Byz. : Σάργαντις (? gen.), St. Byz. : Σεμίραμις, Arc. 32. 3 : Σισίγυλις (?) St. Byz. : Στεῖρις, Paus. 10. 3. 2 : Σύβαρις (gen. ιος, ιδος, and εως) : Σύρτις (gen. ιος, ιδος, and εως) : Τάλμις, Phot. Bib. 62. 22 : Τάναϊς (gen. ιος and ιδος) : Τεῦθις, Paus. 10. 3. 2 ; the MSS. vary between this and Τευθίς : Τεύωχις (? gen.), St. Byz. : Τίριξις (? gen.), Strab. 319 : Τίσις, St. Byz. : the woman's name Τίσις in Anth. Pal. 6. 274 should be oxytone : Τούκκις (? gen.), Strab. 141 : Τρόπις (?) St. Byz. : Τυῆνις (?) St. Byz. : Τύνις, Strab. 834 : Φάρξιρις (?) Strab. 785 : Φασηλίς, St. Byz. : Ἡρωδιανὸς δὲ μόνος νῆσόν φησι καὶ προπαροξύνεσθαι. τὸ μέντοι ἀγγεῖον οἱ ἐπ' Ἀλεξανδρείας ὀξύνουσι ; in the books it occurs sometimes with one accent and sometimes with the other : Φέρσις, Inscr. : Φρόντις, Hom. Il. 17. 40 : ' quod Φροντίδι potius scribendum esse comparatis aliis hujusmodi femininis recte judicat Lobeck.

Pathol. Proleg. p. 512, de quo dissenserunt grammatici, ut apparet ex scholio Herodiani [Schol. Ven. P. 40] Φρόντιδι ὡς Ἡλιδι Τυραννίων, καὶ ἐπείσθη ἡ παράδοσις, ὁ μέντοι κανὼν ὀξυτονεῖ τὸ Φροντίς (ut Προιτίς et alia), conf. etiam Eustath. p. 907. 12 ; 1063 sq. ;' H. *D.* : Χάρμις (?) St. Byz. : Χίρις, Phot. Bibl. 62. 22 : Χλωρίς : 'Accentus nominis proprii in libris plerumque est Χλῶρις rarius Χλωρίς quod in χωρίς corruptum in codicibus Apollod. 3. 5. 6 : quem accentum probat Lobeck. Pathol. Prol. p. 512,' H. *D.* ; it has an accusative Χλῶριν as well as Χλωρίδα : Χρυσόθεμις, Arc. 32. 4.

651. (*d*) Those in ις (gen. ιτος) retract the accent, as χάρις.

NOTE.—Chœrob. C. 355. 21 : χάρις χάριδος, καὶ χάριτος Δωρικῶς τροπῇ τοῦ Δ εἰς τὸ Τ, ὅπερ καὶ παρ' ἡμῖν ἐπεκράτησε.

652. (*e*) Those in ις (gen. ιθος) are paroxytone, as ἄγλις, βάλλις, Βέλλις, γέλγις, δέλλις, ὄρνις.

NOTE.—Arc. 29. 21 ; 30. 26 ; Theodos. Gr. 94. 17 ; Draco 10. 11 ; 45. 11 : Ἄγλις is oxytone in Chœrob. C. 353. 12, and Brunck and Bekker seem to prefer that accent.

653. (*f*) Those in ις (gen. ῖνος) are oxytone, as Ἀβοριγίς, Ἀβοριγῖνες, ἀκτίς, δελφίς, Ἐλευσίς, Σαλαμίς, Τελχίς.

NOTE.—These also end in ιν, as δελφίν, Σαλαμίν, etc. ; Chœrob. C. 278. 18 ; Arc. 10. 1.

-ΙΝΣ and -ΥΝΣ.

654. Those in ινς (gen. ινθος) and υνς (gen. υνθος) are paroxytone, as ἄδμινς, ἕλμινς, πείρινς, Τίρυνς, Chœrob. C. 66. 31.

-ΕΥΣ.

655. All in ευς, whether simple or compound, are oxytone, without exception, as Ἀχιλλεύς, βασιλεύς, γλυφεύς, γραμματεύς, Ἑρμογλυφεύς, ἱερεύς, Θησεύς, Ὀδυσσεύς, Πηλεύς, ὑπογραμματεύς.

NOTE.—Arc. 93. 4 ; in Æolic these words are barytone, as Ἀχίλλευς, Πῆλυς, Ἄτρευς, Ἄρευς, Chœrob. C. 209. 11 ; 60. 10 ; Eust. 518. 37 ; E. M. 189. 40. On the various forms of the genitive case (eight in number) see Chœrob. E. 70. 16 ; some, oddly enough, wrote ἵππευς for ἱππεύς, A. G. Oxon 1. 345. 13.

-ΟΥΣ.

656. Those in ους = όεις (gen. ουντος) are perispomena, whether they are simple or compound, as Ἀγνοῦς, Ἀχερδοῦς, κοπτοπλακοῦς, Μαραθοῦς, μελιτοῦς, μηλοπλακοῦς, πλακοῦς, Σελινοῦς, σησαμοῦς, Φηγοῦς, Φλιοῦς.

NOTE.—Eust. 277. 13 ; 1114. 2 ; Arc. 93. 6 ; Chœrob. C. 238. 6.

657. The rest are paroxytone, as Οἰδίπους, πολύπους ; except ὀδούς oxytone.

NOTE.—Eust. 277. 13 ; 1114. 2 ; Arc. 93. 6 ; Chœrob. C. 238. 6 ; E. M. 615. 30 : such words as πολύπους have been provided for above, § 575.

-ΥΣ.

658. (*a*) Common substantives in υς (gen. υος, εως) retract their accent, as ἀτράφαξυς, βότρυς, γένυς, γῆρυς, ἔγχελυς, πέλεκυς, πῆχυς, χέλυς ; except oxytone, 1. those in τυς, as ἀγορατύς, γελαστός, διωκτύς, καταπλαστύς, κλιτύς, (yet δίκτυες, Herodot. 4. 192, ἴτυς, μάρπτυς? μίτυς? Arist. H. A. 9. 40. 10, πίτυς, Arc. 92, φῖτυς, together with μάρτυς and its compounds, as αὐτόμαρτυς, ἐπίμαρτυς, ὁσιόμαρτυς, ψευδόμαρτυς, retract the accent) ; and 2. ἀχλύς, δελφύς, εἰλύς and ἰλύς, Ἐρινύς, ἰγνύς, ἰθύς, ἰξύς, ἰσχύς, ἰχθύς, λιγνύς, νηδύς, οἰζύς, ὀσφύς, ὀφρύς, πληθύς, τηθύς.

659. NOTE.—E. M. 565. 9: Ἀχνύς (?) E. M. 182. 1: γρῆϋς or γρηῦς, cf. H. D. s. v. γραῖα; E. M. 440. 16; A. G. Oxon. 1. 182. 25; 3. 237. 16: εἰλύς (ἰλύς), Chœrob. C. 358. 26: ἐλινύες, Polyb. 21. 1. 1; H. *D*.: Ἐρινύς, Arc. 92. 9; E. M. 374. 9: ἰξύς, Chœrob. C. 232. 26: τὸ γὰρ ἰξύς, σημαίνει δὲ καὶ αὐτὸ τὴν ῥάχιν, εἰ καὶ παρατέθειται ὁ Ἡρωδιανὸς ἐν τῷ Ὀνοματικῷ ὡς περισπώμενον, ἀλλ᾿ οὖν οὐ περισπᾶται ἀλλ᾿ ὀξύνεται, ὥς φησιν ἐν τῇ Καθόλου: cf. Arc. 92. 14: ἰσχύς has υ short in Pind. N. 11. 41; cf. L. S. s. v.: Ἴσχυς is a proper name: ἰχθύς, ʻde accentu Arc. 91. 11: τὸ ἰχθῦς περιεσπάσθη ἀλόγως. Herod. π. μ. λ. 31. 5: οὐδὲν εἰς ΥΣ λῆγον ἀρσενικὸν ὑπὲρ μίαν συλλαβὴν μὴ ἔχον ὑποκοριστικὴν ἔννοιαν περισπᾶσθαι θέλει ...... ὥστε εἰ περισπᾶται τὸ ἰχθῦς ἔστω θηλυκόν· εἰ δ᾿ ἀρσενικόν ἐστιν, ὀφείλει ὅμοιον εἶναι τῷ στάχυς, βότρυς:ʼ H. *D*.: κλιτύς, Schol. Ven. Π. 390: ἐχρῆν μὲν διὰ τὸ κλιτύας οὐρῆας περισπᾶσθαι τὸ κλιτῦς, ἀνεγνώσθη δὲ κατ᾿ ὀξεῖαν τάσιν ἐν ἐγκλίσει, ὁμοίως τῷ κ ν η μ ῖ δ α ς ῥ α π τ ὰ ς δ έ δ ε τ ο, γ ρ α π τ ὺ ς ἀ λ ε ε ί ν ω ν (Od. 24. 228). σχόλιον· ἐν μέντοι τῇ Ὀδυσσειακῇ προσῳδίᾳ φανερῶς τὸ γραπτὺς περισπᾷ, καί φησιν ὅτι εἴη εἰρηκὼς ὡς καὶ τὸ κλιτῦς δεῖ περισπᾶσθαι. ἀμφίβολος οὖν ἐφ᾿ ἑκατέρων ὁ τόνος· εἰ γὰρ τοῖς ἐνταῦθα εἰρημένοις πεισθείημεν, ἐκεῖνο ἀνθέλκει, εἰ δὲ ἐκείνοις, τοῦτο πάλιν ἀντίκειται: νηδύς, Arc. 92. 10; Chœrob. C. 359. 1: οἰζῦς,. Arc. 92. 9: οισύς (??): ὀσφύς: ʻAccentum Herodian. π. μ. λ. 31. 16 et Jo. Alex. 8. 33, Arc. 92. 11 præcipiunt ὀσφῦς: ita liber unus 1. Æsch. [Prometh. 498], qui ὀφρῦν, ceteri ὀσφύν;ʼ *H*. *D*. Reg. Pros. ap. Herm. de emend. rat. Gr. gr. p. 450: τὰ εἰς ΥΣ εἴτε ἀρσενικὰ εἴτε θηλυκά, ὀξύνονται [?], ταχύς, βραδύς, ἰχθύς, χλαμύς. τὸ μέντοι ὀσφὺς εὗρον παρὰ τοῖς παλαιοῖς περισπώμενον· ἀλλὰ κατὰ συνήθειαν ὄξυνε: cf. Eust. 1859. 14: ὀφρύς: ʻAccentum ὀφρῦς præcipit non solum Arc. 92. 11, sed ipse Herod. π. μ. λ. 31. 15; alterum ὀφρύς, qui non infrequens in libris, neuter videtur cognitum habuisse;ʼ H. *D*.: πληθύς, Arc. 92. 9; Chœrob. E. 67. 8: it will be seen that the exceptions are for the most part feminines with a long final syllable; cf. Arc. 92. 9; Chœrob. C. 231. 32; 357. 18: ἔγχελυς is sometimes found as ἐγχέλυς; on which and the various forms of the word see H. D. s. v. and Göttling, Accent, p. 261.

660. Proper names in υς (gen. υος, εως) retract, as Ἅλυς, Ἕρπυς, Καλαμόδρῦς, Λίβυς, Πόλτυς, Ῥαδάμανθυς; except Τηθύς oxytone.

661. NOTE.—Herod. π. μ. λ. 32. 35. The relative passage in Arc. 91. 9 stands thus in Barker's edition: τὰ εἰς ΥΣ πολυσύλλαβα κύρια ἢ προσηγορικὰ βαρύνεται, πόλτυς, βότρυς, ἔρπυς, ἅλυς. The Paris MS. 2603 adds ἢ ἐθνικά after the word προσηγορικά, and this Schmidt has corrected into μὴ ἐθνικά, adding

'Correxi ope Herod. St. Byz. 207. 12 ubi Γηλύς· ἔθνος—ὀξύνεται δέ. The emendation may be good, but the following exceptions occur: Δαψολίβυες: Μάζυες, St. Byz.: Λίβυς, St. Byz.; A. G. Oxon. 1. 147. 18: Μάκρυες, St. Byz.; Μάχρυες, Ptol. 4. 3. 26: Βλέμμυες, Ptol. 4. 7. 31 (Βλέμνες, St. Byz.) and others: Βαθύς, a river so called, Ptol. 3. 4. 4, is no exception, since the name was Βαθὺς ποταμός: on Βρίηπυς see Schol. Ven. Ν. 521; Ἰχθύς, as the name of a place, is oxytone in Thucyd. 2. 25.

662. (*b*) Diminutives in υς (gen. υ) are perispomena in all cases, as ἀπφῦς, Διονῦς, Καμμῦς, Καρδῦς, Κλαυσῦς, Λαρδῦς.

NOTE.—Arc. 92. 13; Joh. Alex. 8. 34; Herod. π. μ. λ. 31. 6; Chœrob. C. 62. 27; 123. 3 (in which passage some are falsely oxytone); 225. 1; 232. 14.

663. (*c*) Those in υς (gen. υδος) are oxytone, as δαγύς, κροκύς, πηλαμύς, χλαμύς.

NOTE.—Arc. 22. 1; Chœrob. C. 358. 21; 359. 17; 232. 3: Πάλαμυς Παλάμυος· τὸ γὰρ Παλάμυδος διὰ τοῦ ΔΟΣ κλιθὲν παρὰ Αἰσχύλῳ ἡμάρτηται. ἔστι δὲ ὄνομα κύριον βασίλεως: words like ἔπηλυς, ὅμηλυς are adjectives.

664. (*d*) Those in υς (gen. υθος) retract the accent, as κόρυς, κῶμυς; except ἀγνύς oxytone.

NOTE.—Chœrob. C. 358. 1; 359. 17: δεῖ δὲ σημειώσασθαι ἐν τῷ κανόνι τὸ ἀγνὺς ἀγνῦθος, τοῦτο γὰρ ὀξύτονον ὄν, καὶ μακρὸν ἔχον τὸ ΥΣ, διὰ τοῦ ΘΟΣ ἐκλίθη καὶ οὐ διὰ καθαροῦ τοῦ ΟΣ. Ἀγνῦθες δὲ λέγονται οἱ λίθοι οἱ περιφερεῖς καὶ τετρη-[μ]μένοι οἱ κρεμάμενοι ἐν τοῖς ἱταρίοις (μιταρίοις); cf. Pollux 7. 36; ἄγνυθες is therefore an error.

-ΩΣ.

665. (*a*) Those in ως (gen. ωος or ω) are paroxytone, as Ἄθως, ἕως, ἥρως, μήτρως, Μίνως, πάτρως.

NOTE.—Arc. 94. 10; Chœrob. C. 65. 8; Schol. Ven. Γ. 122: according to Chœrob. C. 360. 25, ἄλωος, as a genitive of ἅλως, is a modern blunder (πταῖσμα νεωτερικόν ἐστι): Ἀπολλώς Ἀπολλῶ ὄνομα κύριον Ἀττικῶς (Act. Apost. 18. 24), Suid.

666. (*b*) Those in ως (gen. οος) are oxytone, as αἰδώς, ἠώς, Arc. 94. 11. The Æolic form of ἠώς is αὔως.

667. (*c*) Those in ως (gen. ωτος) are paroxytone, as γέλως, ἔρως; except εὐρώς and ἰδρώς oxytone.

NOTE.—The proper name Ἀραρώς retains its participial accent, cf. Arc. 93. 16: εὐρώς and ἰδρώς, Arc. 93. 16; Schol. Ven. Δ. 27: δίκερως, ῥινόκερως, φίλερως, κλαυσίγελως are incorrect when they form their genitive in ωτος, yet they are found with those accents; Ὑποδεδιώς, used by Aristoph. Aves 65 as the name of a bird, is, of course, nothing but a perfect participle.

-Ω.

668. Those in ω are oxytone, as ἠχώ, Ἐρατώ, Πυθώ, Σαπφώ.

NOTE.—Arc. 116. 1; Schol. Ven. Ι. 240: Ἀκενιππῶ or Ἀκινιππῶ, a city in

Spain, which is quoted by Pape and H. D. from Ptol. 2. 4, 15, is printed Ἀκινίππω in Nobbe's edition; it is barbarous both in form and accent.

669. *Compound Substantives.*—Except in cases specially mentioned above, all compound substantives of the Third Declension retain the accent of their last factor.

Oblique Cases.

670. The general rule is observed, as εἰκών, εἰκόνος, εἰκόνι, εἰκόνα; Βαβυλών, Βαβυλῶνος, Βαβυλῶνι, Βαβυλῶνα; Ἕλλην, Ἕλληνος, Ἕλληνι, Ἕλληνα, Ἕλληνες, Ἑλλήνων, Ἕλλησιν except—

1. Γυνή (or properly γύναιξ), which, in the genitive and dative of all numbers, is accented like a monosyllable, and is paroxytone in the vocative singular, hence—*Singular* γυνή, γυναικός, γυναικί, γυναῖκα, γύναι : *Dual,* γυναῖκε, γυναικοῖν : *Plural,* γυναῖκες, γυναικῶν, γυναιξί, γυναῖκας, γυναῖκες.

2. (*a*) The syncopated genitives and datives (except the dative plural) of ἀνήρ, γαστήρ, θυγάτηρ, μήτηρ, πατήρ, take the accent on their last syllable, as ἀνδρός, ἀνδρί, ἀνδροῖν, ἀνδρῶν; γαστρός, γαστρί, γαστρῶν, γαστέρας; θυγατρός, θυγατρί, θυγατροῖν, θυγατρῶν; μητρός, μητρί; πατρός, πατρί, πατροῖν (?) πατρῶν. This rule does not apply to their compounds, e. g. Δημήτηρ in all cases throws the accent as far back as possible, as Δημήτερος Δήμητρος, Δημήτερα Δήμητρα. When not syncopated, the cases of θυγάτηρ and μήτηρ are paroxytone, as θυγατέρος, θυγατέρι, θυγατέρα, θυγατέρες, θυγατέρων, θυγατέρε, θυγατέρες; μητέρος, μητέρι μητέρα, μητέρες, μητέρων, μητέρε, μητέρας.

(*b*) The accusatives ἄνδρα ἄνδρας, ἄρνα ἄρνας, θύγατρα θύγατρας, retract the accent, as also do the nominatives ἄνδρες ἄνδρε, ἄρνες, θύγατρες.

(*c*) The datives ἀνδράσι, ἀρνάσι, θυγατράσι, μητράσι, πατράσι, υἱάσι, and, according to Aristarchus, ἀστράσι, are paroxytone; those in εσσι retract their accent, as ἄρνεσσι, κύνεσσι.

(*d*) The following cases are also irregular; ἀρνός, ἀρνί, ἀρνῶν, from ἈΡΗΝ; γουνός, γουνί from γονύ; δορός, δουρός, δορί, δουρί from δόρυ; κυνός, κυνί, κυνοῖν (?), κυνῶν, κυσί from κύων. All these are accented, in these cases, as if they came from monosyllabic nominatives.

3. The vocatives ἄνερ, δᾶερ, Δήμητερ, εἶνατερ, θύγατερ, μῆτερ, πάτερ, and σῶτερ retract their accent.

4. Vocatives in ου, οι, and ευ, from oxytones or perispomena, are perispomena, as βοῦς βοῦ, Λητώ Λητοῖ, Πηλεύς Πηλεῦ, πλακοῦς πλακοῦ.

5. Vocatives in ον, from compound proper names in ων, retract the accent, as Ἀγάμεμνον, Ἀριστόγειτον; the same is the case with Ἄμφιον, Ἄπολλον, and Πόσειδον.   Other simple proper names, together with Λακεδαῖμον, and those in φρον (from φρην), keep the accent on the penultimate, as Ἰκετᾶον, Λυκόφρον, Μαχᾶον, Νοῆμον, Φιλῆμον.

6. Vocatives in ες, from compound proper names, also retract, as Ἀριστότελες, Δημόσθενες, Σώκρατες; except those in ηρες (ηρης), ωδες (ωδης), ωλες (ωλης), ωρες (ωρης), as Λειῶδες, Διῶρες.

7. Those forms in which a contraction takes place are accented according to the general rule (§ 20); except the accusative in ω=οα, from nouns in ώ, which is *oxytone*, not perispomenon, as ἠχόα ἠχώ, Σαπφώ Σαπφόα Σαπφώ, and τριήρων= τριηρέων, for which τριηρῶν also occurs.

671. Note 1.—The genuine nominative of γυναικός does not occur except in the grammarians, but ἀγύναιξ was used by Sophocles; Chœrob. C. 307. 12: ὁ γύναιξ εὐθεῖα ἐπιλέλοιπεν. Ἐν δὲ τῇ συνθέσει, ἐπειδὴ γίνεται ἀρσενικοῦ γένους, ἀναδέχεται τὴν εἰς ΑΙΞ κατάληξιν, οἷον

ὡς ὢν ἄπαις τε καὶ ἀγύναιξ, καὶ ἀνέστιος [τε κἀγύναιξ κἀνέστιος] παρὰ Σοφοκλεῖ ἐν Ἀθάμαντι.

On the cases of the word see Joh. Alex. 10. 20; 11. 26: Arc. 128. 7; Chœrob. C. 329. 9; 404. 17; 417. 35; 420. 12; 445; E. M. 457. 25.

672. Note 2.—On the syncopated words in ηρ see Arc. 128. 3; Joh. Alex. 10. 21; 11. 28; Chœrob. C. 318. 24; 346. 19 sqq.; E. 8. 25; 134. 24: when not syncopated, the masculines are regular; the feminines μήτηρ, θυγάτηρ are accented as if the nominative were oxytone, e. g. μήτηρ, μητέρος, μητέρα, θυγατέρος, θυγατέρι, etc., except that the vocative sing. retracts.

According to Eust. 1388. 50; Chœrob. C. 272. 25; 431. 15; Joh. Alex. 10. 25, the genitive of εἰνάτηρ is εἰνάτερος, and therefore εἰνάτερες in Hom. Il. 22. 473 should be εἰνάτερες, as it is in Eust. 1281. 2, and as it is expressly stated to be in Schol. Ven. ad loc. A comparison of the places quoted shows that this was Herodian's accent.

As to their dative plural, Chœrob. C. 463. 7 remarks: αἱ μέντοι, φησὶ [sc. Theognostus] πλεονάσασαι δοτικαὶ πληθυντικαὶ τῷ Α παροξύνονται, οἷον πατρὶ πατράσι, θυγατρὶ θυγατράσιν, ἀνδρὶ ἀνδράσιν, υἷι υἱάσιν. Ἔστι γὰρ υἷις υἷος υἷι καὶ κατὰ συναίρεσιν τοῦ Τ καὶ Ι εἰς τὴν ΤΙ δίφθογγον υἷι· καὶ ἐπειδὴ τοῦ Σ προσερχομένου ἀσυντάξια ἤμελλε γίνεσθαι (οὐδέποτε γὰρ μετὰ τὴν ΤΙ δίφθογγον σύμφωνον εὑρίσκεται ἐπιφερόμενον, οἷον μυῖα, ἅρπυια, υἱός) τούτου χάριν ἐπλεόνασε τὸ Α καὶ γέγονεν υίάσιν. Αἱ μέντοι μεταπεπλασμέναι δοτικαὶ πληθυντικαὶ προπαροξύνεσθαι θέλουσιν, οἷον προβάτοις πρόβασιν, ἐγκάτοις ἔγκασιν, ἄστροις ἄστρασιν, ὑπεσταλμένου τοῦ ἀρῶξιν ὥσπερ παρὰ Σοφοκλεῖ ἐν Ἀχιλλέως Ἐρασταῖς,

ὁ δὲ ἔνθ᾽ ὅπλοις ἀρῶξιν Ἡφαίστου τεχνίτου.

Schol. Ven. X. 28: πολλοῖσι μετ᾽ ἄστρασιν· Ἀρίσταρχος ὡς πατράσιν. ἄμεινον δὲ προπαροξύνειν, ὥσπερ καὶ τοῖς πλείοσιν ἔδοξε καὶ Φιλοξένῳ, ἵν᾽ αὐτῆς τῆς πτώσεως, λέγω δὲ τῆς δοτικῆς, μεταπλασμὸν λάβωμεν: cf. Arc. 138. 5. This amounts to saying that heteroclite datives in ασι are proparoxytone: and to those mentioned by Chœrob., Eust. 677. 10 adds ὀνείρασι, μήλασι. But why it should be assumed that ἄστρασι is from ἄστρον, and not from ἀστήρ, I do not know; Eust. 677. 10 allows that, if it were, it would be paroxytone.

673. NOTE 3.—*Contracted Substantives.* The word Ἡρακλῆς may be taken as a good example of all the ordinary contracted forms: it is thus declined by the grammarians :—

Sing. Nom.	Ἡρακλέης	Ἡρακλῆς		
Gen.	Ἡρακλέεος	Ἡρακλέους		
	Ἡρακλέεος	Ἡρακλῆος		
	Ἡρακλέος	(Ἡρακλοῦς)		
Dat.	Ἡρακλέεϊ	Ἡρακλέει		
	Ἡρακλέει	Ἡρακλῆϊ		
	Ἡρακλέϊ	Ἡρακλεῖ		
Accus.	Ἡρακλέεα	Ἡρακλέα	Ἡρακλέη	Ἡρακλῆ
	Ἡρακλέεα	Ἡρακλῆα		
		Ἡρακλέην	Ἡρακλῆν, *Attic.*	
Voc.	Ἡράκλεες (§ 676)	Ἡράκλεις		
		Ἥρακλες (§ 676)		
		Ἡρακλέη and Ἡρακλῆ, *Attic.*		

Dual Nom. and Accus.	Ἡρακλέεε	Ἡρακλέη	Ἡρακλῆ
	Ἡρακλέεε	Ἡρακλῆε	
	Ἡρακλέε	Ἡρακλῆ	
Gen. and Dat.	Ἡρακλεέοιν	Ἡρακλέοιν	
	Ἡρακλεέοιν	Ἡρακλήοιν	
	Ἡρακλέοιν	Ἡρακλοῖν	

Plural Nom.	Ἡρακλέεες	Ἡρακλέεις	
	Ἡρακλέεες	Ἡρακλῆες	
	Ἡρακλέες	Ἡρακλεῖς and *Attic* Ἡρακλαί	
Gen.	Ἡρακλεέων	Ἡρακλεῶν	
	Ἡρακλεέων	Ἡρακλήων	
	Ἡρακλέων	Ἡρακλῶν	
Dat.	Ἡρακλέεσι	Ἡρακλῆσι	
	Ἡρακλέσι		
Accus.	Ἡρακλέεας	Ἡρακλέας	Ἡρακλᾶς
	Ἡρακλέεας	Ἡρακλῆας	
	Ἡρακλέας	Ἡρακλεῖς	
Voc.	Ἡρακλέεες	Ἡρακλέεις	
	Ἡρακλέεες	Ἡρακλῆες	
	Ἡρακλέες	Ἡρακλεῖς	

On the vocative Ἡρακλες see Apoll. de Adv. 570. 15, and on the other cases Chœrob. C. 170. 22 sq.

Such contractions as διογενέος διογενεῦς, Ὀδυσσέος Ὀδυσσεῦς, Ἰδομενέος Ἰδομενεῦς, are perfectly regular though uncommon: Schol. Ven. I. 106; Chœrob. C. 428. 15.

674. NOTE 4.—Τριήρων: although the MSS. of Thucydides generally agree in having τριήρων, the correctness of the accent may be doubted: the following passages show that Aristarchus had no very just grounds for making it, and others like it, barytone: Joh. Alex. 19. 13: αἱ δὲ εἰς ΕΙΣ εὐθεῖαι συνηρημέναι εἰσὶ καὶ περισπῶσι τὰς ἰδίας γενικάς, ὡς ἤδη εἴπομεν, Σωκράτεις Σωκρατῶν, Δημοσθένεις Δημοσθενῶν. Τὸ δυσῶδον καὶ εὐῶδον τῷ λόγῳ μὲν περισπασθήσονται, φασὶ δὲ τὸν Ἀρίσταρχον ταύτας καὶ τὰς ὁμοίας βαρύνειν, ἀπατηθέντα, ὡς ὁ Ἡρωδιανός φησιν, ἐκ τοῦ οἴεσθαι τὰς ἐντελεῖς γενικὰς αὐτῶν προπαροξύνεσθαι, εὐώδεων, ὡς πόλεων, κακῶς· μόναι γὰρ αἱ ἀπὸ τῶν εἰς ΙΣ ὑπάρχουσιν αἱ προπαροξυνόμεναι, πόλεων, μάντεων, καὶ δύο ἀπὸ τῶν εἰς ΥΣ, πελέκεων, πήχεων· αἱ δὲ λοιπαὶ πᾶσαι βαρύτονοι οὖσαι πρὸ μιᾶς ἔχουσι τὸν τόνον: Chœrob. C. 459. 15: τὸ τριηρῶν περισπωμένως οἱ Ἀθηναῖοι κατ' ἀκολουθίαν ἀναγινώσκουσι· τινὲς δὲ καὶ τοῦτο παρ' αὐτοῖς βαρυτόνως ἀναγινώσκουσιν, οἷον τῶν τριήρων: Theodos. Can. 1006. 22: αἱ εἰς ΕΣ εὐθεῖαι συνηρημέναι ὅταν ἔχωσι τὰς γενικὰς συναιρεθείσας, περισπῶσιν αὐτάς, εὐγενῶν Δημοσθενῶν. τὸ δυσῶδον Ἀρίσταρχος ἀλόγως ἐβάρυνε, καὶ τριήρων φασί τινες Ἀττικοὺς βαρυτόνως λέγειν: Arc. 136. 21: τὸ δὲ δυσῶδον παραλόγως ἐβαρύνθη. καὶ τὸ τριήρων, οἱ μὲν βαρύνουσιν, οἱ δὲ περισπῶσιν: ‘Ap. Thucyd. consentire videntur libri in τριήρων, qui apud alios variant, interdum etiam tertiam inferentes formam τριηρέων vel τριήρεων, ut apud Xenoph. H. Gr. 1. 4. 11; Demosth. p. 306. 22, et alibi, de qua Oudendorp ad Thom. p. 860: Τριήρεος λέγε καὶ μὴ τριήρους, τριήρων καὶ μὴ τριηρῶν, quibus addit solutas formas genit. proparoxytonas esse: τριήρεων (ut est apud Ducam Hist. p. 79 B; 123 D; 124 B) γὰρ καὶ συνήθεων καὶ κακοήθεων λέγομεν: sed recte τριηρέων scribi apud Herodot. 7. 36. 89, falsumque esse accentum proparox. animadvertit Göttling ad Theodos. p. 224 sq.: genit. dual. τριήροιν Xenoph. H. Gr. 1. 5. 19,’ *H. D.*: but there does not seem to be any warrant in the grammarians for τριήροιν.

675. NOTE 5.—Though words in ω (gen. ους) make their accusative singular in ώ contrary to rule, as Σαπφόα Σαπφώ not Σαπφῶ, they are regular in their other cases, as Σαπφόος Σαπφοῦς, Σαπφόϊ Σαπφοῖ: those in ως (gen. οος) on the other hand are quite regular, αἰδώς, αἰδόος αἰδοῦς, αἰδόϊ αἰδοῖ, αἰδόα αἰδῶ; so ἠῶ; Joh. Alex. 12. 31: ἡ δὲ ἠῶ καὶ αἰδῶ συνῄρηνται ἀπὸ τῆς ἠόα καὶ αἰδόα, ὅθεν περισπῶνται. ἀλλὰ καὶ τὴν Λητὼ καὶ τὴν Ἐρατὼ καὶ Κλειὼ καὶ τὰς παραπλησίους ἀπὸ τῶν εἰς Ω εὐθειῶν τῆς Λητὼ Κλειὼ Ἐρατώ, συνῃρημένας ἀπὸ τῆς Λητόα Κλειόα Ἐρατόα δέον περισπᾶν, ὀξύνομεν διὰ τὴν συνέμπτωσιν τῆς εὐθείας. ὅτε γὰρ πτῶσις ἑτέρᾳ πτώσει συνεμπέσῃ κατὰ τὸν αὐτὸν ἀριθμόν, πάντως καὶ ὁμοτονεῖ: thus also Chœrob. C. 334. 5; Schol. Ven. I. 240: and this was the practice of Aristarchus; Dionysius Sidonius, however, read αἰδώ, while Pamphilus circumflexed all such accusatives in ω, as Λητῶ, Πυθῶ, etc.; Schol. Ven. B. 262: Ἀρίσταρχος περισπωμένως ἀναγινώσκει [sc. τά τ' αἰδῶ ἀμφικαλύπτει] ὁμοίως καὶ τό, ἠῶ δῖαν ἔμιμνε, καὶ ἡμεῖς δὲ αὐτῷ συγκατατιθέμεθα· Διονύσιος δὲ ὁ Σιδώνιος ὀξυτονεῖ. Πάμφιλος δὲ πάσας τὰς τοιαύτας αἰτιατικὰς περισπᾷ· Λητῶ γὰρ δ' ἤλκησε, καὶ Πυθῶδ' ἐρχομένην· ἐπεί, φησί, Λητόα ἐστὶ καὶ Πυθόα. Διονύσιος δὲ ὁ Θρᾷξ φησι κακῶς ἀνεγνωκέναι τὸν Ἀρίσταρχον κατὰ τὸν περισπώμενον τόνον, τὸ μὲν αἰδῶ καὶ ἠῶ, τὰ δὲ ἄλλα κατ' ὀξεῖαν τάσιν, Πυθώ, Λητώ· ἐχρῆν γάρ, φησιν, ὁμοίως ἀνεγνωκέναι. οὐκ εὖ δὲ μέμφεται τῷ Ἀριστάρχῳ, εἴγε ἤδη διάφοραι αἱ εὐθεῖαι, ἠώς, αἰδώς, Λητώ δὲ καὶ Πυθώ. ἔστιν οὖν λόγος ὑπὲρ τῆς Ἀρισταρχείου ἀναγνώσεως, καὶ τῆς κατεγνωσμένης προσῳδίας οὗτος, ὅτι ἐχρῆν μὲν τὸ Πυθὼ περισπᾶσθαι, ἐπειδήπερ Πυθόα ἐστί, καὶ τοῦτο ἀπῄτει ἡ συναλοιφή· ἀλλὰ πάλιν τὸ πτωτικὸν Ω ἀπέστραπται τὸν περισπώμενον τόνον· κατὰ τοῦτο ὠξύνετο. ταύτῃ γοῦν καὶ τοῦ χρυσοῦς περισπωμένου τὸ δυϊκὸν ὀξύνομεν. οὕτως ἀποδείκνυται ὅτι καὶ ἡ καλῷ δοτικὴ εἰς Ι λήγει, καὶ οὐκ εἰς Ω. δεύτερος δὲ λόγος ἀληθής ἐστιν, ὡς εὐθεῖα καὶ αἰτιατικὴ ὁμόφωνος οὖσα κατὰ φωνὴν ἐν τῷ αὐτῷ ἀριθμῷ πάντως καὶ τὸν αὐτὸν τόνον ἀποφέρεται, οἱ ταχεῖς τοὺς ταχεῖς. εἰ δὲ ἡ εὐθεῖα ὀξύνεται, πάντως καὶ ἡ αἰτιατική. διὰ τοῦτο οὖν ἡ μὲν αἰδῶ αἰτιατικὴ καὶ ᾐῶ, μὴ κρατούμεναι ὑπὸ τῆς συνεμπτώσεως κατὰ τὴν εὐθεῖαν, περισπῶνται, κατεχύμεναι τῷ λόγῳ τῆς συναλοιφῆς, οὐχ ὑπὸ τοῦ πτωτικοῦ χαρακτῆρος. ἡ δὲ Λητὼ καὶ Πυθώ, καθάπερ κατεχόμεναι ὑπὸ τῆς συνεμπτώσεως τῆς φωνῆς, κατέχονται καὶ τῷ τόνῳ.

The Ionic accusative of these words in οιν or ουν is perispomenon, as Λητοῖν, Σαπφοῖν, Ἰοῦν ; the Æolic has Λήτω, Σάπφω, according to the constant practice of that dialect ; Chœrob. C. 333. 20.

676. NOTE 6.—*Vocative Case.* On the Vocatives in ov, οι, εν, from oxytones or perispomena, see Chœrob. C. 241. 29 ; 250. 10 ; Joh. Alex. 13. 24.

On ἄνερ, πάτερ, μῆτερ, Δήμητερ, θύγατερ, εἴνατερ, δᾶερ, σῶτερ, see Joh. Alex. 14. 4 ; Chœrob. C. 437. 15 ; Schol. Ven. Z. 355 ; Chœrob. C. 431. 26 : τὸ δὲ σῶτερ ψευδαιολικόν ἐστι, καὶ τούτου χάριν συνέστειλε τὸ Η εἰς τὸ Ε ἐν τῇ κλητικῇ καὶ ἐβαρύνθη· οἱ γὰρ Αἰολεῖς ἔθος ἔχουσι πολλάκις συστέλλειν τὸ Η εἰς τὸ Ε ἐν τῇ κλητικῇ καὶ ἀναβιβάζειν τὸν τόνον οἷον ὁ τριβολέτηρ ὦ τριβόλετερ. (ἔστι δὲ εἶδος ἀκάνθης). Διὰ τοῦτο δὲ εἴρηται ψευδαιολικόν, ἐπειδὴ οὐκ ἔστι κυρίως Αἰολικόν· οἱ γὰρ Αἰολεῖς τότε συστέλλουσι τὸ Η εἰς τὸ Ε ἐν τῇ κλητικῇ, ἡνίκα μὴ μακρᾷ παραλήγεται, οἷον ὁ τριβολέτηρ ὦ τριβόλετερ· ἡνίκα δὲ μακρᾷ παραλήγεται, οὐ συστέλλουσι τὸ Η ἐν τῇ κλητικῇ εἰς τὸ Ε οἷον ὁ χρηστήρ (sic).

Joh. Alex. 14. 5 mentions αἰνόπατερ (Æschyl. Choeph.) as the vocative of αἰνο-πάτηρ, and adds, τὸ κυβερνᾶτερ ἀπὸ ὀξυτόνου τοῦ κυβερνατὴρ γενόμενον προπερισπάσθη : the former may be compared with Δήμητερ.

On the vocatives in ov and ες see Joh. Alex. 13. 29 ; 14. 9 ; Chœrob. C. 435. 18 ; E. M. 436. 18.

Παντόκρατορ for παντοκράτορ is false, though some wrote it so, Chœrob. C. 437. 21 ; Schol. Ven. A. 149 ; Γ. 182 ; E. M. 684. 51 ; 130. 32. The proper name Παλαίμων makes Παλαῖμον, and so Εὐδαῖμον to distinguish it from εὔδαιμον the adjective ; Chœrob. C. 438. 26 ; A. G. Oxon. 1. 17. 29.

677. NOTE 7.—Apocope does not influence the accent, hence κυκεῶνα κυκεῶ, ἰδρῶτα ἰδρῶ, αἰῶνα αἰῶ, Ἀπόλλωνα Ἀπόλλω, Ποσειδῶνα Ποσειδῶ, ἥρωα ἥρω, ἰχῶρα ἰχῶ· Schol. Ven. Λ. 641 ; Chœrob. C. 423. 33. Some very curious examples of apocope are to be found in a place where one would hardly expect to find them, namely, in Strabo, 364.

678. NOTE 8.—In such words as εἰκών, ἀηδών, χελιδών, etc., which have a double inflexion, each mode of declension follows the rules given above, e. g. εἰκών, εἰκόνος, εἰκόνι, εἰκόνα retains the accent according to § 670, but if it is declined like Λητώ, we have εἰκοῦς, accus. εἰκώ, accus. plur. εἰκούς· Eust. 829. 1.

679. NOTE 9.—Some persons wished to oxytone the Attic genitive singular of such words as γῆρας, κέρας, κρέας, e. g. γηρώς, κερώς, κρεώς, but Herodian condemned such an accentuation as violating the law of contraction, κρέαος from κρέατος, κέραος from κέρατος can by rule only become κρέως, κέρως, Chœrob. C. 387. 9 : κρεῶν or κρειῶν and the like are regular, the Ionic form being κρεάων, Chœrob. C. 387. 9 ; Schol. Ven. Λ. 551.

680. NOTE 10.—The genitive χοῶς is by some written χοώς, but, as it seems to me, without reason and against authority ; the word from which it comes is inflected in two ways; χόος, contracted χοῦς like βοῦς, makes its cases χοός, χοΐ, χόον or χοῦν and χόα [χόε, χοοῖν], χόες, χοῶν, χουσί, χόας; the other χοεύς makes χοέως (like βασιλέως) and the contraction of this must be χοῶς, not χοώς, χοέϊ or χοεῖ, χοέα or χοᾶ, χοέες or χοεῖς, χοέων or χοῶν, χοεῦσι, χοέας or χοᾶς, or χοεῖς; Chœrob. C. 241. 10; see especially Lob. Par. 233-4.

681. NOTE 11.—The genitive in εως pure, from nouns in ευς, is constantly contracted in Attic into ῶς, as Ἐρετριεύς Ἐρετριέως Ἐρετριῶς, Στειριέως Στειριῶς Ἡειραιέως Πειραιῶς, so also the accusatives Ἐρετριέα, Πειραιέα, Στειριέα become Ἐρετριᾶ, Πειραιᾶ, Στειριᾶ, Chœrob. C. 214. 3.

682. NOTE 12.—*Cases in* θε *and* φι.—They follow rules given above, §§ 219; 555, as ὄχεσφι, ναῦφιν, κρῆθεν.

683. NOTE 13.—*Metaplasmus.* In such forms as ἀλκί for ἀλκῇ, etc. the rules of the declensions to which they apparently belong are observed, as θέραπες for θεράποντες, κλαδί, κλάδεσι, κρόκα, λιτί, λῖτα, νίφα, ὑσμῖνι, ἀνδραπόδεσσι, πρόβασι: ἰῶκα, Hom. Il. 11. 601, forms an exception: Schol. Ven. E. 299: ἀλκί ὡς σαρκί, καὶ ἔστι κατὰ μεταπλασμὸν ἀπὸ τοῦ ἀλκῇ. τινὲς δὲ ἀπὸ τοῦ ἀλκίς [sic] Αἰολικοῦ αὐτό φασιν· τοῖς γὰρ εἰς Η παράκειται τὰ εἰς ΙΣ, ὡς ἑορτή καὶ ἑορτίς καὶ ἐν ὑπερθέσει ἐροτίς. ὤφειλε δὲ ἐκτείνειν τὸ Ι. εἴτε ἀπ᾽ εὐθείας τῆς ἄλξ πεποίηται, ὡς οἴεται ὁ Ἀσκαλωνίτης. Τρύφων δὲ ἐν τῷ πρώτῳ περὶ τῆς ἀρχαίας ἀναγνώσεώς φησιν ὅτι Ἀρίσταρχος λέγει ὅτι ἔθος αὐτοῖς ἐστι λέγειν τὴν ἰωκὴν ἰῶκα καὶ τὴν κρόκην κρόκα καὶ τὴν ἀλκὴν ἄλκα ὡς σάρκα. εἰ δὲ σάρκα ὡς ἄλκα καὶ ἀλκί ὡς σαρκί; cf. Schol. Ven. Σ. 352; O. 320; Matthiä Gr. Gr. § 92.

Attic Declension.

684. The εω in the Attic genitive singular εως, genitive and dative dual εῳν, and genitive plural εων, is reckoned as one syllable for the accent, in masculine and feminine nouns ending in ις (gen. ιος), and in πέλεκυς, πῆχυς, πρέσβυς, as πελέκεως, πελέκεῳν, πελέκεων; πήχεως, πήχεῳν, πήχεων; πόλεως, πόλεῳν, πόλεων.

685. NOTE 1.—Chœrob. C. 194. 16: ἰστέον δὲ ὅτι οἱ Ἀττικοὶ ἐπὶ τῶν τοιούτων, τουτέστι τῶν εἰς ΙΣ τῶν διὰ καθαροῦ τοῦ ΟΣ κλινομένων, τρέπουσι τὸ Ο εἰς Ω ἐν τῇ γενικῇ καὶ τὸ παραλῆγον φωνῆεν εἰς Ε μεταβάλλουσιν, οἷον μάντις μάντιος μάντεως, ὄφις ὄφιος ὄφεως, πόλις πόλιος πόλεως, καὶ φυλάττουσι τὸν αὐτὸν τόνον, τουτέστιν ὃν εἶχον πρὸ τῆς τροπῆς. Chœrob. C. 196. 35: ἰστέον ὅτι τὸ μὲν ὄφεων προπαροξύνεται... ἡ δὲ ὀφίων οὐ προπαροξύνεται: Chœrob. C. 460. 30. Joh. Alex. 19. 4: αἱ εἰς ΕΣ ὑπὲρ δύο συλλαβὰς εὐθεῖαι βαρύνουσι τὰς γενικάς, Αἴαντες Αἰάντων, ἑβδομάδες ἑβδομάδων, εὐσεβέες εὐσεβέων, στάχυες σταχύων, ὀσφύες ὀσφύων. ἐδεῖ οὖν καὶ τὸ πόλεων, μάντεων, πελέκεων, καὶ τὰ τούτοις παραπλήσια πρὸ μιᾶς ἔχειν τὸν τόνον. Ἀλλ᾽ Ἀττικούς φασι προπαροξύνειν ταῦτα, ἅπερ ἐστὶν ἀπὸ τῶν εἰς ΙΣ εὐθειῶν, καὶ ἔτι δύο ἀπὸ τῶν εἰς ΥΣ, τό τε πήχεων καὶ πελέκεων .... Αἱ δὲ εἰς ΕΙΣ συνῃρημέναι εἰσὶ καὶ περισπῶσι τὰς ἰδίας γενικάς, ὡς ἤδη εἴπομεν, Σωκράτεις Σωκρατῶν, Δημοσθένεις Δημοσθενῶν. Τὸ δυσῶδον καὶ εὐῶδον τῷ λόγῳ μὲν περισπαθήσονται, φασὶ δὲ τὸν Ἀρίσταρχον ταύτας καὶ τὰς ὁμοίας βαρύνειν, ἀπατηθέντα, ὡς ὁ Ἡρωδιανός φησιν, ἐκ τοῦ οἴεσθαι τὰς ἐντελεῖς γενικὰς αὐτῶν προπαροξύνεσθαι, εὐώδεων, ὡς πόλεων. κακῶς· μόναι γὰρ αἱ ἀπὸ τῶν εἰς ΙΣ ὑπάρχουσιν αἱ προπαροξυνόμεναι, πόλεων, μάντεων καὶ δύο ἀπὸ τῶν εἰς ΥΣ, πελέκεων, πήχεων· αἱ δὲ λοιπαὶ πᾶσαι βαρύτονοι οὖσαι πρὸ μιᾶς ἔχουσι τὸν τόνον, ὡς πρόκειται. Mœris 260: μάντεων, τὴν πρώτην προπαροξυτόνως, Ἀττικῶς. τὴν δευτέραν παροξυτόνως, Έλληνες. Πήχεων is often, though wrongly, written πηχέων in Attic writers. On πρέσβεως, E. M. 687. 17; the nominative dual of this word πρέσβη (=πρέσβεε) is said by Chœrob. C. 440. 25 to be barytone in the orators, but perispomenon in a passage of Aristophanes, ἤκετον πρεσβῆ δύο; as though from a nominative πρεσβεύς: I cannot find a passage where it occurs, and so am unable to say whether any of our editions preserve traces of so strange an accent. Joh. Alex. 14. 20: ὅτε δὲ μή ἐστι ῥητὴ ἡ εἰς A αἰτιατική, τότε τῇ εἰς ΟΣ γενικῇ ὁμοτονεῖ τὸ δυϊκόν, ταχέος ταχέε, πήχεος πήχεε. Τὰ δύο εε εἰς η συναιροῦσιν Ἀθηναῖοι.

    ἐγὼ δέ τοι πεπόνηκα κομιδῇ τῶ σκέλη ... χορεύων
    καὶ πρός γε τούτοις ἤκετον πρέσβη [sic] δύο.

686. Note 2.—The plural of ἔγχελυς is in Attic declined like πῆχυς, hence ἐγχέλεων, Chœrob. C. 357. 32: τὸ γὰρ παρὰ Ἀριστοφάνει [Nub. 559],

    τὰς εἰκοὺς τῶν ἐγχέλεων τὰς ἐμὰς μιμούμενοι,

ὡς ἀπὸ τοῦ ἡ ἐγχέλις (sic) ἐγχέλεως; on the different forms of this variable word see H. D. Ὀρνέων for ὀρνέων (from ὄρνεον) is an error common to several grammars: 'Quod autem ad ὄρνις Buttmannus (Gramm. vol. 1. p. 236) refert ὄρνεων ap. Aristoph. Av. 291 (295), 305, ipsius est error, quum ὀρνέων sit illis ceterisque locis ab nom. ὄρνεον. Eodem modo peccatum in fragmentis Callimachi ex libro Περὶ ὀρνέων p. 468-9 ed. Ern., ubi constanter scriptum ὄρνεων, quum ὀρνέων sit in locis scriptorum omnibus illis citatis;' L. Dindorf ap. H. D.

687. Note 3.—Whether such forms as σινάπεως, ἄστεως are rightly accented the Greek grammarians do not say: probably they are, but in the other cases the ω is long; hence ἀστέων not ἄστεων; see Kühner, G. G. 1. 345.

2. Simple Adjectives.

(a) *With a Vowel Characteristic.*

688. Those which form their genitive in os pure are oxytone, as αἰπύς, ἀκριβής, ἀληθής, βραδύς, δασύς, ἡδύς, θρασύς, νεαλής, στρηνής, ψευδής, ὠκύς; except 1. those in ις (gen. ιος), as ἄϊδρις, εὖνις, ἦνις, ἴδρις, νῆστις; and 2. ἄκικυς, ἥμισυς, θῆλυς, πλήρης, which retract their accent.

689. Note.—Ἄκικυς strictly belongs to the compound adjectives: ἥμισυς, Arc. 91. 15: its other cases are not unfrequently misaccented, as ἡμίσεα for ἡμισέα, Ionic=ἡμίσεια; ἡμίσεας for ἡμισέας, etc.: θῆλυς, Arc. 91. 16; Schol. Ven. E. 269: it is held by some that θάλεια implies a masculine θάλυς: μῶλυς, Hesych.: νέκυς or νέκυρ, Laced., Hesych., may with more propriety be considered a substantive: πλήρης, Arc. 25. 4; 117. 14: πραΰς was by some written πρᾶϋς, A. G. Oxon. 1. 345. 13: πρέσβυς, Arc. 91. 16, for which the dialectic forms πρέσγυς Doric, πρεῖγυς Cretan, and σπέργυς are mentioned: on ταρφειάς or ταρφείας see E. M. 747. 20, and above § 383: τέρυς (?) Hesych.: φόλυς (?) Herod. π. μ. λ. 32. 34 is probably a substantive. The Epic χέρηϊ, χέρηα, and χέρηες have been derived by some grammarians from a supposed form χέρης, but there is no necessity for doing so; cf. H. D. s. v. χείρων: λιγύς the adjective must be distinguished from Λίγυς, *Ligurian,* Eust. 96. 7: ὀξυνομένου δὲ τοῦ λιγὺς ἐπὶ τοῦ ὀξέως, τὸ Λίγυς κύριον καὶ τὸ ἀπ' αὐτοῦ ἐθνικὸν βαρύνεται πρὸς διαστολὴν τούτου.

(*b*) *With a Consonantal Characteristic.*

690. Those with a genitive in *os* impure retract the accent, as
ἀστερόεις, μέλας, μνήμων, πένης, τάλας, χαρίεις; except oxytone,
.1. ἀργής, γυμνής, ἑκών, ψιλής; those in *as* (gen. αδος), as ἁλμάς,
ἀμβολάς, ἐρημάς, θυιάς, μανιάς, πεδιάς, and 2. those in *ις* (gen.
δος), from masculines in ης, which follow the rule given for
substantives above, § 644; hence ἀγυιᾶτις (ἀγυιάτης), αἰγιαλῖτις
(αἰγιαλίτης), δεσμῶτις (δεσμώτης), δεσπότις (δεσπότης), ἑστιῶτις,
ζεφυρῖτις, ἠπειρῶτις, λιμενῖτις, ποινῆτις, πρεσβῦτις, but Περσίς
and Σκυθίς are oxytone. In many cases there is no corresponding masculine form in use, while in most instances it is
difficult, in some impossible, to distinguish substantives from
adjectives.

NOTE I.—Ἀργής, Arc. 23. 21: its genitive is either ἀργῆτος or ἀργέτος: γυμνής,
see § 635: ἑκών, Arc. 178. 7; Schol. Ven. M. 379: καρβάν, Chœrob. C. 68. 18
χερνής, Chœrob. C. 55. 2: ψιλής, κουρής, Chœrob. C. 55. 2; cf. § 636, above.

NOTE 2.—Κεράστις, *cornuta*, Æschyl. Prom. 674, where Dindorf reads κεραστίς
rightly, for Arcadius 35. 19 expressly says that it is oxytone: φαινολίς, Hom.
Hym. in Cer. 51 should be φαινόλις like μαινόλις.

691. Those which suffer contraction are regular, as αἰγλήεις,
αἰγλᾶς, ἀλκάεις, ἀλκᾶς, ἀργήεις, ἀργᾶς, τιμήεις τιμῆς, ἀμνοκόων,
ἀμνοκῶν; Eust. 775. 45; Schol. Ven. M. 201; 360.

692. The monosyllabic πᾶς is perispomenon in the nominative
singular, masculine and neuter, oxytone in the genitive and
dative singular of the same genders (the feminine πᾶσα follows the rules of the First Declension); in all other cases it
retracts its accent, hence πᾶς, πᾶσα, πᾶν; παντός, πάσης;
παντί, πάσῃ; πάντα, πᾶσαν, πᾶν; πάντε, πάσα; πάντοιν, πάσαιν;
πάντες, πᾶσαι, πάντα; πάντων, πασῶν; πᾶσι πάσαις; πάντας,
πάσας, πάντα. Its compounds retract their accent, as ἅπας,
ἀνάπας, σύμπας, A. G. Oxon. 1. 405. 5; 2. 406. 27.

693. The comparative and superlative degrees throw the accent as far back as possible, as βελτίων, βέλτιον; ἡδίων, ἥδιον;
E. M. 235. 1; Theog. Can. 118. 34; A. G. Oxon. 1. 98. 25.

694. *Oblique Cases.*—The general rule is observed, except
that the genitive plural feminine in adjectives of three terminations is perispomenon (see § 216), as ἥμισυς, ἡμίσεια, ἥμισυ;
ἡμίσεος, ἡμισείας; ὀξύς, ὀξεῖα, ὀξύ; ὀξέος, ὀξείας; ὀξέϊ or ὀξεῖ,

ὀξεία; ὀξύν, ὀξεῖαν, ὀξύ; ὀξέων, ὀξειῶν, etc. The feminines of λιγύς and ἐλαχύς are proparoxytone, λίγεια and ἐλάχεια.

695. NOTE.—The final a of the feminine singular is short, except in some dialectic (Ionic) forms, as ὠκέᾱ: πολέσι, πολέσσι, πολέεσσι is regular as a case of πολύς.

On λίγεια and ἐλάχεια see Arc. 95. 23; E. M. 565. 9; Eust. 1586. 13; the name of the Siren Λίγεια is also proparoxytone.

The old grammarians are not agreed as to the accent of Αἶπυ in Hom. Il. 2. 592; Aristarchus and Apollodorus made it oxytone, Pherecydes Atheniensis understood εὔκτιτον as the name of the city and αἰπύ as the epithet; some distinguish Αἶπυ the town from αἰπύ the adjective; Ptolemæus Ascalonites took Αἰπύ for a proper name, and retained the adjectival accent; Schol. Ven. B. 592; St. Byz. s. v. has Αἶπυ, and that seems the best mode of writing the name: αἴπεια also has a substantival tone, St. Byz. s. v.: Eust. 743. 21: βαθεῖα on the contrary has the accent of an adjective; see above, § 105.

On ἀληθές, ἐπάναγκες, ἐπίτηδες, χάριεν, which are used adverbially, see below, § 832 note.

3. COMPOUND ADJECTIVES.

(a) *With a Vowel Characteristic.*

696. Those from barytones remain unchanged as to the accent, perispomena therefore remain unaltered, as πλήρης, ἡμιπλήρης, φιλοσοφοκλῆς.

697. Those in ευς are oxytone; those in υς and ις retract the accent, as ἰξοφορεύς, λιμοφορεύς, ὠμοβοεύς, ὠμοβορεύς; ἀγάσταχυς, ἀγλαόβοτρυς, ἄδακρυς, ἄδρυς, ἄθηλυς, ἄνιχθυς, ἄτραχυς, εὔβοτρυς, ἰσόνεκυς, λεύκοφρυς, πολύδακρυς, ὑπέρηδυς, ἄϊδρις, πολύϊδρις.

NOTE.—Arc. 91. 18; 21. 16; E. M. 333. 21; 518. 30; Schol. Ven. B. 764; N. 521; Eust. 833. 38; 340. 21: Ἀβαθύς, μελαμβαθύς, νευροπαχύς, ἐπευθύς, μεσευθύς, are all false, either in form or accent; see especially Lob. Phryn. 533 sqq.; the same is true of ἀπιχθύς for ἄπιχθυς, cf. Eust. 1720. 24, ἐντραχύς, περιθαρσύς, προβαθύς, τριβραχύς, ὑπαμβλύς, which are all properly proparoxytone; in Apollon. Rhod. 4. 283 we have εὐρύς τε προβαθύς τε where πρόβαθύς τε is the proper reading: ἀρσενόθηλυς in Chœrob. C. 63. 1 is sufficiently refuted by ἄθηλυς in Eust. 833; ποδῶκυς has no existence.

698. Adjectives in ης are oxytone, as ἀαγής, ἀγχιβαθής, ἀναιδής, ἀψευδής, βαρυαλγής, γηγενής, δυσαής, δυσαλθής, ἐπαχθής, εὐαγής, θυμοδακής, λειτουργής, λυσιμελής, ποδηνεκής; except paroxytone, 1. αὐθάδης, αὐτάρκης, εὐτείχης (?), ποδάρκης, ποδώκης, and, as above mentioned, compounds from barytone words (§ 644); 2. those in αντης, ηθης (from ἦθος and ἀληθής), ηκης (from ἄκη or ἀκή), ηρης, κητης (from κῆτος), μεγεθης, μηκης (from μῆκος), πηχης (from πῆχυς), στελεχης, τηρης (from τηρέω), ωδης, ῳδης, and ωλης, which are paroxytone, as ἀνάντης, ἐνάντης, κατάντης; ἀήθης,

ἀναλήθης, εὐήθης, μισαλήθης, συνήθης, φιλαλήθης; ἀήκης, νεήκης,
τανυήκης; ἀνήρης, λιχμήρης, μεσσήρης, μονήρης, τριήρης, χαλκήρης;
βαθυκήτης, μεγακήτης; εὐμεγέθης, παμμεγέθης, ὑπερμεγέθης; ἑτερο-
μήκης; πενταπήχης, τετραπήχης, τριπήχης; βραχυστελέχης, μακρο-
στελέχης, μονοστελέχης; δεμνιοτήρης, νυκτοτήρης; ἀλσώδης, ἱνώδης,
πετρώδης, στοιχειώδης; ἐξώλης, πανώλης, προώλης.   Those in ετης
(from ἔτος) are paroxytone in Attic, as διέτης, τριέτης, δεκέτης.

699. Note I.—Chœrob. C. 52. 4: τὰ ἀπὸ τῶν εἰς ΟΣ οὐδετέρων εἰς ΗΣ γινόμενα σύνθετα τότε βαρύνονται, ἡνίκα ὦσι κύρια, οἷον σθένος, Δημοσθένης Δημοσθένους,
γένος Διογένης Διογένους, νεῖκος Πολυνείκης Πολυνείκους, κλέος Ἡρακλέης καὶ κατὰ
κρᾶσιν Ἡρακλῆς Ἡρακλέους, καὶ ὅταν ὦσιν ἀπὸ τρισυλλάβου οὐδετέρου σύνθετα, οἷον
στέλεχος εὐστελέχης, μέγεθος παμμεγέθης, καὶ ὅταν ὦσιν ἀπὸ δισυλλάβου οὐδετέρου
σύνθετα ἔχοντα ἐν τῇ παραληγούσῃ τὸ Η ἐπιφερομένου ἀφώνου· ἄφωνα δέ εἰσιν ἐννέα
β, γ, δ, κ, π, τ, θ, φ, χ. Ἔστωσαν δὲ παραδείγματα τοῦ κανόνος ταῦτα, κῆτος μεγακήτης, ἦθος κακοήθης, μῆκος ἐπιμήκης· ... ἐὰν δὲ μηδὲν ἐκ τούτων τῶν τριῶν ἔχωσι
... ὀξύνεσθαι θέλουσιν, οἷον μένος εὐμενής, γένος εὐγενής, εἶδος δυσειδής, κλέος
δυσκλεής, τεῖχος εὐτειχής· ἔχει γὰρ τοῦτο ἄφωνον ἐπιφερόμενον, φημὶ δὲ τὸ Χ, ἀλλ᾽
οὐ παραλήγεται τῷ Η; δῆνος δυσδηνής (δήνεα δέ εἰσι τὰ βουλεύματα), τοῦτο γὰρ
παραλήγεται τῷ Η ἀλλ᾽ οὐκ ἔχει ἐπιφερόμενον ἄφωνον, τὸ γὰρ Ν ἡμίφωνον ἐστίν,
ἔτος διετής. ταῦτα δέ φημι παρὰ τὸ ἔτος παρ᾽ ἡμῖν μὲν ὀξύνονται κατὰ τὸν προειρη-
μένον κανόνα. παρὰ δὲ τοῖς Ἀθηναίοις βαρύνονται; cf. E. M. 393. 6.

700. Note 2.—On those in -αντης see Chœrob. C. 54. 25; Mœris 207: κάταντες, τὴν πρώτην ὀξυτόνως, Ἀττικῶς. τὴν τελευταίαν ὀξέως, Ἑλληνικῶς: -ηθης,
Chœrob. C. 177. 2: τὸ δὲ ἀληθὲς διὰ τοῦτο ἐν τῇ συνθέσει βαρύνεται, οἷον φιλαλήθης,
μισαλήθης, ἐπειδὴ τὰ διὰ τοῦ ΗΘΗΣ σύνθετα ἀπ᾽ ὀνόματος βαρύνεσθαι θέλουσιν, ἦθος
εὐήθης συνήθης κακοήθης, οὕτως οὖν καὶ ἀληθὴς φιλαλήθης μισαλήθης: Chœrob. C.
175. 24; Eust. 897. 40; Philem. Lex. p. 110. § 262; Arc. 28. 4; 27. 14; Schol.
Ven. M. 164: yet παναληθής is quoted by H. D. from Æschyl. S. c. T. 724; Plat.
Rep. 583 B: it also occurs in Anth. Pal. 5. 296. 5, and the adverb in ὣς in
Æschyl. Supp. 85; Suid. s. v. Ἀτρέπτως, etc.; but παναλήθης is undoubtedly the
correct accent, see E. M. 435. 57: ἐπαληθής, Amphiloch. p. 99 D, *H. D.*, who
rightly observe 'rectius scribitur ἐπαλήθης:' those in γηθης (γηθέω) are regular,
as ἐριγηθής, εὐγηθής, δαφνογηθής, λυρογηθής: so those in μηθης, as ἐπιμηθής,
προμηθής: and those in πληθης, as ἐμπληθής, ἁμαξοπληθής, βουπληθής, γυναι-
κοπληθής, ζαπληθής, θυμοπληθής, ἰσοπληθής, κενταυροπληθής, κοινοπληθής,
κοσμοπληθής, λευκοπληθής, μυριοπληθής, οἰνοπληθής, ὁμοπληθής, παμπληθής,
περιπληθής, πολυπληθής, ἀρσενοπληθής: H. D. have διπλήθης, and quote Nicand.
Al. 153: ἢ καὶ σιραίοιο πόσιν διπληθέα (scr. διπλήθεα) τεύξαις: this seems to be a
slip of the pen, for διπληθής is quite right: πυριπλήθης, *H. D.*, is an error, the
word is rightly oxytone in Eusebius: ὑπερπλήθης is quoted from Pseudo-Demosth.
p. 802. 25, but it is unquestionably wrong, though MSS. do vary occasionally
between χειροπληθής and χειροπλήθης, so also παμπλήθης, no doubt from a
confused idea that all compound adjectives in ηθης were paroxytone, a notion
which has led moderns as well as ancients into numerous errors of accentuation:
those in σκηθης are regular, as ἀσκηθής, πανασκηθής.

701. Note 3.—ηκης, see Chœrob. C. 48. 1; Schol. Ven. Il. 768; Eust. 939. 14,
whence it appears that some (i. e. Ptolemæus Ascalonites, cf. Schol. Ven. N. 391)
were for making νεήκης oxytone, but the tradition barytoned it and others of that
termination: so some wrote πυριήκης, others πυριηκής, Eust. 1635. 64: πετράκης,

Orph. Lith. 228, is perhaps a substantive: λεπτηκής in Hesych. is of doubtful origin, the last editor reads λεπτήκης: Lob. Ajax 173 has collected several examples of false accents affixed to adjectives in ηκης.

-ηρης.—Although the adjectives in ηρης from ἄρω are paroxytone, those in ἄρης are oxytone: Arc. 26. 9; Schol. Ven. Γ. 316; I. 336; E. M. 458. 27: the inconsistency of accenting θυμήρης in one way and θυμαρής in another appears to have struck even the Greeks themselves, cf. Eust. 754. 60; 1946. 35: χαλκοάρης seems to be paroxytone in Pindar, but no doubt wrongly: the following exceptions occur:—ἀπηρής, E. M. 122. 6; A. G. Oxon. 1. 84. 10: παναπηρής, ἀριηρής, ἀσηρής (?) ἀτηρής (?) ἀχθηρής, ἀχηρής, δυσβηρής or δυσβήρης, πενταετηρής: they are all more or less doubtful: cf. Lob. Prol. 268.

702. NOTE 4.—κητης, see Chœrob. C. 52. 13; Schol. Ven. N. 63; Eust. 920. 46; Arc. 117. 23: -μεγεθης, Schol. Ven. Π. 57; Chœrob. C. 52. 13: -μηκης, Chœrob. 52. 13: δουρεμηκές, Hesych., is corrupt, cf. H. D. s. v.: -πηχης, Arc. 27. 26: -στελεχης, Schol. Ven. H. 57; L. S. have ἀστελεχής (?) from Theophrastus: it should be paroxytone: -ωδης, these are all paroxytone, whatever their derivation, as εὐώδης, δυσώδης, πετρώδης, προσῴδης (οἰδάω), προσώδης (ὄζω), Arc. 25. 22; 117. 15; Schol. Ven. I. 336; E. M. 458. 29: -ωλης, Arc. 117. 19: -ωρης, Arc. 26. 1: ἔτ ιτὰ διὰ τοῦ ωρης [sc. βαρύνεται] Διώρης Λυκώρης ὅπερ Καλλίμαχος ὀξύνει: Arc. 117. 18, νεώρης and αὐτώρης are said to be paroxytone: Chœrob. C. 54. 6 adds ὑληώρης, and 436. 27, ὑλώρης: γέωρες or γεῶρες in Hesych. and Suid. are false, both in form and accent, cf. H. D. s. v. γειῶραι: εὐρυχωρής is oxytone in Strab. 200; Paus. 3. 19. 1; Diod. Sic. 19. 94; 20. 29, quoted by H. D.; also in Paus. 1. 44. 6: I find no instance of this as a paroxytone: στενοχωρής, Arist. de Gen. An. 3. 4. 5: κατωρής in Hesych. is doubtful: νεωρής is oxytone in all the places quoted by H. D., Soph. Elect. 901; Œd. Col. 730; Plut. Mor. 112 D; Stob. Flor. 104. 11: ὑληώρης is oxytone in Nicand. Ther. 55 in all the MSS. but one: these are all the words of this termination that I have noted, and it appears that our books in every instance contradict the rules of the grammarians:—who shall decide?

703. NOTE 5.—ετης: those in ετης, from ἔτος, are oxytone in the common dialect, but paroxytone in Attic, as διετής, τριετής, δεκετής, πετραετής: Attic διέτης, τριέτης, Chœrob. C. 52. 25; Pollux 1. 54; E. M. 765. 21: but the Attics declined them after the first declension, not after the third, Chœrob. C. 151. 32: yet the same author, 437. 3, says that the vocative singular of these compounds was oxytone in the common dialect, as τριετής, τριετές, πενταετής, πενταετές, but proparoxytone in Attic, as πεντάετης, πεντάετες, ἑξάετης, ἑξάετες: οἰέτης and ἑξέτης in Homer are barytone, Eust. 340. 40; E. M. 617. 14; Schol. Ven. Π. 57: reference to the following passages, Philem. Lex. p. 28. § 75; Schol. Ven. B. 765; Göttling, Accent. p. 324; Lob. Phryn. 407; Ammon. p. 136, will show that both the form and accent of these words is involved in almost inextricable confusion; thus much seems clear, 1. that when declined in ης, gen. ου, they are paroxytone; 2. that however declined, they are in Attic also paroxytone; and 3. that in the common dialect they are oxytone when belonging to the third declension.

704. NOTE 6.—Those in μηδης seem to vary, for ἀλιμηδής, κακομηδής, πυκιμηδής are oxytone, (though πυκιμηδής, Hom. Od. 1. 438 is πυκιμήδης, Hom. Hym. in Cererem 153, and in Hesych.), while δολομήδης, θρασυμήδης, σκοτομήδης, ψοφομήδες are paroxytone; the inconsistency perhaps arises from the different views taken as to their origin, some deriving them directly from μήδομαι, others making them *paronyma* from μῆδος; it is however an error to say, as some do, that all derivatives from neuter nouns are paroxytone, e. g. δολιχεγχής is expressly made oxytone by Schol. Ven. Φ. 155, though some wrote δολιχέγχης: χαλκέγχης is probably false for χαλκεγχής; cf. H. D. s. v.

705. NOTE 7.—The following, if correct, are violations of the rule :—Ἀβακής, which is quoted from Sappho by E. M. 2. 45, cannot be right in Æolic ; it should be paroxytone, as it is in Hesych. : 'Apud. Theocr. I. 27 κισσύβιον ἀμφῶες ... unde citat Herodian. Περὶ μον. λέξ. p. 14. 33 [cf. E. M. 93. 7]. Ubi Lehrsio p. 46 ἀμφαὴς ἀμφωές scribendum videtur. Ἀμφώεις ponit Etym. M. p. 639, 6 ;' H. D. : ἀνεμώκης, Eurip. Phœn. 164, Theoc. Fistula, and elsewhere. This and ποδώκης are the only ones in ωκης : ἀόρχης, Dio Cass. 75. 14, H. D. : with the exception of μόνορχις (and μονόρχης ?) other words of this termination belong to the first declension, e. g. ἐνόρχης, τριόρχης, ὑποτριόρχης ; the passage in Dio Cass. is suspicious : ἀπέσκης, Soph. Frag. 552 = 87 ed. Didot is false for ἀπεσκής : ἀρθροκήδης is quoted from Lucian Tragop. 15, where however Jacobitz has the right accent, ἀρθροκηδής, like λαθικηδής, cf. E. M. 555. 4 : ἀρισκύδης (?) Callim. Frag. 108 ; *L. S.* : αὐθάδης, Chœrob. C. 54. 25 ; Arc. 117. 25 : αὐτάρκης, Chœrob. C. 54. 25 ; Arc. 117 25 : all others are oxytone, as βιαρκής, διαρκής, ὀλιγαρκής, γυιαρκής, ἐπαρκής, ἐξαρκής, etc., except ποδάρκης, on which see below : εὐρυσάκης only occurs as a proper name, as an adjective it would be oxytone, like φερεσσάκης : εὐρυστήθης, Arist. H. A. 9. 50. 12 may be correct, see the passage from Chœroboscus quoted above, § 699 : εὐηχής is falsely paroxytone in Callim. Del. 296 ; all in ηχης (ἠχώ or ἦχος) are oxytone, as διηχής, δυσηχής, ὀξυηχής (not ὀξυήχης), βαρυηχής, γλυκυηχής, etc., cf. E. M. 564. 53 : εὐρώγης (?) Anth. Pal. 6. 190 : εὐτείχεα was by tradition proparoxytone, but Schol. Ven. Π. 57 observes that it should be paroxytone ; cf. A. G. Oxon. I. 158. 20 : (Θεοτείχης is also paroxytone in Anth. Pal. Append. 214 ; αἱρεσιτείχης belongs to the first declension) ; but the grammarians also refer εὐτείχεα not to εὐτειχής, but to εὐτείχεος ; εὐτειχής is oxytone in all the un-Homeric passages quoted by H. D. except one, Theog. 1209, πόλιν εὐτείχεα Θήβην, and there some read εὐτειχέα, like εὐτειχέα δόμον in Pind. Nem. 7. 46, and it is expressly stated to be so accented by Chœrob. C. 52. 21 : it appears that some grammarians wrote ζάης for ζαής, Schol. Ven. Μ. 157 : ζαὴς ὡς ὑγιής· οὕτως καὶ ὁ Ἀσκαλωνίτης. παραιτητέον δὲ τοὺς βουλομένους βαρύνειν, ἴσως πλανηθέντας ἐκ τῆς αἰτιατικῆς τῆς εἰς Ν περατωθείσης : θεοσυλής, Suid., is, as H. D. observe, a false accent ; the word belongs to the first declension : καταλσής, Strab. 238, εἰς φάραγγα βαθεῖαν καὶ καταλσῇ, where some read κατάλσῃ : κατάρης ἄνεμος is quoted by Eust. 603. 35 from Alcæus and Sappho ; as Æolic it seems to be right : μενέγχης, Anth. Pal. 7. 255 : κυανέη καὶ τούσδε μενέγχεας ὤλεσεν ἄνδρας Μοῦσα : probably μενεγχέας is to be read : ναυκράτης in Herodot. 5. 36 is more properly a substantive ; the accusative ναυκράτην occurs in Eust. 1490. 19, where it seems to have more the character of an adjective ; the other compounds, when belonging to the third declension, are oxytone, as ἀκρατής, ἐγκρατής, etc. : ναυτάρης is a barbarous word, see H. D. : πετράκης (or πετρήκης), see above, § 701 : πολυδήνης, Hesych., should certainly be oxytone, like δυσδηνής, Chœrob. C. 52. 23 : ποδάρκης, Arc. 117. 26, sometimes falsely oxytone, e. g. Pind. Pyth. 5. 45 ; Olymp. 13. 38 : ποδώκης, Apion and Herodorus, while they allowed that this as an epithet of Achilles was barytone, seem to deny that it was so in any other collocation, Eust. 340. 21 ; Schol. Ven. B. 764 : πυρικαίης, Anth. Pal. 6. 281, has been corrected into πυρικαής : τετραένης (?) 'Theocr. 7. 147 : τετράενες δὲ πίθων ἀπελύετο κρατὸς ἄλειφαρ : sic enim accentus ponitur in libris et ap. Gregor. Cor. p. 273 : Callimacho Apoll. 57 : τετραέτης τὰ πρῶτα θεμείλια Φοῖβος ἔπηξε, Santenius refert Valckenarium restituisse τετραένης ;' H. D.

706. Barytones retract the accent in the vocative and neuter singular, as ἐπιμήκης, ἐπίμηκες, εὐμήκης, εὔμηκες, κακοήθης, κακόηθες, παμμεγέθης, παμμέγεθες, συνήθης, σύνηθες, so μισάληθες, φιλάληθες ; except those in ήεις, ώδης, ώης (?) ὤλης, ὤρης, and ήρης, which follow the general rule, as ἀμφῶες, αὐτῶρες, νεῶρες, εὐῶδες, ἐξῶλες, πανῶλες, ξιφῆρες, χαλκῆρες.

707. NOTE 1.—Arc. 117.9; Joh. Alex. 13. 30; Chœrob. C. 436. 28 ; Chœrob. E. 19. 6; Schol. Ven. Σ. 519; Theog. Can. 118. 23 : πᾶν εἰς ΕΣ λῆγον οὐδέτερον, πλὴν τοῦ Κυνόσαργες, τὴν μονογενείαν οὐ προσίεται, ἀκολουθεῖ γὰρ τὰ πάντα καὶ κατὰ τόνον καὶ κατὰ γραφὴν τῇ κλητικῇ τοῦ ἀρσενικοῦ· οἷον ὦ εὔμηκες, τὸ εὔμηκες· ὦ εὔηθες, τὸ εὔηθες· ὦ ἀσθενές, τὸ ἀσθενές : Joh. Alex. 13. 35 : τὸ αὔταρκες καὶ αὔθαδες φησὶν ὁ Ἡρωδιανὸς μὴ ἔχειν ἀφορμὴν προπαροξύνεσθαι : Theodos. Can. 1004. 17 : ἀναβιβάζουσι δὲ τὸν τόνον ἐπὶ τῆς κλητικῆς καὶ τὰ εἰς ΗΣ κύρια σύνθετα, Διόμηδες, Ἀριστόφανες, καὶ τὰ παρ' οὐδετέρων ἐσχηματισμένα εἰς ΗΣ, εὔμηκες, κακόηθες· παραλόγως γὰρ ἐβαρύνθη τὸ αὔταρκες, αὔθαδες, κάταντες : on this Chœroboscus, C. 437. 6, thus comments : δεῖ δὲ γινώσκειν ὅτι τὰ παρὰ τὸ ἀντῶ καὶ τὰ παρὰ τὸ ἀρκῶ καὶ τὰ παρὰ τὸ ἄδειν (ὃ σημαίνει τὸ ἀρέσκειν) καὶ τὰ παρὰ τὸ ἀκὴ (ὃ σημαίνει τὴν ὀξύτητα τοῦ σιδήρου), βαρυτονούμενα κατὰ τὴν εὐθεῖαν, ἔχουσι τὴν κλητικὴν προπαροξύτονον, οἷον κατάντης κάταντες, προσάντης πρόσαντες, αὐτάρκης αὔταρκες, ὀλιγάρκης ὀλίγαρκες [the neuter of this is oxytone in Lucian Tim. 54], αὐθάδης αὔθαδες, τανυήκης τανύηκες, ἀμφήκης ἄμφηκες. Οὕτω γὰρ κάλλιόν ἐστι λέγειν ὅτι χαρακτῆρι ταῦτα ὑποπίπτουσιν, καὶ μὴ σημειοῦσθαι ὡς ἐποίησεν ὁ παρὼν τεχνικός ; cf. Chœrob. C. 52. 5 sq.; Kühner, G. G. I. 376, quotes ξυρῆκες from Eurip. Eléct. 335, and ξυρηκές from Eurip. Phœniss. 375 = 372, ed. Nauck, who prints ξυρῆκες, but it is doubtful whether such accents are correct.

708. NOTE 2.—According to Arc. 117. 25 the neuter of ποδάρκης is oxytone, ποδαρκές : the same thing is asserted by E. M. 678. 3, who adds that its vocative is proparoxytone, πόδαρκες ; cf. A. G. Oxon. 1. 348. 16 ; ποδῶκες in Æschylus, S. c. T. 623. ed. Didot, from ποδώκης is probably correct.

709. NOTE 3.—The words in ετης (cf. § 703), when oxytone, are also oxytone in the vocative, as τριετής, τριετές : when paroxytone, the vocative and the neuter are proparoxytone, as τριέτης, τρίετες ; Chœrob. C. 436. 33.

710. NOTE 4.—*Genitive Plural.* The genitive plural, when contracted, is perispomenon, as εὐμηκῶν (= εὐμηκέων), εὐσεβῶν, except those in ωδης, which are paroxytone according to Aristarchus, though his accentuation was denounced as absurd by many, hence δυσώδων, εὐώδων, τριήρων (or τριηρῶν, see § 674), αὐτάρκων (and αὐταρκῶν) in Attic, together with συνήθων and κακοήθων ; our books vary, but are said to be tolerably consistent in circumflexing the gentive plural of those in ὠδης ; cf. Kühner, G. G. 1. 375. It does not appear that the grammarians extended this to all words in ηθης and ηρης, as Göttling, Accent. p. 327, seems to think ; cf. Chœrob. C. 459. 11 ; Joh. Alex. 19. 13 ; Arc. 136. 21.

711. NOTE 5.—*Neuter of Adjectives used as Substantives.* The neuter singular of adjectives in ης, when used exclusively as a substantive, loses its adjectival accent and becomes proparoxytone, as Κυνόσαργες, ὄμαργες, πεύκαες, ῥώπαες : Arc. 124. 7. For exceptions to this see § 576.

712. NOTE 6.—*Syncopated Forms.* Epic syncopated forms in εα = εεα from words in εης, keep the accent on the ε, as δυσκλέα = δυσκλεέα from δυσκλεής : so also εὐκλέας = εὐκλεέας, εὐκλέα = εὐκλεέα, εὐκλέων = εὐκλεέων. When contracted the general rule is observed, as ἀκλέα, ἀκλεᾶ, ὑγιέα, ὑγιᾶ, etc. : cf. Matthiä, Gr. Gr. § 113. 1 ; Eust. 187. 12 ; Schol. Ven. B. 115 ; Θ. 441 ; Κ. 281. The ways in which such words are contracted must be learnt from some good Greek grammar ; the accentuation is always regular, e. g. εὐκλείας = εὐκλεέας or εὐκλέας, Schol. Ven. K. 281 ; Lob. Path. 1. 263 : heteroclite forms, like ἔμπλεα = ἔμπλεον, Nicand. Alex. 164, are accented differently by different editors ; cf. Lob. Path. 1. 266 ; Ἡρακλες (on which see § 675) is hardly an exception.

(b) With a Consonantal Characteristic.

713. Those with a consonant for their characteristic retract the accent when their second factor consists of more than one syllable, as διχόμηνις, δυστάλᾱς, εὔακτιν, εὔπολις, θεοκρήπις, ἵππουρις, κάτηλυς, κισσοχίτων, λεύκασπις, λιπόπατρις, μισαλάζων, πάμμεγᾰς, πολυγλώχιν, χαλκογλώχιν; except *oxytone*, 1. those in ας (gen. αδος), as περιδρομάς, πολυδειράς, συμπληγάς, χαλκεμβολάς, χαμαιευνάς; 2. those in ις which are exclusively feminine, as ἀγελῆϊς, εὐπλοκαμίς, Παναχαιΐς; 3. *perispomena*, those in ωπις, as βλοσυρῶπις, δολῶπις, ἑλικῶπις, εὐρυῶπις, κοιλῶπις, κυνῶπις. Those in ις (or τις) derived from or implying masculine forms in ης (or της) follow the rules given above, § 644, as ἡεροφοῖτις, προθῆϊβις. Those in ξ are always accented on the penultimate, according to § 620, as αἰγιδίωξ, θηριδίωξ, κατῶρυξ, ὁμῆλιξ; E. M. 451. 22.

714. *Oblique Cases.*—These are regular, except that neuters and vocatives in ον retract the accent, as ἐνοσίχθων, ἐνόσιχθον, εὐδαίμων, εὔδαιμον, κυλλοποδίων, κυλλοπόδιον, ὀλβιοδαίμων, ὀλβιόδαιμον; but those in φρον follow the general rule, as δαΐφρων, δαΐφρον.

715. NOTE 1.—Chœrob. C. 437. 35: τὰ εἰς Ω σύνθετα διὰ τοῦ Ω, δηλονότι, ὅταν ἔχωσι τὴν κλητικὴν εἰς ΟΝ διὰ τοῦ Ο, προπαροξύνονται κατὰ τὴν κλητικὴν ὑπὲρ δύο συλλαβὰς ἔντα οἷον ... ὀλβιοδαίμων ὦ ὀλβιόδαιμον, κυλλοποδίων ὦ κυλλοπόδιον : Chœrob. C. 438. 18 : σημειοῦται δὲ ὁ τεχνικὸς καὶ λέγει χωρὶς τῶν παρὰ τὸ φρήν· ταῦτα δὲ πρὸ μιᾶς ἔχουσι τὸν τόνον ἐν τῇ κλητικῇ καὶ οὐ προπαροξύνονται, οἷον ὦ δαΐφρον, ὦ περίφρον : Joh. Alex. 14. 7 ; A. G. Oxon. 1. 17. 16.

716. NOTE 2.—Eust. 26. 29 : βαρύνεται δὲ τὸ εὐκνῆμις κανόνι τοιούτῳ· τὰ εἰς ΙΣ θηλυκὰ ὀξύτονα εἰ μὲν ἐν τῇ συνθέσει φυλάσσει τὸ θηλυκὸν μόνον γένος, καὶ τὸν αὐτὸν τόνον φυλάσσει, οἷον· σκελίς, περισκελίς. εἰ δὲ μεταληπτικὰ γίνονται καὶ ἀρσενικοῦ γένους, μεθίστανται εἰς βαρεῖαν τάσιν, οἷον· ἐλπὶς δύσελπις. τοῦτο γὰρ κοινόν ἐστι τῷ γένει. ταύτῃ τοι καὶ τὸ καταιγὶς ὀξύνεται ὡς μονογενές· τὸ δὲ μελάναιγις βαρύνεται. οὕτω δὲ καὶ τὸ κλῇς εὐκλῇϊς, κνημὶς εὐκνῆμις. ὁμοίως καὶ ψηφὶς πολυψήφις : thus also πολυκλῆϊς, Eust. 174. 8, though some made it oxytone, Schol. Ven. B. 175 ; see also E. M. 518. 32 ; Philem. Lex. p. 40. § 97 ; Eust. 1437. 50 : σκοπητέον δὲ μή ποτε φαῦλα τῶν ἀντιγράφων ἐν οἷς ὀξύνεται ἡ εὐπλοκαμίς· δέον γάρ, ὥσπερ κρηπὶς μελαγκρῆπις, ψηφὶς πολυψήφις......κνημὶς εὐκνήμις, οὕτω καὶ πλοκαμὶς εὐπλοκάμις : Ἁλικρηπίς and εὐκρηπίς are almost certainly wrong for ἁλικρῆπις, εὐκρῆπις ; Schol. Ven. T. 87 ; Ω. 318 ; E. M. 83. 53 ; A. G. Oxon. 1. 230. 1.

717. NOTE 3.—The extreme difficulty of distinguishing substantives from adjectives must serve as some apology for the vagueness of the rule above given: the following real or apparent exceptions to it may be worth noting: λοξοτρόχις, Anth. Pal. 9. 191 : παμμῆτις is quoted by H. D. from Theoph. ad Autol. 2. p. 74 (108 Wolf.) ; but it should be πάμμητις, like πάμμηνις, for all in μητις are *proparoxytone*, Moschop. ad Hes. Op. 23. p. 64. Gaisf. ; cf. also E. M. 518 : ἀπειρωδίν in Stephanus is a mistake, as are πολυαυχήν and πυριγλωχίν, which are all paroxytone : λιπερνής, Diod. Sic. 12. 40 is paroxytone in Photius : φιλοκηδεμών,

Xenoph. Ages. 11. 12, ought by analogy to be paroxytone : βαθυπυθμήν, E. M. 696. 34 is incorrect, it should be βαθυπύθμην like ἀπύθμην, and ὀλιγοπύθμην, Theog. Can. 86. 14 : μισοκαῖσαρ (?) Plut. 1. 987 : προπρεών, Pind. Nem. 7. 126, a false accent and quite contrary to analogy, Theog. Can. 29. 8.

According to Arc. 18. 24, λητροβαστάξ (or λιτροβαστάξ) and νεκροβαστάξ are oxytone, but the latter word is paroxytone in Chœrob. C. 303. 34 ; 304. 2. 14, and in E. M. 270. 30.

718. Those of which the last factor is *monosyllabic* fall into two classes, according as the monosyllable is derived from a substantive or from a verb.

Last Factor derived from a Substantive.—These are accented on the penultimate, as περίφρων, πρόφρων, σώφρων ; μακρόχειρ, μελαινόρριν, οὐλόθριξ, μακρόρρις, μελαινόφλεψ ; Αἰθίοψ, ἦνοψ, μέροψ, νῶροψ, οἶνοψ, στέροψ, χάροψ ; δίπλαξ, τρίπλαξ ; ἀλλόχρως, λευκόχρως, μονόχρως, ῥοδόχρως ; ἀρτίπος, ἀελλόπος (Eust. 768. 48) ; except those in ωψ, which are oxytone, as ἀγλαώψ, αἱματώψ, ἀμβλώψ, βοώψ (also the name of a fish), γλαυκώψ, γοργώψ, δεινώψ, εὐώψ, κελαινώψ· λιπαρώψ, μονώψ, ταυρώψ, χαρώψ, but ἑλίκωψ, εὐρύωψ (?), κύκλωψ, μήλωψ, μύωψ, νυκτάλωψ, and πολύωψ (?), are paroxytone.

719. NOTE.—Arc. 94. 15 : τὰ εἰς Ψ πολυσύλλαβα ἔχοντα πρὸ τοῦ Ψ Ο ἢ Ε βαρύνεται. Πέλοψ, Δρύοψ, μέροψ, βούκλεψ [sic], τυρόκλεψ. Those in χρως are occasionally oxytone, e. g. κελαινοχρώς, μελαγχρώς, Arist. H. A. 9. 41. 1 ; μελαινοχρώς, μελανοχρώς, μολιβδοχρώς, μολυβδοχρώς, μολυβοχρώς, οἰνοχρώς, πελαργοχρώς, Lycoph. 24, but such accents are unquestionably false ; Arc. 93. 21 : τὰ εἰς ΩΣ σύνθετα ἀπὸ τῶν εἰς ΩΣ μονοσυλλάβων παροξύνεται· ζώς ἀείζως, χρώς λευκόχρως. τὸ μέντοι ὑποδμὼς ὀξύνεται ὡς παρέλκουσαν ἔχον τὴν ὑπό.

Words in ωψ.—Arc. 94. 22 : τὰ εἰς ΩΨ πολυσύλλαβα κύρια ὄντα ἢ προσηγορικὰ βαρύνονται· Κύκλωψ ἴωψ μώλωψ. σεσημείωται, ὥς τινές φασι, τὸ εὐρώψ ὀξυνόμενον. τὰ μέντοι ἐπιθετικὰ ὀξύνεται, ὑπεσταλμένων τῶν ὑποπεπτωκότων κυρίοις, ἢ τῶν ἰδιαζόντων· μονώψ (ὁ μονόφθαλμος) κελαινώψ, τυφλώψ. τὸ δὲ ἑλίκωψ καὶ μύωψ (ὁ μυὸς ὀφθαλμοὺς ἔχων) βαρύνεται, ὥσπερ τὸ κύκλωψ καὶ κέκρωψ [leg. κέρκωψ] (ὁ δόλιος) καὶ ἴωψ ὁ κυνίσκος ; Schol. Ven. I. 503 ; cf. Eust. 1279. 17 ; 768. 40 ; 1388. 64 ; Lob. Ajax 338 : ἄζωψ (?) αἱ ξηραὶ ἐκ τῆς θεωρίας, Hesych. : αἱμάλωψ or αἱμαλώψ (?) is used both as a substantive and an adjective : κεραώψ is falsely κεράωψ in Manetho 4. 91 ; H. D. : μονώψ is also found paroxytone, but wrongly : νυκτάλωψ, Eust. 768. 40 : πολύωψ, Anth. Pal. 6. 65. 9 ; 9. 765 : φίλωψ (?)=φίλος, Hesych., is perhaps not an instance coming under this rule : Περιγλώξ, a variant in Hes. Scut. 398 L. S., if a genuine word, is undoubtedly false in accent, and to περιστίξ in Nonnus 2. 170 the like remark applies ; concerning the latter Lobeck (Par. 280) says, ' adjectivum περίστιξ [it is περιστίξ in the passage referred to] eximitur 'mutata interpunctione φρουραὶ δὲ περὶ στίχες ἦσαν Ὀλύμπου ; ' on ὑποδμώς see above, § 575.

720. *Last Factor derived from a Verb.*—Those the latter half of which is derived from a verb, and short by nature, take the accent on the penultimate, as κατῶβλεψ (used as a substantive); ἄζυξ, δίζυξ, ἐτερόζυξ; βοὔκλεψ, τυρόκλεψ; αἰγίλιψ, χέρνιψ (used as a substantive); ἐπίτεξ; αἰγότριψ, ἀλότριψ, ἀστύτριψ, εὔτριψ, οἰκότριψ, πεδότριψ; οἰνόφλυξ, πρόσφυξ; except those in as and αξ, which are oxytone, as ὀρειβάς, ὀροβάς; κυνοσπάς, λυκοσπάς, νεοσπάς; παραστάς, χοροστάς; ἀποφράς; ἀποσφάξ, διασφάξ (not διάσφαξ, cf. Arc. 18. 22), ὑποσφάξ.

721. NOTE.—According to Arc. 94. 13, πελεθοβάψ and πλινθοβάψ are oxytone; on κατῶβλεψ see Arc. 94. 15 ; Eust. 1401. 16 : ἐφευροκλέψ and νακοκλέψ occur as oxytone in the text of Theog. Can. 97. 30, but they should be paroxytone; cf. Arc. 94. 16 ; Lob. Par. 292 : βλεφαροσπάξ, for which the corrupt form βλεφαροπάξ occurs in Draco 19. 10, is also oxytone ; cf. Göttling, Accent. p. 333 : νυμφόβας, Hesych., a false accent for νυμφοβάς : χοροστάς, St. Byz. s. v. Λίμναι. What part of speech προτύψ (sic), Phot. Bib. 532. 5 may be, I know not; possibly it is an adverb.

722. When the last factor is derived from a verb, and by nature long, these adjectives are oxytone, as ἀβλής, κεραυνοβλής, νιφοβλής; κυνοβλώψ᾿ παραβλώψ᾿ ὑποβλώψ; ἀβρώς᾿ ἡμιβρώς, παιδοβρώς; ἀγνώς᾿ ἀλλογνώς; ἀδμής, νεοδμής, σιδηροδμής; ὀσφυήξ; εὐθήξ, νεοθήξ; δασπλής; ἡμιθνής, λιμοθνής, νεοθνής, χειμοθνής; κατακλώς; ἀκμής, δουρικμής, μεγαλοκμής; εὐκράς, μελικράς, νεοκράς; ἀρματοπήξ, κρυσταλλοπήξ; αἰνοπλήξ, ἀκανθοπλήξ, κεραυνοπλήξ; δασπλής; ἀπτήν; ἀπτώς; ἀρρώξ, διαρρώξ, καταρρώξ; ἀεισκώψ; ἀστήν; φυλλοστρώς; ἰθυτμής; ἀποτμήξ; ἀμφιτρής; θυλακοτρώξ, κυαμοτρώξ, φυλλοτρώξ; ἀτρώς.

723. NOTE 1.—Lobeck (Phryn. 611) thinks that all these words are paroxytone, and on the strength of an improbable emendation which he makes in the Venetian Scholia (B. 755) claims the authority of Aristarchus for his opinion : but the following passages from the grammarians will show that he is not justified in doing so, for it is incredible that they should have conspired to teach a doctrine directly at variance with that of the arch-critic without taking more frequent notice of his theories than they have done; E. M. 358. 2 : ἐπιβλής᾿ ... τὰ εἰς ΗΣ λήγοντα ἀρσενικὰ σύνθετα ὑπάρχοντα, ἔχοντα ἐν τῷ τέλει μίαν συλλαβὴν τοῦ ῥήματος, καὶ διὰ τοῦ ΤΟΣ κλινόμενα, ἅπαντα ὀξύνονται· οἷον, προβλής, ἡμιθνής, ἀδμής, ἀσπιδοβλής. παρὰ Ἀριστοφάνει οἱ μὲν βαρύνουσι, ὅτι δοκός ἐστιν· οἱ δὲ ποιότης δοκοῦ· οὐ γὰρ βαρύνεται. οὐ γάρ ἐστι βλὴς μονοσύλλαβον καθ᾿ ἑαυτὸ ἐπὶ ταύτης τῆς ἐννοίας, ἵνα ἐν τῇ συνθέσει βαρύνεται· ὥσπερ τὸ Κρής, ἐτεόκρης: cf. Lob. Par. 82 : Eust. 629. 56 : ὀξύνεται δὲ (βουπλήξ) κανόνι τοιούτῳ. τὰ κατὰ παρακείμενον συντεθειμένα ὀνόματα εἰς ΗΣ ἢ εἰς Ξ λήγοντα ὀξύνονται, κἂν μίαν φυλάττῃ τοῦ ῥήματος συλλαβήν, οἷον ἀδμής, ἀβλής, ἡμιθνής, κυαμοτρώξ, βουπλήξ, σεσημείωται τὸ ὕσπληξ. ἐν δὲ ῥητορικῷ λεξικῷ εὕρηται καὶ ὀρθοπλήξ ἵππος, ὁ ὀρθὸς αἰρόμενος καὶ πλήσσων. προφέρεται δὲ καὶ ἀκανθοπλήξ καὶ νωτοπλήξ καὶ οἰστροπλήξ, ὡς τό, τῆς οἰστροπλήγος ἄλσος Ἰνάχου κόρης, καὶ μεθυπλήξ, ὡς Καλλίμαχος, τοῦ μεθυπλῆγος φροίμιον Ἀντιλόχου. περίεργον οὖν, φασί, λέγειν ὅτι τὰ μὲν δραστικὰ ὀξύνονται· τὰ δὲ παθητικὰ βαρύνεται, πάντα γὰρ οἱ Ἀττικοὶ ὀξύνουσι δίχα τοῦ ὕσπληξ: Eust. 1359. 8 : ὀξύνεται δὲ ὁ ἐπιβλὴς ὡς τὸ προβλής, ἡμιθνής, ἀδμής. τὰ γὰρ εἰς Σ λήγοντα ἀρσενικά, σύνθετα ἔχοντα ἐν τῷ τέλει μίαν συλλαβὴν τοῦ ῥήματος, καὶ διὰ τοῦ ΤΟΣ κλινόμενα, ὀξύνεται.

διὸ καὶ παρὰ Ἀριστοφάνει τό, ὁ μέγας οὗτος κολακώνυμος ἀσπιδαποβλής, ὅ ἐστι
ῥίψασπις, καίτοι ἐκ τριῶν συγκείμενον λέξεων, ὅμως ὀξύνεται. οὐ καλῶς οὖν, φασί, τὸ
ἐπιβλὴς βαρύνει Ἀρίσταρχος: Eust. 1401. 11 : παρὰ δὲ τραγικοῖς καὶ κωμικοῖς παροξυτόνως εὔρηται χερνίβα. Εὐριπίδης, εἰς χερνίβος βάψειεν Ἀλκμήνης γόνος ... χρὴ
μέντοι φησὶ [? φασὶ] προπαροξυτόνως προφέρεσθαι. τὰ γὰρ τοιάδε ῥηματικὰ σύνθετα
εἰς ψ λήγοντα φυλάττοντα παραλήγουσαν παρακειμένου παθητικοῦ δηλαδὴ λεγομένου
διὰ τῶν δύο M ἐξ οὗ καὶ γεγόνασι βαρύνονται. λέλειμμαι λέλειψαι, αἰγίλιψ, τέτριμμαι
τέτριψαι οἰκότριψ, κέκλεμμαι βοόκλεψ. βέβλεμμαι κατώβλεψ (sic) οὗτως οὖν καὶ
νένιμμαι χέρνιψ : Epicharmus used χειρόνιψ, Eust. 1401. 11 ; Chœrob. C. 49. 5 : τὰ
εἰς Σ λήγοντα ὀξύτονα σύνθετα ἀπὸ ῥημάτων, μίαν συλλαβὴν φυλάττοντα τοῦ παθητικοῦ παρακειμένου, διὰ καθαροῦ τοῦ ΤΟΣ κλίνονται, οἷον κέκραται, χαλκοκρὰς χαλκοκρά-
τος, νεοκρὰς νεοκράτος, ὁ νεωστὶ κεκραμένος, ὁ χαλκῷ κεκραμένος, βέβληται, ἀβλὴς
ἀβλήτος, προβλὴς προβλήτος, τέθνηκα, ἡμιθνής, ἡμιθνήτος. Τοῦτο δέ, φημὶ δὴ τὸ
τέθνηκα τῇ μὲν φωνῇ ἐστιν ἐνεργητικόν, τῷ δὲ σημαινομένῳ παθητικόν, πάθος γὰρ
σημαίνει· τοιοῦτον ἐστὶ καὶ τὸ πέπτωκα, ἐξ οὗ γίνεται τὸ ἁπτὼς ἁπτῶτος, πάλιν,
τέτρωμαι, ἀτρὼς ἀτρῶτος· ἰδοὺ γὰρ ταῦτα πάντα μίαν συλλαβὴν ἐφύλαξαν τοῦ παθητικοῦ παρακειμένου, καὶ διὰ καθαροῦ τοῦ ΤΟΣ ἔχουσι τὴν γενικήν; cf. Philem. Lex.
p. 3. § 1 ; p. 27. § 72 ; Arc. 24. 28 ; 18. 18 ; 19. 5 ; 95. 19, etc.

724. NOTE 2.—βλης, E. M. 358. 2 : -βλως, ἀγχιβλώς· ἄρτι παρών, E. M. 15. 36,
is a strange form, but the accent is in accordance with analogy : -βλώψ, Eust. 768.
39 ; Schol. Ven. I. 503 : -βριξ, ἀβρίξ ἐγρηγορώς, Hesych. : -βρως, τριχοβρώς seems
to have fluctuated between an adjectival and substantival accent, for it is observed
by Schol. Aristoph. Ach. 1176 = 1110 : τριχόβρωτες, σῆτες· θρίψ σκώληξ κατεσθίων
τὰς τρίχας· καὶ προπερισπωμένως δὲ λέγεται τριχοβρῶτες : both accents occur in the
books. All the rest in βρως are oxytone : -γνως, ἀριγνώς is paroxytone in Pind.
Nem. 5. 21, but wrongly, cf. ἀγνώς, ἀλλογνώς, and Lob. Par. 181 : ἀβρόδαις,
Athen. 4. E, is probably not a verbal derivative : -δμης, E. M. 358. 2 : -δρας,
-δρης, ὑποδράς and ὑποδρής are of somewhat doubtful origin, see H. D. s. v.
ὑπόδρα.

725. NOTE 3.—θηξ, εὐθήξ and φιλοθήξ, Theog. Can. 40. 24 : νεοθήξ, Anth.
Pal. 7. 181, are sometimes made paroxytone by modern writers, e. g. by Lobeck
Phryn. 611 ; Par. 279 and others, but without authority, and contrary to analogy :
-θλιψ, χοιρόθλιψ, Aristoph. Vesp. 1364, is probably a wrong accent ; it is difficult
to determine whether this word is intended by Chœrob. C. 88. 16, who writes
χοιρόθριψ, and by Theog. Can. 98. 2, or a different one : -θνης, Chœrob. C. 49. 5 :
-κλως, the only word of this termination of which I have any note is κατακλῶθες,
Hom. Od. 7. 197 : -κλωψ, βιαιοκλώψ is oxytone in Lycoph. 548, though γυναικό-
κλωψ is paroxytone in the same author, 771 : ἀρχίκλωψ and ὀψίκλωψ are also
paroxytone in the books, but according to Arcadius 94. 22 they ought to be
oxytone if really adjectives : -κμης, E. M. 49. 27 : -κρας, according to Eust. 1559.
50, ἁλίκρας is barytone, and in the same passage he mentions χαλκόρας, but
the latter is expressly stated to be oxytone in several passages of Chœroboscus,
e. g. C. 49. 6 ; 141. 17 : thus also νεοκράς, εὐκράς (for which εὔκρας sometimes
occurs), μελικράς, μελισσοκράς (or μελισσόκρας? Hesych.) ; on the whole there
seems to be more authority for making words of this termination oxytone than
paroxytone, Chœrob. C. 416. 13 : καὶ πάλιν ἐστὶ τὸ μελίκρατον καὶ τὸ χαλκόκρατον,
τοῦ μελικράτου καὶ τοῦ χαλκοκράτου, τῷ μελικράτῳ καὶ τῷ χαλκοκράτῳ· καὶ γίνεται
κατὰ μεταπλασμὸν τῷ μελίκρατι καὶ τῷ χαλκοκράτι, καὶ προπαροξύνονται· ἐὰν δὲ
εὑρεθῶσι προπερισπωμένες αἱ δοτικαὶ αὗται, τῷ μελικράτι καὶ τῷ χαλκοκράτι, γνῶθι
ὅτι ἀπὸ τοῦ ὁ μελικρὰς καὶ ὁ χαλκοκρὰς γίνονται, καὶ οὐ κατὰ μεταπλασμὸν γεγόνασιν
ἀλλὰ κατὰ ἀκόλουθον κλίσιν, οἷον μελικρὰς μελικρᾶτος μελικρᾶτι, χαλκοκρὰς χαλκο-
κρᾶτος χαλκοκρᾶτι.

726. NOTE 4.—πηξ, substantives in πηξ appear to be generally paroxytone, adjectives oxytone, as ἀντίπηξ, διάπηξ, ἐπίπηξ, κάπηξ, κατάπηξ (?) but ἀρματοπήξ, κλινοπήξ, κρυσταλλοπήξ, ξυμπήξ, Theog. Can. 40. 22: -πληξ, in those ending with πληξ (as perhaps with other words similarly formed) some grammarians distinguished the active and passive significations by a difference of accent, thus in Philem. Lex. p. 27. § 72, βουπλήξ is oxytone, παράπληξ, κατάπληξ paroxytone: Phavorinus also distinguishes βουπλῆγες, οἱ πλήσσοντες τοὺς βύας from βούπληγες, οἱ πληγέντες ὑπὸ τῶν βοῶν, but Chœroboscus (C. 308. 26), a much better authority, makes them oxytone, εἰ δέ εἰσι σύνθετα, ἀπὸ ῥήματος δηλονότι, διὰ τοῦ Γ κλίνονται, καὶ φυλάττουσι μίαν συλλαβὴν τοῦ ῥήματος ἐξ οὗ γίνονται, οἷον πλήξω, οἰστροπλήξ . . . παραπλήξ . . . λαοπλήξ . . . ἀκανθοπλήξ . . . βουπλήξ. Ταῦτα δὲ πάντα σύνθετα ἀπὸ ῥήματος, ὀξύτονά εἰσι καὶ ἐπίθετα καὶ κοινὰ τῷ γένει . . . τὸ μέντοι ὕσπληξ καὶ ἀντίπληξ βαρύνονται, ἐπειδὴ προσηγορικά εἰσι, καὶ μόνου θηλυκοῦ γένους εἰσί: in accordance with this rule we find ἀντιπλήξ, Soph. Ant. 592: ἁπλήξ (though that is sometimes wrongly paroxytone) and λινοπλήξ, Theog. Can. 40. 21: κυματοπλήξ, μεθυπλήξ: in Eust. 1837. 39 we have γαστερόπληξ, which, if not an adjective, may be correct: so also καταπλήξ may perhaps be paroxytone when a substantive; cf. Arc. 19. 5 -πτην, ἀπτήν, E. M. 133. 38; Arc. 8. 19: -πτωξ, ἀπτώξ, πολυπτώξ, Theog. Can. 41. 11; Chœrob. C. 176. 5: -πτως, ἀπτώς, Arc. 93. 20; Chœrob. C. 49. 13; 65. 7.

727. NOTE 5.—ρηξ, μονορρήξ, Hesych.; -ρωξ, there seems to have been some difference of opinion as to the accent of ἀπορρώξ, for we read in Schol. Ven. B. 755: ἀπορρὼξ δέ, ὀξυτόνως μὲν, ἡ ἀπορροή· βαρυτόνως δὲ τὸ ἀπόρρηγμα: but in another scholium, Ἀρίσταρχος ὀξυτόνως, ὡς θυλακοτρώξ. καὶ ἡ σύνθεσις δὲ τοῦτο ἀπαιτεῖ, ὅ τι ἂν σημαίνῃ, εἴτε πάθος, εἴτε ἐνέργειαν, where for ὀξυτόνως Lobeck (Phryn. 611) would read παροξυτόνως: but I find no authority declaring that Aristarchus barytoned these adjectives as Lobeck seems to think he did: at any rate, Herodian considered both ἀπορρώξ and θυλακοτρώξ oxytone, cf. Arc. 19. 10, and those in ρωξ from ῥήγνυμι are regularly ὀxytone in the books, as ἀμφιρρώξ, ἀρρώξ, A. G. Paris. 1. 396. 26, διαρρώξ, καταρρώξ, λοφορρώξ, περιρρώξ, ὑπορρώξ, while those formed from ῥώξ, *a grape* or *olive*, are paroxytone, as κυκλόρρωξ, μεγαλόρρωξ, μικρόρρωξ, πυκνόρρωξ, though φιλόρρωξ is falsely oxytone in Auth. Pal. 7. 22: πνευμόρρωξ from ῥήγνυμι is regular, being a substantive: -σκωψ, ἀεισκώψ, Arist. H. A. 9. 28. 1 (where one MS. has ἀεὶ σκῶπες), if genuine, is an adjective used as a substantive: 'in Aristotele ed. Schneider. ἀεισκῶπες properispomene, ut ἀειναῦται [this is of course not a parallel case] et ἀεισκωπῶν perispomene: in Athenæo et Eustathio proparoxytone ἀείσκωπες, et paroxytone ἀεισκώπων editum, et ita Schneider in Lex. et Ælian,' *Fix* ap. H. D.: -στην, on ἀστήν see Lob. Phryn. 466: -στρως, φυλλοστρώς, Anth. Pal. 9. 338.

728. NOTE 6.—τηξ, μολιβδοτήξ, Chœrob. C. 309. 11: τὸ μολιβδοτήξ, ὥς φησιν Ἡρωδιανὸς ἐπὶ τῇ Καθόλου, τινὲς δὲ βαρύνουσι παραλόγως: no trace of this word remains in the epitome of Arcadius, though it occurs, together with κεραμοτήξ, in Theog. Can. 40. 23: -τμης, ἰθυτμής, Schol. Ven. Π. 44: -τρής, ἀμφιτρής, ἡμιτρής, Chœrob. C. 174. 7: -τρωξ, Eust. 1922. 10; Chœrob. C. 83. 26: -τρως, Chœrob. C. 49. 13.

Barbarous Words.

729. In general those barbarous or un-Hellenic nouns which exhibit a termination identical with that of any true Greek substantive or adjective, follow the rules already given for them, as Βαγράδας, Ptol. 4. 3. 16–18, Βουζάρα, Κίρνα, Μάμψαρον, Σισάρα, though there are numerous examples to the contrary. Those, on the other hand, which have an utterly un-Hellenic form are for the most part oxytone, as ᾿Αβέλ (or ῎Αβελ, Theodos. Gramm. 92. 19), ᾿Αβραάμ, ᾿Αδάμ, ᾿Αλιλάτ, ᾿Ασμάχ, Δαβίδ, ᾿Ελιφάτζ, Θαμύζ, Ἰωσήφ, ᾿Ισαάκ, Λώτ, Μελχισεδέκ, Μιχαήλ, Μωΰθ, Νηΐθ, Νεούτ, Νεσόγ, οἰόρ, Οὐροτάλ. Πνούψ ῾Ριούρ, Σαβαώθ ; but there are a large number of exceptions, e. g. Πατένεϊτ, Schol. Plat. Tim. 22 B; Ζυφᾶ or Ζίφαρ, Ptol. 4. 9. 6; Σούβουρ, Ptol. 4. 1. 13; ᾿Ιγίλγιλι, ᾿Ιγιλγίλει, or ᾿Ιγιλγιλεῖ; ᾿Ασισάραθ or ᾿Ασσαράθ, Ptol. 4. 2. 11; Τουσιατάθ or Τουσιάγαθ, Ptol. 4. 2. 31; Θεῦθ, Plat. Phædr. 274 B, but Φθούθ, Ptol. 4. 1. 3. It would be a waste of time and space to catalogue the vagaries of Greek scribes; they show a general disposition to write barbarous words oxytone, but it is only a disposition, which is often checked by their learning or their ignorance.

CHAPTER V.

ACCENTUATION OF PRONOUNS AND NUMERALS.

730. *Personal Pronouns.*—In Attic the personal pronouns are oxytone in the Nominative, Dative, and Accusative singular (except οἷ perispomenon), and in the Nominative dual; perispomenon in the Genitive singular, Genitive and Dative dual; except σφωΐν oxytone, and in all cases of the plural, except σφέα and σφίσι paroxytone, hence—

SINGULAR.

Nom.	..	ἐγώ		σύ	ἴ
Gen.	..	ἐμοῦ	μοῦ	σοῦ	οὗ
Dat.	..	ἐμοί	μοί	σοί	οἷ
Accus.	..	ἐμέ	μέ	σέ	ἕ

DUAL.

| Nom. Accus. | νώ | | σφώ | σφωέ |
| Gen. Dat. | νῷν | | σφῷν | σφωΐν |

PLURAL.

Nom.	..	ἡμεῖς	ὑμεῖς	σφεῖς	Neut. σφέα.
Gen.	..	ἡμῶν	ὑμῶν	σφῶν	
Dat.	..	ἡμῖν	ὑμῖν	σφίσι	
Accus.	..	ἡμᾶς	ὑμᾶς	σφᾶς	Neut. σφέα.

Νίν, μίν, and σφέ are oxytone. Those printed in thick type are enclitics.

When γε is added to the Nominative or Dative of ἐγώ the accent is thrown upon the first syllable, as ἔγωγε, ἔμοιγε; if written as two words, the general rule for enclitics holds, hence ἐγώ γε, ἐμοί γε, ἐμέ γε.

731. NOTE.—For the accent of several of the dialectic forms mentioned below there is no authority except the practice of the books. In the text of Apollonius some are left without any accent.

Singular: Nominative.—Ἐγώ, Attic; ἐγών Doric; ἰών (or ἰάν) Bœotian, σύ, ἴ, τύ, τού, τούν, are oxytone, Arc. 178. 19; Apoll. Pron. 63. 64: Greg. Cor. p. 263, Schäf. ἐγώνη, ἐγώνγα, ἐγώγα, ἰώγα, τούγα, ἰώνγα, ἰώνει, τύνη are paroxytone. According to Greg. Cor. p. 261 Schäf. the Æolians said ἐγῶν, but he is probably mistaken, ἔγω or ἔγων being the form proper to their dialect.

Genitive.—Perispomena: ἐμοῦ τεοῦ ἑοῦ (or ἕου (?) Apoll. Synt. 130, cf. Pron. 107) μοῦ σοῦ οὗ, ἐμεῦ σεῦ εὗ μεῦ τεῦ, ποῦ, ἐοῦ, ἐμεῦς τεῦς, ἐμοῦς τεοῦς τιοῦς ἑοῦς, ἐμῶς; properispomena, ἐμοῖο τεοῖο ἑεῖο, ἐμεῖο σεῖο εἶο; paroxytone, ἐμέο σεό τέο ἕο, ἐμέθεν μέθεν σέθεν ἕθεν, ἐμέος τέος, ἐμείως ἐμείω τίως τίος: Apoll. Pron. 94 sq.; Joh. Alex. 23. 14; Arc. 179. 19.

Dative.—Oxytone, ἐμοί σοί μοί τοί, ἐμίν τίν ἵν or ἵν σφίν, τεῖν εῖν, ἐμύ: in Æolic ἔμοι was barytone, Apoll. Pron. 104; paroxytone, ἐμίνη τίνη ἐμίνγα. Οῖ is perispomenon, Joh. Alex. 23. 9: Schol. Ven. I. 392; Λ. 201; Arc. 178. 20; Apoll. Pron. 103: ἐπὶ δὲ τοῦ ᾗ ὀλίγον οῖ παῖδα περισπῶμεν. ὅθεν ὡς παράλογον ὁ Σιδώνιος ὤξυνεν, ᾗ αἱ ὁμοιοκατάληκτοι καὶ ὁμότονοι κατὰ πᾶν πρόσωπον.

Accusative.—Oxytone, ἐμέ μέ σέ τέ ἕ, ἐμεῖ τεῖ, τίν μίν νίν, τύ σφέ. Ἑέ is also oxytone, Schol. Ven. Ω. 134, though some wrote ἕε, Apoll. Pron. 107; Synt. 134.

732. *Dual: Nominative and Accusative.*—Oxytone, νώ σφώ, σφωέ; properispomena, νῶϊ νῶε, σφῶϊ, Arc. 178. 23; 179. 5; Joh. Alex. 23. 24; Schol. Ven. E. 219; Κ. 546; S. V. A. 574.

Genitive and Dative.—Perispomena, νῶν σφῶν; properispomena, νῶϊν σφῶϊν, Joh. Alex. 23. 34: αἱ τοῦ τρίτου προσώπου ὀξύνονται πᾶσαι, καὶ ἐγκλίνονται πᾶσαι, αἰτιατικῆς μὲν σφωέ·

τίς γάρ σφωε θεῶν ἔριδι ξυνέηκε μάχεσθαι;

εὐθεῖα γὰρ τούτου οὐκ ἔστι· διότι οὐδὲ μία [εὐθεῖά ἐστιν ?] ἀντωνυμίας ἐγκλινομένης. γενικῆς δὲ καὶ δοτικῆς σφωΐν·

καί σφωιν δὸς ἄγειν.

τόνῳ μὲν γὰρ μόνῳ τῆς τοῦ δευτέρου διήνεγκεν. ὥστε ὅτε μὲν περὶ Ἀθηνᾶς καὶ Ἥρας Ζεὺς πρὸς τὴν Ἴριν φησίν, ἐγκλιτικῶς ἀναγινώσκομεν·

γυιώσω μέν σφωϊν ὑφ᾽ ἅρμασιν ὠκέας ἵππους·

Τρίτου γὰρ προσώπου. ὅτε (δὲ) πρὸς αὐτὰς ἡ Ἴρις, ὀρθο[τονεῖται καὶ] προπερισπῶνται [προπερισπᾶται ?]·

γυιώσειν μὲν σφῶϊν ὑφ᾽ ἅρμασιν ὠκέας ἵππους·

cf. Apoll. Pron. 115; Arc. 179. 5; Joannes Charax ap. A. G. 1153: ἐγκλίνονται δὲ ἀεὶ αἱ τοῦ τρίτου δυϊκαί,

ἀλλ᾽ εἴπ᾽ εἰ σφῶϊν καταλύσομεν ὠκέας ἵππους·

καί

τίς γάρ σφωε θεῶν ἔριδι;

Σφωΐν therefore of the Third person must be distinguished from σφῶϊν of the Second.

733. *Plural: Nominative.*—Perispomena, ἡμεῖς ὑμεῖς σφεῖς; paroxytone, ἡμέες ὑμέες, ἄμμες ὕμμες, σφέα; oxytone, ἀμές ὑμές, Greg. Cor. p. 238, ed. Schäf., but in two MSS. it is ὕμες; οὑμές; Arc. 179. 6; Joh. Alex. 24. 12; Apoll. Pron. 119.

Genitive.—Perispomena, ἡμῶν ἀμῶν ὑμῶν σφῶν; paroxytone, ἡμέων ὑμέων σφέων, ἡμείων ὑμείων σφείων, ἀμμέων ὑμμέων, ἀμίων, Arc. 179. 7; Joh. Alex. 24. 13; Apoll. Pron. 121.

Dative.—Perispomena, ἡμῖν ἀμῖν ὑμῖν οὑμῖν; oxytone, σφί σφίν φίν ψίν; paroxytone, ἄμμι ὕμμι, ἀμμέσι, σφίσι ἄσφι: when enclitic the Doric ἀμῖν shortens the ι and becomes properispomenon or oxytone ἀμίν, E. M. 84. 15; Apoll. Pron. 123: the enclitic ἡμιν is also properispomenon, E. M. 84. 15; cf. Joh. Alex. 24. 19; Arc. 179. 7; A. G. Oxon. 1. 188. 1.

Accusative.—Perispomena, ἡμᾶς ὑμᾶς σφᾶς (or σφάς, Arc. 179. 8); paroxytone, ἡμέας ὑμέας σφέας, σφέα, ἄμμε ὕμμε, ἄσφε; oxytone, ἀμέ ὑμέ σφέ ψέ, νίν; Arc. 179. 11; Joh. Alex. 24. 13; Apoll. Pron. 126 sq.

Besides those here mentioned there are sundry other forms of very rare occurrence, and more or less doubtful accentuation, which, it was thought, might be omitted; see Ahrens de Gr. ling. Dialect. 1. p. 123 sq.; 2. p. 287 sq.; Kühner, G. G. 1. 446-460.

734. NOTE.—On ἔγωγε and ἔμοιγε, see Joh. Alex. 23. 6; Schol. Ven. A. 173, 174; Ξ. 396; E. M. 613. 50; Apoll. de Adv. 594. 7.

According to the grammarians the oblique cases of ἡμεῖς and ὑμεῖς are under certain conditions enclitic; for these, together with the other enclitic pronouns, see Chap. 9.

735. *Reflexive and Reciprocal Pronouns.*—The reflexive pronouns are accented exactly like αὐτός, e. g. ἐμαυτοῦ, -ῆς; ἐμαυτῷ, -ῇ; ἐμαυτόν, -ήν; σεαυτοῦ, etc. The reciprocal ἀλλήλω is paroxytone in all cases and numbers.

736. *Possessive Pronouns.*—They are all oxytone, as ἐμός, ἀμός, σός, τεός, ἀμός, ὑμός, ἐός, ὅς; except those in ρος, which are proparoxytone, as ἡμέτερος, ὑμέτερος, σφωΐτερος, νωΐτερος, σφέτερος. In the oblique cases they follow nouns of the Second Declension.

NOTE.—Arc. 179. 22; Joh. Alex. 25. 13: the Æolic forms ἄμμος and ὕμμος are barytone; cf. Apoll. de Pron. 144.

737. The pronominal adjectives in δαπος are oxytone, as ἡμεδαπός, ὑμεδαπός (ἀλλοδαπός, παντοδαπός, τηλεδαπός), Joh. Alex. 25. 27; Arc. 179. 19. See above, § 403.

738. *Relative Pronoun and Article.*—The relative ὅς is oxytone in the nominative and accusative of all numbers, and perispomenon in other cases: the article is accented in the same manner, except that the nominative of the masculine and feminine, singular and plural, has no accent at all, as ὁ, ἡ, οἱ, αἱ: the dual is oxytone, as τώ τά.

739. Note.—The Epic ὄου and ἔης for οὗ and ἧς are paroxytone, E. M. 614. 5;
Lob. Path. 1. 61 : the Doric forms τός, τή, τοί, ταί are oxytone. According to the
grammarians ὁ, ἡ, οἱ and αἱ of the prepositive article are also *oxytone,* e. g. Arc.
178. 12 : αἱ εὐθεῖαι καὶ αἰτιατικαὶ τῶν ἄρθρων ὀξύνονται, ὁ, τόν, οἵ, τούς, ἥ : Joh.
Alex. 22. 26: πᾶν ἄρθρον ὀξύνεται, χωρὶς τῶν γενικῶν καὶ δοτικῶν· αὗται γὰρ περισπῶνται: A. G. 1153, but the printed books (and, I suppose, MSS. also) leave
these four words unaccented. The dialectic varieties of both relative and article
in the masculine and neuter are accented like the corresponding forms of the Second
Declension, those of the feminine like the parallel forms of the First, as τοῖο, τεῦ,
τάων, τοῖσι.

740. *Demonstrative Pronouns.*—Of these, αὐτός is oxytone and
ἕκαστος proparoxytone (see above, § 407), the rest take the accent on the penultimate, as ἄλλος, ἐκεῖνος, κεῖνος, οὗτος, τόσος:
the compound ὅδε is accented on the penultimate, and like the
relative, as ὅδε ἥδε τόδε, τοῦδε τῆσδε τῷδε. The compounds
in οντος are all perispomena in the Nominative singular, as
τηλικοῦτος, τοιοῦτος, τοσοῦτος, τυννοῦτος.

741. Note.—Cf. Chœrob. E. 76. 8; Arc. 179. 10; Joh. Alex. 24. 22. It is
to be noted that some grammarians wrote οἶδε for οἵδε, τῶδε for τώδε, and τοῦσδε
for τούσδε, but as these words are mere parathetic compounds, such an accentuation
is contrary to analogy, nor has it been followed; Schol. Ven. I. 167; Herodian ap.
Schol. Ven. Θ. 109; A. G. 1236. The Epic τοῖσδεσι or τοίσδεσσι is circumflexed
contrary to rule (§ 12); Eust. 818. 37; 1433. 61; 1902. 55: yet Schol. Odyss. N.
258 : προπαροξυτονητέον τὸ τοίσδεσσι : cf. Lob. Path. 2. 242, who shows that editors
and editions are very inconsistent.

742. The indefinite δεῖν, Attic δεῖνα, is accented on the penultimate in all cases, as δεῖνος, δεῖνι, δεῖνα, δεῖνες, δείνων, δεῖνας,
Joh. Alex. 25. 9; another form, δείνατος, δείνατι, was also in
use, see Trypho ap. Apoll. Pron. 76. Τις, *some one,* is enclitic;
when orthotone it is oxytone in all cases, except that the genitive
dual and plural, τινοῖν, τινῶν, are circumflexed; for further
details, see Chap. 9. The dialectic form τέων is paroxytone;
τίς, *who?* keeps the accent on ι through all cases and numbers,
as τίς τί, τίνος, τίνι, τίνα, etc., A. G. Oxon. 1. 405. 9. The other
indefinite pronominals are oxytone, as ποιός, ποσός; except πηλίκος paroxytone, the correlative forms of these are all accented
on the penultimate, as πόσος, τόσος, ὅσος; ποῖος, τοῖος, οἷος;
πηλίκος, τηλίκος, ἡλίκος. Πότερος (ὁπότερος), ἑκάτερος and ἕκαστος
are proparoxytone.

743. The prefix ὁ causes no alteration in the accent, hence
ἡλίκος ὁπηλίκος, ποῖος ὁποῖος, πόσος ὁπόσος, πότερος ὁπότερος.
In the parathetic compound ὅστις the former part of the word
is alone accented, and is identical with ὅς ἥ ὅ throughout with

an unaccented τις, τινος, etc. appended, hence ὅστις, ἥτις, ὅ τι, οὗτινος ἧστινος, ᾧτινι ᾗτινι, ὅντινα ἥντινα ὅ τι, ᾧτινε ἅτινε, οἷντινοιν αἷντινοιν, οἵτινες αἵτινες ἅτινα, ὧντινων, οἷστισι αἷστισι, οὕστινας ἅστινας : the contracted forms ὅτου, ὅτῳ, ὅτων, ὅτοις, and ἅττα are all paroxytone.

The Suffixes γέ, δή, ή, οὖν, δέ, πέρ, *and* ἱ.

744. **γέ.** With the Personal Pronouns of the first and second person this enclitic may form one word, and when it does, ἐγώ and ἐμοί become (as already noticed) proparoxytone; in all other cases the accent remains unaltered, as ἐμοῦγε, ἐμέγε, σοῦγε, σοίγε. The Spartan ἔγωγα also appears to have been proparoxytone, but the Bœotian ἐγώνγα and ἰώνγα are paroxytone.

745. NOTE.—E. M. 613. 50; Schol. Ven. Ξ. 396: οὔτε πυρὸς τόσσος γε πέλει βρόμος αἰθομένοιο. Ἀρίσταρχος φυλάσσει τὴν ὀξεῖαν ἐπὶ τῆς ΤΟΣ συλλαβῆς· ὁ δὲ Τυραννίων, τοσσός γε ἀνέγνω, τὴν ΣΟΣ συλλαβὴν ὀξύνων, οὐκ εὖ· ὁ γάρ γε οὐκ ἀλλάσσει τὸν τόνον τῶν πρὸ ἑαυτοῦ λέξεων. εἰ δέ τις λέγοι ἐπέκτασιν εἶναι μὴ σύνδεσμον, ἴστω ὅτι τὸ ἐναντίον χωρήσει· ἡ γὰρ διὰ τοῦ γε ἐπέκτασις τρίτην ἀπὸ τέλους ἐποίει τὴν ὀξεῖαν, ἔγωγε, ἔμοιγε.

746. **δή.** All pronouns compounded with δή are oxytone, with δήποτε proparoxytone, and with οὖν perispomena, as ὁστισδή, ὁστισδήποτε, ὁστισοῦν ἡτισοῦν ὁτιοῦν, οὑτινοσοῦν ὁτουοῦν ἡστινοσοῦν, ᾧτινιοῦν ὁτῳοῦν, ὁποσοσδή, ὁποσοσοῦν ὁσοσδήποτε ὁπηλικοσοῦν. It will be seen that these words follow the general rule for the accentuation of parathetic compound particles, see below, Chap. 7.

747. **ή** **and** **ἱ.** Those in η and· ι are oxytone, as ὁτιή, δηλονοτιή, τιή, οὑτοσί τουτί, ἐκεινωνί τουτουί ὁδί τουτοδί ταυταγί οὑτοιί αὑταιί, Arc. 179. 15.

748. **δέ.** All those compounded with the enclitic δε are accented on the penultimate, as ὅδε, ἥδε, τόδε, τοιόσδε τοσόσδε τηλικόσδε, Joh. Alex. 34. 15 ; Apoll. de Adv. 590 ; τοιοῦδε, τοιῷδε, Apoll. de Adv. 591. 617 ; E. M. 341. 35 ; 613. 50 ; the parathetic compound τῴδε is paroxytone.

749. NOTE.—Schol. Ven. B. 346: ἕν ἐστι τὸ τοῦσδε· διὸ προπερισπαστέον, modern editors write τούσδε ; Schol. Ven. Θ. 109 : τῴδε· παροξύνεται τὸ τῴδε παραλόγως· ἀληθὲς γὰρ ὡς ὅτι τὰ διὰ τοῦ ΔΕ ἐπεκτεταμένα, εἰ ἔχοι πρὸ τέλους φύσει μακράν, προπερισπᾶται. ὅπερ ὤφειλε κἀπὶ τοῦ τῴδε δὲ νῶϊ εἶναι, ἀλλ᾽ ὅμως πάλιν ἐπεκράτει καὶ ἐπὶ τούτου πρὸ τέλους ἡ ὀξεῖα. ταῦτα ὁ Ἡρωδιανὸς ἐν τῇ Ζ, ὅπου περὶ τοῦ ἰῷ διαλαμβάνει : cf. Schol. Ven. Λ. 432.

750. περ follows the rule for enclitics, hence ὅσπερ ἥπερ ὅπερ, οὗπερ ἧσπερ, ὅσοσπερ, οἷόσπερ (see Chap. 9).

NOTE.—Μῆτις and οὖτις, μήτι and οὖτι obey the general rule for parathetic compounds. The compounds of πᾶς retract the accent, as σύμπας, ἅπας, πρόπας, παντάπασι. The Doric circumflexed the genitive plural of all barytone pronouns, as τηνῶν, ἀλλῶν, Apoll. de Pron. 41.

Numerals.

751. DEFINITE NUMERALS.—*Substantives* are oxytone, as μονάς, δυάς, τριάς, see § 630.

752. *Adjectives.* (*a*) *Cardinals.*—Monosyllables, when long, are perispomena, when short, oxytone, as εἷς, τρεῖς, ἕν, ἕξ. Those consisting of more than one syllable draw the accent as far back as possible; except ἑπτά, ὀκτώ, and ἑκατόν oxytone, and ἐννέα paroxytone, as δύο, τέσσαρες, πέντε, δέκα, ἕνδεκα, δώδεκα, εἴκοσι, τριάκοντα, διακόσιοι, χίλιοι, τετρακισχίλιοι, μύριοι.

In compounds with καί the accent is placed as near that word as possible; without καί the accent of the last number is alone retained, as τρισκαίδεκα, τεσσαρακαίδεκα, but δεκατρεῖς, δεκατέσσαρες, δεκαπέντε, εἰκοσιέξ, εἰκοσιοκτώ, δεκατρία, εἰκοσιεννέα; ἕνδεκα and δώδεκα are excepted.

Compounds with prepositions seem to retract the accent, as διάπεντε, σύνδυο, σύντρεις, σύμπεντε.

753. *Declension of the first four Numerals.*—Εἷς (or Epic ἔεις) is declined in the singular like a monosyllabic substantive of the Third Declension, εἷς, ἕν, ἑνός, ἑνί, ἕνα, ἕν: the same is the case with the compounds οὐδείς μηδείς; except that in the nominative masculine the acute is substituted for the circumflex, οὐδέν μηδέν, οὐδενός μηδενός, οὐδενί μηδενί, οὐδένα μηδένα; but the genitive and dative plural are οὐδένων μηδένων, οὐδέσι μηδέσι, not οὐδενῶν οὐδεσί, though it appears that some preferred the latter forms.

NOTE.—Arc. 134. 6; E. M. 305. 10; 639. 30; A. G. 1267; Theog. Can. 134. 14; Herod. π. μ. λ. 18. 30; Apoll. de Adv. 557. 26; A. G. Oxon. 1. 134. 26.

754. The feminine μία (οὐδεμία μηδεμία), ἴα, and ἴη, are perispomena in the genitive and dative singular, μιᾶς μιᾷ, οὐδεμιᾶς οὐδεμιᾷ, ἰᾶς ἰᾷ, ἰῆς ἰῆ; the Epic ἴος is perispomenon in the dative masculine ἰῷ.

755. NOTE.—Schol. Ven. Z. 422: ἰῷ ὡς σοφῷ Ἀρίσταρχος· καὶ ἐπεκράτησεν αὐτοῦ ἡ ἀνάγνωσις. ἐκεῖνο μέντοι ἀναγκαῖον προσθεῖναι, ὅτι τὸ ἴα βαρυτόνως ἀνέγνω

ὁ ἀνὴρ καὶ τὸ μία· οὐδ' ἵα γῆρυς (Il. 4. 437) καὶ μία δ' οἵη (Il. 18. 565) τὰς
μέντοι δοτικὰς περιέσπασεν ἱῇ ἄρα γινόμεθ' αἴσῃ (Il. 22. 477) καὶ ἱῇ δ' ἐν
νυκτὶ γένοντο (Il. 18. 251), καὶ φασί γε τὸ τοιοῦτο εἶδος Ἰώνων εἶναι. τινὲς δὲ
ἐτόλμησαν λέγειν αὐτὸ Ἀττικόν, λέγω δὲ τὸ ἐπὶ τῶν τοιούτων θηλυκῶν καταβιβασμὸν
γίνεσθαι τόνου : Schol. Ven. Π. 173; A. G. Oxon. 1. 134. 20; Joh. Alex. 10. 32;
E. M. 472. 46.

756. Δύο and τρεῖς, τρία, together with ἄμφω, are accented, in
the genitive and dative plural, like monosyllabic substantives,
hence ἀμφοῖν, δυοῖν δυεῖν δυσί, τριῶν τρισί, Arc. 132. 6; δυοῖσι
and τριοῖσι are properispomena ; τέσσαρες is quite regular.

757. Note.—The following observation occurs in E. M. 754. 32 : τέτρασι· τὸ
παροξύτονον, ἐντελές, οἷον τετράσιν. ἢ ἐκ τοῦ τέσσαρι, τέταρσι· ἀποβολῇ καὶ ὑπερθέσει, τέτρασι : the meaning is not clear to me ; τετράσι would be the regular dative plural of τετράς ; and τέτρασι from τέτταρες or τέσσαρες is quoted by Matthiä
Gr. Gr. § 140, from Pind. Ol. 10. 83 ; Nem. 8. 117 : μύριοι, *ten thousand*, is proparoxytone : μυρίοι, *an indefinite multitude*, paroxytone; cf. § 377.
It is said that χιλίων, the genitive plural of χίλιοι, was perispomenon in Attic,
Joh. Alex. 18. 6 ; the later Attic circumflexed the genitive plural of numerals in
ας, as χιλιαδῶν, μυριαδῶν, which in the common dialect were χιλιάδων, μυριάδων :
Chœrob. C. 458. 26; Arc. 136. 3 : 'Genitivus pluralis χιλιαδέων vulgo scriptus
est ap. Herodot. 7. 28, quod χιλιάδων scribendum ex libris melioribus ostendi in
Comment. De dialecto, p. 14 ;' H. D.

758. (*b*) *Ordinals.*—Those in στος are oxytone, whether compound or simple, the rest retract the accent, as πρῶτος, δεύτερος, τρίτος, ὄγδοος, ἑνδέκατος, ὀκτωκαιδέκατος, but εἰκοστός, ἑπ-
τακισχιλιοστός, τεσσαρακοντακαιπεντακισχιλιοστός, Arc. 84. 1 ;
Chœrob. E. 133. 4.

759. (*c*) *Multiplicatives* in οος are paroxytone, as ἁπλόος
ἁπλοῦς, δεκαπλόος δεκαπλοῦς ; see above, § 401.

760. (*d*) *Proportionals* in ιος are proparoxytone, as διπλάσιος ;
see above, § 375.

761. (*e*) Numeral adjectives in αιος are properispomena, as
δευτεραῖος, τριταῖος, see above, § 378.

762. *Indefinite Numerals.*—These are all discussed under other
heads : ἄλλος, § 390 ; ἀμφότεροι, §§ 405, 742 ; ἕκαστος, § 408 ;
ἑκάτερος, §§ 404, 742 ; ἕτερος, § 405 ; ἔνιοι, § 375 ; ὀλίγος, § 366 ;
οὐδείς μηδείς, § 753 ; οὐδέτερος μηδέτερος, § 404 ; οὔτις μήτις,
§ 750 ; πᾶς, § 692 ; παῦρος, § 404 ; πολύς, § 688 ; πότερος, §§
404, 742 ; τις τινες § 742.

For the accentuation of Numeral Adverbs see Chap. 7.

CHAPTER VI.

ACCENTUATION OF VERBS AND PARTICIPLES.

763. In general, verbs throw the accent as far back as possible, and most of the exceptions to this rule may be satisfactorily accounted for by keeping in mind the assumed origin of the several verbal forms. It cannot be too strongly insisted on that all rules for the accentuation of verbs are likely to mislead, unless constant attention is paid to the various, and sometimes puzzling, changes to which such forms are liable. For information on this point recourse must be had to some good Greek grammar.

NOTE.—Chœrob. 493. 27 : πάντα τὰ ῥήματα ἀποστρέφονται τὴν ὀξεῖαν τάσιν, καὶ πάντα βαρύνονται ἢ δυνάμει ἢ ἐνεργείᾳ, ἐνεργείᾳ μὲν οἷον λέγω, γράφω, τύπτω· δυνάμει δέ, ὡς πάντα τὰ περισπωμένα οἷον ποιῶ, βοῶ, χρυσῶ, νοῶ, ταυτὰ γὰρ δυνάμει βαρύτονα εἰσί. Herodian devoted a considerable part of the 16th book of the Καθολικὴ Προσῳδία to determining the accent of the present indicative of verbs, that is, in settling which were, and which were not, barytone; but it has been thought unadvisable to increase the bulk of the present volume by doing so, especially as a comparatively superficial knowledge of the language necessarily implies an acquaintance with the fact. It may however be noticed that the different dialects varied, e. g. ἀλέξω, ἔψω, αὔξω, ἕθω, ῥόφω were barytone in Attic, but perispomena in the Common dialect, Chœrob. C. 483. 15; 490. 32. So some grammarians wrote βαρυστεναχῶν, though Aristarchus, with more reason, considered it to be barytone, Schol. Ven. A. 364 : γεγώνειν was the accent of Ptolemæus Ascalonites, but γεγωνεῖν that of Aristarchus; in later Greek it occurs in both forms, Schol. Ven. M. 337.

764. The accent given in the following rules is for *Tenses*, that of the First Person Singular, or, in the case of the Imperative, the Second Person Singular; for *Participles*, that of the Nominative Singular Masculine, and it is to be understood that the accent remains unchanged on the same syllable, counting from the beginning of the word, throughout all inflexions, subject to the general laws; unless it is said to be retracted, when in all forms it recedes as far from the end as possible, irrespective of the place which it holds in the first or second person singular, e. g. the Aorist Passive Subjunctive is perispomenon, as τυφθῶ, hence τυφθῇς, τυφθῇ, τυφθῆτον, τυφθῶμεν, τυφθῆτε, τυφθῶσι, where it will be noticed that the accent remains on the second syllable from the beginning of the word: again, the Perfect Participle Active is oxytone, τετυφώς· hence τετυφυῖα (§ 13), τετυφός, τετυφότος, τετυφυίας, τετυφότι, τετυφυίᾳ, τετυφότες, τετυφυῖαι. The Imperfect passive retracts, as ἐτυπτόμην, ἐτύπτεσο, ἐτύπτεο or ἐτύπτου, ἐτύπτετο, ἐτυπτόμεθον, etc., except that the Feminine Genitive Plural in σων or ιων from participles is always perispomenon, as τύψας, τύψασα, τύψαν, τυψασῶν, not τυψάσων, τετυφυιῶν, not τετυφυίων.

It must also be remembered that the final αι and οι of the Optative are considered long for the accent, as ἀκούσαι, ποιήσαι, but ἀκοῦσαι, ποιῆσαι are infinitives, Schol. Ven. H. 129; Chœrob. C. 764. 17 sq.; and above, § 16.

Simple Verbs.

765. All uncontracted monosyllabic participles are oxytone, as βάς, δύς, πλώς, πτάς, σβείς, σχών, φθάς, φύς: those contracted, like δοῦν for δέον, do not come under this rule.

766. All monosyllabic verbs are oxytone when naturally short, and perispomena when naturally long, as βάν, στάν, φθάν; ἔς, θές, σχές, φρές· δός; βῆς, βῆ, στῆ, φθῆ; σχῶ; except oxytone χρή, *it behoves*; φής, *thou sayest* (φῆς is the Indicative Aorist for ἔφης), and φή for φησί, *he says* (φῆ is Indicative Aorist for ἔφη).

767. All other forms of the simple verb retract the accent, as τύπτω, τύπτετον, ἐτυψάμην, ἐτύψασο, ἐτύψαο, ἐτύψω, τύψᾱς, τύψασᾰ, τυψάσαιν (τυψασῶν § 216), τυπτόμενος, τυπτομένη, τυπτόμενον, τυπτομένων (masculine, feminine, and neuter), τίθημι, τίθεμαι; except

Oxytone :—

1. The Present Indicative of εἰμί, *I am*; φημί, *I say*, and ἠμί (but εἶ or εἶς and φῆσθα are regular), as εἰμί ἐμμί, ἐσσί ἐστί ἐντί, ἐστόν, ἐσμέν εἰμέν εἰμές ἐμέν, ἐστέ, εἰσί ἐντί (but ἔασι and ἔοντι are proparoxytone); φημί φής φησί, φατόν, φαμέν, φατέ, φασί.

2. The Imperative Second Person Singular of φημί, φαθί: the other persons are regular.

3. Aorist Participles in ων, as βαλών, λαβών.

4. Perfect Participles in ως, as τετυφώς (υῖα, ός), πεπλεχώς (υῖα, ός).

5. The Active Present and Second Aorist Participles of verbs in μι and all Passive Aorist Participles in εις, as τιθείς, θείς; ἱστάς, στάς; διδούς, δούς; δεικνύς; πεισθείς, πλακείς, τυφθείς.

6. The Imperatives εἰπέ, ἐλθέ, εὑρέ in the Common dialect, and ἰδέ and λαβέ in Attic.

7. The Participles in ἐών, ὤν, ἰών, κιών, and χρεών.

Perispomenon :—

1. The contracted Future in ω (that of verbs with a liquid characteristic, and the so-called Attic Future), together with its Active Participle and Infinitive, as σκεδῶ, σκεδῶν, σκεδεῖν; σπερῶ, σπερῶν, σπερεῖν; τυψῶ, τυψῶν, τυψεῖν. The Optative of such futures is properispomenon, as σπερῶ σπεροῖμι, φανῶ φανοῖμι; the Attic forms in οιην are regular, as φανοίην φανοίης, but the syncopated forms φανοῖτον, φανοῖμεν, φανοῖτε, φανοῖεν are properispomena.

2. The Active Subjunctive of Verbs in μι, and the Subjunctive of Passive Aorists, as διδῶ, ἱστῶ, στῶ, τιθῶ, τυπῶ, τυφθῶ, except ἴω, ἴῃς, ἴῃ, etc., from εἶμι. When resolved, these forms follow the general rule, as ἔω ἔῃς ἔῃ εἴῃ, ἱστέω ἱστέῃς, τυφθέω τυφθέῃς.

3. The Second Person Singular of the Aorist Imperative in ου, as βαλοῦ, λαβοῦ; the remaining persons are regular, as λαβέσθω, λαβέσθων, λάβεσθε, λαβέσθωσαν, λαβέσθων. Ἰδού is oxytone when used as an interjection.

4. The Second Aorist Infinitive in ειν, as βαλεῖν, λαβεῖν, together with the anamolous ἐχρῆν, and χρῆν.

The following take the accent on the penultimate, and are consequently either

Paroxytone or Properispomenon :—

1. The Third Person Plural Present Indicative of verbs in μι when contracted, as τιθέασι τιθεῖσι, ἱστάασι ἱστᾶσι, διδόασι διδοῦσι, δεικνύασι δεικνῦσι.

2. The Third Person Plural of the Syncopated Perfect in ασι, as βεβάασι βεβᾶσι, τεθνάασι τεθνᾶσι.

3. The contracted and Doric Future in ουμαι, with its Infinitive, as πεσοῦμαι, πλευσοῦμαι, κομιοῦμαι κομιεῖσθαι, τυψοῦμαι τυψεῖσθαι.

4. The Subjunctive and Optative of the Perfect Passive, as βεβλῶμαι, κεκλήμην (κεκλῇο, κεκλῇτο), κεκτῶμαι κεκτώμην· κεκτήμην; μεμνῶμαι μεμνήμην; τετμῶμαι. When resolved they follow the general rule, as μεμνέῳτο.

5. The Passive and Middle Subjunctive and Optative of verbs in μι, as ἱστῶμαι ἱσταίμην, (ἱστῇ ἱστῆται, ἱστώμεθον ἱστῆσθον, ἱστώμεθα ἱστῆσθε ἱστῶνται); except δύναμαι, ἐπίσταμαι, κρέμαμαι, and those in οιμην, which retract the accent, as δύνωμαι, δύνῃ δύνηται, ἐπισταίμην ἐπίσταιο, τιθοίμην τίθοιο.

6. The syncopated plural of the Optative Passive Aorist, as τυφθεῖμεν, τυφθεῖτε, τυφθεῖεν; and the syncopated plural of the Active Optative of verbs in μι, as ἱσταῖμεν, ἱσταῖτε, ἱσταῖεν.

7. The First Aorist Active Participle in ας, as ποιήσας (ποιήσασα, ποιῆσἄν), τύψας.

8. The Perfect Passive Participle, as τετυμμένος τετυμμένη, τετυμμένον, τετυμμένοι, τετυμμέναι, τετυμμένα. Several old forms are excepted, as ἀλαλήμενος, ἀλιτήμενος. Ἐσσύμενος, ἥμενος, κείμενος are present in signification. For ἀκαχήμενος, ἀκάχμενος, and others (on which, see § 788), we also find the regularly accented forms.

9. The Infinitive of the First Aorist Active, as πεῖσαι, πλέξαι, ποιῆσαι, σπεῖραι, τύψαι.

10. All Infinitives in ναι and μεν (but not those in μεναι), as δεικνύναι, διδόναι δοῦναι, ἱστάναι στῆναι, πεισθῆναι, τετυφέναι, τυφθῆναι, τραπῆναι, τιθέναι θεῖναι, ἐλθέμεν.

11. The Aorist Infinitive in εσθαι, as γενέσθαι, πιθέσθαι.

12. The Perfect Infinitive in θαι, as πεπαῦσθαι, πεπεῖσθαι, πεπλέχθαι, τετύφθαι, δέχθαι, together with the anomalous forms ἧσθαι and κεῖσθαι.

13. The Second Aorist Infinitive Middle of verbs in μι, as δόσθαι, θέσθαι, στάσθαι. This rule is only important in respect to compound verbs.

768. Verbs in ω pure, when uncontracted, are accented exactly like those in ω impure, but when contracted, the general rule (§§ 20, 21) must be observed; hence τιμάω τιμῶ, τιμάεις τιμᾷς, ἐτίμας ἐτίμα. When any of these contracted syllables are resolved, the accent recedes, as χρῆται χρέεται, χρῶνται χρέωνται.

The Epic epenthesis of *a, o,* or *ω,* also causes the accent to fall back, as ὁράᾳς, ὁρώωσι, ἀρόωσι, εὐχετάασθαι, ἱστῶ ἱστέω, τιθῶ τιθέω, διδῶ διδώω, στῶ στέω στείω, θῶ θέω θείω, στήῃς στήῃ, θήῃς θήῃ, θεῖτο θέοιτο.

Verbs in ω.—*Active Voice.*

769. Note 1.—*Monosyllabic Forms.* The old grammarians consider χρή to be rather an adverb than a verb. It must not be confounded with χρῆ Ionic for ἐχρῆ, nor with χρῆ or χρᾷ from χράω, Arc. 174. 3; Chœrob. C. 494. 29; Schol. Ven. A. 216–17; E. M. 128. 15; Apoll. Syut. 238. 16; de Adv. 538. 13 sq.: φῄς is remarkable both for its accent and for the ι *subscriptum,* E. M. 792. 14: cf. Chœrob. C. 497. 16, where it is falsely written φῇς: φή, Joh. Alex. 21. 14: φησί, ὅπερ, πάλιν ἀποκοπὲν ὀξύνεται: τὸ γὰρ φὴ ἀντὶ τοῦ φησί: Apoll. Synt. 238. 25; de Adv. 543 (by an error this page is printed 553 in Bekker's edition). On the accentuation of monosyllabic verbal forms generally see Arc. 148. 18; 149. 3; 166. 23; 172. 21; Chœrob. C. 494. 8, who asserts that there are only thirty-two verbal oxytones in the language.

770. Note 2.—*Indicative Mood.* P r e s e n t. In the second person singular the Doric frequently has ες for εις, as συρίσδες for συρίζεις, and such forms probably keep the accent on the penultimate, but I am not aware that any of the ancient grammarians assert as much; cf. Kühner, G. G. 1. 555.

771. Note 3.—I m p e r f e c t and A o r i s t s. According to the general rule the accent will be placed as near the augment as possible; in Doric, however, the third person plural in ον and αν was *paroxytone*: Greg. Cor. p. 316, Schäf.: παροξυτονοῦσι (sc. the Dorians) καὶ τὰ τρίτα πρόσωπα τῶν πληθυντικῶν ἐπὶ τῶν ἀορίστων τὰ λήγοντα εἰς ΑΝ, ἐστάσαν ἐφάσαν ἔλυσαν ἐδείραν ἔκραξαν· ὡσαύτως καὶ τὰ εἰς ΟΝ λήγοντα παροξυτονοῦσιν ἔλαβον ἔφαγον ἔλεγον ἔτρεχον: Joh. Alex. 3. 16. The same thing is also asserted by other grammarians. Göttling, when speaking of this rule (Accent. p. 47), writes ἐδείραν perhaps from inadvertence, but contrary as ἐδείραν is to ordinary rules, it may be correct, since it is remarked by Chœrob. C. 651. 15: πολλάκις οἱ Δωριεῖς ἐναλλαγὰς ποιοῦνται τόνων πρὸς τὴν κοινὴν διάλεκτον· καὶ γὰρ τὰς παρ' ἡμῖν προπερισπωμένας λέξεις αὐτοὶ παροξύνουσιν, οἷον πᾶνες πάνες, αἶγες αἴγες, φῶτες φώτες καὶ πάλιν τὰς παρ' ἡμῖν βαρυτόνους λέξεις αὐτοὶ πολλάκις περισπῶσι· τὸ γὰρ πάντων καὶ παίδων παντῶν καὶ παιδῶν λέγουσι περισπωμένως.

772. Note 4.—Ἐχρῆν is perispomenon, Arc. 169. 2: cf. Kühner, G. G. 1. 667: modern grammarians do not appear to have quite made up their minds about this form. Göttling, Accent. p. 46, regards it as an infinitive; Kühner, as the union of the substantive χρή and ἦν: χρῆν is also perispomenon, according to the general rule.

773. Note 5.—F u t u r e. On those from verbs with a liquid characteristic, see Arc. 166. 10; Chœrob. C. 635. 20; 643. 17; on the Attic in ἰῶ = ίσω from verbs in ίζω, Chœrob. C. 647. 3; E. M. 51. 30; Greg. Cor. p. 173, Schäf. The other Attic contracted futures follow the same rule, as σκεδάζω σκεδῶ, τελέω τελῶ (ὁμόσω ὁμῶ).

The Doric future is always perispomenon, as λεξῶ, ποιησῶ, Chœrob. C. 540. 31: πάντας γὰρ τοὺς ὁριστικοὺς μέλλοντας περισπῶσιν οἱ Δωριεῖς, οἷον γραφῶ, Chœrob. C. 651. 9; Arc. 166. 13; Greg. Cor. p. 235. 276, Schäf. 'This contraction seems to have originated in an old future in σιω and σιομαι, which is found in some forms, as

πραξίομες for πράξομεν, χαριξιόμεθα for χαριούμεθα, προλειψίω for προλειψω,'
Donaldson, Greek Grammar, p. 252.

The Æolic future is barytone, as κέρσω = κερῶ, φθέρσω = φθερῶ, Chœrob. C.
545. 21.

It would appear from Schol. Ven. Λ 454 that the futures in νω = ύσω were
occasionally circumflexed; thus Alexion wrote ἐρυοῦσιν in the above passage, but
Aristarchus ἐρύουσιν, remarking that it is a present used for a future.

774. NOTE 6.—*Imperative Mood.* The words ἐλθέ, εὑρέ, εἰπέ are oxytone in
the Common dialect (Göttling says in *all* dialects), and ἰδέ, λαβέ only in Attic:
Schol. Ven. Α. 85: τρία εἰσὶ τὰ ἐν τῇ κοινῇ ὀξυνόμενα, ἐλθέ, εὑρέ, εἰπέ· ἰδίως δὲ καὶ
μακρᾷ παραλήγονται. Ἀττικοὶ δὲ καὶ ἐπὶ βραχυπαραλήκτων ὀξύνουσι τὸ ἰδέ καὶ
λαβέ: Arc. 148. 26: τὸ δὲ λάβε καὶ ἴδε παρ' ἡμῖν μὲν βαρύνονται, παρὰ δὲ Ἀττικοῖς
ὀξύνονται: so also Chœrob. C. 495. 29: in composition, however, the accent recedes,
as κάτελθε, ἔξειπε, ἔφευρε, Joh. Alex. 21. 10; Arc. 173. 29; Apoll. Synt. 329. 5:
the remaining persons are regular, ἐλθέτω, ἔλθετον, etc.: Chœrob. C. 754. 23:
λέγουσι δέ τινες ὅτι καὶ τὸ φάγε καὶ πίε οἱ Ἀττικοὶ φαγέ καὶ πιέ λέγουσιν ὀξυτόνως,
ὅπερ οὐκ ἐπεκράτησεν: Schol. Plat. Rep. 514 A; Phædon. 72 A.

775. NOTE 7.—There is some doubt as to the accent of εἶπον = εἰπέ: according
to Arc. 169. 18 it is properispomenon; according to Joannes Charax ap. Varini
Eclog. p. 172. 30 it is a Doric second aorist and oxytone; cf. Lob. Phryn. 348;
E. M. 302. 32; Chœrob. C. 747. 10 sq.; 755. 9: on the whole εἶπον seems the
better way of writing it: Chœrob. C. 752. 7: ἰστέον δὲ ὅτι οἱ Συρρακούσιοι μετα-
ποιοῦντες εἰς ΟΝ τὰ προστακτικὰ τοῦ β' ἀορίστου, τὸν τόνον φυλάττουσι τῶν κοινῶν
προστακτικῶν, οἷον λάβε λάβον, νύγε νύγον, ἄνελε ἄνελον· ὅθεν δηλονότι τὸ εἶπον
προστακτικόν, ὡς παρὰ Μενάνδρῳ,

εἶπον δὲ τί ποιεῖν μέλλετε,

ἀντὶ τοῦ εἰπέ, ἀορίστου τοῦ εἶπα προστακτικόν ἐστιν, ὥσπερ ἔτυψα τύψον, ἔλουσα
λοῦσον. Εἰ γὰρ ἦν β' ἀορίστου Συρρακουσίων ἔθει, ὀξυτονεῖσθαι εἶχε ὁμοίως τῷ κοινῷ
προστακτικῷ τῷ εἰπέ.

776. NOTE 8.—*Optative Mood.* The optative of circumflexed futures is properispomenon, as σπερῶ σπεροῖμι, φανῶ φανοῖμι: the Attic forms in οιην are
regular, as φανοίην, φανοίης, φανοίη, φανοίητον, φανοίητην, φανοίημεν, φανοίητε
φανοίησαν, but the syncopated forms φανοῖτον, φανοῖμεν, φανοῖτε, φανοῖεν are properispomena; Chœrob. 780. 15.

777. NOTE 9.—*Infinitive Mood.* The infinitive of the **circumflexed future**
is perispomenon, as σπερῶ, σπερεῖν, φανῶ, φανεῖν, κομιῶ, κομιεῖν: τυψεῖν, *Doric*,
Arc. 166. 11.

The infinitive of the **First Aorist** active is always accented on the penulti-
mate, as ποιῆσαι, πειρῆσαι, διαπέρσαι, ἀκοῦσαι, ἀγγεῖλαι· κῆαι: Schol. Ven. A. 302;
Δ. 53; O. 159; T. 81; Φ. 336: hence may be distinguished ποιῆσαι, Infinitive
First Aorist: ποίησαι, Imperative First Aorist middle: ποιήσαι, third person
singular First Aorist Optative active: in dissyllabic forms the Infinitive and
Imperative cannot be thus distinguished, e. g. λῦσαι may be either one or the
other, but λύσαι is the Optative, because there αι is long; Chœrob. C. 763. 31 : in
E. M. 391. 16 we have ποίηαι (*sic*) given as a dialectic (Argive, Lacedæmonian,
Pamphylian, etc.) form of ποιῆσαι.

The **Perfect Active** is paroxytone, as τετυφέναι: Arc. 173. 23.

The **Second Aorist Infinitive Active** in ειν is perispomenon, as βαλεῖν, ἀγα-
γεῖν, θανεῖν, ἑλεῖν, ἐλθεῖν, δραμεῖν, εἰπεῖν, πεπιθεῖν: (when resolved into εειν it

becomes paroxytone, as ἰδέειν = ἰδεῖν, Schol. Ven. Γ. 236); Arc. 173. 29; Schol. Ven. I. 184.

Several of these forms were regarded by some of the old grammarians as presents and not as aorists, and accordingly they make them paroxytone instead of perispomenon, e. g. θίγειν for θιγεῖν, ὄφλειν for ὀφλεῖν; cf. Veitch, Greek Verbs, p. 507: πέφνειν, Aristarchus and Herodian; but Tyrannion with more reason considered it a Second Aorist, and wrote πεφνεῖν, Schol. Ven. Π. 827; E. M. 187. 9; Arc. 173. 22; Chœrob. C. 730. 9: πίτνειν or πιτνεῖν; cf. Veitch, Greek Verbs, p. 541: σχέθειν, Arc. 155. 27; 156. 24: Göttling, Accent. p. 57, denies the existence of a present σχέθω, Arcadius, however, 156. 24, distinctly asserts it: ἐνισπεῖν (Schol. Ven. Η. 52) and ἐνειπεῖν according to Göttling are paroxytone in a few good MSS: Schol. Aristoph. Nub. 38: καταδαρθεῖν οἱ Ἀττικοὶ παροξύνουσι καταδάρθειν, but Göttling is of opinion that the scholiast has confounded καταδαρθεῖν with καταδάρθαι.

778. Note 10.—In Doric these infinitives end either in ην or εν, as ἰδῆν δραμῆν for ἰδεῖν δραμεῖν: λαβέν ἐλθέν for λαβεῖν ἐλθεῖν: but it is not clear how they accented them, but as they certainly oxytoned the present in εν = ειν, it is probable that they did so in this tense, Chœrob. C. 495. 32: πολλὰ εὑρίσκομεν, καὶ μάλιστα παρὰ τοῖς Δωριεῦσι, κατὰ πάθος ὀξυνόμενα· τὸ γὰρ δασμοφορεῖν ἀποβάλλει τὸ Ι παρὰ τοῖς Δωριεῦσι, καὶ γίνεται ἐν ὀξείᾳ τάσει δασμηφορέν: so also ποιέν = ποιεῖν, Chœrob. C. 651. 23; Arc. 148. 15; cf. Greg. Cor. p. 299, Schäf.: Greg. also has ἐλθῆν, λαβῆν, ἰδῆν as Æolic (p. 587), which are probably wrong.

779. Note 11.—*Participles.* That of the First Aorist Active in ᾱς is quite regular, as τελέσας, τύψας, ἐλάσας, ποιήσας, Arc. 176. 26; Joh. Alex. 22. 11.

The Doric forms in αις are also regular, as ἐλάσαις = ἐλάσας, though that dialect sometimes shortens the last syllable, and when that happens it is uncertain whether a change of accent took place or not; they may have written δήσᾰς for δήσας: δήσᾰς occurs in A. G. 1182.

The Perfect Active Participle is oxytone, as τετυφώς, τετυφυῖα, τετυφός, τετυπώς, ἑστώς, βεβώς, εἰδώς, Arc. 177. 1; Chœrob. C. 565. 9; 826. 16; Greg. Cor. p. 581, Schäf. has absurdly enough πεποιηώς, τεθνηώς, τετιηώς as Æolic, though he says, p. 621: ὅσαι δὲ μετοχαὶ ὀξύτονοι εἰς ΩΣ καταλήγουσι, διὰ τοῦ Ν παρ' ἐκείνοις ἐκφέρονται· εἰρηκώς εἰρήκων, νενοηκώς νενόηκων.

The proper name Ἀραρώς retains its participial accent: the Schol. Ven. B. 316 remarks that ἀμφιαχυῖα is properispomenon, as though there were some who thought otherwise.

The Second Aorist Active Participle is oxytone, as λαβών, τυπών, φαγών, δραμών, Arc. 176. 22; Joh. Alex. 22. 8; Chœrob. C. 561. 6; 619. 10: of course those who held that ἔπεφνον, ἔπιτνον, ὦφλον, ἔθιγον, ἔσχεθον were not aorists (see above, § 777), wrote πέφνων, Chœrob. C. 620. 29; E. M. 356. 4, πίτνων, ὄφλων, θίγων, σχέθων for πεφνών, etc.: there was a difference of opinion concerning the following:—ἀπαφών was by some written ἀπάφων as a present: βιβάσθων, Tyrannion considered this to come from a pure verb, and therefore accented it βιβασθῶν, while others equally mistaken thought it a second aorist, and wrote βιβασθών, Schol. Ven. N. 809: ἐρυγών, Schol. Ven. Υ. 406, not ἐρύγων: ἰάχων, Tyrannion made this ἰαχῶν, Schol. Ven. E. 302; Ξ. 421, and others ἰαχών (?): ἴσχων, or, as others thought, ἰσχών, but wrongly, Schol. Ven. E. 798: κελάδων seems to have been considered an aorist by some grammarians, Schol. Ven. Φ. 16.

Ἐών and ὤν, ἰών, κιών, and ἐκών are oxytone, though not aorists, Chœrob. E. 149. 25; C. 819. 7.

The Second Future Participle is contracted and circumflexed, as τυπῶν, and also those from liquid verbs, as μιανῶν, Chœrob. C. 823. 8.

PASSIVE AND MIDDLE VOICE.

780. NOTE 12.—*Indicative Mood.* Future. The future middle in ουμαι is always properispomenon, as πεσοῦμαι, θευσοῦμαι, λωβησοῦμαι Doric, Greg. Cor. p. 276, Schäf. ἐσσεῖται = ἔσται, Schol. Ven. B. 393 ; cf. Apoll. Synt. 274. 18.

781. NOTE 13.—**Perfect and Pluperfect.** When contracted, such forms as εἰλύαται become properispomena according to rule, εἰλῦται, though by some this was written εἴλυται, as if from εἴλυμι, Schol. Ven. M. 286 ; so εἰρύετο was written εἰρῦτο by Tyrannion, but εἴρυτο by Aristarchus, and the latter is pronounced correct by Schol. Ven. Π. 542 ; E. M. 304. 12.

782. NOTE 14.—**Aorist Passive.** According to the Schol. Theocr. 7. 60, Callimachus made the short forms in εν = ησαν paroxytone : ἐφίλαθεν, ἐφιλήθησαν ἢ φιλοῦνται. ἔστι δὲ Αἰολικόν, ὡς καὶ τὸ ἐκόσμηθεν. Καλλίμαχος δὲ τοῦτο παροξύνει. Ἐφιλάθεν appears strange, but might be correct, cf. above, § 771. Göttling (Accent. p. 70) thinks he may refer to ἐλίφθεν or ἔλειφθεν, Hymn. in Cer. 93, but considers any deviation from the ordinary accent as an error, and accordingly he blames Wolf for writing ἐτράφεν in Hom. Od. 10. 417, adding, 'it is true the Schol. Ven. Φ. 279 says ὡς ἐνθάδε γ' ἔτραφ' ἄριστος· παροξυτονητέον. τὸ γὰρ τέλειόν ἐστιν ἐτράφη καὶ μέμνηται αὐτοῦ ὁ Ἡρωδιανὸς ἐν τῇ ἀρχῇ τῆς ξ ὅπου διαλαμβάνει περὶ τοῦ διχθάδι· ἢ μεθ' ὅμιλον, καὶ λέγει ὅτι συναλοιφὴν πέπονθε διὰ τοῦ η· δεῖ οὖν διὰ τοῦ γ γράφειν ὅς ἐνθάδε, εἶτα ἐτράφετ' ἄριστος, οὐχ ὡς οἱ πολλοὶ τέτραφ' ἄριστος ἀπὸ τοῦ τ ποιοῦντες τὴν ἀρχὴν τοῦ ῥήματος καὶ προπαροξύνοντες. But the Schol. Ven. seem to have read ἐνθάδε γε τράφ' ἄριστος in this passage.' Cf. Kühner, G. G. 1. 532.

783. NOTE 15.—*Imperative Mood.* Second Aorist. The second person singular of the Aorist Middle in ου (or ευ), whether simple or compound, is perispomenon in Attic and in the common dialect (?) ; when resolved the general rule comes into operation, as παραβαλοῦ, καθελοῦ, A. G. 470, πυθοῦ, πυθεῦ, γενοῦ, but πύθεο, γένεο, not πυθέο and γενέο, as they are sometimes written. All the other persons of this tense are regular, as γενοῦ, γενέσθω, γένεσθε. 'The accentuation of γενέσθε, which Blomfield and Wellauer on Æsch. Pers. 176 give as undoubtedly correct, is wrong. For πιθέσθε, λαβέσθε, as Tyrannio Il. 18. 266, wrote them, belong according to the Schol. Ven. [i. e. S. V.] only to the later Ionic.' Göttling, Accent. p. 55. The grammarians frequently remark on the strangeness of the Attic accent. Schol. Aristoph. Plut. 103 ; Suid. s. v. ἀναβαλοῦ; Chœrob. C. 756. 8 ; 767. 5 ; Theodos. Can. 1030. 22.

Traces of an older and more regular accentuation are to be found. Göttling mentions the following :—ἔλευ, Hesiod. Theog. 549 : πύθευ, Herodot. 3. 68 : ἀμβάλευ, Theocr. 10. 22 : τράπου, Aristoph. Ran. 1246 ; this is noted as a special exception, together with ἐπιλάθου and ἀφίκου by Phavorinus 1144. 10 ; 1152. 17 : ἀφίκευ, Theocr. 11. 42 : ἀφίκου, Aristoph. Eq. 584 : ἐνέγκου, Soph. El. 178 ; Œdip. Col. 470 (ἐνεγκοῦ is printed by E. A. I. Ahrens and by Dindorf): ἵκου Eurip. Orest. 1230 ; Eurip. Iph. Aul. 1626 ; to which Kühner, G. G. 1. 554 adds ἐπίσπου, Plat. Theaet. 169 A, which is hardly an example of the rule, for in every example quoted by the grammarians the verb is dissyllabic, never monosyllabic, and it is likely enough that when the verb is monosyllabic, like σποῦ, its compounds retract the accent when united to a dissyllabic preposition after the analogy of similar forms from verbs in μι ; see § 819 : in Soph. Œd. Col. 1495, Hermann and Bothe have ἵκου, Dindorf and others ἱκοῦ. Göttling would read τραποῦ, ἀφικεῦ, ἐνεγκοῦ, and ἱκοῦ, but ἀφίκευ is doubtless correct in Theocritus.

784. NOTE 16.—Ἰδού, when used as an interjection, is oxytone, Arc. 183. 25; Chœrob. E. 10. 14; 109. 9. According to Herodian ap. Chœrob. C. 628. 27, as the imperative of εἰδόμην it is *barytone*: λέγει γὰρ ὁ Ἡρωδιανὸς ὅτι τὰ προστακτικὰ τοῦ δευτέρου ἀορίστου οὐ πάντη περισπῶνται, καὶ παρατίθεται τὸ ἀφίκου βαρυνόμενον καὶ τὸ ἰδου. There can be no doubt that ἰδοῦ, which Göttling and others give, is a false form.

785. NOTE 17.—*Subjunctive Mood.* Passive Aorists. On their accent see Arc. 167. 12; Chœrob. C. 795. 32; 811. 30.

Passive Perfect.—The Subjunctive (and Optative) of the Perfect Passive as special forms only occur in 'certain trisyllabic perfects, particularly of those which have a present signification,' Donaldson, Greek Grammar, p. 261; when contracted they take the accent on the contracted syllable, Arc. 170. 24, as κεκτῶμαι, βεβλῶμαι, τετμῶμαι, μεμνῶμαι, and probably καθῶμαι (see § 813). Of κεῖμαι, the resolved or uncontracted forms like κέωμαι, κέηται, seem to be the only ones that occur; κῶμαι and κῆται are doubtful; cf. Veitch, Greek Verbs, p. 359.

The other tenses of the subjunctive follow the general rule, such forms therefore as ἀρχῶμαι for ἄρχωμαι, or βουλῶμαι for βούλωμαι are barbarisms, and as such they are condemned in the tract Περὶ βαρβαρισμοῦ ap. Valcken. Ammon. p. 196. Thus also, though perhaps with more reason, some wrote ἐπαυρῆαι for ἐπαύρηαι, Schol. Ven. O. 17, and ἰκῶμαι for ἴκωμαι, Schol. Ven. X. 123.

786. NOTE 18.—*Optative Mood.* Passive Aorists. These are regular, except that the syncopated forms of the plural are properispomenon, as τυφθείην, τυφθείης, τυφθείη—τυφθειήτην—τυφθείημεν and τυφθεῖμεν, τυφθείητε and τυφθεῖτε (τυφθείησαν), τυφθεῖεν; τυπεῖμεν, τυπεῖτε, τυπεῖεν, Schol. Ven. Γ. 102; on the mistaken form ἐπίσχοιες = ἐπισχοίης see Dindorf's note on Schol. Ven. Ξ. 241.

Perfect Passive.—These, like their Subjunctives, take the accent on the contracted syllable; when resolved, they are regular, as κεκτῴμην, κεκτῷο, κεκτῷτο —κεκτῴμεθον, κεκτῷσθον, κεκτῴσθην—κεκτῴμεθα, κεκτῷσθε, κεκτῷνται: so also κεκλῄμην, μεμνῄμην, but μεμνεῴμην, μεμνέῳτο, E. M. 578. 56, μεμνέοιτο, μεμνῷτο, Schol. Ven. Ψ. 361, and probably καθῄμην, καθῇο, etc.; cf. Arc. 170. 24; 172. 6; Chœrob. C. 806. 26; Theodos. Can. 1033. 17; A. G. Paris. 3. 292. 22. Buttmann, recognising no contraction, would write κέκλῃο and μέμνῃο, but the ancients are clear upon the point; Suidas, s. v. μεμνῇτο· οὕτω προπερισπωμένως ὡς Ἡρωδιανὸς ἐν τῇ Ὁμηρικῇ προσῳδίᾳ· καὶ Ἀριστοφάνης Πλούτῳ· ἵνα τοὐμὸν ἱμάτιον φορῶν μεμνῇτό μου. Göttling observes that in some MSS. of Plato Legg. 776 B; 931 D, κέκτητο is found without ι *subscript*, and at p. 920 [?] in one MS. κεκτῆται.

'The same rule is to be applied to other words besides the three already mentioned; at least δέδημαι δεδήμην is quoted by Theodos. Alex. p. 1033 Bekk. Anecd. The Optative of κάθημαι occurs in Aristoph. Ran. 947, 1073, accented and formed thus, καθοῖτο, ἐπικαθοῖτο, which however may just as well be a Second Aorist. Without noticing these passages Buttmann (Ausf. Gr. gr. 1. 546) has accented it κάθοιτο. If we compare Aristoph. Lys. 149, where εἰ γὰρ καθήμεθα is certainly correct, the conjecture of Dobree on Aristoph. Plut. 992 might be accepted, to write καθῆτο and ἐπικαθῆτο in the passages quoted from Aristophanes if these forms are really Perfects and not Aorists. Most of the MSS. of Plat. Theag. 130 also read καθήμην (καθῄμην?) for καθοίμην. The form μεμνέῳτο (Il. 23. 362) has changed its characteristic α into the Ionic ε, and lengthened the connective vowel ο into ω, which, though regular in μεμνεώμεθα (Herodot. 7. 47), is exceptional in the Optative;' Göttling, Accent. p. 66.

787. NOTE 19.—*Infinitive Mood.* Future Middle in εισθαι is properispomenon, as σπερεῖσθαι.

Passive Aorists are properispomena, as τυφθῆναι, τυπῆναι, Arc. 173. 13 : thus also the Doric infinitives in ημεν, as αὐξηθῆμεν.

The accentuation of the Æolic forms like στεφανωθην, εἰσενεχθην, ἐνταφην is doubtful; some write στεφανωθῆν, others στεφανώθην.

Second Aorist Middle in εσθαι is always paroxytone, as ἱκέσθαι, ἐπιπτέσθαι, ἀποσχέσθαι, πιθέσθαι, ἰδέσθαι, ἀρέσθαι, λιπέσθαι, πεφιδέσθαι, ἐπισπέσθαι; Schol. Ven. A. 19; Δ. 126; H. 282; Π. 47. 88; Φ. 101; Chœrob. C. 734. 16: the following verbs are differently accented by different grammarians, according as they were deemed presents or aorists: ἀντέσθαι, Tyrannion, but wrongly, for it is certainly a present, Schol. Ven. O. 698: διέσθαι is also obviously wrong for δίεσθαι, Schol. Ven. M. 276: ἐρέσθαι, Chœrob. C. 732. 9: σεσημείωται τὸ ἔρεσθαι δευτέρου μέσου ἀορίστου ὃν καὶ προπαροξυνόμενον, περὶ οὗ ἐστιν εἰπεῖν ὅτι ἐξηκολούθησε τῷ δέρεσθαι καὶ φέρεσθαι καὶ στέρεσθαι, ἅτινά εἰσιν ἐνεστῶτος καὶ παρατατικοῦ καὶ ἐκ τοῦ ἐναντίου δὲ σεσημείωται τὸ λιτέσθαι ἐνεστῶτος καὶ παρατατικοῦ ὃν καὶ παροξυνόμενον ...... Κάλλιον δέ φησιν Ἡρωδιανὸς ἐν τῇ Καθόλου ἠκολούθησε τῷ λιπέσθαι ἱκέσθαι θέσθαι ἰδέσθαι ἅτινά εἰσι δευτέρου μέσου ἀορίστου: λιτέσθαι was thus accented according to the tradition, but Ptolemæus Ascalonites wrote λίτεσθαι, Schol. Ven. Π. 47: it would appear from the special directions given in Schol. Ven. A. 19; Π. 88, for the accentuation of ἀρέσθαι and ἱκέσθαι that some were inclined to look upon them as presents.

The Perfect Passive Infinitive always takes the accent on the penultimate, as τετύφθαι, πεποιῆσθαι, πεπλέχθαι, πεπεῖσθαι, ἐσπάρθαι, πεπαῦσθαι, Chœrob. C. 732. 2.

Ἧσθαι and κεῖσθαι are accented as perfects, e. g. παρῆσθαι, ἐπικεῖσθαι.

It seems that the Æolic followed the general rule, and made this infinitive proparoxytone, an accentuation which has been retained in some of the older verbs, especially those in οθαι; the following examples occur : ἀκάχησθαι and ἀλάλησθαι, which, according to Arc. 170. 4, are Æolic presents, but ἀκαχῆσθαι was also written Schol. Ven. T. 335 : ἐγρήγορθαι was Herodian's accent, Chœrob. C. 732. 22; cf. E. M. 312. 45, where the following are also mentioned : ἐφθορθαι, μέμορθαι, τέτορθαι; Schol. Ven. K. 67.

788. NOTE 20.—*Participles.* Passive Aorists are oxytone, as τυφθείς τυπείς, Arc. 177. 5.

Perfect Passive. On their accent see Arc. 177. 10; Joh. Alex. 22. 17: several, however, which are perfect passive participles in form are *proparoxytone*, and this is particularly the case when the perfect signification has disappeared, e. g. ἀκαχήμενος, Arc. 177. 10; E. M. 56. 25 (or ἀκαχημένος, Chœrob. C. 837. 17): ἀκάχμενος, E. M. 45. 51 (or ἀκαχμένος, Chœrob. C. 837. 17), and ἀκηχέμενος (?): ἀλάλήμενος, E. M. 56. 25 : ἀλιτήμενος, Hom. Od. 4. 807 : ἀρηρέμενος, Apollon. Rhod. 3. 382 : ἀρήμενος and ἀρημένος seem equally correct, Eust. 1838. 15: ἠρήμενος, which is mentioned by Phavorinus, 273. 47, as another form of the same word is questionable, and perhaps only a typographical error: ἄσμενος, Arc. 177. 15: ἐληλάμενος, Apoll. de Conj. 500. 19; de Adv. 545. 549; E. M. 45. 51; Apollon. Rhod. 2. 231, yet ἐληλαμένος is said to occur, and we have ἐξεληλαμένα in Herodot. 7. 84: ἐσσύμενος and σύμενος, ἥμενος, κείμενος, though perfect in form, are present in meaning: πεπτάμενος, Apollon. Rhod. 2. 407; Schol. Apollon. Rhod. 2. 1274; πεπτάμενον Ἡρωδιανὸς παροξύνει·

789. NOTE 21.—The words ἄλμενος, ἄρμενος, βλήμενος, δέγμενος (Chœrob. C. 837. 14; E. 44. 16, δεδεγμένος however is paroxytone), ἐμπλήμενος, ὅρμενος, κτάμενος, οὐτάμενος, though sometimes called perfects, should rather be regarded as aorists; see Joh. Alex. 22. 19: Pamphilus made οὐτάμενος paroxytone, but Aristarchus and most others proparoxytone, Schol. Ven. Λ. 658, on the ground that when σ is omitted before the termination of a word the accent recedes, hence οὐτασμένος, but οὐτάμενος, δεσποστής δεσπότης, ἐργαστής ἐργάτης, or, on the more general principle still, that syncope causes a recession of the accent, as θυγατέρα θύγατρα, ἁρμόσαντες ἄρσαντες, ὁμόπατροι ὄπατροι, E. M. 457. 25; Chœrob. C. 836. 32: according to Herodian οὐτάμενος and ἐληλάμενος are present participles from the verbs οὔτημι, ἐλήλημι, E. M. 45. 51; 330. 42; 644. 50: Apoll. de Adv. 545; 549; de Conj. 500; Chœrob. C. 837. 19.

790. NOTE 22.—The accent remains on the same syllable, counting from the beginning of the word, as long as the general laws permit, except that 1. the feminine genitive plural in σων and ιων is perispomenon, 2. the feminine nominative plural in μεναι is proparoxytone (except that of the perfect, which is paroxytone); e. g. τύψας τύψασα τύψαν, τύψαντος τυψάσης, τύψαντι τυψάσῃ, τύψαντα τύψασαν τύψαν; τύψαντε τυψάσα, τυψάντοιν τυψάσαιν; τύψαντες τύψασαι τύψαντα, τυψάντων τυψασῶν, etc.: τετυφώς τετυφυῖα τετυφός, τετυφότος τετυφυίας; τετυφότες τετυφυῖαι τετυφότα, τετυφότων τ ε τ υ φ υ ι ῶ ν; τυπτόμενος τυπτομένη τυπτόμενον, τυπτομένου, τυττομένης: τυπτομένων, as the genitive plural, may be either masculine, feminine, or neuter. In Doric, however, all feminines in αν = ων from masculines in ος are circumflexed, as φαινομενᾶν for φαινομένων, A. G. 1261; the participles in αν = άων are also perispomena, as γελᾶν = γελάων, ῶν, σιγᾶν, ἐλᾶν, Greg. Cor. p. 315, Schäf.

791. NOTE 23.—*Epic Forms.* The Epic parenthesis of α, ο, or ω also causes the accent to fall back, as ὁρᾷς ὁράᾳς, μενοινᾷ μενοινάᾳ, ὁρῶ ὁρόω, δρῶσι δρώωσι, ἡβῶντα ἡβώοντα, ἡβῷμι ἡβώοιμι, ἀροῦσι ἀρόωσι, δῃϊοῖεν δηϊόῳεν, εὐχετᾶσθαι εὐχετάασθαι, Schol. Ven. Z. 268, though some would write εὐχεταᾶσθαι, which is wrong, because the second of the two α's is short; at least such was the opinion of Aristarchus and Ptolemæus Ascalonites, μηχανάασθαι, αἰτιάασθαι, ἐδριάασθαι, μνάασθαι. On the theory of these parenthetic letters, if indeed such be their true nature, see Göttling, Accent. p. 97 sq.; Lob. Rhem. 173 sqq. It is mentioned in Schol. Ven. I. 393, that Tyrannion accented σοῶσι for σόωσι, and νοῶσι for νόωσι: ἐᾷ in Hom. Il. 5. 256 was written ἔα by some of the grammarians (cf. Schol. Ven. ad loc.), who regarded it as an apocope of ἐᾷ: οὖτᾰ and ἔκτᾰ are regular in accent, though somewhat strange in form.

792. NOTE 24.—The forms in which the characteristic and connective vowels are contracted and the ending left unaltered are accented differently by different grammarians, some throwing the accent back and others following the general rule, e. g. νέεαι would, according to the general rule of contraction, become νέῃ, but in the Epic dialect it contracts the characteristic and connective vowels εε, νεῖαι, μυθέεσαι μυθέεαι, μυθέῃ or μυθῇ, Epic μυθεῖαι, αἰδέεο αἰδεῖο, ὁράεαι ὁρῆαι, ὁράετο ὁρῆτο: and supposing this to be the true account of their origin, such an accentuation appears to be the best: but even in antiquity some wrote them μύθειαι αἴδειο ὄρηαι: Eust. 1361. 35: τὸ δὲ αἰδεῖο θεούς, ὅ ἐστιν αἰδέσθητι, ὡς εὐκτικὸν μὲν οὐκ εὐχερῶς ἂν συμβιβασθείη, τὰ γὰρ εἰς ΜΗΝ περισπώμενα εὐκτικὰ οὐ τοιαύτῃ διφθόγγῳ παραλήγονται, ὡς δῆλον ἐκ τοῦ ποιοίμην ποιοῖο, χρυσοίμην χρυσοῖο, βοῴμην βοῷο, οἷς ἀναλόγως ὤφειλεν εἶναι καὶ αἰδοίμην αἰδοῖο, ἢ γοῦν ἀλλὰ καὶ ἀπὸ τοῦ αἴδω βαρυτόνου ἐχρῆν αἰδοίμην αἴδοιο εἶναι, ὡς τυπτοίμην τύπτοιο· ἴσως οὖν ἐκ προστακτικοῦ τοῦ αἴδεο, οἷον τάδε τ' αἴδεο καὶ μ' ἐλέησον, γένονε τὸ αἰδεῖο ἐπενθέσει τοῦ Ι, καὶ ἅμα καταβιβασμῷ τοῦ τόνου πρός τινα ἔμφασιν εὐκτικοῦ, ἄλλως γὰρ οὐκ ἦν ἀνάλογος οὐδὲ ἡ τοῦ αἴδειο προπαροξυτόνησις: cf. E. M. 621. 32; Lob. Path. 1. 274.

793. Note 1.—*Indicative.* Present: on the accent of the third person plural see Schol. Ven. B. 255; Γ. 152; Λ. 270; Π. 262; Chœrob. C. 860-1: on φασί see Schol. Ven. Λ. 270: on ἔασι, A. G. Oxon. 1. 381. 34, this is said to be enclitic and *oxytone*, A. G. Oxon. 1. 186. 27, no doubt the word there is a false reading for ἐσσί.

The Doric forms in ντι are accented in the books in different ways, e. g. ἀνιέντι διδόντι, ἐπιτίθεντι ἐξιστᾶντι ἐγκιρνᾶντι; they should probably be proparoxytone, though it does not seem that the grammarians give any express rules about them: from Eust. 1557. 44 it might perhaps be inferred that they keep the accent on the same syllable as the corresponding form in εισι, as ἱέντι ἱεῖσι, τιθέντι τιθεῖσι, but in Æolic they would naturally retract the accent, and therefore ἐντί for ἔντι, which he mentions as an Æolic form, is probably a mistake.

Ἄεισι, in Hesiod. Theog. 875, is right, if it be a singular, but, if plural, it should be ἀείσι: cf. Phav. 42. 30: τὸ τρίτον τῶν πληθυντικῶν, ἄεισιν Αἰολικώτερον, ἐχρῆν ἀείσιν, ὥσπερ ἱεῖσιν: it is to be observed that ἴασι is from εἶμι and ἰᾶσι = ἱέασι from ἵημι, thus also ἐξίασι (ἔξειμι), ἐξιᾶσι (ἐξίημι): Chœrob. C. 860. 2; 861. 5: ἴσασι (Doric ἴσαντι), the third person plural of οἶδα, is proparoxytone.

On φῆσθα, Schol. Ven. Φ. 186; S. V. Φ. 186: προπερισπαστέον τὸ φῆσθα· παρατατικοῦ γάρ ἐστι· ὁ δὲ Τυραννίων βαρύνει ὡς ἐνεστῶτος: on διδοῖσθα for διδοῖς = δίδως it is noted by S. V. T. 270: οἱ μὲν βαρύνουσιν [sc. τὸ δίδοις] ὡς Αἰολικόν, ἀπὸ τοῦ δίδοιμι, δίδοις δίδοισθα ὡς τίθησθα· οἱ δὲ περισπῶσιν, ἐπέκτασιν εἶναι οἰόμενοι ἀπὸ τοῦ διδοῖς.

The Æolic verbs ἐλευθερῶμι and δοκιμῶμι are thus accented in the text of Chœrob. C. 843. 31, and γελαῖμι, Chœrob. C. 844. 2.

Syncopated forms like μέθιεν = μεθίεσαν, Third Person Plural Imperfect Active, retract the accent in accordance with a principle generally observed in Greek: A. G. Oxon. 2. 346. 27: αἱ ἐκθλίψεις καὶ αἱ συγκοπαὶ ἀναβιβάζουσι τοὺς τόνους: μεθίεν therefore, as some write it in Hom. Od. 21. 377, is an error.

Syncopated perfects and pluperfects are regular and retract the accent, as τέθνᾰμεν, τέθνᾰτε: the third person plural from roots in αω ending in άασι (Ionic έασι) is contracted into ᾶσι, as βεβάασι βεβᾶσι, ἑστάασι ἑστᾶσι, τεθνάασι τεθνᾶσι.

794. Note 2.—*Subjunctive Mood.* The Subjunctive Active is perispomenon in the singular, and properispomenon in the dual and plural when contracted: when resolved they throw back the accent; those in υμι being in general incapable of contraction are accented like the forms in ω: hence ἱστῶ ἱστῇς ἱστῇ, ἱστῆτον, ἱστῶμεν, ἱστῆτε ἱστῶσι, ἱστέω ἱστέῃς ἱστέῃ, τιθῶ τιθέω, διδῶ διδώω, στῶ στέω στείω, θῶ θέω θείω, δῶ δώω, στήῃς θήῃς, but δεικνύω δεικνύῃς δεικνύῃ, etc.: Chœrob. C. 795. 13; Theodos. Can. 1057. 23.

The Subjunctive Active of ἵημι and its compounds is occasionally found in MSS. with a false accent, e. g. ἀφίω for ἀφιῶ (ἀφιέω), ἀφίωμεν for ἀφιῶμεν, ἀφίωσι for ἀφιῶσι (Aristoph. Lys. 157; Plat. Phædo 90 E), ἵω for ἱῶ = ἱέω: cf. E. M. 467. 42: ἔστι τὸ ῥῆμα ἱέω ἱῶ πρώτης τῶν περισπωμένων.

Ἑῶμεν in Hom. Il. 19. 402 is strange: if the Second Aorist Subjunctive of ἵημι, it should be ἕωμεν: if from ἐάω, ἐῶμεν, both of which are unsatisfactory: Dr. Veitch, Greek Verbs, p. 121 thinks that it may be a Second Aorist of ἄημι = ἄω: in some editions it is printed ἕωμεν.

Εἰδῶ was circumflexed by Aristarchus, and such was the prevailing accentuation, Schol. Ven. Ζ. 150; Arc. 167. 10; Chœrob. C. 796. 32, but εἴδω, εἴδωμεν frequently occur in the MSS. of Aristotle: this variation in the accent arose from a difference of opinion amongst grammarians, some thinking that εἴδω was a mute verb, while others held it to be a pure one; cf. Chœrob. C. 878. 10.

The shortened forms of the Subjunctive retract the accent, as εἴδομεν, Chœrob. C. 797. 30, though it is said that Pamphilus wrote εἰδόμεν, Schol. Ven. A. 363.

The Subjunctive, Passive and Middle, is properispomenon, except the second person singular perispomenon, and the first person dual and plural proparoxytone, as ἱστῶμαι ἱστῇ ἱστῆται, ἱστώμεθον ἱστῆσθον, ἱστώμεθα ἱστῆσθε ἱστῶνται, θῶμαι θῇ θῆται, θώμεθον θῆσθον, θώμεθα θῆσθε θῶνται: but δύνωμαι and ἐπίστωμαι retract the accent: so δύνηαι, for which however Tyrannion wrote δυνῆαι, Schol. Ven. Z. 229: and this is not unfrequently the case with other verbs, especially in Attic: Chœrob. C. 806. 29: τὰ εἰς ΜΙ δὲ κατὰ τὸν ἐνεστῶτα καὶ παρατατικὸν τῶν ὑποτακτικῶν τῶν παθητικῶν προπερισπῶνται οἷον ἐὰν τιθῶμαι, ἐὰν ἱστῶμαι, ἐὰν διδῶμαι· χωρὶς εἰ μήπω εὑρεθῇ τὸ ἐνεργητικὸν ὁριστικὸν ἐν χρήσει, τότε παθητικὸν τὸ ὑποτακτικὸν προπαροξύνεται, οἷον ἐὰν δύνωμαι, ἐὰν κρέωμαι, ἐὰν ἐπίστωμαι, ὃ σημαίνει τὸ γινώσκω· οὐκ ἔστι γὰρ τὸ δύνημι ἐν χρήσει, ἢ τὸ κρέμημι, ἢ τὸ ἐπίστημι: the same rule is given by Arc. 171. 3 and others: the following instances of a retracted accent are quoted by Göttling: κέρωνται, Hom. Il. 4. 260, an accent attested by Schol. Ven. ad loc.: ἵστωμαι, cf. Schäf. App. ad Demosth. 5. p. 180: ἵστηται in one MS. of Thucyd. 2. 97.

795. NOTE 3.—*Optative Mood.* The optative first person singular is paroxytone, and the accent is retained on the same syllable, subject, of course, to the general rules; hence ἱσταίην ἱσταίης ἱσταίη—ἱσταιήτην or ἱσταίτην—ἱσταίημεν or ἱσταῖμεν, ἱσταίητε or ἱσταῖτε, ἱσταῖεν· θείην θείης θείη—θειήτην or θείτην—θείημεν or θεῖμεν, θείητε or θεῖτε, θεῖεν, and in the passive ἱσταίμην ἱσταῖο ἱσταῖτο—ἱσταίμεθον ἱσταίσθην ἱσταίμεθα ἱσταῖσθε ἱσταῖντο—θείμην θεῖο θεῖτο—θείμεθον θείσθην—θείμεθα θεῖσθε θεῖντο; except δυναίμην and ἐπισταίμην, which throw the accent as far back as possible, as δυναίμην δύναιο δύναιτο—δυναίμεθον δυναίσθην—δυναίμεθα δύναισθε δύναιντο (Arc. 171. 20–172. 13), together with ὀναίμην ὄναιο ὄναιτο, etc., and those in οιμην, as τιθοίμην τίθοιο τίθοιτο, διδοίμην δίδοιτο, ὀνοίμην ὄνοιο ὄνοιτο, Eust. 932. 23.

The contracted forms of verbs in νμι are accented in precisely the same manner: as δαινύμην δαινῦτο, Schol. Ven. Ω. 665: λελῦτο (?) or λελῦντο, Hom. Od. 18. 238 (for which Eust. 1845. 6 has λέλυτο), φθίμην, φύην δύην.

796. NOTE 4.—*Imperative Mood.* The Imperative is regular, τίθετι, τίθει, τιθέτω—τίθετον, τιθέτων—τίθετε, τιθέτωσαν or τιθέντων: στῆθι (or -στα), στήτω—στήτον, στήτων—στῆτε, στήτωσαν or στάντων: Passive, ἵστασο or ἵστω, ἱστάσθω—ἵστασθον, ἱστάσθων—ἵστασθε, ἱστάσθωσαν or ἱστάσθων: θέσο or θοῦ, θέσθω—θέσθον, θέσθων—θέσθε, θέσθωσαν or θέσθων: but in *Attic* φαθί is oxytone, Arc. 172. 27; Joh. Alex. 21. 13; Varin. Eclog. 436. 29, and such was its usual accent, though it was considered by Herodian to be contrary to analogy, cf. Schol. Aristoph. Equit. 22; Apoll. Synt. 264. 3; A. G. Oxon. 2. 468. 9: the form φᾶθι, mentioned by Draco 58. 1, is very strange, for in Attic the a is short.

Ἔστε, the second person plural Imperative of εἰμί, would almost appear to have been oxytoned by some grammarians, Apoll. Synt. 263. 5: but there is no warrant whatever for such an accent, Chœrob. C. 744. 3: μάρτυροι ἐστέ therefore in some editions of Hom. Il. 3. 280 is false for μάρτυροι ἔστε or μάρτυροί ἐστε; cf. Schol. Ven. ad loc.

797. NOTE 5.—*Infinitive Mood.* The active infinitives in ναι and μεν (except those in μεναι) take the accent on the penultimate, as τιθέναι τιθέμεν, διδόναι διδόμεν, θεῖναι θέμεν, δοῦναι δόμεν, στῆναι στῆμεν, ἐξῆμεν, δῦναι δῦμεν (ἐκδύμεν,

Schol. Ven. Π. 99), δεικνύναι, διδοῦναι ; but ἱστάμεναι, διδόμεναι, τιθέμεναι, δεικνύ-
μεναι, θέμεναι, δόμεναι, στήμεναι, δύμεναι ; εἶναι, ἔμεν, εἶμεν, ἔμμεναι, ἤμεναι, ἰέναι,
ἴμεν, ἴμεναι ; thus also the perfects βεβάναι, γεγάμεν, δεδιέναι, τεθνάναι, ἑστάναι,
τετλάναι, Chœrob. C. 735. 15 ; those with a short penultimate are sometimes found
perispomena, wrongly of course, as μεθεστάναι : τεθνάναι (?) in Æschyl. Ag. 539
ed. Didot may be a contraction for τεθναέναι.

The Passive and Middle Infinitives retract the accent, except that of the
Second Aorist middle, which is paroxytone, as στάσθαι, θέσθαι, δόσθαι ; yet πρία-
σθαι is proparoxytone, see Veitch, Greek Verbs, p. 563 : for φάσθαι Heraclides wrote
φᾶσθαι, holding the a to be naturally long, Varin. Eclog. 437. 29.

798. Note 6.—*Participles.* The participles of the Present and Second
Aorist Active are oxytone in the masculine and neuter, and properispomena in
the feminine, as τιθείς τιθεῖσα τιθέν, στάς στᾶσα στᾶν, διδούς διδοῦσα διδόν, Arc.
177. 3 ; Chœrob. C. 736. 4 : ἴσας from ἴσημι is barytone, Arc. 176. 27 ; E. M.
476. 12 ; Apoll. de Adv. 587. 9.

Ὤν ἐών (οὖσα), ὄν ἐόν from εἰμί, and ἰών (ἰοῦσα) ἰόν from εἶμι are also oxytone,
Chœrob. C. 798. 12. The dialectic forms of ὤν seem to be properispomena in the
feminine, as ἐοῦσα, ἐοῖσα, εὖσα, but the Doric ἔασσα is proparoxytone. For ἐᾶσα
Timæus Locr., Göttling Accent. p. 95 considers ἔασα to be the correct accent,
but his reasons are not satisfactory. Βιούς and διδούς are said to make their
neuters in οὖν, βιοῦν, διδοῦν, Reg. Pros. ap. Herm. de emend rat. Gr. gr. No.
161. p. 457, and they also declare that the oblique cases of ζευγνύς and δεικνύς are
properispomena.

On the monosyllabic forms see above, § 769.

799. *Syncopated Forms.*—In Ionic and Epic εο for έεο, and εαι
for έεαι, are paroxytone according to some authors, as ἀνακοινέο=
ἀνακοινέεο, μυθέαι=μυθέεαι, Eust. 1441. 35, ἐποιέο=ἐποιέεο, φο-
βέαι=φοβέεαι, φιλέο=φιλέεο, but it is highly probable that
others made them proparoxytone, e. g. ἔκλεο, which however
was accented ἐκλέο by Ptolemæus Ascalonites, Schol. Ven. Ω.
202 : τὴν ΚΛΕ συλλαβὴν ὀξυτονεῖ ὁ Ἀσκαλωνίτης ἡγούμενος τὸ
πλῆρες εἶναι ἐκλέου. οὐκ ἔστι δέ, ἀλλ᾽ ἐκλέεο τετρασυλλάβως. καὶ
δῆλον ὅτι εἴτε συγκέκοπται ἢ ὀξεῖα εἴτε ἡ βαρεῖα ἢ μετὰ
τὴν ὀξεῖαν, ὀφείλει πάλιν τρίτη ἀπὸ τέλους ἡ ὀξεῖα φυ-
λάττεσθαι. οὐδὲ γὰρ ὁ χαρακτὴρ κωλύει. τὸ μέντοι σὺ δ᾽
αἴδεο καί μ᾽ ἐλέησον καὶ τὰ τοιαῦτα πρώτης ὄντα συζυγίας τῶν
περισπωμένων ἄλλης ἀναλογίας ἔχεται. Eust. 1518. 54 : τὸ δὲ
πωλέαι......παροξύνεται,...εἰ μή τις ἴσως καὶ τοῦτο καὶ ἐκεῖνο
[sc. μυθέαι] προπαροξύνειν ἐθέλει, ὡς ἀναδραμόντα εἰς ὁμοιότητα
τοῦ τύπτεται λείβεται καὶ τῶν ὁμοίων.

800. Note 1.—Lobeck, Path. 1. 273, in commenting on the passage from the
Venetian Scholia quoted above, says : 'certissimum vero syncopæ documentum
est imperativus χρέο, quo scriptores ionici utuntur sæpius. Nec aliter conformati
sunt imperativi verborum circumflexorum φοβέο, ἀκέο, ἐξηγέο, quorum in accentu
Herodoti libri plerumque concordant v. Bredov. p. 375. His simile est αἴδεο
Theogn. 1334, dissimile vero ἤγεο in Chœrili versu apud Aristot. Rhet. 3. 14. p.

1414. 16, codicum consensione summa munitum, idemque in duobus Anthologiæ locis 9. 403 et 12. 119, ubi Jacobsius ex Schaeferi decreto ἡγέο edidit; ὑφάγεο, Theocr. 2. 101, Ahrensius in ἀφαγέο mutavit, sed intactum mansit μίμεο in versibus Simonidi adscriptis p. 57. ed. Schneidew. His non cliticam vocalem subductam esse sed eam quæ in substantia verbi continetur, cognoscitur ex imperativo tertiæ conjugationis ἀνακοίνεο, quem Buttmannus Gramm. § 105. 8, tacite paroxytonon fecit.'

801. NOTE 2.—The Doric Infinitives in εν = εῖν from pure verbs are oxytone, see above, § 778, those in εν = ειν are said to be paroxytone, as συρίσδεν = συρίζειν, which amounts to saying that they elided ι and suffered the accent to stand where it was before the elision; thus also the second person singular, as συρίσδες = συρίζεις, ποιές = ποιεῖς, Apoll. de Pron. 119 A.

802. NOTE 3.—*Æolic Forms.* There are several Æolic verbs concerning the accent of which there is a difference of opinion. Beyond the general statement that all verbs are barytone in this dialect there is little or nothing to be found in the old grammarians on the subject. Modern writers have accented them in accordance with the theories which they entertain of their origin. Göttling (ad Theodos. Gramm. 227), for instance, explains γελαις as a contraction of γελ-α-ε-ες, where α is the characteristic and ε the connective vowel, accordingly he considered the final syllable ις to be long, and wrote γελάϊς; βοάϊς. In his treatise on Accentuation (p. 107) he assents to Neue's opinion, and holds that the Æolic conjugated these verbs, γέλαιμι γέλαις γέλαι. But there is no proof that this dialect regulated the accent of its verbs by any consideration of characteristic or connective vowels; it is quite possible that the accent might be at variance with any theory, even with a true one, if such could be found.

The infinitives in ην = εῖν are all barytone, e. g. κάλην = καλεῖν, φίλην = φιλεῖν: Greg. Cor. p. 619, ed Schäf.: τὰ ἀπαρέμφατα ῥήματα τὰ εἰς ΕΙΝ καταλήγοντα αὐτοὶ (sc. Æolians) διὰ τοῦ ΗΝ ἐκφέρουσι βαρυτονοῦντες, φιλεῖν φίλην, καλεῖν κάλην, φρονεῖν φρόνην; the infinitives in ις are paroxytone in the text of Greg. Cor. p. 619, as γελάϊς = γελᾶν, πεινάϊς = πεινᾶν, ὑψόϊς = ὑψοῦν, ὀρθόϊς = ὀρθοῦν, χρυσόϊς = χρυσοῦν; and also the participles in εις, as κάλεις = καλῶν.

803. NOTE 4.—In Attic the connective vowel is rejected in the third person singular of ἔσομαι from εἰμί, as ἀπέσται, ἐπέσται; all such forms are paroxytone; Lob. Path. 1. 275. According to Schol. Ambros. in Odyss. Υ. 311, τέτλαμεν first person plural is *paroxytone,* but in the books it is proparoxytone. Ἔγεντο Dor. = ἐγένετο, Greg. Cor. p. 203, ed. Schäf.

COMPOUND VERBS.

804. Composition does not affect the accent of Infinitives, Participles, the Perfect Passive, the Passive Aorist, or of the Second Person Singular of the Second Aorist Middle, as βαλεῖν καταβαλεῖν, γενέσθαι ἐπιγενέσθαι, βεβληκέναι καταβεβληκέναι, τιθέναι συντιθέναι; ἀποτρέπων ἀποτρέπουσα ἀποτρέπον, ἀποτραπών ἀποτραποῦσα ἀποτραπόν, ἀποτετραμμένος, ἀποτρεφθῶ ἀποτρεφθῇ, ἀποτραποῦ; συντιθείς.

805. Monosyllabic oxytones become paroxytone, as δός ἀπόδος, ἔς συμπρόες ἄνες, θές περίθες ἐπίθες, σχές ἐπίσχες, χρή ἀπόχρη.

806. The Second Person Singular of the Second Aorist Middle of verbs in μι is perispomenon if it forms a dissyllable, and retracts the accent if it consists of more syllables than two, as ἐνθοῦ, προδοῦ, προοῦ, but ἀπόθεσο ἀπόθεο ἀπόθου, ἔνθεο, κατάθεσο κατάθεο κατάθου, πρόδοσο, πρόεσο πρόεο; the other persons of this tense throw the accent back, as προέσθω, πρόεσθον.

807. The accent of the simple verb is retained in the Subjunctive and Optative of verbs in μι, as ἀναβῇ, ἀνίης, ἀποδιδῶ, ἀποθείμην, ἀποθεῖο, ξυνῶ ξυνῇς; except the Second Aorist Middle, which retracts the accent, as δῶμαι ἀπόδωμαι, θῆται ἐπίθηται, θῶμαι ἐπίθωμαι: yet the Aorist of ἵημι retains the accent of the simple verb, as προῶμαι, προῆται.

808. Dissyllabic Imperfects, Aorists, Perfects, and Pluperfects retain their accent in the Indicative Mood, when they are augmented, and retract it when they are not, as εἶπε κατεῖπε ἐξεῖπε, εἷλον ἀνεῖλον, ἧκε ἀνῆκε, ἔβαν ἐπέβαν; trisyllables necessarily remain unaltered, as ἔειπε ἐξέειπε, ἔηκε συνέηκε, ἔαξα κατέαξα, ἔῳξα ἀνέῳξα, ἀνῷξα, ἐνῆσαν, but ἔνεσαν. The grammarians except from this rule ὑπόεικον, ὑπόειξεν, and the compounds of οἶδα, as σύνοιδα.

809. With these exceptions, compound verbs throw the accent as far back as possible, as ἔφευρε, κάτειπε (Imperative), κάθευδε, σύμφημι, σύνεσμεν, σύνεισι, πάρεισι, yet the Third Person Plural of the Active Present of verbs in μι is properispomenon when contracted, as ἀποδιδοῦσι, ἀφιστᾶσι.

810. The anomalous perfects κεῖμαι and ἧμαι, when compounded, deviate from the rule given above. The Infinitives κεῖσθαι and ἧσθαι are always properispomena, but in all other forms the accent is retracted, as κατακεῖσθαι, κατάκειμαι, κατάκεισο. In the Present Indicative, and in the Imperative of ἧμαι, the accent recedes, as κάθημαι, κάθηται, κάθησο, κάθου. This is also the case with the Imperfect (Pluperfect) when it has the syllabic augment, as ἐκαθήμην, ἐκάθητο; but when it has not, η seems to be regarded as a temporal augment, and the accent does not recede beyond it, as καθήμην, καθῆσο. In the Subjunctive καθῶμαι, καθῆται, καθῆσθε, καθῶνται seem to be better attested than κάθωμαι, κάθηται, etc.

811. Note i.—Chœrob. C. 732. 31 : *οὐδέποτε ἀπαρέμφατα συντιθέμενα τοὺς* τόνους ἀναβιβάζουσιν, οἶον ἰδεῖν συνιδεῖν, πλεῖν συμπλεῖν, σπᾶν περισπᾶν, χεῖσθαι συγχεῖσθαι, τετύφθαι προτετύχθαι [leg. προτετύφθαι] ἵκεσθαι (sic) ἀφίκεσθαι . . . ἀποχέσθαι, ὀλέσθαι ἀπολέσθαι, δόσθαι ἀποδόσθαι, σχεῖν ἐπισχεῖν, σπεῖν ἐπισπεῖν, θῆσθαι [leg. ἧσθαι] καθῆσθαι, κατακεῖσθαι, διακεῖσθαι, παρακεῖσθαι, περικεῖσθαι : Chœrob. C. 733. 10 : αἱ δὲ μετοχαὶ συντεθειμέναι οὐκ ἀναβιβάζουσι τοὺς τόνους, οἶον πτὰς ἀποπτάς, δοὺς ἀποδούς· ἐὰν γὰρ ἀναβιβάσωσι τοὺς τόνους οὐκέτι μένουσι μετοχαί, ἀλλὰ γίνονται ὀνόματα, οἶον τλάς Ἄτλας, βάς Ἄβας, φάς Περίφας, χωρὶς τῆς ἀεκὼν [leg. ἑκών] δέκων, αὕτη γὰρ καὶ τὸν τόνον ἀνεβίβασε καὶ ἔμεινε μετοχή· ἥτις καὶ ἄκων γίνεται, κράσει τοῦ Α καὶ Ε εἰς Α μακρόν : and the reason assigned is that participles are not synthetic but parasynthetic compounds ; cf. Chœrob. C. 817. 34 ; Arc. 178. 3 : E. M. 92. 3 ; Apoll. Synt. 330. 4 ; Schol. Ven. P. 190.

812. NOTE 2.—Schol. Ven. Ω. 388 : ἔνισπες ὡς ἔδραμες· ἔστι γὰρ ὁριστικὸν ἐκ τοῦ ἤνισπες τὴν ἄρχουσαν συστείλαντος. τὸ μέντοι προστακτικὸν πρὸ τέλους ἔχει τὴν ὀξεῖαν σὺ δ' ἀληθῶς ἐνίσπες ὁμοίως τῷ ἐπίσχες, καὶ δῆλον ὅτι ὅπου μὲν τὸ Ι ἐστι τῆς προθέσεως, ὅπου δὲ τοῦ ῥήματος. τὸ μέντοι ἄνευ τοῦ Σ προστακτικὸν προπαροξύνεται, λέγω δὲ τὸ νημερτές μοι ἔνισπε. The imperatives κάτασχε and πάρασχε are proparoxytone, there being no form σχέ. 'There can be no doubt that ἐπίσχε in Hes. Scut. 446 ought to be accented ἔπισχε, since it must be derived from ἐπίσχω, and not from ἐπέχω ;' Göttling, Accent. p. 45 ; A. G. Oxon. 2. 405. 20 ; Lob. Path. 2. 208.

813. NOTE 3.—*Compounds of* κεῖμαι *and* ἧμαι. The anomalous perfects κεῖμαι and ἧμαι, when compounded, deviate from the rule given above. The infinitive κεῖσθαι is always properispomenon in composition, as κατακεῖσθαι, ἐπικεῖσθαι, Chœrob. C. 732. 31, but in all other forms it retracts the accent, as κατάκειμαι, κατάκεισαι, κατάκειται ; κατακῆται, κατακέωνται ; κατάκεισο, κατακείμενος, E. M. 483. 32 ; Arc. 170. 8 ; Chœrob. C. 591. 23 ; A. G. Oxon. 2. 382. 5.

In the present indicative and in the imperative of ἧμαι the accent recedes, as κάθημαι, κάθησται, κάθηται ; κάθησο or κάθου, καθήσθω, E. M. 483. 32 ; Chœrob. C. 591. 32 : and this is also the case with the imperfect (pluperfect) when it has the syllabic augment, as ἐκαθήμην, ἐκάθησο, ἐκάθητο, ἐκάθηστο (?), ἐκάθησθε, ἐκάθηντο, but when it has not, η seems to be regarded as a temporal augment, and the accent, according to the general rule, does not recede beyond it, as καθήμην, καθῆσο (κάθησο is the imperative, Schol. Ven. A. 565), καθῆτο or κάθητο (?), καθῆστο, E. M. 483. 50 ; Schol. Ven. A. 569, καθήμεθον, καθήμεθα, καθῆσθε (κάθησθε is the present), καθῆσθε, καθῆντο ; the books present sundry instances in which this rule is violated.

In the Subjunctive καθῶμαι, καθῆται, καθῆσθε, καθῶνται seem to be better attested than κάθωμαι, etc., cf. Veitch, Greek Verbs, p. 347. On the Optative, see § 786. The Infinitive is always properispomenon, and the participle proparoxytone, as καθῆσθαι, E. M. 483. 44, καθήμενος.

814. NOTE 4.—*Subjunctive and Imperative Middle Aorist.* The accent is retained unchanged in the subjunctive of the passive aorists for obvious reasons, the termination being -θέω, -θέῃς, -θέῃ, etc., contracted into -θῶ, -θῆς, -θῇ.

The second person singular of the Second Aorist Middle Imperative retains its accent, though probably only in Attic, as παραβαλοῦ, καθελοῦ, ἀφελοῦ, A. G. 470. 8.

815. NOTE 5.—Every monosyllabic subjunctive in ω from a tense having a participle in ων retracts the accent in composition, as σχῶ (σχών), κατάσχω, κατάσχωμεν, σπῶ (σπών), ἐπίσπω, Arc. 174. 10 ; E. M. 495. 2 ; Chœrob. C. 798. 24 ; E. 92. 26 ; Göttling observes that ἀντισχῇ in Thucyd. 1. 65, ed. Bekk. Berol. 1821 is false.

816. Note 6.—Chœrob. C. 591. 6 : πᾶς παρῳχημένος ὁριστικὸς ἀπὸ φωνήεντος ἀρχόμενος καὶ ἀπὸ φύσει μακρᾶς τὸν αὐτὸν τόνον φυλάττει ἐν τῇ συνθέσει χωρὶς τοῦ ὑπόειξεν . . . καὶ τοῦ εἶκον ὑπόεικον . . . Ἐστωσαν δὲ παραδείγματα τοῦ κανόνος ταῦτα· εἶχον κατεῖχον, εἶπον προσεῖπον, ἦλθον συνῆλθον, εὗρον ἐφεῦρον, ᾖψα συνῆψα, εἶδον συνεῖδον, ἶγμαι ἀφῖγμαι, εἶκον ὑπεῖκον, εἶξεν ὑπεῖξεν· οὕτως οὖν καὶ οἶδα συνοῖδα ὤφειλεν εἶναι, ἀλλ' ὡς εἴρηται Αἰολικῶς ἀνεβίβασε τὸν τόνον καὶ γέγονε σύνοιδα προπαροξυτόνως, ὥσπερ καὶ τὸ δεύτερον τοῦτο πρόσωπον τοῦ οἶδα κάτοισθα, yet κατοῖσθα proporispomenon is given as the Attic form in A. G. Oxon. 1. 220. 13; but κάτοισθα, A. G. Paris. 3. 365. 35, and that is the accent of the books; E. M. 483. 50; 484; Schol. Ven. A. 611; Φ. 244; Arc. 174. 21; E. M. 778. 30: πᾶς παρῳχημένος χρόνος τὸν προσγινόμενον αὐτῷ χρόνον ἀποβαλών, ἐν τῇ συνθέσει προπαροξύνεται· οἷον εἶχον κάτεχον: Schol. Ven. Γ. 426: κάθιζ'· συστέλλειν δεῖ τὸ Ι, καὶ προπαροξύνειν τὸ κάθιζε. ὅσα γὰρ παρῳχημένου χρόνου ῥήματα βραχυκατάληκτα ἐνέλειψε χρόνῳ κατὰ τὸ ἄρχον, ταῦτα συντιθέμενα, ἀναδίδωσι τὸν τόνον· εἶχον συνεῖχον· ἀλλ' ἐπεὶ ἐγένετο ἔχε, ἀνεδόθη ὁ τόνος· νύξ δὲ μάλα στυγερὴ κάτεχ' οὐρανόν. οὕτως ἷζε κάθιζε· Νέστωρ τ' αὖ τοτ' ἐφίζεται. On κάθηρεν and ἐκάθηρε, see Schol. Ven. Ξ. 171.

Göttling mentions the following instances in which this rule is violated:— Ἀνέλκεν, Hom. Il. 13. 583 (ἄνελκεν, Dind.): ἐπᾶλτο, Hom. Il. 13. 643; 21. 140, this is hardly to be considered an exception : ἐπίεσται, Herodot. 1. 47, is, according to Göttling, an Ionic perfect from ἐφέννυμι, and should therefore be ἐπίεσται; cf. Veitch, Greek Verbs, p. 252 : ἐσίδον for ἔσιδον is not uncommon in MSS.: κατέχε, Hom. Il. 3. 243 (κάτεχεν, Dind.); Od. 13. 269, and elsewhere, is false for κάτεχε: μεθίεν, Hom. Od. 21. 377, cf. § 793: περιχεῦεν is undoubtedly wrong, though it stands so accented in Hom. Od. 3. 437, cf. ἐπέχευεν, Chœrob. C. 591. 23.

817. Note 7.—Καθίζω, καθεύδω, *et similia.* The compounds of verbs beginning with a long vowel or diphthong, which sometimes take the augment before the preposition and sometimes after it, as καθίζω, ἐφίζω, καθεύδω, are in appearance at least somewhat irregular : where the augment is evident, and placed *after* the preposition, there can be no doubt that they obey the general rule, as καθηῦδον, and whenever the penultimate of such forms is naturally long, it accords best with the statements of the old grammarians to place the circumflex upon it, of course only in the past tenses of the indicative mood, as καθεῦδον, E. M. 483. 44, or as Zenodotus wrote, ἐκαθεῦδον, Schol. Ven. A. 611 : at the same time it must be observed that κάθευδον and ἐκάθευδον are frequently found in the books, though the former is expressly condemned by E. M. 484.

The compounds of ἴζω differ on account, as it is said, of the variation in quantity to which the penultimate is liable, for instance, Chœroboscus (C. 591. 25), after enunciating the rule quoted above, § 816, adds: ἀπὸ φύσει δὲ μακρᾶς πρόσκειται διὰ τὸ ἴζε ἔφιζε

Νέστωρ αὖτις ἔφιζε,

τοῦτο δὲ τὸ ἔφιζε κοινῶς μὲν φύσει μακρὸν ἔχει τὸ Ι, ἐξ οὗ ἐφῖζε προπερισπωμένως, Ἰωνικῶς δὲ ἢ ποιητικῶς συστέλλει αὐτό, τουτέστιν θέσει μακρὸν αὐτὸ ἔχει ἐξ οὗ τὸ ἔφιζε προπαροξυτόνως: and in accordance with this we have κάθιζε made proparoxytone by Schol. Ven. Γ. 426, and E. M. 484. 13 adds that ἔφιζε is Attic as well as poetic.

Compound Verbs in μι,

818. Note 1.—All oxytone verbs become barytone in composition, E. M. 128. 15; Schol. Ven. A. 577; E. 477; H. 362; Arc. 175. 24; Lob. Ajax 168: 'Anabibasmum toni in hoc verbo [sc. φημί] et cognatis παράφημι, ἀπόφημι, legitimum et

ubique servatum mirum est a Grammaticis identidem præscribi: Schol. Ven. I.
577; 7. 362; Arcad. p. 173; E. M. s. 'Απόχρη et s. 'Ένειμεν, nihil autem præcipi
de secunda persona, cujus accentus fluctuat: ξύμφης, Plat. Hipparch. 232 B;
Soph. 236 D; 237 D, quibus in locis codd. complures aut συμφῆς aut συμφής
exhibent: ξυμφής legitur Lach. 199 A: σύμφης, Hipparch. 232 A: ἀντιφῆς, Gorg.
501 C: οὐδὲ σὺ φής (cod. σύμφης) οὔτε ἀπόφης, Protag. 360 D, tres codd. ἀποφῆς:
Anecd. p. 409, ἀντιφῆς ἀντὶ τοῦ ἀντιλέγεις, pro quo rectius ἀντιφής legitur apud
Suidam: σύμφαθι, Xen. Cyr. 4. 5. 34; Plato Gorg. p. 500 E; Rep. 7. 523 A, cujus
simplex acui vult Joannes p. 21. 17, quanquam non magis inclinatur, quam
persona indicativi secunda:' the passages quoted by Lobeck merely prove that the
scribes did not know how to accent their own language in all cases.

819. NOTE 2.—*Imperative Mood.* Chœrob. C. 494. 21; E. M. 99. 34; Chœrob.
E. 102. 9; Etym. Gud. s. v. ἀνάστηθι; Arc. 174. 1.

On the accent of the second person singular Imperative Second Aorist Middle,
see Phav. 1571. 1; E. M. 688. 38: προοῦ ... περισπᾶται· ἡνίκα γὰρ συντεθῇ μετὰ
μονοσυλλάβου προθέσεως, περισπᾶται, οἷον προοῦ· ἡνίκα δὲ μετὰ δισυλλάβου βαρύνεται, ἀπόθου, κατάθου: this singular rule is sometimes violated in the books, and
Göttling Accent. p. 90 mentions the following examples:—ἔνθου, Aristoph. Eq. 51:
πρόσθου, Soph. Trach. 1224: περιδοῦ, Aristoph. Eccles. 121, for which the correct
form, περίδου, occurs in the same author, Nub. 634; Ach. 737; Suid. s. v.

820. NOTE 3.—*Subjunctive Mood.* E. M. 495. 2; Chœrob. E. 92. 26; A. G.
Oxon. 2. 334. 20: it has been observed above, § 794, that the subjunctive of com-
pounds from ἵημι is occasionally found misaccented: πρόσθητε for προσθῆτε, Eurip.
Heracl. 476 (cf. Elmsley ad loc.) is another instance of a similar error.

Πρόωμαι or πρόηται for προῶμαι and προῆται (ἵημι) are almost certainly errors:
cf. Phav. 1397. 57; Göttling Accent. p. 82: on συνῶ, παρῶ, cf. Chœrob. C. 798. 26.

As to the Second Aorist Middle, there seems to have been a difference of
opinion: according to E. M. 459. 48: πᾶν ὑπερτρισύλλαβον εἰς ΜΑΙ λῆγον ἐπὶ
τοῦ δευτέρου μέσου ἀορίστου, ἐν τῇ συνθέσει ἀναβιβάζουσι [leg. ἀναβιβάζει] τὸν
τόνον· δῶμαι ἀπόδωμαι, σχῶμαι ἀπόσχωμαι: A. G. Oxon. 2. 344. 29: πᾶν ὑποτακτικὸν
εἰς ΜΑΙ λῆγον ἐπὶ δευτέρου μέσου ἀορίστου ἐν τῇ συνθέσει προπαροξύνεται· οἷον θῶμαι
ἀπόθωμαι καὶ διάθωμαι: 2. 376. 22: πᾶν ὑποτακτικὸν δισύλλαβον εἰς ΜΑΙ λῆγον ἐπὶ
δευτέρου ἀορίστου, ἐν τῇ συνθέσει προπαροξύνεται· οἷον δῶμαι ἀπόδωμαι· σχῶμαι
κατάσχωμαι· θῶμαι διάθωμαι

φέρε τέκνον διάθωμαι

σχῶμαι, ἀπόσχωμαι καὶ

ἀπόσχωνται πολλοί:

but MSS, though they sometimes exhibit this accentuation, are said more
generally to retain the accent of the simple word: Göttling mentions ἐπιθῆται,
Thucyd. 4. 71 (where however some books have ἐπίθηται), Demosth. Phil. 4. 33;
[Herodian 2. 15. 3]: προσθῇ, Herodot. 6. 109: [προσθῆται, Æschyl. Pers. 531,
ed. Didot]: ἀποδῶμαι, Aristoph. Aves 585, and others.

821. NOTE 4.—*Infinitive Mood.* On the accent of infinitives used as imperatives, see Schol. Ven. A. 302.

CHAPTER VII.

ACCENTUATION OF INDECLINABLE WORDS.

Prepositions.

822. PREPOSITIONS, whether compound or simple, are oxytone, as ἀντί, ἀπό, πρό; σύν; ἀνά; διά, κατά, μετά, ὑπέρ; ἀμφί, ἐπί, παρά, περί, πρός, ὑπό; ὑπέκ, ἀποπρό, ἐπιπρό, ἀπέκ, ἀπέξ, διαπρό, καταί, ὑπαί, ὑπεκπρό, ἄμ = ἀνά; except ἐκ or ἐξ, ἐν, εἰς or ἐς and ὡς, which are usually unaccented.

NOTE.—Arc. 179. 26; Chœrob. E. 14. 29. On the Anastrophe of prepositions, and on the modern practice of leaving ἐκ ἐν εἰς ὡς unaccented, see Chaps. 8 and 9. When the preposition is conjoined with the word following it, it is unaccented, as καδδύναμιν, ἀμβωμοῖσι, cf. Aristarchus ap. Schol. Ven. Θ. 441. In some editions ἀμ βωμοῖσι, ἀμ πεδίον, etc. are found; cf. Kühner, G. G. I. 259.

Conjunctions and Adverbs.

823. *Monosyllables.*—Monosyllabic particles (conjunctions and adverbs) are oxytone, as ἄψ, μάψ; δάξ, λάξ, πύξ; δίς, τρίς; πρίν, μά, νή, πλήν, δήν, γάρ, μέν, δέ, ἄν, καί, μήν; ναί, οὔ, μή; δαί, τώς, ἤ, *or*, except ἦ, *truly*, αὖ, εὖ οὖν and ὦν (γοῦν, μῶν) νῦν, λῖ = λίαν, Strabo 364, and the interrogatives πῆ, ποῖ, ποῦ, πῶς, which are perispomena. Οὐ is unaccented, unless it means *No*, or stands at the end of a sentence: ὡς is also generally proclitic in our editions, see below, § 934.

824. The indefinite particles πώς, ποί, πή, πού, ποθί, ποθέν, ποτέ, πώ, together with γέ, κέ, or κέν, νύ and νύν, πέρ, ῥά, τέ, θήν, θέ, δέ, τοί and τίς τί are enclitics, on which see Chap. 9.

825. The indefinite adverbs ποθί, πού, ποθέν, ποί, ποτέ, ὁτέ, πώς, πώ, πή are enclitic and oxytone, the corresponding interrogatives, dependent interrogatives, demonstratives and relatives are all orthotone, monosyllables being perispomena, with the exception of τώς oxytone, and ὡς unaccented; the rest take the accent on the penultimate, as ποῦ, ποῖ, πῶς, πῆ, οὖ, οἶ, ῇ, πόθεν, πότε, πηνίκα, τότε, τηνικάδε, τηνικαῦτα, οὕτω, τῇδε, ταύτῃ, ὧδε, ὅθεν, ὅτε, ἡνίκα, ὅπου, ὁπόθεν, ὅποι, ὁπότε, ὁπηνίκα, ὅπως, ὅπη, ὁπόσε, τόθεν, τόθι, Joh. Alex. 31. 2; 34. 3. On ὡς see below, § 934.

826. NOTE.—Arc. 184. 15 sqq.: αὖ, Arc. 185. 2; Joh. Alex. 40. 11: μῶν, E. M. 596. 26; Joh. Alex. 40. 26: οὖν, Arc. 185. 7; Joh. Alex. 40. 11: ἤ and ἦ, E. M. 415. 43: ὅτι τὸν Η σύνδεσμον ἐξ διαφόρως σημαίνει φησὶν Ἡρωδιανός· περισπώμενον, τρία· καὶ βαρυνόμενον τρία. περισπώμενος μὲν γὰρ, ἔστι παραπληρωματικός, βεβαιωτικός, διαπορητικός· βαρυνόμενος δὲ, ἔστι διαζευκτικός, παραδιαζευκτικός, διασαφητικός: in other words, ἤ, *or*, is oxytone; ἦ, *verily*, perispomenon, cf. Arc. 185. 8; Schol. Ven. Ven. A. 77; 190; 219; 229; 232; B. 272; 368; Joh. Alex. 40. 35 sq.: οὐ, and οὐκ, Schol. Ven. Δ. 539; Arc. 183. 26; Joh. Alex. 32. 21; see Chap. 9: ἐπεὶ ἤ, E. M. 356. 18: περισπᾶται τὸ Η ἀντὶ τοῦ δὴ παραπληρωματικοῦ. ὁ Η σύνδεσμος μετὰ τοῦ ἐπεί, περισπᾶται ἐν μέσῃ φράσει. τὸ δὲ τίη εὐθίνεται [leg. τιή ὀξύνεται], cf. E. M. 414. 54; Joh. Alex. 42. 16; Schol. Ven. A. 156, ἐπειή· περισπαστέον τὸ Η· ἔστι γὰρ βεβαιωτικός: Schol. Ven. Υ. 251; Eust. 73. 18; in modern editions, however, when the two words are written as one it is usual to make it oxytone, ἐπειή, though there does not seem to be any ancient authority for doing so: τίη or τιή, Eust. 118. 36: σημείωσαι δὲ ὅτι οἱ παλαιοὶ ἐν μὲν τῷ ἐπειή .... περισπῶσι τὸ Η τῆς ληγούσης, ἐνταῦθα δὲ βαρύνουσιν ἐγκλίνοντες, ὡς ἐν τοῖς Ἀπίωνος καὶ Ἡροδώρου φέρεται. οἱ δὲ Ἀττικοὶ ὀξυτόνως λέγουσι τιή καὶ ὁτιή: νῦν, and νύν, νύ, νῦν is a temporal adverb, *now, at this time*, and has the υ long: νύν generally with a short υ is an inferential particle, *then* or *now, therefore*, and is by the Greek grammarians considered an enclitic, Schol. Ven. A. 421: ἀλλὰ **σὺ** μὲν **νῦν νηυσὶ παρήμενος· τὸ νῦν ἀντὶ τοῦ** δή, διὸ καὶ Τυραννίων ἠξίου ὀξύνειν αὐτό, ο ὐ κ ε ὖ: Schol. Ven. Γ. 97: τὸ νῦν περισπαστέον, κἂν παρέλκῃ παρὰ τῷ ποιητῇ: S. V. Φ. 428: ἀεὶ τὸ νυν φυλάσσον τὸν χρόνον καὶ τόνον φυλάσσει· εἴ που δὲ συσταλῇ διὰ μέτρον, ἐγκλίνεται: Arc. 182. 8: περισπᾶται δὲ καὶ ὅσα ἔχει δίχρονον ἐκτεταμένον, ἃ, νῦν, γρῦ, κρῖ, ὁπότε ἐκτείνεται· ὁπότε δὲ συστέλλεται, ὀξύνεται: cf. Joh. Alex. 31. 10; Charax ap. A. G. 1155: τὸ νῦν ἐπίρρημα ὂν περισπᾶται, σύνδεσμος δὲ ὢν καὶ συστέλλεται καὶ ἐγκλίνεται: S. V. Υ. 251: ὁ Η τῷ μὲν ΤΙ ὑποτασσόμενος ὀξύνεται, τῷ δὲ ἐπεί περισπᾶται: ὅταν, cf. Schol. Ven. A. 519, when not written as one word, it is ὅτ' ἄν, according to rule.

827. NOTE 2.—Οὔκουν, Ammon. p. 105: οὔκουν παροξυτόνως μέν, ἀποφαντικὸν, ἴσον τῷ οὐχιοῦν. οἶον, οὔκουν ἀπιστεῖν [εἰκός]. περισπωμένως δὲ, συλλογιστικός ἐστι σύνδεσμος· καὶ σημαίνει κατάφασιν. A. G. 57. 10; Apoll. de Conj. 525. 28: in other words, οὔκουν is paroxytone when it means *certainly not, therefore not*, or *nonne*, and perispomenon when it means *ergo, therefore*, the accent being placed on that part of the word which is emphasised; cf. Joh. Alex. 40. 30. Kühner (Excursus 3. ad Xenoph. Memorab. p. 513 sq.), after an elaborate examination of the various senses in which this particle is used, concludes with the words 'ut igitur disputationis nostræ summam paucis complectamur, οὐκοῦν particula scribenda est οὐκοῦν, ubi significat 1. nonne igitur? nonne ergo? 2. ergo, igitur;—οὔκουν contra ubi significat 1. non ergo, non igitur in conclusione negativa;—2. nullo modo, neutiquam, nequaquam, haudquaquam in responsione fortiter negante;—3. non igitur? in interrogationibus affectus plenis.'

828. Conjunctions consisting of more than one syllable generally throw the accent as far back as possible, as ἄρα, ἆρα, ἄχρι, δῆτα, εἶτα, ἕνεκα, ἔνθα, ἤδη, ἵνα, ὄφρα, τόφρα; except ἀλλά, the indefinite ποθί, ποθέν, ὁτέ, τοτέ, and αὐτάρ, ἀτάρ oxytone.

829. Note.—Ἀλλά, Chœrob. E. 63. 22, is so accented to distinguish it from the adjective ἄλλα : ὁτέ, Schol. Ven. A. 493 : ἀλλ' ὅτε δή ῥ' ἐκ τοῖο· Ἀρίσταρχος ὁτεδή ὡς δηλαδὴ παραλόγως. Πάμφιλος δὲ τὸ ὁτε κατ' ἰδίαν ἀναφορικόν, ἀναλόγως· διαφέρει γὰρ τὸ ὅτε ὀξυνόμενον κατὰ τὴν πρώτην τοῦ ὁτέ ἀορίστου· ὥστε ἐὰν θελήσῃ ὁ Ἀρίσταρχος ἀναγινώσκειν ὁτεδή ὡς δηλαδή, πρῶτον τὴν μὴ οὖσαν χρῆσιν παρὰ τῷ ποιητῇ παραλήψεται· δεύτερον, τὸ σημαινόμενον παραφθείρει—τὸ δὲ τοῖο προπερισπαστέον· τὸ γὰρ τοῦ Θεσσαλικῶς παραυξηθέν, ἐγίνετο τοῖο, ὡς καλοῦ καλοῖο. ἀποφήνασθαι δεῖ ὅτι ὁ Ἡρωδιανὸς ἐν τῇ Ἰλιακῇ προσῳδίᾳ διαλαμβάνων περὶ τοῦ ἀλλ' ὅτε δή ῥ' ἐκ τοῖο λέγει ὅτι τοῦ ὁτέ ὀξυτόνου ἀορίστου οὐκ ἔστιν ἡ χρῆσις παρὰ τῷ ποιητῇ· ἐν μέντοι τῷ ἐννεακαιδεκάτῳ τῆς Καθόλου τὸ ὡς Ἕκτωρ ὁτὲ μὲν μετὰ πρώτοισι φάνεσκεν, ὀξυτόνως δεῖν φησὶν ἀναγινώσκεσθαι : αὐτάρ, Schol. Ven. Γ. 1 : ζητεῖται δὲ πῶς δεῖ τὸν αὐτὰρ σύνδεσμον προφέρεσθαι, πότερον ὀξυτόνως ἢ βαρυτόνως; οἱ μὲν οὖν ὀξυτόνως ἀνεγνώκασιν, ὡς Καλλίμαχος· οἱ δὲ βαρυτόνως λόγῳ τῷδε· πᾶσα λέξις εἰς ΑΡ λήγουσα βαρύνεται οἷον ἄφαρ, εἶθαρ, μάκαρ, δάμαρ, στέαρ, οὖθαρ. ῥητέον δὲ ὅτι οὐδεὶς συμπλεκτικὸς, ἢ περισπᾶται, ἢ βαρύνεται· πάντες δὲ ὀξύνονται : so E. M. 172. 29 ; Chœrob. C. 134. 25.

General Rule for the Accentuation of Compound Particles.

830. By far the greater number of compound particles are formed by the simple juxtaposition of their parts. The accent of the last factor (when not an enclitic) is retained, as ἀπό-δίς, δι-ὅτι, ἐπί-δήν, ἐπί-το-πλέον, ἐπί-τρίς, ἐσ-ἄρτι, ἦ-μέν, καθ-ὅτι, μηδ-ὅλως, οὐκ-ἔτι, οὐκ-οὖν, πρόσ-ἔτι, τά-νῦν, τοί-γάρ-οὖν, become ἀποδίς, διότι, ἐπιδήν, ἐπιτοπλέον, ἐπιτρίς, ἐσάρτι, ἠμέν, καθότι, μηδόλως, οὐκέτι, οὐκοῦν, προσέτι, τανῦν, τοιγαροῦν ; ὁπητιοῦν ; ἤγουν = ἤ γε οὖν is slightly irregular in appearance ; except ἐπειή not ἐπειῆ, ὅταν not ὁτάν, though ἐπάν, ἐπειδάν, etc., are regular. When the last factor is an enclitic, the accent of the former part of the word is retained, as αἴ-τέ, εἴ-τέ, δή-πού, εὖ-τέ, ἦ-τοί, μή-τίς, τοί-ννν, ὥσ-πέρ, ὥσ-τε, become αἶτε, εἶτε, δήπου, εὖτε, ἦτοι, μήτις, τοίνυν, ὥσπερ, ὥστε ; thus also ἀμηγέπη, ἀμηγέπου, δήπουθεν, οὔτιπω, τοιγάρτοι. As these are mere parathetic compounds, the law respecting the circumflex (§ 12) is not observed. Reference to the succeeding sections will show that this rule is not unfrequently violated.

831. Note.—Eust. 118. 34: σημείωσαι δὲ ὅτι οἱ παλαιοὶ ἐν μὲν τῷ, ἐπειῆ, καθὰ καὶ προείρηται, περισπῶσι τὸ ἤ τῆς ληγούσης. ἐνταῦθα δὲ βαρύνουσιν ἐγκλίνοντες, ὡς ἐν τοῖς Ἀπίωνος καὶ Ἡροδώρου φέρεται. οἱ δὲ Ἀττικοὶ ὀξυτόνως λέγουσι τιή καὶ ὁτιή. Nothing can be more capricious than the way in which words thus compounded are written ; see Lobeck's dissertation De Parathesi, in Lob. Path. I. 566 sqq.

832. Cases of substantives or adjectives in common use, when used adverbially, generally retain their substantival or adjectival accent, as ἀκήν, ἀκμήν, ἐθελοντήν, ἑκοντήν, πεζῇ, πυκινά, πυκνά, σαφέα, ταχέα, ὠκέα; and compounds with prepositions generally retain the accent of their last factor according to the rule given above, § 830, as ἐκπαντός, ἐξαρχῆς, ἐξίσης, ἐπανάγκης, ἐπίσης, ἐσύστερον, καθαυτό, καθεῖς, μεταύριον, etc. But there are exceptions, as, for instance, ἄληθες, ἀλλά, χάριεν, and many others.

NOTE.—E. M. 358. 49 : κανὼν γὰρ ἐστὶν ὁ λέγων, ὅτι τὰ ἀπὸ ὀνόματος εἰς ἐπιρρηματικὴν σύνταξιν μετενηνεγμένα, ὁμοτονοῦσιν· οἷον ἐπιεικές, ὡς ἐπιεικές· συνεχές, διαμπερές, ἀτρεκές. τὸ δὲ ἄληθες ἀντὶ τοῦ ἀληθῶς παρὰ Ἀττικοῖς, οὐχ ὁμότονον. ὁμοίως καὶ τὸ ἐπάναγκες· καὶ τὸ χάριεν, ἀντὶ τοῦ χαριέντως. Thus also ἐπίτηδες, E. M. 366. 26 ; though that accent is declared to be false by S. V. A. 142. Editors are very inconsistent in writing these words, καθ' ὅλου and καθόλου, διακενῆς and διὰ κενῆς, ἐπίσης and ἐπ' ἴσης and the like are constantly to be met with ; see Lob. Path. 1. 600.

Adverbs.

-A.

833. The final syllable is generally, though not always, short, and the accent is, with comparatively few exceptions, thrown back, see Apoll. de Adv. 560. 22–563.

834. (*a*) Those in εα and ρα are paroxytone, as λιγέα, ῥέα, σαφέα, ταχέα, ὠκέα ; λάθρα, σφόδρα, ὑπόδρα ; except τήμερα and ὑπέρμορα proparoxytone.

NOTE.—See Eust. 88. 31 ; Apoll. de Adv. 563. 4 : κατωκάρα, Schol. Aristoph. Pac. 153 : κατωκάρα λέγεται Ἀττικῶς, οὐ διῃρημένως ἀλλ' ὑφ' ἕν . . . ἐπίρρημά ἐστι σύνθετον καὶ σὺν τῷ Ι γράφει Ἡρωδιανός : in Joh. Alex. 29. 24 it is written as two words κάτω κάρα ; cf. Lob. Path. 1. 589 : ἀντιπέρα is a spurious form, which has no existence in genuine Greek : ποθέσπερα and ὑπέρμορα are cases of the adjectives ποθέσπερος (προσέσπερος) and ὑπέρμορος ; on ὑπόδρα see Apoll. de Adv. 548. 1 ; Joh. Alex. 33. 24.

835. (*b*) Those in δα, with corresponding forms in δον, are oxytone, as ἀναφανδά, αὐτοσχεδόν αὐτοσχεδά, καναχηδόν καναχηδά, ῥοιζηδά, χανδόν χανδά ; names of games in ινδα are paroxytone, as βασιλίνδα, ληκίνδα, μυΐνδα, ὀστρακίνδα ; the rest in δα retract the accent, as ἀνάμιγδα, ἄπριγδα, κρύβδα, κύβδα, μίγδα, φύγδα.

NOTE.—See Apoll. de Adv. 562. 10, he mentions that some persons thought that μίγδα should be oxytone, but condemns their opinion : Joh. Alex. 33. 6 : τὰ γύδα [χύδα, Dind.] οἱ μὲν ὤξυναν, οἱ δὲ ἐβάρυναν, ὅπερ καὶ ἐπεκράτησεν. On those in ινδα, cf. Philem. Lex. § 133. p. 50 ; Joh. Alex. 32. 35 ; A. G. 1353.

836. (*c*) Numerals in θα are oxytone, as διχθά, τετραχθά, τριχθά; the rest in θα retract the accent, as ἔμπροσθα, ἔνθα, ἤλιθα, λάθα, μίννθα, ὀλίγυννθα, πρόσθα, ὑπόγνυθα; except δηθά, καθά (καθάπερ) oxytone, and ἐνταῦθα properispomenon.

NOTE.—On those in χθα, see Etym. Gud. 535. 44; Joh. Alex. 33. 7; E. M. 768. 36: on the rest, Apoll. de Adv. 563. 24 sq.; E. M. 341. 40: on ἐνταῦθα, Joh. Alex. 33. 10.

837. (*d*) Those in μα and ξα are oxytone, as μά, θαμά, Joh. Alex. 29. 4, μηδαμά, οὐδαμά, διξά, πενταξά, τριξά; except the paroxytones, ἀτρέμα, ἠρέμα, ὑπηρέμα, and ἅμα, σύναμα, εὔστομα, which retract the accent.

NOTE.—Ἅμα, Arc. 184. 6; Chœrob. E. 123. 18; in Doric it is perispomenon, Schol. Pind. Pyth. 3. 36: τὸ ἁμᾶ, ὡς Ἡρωδιανός φησιν ἐν τῇ ιθ′, οἱ Δωριεῖς περισπῶσι, καὶ τὸ παντᾶ, ὥσπερ καὶ τὸ κρυφᾶ παρὰ Πινδάρῳ. Τοιοῦτον δέ ἐστι τὸ ἁμᾶ περισπώμενον ἀπὸ τοῦ ἁμῇ γινόμενον. Ζητεῖται δὲ ἐν τῷ περισπωμένῳ ἁμᾶ εἰ προστεθήσεται τὸ Ι: 'Callim. Lav. Min. 75: Τειρεσίας δ' ἔτι μῶνος ἅμαι κυσίν, quod ἁμᾶ scribendum animadvertit Ahrens. Dial. vol. 2. p. 372, ubi rectius addi disputat ι quam omitti;' L. Dindorf ap. H. D. The compound σύναμα is also written divisim σύν ἅμα, and sometimes συνάμα: ἀτρέμα, Apoll. de Adv. 570. 33; Joh. Alex. 30. 22; 33. 23: εὔστομα is a mere adjective: ἠρέμα, Apoll. de Adv. 562. 4; Joh. Alex. 30. 21: ὑπηρέμα is somewhat doubtful, in Dion. Per. 1122 at least, ὑπ' ἠρέμα is as good: θαμά, Joh. Alex. 29. 4: μά, Arc. 181. 24: μηδαμά and οὐδαμά are frequently perispomena in the books, but wrongly, see Apoll. de Adv. 565. 6: ὁμᾶ = ὁμοῦ, Hesych.: παραχρῆμα, cf. § 832: on those in ξα, see Eust. 22. 10.

838. (*e*) The rest throw the accent back, as σύρβα; λίγα, μίγα (σύμμιγα, ἄμμιγα), σῖγα; ἔμπεδα, μίγδα, περίχυδα; διχάδεια, καταλοφαδία, κρυφάδεια, ῥεῖα, τροπάδεια; ἄνασκα, ἔνεκα, ὁθούνεκα, ἦκα, προῖκα, πύκα, ὦκα; κατακέφαλα, μάλα (πώμαλα); ἐξάπινα, ἐπέκεινα, πρόπρυμνα; ἐπίσκοπα; ἄντα (but εἴσαντα, ἔσαντα, ἐσάντα or divisim ἐς ἄντα, ἄναντα, κάταντα, πάραντα are proparoxytone, Joh. Alex. 32. 34), κάρτα, νέωτα, ὤκιστα; κρύφα, μέσφα, ῥίμφα, σάφα; διάτριχα, ἔξοχα, ἔπταχα, ἤσυχα, νύχα, τάχα, τέτραχα; αἶψα: except ἀντία, and all in ικα, which are paroxytone, as ἡνίκα, τηνίκα, πηνίκα, ὁπηνίκα, αὐτίκα, μεταυτίκα; ἀλλά, θαμινά, πυκινά, πυκνά, χθιζά oxytone; and ἐνταῦθα, ἐνθαῦτα, τηνικαῦτα properispomena.

839. NOTE I.—E. M. 75. 18; 768. 36; 821. 14; Schol. Ven. B. 655; Joh. Alex. 29. 2; 32. 34; 33. 19: Ἀνόπαια, Schol. Hom. Od. 1. 320: ὁ μὲν Ἀρίσταρχος ἀνόπαια προπαροξυτόνως ἀναγινώσκει ὄνομα ὄρνιθος λέγων, ὁ δὲ Ἡρωδιανὸς ἀνοπαῖα ἀντὶ τοῦ ἀοράτως, ἵν' ᾖ οὐδέτερον πληθυντικόν, ὡς τὸ πυκνὰ μάλα στενάχων (Il. σ. 318)· διὸ καὶ προπερισπαστέον φησίν: ἀκᾶ, Pind. Pyth. 4. 277: ἀλλά, Joh. Alex. 40. 2: ἐνθαῦτα, Ionic = ἐνταῦθα: ἐνιόκα, Doric = ἐνιότε: ἐτά and ἐτεά, Joh. Alex. 29. 5: καταπόδα is better written as two words, κατὰ πόδα: for κατένωπα, which was the accent of Alexion and Herodian, Aristarchus wrote κατενῶπα, Schol. Ven. O. 320, others κατ' ἐνῶπα: cf. Lob. Par. 169; A. G. Paris. 3. 20. 28: πεσδᾶ, Dor. = πεζῇ: προσχρῶτα, συγχρῶτα, Lob. Phryn. 414: συμπρῶτα, ταπρῶτα, cf. above, § 832: πυκινά and πυκνά, like θαμινά, χθιζά, etc., are cases of adjectives: τρόπα,

Joh. Alex. 32. 32 : καὶ τὸ τροπάδε (sic) ὀφείλει βαρύνεσθαι, ἔστι δὲ παιδιά. τινὲς δὲ ὤξυναν : on ὀψιχᾶ, Byzantine for ὀψέ, Hesych., see Lob. Phryn. 51 : on those in ικα, Joh. Alex. 33. 25 : in εια, A. G. 1364 ; Joh. Alex. 33. 19.

Doric varies from the common dialect in the accentuation of some of these adverbs, e. g. παντᾷ, ἀλλᾷ = πάντῃ, ἄλλῃ, Apoll. de Adv. 586, ἀμᾶ for ἄμα, see above, § 837, διχᾷ, τριχᾷ for διχῇ and τριχῇ, κρυφᾶ for κρύφα : Ahrens (De dialect. Gr. ling. 2. p. 34) seems to go beyond the evidence when he asserts that 'adverbia in ᾳ locum *in quem* significantia vel modum, quæ a pronominibus derivantur, perispomena sunt, ut ἀλλᾷ, παντᾷ, quanquam vulgo paroxytona ἄλλῃ πάντῃ ;' cf. Ahrens De Dial. Gr. ling. 2. p. 372.

-E.

840. Adverbs in ε retract the accent, as τῆλε (ἀποτῆλε), κεῖσε, πόσε, ὧδε, ὅτε, *when*, ἐνίοτε, ἄλλοτε, πάντοτε, ἀπάντοτε, ἑκάστοτε, μηδέποτε, μήποτε, μήκοτε, εὖτε, αἶδε, εἴθε ; except ὀψέ (ἀποψέ, ἐποψέ, εἰσοψέ), and the Doric ἀέ = ἀεί oxytone, ἠέπερ paroxytone, and those in δε, θε or θεν, ζε and σε, which require special rules.

NOTE.—Joh. Alex. 33. 27 : ὀψέ, Joh. Alex. 33. 36 ; E. M. 646.8 : ἀποψέ, Apoll. de Synt. 336. 27 : on εὖτε or ηὖτε, see Apoll. de Adv. 558. 5 : the latter is written ηὖτε in Joh. Alex. 33. 29 : αἶθε and εἴθε, Joh. Alex. 33. 33 : τὸ δὲ εἴθε καὶ αἶθε βαρύνεται μέν, οὐ προπερισπᾶται δέ, ὡς τὸ τῆλε καὶ ὧδε, ἀλλὰ παροξύνεται, ὅτι περιττή ἐστιν ἡ θε συλλαβή : cf. Schol. Ven. K. 292 : ἐξότε, εἰσότε (εἰσόκε) and δηλονότε should rather be written as two words, see Lob. Phryn. 46 : οἰόντε is also better οἷόν τε.

841. *Adverbs in* θεν, θε, θι, φι, φιν.—As they are governed by the same rules, it will be convenient to include those in φι, φιν and θι with the rest.

(*a*) All with a naturally short penultimate are paroxytone, as Ἀβυδόθεν, αὐτόθεν, ἐγγύθεν, Κυπρόθεν, Μεγαρόθεν, μηκόθεν, ὅθεν, οὐρανόθεν, πατρόθεν Πλαταιόθεν, πόθεν, Τιθραντόθεν, τόθεν, τριχόθεν, Φηγουντόθεν, χαμόθεν ; ἀγρόθι, ἀγχόθι ; ἐσχαρόφι, οὐρανόφι, πτυόφι ; νηδυιόφιν : except proparoxytone, ἄλλοθεν, ἀνέκαθεν (ἄγκαθεν ἔκαθεν), ἄποθεν, ἑκάστοθεν (but ἑκασταχόθεν), ἔκτοθεν, ἔνδοθεν, ἔντοθεν, ἔξοθεν, οἴκοθεν, ὄπιθεν (ἐξόπιθεν), πάντοθεν (or παντόθεν), πάροθεν (προπάροιθεν), πρόσσοθεν ; ἔνδοθι, οἴκοθι.

842. NOTE.—Joh. Alex. 34. 30 ; Apoll. de Adv. 605. 10 ; Schol. Ven. B. 75 ; A. G. Oxon. 1. 318. 4 ; Eust. 174. 16 : τὸ δὲ ἄλλοθεν σημειῶδές ἐστι τοῖς παλαιοῖς ὡς προπαροξυνόμενον, οἳ καὶ λέγουσι κανόνα τοιοῦτον· τὰ εἰς ΘΕΝ ἐπιρρήματα τῷ Ο μόνῳ παραληγόμενα παροξύνονται, Κυπρόθεν, Ἰλιόθεν, Αἰνόθεν, Ἀβυδόθεν. τὸ ἄλλοθεν, πάντοθεν, οἴκοθεν προπαροξύνονται, διότι ἀόριστά εἰσι καὶ κοινὴν τόπου σημασίαν ἀναδέχονται, ἕτεροι δέ φασιν ἁπλῶς ὡς πάντα τὰ εἰς ΘΕΝ [leg. οθεν] παροξύνονται χωρὶς τῶν ῥηθέντων τριῶν ὡς σεσημειωμένων : but in 918. 41 he excepts οἴκοθεν, ἔνδοθεν, ἄλλοθεν, ἑκάστοθεν, ἀπόπροθεν, ἔκτοσθεν (leg. ἔκτοθεν) πάντοθεν : Schol. Ven. N. 28 : ταῦτά εἰσι τὰ εἰς ΘΕΝ τῷ Ο παραληγόμενα καὶ προπαροξυνόμενα ἐπιρρήματα, οἴκοθεν, ἄλλοθεν, ἔνδοθεν, ἔκτοθεν, ἑκάστοθεν, ἀπόπροθεν, πάντοθεν: Schol. in Dionys. Thrac. 945. 22: τὰ εἰς ΘΕΝ τῷ Ο παραληγόμενα παροξύνεται, οἷον οὐρανόθεν, Ἰλιόθεν, εἰ μὴ παρὰ πρόθεσιν γένοιτο, οἷον παρὰ πάροθεν καὶ πλεονασμῷ τοῦ Ι πάροιθεν· ἢ ἀπὸ ἐπιρρήματος ἐκ προθέσεως γενομένου, οἷον ἔνδοθεν, ἔξοθεν παρὰ Στησιχόρῳ, πρόσσοθεν παρ' Ὁμήρῳ—τούτων δὲ τῶν δύο τὰ ἀνάλογα διὰ τοῦ Ω—ἔκτοθεν, ἔντοθεν, ἃ καὶ ἐν τῷ Σ λέγεται· ἢ ἀπὸ ὀνομάτων ἐπιμεριζομένων, ἄλλοθεν, ἑκάστοθεν. Σεσημείωται τὸ οἴκοθεν, πάντοθεν, ὅτι μηδεμίαν τοιαύτην ἔχει παρατήρησιν: on πάντοθεν or παντόθεν, see Apoll. de Adv. 605. 16: ἔκαθεν and ἀνέκαθεν, Joh. Alex. 35. 26: οἴκοθεν and οἴκοθι, E. M. 25. 12: besides these several others occur in the books proparoxytone, but some of them are not improbably mistakes, e. g. ἄκροθεν, Nicand. Ther. 337, should be ἀκρόθεν, as it is in Arist. Physiog. 6. 20, like ἀκρόθι in Arat. 308: διάπροθι, Nicand. Alex. 3, where one MS. has διὰ προθι (*sic*), but ἀπόπροθι and ἀπόπροθεν in Homer are proparoxytone, as are ἔκπροθεν and ἔμπροθεν: πρέμνοθεν can hardly be defended: and ἄντροθε should be ἀντρόθε: the Doric ἔμποθεν = ἔμπροσθεν is proparoxytone in Greg. Cor. p. 263, ed. Scháf.

843. (*b*) Those with a penultimate long either by nature or position throw the accent back, except such as are derived from words accented on their last syllable, which are properispomena, as ἀπάνευθε, ἀπάτερθε, ἔκτοσθε, νέρθε, ὕπερθε; ἀμφοτέρωθεν, ἔνθεν, ἔξωθεν, ἐπόπισθεν, ἔωθεν, θύραθεν, κεῖθεν, κρῆθεν, ξένηθεν, ὄπισθεν, πρόσθεν, πρώραθεν; κεῖθι, ὁποτέρωθι; ἶφι, νόσφι, ὄρεσφι; Ἀθήνηθεν, Θήβηθεν, Λυκίαθεν, Ὀλυμπίαθεν; but ἀγορή ἀγορῆθεν, ἀρχή ἀρχῆθεν, Πλαταιαί Πλαταιᾶθεν; Ἀγρυλῆθεν, γῆθεν, ἐκεῖθεν, Θεσπιᾶθεν. Ἐντεῦθεν and ἀπεντεῦθεν also are properispomena.

844. NOTE 1.—E. M. 13. 4; Joh. Alex. 34. 30; Apoll. de Adv. 574. 7; 604: Ἀπονόσφι is also written ἀπὸ νόσφι: κατακρῆθεν, on which see E. M. 387. 20; Schol. Ven. Π. 548, and ἀποκρῆθεν are dubious forms from κατὰ κρῆθεν, ἀπὸ κρῆθεν: the following false accentuations in Stephanus Byz. are noted by Göttling p. 350: Ἀμφισσῆθεν, Ἀρπινῆθεν, Ἀσκρῆθεν, Θόραθεν (Θοραί), Μουνυχιᾶθεν, Νεμεῆθεν, Πλωθειᾶθεν (Πλωθειᾶθεν might be correct from Πλωθειά, see above, § 98), Πρασίαθεν (this may be right if from Πρασία, see above, § 98), Πτελεᾶθεν: he also quotes Κρητῆθεν from Plut. Thes. 19 (where it does not occur) for Κρήτηθεν, Hom. Il. 3. 223: Κεφάληθεν for Κεφαλῆθεν, as a reading of some MSS. in Demosth. in Neær. p. 1368, and Οἴηθεν from Suidas.

St. Byz. s. v. Αἰγιλία· ὁ δημότης Αἰγιλιεύς, τὰ τοπικὰ Αἰγιλιᾶθεν, Αἰγιλιάδε Αἰγιλιοῖ: Ἀχαρνῆθεν is well established, though irregular: St. Byz. s. v. Ἀχάρνα· Ἡρωδιανὸς Ἀχάρνεις βαρύτονον· τὰ τοπικὰ ὡς ἀπὸ ὀξυτόνου Ἀχαρνῆθεν· μήποτε δ' ἀπὸ Ἀχαρνεὺς ἡ παραγωγή: Δεκελειᾶθεν, St. Byz., or Δεκελεῆθεν, Herodot. 9.73: Κριῶθεν for Κριώαθεν is regular, Theog. Can. 157. 10; St. Byz.

845. NOTE 2.—There seems to be some difference of opinion as to the proper accentuation of the Doric forms τηλωθεν, τουτωθεν, τηνωθεν, and ἀλλωθεν: Göttling Accent. p. 351 makes them proparoxytone: τηνῶ is circumflexed in the best MSS. of Theocritus 3. 10, though some have τήνω, and τηνῶθεν (*sic*): in Theocr. 3. 25 one MS. has τήνω, another τηνῶ, and the rest τῆνα: ἄλλωθεν has now given way to the MS. reading ἄλλοτε: cf. Ahrens de Dial. Gr. ling. 2. p. 374: on the whole I am inclined to think that Göttling is mistaken, and that these words ought to be properispomena: but there is no decisive evidence on the point.

Χαμᾶθεν (or χαμαῖθεν), Apoll. de Adv. 600. 4; Eust. 999. 22, from χαμαί, is not uncommonly found paroxytone, though such an accent is false, as the penultimate is long.

846. *Adverbs in* δε *and* ζε. A considerable number of adverbs are formed by adding the particle δε to nouns.

(*a*) When the subtraction of δε does not leave an actual accusative case, those in αδε are proparoxytone, as Ἀνακαια-δε Ἀνακαίαδε, οἰκα-δε οἴκαδε, ἄγραδε, φύγαδε, Αἰξώναδε, Θήβαδε, Παλλήναδε.

NOTE.—Joh. Alex. 34. 5 ; Apoll. de Adv. 594. 25 ; 616.19 ; Schol. Ven. Π. 697: φύγαδε· τοῦτο οὐκ ἰσοδυναμεῖ τῷ εἰς φυγήν, ὡς τὸ ἦ καὶ ὁ μὲν φύγαδ' αὖθις ὑποστρέψας (Il. 11. 446)· ἀντὶ γὰρ αἰτιατικῆς, οὐ μετὰ τῆς εἰς. διὸ καί τινες ὑπέλαβον μὴ καὶ δύο μέρη λόγου ἐστίν, ἤτοι κατὰ μεταπλασμὸν γενομένης τῆς αἰτιατικῆς ποιητικῶς, ὡς σκέπην σκέπα, φυγήν φύγα, ἢ ὡς οἴεται ὁ Ἀσκαλωνίτης ἀπ' εὐθείας τῆς φύξ, ὡς Στύξ Στύγα, τοῦ ΔΕ ἐνθάδε παρέλκοντος. ἡ ἐπίρρημά ἐστι ταὐτὸ σημαῖνον τῇ αἰτιατικῇ ὡς καὶ ἄλλα παραγωγὰ ἐπιρρήματα ἰσοδυναμοῦντα τοῖς πρωτοτύποις, Ἴδη θ ε ν μεδέων (Π. 3. 276)· δόρυ δ' ἔκβαλεν ἔκτοσε χειρός (Od. 14. 277)· ἀλλ' οὖν γε ὡς ἂν ἔχῃ, οὐκ ἐναντιοῦται τὸ τοῦ τόνου· ἤτοι γὰρ δύο τόνοι ἔσονται φύγαδέ, ὡς Οὐλυμπόνδε, ἢ εἷς, ὡς ἄγραδε. τὸ γοῦν ἄλαδ' ἐλκομενάων (Π. 14. 100), δύναται καὶ δύο μέρη λόγου εἶναι, ὡς οἰκόνδε, ἐντελοῦς οὔσης τῆς αἰτιατικῆς, ἢ πάλιν κατὰ παραγωγήν, ὡς ἄγραδε, ἄλαδε. ταῦτα ὁ Ἡρωδιανὸς ἐν τῷ ιθ' τῆς Καθόλου: cf. Schol. Ven. Θ. 157.

847. (*b*) When the subtraction of δε leaves an actual accusative or genitive case, the particle merely acts as an enclitic (see Chap. 9.), and the former accent, if there should happen to be two, is dispensed with, as ἅλα-δε, πόλιν-δε, Βραυρῶνά-δε Βραυρωνάδε, Μέγαρά-δε Μεγαράδε, οἶκόν-δε οἰκόνδε, Ὄλυμπόν-δε Ὀλυμπόνδε, ὄρθιά-δε ὀρθιάδε, Ἀϊδόσδε, Πυθώδε, not Πυθῶδε, since the word is a mere parathetic compound.

NOTE.—Joh. Alex. 34. 4: τὰ εἰς ΔΕ ἐπιρρήματα, τὴν εἰς τόπον σχέσιν σημαίνοντα, τρίτην ἀπὸ τέλους ἔχει τὴν ὀξεῖαν, οἴκαδε, ἄγραδε, ἅλαδε, Παλίναδε [Παλλήναδε ?] φύγαδε. τὸ οἶκον δέ, ἀγρὸν δέ, δύο μέρη λόγου, τὴν ἰδίαν ἕκαστον ἔχον προσῳδίαν, ἰσοδυναμοῦντα τοῖς ἐπιρρήμασι, τὸ ἀγρόνδε τῷ ἄγραδε, τὸ οἰκόνδε τῷ οἴκαδε: but οἶκον δέ seems to be an error, οἰκόνδε or οἰκόνδε being the only correct forms: see Apoll. de Adv. 592. 16, who discusses this and similar combinations at considerable length.

848. Those in ζε are proparoxytone, unless derived from oxytone nouns, when they are properispomena, as Ἀθήναζε, ἔραζε, θύραζε, Οἰνόηζε, Ὀλυμπίαζε, Ἀχαρνῆζε, Κεφαλῆζε, χαμᾶζε.

NOTE.—Joh. Alex. 34. 17: τὰ εἰς ΖΕ, εἰ μὲν ἔχει πρὸ τέλους βραχὺ τὸ Α, τρίτην ἀπὸ τέλους ἔχει τὴν ὀξεῖαν οἷον ἔραζε, θύραζε, Ἀθήναζε, Ὀλυμπίαζε. τὰ δὲ φύσει μακρὰ παραληγόμενα προπαροξύνεται ἢ προπερισπᾶται· προπαροξύνεται μὲν ὅσα ἔχει βαρύτονον τὸ πρωτότυπον, ὡς παρὰ τὸ Οἰνόη τὸ Οἰνόηζε, προπερισπᾶται δὲ τὰ ἀπὸ ὀξυτόνων ὡς παρὰ τὸ Ἀχαρνὲς (sic) τὸ Ἀχαρνῆζε, Κεφαλὴ Κεφαλῆζε, χαμαὶ χαμᾶζε: Schol. Ven. Γ. 29 ; A. G. Oxon. 3. 293. 2 ; 3. 297. 18: τὸ χαμᾶζε δὲ προπερισπώμενον εὗρον, ἀλλ' ἡ συνήθεια παροξύνει: cf. E. M. 806. 9;

Schol. Ven. Γ. 29 : 'Αθμονῆζε and 'Αθμονῆσι, from 'Αθμόνη, St. Byz.: Θριῶζε (and Θριῶθεν), Joh. Alex. 34. 27 ; St. Byz. s. v. Θριά, with Κριῶζε, St. Byz., form apparent exceptions, which Göttling explains by supposing an old genitive case Θριῶς and Κριῶς from Θριώ and Κριώ, and hence Θριῶσ-δε, Κριῶσ-δε : 'Αληθένδε, St. Byz. s. v. 'Αλαί 'Αραφηνίδες is a very strange form, if genuine : Göttling's explanation of it (Accent. p. 359) is not satisfactory.

849. All other adverbials in δε are accented on the penultimate, as διχάδε, ἐνθάδε, ἐνθένδε, τεῖνδε, τημόσδε, τηνικάδε, τοιῇδε, τοιόνδε, τοσόνδε, τυῖδε, ὧδε. The conjunctions μηδέ, οὐδέ are oxytone.

NOTE.—Πηνικάδε is twice written πηνίκαδε in Joh. Alex. 34. 12, but wrongly: E. M. 341. 35 : on ἐνθάδε see Schol. Ven. Υ. 390 ; E. M. 416. 20 ; ἐπίταδε for ἐπιτάδε or ἐπὶ τάδε is doubtful.

850. Adverbs in σε are accented like the corresponding forms in θε, as αὐτόσε, ἑτέρωσε (ἑτέρωθεν), ἐκεῖσε (ἐκεῖθεν), κεῖσε, κυκλόσε (κυκλόθε), μηδαμόσε, ὁποτέρωσε (ὁποτέρωθε), οὐδαμόσε, πανταχόσε, πεδιόσε, πόσε, Ἑρμόσε, 'Οθριῶσε ; but ἄλλοσε (ἄλλοθεν), ἔκτοσε (ἔκτοθεν), πάντοσε (πάντοθεν).

NOTE.—Apoll. de Adv. 620. 17 ; Joh. Alex. 34. 24 ; Schol. Ven. Π. 515.

-H.

851. Those in η or ῃ retain the accent of the word from which they are derived, as ἄλλη, ἀμῆ (or ἀμῇ), διπλῆ, ἐνωπῆ, ὀμῆ, πάντῃ, πεζῇ, ταύτῃ, τριπλῆ ; all in χη are perispomena, as ἀλλαχῇ, ἀπανταχῇ, πενταχῇ, πολλαχῇ.

852. NOTE 1.—It may perhaps be found more convenient to remember that all proper adverbs in η or ῃ are perispomena, except ἀπάντῃ, πάντῃ, ἄλλη, ἑτέρῃ, λάθρῃ, πανσυδίῃ or πασσυδίῃ, and ταύτῃ. The monosyllabic conjunctions are oxytone, as νή, μή, δή (δηλαδή ἐπειδή, see above, § 830), ἤ, but ῇ, *verily*: conjunctions not monosyllabic are paroxytone, as ἤδη : πῆ (κῆ), πή, ὅπη, etc., have been already noticed above, § 825 : Joh. Alex. 31. 11 : τὰ μέντοι τὸ Η ἔχοντα μονοσύλλαβα, μὴ προσκειμένου τοῦ Ι, ὀξύνεται, ὡς καὶ ἤδη εἶπον, νή, μή· πλὴν τοῦ δῆ καὶ τοῦ ῇ ἰσοδυναμοῦντος τῷ ὡς, ῇ Θέμις ἐστι· φῇ ἀντὶ τοῦ καθάπερ,

φῇ νέος οὐκ ἀπάλαμνος,

but what he means by saying that δή is not oxytone I cannot imagine. On ἀμηγέπη see Joh. Alex. 29. 13 : on those in χῇ, Joh. Alex. 30. 23 : on ὀμῇ, Schol. Ven. O. 209.

853. NOTE 2.—For ἀμαρτῇ, which was the accentuation of Herodian, of Ptolemæus Ascalonites, and most other grammarians, Aristarchus wrote ἀμαρτή without ι *subscriptum* and oxytone. He thought it a shortened form from ἀμαρτήδην, but both it and ἀμαρτῇ were usually, and as it seems correctly, made perispomena ; Schol. Ven. E. 656 ; Φ. 162 ; E. M. 78. 22 ; Eust. 592. 16 ; 1229. 18 ; Joh. Alex. 29. 12 ; Arc. 183. 6 : for ἡσυχῇ some grammarians wrote ἡσύχῃ, on the principle that these adverbs correspond in accent with the genitive plural of the words from which they are derived, and as ἥσυχος makes ἡσύχων the adverb,

R

ἡσύχως, would be barytone, and consequently ἡσύχῃ. But in this case at least the analogy does not hold good, for ἡσυχῶς is usually circumflexed like other adverbs in χως (Theog. Can. 164), and therefore ἡσυχῇ would be the better form; cf. Apoll. de Adv. 586. 19; Joh. Alex. 30. 23 : on παντᾷ *Doric* = πάντῃ, see § 839 : χρή, which the Greek grammarians consider to be an adverb, see Apoll. de Adv. 538. 13, and above, § 769.

-I (AI, EI, OI).

854. Monosyllables are oxytone, as δαί, καί, ναί (on οῖ, ποῖ, etc., (see § 825): dissyllables and their compounds are accented on the penultimate, as ἄρτι, ἀπάρτι, ἐσάρτι; αὖθι, καταῦθι; ἔτι, εἰσέτι, ἐξέτι, μηκέτι, οὐκέτι, προσέτι; ὅτι, δηλονότι, διότι, καθότι; ἄγχι, ἄχρι, ἦρι, ἦχι, μέχρι, οἴκει, ὄψι, πάγχι, χῶρι; ἄμαι, πάλαι, the compounds of which retract the accent, as πρόπαλαι, τρίπαλαι; except ἀεί, ἐπεί (see above, § 830), πρωΐ in Attic, χαμαί oxytone, and ἐκεῖ perispomenon. On those in οι, see below, § 858.

855. NOTE 1.—Joh. Alex. 32. 15 : τὸ εἰ ὀξύνεται ὁμοίως τῷ συνδέσμῳ, εἴγ' ὤφελες· τὸ γὰρ στοιχεῖον περισπᾶται : it is, however, like the Doric αἰ, left unaccented in our editions, though οἰονεί, ὡσανεί, ὡσπερεί, ὡσεί, and the like are oxytone : ἄϊ, Æolic = ἀεί, is paroxytone, Theog. Can. 3. 8 : ἀπάρτι, or ἀπ' ἄρτι = ἀπὸ τοῦ νῦν, must be distinguished from ἀπαρτί = ἀπηρτισμένως, τελείως, ἀκριβῶς, Schol. Aristoph. Plut. 388; Joh. Alex. 37. 10 : τὸ δὲ ἀπαρτὶ παρ' Ἀθηναίοις ὀξύνεται : cf. Lob. Phryn. 21 : on πάλαι and its compounds see Joh. Alex. 36. 22; Chœrob. C. 402. 3 : Theog. Can. 158. 31 : on ὄψι, E. M. 646. 8 : οἴκει and χαμαί, Joh. Alex. 36. 21–32 : χῶρι is perispomenon, though χωρίς is oxytone, Apoll. de Adv. 548. 31 : πρωΐ, E. M. 607. 21 : καὶ τὸ πρωΐ ἀναλογώτερόν ἐστι παρὰ τῷ ποιητῇ βαρυνόμενον, πρῶϊ δ' ὑπ' ἠοῖ : E.M. 692. 12 : πρωΐ ὅπερ οἱ μὲν ποιηταὶ βαρύνουσιν· οἷον, Πρῶϊ δ' ὑπ' ἠοῖ—οἱ δὲ κοινοὶ καὶ Ἀττικοὶ καὶ Ἀθηναῖοι ὀξύνουσιν : cf. Theog. Can. 159. 26 : ὕψι, Schol. Ven. N. 140 : ὕψι ὡς οἴκοθι[?] καὶ ἄγχι ὥς φησι Πτολεμαῖος· τινὲς δὲ τοῦτο ὀξύνουσι, ὑψί : cf. Apoll. de Adv. 545. 18 : ἀκαῖ (?) is a doubtful form.

856. NOTE 2.—Doric adverbs of place in ει are perispomena, as τηνεῖ, τουτεῖ, πεῖ, αὐτεῖ, Joh. Alex. 36. 33; Theog. Can. 159. 7, who includes ἐκεῖ among them; Apoll. de Adv. 542. 30; Synt. 238. 8.

857. *Iota paragogicum* always takes the accent, as δευρί, εἰνί, ἐνθαδί, ἐνί, ἐντεῦθεν, ἐντευθενί, νῦν, νυνί, νυνμενί, οὐκί, οὐχί, οὑτωσί, τουτί, ὡδί; except ναίχι paroxytone.

NOTE.—Apoll. de Adv. 571. 4; E. M. 607. 20; 646. 10 : ναίχι, Joh. Alex. 37. 5; Arc. 183. 11; A. G. 1161; Matthiä (Gr. Gr. T. 1. § 261 d. p. 454) denies that either οὐχί or ναίχι, which he wrongly accents ναιχί (cf. Schol. Ven. K. 292), is a case of ι *paragogicum* : μήχι, A. G. 108. 14, and νήχι, are both doubtful.

858. Those in οι are perispomena, as ἁρμοῖ, βυθοῖ, ἐνταυθοῖ, οὐδαμοῖ, Ἀθμονοῖ, Ἰσθμοῖ, Μεγαροῖ, Παιανιοῖ, Σφιγγοῖ, Φρεαρροῖ; except dissyllables from barytone primitives, which are paroxytone, as ἔνδον ἔνδοι, ἔξω ἔξοι, μέσοι μέσσοι, οἶκος οἴκοι, ὅποι, πέδον πέδοι.

NOTE.—A. G. 944. 30 ; Schol. Ven. Φ. 122 ; Joh. Alex. 36. 1 ; Arc. 183. 16 ; Ἔνδοι, Apoll. de Adv. 610. 25, some wrote ἐνδοῖ, E. M. 663. 30 ; Eust. 140. 15; 722. 62 : ἔξοι, E. M. 663. 32, is written ἐξοῖ, Eust. 140. 15 : οἴκοι, Arc. 183, 16 : οἴκοι δὲ ἀντὶ τοῦ εἰς τὸν οἶκον παροξύνεται : Apoll. de Adv. 588. 21 : ὅποι, Arc. 182. 8 ; πέδοι, A. G. 945. 2 ; Joh. Alex. 36. 8 : μέσοι, Æolic, Apoll. de Adv. 610. 31; μέσσοι, Æolic, Apoll. de Adv. 589. 3.

859. Those in σι retain the accent of their primitives, as θύρᾱ-σι, Ἀθήνη-σι, Ὀλυμπίᾱ-σι, Πρασιά-σι become θύρασι, Ἀθήνησι, Ὀλυμπίασι, Πρασιᾱσι (§ 98), παντάπασι (ἄπασι), ὦρασι (ὦρα), Ἐλαιοῦσι (Ἐλαιοῦς), Ἐλευσινίσι (Ἐλευσινίς).

860. NOTE 1.—Joh. Alex. 35. 28 : τὰ εἰς ΘΙ καὶ εἰς ΣΙ τὸν τῶν εἰς ΘΕΝ ἐπιρρημάτων ἔχει τόνον, οἷον οἴκοθεν οἴκοθι, ἀγρόθεν ἀγρόθι, Ὀλυμπιᾶθεν, Ὀλυμπιᾶσιν [leg. Ὀλυμπίαθεν, Ὀλυμπίασιν, cf. 35. 14], Ἀλωπήκηθεν Ἀλωπήκησιν [? leg. Ἀλωπεκῆθεν Ἀλωπεκῆσι] : Ὀλυμπίασι, Schol. Aristoph. Vesp. 1382 : νῦν προπαροξύνεται· λέγεται γὰρ περὶ τόπου. ἐὰν περὶ πράγματος ᾖ δηλοῦσα ἡ λέξις, οἷον ὡς εἰ λέγοι τις δέκα Ὀλυμπιᾶσιν ἐφεξῆς ἐνίκησεν ὁ δεῖνα προπερισπᾶται. γίνεται γὰρ τὸ μὲν ἀπὸ τοῦ Ὀλυμπία Ὀλυμπίασι, τὸ δὲ ἀπὸ τοῦ Ὀλυμπιάς Ὀλυμπιᾶσι ; but has the dative plural of Ὀλυμπιάς a long penultimate? cf. A. G. Oxon. 1. 388. 8 ; Lob. Path. 2. 251.

861. NOTE 2.—Many adverbs of this termination are found in the books wrongly accented: Göttling mentions Μουνυχιάσι or Μουνυχιᾶσι for ίασι, Πρασίησι, St. Byz. for Πρασιᾶσι (but Πρασίασι may be correct, cf. § 98): Πλαταιάσι, Paus. 3. 5 (where Dindorf has the correct form Πλαταιᾶσι), Θριάσι for Θριᾶσι ; Δεκελειᾶσι from Δεκέλεια : on this St. Byz. says, Δεκέλεια ... ὁ δημότης Δεκελειεύς, τὸ τοπικὸν Δεκελειᾶθεν· τὰ γὰρ ἀπὸ ὀξυτόνων εἰς Α ἢ εἰς Η γιγνόμενα διὰ τοῦ ΗΘΕΝ ἢ ΑΘΕΝ προπερισπᾶται. παρὰ δὲ Καλλιμάχῳ Δεκελειόθεν Δεκελειάζε Δεκελειᾶσι. But it is questionable whether any such form as Δεκελειά exists ; there is Δεκελέη, which might be contracted Δεκελῆ, from which we should get Δεκελῆθεν and Δεκελῆσι. Ἀμαξαντειᾶσιν from Ἀμαξάντεια, St. Byz., and in the same author, Ἐρικειᾶσι, Πτελεάσι, Ἐρχιᾶσι, Ἑκαλῆσι, Ἐρεχθιᾶσι, Κρωπᾶσι, Τρινεμεάσι, Ἀνακαιᾶσιν, Suid. Κριῶσι (perhaps for Κριώασε, cf. A. G. 1423), St. Byz., and Ἀραφηνῆσι (Göttling conjectures Ἀραφηνίσι) are doubtful.

862. Those in ακι for ακις are paroxytone, as θαυμάκι· Joh. Alex. 37. 13, πολλάκι (πολλάκις), τουτάκι.

For those in φι and θι, see above § 841.

The remaining adverbs in ι are oxytone, as ἀθρηνί, ἀκραεί, ἀμεταστρεπτί, ἀμυθητί, ἀνοιμωκτί, αὐτοεθνεί, αὐτοχειρεί, ἀωρί, νεωστί, πανοικεί, προταινί, παγγυναικί, Δωριστί, Ἑλληνιστί, Ἰαστί, Συριστί ; except ἀμέλει, ὀσημέραι paroxytone, ὀσῶραι properispomenon, and ἔκητι, ἀέκητι, ἔναντι, ἀπέναντι, κατέναντι, πέρυσι, προπέρυσι proparoxytone.

863. NOTE.—A. G. Oxon. 1. 124. 21 : Ἀμέλει, though used as an adverb, is the imperative of ἀμελέω, Theog. Can. 165. 11 : ἔκητι, ἀέκητι, Apoll. de Conj. 498. 31 ; de Adv. 553. 17; Joh. Alex. 37. 10 : ἔμπαλι = ἔμπαλιν : ὀσημέραι and ὀσῶραι = ὅσαι ἡμέραι, ὅσαι ὦραι : πέρυσι, Schol. Ven. Π. 324.

The Æolic adverbs in νι are barytone, as τηλύϊ, ἀλύει, ἀτερύει, Theog. Can. 160. 7.

Ἁλιμοῦντι, St. Byz., Ἀναγυροῦντι, St. Byz., and Μαραθῶνι, Aristoph. Eq. 781, are mere dative cases, and as such they naturally retain their proper accent.

-N.

864. On those in θεν, φιν, see above, § 841.

(*a*) Adverbs in ν throw the accent back, as ἄγαν, ἄγδην, αἴγδην, ἀκέων, ἄντην, ἀπριάτην, ἆσσον, αὔριον, ἐπαύριον, σήμερον, βύζην, ἐξάπινον, ἐπίκλην, λίᾶν, ὑπερλίαν, μάτην, πάλιν, ἔμπαλιν, πέραν, ἀντιπέρᾶν, πρώην ; except oxytone, those in δον and δων, and those from oxytone primitives, as ἀκτινηδόν, ἐθνηδόν, κριδόν, διακριδόν, κυνηδόν, λυκηδόν, σχεδόν (but ἔμπεδον and ἔνδον are barytone), δηρόν, ἐλεόν, ἐτεόν ; ἐκποδών, ἐμποδών, προποδών ; ἀκήν (ἀκή), ἀκμήν (ἀκμή), ἐθελοντήν (ἐθελοντής), ἐκοντήν (ἑκοντής). The word αἰέν (ἐσαιέν) is also oxytone.

865. (*b*) Cases of substantives and adjectives, when used adverbially, retain the accent of the original word, as ἀκήν, ἀκμήν, ἄλλην, ἀντίον, ἀπαντίον, ἀρχήν, ἰθεῖαν, δωρεάν, ἱμονιάν, κάλλιον, μακράν, νεῖον, πασυδίην, πλησίον, προφθαδίην, σχεδίην, τυχόν, ὑπέρμορον ; except χάριεν *Attic*, proparoxytone, and αὐθημερόν oxytone.

866. (*c*) Those consisting of a preposition or article and an accusative case retain the accent of the last factor (see above, § 832), as ὑφέν ; ἀνόπιν, εἰσόπιν, κατόπιν, μετόπιν, ἐξόπιν, κατάντησιν, κατάντηστιν, ἐπιπλεῖον, ἐπιπλέον, ἐπιτοπλέον, ἐπιτοπλεῖστον, ἐσύστερον, ἐφόσον, καθαυτόν, κατεναντίον, παρᾶσσον, τοαρχαῖον, τοπλέον, τοπρῶτον ; but compounds with παν are paroxytone, except those in πάμπαν, which are proparoxytone, as εἰσάπαν, ἐπίπαν, καθάπαν, παράπαν, περίπαμπαν, τοεπίπαν ; τοπάν (or τὸ πᾶν) is oxytone. These words are frequently written separately, and in some cases at least it is far better to do so.

867. NOTE.—On adverbs in δόν, see Apoll. de Adv. 550. 6 ; 609. 28 ; 611. 1 ; Eust. 1062. 31 ; Herod. π. μ. λ. 46. 7 ; they retain their accent in composition, as παρακλιδόν, αὐτοσχεδόν, S. V. H. 273 : ἡμερολεγδόν, Arist. H. A. 6. 21. 3, not ἡμερόλεγδον, as in E. M. 429. 40, and in some editions of Æschyl. Pers. 63 : ἀδεμάν, ὅταν, Κρῆτες, Hesych.: on ἔνδον and ἔμπεδον, see Theog. Can. 162. 8 ; Herod. π. μ. λ. 25. 14 ; Joh. Alex. 38. 3 ; E. M. 204. 52 ; on those in δην, Joh. Alex. 37. 33 ; Apoll. de Adv. 611. 23 ; Göttling, Accent. p. 344, notes that ἐκοντήν and ἐθελοντήν, on which see Joh. Alex. 37. 36, are falsely paroxytone in A. G. 1368 : on ἀκμήν, Joh. Alex. 29. 23 : αἰέν, Theog. Can. 161. 29 ; Joh. Alex. 33. 36 : ἐξόν, Chœrob. E. 89. 27 : αὐθωρόν seems to be oxytone in all the places quoted in

H.ʼD. : **εὐθυωρόν** in Suidas is probably incorrect; H. D. quote it from Procop. Goth. 4. p. 665 A, but it is rightly proparoxytone in Ælian, H. A. 7. 5 : **αὐθημερόν** is oxytone, Joh. Alex. 50. 24 ; Chœrob. E. 89. 27 : on **πάμπαν** and **παντάπασι**, see Joh. Alex. 30. 27 : **πανημερόν** is also oxytone in Herodot. 7. 183 : on **πέραν** and **ἀντιπέραν**, Joh. Alex. 29. 28 : on the Doric form **δοάν**=**δήν**, which is oxytone contrary to rule, see Joh. Alex. 37. 31 : **πρῶϊν**, Joh. Alex. 32. 7 : τὸ μέντοι πρῷ μονοσύλλαβον παρ' Ἀττικοῖς ὀξύνεται· ἐπεὶ ἐκ τοῦ πρωΐ δισυλλάβου ὀξυνομένου κατὰ συναίρεσιν γέγονε. τὸ δὲ πρῶϊν προπερισπᾶται . . . ἐπεὶ ἐκ τοῦ πρώην.

On **χάριεν**, which the Attic distinguished from the neuter singular **χαρίεν**, see Joh. Alex. 30. 17 ; Apoll. de Adv. 570. 27 ; Ammon. p. 117 ; E. M. 358. 55 ; 807. 15, but the distinction is sometimes neglected, cf. H. D. s. v.

Κραγόν, Schol. Aristoph. Eq. 485 : Ἀρίσταρχος ὀξυτόνως ἀντὶ τοῦ κραυγαστικῶς, καὶ Ἡρωδιανὸς ἐν Ἀττικῇ προσῳδίᾳ.

-Ξ.

868. Adverbs in ξ are oxytone, as ἀλλάξ, ἀπαλλάξ, ἐναλλάξ, παραλλάξ, αὐτοδάξ, διαμπάξ, ἐπιτάξ, εὐράξ, λάξ, μονάξ, ὀκλάξ ; ἀβρίξ, ἀναμίξ, ἀπρίξ, ἐπιμίξ, κουρίξ, μεταμίξ, πλίξ ; γνύξ, ἐπιβλύξ, προνύξ, πύξ ; except **ἅπαξ** (εἰσάπαξ, ἐφάπαξ, καθάπαξ, προσάπαξ), and **πέριξ** paroxytone.

NOTE.—Apoll. de Adv. 544. 32 ; 548. 9 ; E. M. 781. 47 ; S. V. A. 148 ; Schol. Ven. Λ. 251 ; Ξ. 60 ; Eust. 249. 33 ; 842. 43 ; 966. 63. Besides **ἅπαξ** and **πέριξ**, Joh. Alex. 38. 9 mentions **πάρεξ** (πάραξ cod.): Herod. π. μ. λ. 25. 20 : οὐδὲν εἰς ΕΞ ἐπίρρημα βαρυνόμενον ἐκ δύο προθέσεων συνεστηκὸς, ὅπερ καὶ γενικῇ θέλει συντάττεσθαι, ἀλλὰ μόνον τὸ πάρεξ. καὶ γὰρ ἡ συνήθεια οὕτως ἔσθ' ὅτε φησί, πάρεξ Ἀπολλωνίου· ὃν τρόπον καὶ Ἡρόδοτος ἐν τῇ τετάρτῃ ἔφη, πάρεξ τοῦ τε Σκυθίου ἔθνεος. παρὰ μέντοι τῷ ποιητῇ ἕτερόν ἐστι τὸ ὀξυνόμενον. ἀλλὰ παρὲξ τὴν νῆσον ἐλαύνετε· παρὲξ περιμήκεα δῶρα. εἴρηται δὲ περὶ αὐτοῦ ἐν τῇ Ὁμηρικῇ προσῳδίᾳ: Schol. Ven. I. 7 : Τυραννίων δὲ ἐν μέρος λόγου ἤκουσεν, ἵν' ᾖ ἐπίρρημα καὶ βαρύνει· καὶ ἔχει λόγον, ὡς Ἡρόδοτος ἐν δ' (c. 46) πάρεξ τοῦ Σκυθικοῦ ἔθνους. παρὰ δὲ τῷ ποιητῇ τὸ παρέξ δύο μέρη λόγου εἰσὶ καὶ ἐγκλίνονται αἱ δύο προθέσεις : cf. Apion and Herodorus ap. Eust. 732. 39. Apparently Herodian wrote **πὰρ ἐξ** in Homer, later editors have been content with **παρέξ**. In A. G. 1428 the adverb **ὕρραξ** (?) is barytone.

-O.

869. All particles in o (there are no proper adverbs), both simple and compound, are oxytone, as **διό, καθό, καθαυτό, πρό, ἀποπρό, διαπρό, προπρό** ; except **δεῦρο** properispomenon.

NOTE.—Apoll. de Synt. 332. 19 : on **δεῦρο** and its various forms, Herod. π. μ. λ. 26. 31 ; the barbarism **ἐξόπιστο**=**ἐξόπισθεν** is proparoxytone.

-P.

870. Those in ρ take the accent on the penultimate, as **αὐτῆμαρ, ἐννῆμαρ, ἐξῆμαρ, πανῆμαρ, ἄφαρ, εἶθαρ, ἐπίκαρ, ἴκταρ, πρόπαρ, ὕπαρ ; νύκτωρ** ; except **αὐτάρ** and **ἀτάρ** oxytone.

NOTE.—Joh. Alex. 30. 27 ; 38. 10 ; Arc. 184. 9 ; E. M. 172. 30 ; 343. 50 ; Schol. Ven. Γ. 1 ; Ω. 657 ; Chœrob. E. 134. 25 ; A. G. Paris. 3. 8. 15 : ζητεῖται δὲ πάλιν πῶς τὸν ἀτὰρ σύνδεσμον δεῖ προφέρεσθαι, πότερον ὀξυτόνως ἢ βαρυτόνως, οἱ μὲν γὰρ φησιν ὀξυτόνως ἀνεγνώκασι ὡς Καλλίμαχος, οἱ δὲ βαρυτόνως, λόγῳ τῷδε· πᾶσα λέξις εἰς AP λήγουσα βαρυτονεῖται, οἷον ἄφαρ, εἶθαρ, δάμαρ, στέαρ, οὖθαρ· ῥητέον δὲ ὅτι οὐδεὶς συμπλεκτικὸς ἢ βαρύνεται ἢ περισπᾶται, πάντες δὲ ὀξύνονται.

-Σ.

871. (*a*) αs. Those in αs are oxytone, as ἀγκάς, ἀνδρακάς, ἑκάς, ἀνεκάς, ἐντυπάς; except ἀντιπέρας, καταντιπέρας, ἀτρέμας, ἔμπας, πέλας paroxytone.

NOTE.—῞Ααs, cras, a Bœotian word, Hesych.; according to Schol. Ven. ad loc. Zenodotus wrote ἄας δὴ καὶ μᾶλλον in Il. 8. 470: ἄλιας=ἅλις in Hipponax, Joh. Alex. 38. 14; E. M. 63. 18: ἀτρέμας, Joh. Alex. 38. 14; E. M. 63. 18: πέλας, Joh. Alex. 38. 14; according to E. M. 63. 21 ἐμπάς is oxytone, but it never occurs with that accent in our books: κατάκρας is perhaps better written κατ' ἄκρας: καταμόνας and παραπόδας are better written as two words; Apoll. de Adv. 570. 25: καὶ τὸ ἐντυπάς, ἑκάς, ἀνεκάς, ἅπερ Ἀττικοὶ οὐ δεόντως ἀναβιβάζουσιν.

872. (*b*) ες. Ἀές and αλές=ἀεί, χθές, ἐχθές, προχθές (not πρόχθες), προυχθές, are oxytone; τῆτες (σῆτες, σάτες) barytone. The rest are merely adjectives of the Third Declension used adverbially, and retain their adjectival accent, as ἀεικές, ἐπιεικές, ἀκλέες=ἀκλεέες, ἀμπερές, ἀμφίετες, αὐτόετες (see above, § 709), ἀσπερχές, διαμπερές, νωλεμές. The Homeric εἰνάνυχες is only another form of ἐννέα νύχες or ἐννεάνυχες. In Attic the adverbs ἄληθες, ἐπάναγκες, ἐπίτηδες, and ἐξεπίτηδες are proparoxytone.

NOTE.—Joh. Alex. 30. 1; A. G. 376. 7; Herod. π. μ. λ. 47. 3; E. M. 62. 51; 358. 53; 366. 26; Schol. Aristoph. Eq. 89; yet we find S. V. A. 142 saying, τὸ ἐπιτηδὲς ὀξυντέον ἀπὸ τοῦ ἐπιτηδεῖς γάρ. τὰ δὲ ὀνοματικὰ ἐπιρρήματα τὸν αὐτὸν τοῖς ὀνόμασι φυλάσσει τόνον: Göttling, Accent. p. 348, mentions βιόπλανες, but it seems to be an error on his part, the word is oxytone; cf. Callimachus ap. Chœrob. C. 447. 13.

873. (*c*) ης. Adverbs in ης are, with the exception of ἔμπης (and ἑξῆς, ἐφεξῆς, ἐπεξῆς, παρεξῆς), genitive cases of nouns belonging to the First Declension; they retain the accent of the words from which they are derived, as ἀίφνης, ἐξαίφνης, ἀπαρχῆς, διακενῆς, ἐξαπίνης, ἐξαυτῆς, ἐξείης, ἐφεξείης, ἐξίσης, ἐπανάγκης, ἐπικοινῆς.

NOTE.—Theog. Can. 163. 3: ἐξείης ἀφ' οὗ τὸ ἑξῆς περισπώμενον: Joh. Alex. 38. 16: on ἔμπης, Apoll. de Adv. 564. 23.

874. (*d*) ις. *General Rule.*—All simple adverbs in ις are oxytone, except dissyllables, those in ἄκις, ἄδις, υδις and ἄνδις, which are barytone: compounds keep the accent of the simple words from which they are derived.

Special Rules.—Monosyllables in ις with their compounds are oxytone, as δίς, ἀποδίς; τρίς, ἀποτρίς, ἐπιτρίς, ἐστρίς. Καθεῖς is remarkable.

875. Dissyllables and their compounds are accented on the penultimate, as ἄλις, ἄνις, αὖθις, εἰσαῦθις, ἐξαῦθις, μεταῦθις, ἄχρις, λέχρις, μεταῦτις, μέχρις, μόγις, μόλις; except ἀμφίς and χωρίς oxytone.

NOTE.—Joh. Alex. 38. 19; E. M. 114. 35; 607. 22; Schol. Ven. Π. 324.

876. Those in ακις are paroxytone, as δεκάκις, ὀλιγάκις, πλεισάκις, πλεονάκις, πολλάκις, τοσαυτάκις, Joh. Alex. 38. 24; Theog. Can. 163. 13; ἄμακις· ἅπαξ· Κρῆτες, Heschy. is proparoxytone.

877. Trisyllables in ἄδις are paroxytone, as ἐσχάδις, κρυφάδις, μιγάδις, ὀκλάδις, πτακάδις, φυγάδις, χαμάδις; except οἴκαδις proparoxytone, and ὠμαδίς oxytone. The Doric adverbs in ανδις are also paroxytone, as ἀγράνδις, Ὀλυμπιάνδις, χαμάνδις.

NOTE.—Joh. Alex. 38. 25; A. G. 1303; 1317; Theog. Can. 163. 20: ὠμαδίς is spelled ὁμαδίς in E. M. 806. 7.

878. Those in υδις are proparoxytone, as ἄλλυδις, ἄμυδις.

NOTE.—Joh. Alex. 38. 31; Eust. 732. 30; Schol. Ven. I. 6; Υ. 114; Theog. Can. 163. 28.

879. Those in δις, when consisting of more than three syllables, or with a long penultimate, and all other adverbs in ις, are oxytone, as αἰφνηδίς, ἀκροπουδίς, ἀμοιβαδίς, ἀμφιουδίς, ἐ βολαδίς, ἐπιουδίς, κατωμαδίς, κλωπηδίς, λαθρηδίς, στοιχηδίς, ἀμφικελεμνίς, αὐτονυχίς, ἐγκοιτίς, κραταιΐς, λικριφίς, παμπηδονίς, σολικρίς; except πέρυτις.

NOTE.—Schol. Ven. Ξ. 463; Joh. Alex. 38. 28; A. G. 1310; 1319; Theog. Can. 163. 13: in Herod. π. μ. λ. 46. 15 ἀμφουδίς is proparoxytone: κραταιΐς, Schol. Hom. Odyss. 11. 597: ὁ μὲν Ἀρίσταρχος καὶ Ἡρωδιανὸς ὀξυτόνως κατὰ συστολὴν, ὡς λικριφίς, ἀμφουδίς, ἐπιρρηματικῶς, ὁ δὲ Ἀσκαλωνίτης τὸ πλῆρες κραταιὰ ἴς, οἷον ἰσχυρὰ δύναμις. ᾧ ἐπείσθη καὶ ἡ συνήθεια.

880. (*e*) ος. Those in ος are accented on the penultimate, as ἦμος, πῆμος, ὀπῆμος, ὀππῆμος, τῆμος, κῆγχος or κῆχος, πάρος, τημοῦτος (τημόσδε, see above, § 849); except oxytone, εἰκός (which is really a participle), ἐκτός (παρεκτός), ἐντός, ἐτός, προικός; and proparoxytone ἔναγχος (προσέναγχος) and μέταυτος (?)=μετά.

NOTE.—Theog. Can. 164. 1: τὰ εἰς ΟΣ ἐπιρρήματα ἀπὸ προθέσεως παρηγμένα διὰ τοῦ Ο μικροῦ γράφονται, καὶ ὀξύνονται, καὶ σχέσιν τοπικὴν δηλοῖ μετὰ τῆς εἰς ΟΣ καταλήξεως. οἷον ἐντός, ἐκτός· ὅσα δὲ τοπικῆς ἀπήλακται σχέσεως, καὶ χρόνον, ἢ ἄλλο τι δηλοῖ μετὰ τῆς εἰς ΟΣ καταλήξεως, τὴν βαρύτονον τάσιν ἐπιζητεῖ· οἷον, πάρος ἐπὶ χρόνον, ἦμος ὁμοίως, τῆμος, ὀπῆμος, κῆχος· τὸ ἔναγχος προπαροξύνεται· τὸ εἰκὸς ὀξυνόμενον οὐδέτερον ἦν μετοχὴ οὐδέτερου γένους εἰς σύνταξιν ἐπιρρηματικὴν ἐλθοῦσα·

τὸ γοῦν ἔνδος, ἕζος, βαρύτονα Δώρια : Joh. Alex. 38. 32. Apollonius (de Adv. 595. 5) thinks that ἔναγχος and the Ionic κῆγχος should be oxytone. Ἐκπαντός and παράχρεος are better written as two words.

881. (ƒ) υς. Those in υς are oxytone, as ἐγγύς, εὐθύς᾽ ἰθύς, μεσσηγύς ; except such as begin with a preposition, which are proparoxytone, as ἄντικρυς, ἔνεγγυς, πάρεγγυς, πρόσεγγυς, σύνεγγυς.

NOTE.—Theog. Can. 164. 10 : τὰ εἰς ΥΣ ἐπιρρήματα ὀξύτονα διὰ βραχὺ τοῦ Υ γράφεται ἁπλᾶ ὄντα· τὰ γὰρ παρὰ πρόθεσιν συγκείμενα προπαροξύνονται· οἷον, ἐγγύς, εὐθύς, ἰθύς, μεσσηγύς· τὸ ἄντικρυς, σύνεγγυς, παρὰ πρόθεσιν συγκείμενα προπαροξύνονται· τὸ ἀντικρὺς ὀξυνόμενον ἐκτείνει τὸ Υ· τὸ ἀλλῦς μακρὸν ἔχον τὸ Υ περισπᾶται. Thus also the Doric πῦς is perispomenon, Ammon. 121 : κατιθῦς (?), κατευθῦς, Anna Comn. p. 350 D, H. *D.*, and παρευθῦς, quoted from Dio Cass., are probably erroneous ; cf. Lob. Phryn. 145. On ἄντικρυς see E. M. 114. 35 ; Schol. Ven. Γ. 359 ; E. 100 ; Joh. Alex. 38. 35.

882. (ɡ) ως. Adverbs in ως have the same accent as the genitive plural of the word from which they are derived, as ἀκρονυγῶς, ἀληθῶς (ἀληθῶν), ἀμῶς, ἀπαξαπλῶς, ἁπλῶς (ἁπλῶν), ἀποχώντως, ἀρκούντως, αὐθάδως, αὐτάρκως, ἀφειδείως, βαρέως, γλυκέως, διαψευστῶς, εὔνως (εὔνων § 557), ἡδέως, καλῶς (καλῶν), λεληθότως, μεγάλως, μηδαμῶς, μηδόλως, οἰκότως, οἴως, ὄντως, ὀρθίως (ὀρθίων), πάντως, ποτέρως, πραόνως, πρεπόντως, ῥᾳόνως, τηνάλλως. Adverbs of quantity in χως are perispomena, as διχῶς, τριχῶς, πολλαχῶς, together with ζαφελῶς (ἐπιζαφελῶς) from ζάφελος, and ἀνακῶς from ἄναξ. Αὔτως, ἕως, λέως, ὅμως, *nevertheless*, ὅπως, τείως, τέως, ὡσαύτως, are paroxytone ; ὁμῶς, *equally*, is perispomenon. Καθώς, τώς, ὥς, *thus*, are oxytone ; ὡς, *as*, is proclitic, see Chap. 9.

883. NOTE I.—Joh. Alex. 39. 5 ; Apoll. de Adv. 580. 30 sq. ; Theog. Can. 164. 16 ; Chœrob. C. 459. 17 : καὶ τὸ αὐταρκῶν δὲ παρὰ τοῖς Ἀθηναίοις βαρύνεται κατὰ τὴν ἀκρίβειαν, οἷον αὐτάρκων· καὶ τὸ ἐπίρρημα δὲ τὸ ἐξ αὐτοῦ γινόμενον αὐτάρκως βαρυτόνως ἀναγινώσκεται· καὶ λέγουσί τινες τῶν τεχνικῶν περισπωμένως αὐτὸ ἀναγινώσκειν καὶ τὸ συνήθων δὲ καὶ κακοήθων βαρυτόνως ἐπεκράτησεν ἀναγινώσκεσθαι, οἷον συνήθως καὶ κακοήθως : Joh. Alex. 39. 12 : τὸ δὲ αὐταρκῶς, εὐωδῶς περισπᾷ Ἡρωδιανὸς, ἐπεὶ καὶ τὰς γενικὰς αὐτῶν· τὴν δὲ κακοήθων γενικὴν καὶ αὐθάδων βαρύνειν μεμελετήκασι παραλόγως, αἷς συμβαρύνουσι καὶ τὰ ἐπιρρήματα, κακοήθως, αὐθάδως· ὁ δὲ Ἀρίσταρχος καὶ τὸ νοσώδων ἐβάρυνεν ἀλόγως ; Arc. 136. 23.

On those in χως, see Apoll. de Adv. 585. 31 ; Theog. Can. 164. 20 ; Joh. Alex. 39. 2. Concerning ἡσύχως, there was a doubt whether it should be paroxytone or perispomenon ; there is authority for both accents, but perhaps ἡσυχῶς is the better of the two, cf. Apoll. de Adv. 587. 11.

884. NOTE 2.—On ἐπιζαφελῶς, see Joh. Alex. 39. 18 ; Schol. Ven. I. 516 ; E. M. 408. 23 : ἀτεχνῶς is from ἀτεχνής, and ἀτέχνως from ἄτεχνος, E. M. 163. 1 : on ἕως, τέως, see Joh. Alex. 39. 25 : ὅπως, above, § 825 : ὅμως, Schol. Ven. M. 393.

885. NOTE 3.—*Doric Accentuation of Adverbs in* -ως. Concerning the accent of these adverbs in Doric, I cannot do better than quote the words of Ahrens De dialect. Gr. ling. 2. p. 32 : 'De adverbiorum in ΩΣ exeuntium accentu mira præcipiuntur apud Joannem Grammaticum et qui hunc exscripserunt [1], ea, quæ vulgo sunt perispomena, Doriensibus barytona esse, contra quæ vulgo barytona, in Dorica dialecto circumflexum in ultima habere, ut κάλως, σόφως, et οὐτῶς, παντῶς, αὐτομάτως. Alterum præceptum quatenus verum sit doctissimus Grammaticus Apollonius [2] aperit, corum errorem castigans, qui in universum adverbia vulgo barytona circumflecti apud Dorienses dixerint. Adverbiorum enim in ΩΣ accentum eundem esse, quem Genitivorum pluralium ; itaque Dorienses παντῶς, ἀλλῶς, τηνῶς pronuntiare ut παντῶν, ἀλλῶν, τηνῶν, non φιλῶς vel κουφῶς. Ergo Joannes non recte præcipit de αὐτομάτως, melius de οὐτῶς, quum τουτῶν Doricum sit, accedente præterea Eustathii testimono, qui οὐτῶς ut Doricum affert e Theocr. 10. 47 [3]. In adverbio ὅπως judice Apollonio utraque accentus ratio, ὅπως et ὀπῶς defendi potest [4]. Quid vero de priore illius regulæ parte judicandum est ? Optimi auctores docent, nonnulla adverbia apud Dorienses acutum in ultima habuisse, ut καλώς, σοφώς [5], et apud ipsum Joannem in ea regula, cui hæc adnexa est, pro βαρυτονοῦσι restituendum esse ὀξυτονοῦσι supra monuimus not. 4, quod jam certissime confirmatum vides. Neque tamen omnia adverbia vulgo circumflexa vel, quod Theognostus docet, ab adjectivis ὀξυνομένοις derivata apud Dorienses acutum in fine habuisse, Apollonius significat. Nam et eam regulam, quam proponit, adverbia genitivorum pluralium accentum sequi, ad Doricum dialectum adhibet, vid. not. 14, et nonnulla tantum adverbia, quum enclitica fiant, acutum assumere docet. Itaque pauca quædam, quarum vis ita debilitari posset, ut encliticæ fierent, eo præcepto tangi arbitramur, ut καλώς, σοφώς. Non credimus Joanni de κόμψως et ἅπλως.'

-Υ.

886. (*a*) Adverbs in v from adjectives in vs retain the accent of the latter, as εὐθύς εὐθύ· εὐρύ μεσσηγύ ; of the remainder, the dissyllables and their compounds are accented on the penultimate, as ἄνευ, πάγχυ, ἐπιπάγχυ (?), πάνυ, πρόχνυ, τῆλυ, while those which consist of more than two syllables are oxytone, as ἀντικρύ, καταντικρύ, μεταξύ.

---

[1] J. Gr. 243 a ; Meerm. 657 ; Gr. C. 311 : ὁμοίως δὲ (i. e. βαρυτονοῦσιν) τὰ ποιότητος δηλωτικὰ ἐπιρρήματα, κάλως, σόφως, κόμψως, ἅπλως· τὰ δὲ ὑφ' ἡμῶν βαρύτονα περισπῶσιν· οὐτῶς, παντῶς, αὐτομάτως.

[2] Apoll. de Adv. p. 581 : τὰ προκείμενα τῶν ἐπιρρημάτων ... περισπᾶται ἢ βαρύνεται καθὸ πᾶσα γενικὴ πληθυντικὴ ἤτοι περισπᾶται ἢ βαρύνεται, deinde ἐκ τοῦ Δωριεῖς συμπερισπᾶν τὸ ἐπίρρημα (παντῶς) ἐπεὶ καὶ τὴν γενικὴν παντῶν φασίν. οὕτως ἔχει καὶ τὸ ἀλλῶς καὶ τηνῶς. τοῦτο γὰρ καὶ ἐνίους ἠπάτησεν ἀποφήνασθαι ὡς τὰ παρ' ἡμῖν βαρύτονα τῶν ἐπιρρημάτων περισπῶσι Δωριεῖς· ὅπερ οὐκ ἦν ἀληθές. οὔτε γὰρ τὸ κούφως οὔτε τὸ φίλως οὔτε τὰ τοιαῦτα περισπῶσι.

[3] Eustath. 630. 29 : Δωριεῖς κατὰ τὸ καλῶς, σοφῶς, δυνατῶς φασὶ καὶ οὐτῶς, οἷον· πιαίνεται ὁ στάχυς οὐτῶς. In bono Theocriti libro (Ben. 2) est οὐτῶς.

[4] Apoll. de Adv. 584. 19 : δοκεῖ μοι καὶ κατὰ τὴν Δωρίδα διάλεκτον τῷ μὲν προκατειλεγμένῳ λόγῳ ὅπως ἀναγινώσκειν, οὐδ' ὅπως ἄριστα· τῷ μέντοι μᾶλλον αὐτοὺς συγκαταβιβάζειν τὰ ἐπιρρήματα ὁπῶς, ὥστε ἀμφοτέρας τὰς ἀναγνώσεις λόγον ἔχεσθαι.

[5] Apoll. de Adv. 580. 33 : παρὰ Δωριεῦσιν ἔνια (adverbia in ΩΣ) ὀξύνεται ὥστε (num ὅτε ?) κατ' ἔγκλισιν ἀνεγνώσθη· ἢ ῥα κάλως (corr. καλῶς) ἀποκαθάρασα ἐξελεπύρωσεν, unde nonnulli ὣς Doricum esse putarunt, vid. p. 581. 3 et 583. 20.—Theog. Oxx. 164. 18 (Ann. Bekk. p. 1123) : Δωριεῖς τὰ ἀπὸ τῶν εἰς ΟΣ ὀξυτόνων ἐπιρρήματα ὀξύνουσιν, οἷον σοφὸς σοφῶς, καλὸς καλῶς : Herod. π. μ. λ. 25. 29 : οὐδὲν εἰς ΩΣ λῆγον ἐπίρρημα ὀξυνόμενον ὑπεσταλμένης Δωρίδος διαλέκτου.

(*b*) Those in ου are perispomena, as ἀγχοῦ, ἀμοῦ, αὐτοῦ, διχοῦ, μηδαμοῦ, μοναχοῦ, μυριαχοῦ, ὁμοῦ, πανταχοῦ, πηλοῦ, ὑψοῦ.

887. NOTE.—Theog. Can. 161. 6; Apoll. de Adv. 587. 30; 614. 9; Joh. Alex. 37. 14.   On ἀντικρύ see E. M. 114. 35; Schol. Ven. E. 100; Lob. Phryn. 443: ἔμβραχυ is proparoxytone, not oxytone as it is falsely printed in Joh. Alex. 37. 21; so too in πρόβραχυ: ἐπιβραχύ, καταβραχύ, παραβραχύ, κατευθύ, ἐπιπολύ, ἐπιτοπολύ, καταπολύ, παραπολύ, and the like, should probably be written ἐπὶ βραχύ, κατὰ βραχύ, etc.: on the latter word Lobeck (Phryn. 540) thus writes: 'Καταβραχύς agnoscere videtur Schol. Thucyd. 7. 2. 170.   Sed prius verba Thucydidis ponam ipsa: ἤδη ἐπετετέλεστο τοῖς Ἀθηναίοις ἐς τὸν μέγα λιμένα διπλοῦν τεῖχος πλὴν κατὰ βραχύ τι τὸ πρὸς τὴν θάλασσαν· ad quæ hæc annotat Scholiographus: κατὰ βραχύ τι βαρυτόνως τινὲς ἀναγιγνώσκουσι, ὡς μὴ τὸ ὀλίγον, ἀλλὰ τὸ πετρῶδες ἀκούηται· de quo quæ Bauerus scripsit, nugatoria sunt.   Mihi illud significari videtur, aliquos, utroque conjuncto, πλὴν κατάβραχύ τι scripsisse, *excepto loco quodam vadoso eodemque scruposo* (nisi pro πετρῶδες ille πηλῶδες scripsit).' Πάμπανυ in Dio Cass. is probably false.

On those in ου see Chœrob. C. 429. 22; Joh. Alex. 32. 20: Καθόλου, προύργου, ἄλλου, ὑπερεκπερισσοῦ are hardly to be considered as coming under this rule: on ὅτου (ἐξότου), see above, § 743, and Joh. Alex. 32. 22: on ὅπου, ποῦ, πού, οὗ, οὐ, above, § 825: on ἔῦ = εὖ, Apoll. de Adv. 614. 11: ὑπέρευ is paroxytone: κόχυ and κοχύ both occur in Hesych., but it is doubtful whether the word is an adverb.

-Ω.

888. Those in ω are paroxytone, as ἄνω, κάτω, ἔξω, πρόσω, ἑκατέρω, πορρωτέρω, ἑκαστάτω, ἀνωτέρω, ἄφνω, ὀπίσω, οὕτω; except ἄνεω or ἄνεῳ proparoxytone, and πρῴ, ἐπισχερῴ, ἐνσχερῴ oxytone.

889. NOTE 1.—Theog. Can. 161. 15; Joh. Alex. 37. 22; Apoll. de Adv. 576. 12; E. M. 114. 35: ἀβώ· πρωΐ Λάκωνες, Hesych.: ἄνεω, Apoll. de Adv. 577. 9: ἔτι τὰ εἰς Ω λήγοντα ἐπιρρήματα παροξύνεται, καθὼς ἔχει τὰ προκατειλεγμένα, πρόσω, ἔσω, κάτω, ἐγγυτέρω. σαφὲς οὖν ὅτι, καθὼς προείπομεν, εἰ ἐπίρρημα τὸ ΑΝΕΩΙ, σεσημείωσεται. καὶ εἰ παρεστήσαμεν ὡς τὰ συνεμπίπτοντα ὀνοματικῇ πτώσει ἐπιρρήματα τὴν τάσιν τῶν ὀνομάτων φυλάσσει, σαφὲς ὅτι προπαροξυνόμενον ἕνεκα τοῦ τόνου κατώρθωται. ἐδείκνυτο γὰρ τὸ προκείμενον, ὡς ἀπὸ Ἀττικῆς γραφῆς τῆς ἄνεως ἐσχημάτιστο· ἦν δὲ. τὸ παρὰ Ἀττικοῖς ἄνεως τρίτην ἀπὸ τέλους ἔχον τὴν ὀξεῖαν: cf. also Joh. Alex. 37. 24: ἐπισχερώ, Schol. Ven. Σ. 68; E. M. 365. 14; Apoll. de Adv. 576. 12: πρῴ, Joh. Alex. 32. 7: τὸ μέντοι πρῴ μονοσύλλαβον παρ' Ἀττικοῖς ὀξύνεται· ἐπεὶ ἐκ τοῦ πρωΐ δισυλλάβου ὀξυνομένου κατὰ συναίρεσιν γέγονε.   It is sometimes however written πρῶ, but wrongly.

890. NOTE 2.—The Doric adverbs in ω = οθεν or ωθεν are perispomena, as πῶ, τουτῶ, αὐτῶ, τηνῶ, Apoll. de Adv. 598. 9.; 604. 3.   It is asserted in E. M. 773. 18 that Apollonius oxytoned τουτώ, but the place is corrupt: see Ahrens, de Dial. Gr. ling. 2. p. 134, and the authorities there quoted.

Interjections.

891. As might naturally be expected, Interjections are hardly reducible to any rule.   The following sections comprise all that

I have noted. Suidas, s. v. ἐποποῖ, mentions a large number of Aristophanic interjections.

-A.

892. Ἄππα, πάππα, ἄττα, ἄττατα, ἔα, εἶα, ἴσσα, σίττα, τήνελλα, ψίττα, ψύττα, ὠεία retract the accent, ταττά, οὐά (or οὖά), ὁά (or ὁᾶ), and ὡσαννά are oxytone, and ἇ, βᾶ, παπαπᾶ, or πᾶ πᾶ πᾶ, perispomena.

893. NOTE.—ἇ, Joh. Alex. 31.8 : τὰ ἔχοντα δίχρονον ἐκτεταμένον περισπᾶται· ἇ δειλὲ πάντων· καὶ τὸ βᾶ ἐν τῇ συνηθείᾳ παρὰ ἀρχαίοις ἔκπληξιν δηλοῦν. Suidas draws a distinction between ἁ and ἇ : ἇ ἇ παρ' Ἀριστοφάνει ἐπίρρημα μετ' ἐκπλήξεως καὶ παρακελεύσεως· ἇ ἇ τ ὴ ν δ ᾶ δ α μ ή μ ο ι π ρ ό σ φ ε ρ ε (Plut. 1052). τὸ ἇ ἇ κατὰ διαίρεσιν ἀναγνωστέον, οὐ καθ' ἕνωσιν. ἀλλὰ καὶ ψιλωτέον ἀμφότερα· εἰ γὰρ ἐν μέρος λόγου ἦν καὶ κατὰ σύναψιν ἀνεγινώσκετο, οὐ χρείαν εἶχε τῶν δύο τόνων ἤτοι τῶν δύο ὀξειῶν· καὶ τοῦτο μὲν ἐκπλήξεως ὂν ψιλοῦται· τὸ δὲ ἇ ἇ θαυμαστικὸν δασύνεται, ὡς ἐν ἐπιγράμματί φησιν Ἀγαθίας (A. P. I. 34) ἇ μ έ γ α τ ο λ μ ή ε ι ς κ η ρ ὸ ς ἀ ν ε π λ ά σ α τ ο : Schol. Plat. Hipp. maj. 295 A : ἇ περισπασθὲν δηλοῖ εἴθε· Καλλίμαχος·

ἇ πάντως ἵνα γῆρας.

καὶ τὸ ὦ κλητικόν· Ὅμηρός·

ἇ δειλοί, τί κακῶν ;

σημαίνει δὲ καὶ τὸ πολὺ καὶ μέγα παρ' Ἀρχιλόχῳ·

ἇ ἔαδ' εἶς τε ταύρους.

τό τε ἐν ἴσῳ τῷ ναί, καὶ εἴθε. καὶ ἔτι σχετλιαστικὸν ἀντὶ τοῦ φεῦ ἐπιρρήματος . . . εἰ δὲ ψιλωθείη περισπασθέν, τὸ νῦν σημαίνει. The books vary considerably: εἶα, Eust. 107. 25: δοκεῖ δὲ τὸ ῥηθὲν εἶα παροξύνεσθαι, ὡς κατ' ἐπέκτασιν ἔχον τὸ Α, ὁποῖόν τι καὶ ἐν τῷ ναίχι γίνεται. ὅτι δὲ τὸ εἶα συνεσταλμένην ἔχει τὴν λήγουσαν, ἡ τραγῳδία δηλοῖ ἐν τῷ, ἀλλ' εἶα, τέκνον· καὶ, ἀλλ' εἶα, χώρει· καὶ, ἀλλ' εἶα, φείδου μηδέν. ἐξ ἰαμβικῶν δὲ στίχων ταῦτα εἰσί. σημείωσαι δὲ ὅτι κατὰ τὴν τέχνην τοῦ Γεωργίου προπερισπᾶται τὸ ῥηθὲν εἶα, εἰπόντος, ὅτι τε παρακελευσματικὸν ἐπίρρημά ἐστι, καὶ ὅτι, ὡς ῥέω ῥέα καὶ πλεονασμῷ τοῦ Ι ῥεῖα, οὕτως ἔω τὸ ἐκπέμπω, ἔα, καὶ πλεονασμῷ, εἶα. φέρει δὲ καὶ χρῆσιν τῆς λέξεως κειμένην, φησὶ, παρ' Εὐριπίδῃ ἐν Σολεῖ ταύτην. εἶα δὴ, φίλον ξύλον, ἔκτεινέ μοι σεαυτὸ καὶ γίνου θρασύ. In our books it is in almost every instance properispomenon: ὠεῖα = ὦ εἶα or εἶα, Theodos. Gramm. 79. 18 : τὸ ὠεία μίμημα βαρβάρων ἑλκόντων τι : ταττά, Theodos. Gramm. 79. 14 : εὐά, Theodos. Gramm. 79. 24, Suid., is sometimes written εὖα.

-E.

894. Ἀβάλε = ἇ βάλε, ἄγε, βάλε, ἠνίδε, σίττε, φέρε, are paroxytone, δεῦτε, εὖγε properispomena, ὑπέρευγε proparoxytone, ἐέ, ἔ, ἔ, ἰδέ oxytone.

NOTE.—ἰδέ, 'Atticum esse ἰδέ, non ἴδε, tradunt Schol. Hom. Il. A. 85; Eust. Il. p. 341. 22 ; Moeris, p. 193. In libris scriptis ἰδέ vix reperitur, sed ἴδε;' H. D.

-H.

895. Ἰή and ὠή are oxytone, βῆ, βλῆ (?) perispomena.

NOTE.—Joh. Alex. 29. 18: καὶ τὰ καθαρεύοντα, μὴ δηλοῦντα χρόνον, ὀξύνεται οἷον ἰή, ὠή, ἰωή: Arc. 183. 7; Eust. 751. 59: γάρφουσι γὰρ οἱ παλαιοὶ δίχα παραδειγμάτων, ὅτι πᾶσα λέξις δισύλλαβος ἐν ῥήμασιν, εἰ μὲν ἀπὸ τῆς ἀρχῆς πάθη ἀποκοπήν, περισπᾷ τὴν καταλειπομένην· εἰ δὲ ἀπὸ τοῦ τέλους, ὀξύνει αὐτὴν ἐπιρρηματικῶς δηλαδὴ κατὰ τὸ ὠή, ὁτιή. Both ἰή and ὠή are falsely paroxytone in Theog. Can. 160. 27: βῆ, Eust. 592. 18 (yet it is βή Eust. 768. 13); Suid. βλῆ [? βῆ], Theog. Can. 155. 19: βλῆ μίμημα φωνῆς ἀλόγου ἰσοδυναμοῦν τὸ βλιχᾶσθαι (sic) ὃ καὶ περισπᾶται ... καὶ τὸ φνη [sic φνεῖ?] παρ' Ἀριστοφάνει· ἔστι δὲ καὶ αὐτὸ μίμημα φωνῆς ὀρνέου.

-AI.

896. Ἀτταταῖ, ἀταταταῖ, αἰαῖ, παπαῖ, ῥυπαπαῖ are perispomena, βαβαί, εὐαί, ἰατταταί, οὐαί, ὠαιαί oxytone; αἴ and αῖ seem to be equally good.

897. NOTE.—Schol. in Dion. Thrac. 946. 31: τὰ σχετλιαστικὰ περισπᾶται, τῶν εἰς ΑΙ περισπωμένων, οἷον ἀτταταῖ, οἳ οἳ, ἀοίμοι, οἴμοι. τὸ ὦ πόποι σημειῶδες—παπαῖ γὰρ περισπᾶται—ἐνομίσθη γὰρ ὡς ὄνομα εἶναι· διὸ καὶ ὀνοματικὴν ἔλαβε τάσιν· ὡς γὰρ ὦ φίλοι, οὕτως ὦ πόποι ὦ θεοί. ἔστι δὲ δύο σχετλιαστικὰ ἐπιρρήματα: Theog. Can. 158. 25: τὰ εἰς ΑΙ λήγοντα ἐπιρρήματα ὑπὲρ μίαν συλλαβὴν ὧν καὶ τὰ σχετλιαστικὰ τὰ πλείω ἐστι, διὰ τῆς ΑΙ διφθόγγου γράφεται· οἷον, αἰαί· ἀτταταί· παπαί (sic) ὃ δὲ περὶ ταῦτα τόνος ἀμφίβολος. οἱ μὲν γὰρ ὀξύνουσιν αὐτὰ, οἱ δὲ περισπῶσιν· ἄλογοι γὰρ αὐτῶν λυπουμένων ἢ μεθυόντων φωναί, καθὼς εἴρηται· χαμαί· τοῦτο ὀξύνεται, ὡς καὶ τὸ νυμαί· ὑμαί· ... σημειωτέον δὲ ὅτι τὰ μὲν χρονικὰ βαρύνεται ὡς τοπάλαι· ὕπαι· τὰ δὲ σχετλιαστικὰ περισπᾶται· τὰ δὲ λοιπὰ ὀξύνεται: ΑΙ, Joh. Alex. 32. 24: τὰ τὴν ΑΙ δίφθογγον ἔχοντα ὀξύνεται, οἷον αἲ τάλας, ναί. ταῦτά ἐστι μονοσύλλαβα: Theog. Can. 155. 30: τὰ εἰς ΑΙ λήγοντα ἐπιρρήματα μονοσύλλαβα, τρία ἐστίν· αἴ τὸ δασυνόμενον, ὡς ὅταν λέγωμεν (sic), αἴ τάλας· καὶ αἲ τὸ εὐκτικὸν ... καὶ τὸ ναί ...: A. G. 353. 18: αἲ ψιλούμενον καὶ περισπώμενον τὸ ὄφελον σημαίνει, κατ' ἀποκοπὴν τοῦ αἴθε. δασυνόμενον δὲ ἄρθρον θηλυκὸν ἀναφορικόν. σημαίνει δὲ ἐπίρρημα θρηνητικὸν περισπώμενον καὶ ψιλούμενον, ὃ καὶ διπλασιάζεται. αἲ αἲ τάλαινα: thus also Suidas, Tzetzes in Lycoph. 31: αἲ αἴ, ἐπίρρημα θρηνητικόν, ὃ πάντες οἱ νῦν βαρύνουσι. Στέφανος δὲ καὶ Μελάμπους περισπᾶν ἀξιοῦσι, λέγοντες τουτονὶ τὸν κανόνα. Τὰ εἰς ΑΙ δίφθογγον λήγοντα ἐπιρρήματα, ἂν ἐπὶ τέλους ἔχωσι τὸν τόνον, περισπῶνται. ἰατταταῖ, παπαῖ, αἲ καὶ τὰ ὅμοια. πλὴν τοῦ βαβαί, καὶ τὸ ναί· ἐγὼ δέ φημι καὶ τοῦ οὐαί. Our books vary, and no wonder: ἀτταταῖ (and ἀταταταῖ), Joh. Alex. 36. 12: τὰ δὲ σχετλιαστικὰ τῶν εἰς ΟΙ καὶ εἰς ΑΙ ἄλογον ἔχει τὸν τόνον ἃ μὲν γὰρ αὐτῶν περισπᾶται, ὡς τὸ ὀττοῖ ἔχον συμπαρακείμενον καὶ τὸ ἀτταταῖ, καὶ τὸ οἰοῖ καὶ αἰαῖ σαβοῖ τε, καὶ τὸ αἰβοῖ καὶ τὸ σαβαῖ παρ' Εὐπόλιδι ἐν Βάπταις. τὸ δὲ εὐαὶ παρὰ τῷ αὐτῷ ὀξύνεται εὐαὶ σαβαί. βαρύνεται δὲ τὸ οἴμοι. τὸ δὲ ὦ πόποι δυσὶ τόνοις χρῆται. ἔδει δὲ αὐτὸ δύο περισπωμένας ἔχειν, ἐπεὶ καὶ παράκειται καὶ τὸ παπαῖ: Herod. π. μ. λ. 27. 11: οὐδὲν εἰς ΑΙ λῆγον ἐπίρρημα ὑπὲρ μίαν συλλαβὴν ὀξύνεται· λέγω δὴ τὸ χαμαί· τὰ δὲ τοιαῦτα περισπᾶται, ἀταταῖ, αἰαῖ, παπαῖ: yet ἀτταταί occurs as well as αἰαί: βαί (?) Eust. 768. 13: βαβαῖ, Arc. 183. 18: τὰ εἰς ΟΙ καὶ εἰς ΑΙ σχετλιαστικὰ παραλόγως περισπῶνται· ὀττοτοῖ, εὐοῖ, παπαῖ, ἀταταῖ, πλὴν τοῦ αἴ, οὐαί, βαβαί. παροξύνεται δὲ τὸ οἴμοι, ὤμοι· ἡ δὲ συνήθεια ὀξύνει τὸ παπαῖ καὶ ἀταταί: Etym. Gud. 451. 19; but βαβαῖ is found in the Cod. Clark. of Plato: εὐαί, Joh. Alex. above: ἰαί, Aristoph. Eccl. 1179: ἰατταταί (?): οὐαί, Arc. 183. 18: παπαῖ, A. G.; Arc.; Joh. Alex. above, or παπαί, E. M. 823. 25; Theog. Can. 158. 25: παπαπαῖ or παπαπαῖ: ῥυπαπαῖ, or ῥυπαπαῖ, also occurs as proparoxytone and oxytone: ὠαιαί, Apoll. de Adv. 537. 32: καθάπερ οὖν τῷ πόποι τὸ παπαῖ (sic) παράκειται καὶ τῷ ὀτοτοῖ τὸ ἀταταῖ (sic), οὕτως καὶ τῷ ὠοιοῖ τὸ ὠαιαί, ὅπερ συναλειφθὲν καὶ ἐν βαρείᾳ τάσει γινόμενον παρ' Αἰολεῦσίν ἐστιν ὤαι.

-EI.

898. Φνεί is oxytone, ἄγρει paroxytone.

NOTE.—Ἄγρει is of course only the imperative of ἀγρέω, Joh. Alex. 36. 29; Theog. Can. 159. 6.

-OI.

899. These are generally perispomena, as αἰβοῖ, γοῖ, οἰοιοῖ, οἰμοιμοῖ, εὐοῖ, ἰαιβοῖ, οἰοῖ, ὀτοτοῖ; except κοί, οἴ oxytone, and πόποι paroxytone. Of the rest in ι, ἠνί and ὀί are oxytone, ἴθι paroxytone.

NOTE.—Αἰβοῖ, Joh. Alex. 36. 15: βοῖ, Aristoph. Pac. 1031: γοῖ, Jacobs ad Anthol. T. 12. p. 476: ἐποποῖ, Schol. Aristoph. Av. 58: Σύμμαχος καὶ Δίδυμος προπαροξύνουσιν· οἱ δὲ περισπῶσιν ἵν' ᾖ ἐπίρρημα, ἀντὶ τοῦ ἐποπιστί: Schol. Aristoph. Av. 227 = 228: τὸ δὲ ἐποποί καὶ τὰ τοιαῦτα δεῖ ὀξυτόνως προφέρεσθαι, ὥστε ἦχον ὀρνέου προφέρεσθαι κατὰ μίμησιν, so also Theodos. Gramm. p. 79. 2: εὐοῖ, Apoll. de Adv. 588. 24: καὶ γὰρ τὰ πρωτότυπα θέλει ὁπωσδήποτε περισπᾶσθαι, ὡς ἔχει τὸ οἰμοιμοῖ καὶ τὸ ὀτοτοῖ καὶ τὸ οἰοιοῖ. Φαίνεται ὅτι καὶ τὸ εὐοῖ κατὰ τοῦτο σεσημειώσεται: Arc. 183. 19, but it is oxytone in Theog. Can. 158. 23, and elsewhere: κοί, E. M. 607. 24; Joh. Alex. 36. 36: οἴ ought seemingly to be οἶ according to the passage just quoted from Apollonius: οἴμοι, Arc. 183. 21; Apoll. de Adv. 537. 22, and πανοίμοι: πόποι, E. M. 823. 25; Theog. Can. 158. 10; Joh. Alex. 36. 18; ποποῖ also occurs: σαβοῖ, Joh. Alex. 36. 16: ὤμοι, Theog. Can. 159. 14; Apoll. de Adv. 537. 22: the books vary considerably in the accentuation of many of these words.

-N.

900. Those in ν are oxytone, as ἀμήν, εὐάν, ἤν; except αὖν, βρῦν (and βρῦ) perispomena.

NOTE.—Εὐάν, Theodos. Gramm. 79. 24; E. M. 391. 15; Draco, 9. 19; yet it is paroxytone according to Joh. Alex. 37. 27: it appears from Theog. Can. 161. 30 that the verb εἶεν was made oxytone by some writers: on εὐέν, εὐάν (εὐόί), and the like, see H. D. s. vv.

-Ξ, -Ο, -Π, -Σ, -Τ.

901. Those in ξ, ο, and π are oxytone, as βαβαιάξ, βομβάξ, ἰαταταιάξ, ἰατταταιάξ, ἱππαπαιάξ, πάξ, παπαιάξ, πατάξ, πυππάξ (and πύππαξ), βρεκεκέξ, κόγξ, τοροτίξ, τοτοβρίξ, τυροτίγξ; θρεττανελό, ποποπό, τιό, τορό, τριοτό, ψό (Herod. π. μ. λ. 46. 16); ὄπ, ὠόπ, ὦ ὀπόπ. Φλαττόθρατ and φλαττοθραττόφλατ are paroxytone; ἐές or ἔς is oxytone.

-Υ, -Ω.

902. Those in υ are perispomena, as αὖ αὖ, βδεῦ, βῦ, γρῦ, ἐλελεῦ, εὖ, ἰαῦ, ἰεῦ, κικκαβαῦ, σοῦ, φῦ, μῦ, φεῦ; except ἰδού, ἰού, ἰύ oxytone, and κόκκυ paroxytone; those in ω are oxytone, as ἰτώ· ἰώ, ἰωτώ, ὤ = *alas!* but ὦ κλητικόν is perispomenon.

903. NOTE I.—Theog. Can. 161. 6, where ἀρρυ, ἰυ are mentioned, but they are not accented in the MS : Ἀλεῦ or ἄλευ is a verb : αὖ αὖ (?) Theodos. Gramm. 79. 20 : βαύ, Joh. Alex. 32. 23 : τὸ βαὺ κατὰ μίμησιν κυνὸς ὀξύνεται, βαὺ βαύ : γρῦ, Arc. 182. 9; Chœrob. E. 95. 9; Theog. Can. 155. 29, for which γρύ is a false form : ἐλελεῦ, Joh. Alex. 36. 25; Arc. 183. 23 : εὖ, E. M. 388. 17; Joh. Alex. 36. 25; ὑπέρευ is paroxytone, ὑπέρευγε proparoxytone : ἰδού, Joh. Alex. 32. 21, and above, § 784: ἰύ, Joh. Alex. 37. 16 : ἰού, Joh. Alex. 32. 21 : ἰοὺ ... ὀξύνεται : Theodos. Gramm. 79. 27 : ἰού ἰού ἐπὶ λύπης, τὸ ἰοῦ δὲ ἐπὶ χαρᾶς : Chœrob. C. 429. 9 : σημειούμεθα τρία τινὰ εἰς τὸ Τ καταλήγοντα ἐν διφθόγγῳ καὶ ἐπὶ τῆς τελευταίας συλλαβῆς ἔχοντα τὸν τόνον, καὶ ὅμως μὴ περισπώμενα ἀλλ᾽ ὀξυνόμενα· ἔστι δὲ ταῦτα τὸ ἰδού δεικτικὸν καὶ τὸ ἰοὺ σχετλιαστικόν, καὶ τὸ οὐ ἀρνήσεως δηλωτικόν : cf. Chœrob. E. 10. 14; 109. 9 : μῦ, Theog. Can. 155. 29, is falsely μύ in Theodos. Gramm. 79 : φεῦ, Joh. Alex. 32. 18; 36. 24 : ὑπέρφευ is paroxytone, Joh. Alex. 36. 25.

904. NOTE 2.—Ἰώ, E. M. 365. 14; 481. 12; Schol. Ven. Σ. 68; Joh. Alex. 32. 3; Apoll. de Adv. 576. 12 : ἰωτώ, Theodos. Gramm. 79. 3 : ὤ, 'Etym. M. p. 79. 13 : τὸ ὤ ἡνίκα θαυμαστικὸν λαμβάνεται, ὀξύνεται καὶ χωρεῖ εἰς ἐπιρρηκματ-ικὴν σύνταξιν, οἷον ὦ Ἡράκλεις : Etym. Gud. p. 576. 40 : ὦ κλητικὸν ἐπίρρημα· ὤ ὀξυνόμενον σχετλιαστικόν, ὦ τοῦ ἰδίου, ὦ ἐγώ. Explicatius Thom. M. p. 930 (408 Ritsch.) : τὸ ὦ μετὰ τῆς κλητικῆς οὐδέποτε ὀξύνεται, εἰ καὶ ἔκπληξιν ὁ λόγος ἔχει καὶ θαῦμα, οἷον ὦ Ἡράκλεις, ὦ θαῦμα θαυμάτων. Οὐ γὰρ τὸ ὦ μόνον ἐν τούτοις ἐμφαίνει τὴν ἔκπληξιν καὶ τὸ θαῦμα, ἀλλὰ μετὰ τῶν κλητικῶν. Ὅτε δὲ ἐπάγεται γενική, ἐξ ἀνάγκης ὀξύνεται· τότε γὰρ πάντως ἢ σχετλιαστικόν ἐστιν, οἷον ὦ τῆς ἐμῆς ἀθλιότητος, ἢ θαυμαστικόν, οἷον ὦ τοῦ ξένου μετάλλου. Διὸ καὶ τὴν γενικὴν ἔχει ἐπαγομένην λαμβανομένου ἔξωθεν τοῦ ἕνεκα. Oxytonum ὤ sæpissime servatum in quorumvis scriptorum codicibus, sed ab editoribus non raro in ὦ mutatum : v. Brunck. ad Aristoph. Lys. 836, et Bast. ad Aristæn. p. 209, qui longa experientia edoctum se esse scribit libros MSS. exacte servare discrimen grammaticorum inter ὤ et ὦ ;' H. D.

CHAPTER VIII.

THE ACCENTUATION OF WORDS WHEN STANDING IN A SENTENCE ; MODIFICATIONS OF ACCENT ARISING FROM ELISION, ANASTROPHE, AND CRASIS.

905. WHEN words are combined in a sentence their accent becomes liable to certain modifications, which are governed by the following rules:—

Oxytones become barytone, except before a colon, a full stop, a break in the sense, or an enclitic, as

αἰὲν ἐγὼ τεύχοιμι διαμπερές, εἰσόκ' Ἀχαιοὶ
Ἴλιον αἰπὺ ἕλοιεν Ἀθηναίης διὰ βουλάς.

Τὸν δ' ἀπαμειβόμενος, προσέφη πόδας ὠκὺς Ἀχιλλεύς
θαρσήσας μάλα εἰπὲ θεοπρόπιον ὅ τι οἶσθα.

Here it will be observed that the oxytones αἰέν, ἐγώ, διαμπερές, Ἀχαιοί, αἰπύ, διά receive the grave instead of the acute accent; βουλάς, being followed by a full stop, remains oxytone. In the second example the accent of Ἀχιλλεύς is not inclined, because of the pause in the sense. To this rule there is but one exception, the interrogative τίς, τί, which is always oxytone, as

τίς δ' ὅδε Ναυσικάᾳ, ἕπεται καλός τε μέγας τε
ξεῖνος;

906. Note i.—Chœrob. ap. A. G. 707. 24: ἰστέον δὲ ὅτι πᾶσα λέξις ὀξύτονος ἐν τῇ συνεπείᾳ, ἤγουν ἐν τῇ φράσει, κοιμίζει τὴν ὀξεῖαν εἰς βαρεῖαν, χωρὶς τοῦ τίς: Joh. Alex. 6. 5: πᾶσα ὀξεῖα ἐπὶ τέλους λέξεως οὖσα εἰ μὴ ἐπιφέροιτο μετ' αὐτὴν στιγμή, πάντως ἐν τῇ συμφράσει κοιμίζεται εἰς βαρεῖαν· οἷον

Ζεὺς δ' ἐπὶ οὖν Τρῶάς τε καὶ Ἕκτορα,

τό τε Ζεὺς καὶ ἐπὶ βαρύνεται, ὅτι στιγμὴ μετὰ ταῦτα οὐ τίθεται: Schol. in Dionys. Thrac. 690. 15: ἔστιν οὖν εἰπεῖν ὅτι ἡ στιγμὴ καὶ ἡ ἀνάπαυσις τῆς φωνῆς οὐκ ἐᾷ βαρεῖαν τεθῆναι ἀλλὰ κρουστικωτέραν, ἵν' οὕτως εἴπω, τὴν λέξιν ἀπεργαζομένη ὀξύνεσθαι ταύτην βιάζεται: Schol. in Dionys. Thrac. 689. 23; cf. Arc. 140. 8; Apoll. de Pron. 34 C.

907. Note 2.—Reiz (de Accent. inclinat. p. 56) asks the question, 'An dictio acuta recte gravetur ante comma?' adding, 'loquor de commatibus iis, quibus pronuntiatio sola regitur; non de iis, quæ plerique hodie solent in libris Græcis et Latinis edendis nimium crebra ponere ut imperitioribus construendi negotium facilius reddant:' he is of opinion that commas which mark off real parts in a proposition affect, or ought to affect, the accent like other stops; printed books vary a good deal, and each editor does that which is right in his own eyes.

908. *Elision.*—When, in a word of more than one syllable, an accented final vowel is elided, an acute accent is placed on the preceding syllable, as κείν' ὄχεα κροτάλιζον ἀνὰ πτολέμοιο γεφύρας for κεινὰ ὄχεα: ἆ δείλ' οὐδέ τί τοι θάνατος καταθύμιός ἐστιν for ἆ δειλέ: ὤμ' ἀποταμνόμενον for ὠμὰ ἀποταμνόμενον: κῆφ' ὅτι for καὶ εἰπὲ ὅτι: κάκ' ὀσσόμενος: ἀγλά' ἄποινα: πόλλ' ἐμόγησα: πάντ' ἀγορεύω. From this rule however the particles ἀλλά, οὐδέ, μηδέ, ἠδέ, the enclitics τινά and ποτέ and dissyllabic prepositions are excepted, which lose their accent altogether when their final vowel is elided, as ἀλλ' οὐκ: ἐπ' ὤμων: οὐδ' ἀναθηλήσει: ἅτιν' οὐ πείσεσθαι ὀΐω: ἠδ' ἔτι: παρ' αὐτόν: ἀμφ' ὀβελοῖσιν: ἀπ' ἀθανάτοιο: μηδ' ἐπαγαλλόμενος.

909. Note—Schol. Ven. Λ. 160: λέγει ὁ τεχνικὸς ἐν τῷ ὑπομνήματι τοῦ περὶ παθῶν Διδύμου· τὰ ὀξύτονα ἡνίκα ἐκθλίβηται τὴν ὀξυνομένην συλλαβήν, ἀναπέμπει τὴν ὀξεῖαν ἐπὶ τὴν ὀπίσω συλλαβήν, καὶ ἐὰν ᾖ ἡ ἐκθλιβεῖσα συλλαβὴ ἡ ἔχουσα τὴν ὀξεῖαν βραχεῖα, ἡ δὲ ὀπίσω συλλαβὴ φύσει μακρά, τῷ τονικῷ παραγγέλματι γίνεται περισπώμενον· περισπᾷ γοῦν τὸ δεῖλ', ἐν δὲ τῇ Ὁμηρικῇ προσῳδίᾳ ἐναντιοῦται τούτῳ: Schol. Aristoph. Plut. 143: φήμ' ἐγώ ὅτε ἀναβιβάζεται ὀξεῖα, πάλιν ὀξεῖα ὀφείλει τίθεσθαι· οὐ μὴν περισπωμένη· ἄτοπον γὰρ, ὥσπερ ἐνταῦθα τὸ φήμ' ἐγώ· καὶ τὸ χρῆστ' ἔδρασε· καὶ τὸ δεῖν' ἄττα· καὶ τὰ τοιαῦτα: Schol Ven. P. 201: ζητεῖ ὁ Ἡρωδιανὸς ἐν τῷ Α´ ὑπομνήματι τῷ περὶ παθῶν Διδύμου περὶ τοῦ ᾶ δειλ´, πῶς δεῖ τονίζειν αὐτό, καί φησι, πολὺ δὲ πρότερον παρὰ τῷ ποιητῇ ἐστι τὸ τῆς ἀναγνώσεως, ᾶ δειλ´, οὐδέ τι τοι θάνατος, ἢ ᾶ δειλ´ οὐδέ τι τοι θάνατος. τὸ γὰρ πλῆρές ἐστιν; ᾶ δειλέ· οὐ γάρ, ὡς οἱ ἐξηγησάμενοι, τοῦ δείλαιε ἀποκοπῇ· ἐν ἑτέροις γὰρ αὐτὸς λέγει, ᾶ δειλώ, τί νυ δάκρυ κατείβετον; περιγέγραπται οὖν ἡ ὀξεῖα, εἶτα καὶ ἀνάπαυσις γέγονεν. ἀρά γε οὖν φυλαχθήσεται ἡ ὀξεῖα, ἢ ἐπεὶ περιγέγραπται τὸ φωνῆεν τῆς ὀξείας, περιγέγραπται καὶ ὁ τόνος; τὸ κρινόμενον ἐκεῖνο, ἵνα ἐπιστάμενοι ἀναγνῶμεν· ἕν ἐστιν εἰπεῖν, εἰ ἅπαξ περιγέγραπται τὸ φωνῆεν τὸ ἔχον τὴν ὀξεῖαν, ὁ τόνος γενέσθω τῆς προτέρας συλλαβῆς, οὐχὶ τῆς ἐπὶ τέλους: Schol. Ven. Λ. 441: ᾶ δείλ´· ἐπεὶ μετὰ τὰς προσαγορευτικὰς ἀνάγκη στίζειν, ὡς καὶ ἡ συνήθεια μαρτυρεῖ στίζουσα μετὰ τὴν δευτέραν λέξιν, οὐκ ἔστι δὲ πλήρης, ἀλλὰ συνείληπται, οὕτως δὲ ἡμῶν ἀναγινωσκόντων πεπονθυῖαν τὴν λέξιν βαρβαρισμὸς γίνεται, εἴτε ὀξύνοιμεν εἴτε περισπάσοιμεν, ἀναγκαίως ἐκ πλήρους γράφειν τὴν λέξιν, ᾶ δειλέ, δεῖ, ἵνα καὶ ἡ στιγμὴ καὶ ὁ τόνος ἀναλόγως καὶ Ἑλληνικῶς ἔχῃ· οὕτως δὲ καὶ Ἀρίσταρχος ἔγραφεν ἐκ πλήρους, ὡς Δίδυμος μαρτυρεῖ· τὸ μὲν γὰρ μέτρον οὐκ ἂν δόξαι βλάπτεσθαι τοῦ στοιχείου προστεθέντος, ἐπεὶ ὅταν δέῃ ὑγιὲς αὐτὸ παριστάναι, πάλιν ἀφαιρεθήσεται, ὡς βουκόλε ἐπεὶ οὔτε κακῷ (Od. 20. 227)· ἢ οὐ μέμνῃ ὅτε τ´ ἐκρέμω (Il. 15. 18)· οὕτως δὲ καὶ ἐν τοῖς ἐξῆς ᾶ δειλέ, οὐ μὲν σοί γε (452): it will be seen from these passages that the ancient grammarians were not absolutely unanimous.

According to Schol. Ven. A. 269 Aristarchus retained the accent in μέθ᾽ ὁμίλεον (οὕτως Ἀρίσταρχος τὴν μετὰ φυλάσσειν τὸν τόνον) where others read μεθομίλεον: Aristarchus probably accented the preposition to obviate an ambiguity, which was however hardly likely to arise: cf. below, § 920.

910. *Anastrophe.*—All prepositions consisting of two short syllables, except ἀνά and διά, are paroxytone when placed *immediately* after the noun or verb to which they belong, as Ἰθάκην κάτα for κατὰ Ἰθάκην: ἀκροτάτη δὲ ποδῶν ὕπο σείετο ὕλη: μάχῃ ἔνι κυδιανείρῃ: νηῒ πάρα πρύμνῃ: νεῶν ἄπο καὶ κλισιάων: ᾧ ἔπι πόλλ᾽ ἐμόγησα.

If any word is interposed between the preposition and the word which it governs the accent is not retracted unless the preposition finishes a sentence, as τῷ δ᾽ ἐπὶ Τυδεΐης ἦλθε κρατερὸς Διομήδης: ἦλθε δ᾽ ἐπὶ πτωχὸς πανδήμιος, not τῷ δ᾽ ἔπι nor ἦλθε δ᾽ ἔπι. But τῶν πάντων δ᾽ ἔπτυσε πολὺ κάτα because here κατά finishes the sentence.

911. Note I.—On the Anastrophe of prepositions see Arc. 180. 1; Joh. Alex. 26. 16 sqq.; Chœrob. E. 14; Apoll. de Synt. 304-305: Ptolemæus Ascalonites anastrophised prepositions even when separated by some intervening word from the noun or verb, as ὥσε δ᾽ ἄπο ῥινὸν τρηχὺς λίθος, Hom. Il. 5. 308, on which Schol. Ven. ad loc. observes: οὐχ ὡς οἴεται ὁ Ἀσκαλωνίτης ἀναστραφήσεται ἡ πρόθεσις, ἐπεὶ τὸ ἐξῆς ἐστιν ἀπῶσε· μεταξὺ γὰρ πέπτωκεν ὁ δέ: Hermann and Göttling agree with Ptolemæus, but the old grammarians generally adhere to the rule given above: Schol. Ven. E. 283; Ψ. 377; S. V. E. 405; E. M. 342.8, and Joh. Alex. 27. 24 adds: διὸ σημειοῦνται τὴν παρὰ Πλάτωνι ἀνάγνωσιν, ἀρετῆς δ᾽ αὖ πέρι διότι ἀνεστράφη ἡ πρόθεσις, μεσοσυλλαβοῦντος τοῦ δέ συνδέσμου καὶ τοῦ αὖ. What shocks this ancient grammarian does not shock many modern editors; C. F. Hermann prints ταύτης δὴ πέρι, Plat. de Legg. 676 C: οὗ δὴ καὶ νῦν ἐφέστηκε πέρι τὸ λεγόμένον, Plat. de Legg. 780 D : Nauck has αἰδοῦς δὲ καὐτὸς δυσκρίτως ἔχω πέρι, Eurip. Frag. 367, and such instances might easily be multiplied.

912. NOTE 2.—Διά is not susceptible of anastrophe, because it might be confounded with Δία accusative of Ζεύς, Joh. Alex. 27. 31 ; Arc. 180. 4 ; S. V. P. 522 : nor is ἀνά, which might be confused with ἄνα the vocative of ἄναξ, or with ἄνα for ἀνάστηθι : this was the doctrine (foolish enough, no doubt) of Aristarchus, Schol. Ven. E. 824, Chœrob. E. 14, although it was not universally admitted to be correct, at least as far as regards ἀνά.

Prepositions of three *moræ* are not subject to anastrophe, as ἐνί, προτί, Apoll. de Syut. 309. 15, but ἐνί is, as μάχη ἔνι κυδιανείρη : so καταί, ὑπαί (cf. Schol. Ven. O. 4), ἀντί, ἀμφί, παραί, ὑπείρ, διαί, ἀπαί, πορτί : Joh. Alex. 27. 30 ; Schol. Ven. Θ. 125.

The passage in E. M. 123. 30, in which it is asserted that κατά and περί are not capable of anastrophe, is corrupt, indeed a farrago of contradictory statements. In Chœrob. E. 14. 12 it is gravely stated that κατά is not anastrophised, lest it should be confounded with κᾆτα !

The shortened forms of prepositions like πάρ for παρά are not liable to anastrophe ; Schol. Ven. Σ. 191 : παροισέμεν· Ἀρίσταρχος ἀναστρέφει τὴν πρόθεσιν πρὸς τὸ μὴ ἀμφιβάλλεσθαι τὸν λόγον, καίτοι τῶν συναλοιφομένων μὴ ἀναστρεφομένων, ὡς καὶ Ἀπολλώνιός φησιν. ἐπείσθη δὲ ἡ παράδοσις Ἀριστάρχῳ.

913. The monosyllables ἐκ ἐξ, ἐν εἰν, ἐς εἰς and ὡς, when standing after the word which they govern, *and at the end of a verse*, take the acute, as

ἦ ῥ’ οὐχ οὗτος ἀνὴρ Προθοήνορος ἀντὶ πεφάσθαι
ἄξιος ; οὐ μέν μοι κακὸς εἴδεται οὐδὲ κακῶν ἔξ.

ὡς δ’ ὅτ’ ἀοιδὸν ἀνὴρ ποτιδέρκεται, ὅστε θεῶν ἒξ
ἀείδει δεδαὼς ἔπε’ ἱμερόεντα βροτοῖσιν.

ἀλλ’ ἄγε μηκέτι ταῦτα λεγώμεθα νηπύτιοι ὥς.

τῷ ὅγε οἰνοποτάζει ἐφήμενος ἀθάνατος ὥς.

NOTE.—Joh. Alex. 27. 34 ; E. M. 342. 8. It would appear that some considered such an accentuation to be correct, even when the preposition did not conclude a line, for Schol. Ambros. in Odyss. 3. 137 (καλεσσαμένω ἀγορὴν ἐς πάντας Ἀχαιοὺς) says, βούλονται τῆς ἐς προθέσεως ῥωννύναι τὸν τόνον τινὲς, ἵνα δυνάμει ἀναστροφὴ γένηται κατὰ τὸ ὄρνιθες ὥς : and this is also the opinion of Göttling, Accent. p. 381, and of Hermann, De emend. rat. Gr. gr. p. 102 : W. Christ writes τὰν δ’ ἔπειτ’ ἀνδρῶν μαχᾶν ἐκ παγκρατίου, Pind. Olymp. 8. 59, but it is a doubtful accent ; Kühner, G. G. 1. 259, rejects the doctrine of the old grammarians as irrational, as though that were a good reason to give.

914. When a preposition capable of anastrophe stands between a substantive and its epithet or apposition, the accent is generally thrown back, as ποταμοῦ ἄπο Σελλήεντος : Ξάνθου ἄπο δινήεντος : ἀνθρώπων πέρι μαιομένων, Pind. Olymp. 8. 4 ; γῆν πέρι πᾶσαν, Herodot. 2. 22, cf. 4. 8 ; χρόνον ἔπι πολλόν, Herodot. 2. 133 ; οἱ δὲ μάλ’ αἰεὶ Νίκης ἱέσθην, τρίποδος πέρι ποιητοῖο, Hom. Il. 23. 718,

where Ptolemæus Ascalonites wrote περί, cf. Schol. Ven. ad loc. ; ὑψηλῶν ὀρέων κορυφὰς ἔπι δενδροκόμους, Aristoph. Nub. 278.

915. NOTE 1.—The grammarians are guilty of several unnecessary refinements in this case. Schol. Ven. B. 877 : πᾶσα πρόθεσις μεταξὺ κυρίου καὶ ἐπιθετικοῦ τῷ κυρίῳ ἕπεται κατὰ 'Αρίσταρχον· κατὰ δὲ Πτολεμαῖον, τῷ προσηγορικῷ· κατὰ δὲ 'Απολλώνιον, πάντως ἀναστρέφεται: Schol. Ven. Γ. 240 : Νέεσσ' ἐνὶ ποντοπόροισι· Νικίας ἀναστρέφει· οὐ συμφωνεῖ δὲ τὰ τῆς ἱστορίας αὐτῷ· φασὶ γὰρ 'Αρίσταρχον τοῖς κυριωτέροις συντάσσειν τὰς προθέσεις. Herodian's opinion coincided with that of Apollonius ; cf. Schol. Ven. B. 523 ; 839 ; Δ. 423 ; Joh. Alex. 26. 25 : εἰ δὲ μεταξὺ πέσῃ δύο ὀνομάτων ἡ πρόθεσις, τοῦ μὲν κυρίου ὄντος, τοῦ δὲ προσηγορικοῦ, ἢ ἐπιθετικοῦ καὶ προσηγορικοῦ ἐν πᾶσι τούτοις ἀναστρέφειν δεῖ τὴν πρόθεσιν, ἵνα τῆς ὅλης συντάξεως προηγήσηται· ποταμοῦ ἄπο Σελλήεντος : cf. Chœrob. E. 14 : Tyrannion seems to have carried the principle further still, Schol. Ven. M. 462 : λᾶος ὑπὸ ῥιπῆς· τὴν δὲ πρόθεσιν Τυραννίων ἀναστρέφει, ἵνα τὸ ἐξῆς ὑπάρχῃ ὑπὸ λίθου ῥιπῆς· οὐκ ἀναγκαῖον δέ· τί γὰρ κωλύει φυλάσσεσθαι τὸν τόνον τῆς προθήσεως, καὶ εἶναι ὑπὸ ῥιπῆς λίθου; A. G. Paris. 3. 314. 8; C. F. Hermann prints πολεμικοῦ περὶ βίου in Plat. de Legg. 943 Α, where πολεμικοῦ πέρι βίου is probably more correct, and yet he has τοῦ γυναικείου πέρι νόμου, Plat. Rep. 457 B.

916. NOTE 2.—When the preposition stands between a genitive case and a substantive governing or governed by it, anastrophe does not take place, as in the instance just quoted, λᾶος ὑπὸ ῥιπῆς, or βοῶν ὑπὸ πόσσ' ἐριμύκων, Hom. Il. 21. 497, where Schol. Ven. says : οὐκ ἀναστρεπτέον τὴν πρόθεσιν· ἔχει γὰρ σύνταξιν πρὸς τὴν ἐπιφερομένην δοτικὴν τὴν ποσσίν, ὁμοίως τῷ ὡς ἄρα τῶν ὑπὸ ποσσὶ κονίσαλος ὥρνυτ' ἀελλής (Il. 3. 13) : Schol. Ven. B. 162 : φίλης ἀπὸ πατρίδος αἴης· οὐκ ἀναστρεπτέον τὴν πρόθεσιν, ὡς Τυραννίων καὶ Πτολεμαῖος· ὁπότε γὰρ γενικῇ συντάττεται ἡ ἀπό, τηρεῖ τὸν τόνον· καὶ γάρ τις θ' ἕνα μῆνα μένων ἀπὸ ἧς ἀλόχοιο: Δ. 67 : τινὲς ἀναστρέφουσι τὴν παρά, κακῶς· οὐδέποτε γὰρ ἀναστρέφεται πρόθεσις γενικῇ συντασσομένη πτώσει· ἔστι γὰρ τὸ ἐξῆς παραφέροιο.

917. Prepositions used elliptically for verbs are barytone, as ἄνα for ἀνάστηθι, ἄπο for ἄπεστι, ἔνι for ἔνεστι, ἔπι for ἔπεστι, πάρα for πάρεστι, μέτα for μέτεστι, ὕπο for ὕπεστι.

918. NOTE 1.—Joh. Alex. 28. 5 : πᾶσα δὲ πρόθεσις ῥῆμα σημαίνουσα βαρύνεται·

ἔνθ' ἔνι μὲν φιλότης·
πάρα δ' ἀνήρ, ὃς καταθήσει.

Cf. Schol. Ven. E. 824; A. 174; E. M. 123. 30; 342. 8; S. V. Φ. 110: ἀλλ' ἐπί τοι καὶ ἐμοὶ θάνατος καὶ μοῖρα κραταιή· οὐκ ἀναστρεπτέον τὴν ἐπί· τὸ γὰρ ἐξῆς ἐστιν ἐπί σοι καὶ ἐμοί.

According to the old grammarians, a preposition when used in the sense proper to some other preposition, does not suffer anastrophe: Schol. Ven. E. 824: ὅταν πρόθεσις ἀντὶ ἑτέρας προθέσεως παραλαμβάνηται οὐκ ἀντιστρέφεται : Schol. Ven. A. 258 : πρόθεσις ἀντὶ ἑτέρας προθέσεως παραλαμβανομένη, τὸν ἴδιον τόνον φυλάττει: Schol. Ven. B. 831 ; E. 325 ; but modern editors pay little or no attention to this rule, e. g. Dindorf reads οἷον δὴ καὶ ὅδ' ἦλθε φυγὼν ὕπο νηλεὲς ἦμαρ, Hom. Il. 21. 57, where the Schol. Ven. bids us write φυγὼν ὑπὸ νηλεὲς ἦμαρ.

919. NOTE 2.—Some paroxytoned ἀπό and περί when they stood for ἄποθεν and περισσῶς: Schol. Ven. Σ. 64 : 'Αρίσταρχος φυλάττει τὸν τόνον τῆς προθέσεως· ἔφαμεν δὲ ἐν ἑτέροις ὅτι ἡ ἀπό, ἐὰν συντάσσηται τῇ γενικῇ μὴ μεταξὺ πιπτουσῶν λέξεων καὶ σημαίνῃ τὸ ἄπωθεν, φυλάσσει τὸν τόνον. οὕτως γοῦν ἀνέγνωμεν ἀπὸ πατρίδος ἄνδρα κατακτάς (Il. 13. 696), καὶ οὐκ ἐθέλεσκε μάχην ἀπὸ τείχεος (Il. 9. 353), καὶ γάρ τίς θ᾽ ἕνα μῆνα μένων ἀπὸ ἧς ἀλόχοιο (Il. 2. 292): προσέθηκα δὲ μὴ μεταξὺ πιπτουσῶν λέξεων διὰ τὸ ἄπο πλυνοί εἰσι πόληος (Od. 6. 40): οὐ γὰρ ἐπλησίασε τῇ πόληος γενικῇ, ἀλλὰ μεταξὺ ἀνεδέξατο λέξεις: Schol. Ven. A. 258; B. 292; Δ. 46. 75; I. 353; Ψ. 718: Schol. in Dionys. Thrac. 931. 19, and in such phrases as πέρι κῆρι modern editors frequently obey the directions of the older writers: Kühner, G. G. 1. 261, and others, write πέρι whenever the word is used adverbially, as

καὶ πάντων Τρώων, πέρι δ᾽ αὖ Πριάμοιό γε παίδων.

Hom. Il. 21. 105.

οὕνεκά τοι πέρι δῶκε θεὸς πολεμήϊα ἔργα.

Hom. Il. 13. 727.

He also maintains that unaccented prepositions are oxytone when used as adverbs, as ἐν (=ἔνδον) δέ μιν αὐτὸν Εὖρ᾽, Il. 24. 472; ἐν δὲ λιμὴν εὔορμος, Hom. Od. 4. 358; in both places Dindorf and others leave the preposition unaccented.

920. If the last syllable of a preposition capable of anastrophe, and standing after the word to which it belongs, be elided, it is not accented at all unless it is followed by a stop, or any ambiguity is likely to arise, as

τῇσι παρ᾽ εἰνάετες χάλκευον δαίδαλα πολλά.

Hom. Il. 18. 400.

δῶκε δ᾽ ἄγειν ἑτάροισιν ὑπερθύμοισι γυναῖκα,
καὶ τρίποδ᾽ ὠτώεντα φέρειν· ὁ δ᾽ ἔλυεν ὑφ᾽ ἵππους.
τῷ δ᾽ ἄρ᾽ ἐπ᾽ Ἀντίλοχος Νηλήϊος ἤλασεν ἵππους·

Hom. Il. 23. 512.

But

τῷ κέ τοι ἀγλαΐας γε διασκεδάσειεν ἁπάσας,
τὰς νῦν ὑβρίζων φορέεις, ἀλαλήμενος αἰεὶ
ἄστυ κάτ᾽· αὐτὰρ μῆλα κακοὶ φθείρουσι νομῆες.

Hom. Od. 17. 244.

Here κατ᾽ receives the acute because of the stop after it. In the line στεῦτο γὰρ Ἡφαίστοιο πάρ᾽ οἰσέμεν (Hom. Il. 18. 191) the elided preposition is accented, ἵνα ᾖ παρὰ τοῦ Ἡφαίστου οἰσέμεν, καὶ μὴ νομίζηται τοῦ Ἡφαίστου ὅπλα παροισέμεν, Joh. Alex. 28. 8; Aristarchus ap. Schol. Ven. Σ. 191. 244. 400; B. 150, and above, § 909.

Those used in the place of verbs, however, seem always to retain their accent, as

οὐδέ σ᾽ ἔγωγε
λίσσομαι εἵνεκ᾽ ἐμεῖο μένειν· πάρ᾽ ἔμοιγε καὶ ἄλλοι
οἵ κέ με τιμήσουσι.

Modern editors are, however, not unfrequently neglectful of these rules; for instance Bergk prints

ταυτὶ παθόντες τῶν Ἀθηναίων ὕπο
δῃοῦτε χώραν, ἦς ὕπ' εὖ πεπόνθατε;
Aristoph. Lysist. 1145.

921. NOTE.—Schol. Ven. A. 174: παρ' ἔμοιγε· τὴν παρὰ πρόθεσιν κατὰ τὴν ἄρχουσαν ὀξυτονητέον. καὶ καθόλου ὁπότε σημαντικαί εἰσι ῥημάτων αἱ προθέσεις, τοῦτον τὸν τόνον ἀναδέχονται.

Aristophanes Byzantius even oxytoned prepositions in Æolic, contrary to the genius of that dialect, in order to make them capable of anastrophe; a proceeding on his part which probably shows that his zeal for grammatical propriety outran his respect for philological fact. Apoll. de Synt. 309. 15: διὰ τοῦτο οὐδ' οἱ περὶ τὸν Ἀριστοφάνη ἠξίωσαν βαρύνειν τὰ μόρια κατὰ τὴν Αἰολίδα διάλεκτον, ἵνα μὴ τὸ ἴδιον τῆς προθέσεως ἀποστήσωσι, λέγω τὴν ἀναστροφήν: De Pron. 93 B: ἀδύνατον πρόθεσιν βαρύνεσθαι, χωρὶς εἰ μὴ ἀναστρέφοιτο· οὐδὲ γὰρ Αἰολεῖς τὸν ἐπὶ ταύταις τόνον ἀναβιβάζουσιν.

922. A preposition separated from its verb by *tmesis* retains its accent if it precedes the verb, as

· νήπιοι οἳ κατὰ βοῦς Ὑπερίονος ἠελίοιο ἤσθιον.

ἧμιν ἀπὸ λοιγὸν ἀμῦναι.

If the preposition follows its verb the accent is thrown back, as

τῶν αὖ Πρωτεσίλαος Ἀρήϊος ἡγεμόνευεν,
ζωὸς ἐών· τότε δ' ἤδη ἔχεν κάτα γαῖα μέλαινα.
Hom. Il. 2. 699.

923. NOTE.—Schol. Ven. A. 67; 258; B. 699: some grammarians, however, left the preposition unaccented, as πρίν γ' ἀπο πατρὶ φίλῳ δόμεναι: Villoison, Anecdota Græca, T. 2. p. 130: 'nec prætermittendum in eximio illo Codice Homerico S. Marci cujus infra recensionem dabimus, quique diligentissime ex antiquissimis exemplaribus descriptus fuit, fere semper, et recte quidem, præpositionem, cum a verbo suo disjuncta est, vocabulo quodam interposito, carere accentu, ut in πρίν γ' ἀπο πατρὶ φίλῳ δόμεναι, ubi ἀπο quod vides sine accentu expressum, sic ad verbum suum δόμεναι pertinere indicatur, ut sit ἀποδόμεναι.

Others refined still further, Schol. Ven. Γ. 440: πάρα γὰρ θεοί εἰσι καὶ ἡμῖν· ὀξυτονητέον τὴν πάρα πρόθεσιν κατὰ τὴν ἄρχουσαν. ἔστι δὲ οὐκ ἀναστροφή, ἀλλὰ καθ' ὑπέρβατον κεῖται, διαλελυμένου τοῦ πάρεισιν· εἰκότως τινές φασιν ὅτι οἱ προθέσεις ὅταν κατὰ διάλυσιν λέγωνται πρὸς τὰ ἐπιφερόμενα φυλάσσουσι τοὺς τόνους· κατὰ ταῦρον ἐδηδώς, κατὰ βοῦς Ὑπερίονος ἤσθιον, ἀνὰ δ' ὁ πτολίπορθος Ὀδυσσεὺς ἔστη. ἐχρῆν οὖν καὶ τῆς παρὰ ἐνθάδε, εἰ πρὸς τὸ ἐπιφερόμενον συντάττεται, φυλάσσεσθαι τὸν τόνον· πρὸς οὓς πιθανῶς ὑπαντητέον, ὅτι ἐκεῖνα μὲν ἅπερ ἐτίθεντο, καὶ ἐν τῇ συνθέσει φυλακτικὰ ἐγένετο τοῦ τόνου τῶν προθέσεων, οἷον κατήσθιον, κατεδηδώς. οὐ γάρ τις τῶν προθέσεων τούτων ἐπὶ τὴν ἄρχουσαν συλλαβὴν ἑαυτῆς μετεβίβαζε τὸν τόνον· τὸ δὲ πάρεισι μετεβίβαζεν· ἔνθεν καὶ τὸ κατὰ διάλυσιν οὕτως ἀναγινώσκομεν: according to this only such prepositions retain their accent in elision as were accented on the first syllable when connected with their verb;

cf. Schol. Ven. E. 178: Ἱρῶν μηνίσας, χαλεπὴ δὲ θεοῦ ἐπὶ μῆνις· Ἀρίσταρχος παρολκὴν οἴεται τῆς ἐπὶ ὁμοίως τῷ ἐπισμυγερῶς, καὶ βοῶν ἐπιβουκόλος ἀνήρ. ὅταν δὲ παρέλκῃ ἡ πρόθεσις, οὐ ποιεῖται ἐξαλλαγὴν τόνου. εἰσὶ δὲ οἱ ἀνεγνώκασιν ὁμοίως τῷ, ἐπεὶ οὗτοι ἐπὶ δέος, ἵνα τὸ ἔπεστι σημαίνηται. ἄλλοι δὲ ἐπίμηνις, ἐν μέρος λόγου ποιοῦντες. ἄμεινον δὲ τῷ Ἀριστάρχῳ συγκατατίθεσθαι.

924. Crasis.—In Crasis proper the first word loses its accent, and that of the second is retained, but if the crasis results in a trochee with an accented penultimate, the word is properispomenon, as καὶ ἀγαθός becomes κἀγαθός, καὶ ἁρπάσαι χἁρπάσαι, τὰ ἀρκοῦντα τἀρκοῦντα, ὁ ἄριστος ὥριστος, τὸ ὄνομα τοὔνομα, ἡ ἀλήθεια ἁλήθεια, τῇ ἀγορᾷ τἀγορᾷ, ἐγὼ οἶμαι ἐγῷμαι, ἐγὼ οἶδα ἐγῷδα, ἐγὼ ἔτασσον ἐγώτασσον, but τὸ ὄναρ τοὔναρ not τοὖναρ, τὸ ἔργον τοὔργον, καὶ ὅσοι χὤσοι, τὰ ἔνδον τἄνδον, καὶ ἅμα χἄμα, καὶ ἔτι κἄτι.

Parathetic compounds form an apparent exception to the rule, e. g. καὶ ὅστις being nothing more than καὶ ὅς τις, the two first words coalesce, χὤς, and the addition of τις makes no alteration in the accent χὤστις, in like manner καὶ ὅτι = καὶ ὅ τι becomes χὤτι not χὦτι, καὶ ὥσπερ = καὶ ὥς περ, χὤσπερ.

925. NOTE 1.—Schol. Ven. A. 277: Πηλείδ' ἤθελε· Ἀρίσταρχος ἀποφαίνεται ὡς κατὰ τὴν Ὁμηρικὴν συνήθειαν τὸ ῥῆμα κατὰ τὸν ἐνεστῶτα ἀπὸ τοῦ Ε ἄρχεται· ἀλλὰ μὴν καὶ ἡ κίνησις ἡ τοῦ παρατατικοῦ· ἀλλ' ὅδ' ἀνὴρ ἐθέλει· ἤθελε Μηριόνης. καὶ ἐνθάδε οὖν ἄμεινον τῇ συνηθεστέρᾳ ἀναγνώσει προσέχοντας, ἐπὶ τὴν ΔΗ συλλαβὴν ὀξεῖαν παραλαμβάνειν, ἵνα κρᾶσις ᾖ τοῦ ἔθελε τρισυλλάβου γενομένου, ὡς καὶ συνήθης ἐστὶν ὁ ποιητής. τὸ μέντοι ῥῆμα τῶν παραλόγων κατὰ τόνον ἐστὶ τρισύλλαβον ὄν, ὡς δέδεικται ἐν τοῖς περὶ ῥημάτων: in other words, Aristarchus read Πηλείδῆθελ' for Πηλείδη ἔθελ'.

926. NOTE 2.—Kühner, G. G. 1. 258, asserts that, in cases of aphæresis, if the accented syllable of the second word is cut off, the preceding word is to be marked with the acute, not with the grave, accent, as ἃ μή 'θιγες, Soph. Ant. 546; μή 'ξω, Soph. Aj. 742; ὅτε δή 'γνων Aristoph. Equit. 632; for this rule he quotes no ancient authority, nor is there any: he has seemingly evolved the precept from his sense of the general fitness of things—an unsafe guide in the matter of Greek accents.

927. NOTE 3.—There is much difference of opinion and of practice among modern grammarians and editors as to the accent of words affected by crasis; what crasis is does not seem to be quite clearly determined; H. L. Ahrens has written a learned and somewhat dogmatical tract, ' De Crasi et Aphæresi,' which is only known to me from the reprint of it in Gaisford's Hephæstion, ed. 2. vol. 2. pp. 235–279: the reader may consult it, but it is doubtful whether he will find in it full satisfaction. A clear description of the different forms of synalœphe is contained in Donaldson's Greek Grammar, § 121 sqq.: a more elaborate discussion of the matter will be found in Kühner, G. G. § 50 sqq.: but perhaps the best account is that given by an ancient grammarian (possibly Trypho) in the valuable Ἐπιμερισμοὶ published by Cramer in the A. G. Oxon. 1. 371. 20: cf. Draco 157; Chœrob. C. 846. 6: some obvious corrections have been made in the passage, which is as follows: ἰστέον ὅτι ἡ Συναλοιφὴ γένος ἐστίν· ἔχει δὲ εἴδη ἑπτά· τρία μὲν ἁπλᾶ· τέσσαρα δὲ σύνθετα· καὶ τὰ μὲν ἁπλᾶ ταῦτα· Ἔκθλιψις, Κρᾶσις, Συναίρεσις. καὶ ἔκθλιψις μὲν ἐστιν ἡνίκα εὑρέθη λέξις εἰς φωνήεντα ἢ εἰς φωνήεντα [leg. εἰς φωνῆεν ἢ εἰς φωνήεντα] καταλήγουσα, τῆς ἐπιφερομένης λέξεως ἀπὸ φωνηέντων [leg. φωνήεντος] ἀρχομένης· τότε γὰρ τὸ χασμῶδες καὶ κεχηνῶδες ἐκθλίβεται [ἐκθλίβει τὸ] τέλος τῆς προηγουμένης λέξεως· καὶ ἡνίκα μὲν ὦσιν ἐν παραθέσει δέχονται ἀπόστροφον· οἷον κατὰ ἐμοῦ, κατ᾿ ἐμοῦ· βούλομαι ἐγώ, βούλομ᾿ ἐγώ· κατὰ εὐεργέτου, κατ᾿ εὐεργέτου· ἡνίκα δὲ ὦσιν ἐν συνθέσει οὐ δέχονται ἀπόστροφον· καταέγραφον, κατέγραφον· ἀναέβην, ἀνέβην· καταέρχομαι, κατέρχομαι. διαφέρει δὲ ἡ συναίρεσις [τῆς] κράσεως κατὰ τούτους τοὺς τρόπους· (I) ἡ συναίρεσις περὶ τοῦ I καὶ Υ καταγίνεται προηγουμένη [leg. προηγουμένου] προτακτικοῦ φωνήεντος· οἷον, πάϊς παῖς· ἄϋω αὔω, Δημοσθένεϊ Δημοσθένει· διαστέλλεται δὲ τὸ συνηρημένον ἐκ τοῦ ἐντελοῦς, ἐκ τοῦ μὴ περιστίζεσθαι τὸ I καὶ Τ ἐν τῇ συναιρέσει· δεῖ γὰρ γινώσκειν ὅτι τότε τὸ I καὶ Υ περιστίζεται ἡνίκα προηγεῖται προτακτικὸν φωνῆεν κατὰ διάστασιν· οἷον ἄϋω, πάϊς, Δημοσθένεϊ· ἐπεὶ ὅτε μὴ προηγεῖται προτακτικὸν οὐ δεῖ περιστίζειν αὐτά· οἷον, ἰαχὴ ὑπόπτερος· ἡ δὲ κρᾶσις περὶ πάντα τὰ φωνήεντα καταγίνεται· οἷον Δημοσθένεος Δημοσθένους· τὸ ἐμὸν τοὐμόν· ἱερεὺς ἱρεύς· ἰχθύες ἰχθύς [leg. ἰχθῦς]· βότρυες βότρυς· καὶ ἡνίκα μὲν γένηται κρᾶσις ἐν ἁρμογῇ δύο λέξεων τίθεται κορωνίς· οἷον τὸ ἐμόν τοὐμόν· τὰ ἐμά τἀμά· προέστη προὔστη· ἡνίκα δὲ μὴ γένηται ἐν ἁρμογῇ δύο λέξεων ἡ κρᾶσις, οὐ τίθεται κορωνίς· οἷον νόος νοῦς, Δημοσθένεος Δημοσθένους. (2) ἄλλως τε δὲ ἡ συναίρεσις φυλακτική ἐστι τῶν αὐτῶν φωνηέντων· οἷον πάϊς παῖς· Ἀχιλλέϊ Ἀχιλλεῖ· ἡ δὲ κρᾶσις πάντως ἀλλοίωσιν κατεργάζεται· οἷον, Δημοσθένεος Δημοσθένους· τὸ ἐμόν τοὐμόν· τὰ ἐμά τἀμά. ταῦτα μὲν οὖν εἰσὶ τὰ ἁπλᾶ εἴδη τῆς συναλιφῆς [leg. συναλοιφῆς]· τὰ δὲ σύνθετα εἰσὶ ταῦτα· (1) ἔκθλιψις καὶ κρᾶσις, καὶ [dele] (2). συναίρεσις [καὶ] ἔκθλιψις, καὶ [dele] (3) κρᾶσις καὶ συναίρεσις, (4) [ἔκθλιψις καὶ κρᾶσις καὶ συναίρεσις]. καὶ Ἔκθλιψις μὲν καὶ κρᾶσις ἐστιν ὡς ἐπὶ τοῦ, καὶ ἐγὼ κἀγώ· ἐκθλίβεται γὰρ τὸ I τοῦ καὶ συνδέσμου, καὶ κιρνᾶται τὸ Α καὶ Ε εἰς Α μακρόν. ἔκθλιψις δὲ καὶ συναίρεσις, ὡς ἐπὶ τοῦ, ἐμοὶ ὑποδύμη ἐμοὐποδύνη [leg. ἐμοὔποδύνει]· ἐκθλίβεται τὸ ἰῶτα τῆς ἐμοὶ ἀντωνυμίας καὶ συναιρεῖται τὸ Ο καὶ Υ εἰς τὴν ΟΥ δίφθογγον· κρᾶσις δὲ καὶ συναίρεσις, ὡς ἐπὶ τοῦ ὁ αἰπόλος ὡπόλος· κιρνᾶται γὰρ τὸ Ο καὶ Α εἰς Ω μέγα, καὶ συναιρεῖται τὸ Ο καὶ Ι εἰς τὴν Ω [leg. ΩΙ] δίφθογγον· ἔκθλιψις δὲ καὶ κρᾶσις καὶ συναίρεσις, ὡς ἐπὶ τοῦ οἱ αἰπόλοι ὡπόλοι· ἐκθλίβεται γὰρ τὸ I τῆς ΟΙ, καὶ κιρνᾶται τὸ Ο καὶ Α εἰς Ω καὶ συναιρεῖται τὸ Ω καὶ τὸ ἰῶτα εἰς τὸ Ω [leg. ΩΙ] δίφθογγον.

928. NOTE 4.—How far written speech, especially how far written verse, should express actual pronunciation, is a hard question, which neither ancients nor moderns are able to answer to everyone's satisfaction: many verses now-a-days, both Greek and Latin, are troublesome to read, because fussy editors have a craze for exhibiting the scansion to the eye; Aristarchus had generally more common sense, and valued legibility above most things; forms like διοσημίᾱστι, χρείᾱστι, even if they were diplomatically correct, only confuse and worry: διοσημία 'στι χρεία 'στι are better because clearer: but it is to be hoped that a time will come when all such oddities will be left for the exclusive use of irreclaimable pedants, and then we shall read in comfort χρεία ἐστί, dictum est, not dictŭmst, nor will verse or rhythm suffer in the least by it. Μὴ 'χειν, μὴ 'νοια, for μὴ 'χειν and μὴ 'νοια, are upon any theory monstrous and impossible.

929. NOTE 5.—The accents proper to crasis cannot be authoritatively determined: the old grammarians give us no information on the subject; the scholiast on Tzetzæ Epistolæ ap. A. G. Oxon. 3. 360. 10 says: ὄξυνε τ᾿ ἄλλα, μὴ περίσπα δυστέχνως, and argues that the circumflex can only arise from the acute followed by the grave accent: the scribe of the Bodleian Plato, written A.D. 896, accents this very combination τᾶλλα (see Wattenbach's 3rd plate); the accents which we find in printed books are sometimes perhaps a reproduction of those found in manuscripts, but more often they are the products of modern theories. The rule given in the text represents the practice of some of the most industrious editors, but I must leave others to determine whether industry and diplomatic fidelity generally go together, or whether strict diplomatic fidelity would bring us sensibly nearer to such accents as would have approved themselves to an Aristarchus or an Herodian.

930. NOTE 6.—Wolf, Litter. Analekt. 1. (2). p. 434, maintains that trochees resulting from crasis, having the accent on the penultimate, should be *paroxytone* when no new diphthongal sound arises, or when the second word is not properispomenon; hence he prefers τἄργα, χἄμα to τᾶργα and χᾶμα. The point is a doubtful one, but a general analogy and, as it is said, manuscript authority, are against Wolf's view. The full discussion of his opinion would necessitate the introduction of much that is too purely theoretical to find an appropriate place here. See, however, Göttling ad Theodos. Gramm. p. 221; Schol. Ven. A. 126.

931. NOTE 7.—Göttling, Accent. p. 385, affirms that an enclitic, when it forms a crasis with a word following it, no longer affects the accent of that which precedes it, as δεινά τοι ἄρα becomes δεινὰ τᾶρα, not δεινά τᾶρα, τρισώματος τὰν Γηρυών, not τρισώματός τὰν, ὀξυγλύκειαν τᾶρα. He argues that τοί in τᾶρα can no more influence the accent of the preceding word than it can in τοίγαρ; but all editors are not of his opinion; for instance, Bergk prints βοάσομαί τᾶρα, Aristoph. Nub. 1154; ἀπέλαυσά τᾶρ' ἂν νὴ Δί' ἐλθὼν ἐνθαδί, Aristoph. Aves 1364: Dindorf has τρισώματός τὰν Γηρυών, Æschyl. Agam. 870; ἐμοί τε καὶ σοί τᾶρ' ἐπεύξωμαι τάδε, Æschyl. Choeph. 112: Bergk δεινά τᾶρα πείσομαι, Aristoph. Achar. 323; and Bekker reads ὀξυγλύκειάν τᾶρα κοκκιεῖς ῥόαν, Pollux 6. 80: E. A. J. Ahrens does the same, Æschyl. Frag. 362 = 318 Dindorf. Each one settles the question according to his own fancies, for no ancient authority says a word on the matter: it is probable that Göttling is mistaken, and that his argument is fallacious.

CHAPTER IX.

PROCLITICS AND ENCLITICS.

932. IN conformity with the best Greek manuscripts, though contrary to the express precepts of the ancient grammarians, the following monosyllables are unaccented when they precede the words to which they belong; ὁ ἡ, οἱ αἱ of the prepositive article (ὅ = ὅς, ἥ, οἵ, αἵ, ὅ of the postpositive article or relative pronoun are accented), the relative adverb ὡς, the negative οὐ οὐκ or οὐχ, the conjunction εἰ or αἰ, and the prepositions ἐκ ἐξ, ἐν εἰν, ἐς εἰς ὡς, as ἐκ κεφαλῆς ἐς πόδας: ὁ μάντις ἦν ἐν τῇ τέχνῃ: εἰν Ἀΐδου: σάφα οὐκ οἶδ' εἰ θεός ἐστιν: ὡς ἐκ κακῶν ἐχάρη: εἰς Φωκέας ὡς πρὸς συμμάχους ἐπορεύετο: ἡ οὐ διάλυσις: οἱ ἄνδρες καὶ αἱ γυναῖκες.

Ὡς, *as*, is oxytone when it follows the word to which it belongs, as θεὸς δ' ὡς τίετο δήμῳ. When it stands for οὕτως some make it oxytone, but there seems more authority for writing ὣς, as ὣς or ὣς εἰπών·

Οὐ (or οὐκ), when it means *No*, or stands at the end of a sentence, is oxytone, as

P.   Ζεὺς δ' ἔστ' ἐκεῖ τις, ὃς νέους τίκτει θεούς;

D.   οὔκ, ἀλλ' ὁ Σεμέλην ἐνθάδε ζεύξας γάμοις.

Eurip. Bacch. 467.

B.   νὴ τὸν Δί', αὕτη πού 'στί σοί γ' ἡ Δαρδανίς.

P.   οὔκ, ἀλλ' ἐν ἀγορᾷ τοῖς θεοῖς δᾷς κάεται.

Aristoph. Vesp. 1371.

S. 1.   αἰβοῖ · φέρ' ἄλλην, χἀτέραν μοι χἀτέραν,
καὶ τρῖβ' ἔθ' ἑτέρας. S. 2. μὰ τὸν Ἀπόλλω 'γω μὲν οὔ.

Aristoph. Pax 15.

δίδωμ' ἔκουσα τοῖσδ' ἀναγκασθεῖσα δ' οὔ.

Eurip. Heraclid. 551.

The prepositions are also oxytone under the conditions mentioned above, § 913.

933. Note 1.—'There are in Greek, as in other languages, words so unimportant of themselves that they have no accent of their own, but are associated by the speaker with the really accented word to which they belong, in the same way as if the two formed one word. In Greek, however, a distinction is observed in such words: (1) those which stand *before*, and (2) those which stand *after*, the word that they refer to. The former of these unaccented words are called *proclitics* [by Hermann, not by any ancient authority], and are not furnished by the Greeks with a sign of accent: the others are called *enclitics*. They differ from each other merely by position; for e. g. τοι belongs to both in τοιγάρτοι, the first τοι being proclitic, the second enclitic;' Göttling, Greek Accent. p. 99. This passage expresses the common doctrine concerning the nature of proclitics and enclitics. The Greek grammarians know nothing whatever about proclitics. Ὁ, ἡ, οἱ, and αἱ are oxytone, Joh. Alex. 22. 26; Apoll. de Pron. 62; Arc. 178. 12; Charax, ap. A. G. 1153: so too is εἰ, Arc. 185. 6; Joh. Alex. 40. 17; and οὐ, Arc. 183. 26; Joh. Alex. 32. 21; Chœrob. E. 10. 14; 109. 9; and the prepositions, Arc. 179. 26; Joh. Alex. 25. 31: on the whole subject, see Göttling, Accent. pp. 388–9; Reiz, de Inclin. Accent. p. 43. Dindorf, in his edition of Sophocles, Lips. 1863, reads in Œd. Tyr. 182, ἐν δ' ἄλοχοι, where others leave ἐν unaccented; one cannot help wishing that editors would once for all make up their minds as to the principles on which they mean to accent their Greek.

934. Note 2.—Ὡς. A. G. Oxon. 1. 448. 26: καὶ πότε ὀξύνεται καὶ βαρύνεται τὸ ὡς; ὅτε ἐπὶ τέλους στίχου κεῖται, ὀξύνεται,

ὄρνιθος ὥς (Il. Γ. 2),

καὶ ὅτε προηγεῖται ἐγκλιτικὸν, ἐάντε ἀρχὴ φράσεως, ἐάντε μέσον εἴη,

ὥς μοι καλὰ τὸν οἶτον ἀπότμου παιδὸς ἐνίσποις (Il. Ω. 388).
ὥστε γὰρ ἢ παῖδες νεαροί, χῆραί τε γυναῖκες (Π. Β. 289).
ἀλλ' ὥς τις τούτων τε βέλος καὶ οἴκοθι πέμπει (Π. Θ. 513).

βαρυτονεῖται δὲ ἐν ἀρχῇ τασσόμενον, μὴ ἐπιφερομένου ἐγκλιτικοῦ,

ὣς εἰπὼν πυλέων (Il. H. 1).
ὣς δὲ λέων μήλοισιν (Π. K. 485).
ὣς ἐχάρη Μενέλαος (Il. Γ. 27).

καὶ ἐν μέσῃ φράσει μὴ ἐπιφερομένου ἐγκλιτικοῦ, εἰ μὴ σημαίνει τὸ ὁμῶς ἢ τὸ οὗτως·
ὁπότε γε οὗτως ὑποτάσσοιτο συνδέσμῳ,

ὡς αἰεὶ τὸν ὁμοῖον ἄγει θεὸς ὡς τὸν ὁμοῖον (Od. P. 218).

καὶ

Ἕκτωρ δ' ὡς εἶδε Τεύκρου βλαφθέντα βέλεμνα (Π. Ο. 484).
Ἕκτωρ δ' ὡς οὐκ ἔνδον ἀμύμονα τέτμεν ἄκοιτιν (Π. Z. 374).

Ἀρίσταρχος δὲ παρήνει καὶ Τυραννίων, τὸ ὡς ἐν μέσῃ φράσει περισπᾶν εἰ μὴ ὑποτάσσοιτο συνδέσμῳ, ὡς τὸ καὶ

ἀλλὰ καὶ ὣς ἐθέλω ἐπεὶ ὣς ἄγε νεῖκος Ἀθήνη (Π. Λ. 721).
ἀλλὰ καὶ ὣς ἱππεῦσι μετέσσομαι (Π. Δ. 322).
ἀλλὰ καὶ ὣς ἐθέλω δόμεναι πάλιν εἰ τόγ' ἄμεινον (Π. A. 116).
ἀλλ' οὐδ' ὣς σε ἔολπα ὀνήσεσθαι κακότητος (Od. E. 379).

The last four examples are curious, for in two of them ὡς is preceded by a conjunction, and yet the scribe circumflexes it. Herod. π. μ. λ. 25. 29: ὡς, τώς.
οὐδὲν εἰς ΩΣ λῆγον ἐπίρρημα ὀξυνόμενον, ὑπεσταλμένης Δωρίδος διαλέκτου, ἀλλὰ
μόνον τὸ ὡς, καὶ τὼς ἀνταποδοτικὸν αὐτοῦ ὑπάρχον. οὐκ ἀγνοῶ μέντοι, ὅτι ἐν διαφόρῳ
σημαινομένῳ καὶ διαφόρῳ συντάξει, ἔσθ' ὅτε περισπᾶται: Joh. Alex. 31. 21: τὸ ὡς
ἀεὶ ὀξύνεται, κἂν ἐν ἀρχῇ, κἂν ἐν μέσῳ, κἂν ἐν τέλει ᾖ, πλὴν μόνον ὅτε σημαίνει τὸ
οὗτως καὶ τὸ ὁμῶς· τότε γὰρ περισπᾶται: Arc. 182. 18: καὶ ὡς ἀντὶ τοῦ οὗτως
ὀξύνεται, which passage is probably corrupt; Schol. Ven. A. 116: τὸ ὡς ὁπότε
σημαντικόν ἐστι τοῦ ὁμῶς, περισπᾶται: Schol. Ven. Γ. 159; H. 31; Λ. 720; Eust.
61. 46: ὅτι ἐν τῷ ἀλλὰ καὶ ὣς ἐθέλω δόμεναι πάλιν, περισπᾶται παρὰ τοῖς παλαιοῖς τὸ
ὡς. φέρεται γὰρ ἐν τοῖς Ἡροδώρου καὶ Ἀπίωνος, ὅτι τὸ ὡς ὅτε δηλοῖ τὸ ὁμῶς περισπᾶται: Apoll. de Conj. 523; de Adv. 581, makes some remarks on the accent of
this word which are not very intelligible.

935. For present purposes Enclitics may be described as words
which, under certain conditions, affect the accent of those which
immediately precede them in the same sentence, and frequently lose their own accent altogether. The following is
a list of them:—

(a) *Verbs.*—The Present Indicative of εἰμί and φημί, except
φῄς and εἶ; εἶς and ἐσσί are enclitic.

(b) *Pronouns.*—The indefinite τίς τί in all its forms, including
the Attic τού and τῷ; the personal pronouns μοῦ, μεῦ, μέθεν, μοί,
μέ, τοί, μίν, σφωέ, σφίν, σφέ are always enclitic; the following
are enclitic except under the conditions mentioned below, § 945,
ἡμῶν, ἡμῖν, ἡμᾶς, σοῦ σέο σεῦ τέος, σοί, σέ τύ (but τύ = σύ is

orthotone) ὑμῶν, ὑμῖν, ὑμᾶς, οὗ ἕο εὖ ἕθεν, οἷ, ἕ μίν νίν, σφώ σφωῖν, σφῶν σφέων, σφίσι σφί, σφάς σφέας.

(c) *Particles.*—The indefinites ποτέ, ποθέν, ποθί, πώς, ποί, πή, πού, πώ ; the conjunctives τέ, νύ νύν = δή (νῦν, *now*, is orthotone, see above, § 826), τοί, θήν, πέρ, γέ, κέ, κέν, ῥά. Δε, θε or θεν, when united with the word to which they belong, may also be included.

936. NOTE 1.—The above description does not attempt to express the true nature of an enclitic, but merely marks it off from other words by a property, which is about as much as is done by the older writers: thus Apollonius (de Synt. 97. 26): καλοῦνται οὖν αἱ ἐντελεῖς κατὰ τὴν φωνὴν καὶ τὸν διεγηγερμένον τόνον ὀρθοτονούμεναι, τάχα συνωνυμοῦντος τοῦ ὀρθοῦ καὶ τοῦ ὑγιοῦς· αἱ δὲ τὸν τόνον μετατιθεῖσαι, ὡσπερεὶ ἀπὸ τῶν ἐγκλινόντων τὰ βάρη ἐφ᾽ ἕτερον σῶμα ἐγκλιτικαί: and Herodian (ap. A. G. 1142), ἐγκλιτικὸν δέ ἐστι μόριον, ὃ τὴν ἰδίαν ὀξεῖαν κοιμίζον τὴν προκειμένην βαρεῖαν εἰς ὀξεῖαν μεθέστησιν, ᾧ ἢ δυνάμει ἢ φύσει ἑτέρα βαρεῖα ὑπέρκειται, δυνάμει μὲν ὡς τὸ δώματά μοι, φύσει δὲ καθάπερ ᾿Αρκεσίλαός τε. A. G. Oxon. 1. 186. 16 is one of the best passages on enclitics anywhere to be found, but it contains a ludicrous error; 187. 6: εἰ δέ ἐστι λέξις προπαροξύτονος τότε πίπτουσι δύο τόνοι εἰς τὴν λέξιν εἷς μὲν ὁ Κύριος τόνος: here the grammarian is made to say 'the Lord is one,' whereas what he wrote was εἷς μὲν ὁ κύριος τόνος, ἕτερος δὲ ὁ τῆς ἐγκλίσεως, 'the word receives two accents, one the accent proper to the word, the other that of the enclisis; κύριος τόνος is one of the commonest of technical terms. On the theory of enclitics see Göttling, Accent. p. 390.

937. NOTE 2.—*Enclitic Verbs.* Arc. 142. 6: ἐν δὲ ῥήμασιν ἐγκλίνεται τὸ φημὶ καὶ εἰμί. πεζὸς δ᾽ ἑνδεκά φημι, τόσσον ἐγώ φημι. τούτου τὸ δεύτερον φὴς (sic) ἀνέγκλιτον. τὸ δὲ τρίτον ἐγκλίνεται· τί φησιν οὗτος; ἔσθ᾽ ὅτε καὶ τὰ πληθυντικὰ ἐγκλίνεται. ἔτι καὶ τὸ εἰμί· Διὸς δέ τοι ἄγγελός εἰμι. τὸ δὲ εἶ ἀνέγκλιτον. τὸ δὲ .... ἐστιν ἐγκλίνεται· αἵματός ἐστιν ἀγαθοῦ. τοῦτο δὲ τὸ ἐστίν ἐν ταῖς ἀρχαῖς τῶν λόγων βαρύνεται· ἔστι πόλις Ἐφύρη, καὶ μετὰ τῆς οὐ ἀποφάσεως· οὐκ ἔστιν ἀγαθόν. καὶ μετὰ τοῦ καὶ καὶ ὡς παροξύνεται· καὶ ἔστιν ἰδεῖν, ὡς ἔστιν εἰπεῖν. ὁμοίως καὶ τὰ δυϊκὰ καὶ τὰ πληθυντικὰ ἐγκλίνονται. καὶ ἐσσι δεύτερον ἑνικὸν ἐγκλίνεται· [cf. Herod. π. ε. μ. 1144] σχέτλιός ἐσσι γεραιέ. On φής see Charax, 1152, A. G. 1158, Schol. Ven. P. 174: φή for φησί is also enclitic, Apoll. de Adv. 543. 11; Joh. Alex. 21. 15. The best grammarians made φαμεν, φατε, φασι enclitic, Charax, 1152: τὰ δὲ πληθυντικὰ οὐκ ἐξωμάλισται, ἀλλὰ παρὰ μὲν τοῖς πολλοῖς καὶ μάλιστα τοῖς ἀκριβέσιν ἐγκλίνεται, ἄνθρωπόν φαμεν, ἄνθρωπόν φατε, ἄνθρωπόν φασι, παρὰ τισι δ᾽ οὔ, οἷς ἡ ἀκριβὴς ἀνάγνωσις οὐκ ἐπείσθη: cf. Schol. Ven. O. 735: ἠέ τινάς φαμεν εἶναι ἀοσσητῆρας ὀπίσσω· τὸ φαμὲν ἐντελές ἐστι καὶ ἐνεστῶτα χρόνον σημαίνει· διὸ τὰς δύο συλλαβὰς βαρυτονητέον. When orthotone the dissyllabic forms of φημί and εἰμί in the Indicative Mood are oxytone, Apoll. de Synt. 134. 24, and above, § 767: φημί was considered to be an Æolic form of φῶ, hence Tyrannion barytoned it, e. g. φῆμι γὰρ οὖν κατανεῦσαι, Eust. 1613. 18, and Telephus Pergamenus denied that φημί and ἐστόν were enclitic, Charax, 1152: ἡμί is never enclitic, Charax, 1152.

On the enclitics εἰς (or εἴς or ἦς) and ἐσσί see Herod. π. ε. μ. 1144, Charax, 1151, Joh. Alex. 21. 17: ἔασι is not enclitic; on the other persons of the dual and plural see Arc. 142. 6, Herod. π. ε. μ. 1144. Some grammarians considered their enclisis a mistake, e. g. Heracleides. Eust. 1457. 46: ἡμάρτηται δὲ καθ᾽

Ἡρακλείδην τὸ ἐστέ. ὡς γὰρ οὐ λέγομεν δείκνυστε ἢ φάστε, οὕτως οὐδὲ ἔτι ἐστί. ἔτι δὲ καὶ καθότι ὀξύνεται, οὐδὲν γὰρ τῶν εἰς ΤΕ ληγόντων ὀξυτονεῖται, ἡμαρτημένου τοῦ φατέ· καὶ Ἀρίσταρχος ἁμαρτάνει φησὶν ἐγκλίνας ἐν Ἰλιάδι τὸ, ὑμεῖς μάρτυροί ἐστε. οὐ γὰρ ἀνῄρηταί τι μὴ πρότερον ὀξυτονούμενον. εἰ δὲ ἀνῄρηται τὸ ὀξυτονούμενον, ἄτοπός φησι καὶ ἡ ἔγκλισις. οὕτω δὲ καὶ περὶ τούτων γράψας, ἑτέρωθι λέγει ὅτι τὸ ἐσμὲν ἐστὲ εἰσὶν εἰ καὶ ἡμάρτηται ὀξυτονούμενα, ὅμως ἔπαθον τοῦτο, διὰ τὰ ἐνικὰ οἷς ὀφείλουσιν ὁμοτονεῖν.

938. Ἐστί is paroxytone when it begins a sentence, or when it is immediately preceded by οὐκ, μή, εἰ, ὡς, ἀλλά, καί, or τοῦτο, as ἔστι θεός, ἔστι πόλις Ἐφύρη, οὐκ ἔστιν ἀγαθός, εἰ ἔστι κακός, τοῦτ' ἔστιν ἁμάρτημα, ὡς ἔστι κακὸν ἀμαθία, ἀλλ' ἔστιν εἰπεῖν.

Many modern scholars make ἔστι paroxytone whenever it affirms existence or possibility, as ἔστι δ' ὅπη νῦν ἔστι, Æschyl. Agam. 67 ; κεῖσε μὲν ἔστι (= ἔξεστι) καὶ ὕστερον ὁρμηθῆναι, Hom. Il. 14. 313. It is also usual to write ἔστι whenever it is followed by any relative particles, as ἔστιν οἵ, ἔστιν ὡς, ἔστιν ὅπου: in many editions ἐστί, even when a mere copula, is paroxytone if it begins a verse, as

πέπλον δ', ὅστις τοι χαριέστατος ἠδὲ μέγιστος
ἔστιν ἐνὶ μεγάρῳ, καί τοι πολὺ φίλτατος αὐτῇ.

Il. 6. 271.

939. Note.—Herod. π. ε. μ. 1148 : τὸ ἔστιν ἡνίκα ἄρχει λόγου, ἢ ὅτε ὑποτάττεται τῇ οὐ ἀποφάσει ἢ τῷ καί ἢ εἰ ἢ ἄλλῳ συνδέσμῳ ἢ τῷ ὡς ἐπιρρήματι ἢ τῷ τοῦτο, τηνικαῦτα τὴν ὀξεῖαν ἔχει ἐπὶ τοῦ Ε: Arc. 142.13 ; 147. 23; E. M. 301. 2 ; S. V. A. 63. According to Hermann (de emend. rat. Gr. gr. p. 84) ἐστί is enclitic when it is merely the copula, where consequently it might be omitted, and orthotone whenever it predicates existence or possibility, as κεῖσε μὲν ἔστι (= ἔξεστι) καὶ ὕστερον ὁρμηθῆναι, Il. 14. 313 : ἀλλ' ἔπευ· οὐ γὰρ ἔτ' ἔστιν ἀποσταδὸν Ἀργείοισι μάρνασθαι, Il. 15. 556, in which cases it could not be omitted. Hermann's rule seems reasonable, squares pretty well with what the older grammarians say, and has been followed by several modern editors.

940. The enclitic forms of εἰμί are generally orthotone in modern books when, 1. they begin a sentence or a verse, as ξεῖνος φίλος Ἀργεῖ μέσσῳ Εἰμί, Il. 6. 224 ; 2. when they are separated by a stop from the words to which they belong, as σκολιὸς δὲ ταύτῃ· κατάπερ ὁ Μαίανδρος, ἐστὶ ὁ Νεῖλος, Herod. 2. 29 ; ἐγώ τοι, μῆτερ, εἰμὶ παῖς σέθεν, Eurip. Bacch. 1118, and, 3. in elisions, as τοῦτ' ἐστίν, Demosth. 701 ; 851 ; τί ποτ' ἐστίν, Demosth. 724 ; ἀγαθὸς δ' ἐστίν, but ἀγαθὸς δέ ἐστιν.

941. The enclitic forms of φημί are oxytone in modern editions when they begin a sentence or verse, and when they are separated by a stop from the preceding words, as φασὶν ἀλλήλαις ξυνελθεῖν τὰς τριήρεις εἰς λόγον, Aristoph. Eqq. 1300 ; πολλοί γάρ, φημί, οὐκ ἀγαπῶντες, Lucian. Deor. Concil. 2; ἔα, φημί, τὰ περὶ τῶν Αἰγυπτίων· Lucian. Deor. Concil. 11. But editions and editors differ much as to the accentuation of such combinations. Dindorf and others print καὶ φημὶ κἀπόφημι κοὐκ ἔχω τι φῶ, Soph. Œd. Col. 317.

942. Contrary to the statements of the old grammarians, the indefinite τις is orthotone in modern editions, 1. when it begins a clause, as οὐκ ἡ αὐτὴ ἀρετὴ ἁπλῶς ἂν εἴη πολίτου καὶ ἀνδρός, τινὸς μέντοι πολίτου, Arist. Polit. 3. 4. 9; ἀναγκαῖον δ' ἤτοι πᾶσι τοῖς πολίταις ἀποδεδόσθαι πάσας παύτας τὰς κρίσεις ἢ τισὶ πάσας, οἷον ἀρχῇ τινὶ μιᾷ ἢ πλείοσιν, ἢ ἑτέραις ἑτέρας, ἢ τινὰς μὲν αὐτῶν πᾶσι, τινὰς δὲ τίσιν, Arist. Polit. 4. 14. 3; τίς ἔνδον, ὦ παῖ, παῖ, μάλ' αὖθις, ἐν δόμοις; Æschyl. Choeph. 654; 2. when it begins a verse, as

οὐδέ τι Νηλεὺς
τῷ ἐδίδου, ὃς μὴ ἕλικας βόας εὐρυμετώπους
ἐκ Φυλάκης ἐλάσειε·   Hom. Od. 11. 288;

3. when preceded by the article, in the singular number, as ὁ τὶς ἄνθρωπος, Arist. Cat. 5. 2; ἡ τὶς γραμματική, Arist. Cat. 2. 2, where Bekker notes that cod. B reads ἡ τίς; 4. after a stop, and therefore after a vocative case, as πῶς γὰρ ἄν, ἔφην ἐγώ, ὦ βέλτιστε, τὶς ἀποκρίναιτο; 5. in the combination τινὲς μὲν .... τινὲς δὲ: lastly, 6. when emphatic, as τὸ χρῶμα ἐν σώματι· οὐκοῦν καὶ ἐν τινι σώματι· εἰ γὰρ μὴ ἐν τινὶ τῶν καθ' ἕκαστα, οὐδὲ ἐν σώματι ὅλως, Arist. Cat. 5. 7; but, when τις or τι are equivalent to *somebody*, or *something of importance*, they are enclitic, as εἰ μὲν γὰρ τὰ ἀνόητα ὠρέγετο αὐτῶν, ἦν ἄν τι τὸ λεγόμενον, εἰ δὲ καὶ τὰ φρόνιμα, πῶς λέγοιεν ἄν τι; Arist. Eth. Nic. 7. 2. 4; yet C. F. Hermann prints οὗτοι ἀπόβλητον ἔπος εἶναι δεῖ, ὦ Φαῖδρε, ὃ ἂν εἴπωσι σοφοί, ἀλλὰ σκοπεῖν μὴ τὶ λέγωσι, Plat. Phaedr. 260 A, where others have μή τι. In all other circumstances τις, whether it precedes or follows the word to which it belongs, is enclitic, as

οὐδέ τις οὖν μοι
νηῶν πημάνθη, ἀλλ' ἀσκηθέες καὶ ἄνουσοι.
Hom. Od. 14. 254.

οὐκ οἶδ'· οὐ γάρ πώ τις ἑὸν γόνον αὐτὸς ἀνέγνω,
ὡς δὴ ἔγωγ' ὄφελον μάκαρός νύ τευ ἔμμεναι υἱός.
Hom. Od. 1. 216.

ἦ γάρ οἱ ζωή γ' ἦν ἄσπετος· οὔ τινι τόσση.

Hom. Od. 14. 96.

κλαῖ' ἐπεὶ οὐκ ἄνυσίν τινα δήομεν· ἀλλὰ τάχιστα.

Hom. Od. 4. 544.

εἰ μέν τις τὸν ὄνειρον—οὔ τινι κοσμηθεῖσα—καί τινα Τρωϊάδων—
οὔς τινας μεθιέντας ἴδοι—ἀπαιτῶν γὰρ παρά τινος τῶν μαθητῶν τὸν
μισθὸν ἠγανάκτει. It will be found, however, that editors are
capricious and inconsistent.

943. NOTE I.—See Kühner, G. G. I. 269; Herod. π. ε. μ. 1143; Charax, 1151.
Τευ, like του and τῷ for τινός and τινί, is enclitic, as ἀλλ' οὔ τευ οἶδα: οὔτε σοὶ οὔ
τέ τῳ ἄλλῳ, Herod. π. ε. μ. 1143; Arc. 142. 2; S. V. Φ. 252: αἰετοῦ οἴματ' ἔχων
μέλανος τοῦ θηρητῆρος· Ἀρίσταρχος μέλανός του· ἀγνοεῖ δὲ ὅτι ὁ ποιητὴς τῷ
ἐγκλιτικῷ ΤΟΥ οὐ χρῆται. ἄμεινον οὖν ἄρθρον αὐτὸ ἐκδέχεσθαι. There can, I think,
be very little doubt that many of these modern accents are wrong: ὁ τὶς ἄνθρωπος
for *any individual man*, and all similar combinations, ought to be written ὅ τις
ἄνθρωπος. The modern device of writing τὶς with a grave accent finds no warrant
among the old grammarians, and, even if ὁ τίς is found in a manuscript of the ninth
or tenth century, it is probable that it only represents the pronunciation of the
scribe's age, not that of Apollonius or Herodian.

944. NOTE 2.—*Enclitic Pronouns.* On μου, μοι, με see Arc. 142. 26: on μευ,
Eust. 32. 45: on με, Schol. Ven. Γ. 400; Herod. π. ε. μ. 1144: ἐκ δὲ ἀντωνυμιῶν αἱ μὲν
ἐγείρουσαι τὴν ὀξεῖαν τὴν πρὸ αὐτῶν ἐγκλιματικαὶ καλοῦνται, αἱ δὲ μὴ ἐγείρουσαι ὀρθοτονούμεναι, αἱ μὲν οὖν ἀεὶ ἐγείρουσαι τὴν πρὸ αὐτῶν ὀξεῖάν εἰσιν αἵδε, μεῦ μου, μοί τοί,
μέ μίν, σφίν σφε, σφωέ, . . . αἱ δὲ ποτὲ μὲν ἐγείρουσαι τὴν πρὸ αὐτῶν ποτὲ δὲ μή, σεῦ σέο
σοῦ σοί σέ, εὗ οἷ ἕθεν, σφί σφώ σφίσι σφέας: on μεθέν, Apoll. de Pron. 98 A: σοῦ σοί
σέ, Arc. 143. 3; Apoll. de Pron. 105 A: τοί, Apoll. de Pron. 105 A: ὀρθοτονεῖται δὲ
καὶ παρ' Ἀλκμᾶνι, συνηθῶς Δωριεῦσιν· ἄδοι Διὸς δόμῳ ὁ χορὸς ἁμὸς καὶ
τοί, ϝάναξ: it seems from the same passage that τίν is also enclitic as οὐ γάρ
τιν ὁ φθονερὸς δαίμων: τύ=σέ, as τί τυ ἐγὼν ποιέω, Apoll. de Pron. 68 B; de Synt.
120. 12: 131. 25; Herod. π. ε. μ. 1145: τέος, Apoll. de Pron. 95 C: ἔτι τῇ ἐμέος
ἢ τέος κατ' ἔγκλισιν σύζυγος, ἐκπεφήναντί τεος αἱ δυσθαλίαι, Σώφρον· τὸ
γὰρ ὀρθοτονούμενον κτητικὴν σημαίνει: on οἷ ἕ and μίν see Arc. 143. 4; Apoll. de
Pron. 49 A: μόνως ἐγκλίνονται αἱ τοῦ τρίτου δυϊκαί, καὶ ἡ μίν, αἵ τε μονοσύλλαβοι
σφίν καὶ σφέ, ἥ τε διὰ τοῦ τ τοί, Apoll. de Pron. 107 C: on ἕθεν, Schol. Ven. A.
114; Γ. 128; Arc. 143. 23, some made it always orthotone, Apoll. de Pron. 98 A:
οἱ, Schol. Ven. B. 665; I. 392; Ψ. 387: ἕ, Schol. Ven. Δ. 534; Arc. 143. 4: σφέ
and ψέ, Apoll. de Pron. 49 A; 128 A: on σφωέ and σφωῖν, Schol. Ven. Θ. 402:
γυιώσω μέν σφωϊν ὑφ' ἄρμασιν ὠκέας ἵππους· ἐγκλιτικὴ νῦν ἐστὶν ἡ ἀντωνυμία·
τρίτου γὰρ προσώπου. τὰ δὲ τρίτα δυϊκὰ τό τε σφωέ καὶ σφωῖν ἐγκλιτικά ἐστιν. ὅτε
μέντοι δευτέρου γίνεται τὸ σφῶϊν προπερισπᾶται· ὀρθοτονεῖται γὰρ τὸ γυιώσειν
μὲν σφῶϊν: Schol. Ven. O. 155; Ψ. 281; Arc. 143. 10; Joh. Alex. 23. 34; Apoll.
de Pron. 114 A sq.; 141 B; de Synt. 167. 15: νῶϊν and σφῶϊν are never enclitic,
Arc. 143. 8: on σφῶν, σφίν, σφάς see Apoll. de Pron. 49 A; 125 A; 128 A;
Arc. 143. 17; Schol. Ven. Z. 367; Herod. π. ε. μ. 1146 sq.; Kühner, G. G. I. 263,
asserts that τείν, φίν, ψίν, and ψέ are enclitic, but he quotes no authority for the
statement.

945. The pronouns above mentioned are not always enclitic. They are orthotone,

1. When they begin a sentence, clause, or verse, as

χωρῶ πρὸς ἔργον· σοὶ δ' ἐφίεμαι, θεὰ,
τοιάνδ' ἀεί μοι σύμμαχον παρεστάναι.

Soph. Ajax 116.

σὲ μὲν εὖ πράσσοντ' ἐπιχαίρω.   Soph. Ajax 136.

οὗτος, σὲ φωνῶ τόνδε τὸν νεκρὸν χεροῖν
μὴ συγκομίζειν.   Soph. Ajax 1047.

πορεύσομαι,
σοῦ μὲν τυχὼν ἀγνῶτος, ἐν δὲ τοῖσδ' ἴσος.

Soph. Œd. Tyr. 676.

2. When they are emphatic, or imply a contrast between one person and another, as

δαιμόνι', ἀτρέμας ἧσο, καὶ ἄλλων μῦθον ἄκουε,
οἳ σέο φέρτεροί εἰσι· σὺ δ' ἀπτόλεμος καὶ ἄναλκις.

Hom. Il. 2. 200.

Διὸς δέ τοι ἄγγελός εἰμι,
ὃς σεῦ, ἄνευθεν ἐὼν, μέγα κήδεται ἠδ' ἐλεαίρει.

Hom. Il. 2. 26.

ὡς σοὶ ἐνὶ στήθεσσιν ἀτάρβητος νόος ἐστίν.

Hom. Il. 3. 63.

ἐπεὶ οὔτινά φησιν ὁμοῖον
οἷ ἔμεναι Δαναῶν, οὓς ἐνθάδε νῆες ἔνεικαν.

Hom. Il. 9. 305.

But   ὥς σεο νῦν ἔραμαι καί με γλυκὺς ἵμερος αἱρεῖ,

Hom. Il. 3. 446,

because Paris is not contrasting Helen with any other woman. After ἐπεί, however, enclitic pronouns remain enclitic, even when emphatic, as

δᾶερ ἐπεί σε μάλιστα πόνος φρένας ἀμφιβέβηκεν.

Hom. Il. 6. 355.

3. When preceded by a preposition, as

καὶ τὰ μὲν εὖ δάσσαντο μετὰ σφίσιν υἷες Ἀχαιῶν.

Hom. Il. 1. 368.

διὰ σέ: περὶ σοῦ: ἐπὶ σοί, and after ἕνεκα, as ἕνεκα σοῦ: τις, however, forms an exception, as ἕνεκά του, ἕνεκά τινος: μέχρι του.

4. When they are joined with any case of αὐτός, as

ἐν πρύμνῃ δ᾽ ἄρ᾽ ἔπειτα καθέζετο· πὰρ δὲ οἷ αὐτῷ
εἷσε Θεοκλύμενον.   Hom. Od. 15. 285.

σοὶ δ᾽ αὐτῷ μελέτω, καὶ ἐμῶν ἐμπάζεο μύθων.
                                                Hom. Od. 1. 305.

ἕο δ᾽ αὐτοῦ πάντα κολούει.   Hom. Od. 8. 211.

οὐρῇ δὲ πλευράς τε καὶ ἴσχια ἀμφοτέρωθεν
μαστίεται, ἕε δ᾽ αὐτὸν ἐποτρύνει μαχέσασθαι.
                                                Hom. Il. 20. 170.

5. When οὗ, οἷ, ἕ, ἕο, εὗ, ἕθεν, σφέων, σφίσι, σφέας are resolvable into ἑαυτοῦ, ἑαυτῆς, ἑαυτόν, etc., that is, when they are used in a reflexive sense, as

                    Δηΐφοβος δὲ
ἀσπίδα ταυρείην σχέθ᾽ ἀπὸ ἕο=ἀφ᾽ ἑαυτοῦ.
                                                Hom. Il. 13. 162.

ἢ ὀλίγον οἷ (=ἑαυτῷ) παῖδα ἐοικότα γείνατο Τυδεύς.
                                                Hom. Il. 5. 800.

But   οἱ δέ οἱ (=αὐτῷ) ἐβλάφθησαν, ἄνευ κέντροιο θέοντες.
                                                Hom. Il. 23. 387.

        καὶ γάρ ῥα Κλυταιμνήστρης προβέβουλα
κουριδίης ἀλόχου· ἐπεὶ οὔ ἕθεν (αὐτῆς) ἐστὶ χερείων.
                                                Hom. Il. 1. 113.

Θρήϊκες ἀκρόκομοι, δολίχ᾽ ἔγχεα χερσὶν ἔχοντες,
οἵ ἑ (=αὐτὸν) μέγαν περ ἐόντα καὶ ἴφθιμον καὶ ἀγαυὸν
ὦσαν ἀπὸ σφείων.   Hom. Il. 4. 533.

The ancient critics differed considerably in their opinions about the accentuation of such passages as these, and modern editors do not seem to be always quite sure of their own theories.

According to the grammarians αὐτός is enclitic in Hom. Il. 12. 204,

        κόψε γάρ αὐτον ἔχοντα κατὰ στῆθος παρὰ δειρὴν,
        ἰδνωθεὶς ὀπίσω,

but Dindorf and others read, as Trypho did, κόψε γὰρ αὐτόν.

946. Note 1.—Kühner, G. G. 1. 271, asserts that in Homer when αὐτός is added to a personal pronoun three cases are to be distinguished : 1. both pronouns have a reflexive sense, αὐτός generally following, the personal pronoun is orthotone, as σέο αὐτοῦ, ἕο αὐτοῦ, ἓ αὐτόν: 2. the personal pronoun reflexive, and αὐτός precedes and is emphatic, the personal pronoun is enclitic, as αὐτὸν μέν σε πρῶτα σάω, αὐτόν ... μιν δαμάσσας : 3. the personal pronoun not reflexive, in which case, if emphatic, it precedes and is orthotone, as ἀλλὰ τόδ' ἦμὲν ἐμοὶ πολὺ κέρδιον ἠδὲ οἷ αὐτῷ, or it is enclitic, and αὐτός sometimes precedes, sometimes follows, if the personal pronoun is not emphatic, as αὐτόν με, σε αὐτόν.

947. NOTE 2.—Kühner, G. G. 1. 271, quotes πρός σε from Xen. Sympos. 5. 8, where, however, L. Dindorf rightly has πρὸς σέ : he also declares that, when one preposition is opposed to another, 'the preposition is naturally accented, and the pronoun enclitic, as Xen. Anab. 7. 7. 32 : πολὺ ἂν προθυμότερον ἴοιεν ἐπί σε ἢ σύν σοι,' and so L. Dindorf prints it, but there is no ancient authority for it ; only one passage occurs to me where an old grammarian seems to deny that pronouns after a preposition are always orthotone, and that is Schol. Ven. Φ. 174 : ἀλτ' ἐπί οἱ· ἡ ΟΙ ἀντωνυμία ἀπόλυτός ἐστι καὶ ἐγκλιτική· διὸ τῆς ἐπί προθέσεως τὸ τέλος ὀξύνουσιν : in many modern editions this is printed ἐπὶ οἱ according to rule ; it is a case where two rules are in conflict, for ἐπὶ οἱ would properly mean *against himself,* whereas it here means *against him,* hence it was natural that some should prefer to break another rule and write ἐπί οἱ.

948. NOTE 3.—Kühner, G.G. 1. 172, declares that the unaccented prepositions are united with enclitics, as ἔκ μου, ἔν μοι, εἴς σε, ἔν σοι : he quotes no authority for such an accentuation as this, nor could he do so ; were we strictly to follow the precepts of the old grammarians, all such combinations would be written ἐκ μοῦ, ἐν μοὶ, εἰς σὲ, ἐν σοὶ, and so on ; but in our editions the preposition is left unaccented, and the pronoun is orthotone, e. g. ἐς σέ, Soph. Elect. 954 ; Philoct. 500 : εἰς σέ, Eurip. Androm. 63 ; Iphig. Aul. 480 ; 877 ; Heraclid. 147 ; Phœniss. 435 ; 569 ; Hec. 802 : εἰς ἕ, Hom. Od. 22. 436 ; Il. 23. 203 ; Apollon. Rhod. 2. 467, ed. Hoelzlin.: ἐν σοί, Soph. Œd. Rex 314 ; Œd. Col. 392 ; Trachin. 621 ; Eurip. Alcest. 278 ; Helena 1425 ; Rhes. 859 : ἐκ σοῦ, Eurip. Androm. 1235 ; Hippolyt. 1177 : σὺν σοί, Hom. Il. 10. 290 ; Od. 3. 85 : 13. 391 : σὺν σοί τε καί, Il. 9. 346 : at least, so they stand in Dindorf's editions of Homer and Sophocles, and Nauck's edition of Euripides.

949. NOTE 4.—Apoll. de Pron. 54 A : αἱ ἐγκλιτικαὶ .... ἀρκτικαὶ γινόμεναι, ὀρθοτονοῦνται, ὡς ἐπὶ τοῦ ἐμὲ δ' ἔγνω καὶ προσέειπεν καὶ τῶν παραπλησίων : Apoll. de Pron. 49 B ; Apoll. de Synt. 166. 17 : αἱ ἀρκτικαὶ ἀντωνυμίαι φυσικῶς ὀρθοτονοῦνται· τὸ οὖν σέο δ' ὀστέα πύσει ἄρουρα ἀπανάγνωσμα, εἰ δύναται ἐγκλιθῆναι καὶ μὴ ἐγκέκλιται. ὁμοίως ὅτι καὶ αἱ προθέσεις ὀρθοτονοῦσι τὰς ἀντωνυμίας οὐκ ἄλλην ἄρα τάσιν ἀναδέξεται τὸ ἐξ ἐμεῦ ἢ τὴν ὀρθήν : Arc. 144. 13 ; Schol. Ven. E. 64.

950. NOTE 5.—Arc. 143. 24 : αἱ μὲν οὖν ἐγκλινόμεναι τῶν ἀντωνυμιῶν αὐταί εἰσιν, αἵτινες ὀρθοτονούμεναι μὲν ἀντιδιαστολὴν ἔχουσιν ἑτέρου προσώπου· ἐμοῦ ἤκουσας οὐκ ἄλλου· ἐμοὶ ἔδωκας, οὐκ ἄλλῳ· ἐμὲ ἐδίδαξας, οὐκ ἄλλον. ἐγκλινόμεναι δὲ ἀπόλυτα πρόσωπα δηλοῦσιν· ἤκουσά σου, ἔδωκά σοι· καὶ ἡ μὲν γενικωτάτη αἰτία τῆς ὀρθῆς τάσεως ἡ ἀντιδιαστολὴ τοῦ προσώπου· αὕτη δὲ διαιρεῖται εἰς πλείονα εἴδη· αἵ τε γὰρ διεζευγμέναι ὀρθοτονοῦνται· καὶ ἐμοὶ καὶ Ἀπολλωνίῳ, ἢ ἐμοὶ ἢ Ἀπολλωνίῳ. καὶ μετὰ τοῦ ἕνεκα συνδέσμου· ἕνεκα σοῦ ἕνεκα μοῦ : Schol. Ven. A. 214 ; 294 ; B. 27 : ὃς σευ. ὀρθοτονητέον τὴν σεῦ· ἀντιδιέσταλται γὰρ πρὸς τὸν Ἀχιλλέα· ἢ ὅτι πρόκειται τοῦ ῥήματος ἡ ἀντωνυμία : Schol. Ven. B. 201 : οἱ σέο φέρτεροί εἰσι· οὕτως ὀρθοτονητέον τὴν σέο· ἀντιδιασταλτικὴ γάρ ἐστιν : Schol. Ven. Γ. 63. 160. 446 ; I. 494 : ἀλλὰ σὲ παῖδα, θεοῖς ἐπιείκελ' Ἀχιλλεῦ, ποιεύμην· ἐνθάδε ὀρθοτονητέον, ἔμφασις γὰρ δείξεως: Schol. Ven. Υ. 105; Herod. π. ε. μ. 1145; Apoll. de Synt. 125. 21; 143. 18; de Pron. 44 A.

951. NOTE 6.—When Paris (Π. 3. 446) says to Helen, ὥς σεο νῦν ἔραμαι καί με γλυκὺς ἵμερος αἱρεῖ, the pronoun σέο is enclitic, because he is not contrasting his love for her with that for any other woman, but the same words in the mouth of Zeus (Π. 14. 328) are written ὡς σέο, because he tells Hera that he feels more charmed with her at present than he ever was with Danaë, Semele, and the rest of his favourites; cf. Schol. Ven. ad loc.; Charax, 1152: καὶ τὸ σέο δὲ παρὰ τὸ σοῦ ἐνεκλίθη, ὡς ἐπὶ τοῦ Πάριδος ὥς σεο νῦν ἔραμαι, ἐπὶ γὰρ τοῦ Διὸς, ὀρθοτονεῖται· ἀντιδιαστολὴν γὰρ ἔχει πρὸς ἄλλας γενικάς, ἐπὶ δὲ τοῦ Πάριδος οὐκ ἔστι διαστολὴ πρὸς ἄλλην: cf. Apoll. de Synt. 166. 1.　As might be expected, there are passages where the grammarians differ, e. g. Il. 9. 614, οὐδέ τί σε χρὴ τὸν φιλέειν, ἵνα μή μοι ἀπέχθηαι φιλέοντι: Schol. Ven. I. 614: ὁ Ἀσκαλωνίτης ἀναγινώσκει ἵνα μὴ μοὶ, τὰς δύο βαρυτόνως· οἷον ἵνα μὴ ἐμοί κατ' ὀρθὴν τάσιν. συγκριτικὴ γάρ ἐστι, φησίν, ὡς πρὸς τὸν Ἀγαμέμνονα· καὶ ὑγιῶς φησίν. ἡ μέντοι παράδοσις ἐγκλιτικῶς ἀνέγνω, ἐπὶ τὴν μὴ τὴν ὀξεῖαν τιθεῖσα, ὁμοίως τῷ, μή μοι οἶνον ἄειρε, τῷ μὴ εἶναι ἐν τῇ ἀντωνυμίᾳ τὸ Ε, ἀλλ' ἀποβεβλῆσθαι. καὶ ὁμοιά ἐστιν ἡ πλάνη τῷ ἤ μ' ἀνάειρε τῷ ἢ ἐγὼ σέ καὶ τῷ τάχα δή με διαρραίσουσι καὶ αὐτόν. εἴ γε ἐχρῆν καὶ ταῦτα ὀρθοτονεῖσθαι, ἀλλὰ τῷ μὴ ὁρᾶσθαι κατ' ἀρχὴν τὸ Ε οὕτως ἀνέγνωσαν· τοῦτο γὰρ ἐπακολουθεῖ ταῖς πρωτοτύποις. ἐχρῆν δὲ αὐτοὺς ἐπιγνῶναι ὅτι κρᾶσις δύναται ἐπακολουθεῖν, καὶ οὕτως ῥῶσαι τὴν ὑγιῆ ἀνάγνωσιν.　And again, Il. 1. 396: πολλάκι γάρ σεο πατρὸς ἐνὶ μεγάροισιν ἄκουσα, where S. V. says, Ἀρίσταρχος δὲ τὴν σέο ἐγκλίνει λέγων ἁπλῆν τε εἶναι αὐτήν, καὶ ἀντιδιαστολὴν οὐκ ἔχειν. ὁ δὲ Ἡρωδιανὸς καίτοι, φησίν, ὀφείλουσα ὀρθοτονεῖσθαι, ἵνα λέγῃ σοῦ καὶ οὐκ ἄλλης ἀκήκοα, ὅμως πεπεῖσθαί φησι κατὰ τὴν ἀνάγνωσιν Ἀριστάρχῳ.　Ptolemæus made it enclitic, though for a different reason.　And again, Il. 5. 252, ἐπεὶ οὐδὲ σὲ πεισέμεν οἴω: Schol. Ven. ad loc., ὁ Ἀσκαλωνίτης τὸν δὲ ὀξύνει, ἵνα ἐγκλιτικῶς ἀνάγνω. οὐκ ἀναγκαῖον δὲ, ἀλλ' ὀρθοτονεῖν· καὶ γὰρ δύναται συνδεδέσθαι.

952. NOTE 7.—Custom is the main reason assigned for making an emphatic pronoun enclitic after ἐπεί: Schol. Ven. Z. 355: τὴν δὲ σὲ ἀντωνυμίαν ὀξυτονοῦσι, τουτέστιν ὀρθοτονοῦσιν, ἐπεὶ πρός τί ἐστιν. ἔστι μὲν οὖν ἀληθὲς, ὅτι ἀντιδιασταλτική ἐστι νῦν ἡ ἀντωνυμία· ἡ μέντοι κοινὴ ἀνάγνωσις ἀνέγνω ἐγκλιτικῶς ἀεὶ τὴν τοιαύτην σύνταξιν· ὃ δὲ λέγω τοιοῦτόν ἐστι, τὸ ἐπεί σε εὑρέθη συνεχῶς οὕτως ἀνεγνωσμένον ἐγκλιτικῶς ἀεὶ, μὴ ἐπιφερομένου συνδέσμου, ἐπεί σ' εἴασεν Ἀχιλλεύς, ἐπεί σε πρῶτα κιχάνω, ἐπεί σε φυγὼν ἱκέτευσα, ἐπεί σε λέοντα. οὕτως δὲ καὶ, ἐπεί σε μάλιστα πόνος φρένας. καί μοι δοκοῦσι τῷ πρώτῳ προσώπῳ ἀκολουθεῖν οἱ οὕτως ἀνεγνωκότες, πιθανῶς πάνυ· διὰ γὰρ τῆς φωνῆς τὸ πρῶτον πρόσωπον ἐπιδείκνυται τό τε ὀρθοτονούμενον, καὶ τὸ ἐγκλιτικόν. εἴ γε ἡ ἐμὲ αἰτιατικὴ, ὅτε φυλάσσει τὸ Ε ὀρθοτονεῖται, εἰ δὲ ἀποβάλοι, ἐγκλιτική ἐστιν. εὑρέθη τοίνυν μετὰ τοῦ ἐπεὶ συνδέσμου παρὰ τῷ Ποιητῇ, κατὰ ταύτην σύνταξιν ἀποβάλλουσα τὸ Ε, Ἕκτορ, ἐπεί με κατ' αἶσαν, ἐπεί μ' ἀφέλεσθέ γε δόντες. τούτῳ τοίνυν τῷ λόγῳ πιθανὸν ἂν εἴη κατακολουθήσαντας ἡμᾶς ἀναγινώσκειν ἐγκλιτικῶς, ἐπεί σε μάλιστα: Schol. Ven. K. 574.

953. NOTE 8.—Arc. 144. 5: καὶ αἱ μετὰ προθέσεως δὲ ἀεὶ ὀρθοτονοῦνται, διὰ σὲ, περὶ σοῦ, κατ' ἐμὲ, ἐπὶ σοί: Apoll. de Pron. 52 C: ὁμοίως αἱ προθέσεις παρατιθέμεναι ὀρθοτονοῦσι, κατ' ἐμέ, δι' ἐμέ, περὶ ἐμοῦ.　Διὸ καὶ τοῖς ἀξιοῦσιν ὀρθοτονεῖν τὸ

.... σὺν καὶ τρίτος ἄμιν Ἀμύντας

παρὰ Θεοκρίτῳ συγκαταθετέον. τὰ γὰρ ἐν ὑπερβατῷ κείμενα ὀφείλει τὸν λόγον ἀναδέχεσθαι τῆς κατὰ φύσιν ἀκολουθίας, εἴγε πάλιν τὸ καί μοι καί με ἐνεκλίναμεν, καθὸ οὐ συμπέπλεκται: Apoll. de Synt. 127. 7; Schol. Ven. A. 368: τοῦ σφίσι τὴν πρώτην ὀξυτονητέον, ἐπειδήπερ εἰς σύνθετον ἡ μετάληψις, εἰ καὶ οὐκέτι διηνεκὴς ὁ λόγος. ἔστι γάρ τινα ἐναντιούμενα, τοὺς δ' ἄναγον ζωοὺς σφίσιν ἐργάζεσθαι

ἀνάγκη, καὶ σφίσι δ' αὐτοῖς δαῖτα πένεσθαι. καὶ ὅτι μετὰ προθέσεως
ἐστιν· ὅταν γὰρ πρόθεσις ᾖ μετ' ἀντωνυμίας, ὀρθοτονεῖται ἡ ἀντωνυμία· σ ὺ ν σ ο ὶ δ ῖ α
θ ε ά, π ρ ο τ ὶ ο ἷ δ' ἔλαβον ἔντεα· κατὰ σφέας γὰρ μαχέοιντο· ἀπὸ ἕο κάββαλεν· ἀμφὶ ἓ
παπτήνας, τοῦ Ἄλτης ἐπὶ οἷ μεμαμὼς, ζήτησιν ἔχοντος: cf. Schol. Ven. Δ. 2 ; Χ.
474 ; Ψ. 698. 703 ; Λ. 413 ; Τ. 152 ; Charax, 1154: πολλοὶ δὲ τρόποι εἰσὶν ὀρθοτο-
νοῦντες καὶ προηγουμένης τῆς ὀφειλούσης δέξασθαι τὴν ἔγκλισιν, οἷον αἱ προθέσεις
ὀξύνονται, καὶ ὅμως αἱ μετὰ τούτων ἀντωνυμίαι ὀρθοτονοῦνται, περὶ ἐμοῦ, κατ' ἐμοῦ,
σὺν ἐμοί, ὑπὲρ ἐμοῦ. ὅθεν παρὰ Μενάνδρῳ σημειοῦνται τὸ πρός με ἐγκλιθέν. οἱ δὲ
ἐξηγηταὶ μετὰ τοῦ Ε προφέρονται αὐτό, πρὸς ἐμέ. αἱ μετὰ τῶν συμπλεκτικῶν καὶ δια-
ζευκτικῶν ὀρθοτονοῦνται. τὸ γὰρ ἦ μὲ ἀνάειρε [Π. 23. 724] τὸ Ε συνεκεράσθη μετὰ
τοῦ Η, ἢ ἐμέ—ἢ μέ [? ἢ 'μέ] καὶ τὴν ὀξεῖαν εἰς τὸ Ε φυλάττομεν. τὸ δὲ κ α ί μ ο ι
ὑ π ο σ τ ή τ ω [Π. 9. 160] ὑπέρβατόν ἐστι, καὶ ὑποστήτω μοι, ὡς δείκνυμεν ἐν τῇ ἀντωνυμίᾳ. καὶ εὐλόγως ὀρθοτονοῦνται, ἐπειδὴ ἀντιδιαστολὴν πάντως εἰσφέρουσιν αὗται αἱ
συντάξεις. καὶ μετὰ τοῦ οὕνεκα καὶ ἕνεκα ὀρθοτονοῦνται, ἕνεκα σοῦ, οὕνεκα σοῦ, ἕνεκεν
σοῦ· κακῶς γὰρ ἐγκλίνουσιν : Apoll. de Synt. 125. 22 : ἀνάπαλιν οὖν ὁ ἕνεκα σύνδεσμος, φερόμενος πάντοτε ἐπὶ γενικὴν, μόνως ὀρθοτονεῖ τὴν ἀντωνυμίαν, ἡνίκα τὰς
τούτων γενικὰς συνδεῖ, ε ἵ ν ε κ' ἐ μ ε ῖ ο κ υ ν ό ς τίς γὰρ ἂν θαρρήσειεν Ἑλλήνων ἐγ-
κλίνειν τὸ ἕνεκά μου ; καὶ δῆλον ὡς μόνως πάλιν ὀρθοτονοῦνται, καθὸ συνδεθεῖσαι πρός
τι πτωτικὸν τὸν λόγον ἀνέχουσι.

954. Note 9.—Hermann (de emend. rat. Gr. gr. p. 76) denies that the
purely enclitic forms of pronouns are ever governed by prepositions, and adds,
'etenim ubi illæ pronominum formæ subjunguntur, quæ necessario encliticæ sunt,
non reguntur a præpositionibus, nec si conjunctio præcedit, ad ipsas pertinet
consociatio· vel disjunctio, sed aliunde pendent, atque deponunt in præpositione
vel conjunctione accentum suum, ut *ὑπέρ μου πατρίδος.* Quod in Odyssea est, lib.
8. 488,

> ἢ σέγε Μοῦσ' ἐδίδαξε, Διὸς παῖς ἢ σέγ' Ἀπόλλων,

in eo σὲ non acuitur propter præcedens ἤ, sed quia adjuncto γέ nunquam enclitic-
cum est. Quod si σὲ sine γὲ dixisset, deposuisset accentum, quia ἤ non ad pronomen,
sed ad Musam et Apollinem refertur.'

955. Note 10.—Charax, 1153 : πάλιν αἱ ἔχουσαι ἐπιφορὰν τὴν ἐπιταγματικὴν
ὀρθοτονοῦνται, σὲ αὐτόν, σὲ δὲ αὐτὴν παντί, ἀλλὰ σὲ αὐτόν, εἰ μή που ποιητικῶς
ἐγκλιθῶσιν, ἀ λ λ ά ο ἱ α ὐ τ ῷ. οὐκ ὄφειλεν ἡ οἱ ἐγκλιθῆναι· ἔχει γὰρ τὴν ἐπιταγ-
ματικήν. τινὲς δέ φασι καὶ ἵνα μὴ νομισθῇ ἄρθρον· ὅπερ ψευδές· ἀντωνυμία γὰρ οὖσα
περισπᾶται, ἄρθρον δὲ ὂν ὀξύνεται· ὥστε ποιητικῶς ἐνεκλίθη : Arc. 144. 7 : αἱ μετὰ
τῆς ἐπιταγματικῆς ἀντωνυμίας τῆς α ὐ τ ὸ ς ἀεὶ ὀρθοτονοῦνται· αὐτὸν ἐμέ, αὐτῷ ἐμοί.
ὑπεξαιρείσθωσαν δὲ αἱ παρὰ τοῖς ποιηταῖς μετὰ τῆς ἐπιταγματικῆς παραλόγως ἐγκλινόμεναι. ἀ λ λ ά ο ἱ α ὐ τ ῷ Ζ ε ὺ ς ὀ λ έ σ ε ι ε β ί η ν, καὶ Ε ὐ ρ ύ α λ ο ς δ έ ἑ
α ὐ τ ό ν, καὶ εἴ τινες ἄλλαι μετὰ προθέσεων ἢ συνδέσμων ἐνεγκλίθησαν παραλόγως :
Apoll. de Synt. 137. 2 : ὀρθοτονοῦνται καὶ ὅσαι συντάσσονται τῇ αὐτός ἐπιταγ-
ματικῇ,

> ἦε τι Μυρμιδόνεσσι πιφάσκεαι ἢ ἐμοὶ αὐτῷ,
> σοὶ δ' αὐτῷ,
> οὐδὲ σεῦ αὐτῆς,
>   οὐδ' ἐμοὶ αὐτῷ
> θυμὸς ἐνὶ στήθεσσι σιδήρεος.

τά γε μὴν τοῦ τρίτου οὐκ ἐξωμάλισται, καθότι οὐδ' ἀληθὴς λόγος παρεδείχθη τὸ τὰς
κατὰ τὸ τρίτον πρόσωπον ὀρθοτονηθείσας πάντως μεταλαμβάνεσθαι εἰς συνθέτους.
ὡς γὰρ ἐστι ψευδὴς ὑπόληψις καὶ ὡς οὐκ ἐξωμαλίσθη καὶ ὡς οὐ τόνου ἐναλλαγὴ
αἰτία γίνεται συνθέτου μεταλήψεως, εἰρήσεται κατὰ τὸ ἑξῆς· ἐντεῦθεν οὖν ἐνεκλίθη τὸ

ἀλλά οἱ αὐτῷ

καὶ τὸ

Ζεὺς ὀλέσειε βίην πρὶν ἡμῖν πῆμα γενέσθαι,

Εὐρύαλος δέ ἑ αὐτὸν ἀρεσσάσθω ἐπέεσσιν,

ὠρθοτονήθη δὲ τὸ

ἀμφὶ ἓ παπτήνας·

ἄλογόν τε δοκεῖ τὸ οἷ τ᾽ αὐτῷ, διήκοντος τοῦ λόγου ἐπὶ ἀπάντων ὁμοίως. ἔσται μέντοι ἡ σύνταξις εἰς ἔμφασιν πλείονα διαστολῆς παραλαμβανομένη, ἐ μ ὲ α ὐ τ ὸ ν ἐ τ ί-μ η σ ε, σ ὲ α ὐ τ ὸ ν ἐ μ έ μ ψ α τ ο. ἐν προτάξει γοῦν ἀπάντοτέ εἰσιν αἱ ἀντωνυμίαι, καθὸ ἔχονται τοῦ ὀρθοῦ τόνου, ὥς γε ἐδείχθη κἀν τοῖς προκειμένοις. εἰ μέντοι τὰ τῆς συντάξεως ἀναστραφείη, οἷόν τέ ἐστι καὶ ἐγκλίνεσθαι τὴν ἀντωνυμίαν,

αὐτῷ τοι μετόπισθ᾽ ἄχος ἔσσεται,
αὐτόν σε φράζεσθαι ἄμ᾽ Ἀργείοισιν ἄνωγεν.

οὐ τοῦτο δέ φημι, ὡς οὐχ οἷόν τε καὶ ἐπὶ τῆς τοιαύτης συντάξεως ὀρθοτονεῖν, ἀλλ᾽ ὡς ἀφορμὴν ἔχει ἐγκλίσεως ἡ τοιαύτη σύνταξις,

αὐτόν με πρώτιστα συνοικιστῆρα γαίας
ἔς δέξαι τεμενοῦχον.

But for αὐτῷ τοι, Il. 9. 249, Dindorf reads αὐτῷ σοὶ, and for αὐτόν σε, Il. 9. 680, αὐτὸν σέ; cf. also Apoll. de Pron. 52 A sq.; 57 A; 79 A; 82 A; 147 C; de Synt. 143 sq.; Herod. π. ε. μ. 1145; Schol. Ven. A. 114; Δ. 534; E. 64; I. 392; Ψ. 387: from which passages it appears that, according to many grammarians, the pronoun of the third person, when not used in a reflexive sense, is enclitic, even though αὐτὸς is joined to it; but without entering upon matters of theory it would be impossible to discuss the correctness of their practice. This difference in their opinions however has left its traces in several passages in our books, e. g. ἦ ὀ λ ί γ ο ν ο ἷ π α ῖ δ α ἐ ο ι κ ό τ α γ ε ί ν α τ ο Τ υ δ ε ύ ς (Il. 5. 800), where Schol. Ven. says, τὴν δὲ ἀντωνυμίαν ὀρθοτονοῦσιν, ἐπεὶ εἰς σύνθετον μεταλαμβάνεται: and it is so accented in Apoll. de Pron. 52 B; 53 A: but ἦ ὀλίγον οἷ in Apoll. de Synt. 143. 28, and elsewhere. In the words π έ π λ ο ν ὅ ς ο ἱ δ ο κ έ ε ι χ α ρ ι έ σ τ α τ ο ς ἠ δ ὲ μ έ γ ι σ τ ο ς (Il. 6. 90; cf. 6. 271) the pronoun is enclitic according to Schol. Ven. ad loc., but it seems a doubtful case. The following are also disputed: Il. 9. 680: α ὐ τ ὸ ν σ ὲ φ ρ ά ζ ε σ θ α ι ἐ ν Ἀ ρ γ ε ί ο ι σ ι ν ἄ ν ω γ ε ν: Schol. Ven. ad loc.: ὁ Ἀσκαλωνίτης ὀρθοτονεῖ τὴν σέ, ἐπεί φησιν, ἀεὶ μετὰ τῆς ἐπιταγματικῆς αἱ πρωτότυποι φιλοῦσιν ὀρθοτονεῖσθαι. ἐχρῆν δὲ αὐτὸν ἐπὶ τοῦ πρώτου καὶ δευτέρου προσώπου ὁρίσασθαι, παραιτήσασθαι δέ τινα Ὁμηρικὰ ἄλλως ἀνεγνωσμένα δι᾽ αἰτίαν τινά. κ ε λ ε ύ ε τ έ μ᾽ α ὐ τ ὸ ν ἐ λ έ σ θ α ι. ε ἰ μ ή τ ι ς σ᾽ α ὐ τ ό ν. ἄλλως τε αἱ πρὸ τῆς αὐτός εἰσιν αἱ ὀρθοτονούμεναι, οὐχ αἱ μετὰ τὴν αὐτός. ἐγκλιτικῶς οὖν ἀναγνωστέον: Schol. Ven. K. 242: ε ἰ μ ὲ ν δ ὴ ἕ τ α ρ ό ν γ ε κ ε λ ε ύ ε τ έ μ᾽ α ὐ τ ὸ ν ἐ λ έ σ θ α ι. Ἀλεξίων τὸ Ε τῇ ἀντωνυμίᾳ δίδωσιν οὐ τῷ ῥήματι τελικόν [i. e. he read κελεύετ᾽ ἔμ᾽ αὐτὸν] καὶ δοκεῖ ὀρθοτονεῖν, ὡς εἰ καὶ συνθέτως ἐλέγετο ἐμαυτόν· καὶ τοῦτό γε ἐχρῆν εἶναι· ἀεὶ γὰρ αἱ τοῦ πρώτου προσώπου ἀντωνυμίαι προτασσόμεναι τῆς αὐτός, ὀρθοτονοῦνται. ὁ μέντοι Ἀσκαλωνίτης καὶ Ἀρίσταρχος ἐγκλιτικῶς ἀνεγνώκασιν, ἐπὶ τὴν ΤΕ συλλαβὴν ποιοῦντες τὴν ὀξεῖαν, ἵνα μὴ ὡς ἀκατάλληλον φανῇ τὸ ἐμαυτὸν ἐλέσθαι: Schol. Ven. O. 226: ἀ λ λ ὰ τ ό δ᾽ ἦ μ ὲ ν ἐ μ ο ὶ π ο λ ὺ κ έ ρ δ ι ο ν ἠ δ ὲ ο ἷ α ὐ τ ῷ. ὁ Ἀσκαλωνίτης ἀξιοῖ ἐγκλιτικῶς ἀναγινώσκειν, ἐπεὶ ἀπὸ προσώπου ἐπὶ πρόσωπον ἡ ἀναφορά, καὶ εἰς ἁπλῆ ἡ μετάληψις· ἀντὶ γὰρ τῆς αὐτῷ δισυλλάβου. ἄμεινον δὲ πείθεσθαι τοῖς περισπῶσι, διὰ τὸ ἤδη διαστολὴν γεγηνῆσθαι διὰ τῆς ἐμοί· τὸ γὰρ ἑξῆς τοιοῦτόν ἐστιν, ἐμοὶ καὶ αὐτῷ ἔπλετο, ὥστε ἀπὸ κοινοῦ λαμβάνεσθαι τὸ ἔπλετο ῥῆμα· ὁμοίως δὲ καὶ ἐπ᾽ ἐκείνου κατ᾽ ὀρθὸν τόνον ἀνέγνωμεν τὴν οἷ· Μέντορ, μή σ᾽ ἐπέεσσι παραπεπίθησιν Ὀδυσσεὺς μνηστήρεσσι μάχεσθαι, ἀμυ-νέμεναι δέ οἱ αὐτῷ· καὶ τὸ ἑξῆς ἐστι τοιοῦτον· μὴ πεισάτω σε Ὀδυσσεὺς ἡμῖν μάχεσθαι, αὐτῷ δὲ ἀμύνειν. καὶ καθόλου ἡ οἱ ὁπότε προηγεῖται τῆς αὐτὸς ἀντωνυμίας κατὰ δοτικὴν πτῶσιν ὀρθοτονεῖσθαι θέλει, εἴτε εἰς ἁπλῆν εἴη ἡ μετάληψις, εἴτε καὶ εἰς σύνθετον· διὸ μεμπτέον ἐκείνην τὴν ἀνάγνωσιν, ἀλλὰ οἱ αὐτῷ Ζεὺς ὀλέσσῃ· ἐχρῆν γὰρ διὰ τὴν ἐπιφερομένην ἀντιδιαστολὴν κατ' ὀρθὸν τόνον ἀναγινώσκεσθαι. Passages of this kind might easily be multiplied, but enough have been quoted to show that there is ample warrant for the rule which has been given above.

956. NOTE II.—According to the grammarians the pronouns of the first and second person are enclitic in the oblique cases of the plural when they are not emphatic, and when enclitic they take the accent on their first syllable, as ἔδωκεν ἡμῖν, ἥρπασεν ἥμων: Arc. 139. 15: ἰστέον δέ, ὅτι, ἡνίκα ἔστι λέξις τετράχρονος, οὐκ ἀναπέμπει τῇ προηγουμένῃ λέξει τὸν τόνον, ἀλλὰ τῇ προηγουμένῃ συλλαβῇ· ἄνθρωπος ἥμων, ἔτυψας ἥμας. ἐπειδὴ οὐδέποτε πρὸ τεσσάρων χρόνων τόνος πίπτει: Arc. 143. 11: καὶ τὰ πληθυντικὰ τοῦ τε πρώτου προσώπου καὶ δευτέρου· ἡμῶν ὑμῶν ἡμῖν ὑμῖν ἡμᾶς ὑμᾶς τετράχρονοι οὖσαι, ἐπειδὰν ἐγκλίνωνται τὴν πρώτην συλλαβὴν ὀξύνουσιν· ἤκουσεν ἥμων, ἔδωκεν ἥμιν καὶ ἐπὶ τῶν λοιπῶν ὁμοίως: Arc. 145. 7; Schol. Ven. O. 494: ἀλλὰ μάχεσθ' ἐπὶ νηυσὶν ἀολλέες· ὃς δέ κεν ὕμεως. ἡ ὕμεων ἀντωνυμία ἀπόλυτός ἐστι, καὶ οὐκ ἔχουσα ἀντιδιαστολήν· διὸ τρίτην ἀπὸ τέλους ἔχει τὴν ὀξεῖαν: Schol. Ven. A. 147: ὄφρ' ἥμιν ἐκάεργον ἱλάσσεαι ἱερὰ ῥέξας. ἥμιν ἀντὶ τοῦ ἡμῖν ἀντωνυμίας. ἔστι γὰρ διαλέκτου ἴδιον Δωριέων. αἱ δὲ ἀντωνυμίαι ἡνίκα ὁρισμὸν δηλοῦσι, μένουσιν ἐν τῷ αὐτῷ τόνῳ, οἷον ἡμῖν τόδ' ἔφηνε, καὶ ὑμῖν μὲν νεμεσσῶμαι περὶ κῆρι. ὅτε δὲ ἀπόλυτον ἔχουσι τὸ σημαινόμενον ἐγκλίνονται· εἰ δ' ὕμιν δοκέει τόδε λώτερον· σὺν δ' ἥμιν δαῖτα ταράξῃ. καὶ ὡς ἐνταῦθα: cf. Schol. Ven. A. 214. 579; Γ. 160; Eust. 1112. 34: ἰστέον δὲ καὶ ὡς τὸ οὐ μὰν ἥμιν ἔϋκλεές, δακτυλικῶς ποδιζόμενον μετὰ τὸ οὐ μάν, γράφουσι μέν τινες, οὐ μὰν ἡμῖν εὐκλεές. ἀρέσκει δὲ τοῖς παλαιοῖς ἡ πρώτη γραφή, παρ' οἷς κεῖται ταῦτα· τὸ ἡμῖν ἄμμι λέγουσιν οἱ Αἰολεῖς, βαρύνοντες αὐτὸ καὶ συστέλλοντες τὴν λήγουσαν, Ἀπολλώνιος ἄμμι γεμὴν, νόος ἔνδον ἀτύζεται. Δωριεῖς δὲ ἀμὶν συστέλλοντες τὸ Ι καὶ ὀξύνοντες. Θεόκριτος· πολλαὶ δ' ἀμὶν ὕπερθε κατὰ κρατὸς δονέοντο. Ἴωνες δέ, πολλάκις δὲ καὶ Ἀθηναῖοι προπερισπῶσιν ἐν συστολῇ τοῦ Ι. Ὅμηρος· ὦ φίλοι, οὐ μὰν ἥμιν ἔϋκλεὲς ἀπονέεσθαι. Σοφοκλῆς Οἰδίποδι· ὅπως λύσιν τιν' ἥμιν εὐαγῆ πόροις. Φρύνιχος Μύστῃ· ἐβουλόμην ἂν ἥμιν ὥσπερ καὶ προτοῦ. Ἀττικὰ δὲ παραδείγματα ταῦτα τὰ δύο. οἱ δ' αὐτοὶ παλαιοὶ φασὶ καὶ ὅτι τὸ ἡμεῖς ἅμες λέγουσιν οἱ Δωριεῖς, ἅμμες δὲ οἱ Αἰολεῖς. χρῆσις δὲ τοῦ ῥηθέντος ἥμιν καὶ ἐν Ὀδυσσείᾳ: Eust. 1611. 3; 1670. 4; 1690. 13; Apoll. de Pron. 123 A: ἡμῖν Ἴωνες ᾗ καὶ Ἀττικοί. τὸ ἐγκλινόμενον παρ' Ἴωσι συστέλλει τὸ Ι. σημειῶδες καθὸ αἱ ἐγκλινόμεναι τὸν αὐτὸν χρόνον φυλάττουσι ταῖς ὀρθοτονουμέναις. ἡ ἀμὶν Δωρικὴ ἐγκλινομένη συστέλλει τὸ Ι, ἐν οἷς προπερισπᾶται,

αἱ γὰρ ἀμὶν τούτων μέλοι·

ὀξύνομέν τε

ἀμὶν δ' ὑπαυλήσει μέλος,

Ἀλκμάν· οἰκεῖος ὁ χρόνος πληθυντικῇ διὰ τοῦ Ι ἐκφερομένη: Apoll. de Pron. 124 B: ὑμῖν, πάλιν παρ' Ἴωσι προπερισπᾶται ἐγκλινομένη, καθὸ συστέλλει τὸ Ι. καὶ ἔτι παρὰ Δωριεῦσιν. ὅσαις ὕμιν αἰνέσω, Σώφρων. καὶ ἐν ὀρθῇ τάσει· οὐ μάν τοι δίφρον ἐπημμένον ὑμῖν: Apoll. de Pron. 127 A: τὸ μηδ' ἡμας ὑπεκφύγοι Ἰώνων ἔθει φασὶ συνεστάλθαι κατὰ τὴν ἀπόλυτον σημασίαν: cf. Apoll. de Pron. 79 A; Apoll. de Synt. 135. 22; 166. 11; Charax, 1150: according to a rule given below, § 968, ἥμων ἥμιν and the like cannot stand after a paroxytone or perispomenon: see Hermann de emend. rat. Gr. gr. p. 78 sq., and Kühner, G. G. I. 264, who assent to the doctrine of the older writers; W. Dindorf however (Præf. ad Hom. Iliad. 8vo. Oxon. 1856. p. 21) rejects what he calls the 'inanis subtilitas grammaticorum,' and in Homer makes all such pronouns orthotone, writing ἡμῖν ὑμῖν, where a trochee is required: his practice is certainly convenient; but if we are to reject all that is, or all that seems to be, absurd, in the grammarians, it is to be feared that very little will be left : as they testify, however, in this instance to a fact of which they must have been cognizant, it is difficult to see upon what principle we can refuse to believe them.

957. NOTE 12.—On the enclitic accusative αὐτόν in Hom. Il. 12. 204, κόψε γάρ αὐτον ἔχοντα, see Charax, 1153 ; Apoll. de Pron. 41 C ; Herodian ap. Schol. Ven. M. 204 ; Hermann de emend. rat. Gr. gr. p. 82 : Trypho sensibly wrote the passage κόψε γὰρ αὐτόν, Apoll. de Pron. 77 C.

958. NOTE 13.—On the enclitic indefinite particles πού, ποτέ, ποθί, πή, ποθέν, πώς, πώ, see Arc. 144. 18 ; Schol. Ven. B. 565 ; Γ. 400 ; T. 464 ; Herod. π. ε. μ. 1147 ; Charax, 1154 ; Joh. Alex. 31. 2 : the form πῶποτε mentioned by Arc. 146. 9 is strange, and perhaps corrupt : as an indefinite it is πώποτε in Attic, Apoll. de Pron. 48 B : καὶ καθὸ ἀδύνατον ἐγκλιτικὸν συντεθῆναι, διὸ καὶ παρὰ Ἀττικοῖς τὸ πώποτε ἐσημειοῦτο : Joh. Alex. 31. 6 : ἐκ δὲ τοῦ πω καὶ τοῦ μάλα τὸ πώμαλα προπαροξύνουσιν Ἀθηναῖοι, καὶ ἔτι τὸ πώποτε ἐκ τοῦ πω καὶ τοῦ πότε : cf. A. G. Paris. 3. 186. 6 ; Lob. Path. 2. 296.

959. Ποτέ rarely begins a clause or sentence, but when it does it is oxytone ; in Demosth. 959, Dindorf prints ποτ᾽ εἶχεν ἀγρὸν, εἶτα γε νῦν πολλοί ; others write πότ᾽ εἶχεν. In such expressions as ποτὲ μὲν . . . ποτὲ δὲ, ποτὲ μὲν . . . αὖτις δὲ, and the like, ποτέ is orthotone in our books, as πότερον ἀληθῆ φῶμεν ἀεὶ τοὺς ἀνθρώπους δοξάζειν, ἢ ποτὲ μὲν ἀληθῆ, ποτὲ δὲ ψευδῆ ; Plat. Theaet. 170 C.

960. NOTE 1.—On the particles τέ, κέ, see Arc. 144. 28 ; Herod. π. ε. μ. 1147 ; Schol. Ven. B. 223 : γέ, Arc. 144. 28 ; 139. 14 ; Herod. π. ε. μ. 1147 ; Schol. Ven. Ξ. 396 : οὔτε πυρὸς τόσσος γε πέλει βρόμος αἰθομένοιο. Ἀρίσταρχος φυλάσσει τὴν ὀξεῖαν ἐπὶ τῆς ΤΟΣ συλλαβῆς· ὁ δὲ Τυραννίων, τοσσός γε ἀνέγνω, τὴν ΣΟΣ συλλαβὴν ὀξύνων, οὐκ εὖ. ὁ γὰρ ΓΕ οὐκ ἀλλάσσει τὸν τόνον τῶν πρὸ ἑαυτοῦ λέξεων. εἰ δέ τις λέγοι ἐπέκτασιν εἶναι μὴ σύνδεσμον, ἴστω ὅτι τὸ ἐναντίον χωρήσει· ἡ γὰρ διὰ τοῦ ΓΕ ἐπέκτασις τρίτην ἀπὸ τέλους ἐποίει τὴν ὀξεῖαν ἔγωγε, ἔμοιγε : perhaps Tyrannion wrote τόσσός γε in accordance with the rule mentioned below, § 964 : νύν, νύ, Herod. π. ε. μ. 1147 ; Schol. Ven. A. 421 ; Φ. 428 ; Arc. 139. 13 ; Apoll. de Conj. 525. 19 : it must be distinguished from the temporal adverb νῦν, see above, § 826 : περ, Arc. 139. 13 ; Schol. Ven. Θ. 125 : θήν, Apoll. de Conj. 525. 19 is printed θῆν in Herod. π. ε. μ. 1148 ; Charax, 1155 : ῥά, Herod. π. ε. μ. 1148 : Apoll. de Conj. 525. 19 ; Schol. Ven. Λ. 249 ; τοί, Arc. 139. 13 ; Charax, 1155.

961. NOTE 2.—Besides these, some consider the particle τάρ to be an enclitic, Schol. Ven. A. 93 : οὔταρ. οὔτως ὀξεῖαν ἐπὶ τοῦ ΟΥ· ὁ γὰρ τάρ ἐστι σύνδεσμος ἐπιφερόμενος ἐγκλιτικῶς, ὡς καὶ ἐπὶ τοῦ εἴ ταρ ὅ γ᾽ εὐχωλῆς. οὐ γάρ ἐστιν ὅ τε συμπλεκτικός· εἰ γὰρ ἦν, ἐπεφέρετο ἂν πάλιν ὁ τέ μετὰ ἀποφάσεως : Schol. Ven. A. 65 ; Apoll. de Conj. 522. 4 ; Herod. π. ε. μ. 1147 ; Joh. Alex. 23. 36, and H. D. s. v.

962. NOTE 3.—The following assertion is made by a grammarian in A. G. 1156 : σύνδεσμοι δὲ ἐγκλίνονται μέν δέ τέ γάρ, οἷον ἐγώ μεν, σύ δε, αὐτός τε, ἀλλοί γαρ καὶ τὰ τοιαῦτα : but I know of no other passage in which anything of the kind is said ; that it had a foundation in fact is certain : 'δὲ saepe est encliticum in libris scriptis et edd. vetustis, velut Tzetz. Hist. 3. 308 : οὐ συναφῆς λοιπόν δε τῇ Ἑλένῃ : 6. 687 : Ῥᾷδε καὶ πόνου δίχα δέ· scr. ῥᾳ δέ : 16. 712 sec. cod. : τινὲς λωτόν δε λέγουσι: MS. ap. Lambec. Bibl. Caes. l. 8. vol. 8. p. 232 A; 234 B: Ὧσδε: Chœrobosc. Aldi Hort. fol. 229 verso: Σύνδεσμοι δὲ ἐγκλίνονται μὲν δὲ τὲ γάρ, οἷον ἐγώ μεν, σύ δε . . .' H. D. 2. p. 929 D; that some of the grammarians considered δή as an enclitic, is clear from Eust. 143. 26: οὐκ ἄδηλον δὲ ὅτι τὸ ἦ δὴ λοίγια, τινὲς μὲν ἤδη ἔγραψαν παροξυτόνως, ὡς καὶ προεδηλώθη. τινὲς δὲ τὸ μὲν ἦ ἀντὶ τοῦ ὄντως φασί, τὸ δὲ δή, ἄνευ τόνου προφέρουσιν ὁμοίως τῷ ἐπιδητούτοις: this combination we should now-a-days write ἐπὶ δὴ τούτοις: there is also evidence that μέν in some circumstances at least was an enclitic; ' εἰ γέμεν εἰδείης, e textu Pal. [i. e. the Heidelberg MS. of the 14th century, catalogue of Wilkenius, p. 277]: hoc lemma sumo: simulque observo hanc sollemnem esse in codd. (etiam Arati) scripturam formulæ γὲ μέν quoties vicem gerit particulæ δέ:' Buttmann ad Schol. Hom. Od. E. 206. p. 193: in the Oxford reprint, edited by Dindorf, the whole point of this note is lost by printing εἴ γε μέν; all these peculiarities of the grammarians are neglected by modern scholars, to the great comfort of those who accent their Greek.

Some are also of opinion that οὖν in οὔκουν, γοῦν in ἤγουν, and μάλα in πώμαλα are in some sense enclitics: Apoll. de Conj. 526. 17: δισσὸς οὖν ἐστὶν ὁ οὖν, περισπωμένως μὲν ἐν συλλογιστικῇ ἐκφορᾷ, ὀξυνόμενος δὲ ὅτε ἐστὶ παραπληρωματικός, καὶ δῆλον ὅτι καὶ τῶν ἐγκλιτικῶν, ἵνα καὶ ὁ τόνος τῆς ἀποφάσεως: on the Attic πώμαλα see Joh. Alex. 31. 6, quoted above, § 958.

963. NOTE 4.—One peculiarity in Æolic deserves mention: 'memorabili grammaticorum de dialectis testimonio[1] doceri videtur, eo extensam esse accentus apud Æoles retractionem, ut etiam articulus, cum aliis quibusdam vocibus junctus, harum quasi encliticarum accentum in se reciperet, cujus rei exempla tradunt ὅ σος, τό σον pro ὁ σός, τὸ σόν: accuratiora nunc non licet explorare:' Ahrens de Græcæ ling. dialect. 1. p. 18.

964. Enclitics affect the accent of the word which immediately precedes them in a sentence, according to the following rules:—

An oxytone word followed by an enclitic remains oxytone, the enclitic losing its accent, as ἀγαθός ἐστι, not ἀγαθὸς ἐστι,—αὐτός μοι,—καί σφεας φωνήσας,—πὰρ δέ οἱ ἐστήκει,—ἀπὸ κρατός τε καὶ ὤμων. The so-called proclitics become oxytone, as ὡς φάσαν οἵ μιν ἴδοντο,—ἀλλ' ἔκ τοι ἐρέω.

NOTE—Arc. 140. 3; 145. 7; 146. 6; Charax, 1149. 1151. 1157; Aristarchus and Herodian ap. S. V. B. 330.

965. After a paroxytone word a *monosyllabic* enclitic loses its accent, the paroxytone remains unaltered, as οὕτω που Διὶ μέλλει ὑπερμενέϊ φίλον εἶναι: ἤδη τις εἶπεν: φίλος τις.

According to the older writers, 1. a paroxytone word with a

---

[1] J. Gr. 244 a; Greg. C. 616; Meerm. 662: βαρυτονοῦσι δὲ οὐ μόνον τὰ ὀνόματα, ἀλλὰ καὶ τὰ ἄρθρα, ὅταν ὀνομάτων τάξιν ἐπέχῃ, ὁ σὸς ὅ σος, ἡ σὴ ἥ ση, τὸ σὸν τό σον, quibus J. Gr. addit τῆς σῆς τῆς σης: num forte eodem spectat Apoll. de Synt. 51. 26, ὦ non esse vocativum articuli docens: τί δέ, εἰ περισπᾶται, οὐκ ἐνεκλίθη κατὰ τὰς Αἰολικὰς ἀναγνώσεις ὑπ' Ἀριστάρχου, καθὸ καὶ τὰ ἄλλα τῶν περισπωμένων ἄρθρων?

trochaic ending, when followed by an enclitic, takes the acute on its last syllable, as λάμπέ τε: φύλλά τε καὶ φλοιόν: ὅττί μιν: ἄλλός τις: τυφθέντά τε: 2. a paroxytone word of any form takes the acute on its last syllable when followed by an enclitic pronoun beginning with the letters σφ, as ἔνθά σφεας: ἵνά σφισι δῶκ' Ἐνοσίχθων: πολλάκίς σφεας: τόξά σφεων. Modern editors, however, seem to pay no attention to these directions, for they uniformly write λάμπε τε, φύλλα τε, and so on.

966. Note 1.—Arc. 141. 3; 145. 11; Herod. π. ε. μ. 1143: ἐπὶ δὲ τῶν παροξυτόνων (sc. ἀναπέμπει ἐγκλιτικὸν τὴν ὀξεῖαν ἐπὶ τὴν ὑπερκειμένην βαρεῖαν ἐν τῇ συντάξει) μόνων τῶν τροχαίων, λ ά μ π ε τ ε, φ ύ λ λ ά τ ε κ α ὶ φ λ ο ι ό ν. οὐδέποτε δὲ τοῦτο ἐν σπονδείῳ παρακολουθεῖ, ὡς δὴ ἐπὶ τοῦ Ἀ τ ρ ε ί δ η ς τ ε ἄ ν α ξ ἀ ν δ ρ ῶ ν, Φ ο ί β ῳ θ' ἱ ε ρ ὴ ν ἑ κ α τ ό μ β η ν. ἀ λ λ' ο ὐ δ ὲ ἐ ν ἰ ά μ β ῳ, π ά ρ ο ς γ ε μ ὲ ν ο ὔ τ ι θ α μ ί ζ ε ι ς. ἀ λ λ' ο ὐ δ ὲ ἐ ν τ ῷ π υ ρ ρ ι χ ί ῳ, ὅ τ ι ο ἱ σ υ μ φ ρ ά σ σ α τ ο β ο υ λ ά ς. ἐ ὰ ν δ έ π ο τ ε τ ρ ο χ α ῖ ο ς γ έ ν η τ α ι διπλασιασθέντος τοῦ Τ, ἔσονται ἐπάλληλοι ὀξεῖαι, οἷον ὅ τ τ ί μ ι ν ὡ ς ὑ π έ δ ε κ τ ο. πλὴν εἰ μὴ τὸ ἐπιφερόμενον μόριον δισύλλαβον εἴη ἀπὸ τοῦ Σ Φ ἀρχόμενον· ἀκολουθήσει γὰρ τοῖς παροξυνομένοις οὐκ ἐν μόνῳ τροχαίῳ, ἀλλὰ καὶ ἐν ἄλλοις ποσίν, οἷον ἵ ν ά σ φ ι ν δ ῶ κ' Ἐ ν ο σ ί χ θ ω ν, ἔ ν θ ά σ φ ε α ς ἐ κ ί χ α ν ε ν υ ἱ ὸ ς Δ ο λ ί ο ι ο Μ ε λ α ν θ ε ύ ς, τ ό ξ ά σ φ ε ώ ν τ ι ς ἄ ρ ι σ τ α Κ υ δ ω ν ί ῳ. Arc. 139. 29; 146. 4; Schol. Ven. H. 199; Charax, 1149: ἐν μιᾷ λέξει κατὰ συνέχειαν δύο ὀξείας οἱ παλαιοὶ οὐκ ἐτίθουν· κακοφωνίαν γὰρ ποιοῦσι ... ὅθεν μέμφονται οἱ ἀκριβεῖς τὸν θέσει τροχαϊκὸν ἔχοντα δύο ὀξείας ἐφεξῆς, ἄλλός τις· καὶ εὐλόγως εἰς τὴν ἀρχὴν τῆς Ὀδυσσείας ὁ Ἀρίσταρχος οὐκ ἐβουλήθη δοῦναι εἰς τὸ ἄ ν δ ρ α μ ο ι δύο ὀξείας, ἀλλὰ μίαν εἰς τὸ ΑΝ, φάσκων ἐ ν ἀ ρ χ ῇ π ο ι ή σ ε ω ς π α ρ ά λ ο γ ο ν ο ὐ μ ὴ π ο ι ή σ ω: Charax, 1157.

967. Note 2.—S. V. B. 255: ὅτι οἱ μ ά λ α π ο λ λ ά· τοῦτο οἱ ἐν μιᾷ ὀξείᾳ προενεκτέον ὀξείᾳ. πᾶσα γὰρ δίβραχυς λέξις πρὸ ἐγκλιτικοῦ, οὐκ ἐπιδέχεται ἐπάλληλον ὀξεῖαν, εἰ μὴ ἀντωνυμία ἐπιφέροιτο διὰ τοῦ ΣΦ, σεσημειωμένου τοῦ, ἐ ν θ' ἔ σ ά ν ο ἱ π έ π λ ο ι. Arc. 140. 24; 141. 2; 145. 19; Charax, 1157; Herod. π. ε. μ. 1143; Schol. Ven. Z. 367: ο ὐ γ ά ρ τ' ο ἶ δ' ε ἰ ἔ τ ι σ φ ι ν ὑ π ό τ ρ ο π ο ς ἵ ξ ο μ α ι α ὖ θ ι ς· οὕτως εἰ ἔτι σφιν εἷς τόνος, καίτοι ἐχρῆν δύο, διὰ τὸ ἐπιφέρεσθαι ἀντωνυμίαν ἀπὸ τοῦ ΣΦ ἀρχομένην, ὁμοίως τῷ ὅ θ ι σ φ ι σ ι π έ φ ρ α δ' Ἀ χ ι λ λ ε ύ ς, ἦ ρ χ ε δ' ἄ ρ α σ φ ι ν ἄ ν α ξ ἀ ν δ ρ ῶ ν Ἀ γ α μ έ μ ν ω ν. σεσημείωται οὖν αὕτη ἡ ἀνάγνωσις μόνη ὡς ἐν ἄλλοις ὁ Ἡρωδιανὸς λέγει: Charax, 1154: ὀλίγαι δὲ παρέβησαν τὸν λόγον, οἷον τὸ ἔσαν,

ἐ ν θ' ἔ σ ά ν ο ἱ π έ π λ ο ι.

καὶ πάλιν ἐνταῦθα, ἵνα μὴ νομισθῇ τὸ οἱ ἄρθρον, ὅπερ ἄκαιρον· ὡς εἴπομεν γάρ, ὁ τόνος διέστειλε. καὶ πάλιν

ἵ ν ά σ φ ι σ ι ν ἀ γ ο ρ ή τ ε θ έ μ ι ς τ ε.

καὶ πάλιν

ὅ τ έ σ φ ε α ς ε ἰ σ α φ ί κ η τ α ι,
ἦ ρ χ ε δ' ἄ ρ ά σ φ ι ν.

αὗται παραλόγως ἐνεκλίθησαν, μὴ προηγουμένων ἢ ὀξυτόνων ἢ τροχαϊκῶν. καὶ παρὰ Καλλιμάχῳ τόξού σφεών τις ἄριστα Κυδωνίου· σπονδεῖος γὰρ βαρύτονος προηγεῖται· παραλόγως οὖν ἐπὶ τούτων ἐπεκράτησεν ἡ ἔγκλισις.

968. Note 3.—The grammarians note that these rules are not invariably observed under all circumstances, e. g. ἔλπομαι ἐν Σαλαμῖνι γενέσθαι τε τραφέμεν τε, Hom. Il. 7. 199, was written γενέσθαί τε: Schol. Ven. H. 199: ἀλλεπάλληλοι ὀξεῖαι, κ α ί τ ο ι σ π ο ν δ ε ι α κ ό ν ἐ σ τ ι ν, ἀ λ λ' ἴσως ἵ ν α ἐ κ φ ύ γ ω μ ε ν τὸν διπλασιασμὸν τοῦ ῥήματος, λέγω

δὲ τοῦ τετραφέμεν τε, ὡς καὶ ἐν τῇ Τ τῆς Ὀδυσσείας (320) παραλόγως ἐνέ-
κλίναμεν ἐν τῷ ἠῶθεν δὲ μάλ' ἦρι λοέσσαί τε χρῖσαί τε. The passage ἔνθ' ἔσάν
οἱ πέπλοι, Il. 6. 289, is noted as a remarkable deviation from rule by Schol. Ven.
ad loc., Arc. 145. 16; Charax, 1154. 1157. In modern editions it is printed
ἔσαν οἱ.

969. A dissyllabic enclitic after a paroxytone word is oxytone,
as Ἀτρείδης ἐστί: πολλάκις εἰσί: οὔπω ποτέ: ἤδη φαμέν: φίλοι
εἰσίν: but τινοιν or τινων is perispomenon, ἀνθρώπων τινῶν, ἀν-
θρώποιν τινοῖν.

NOTE.—Arc. 134. 15; 140. 22; 145. 23; 147. 13.

970. A proparoxytone word followed by an enclitic receives
the acute on its last syllable, as ἄγγελός εἰμι: ἤκουσέ μου: ἄνθρω-
ποί εἰσι: κάκιστοί εἰσιν: ἐλάλησέ τις.

NOTE.—Herod. π. ε. μ. 1143; Arc. 145. 23; Schol. Ven. B. 26; Charax, 1157.

971. A properispomenon followed by an enclitic receives the
acute on its last syllable, as οἶκός τε: Σκῶλόν τε Κνημόν τε: ταυτά
με, but dissyllabic enclitics after properispomena ending in ξ or
ψ are oxytone, as φοῖνιξ ἐστίν: κῆρυξ ἐστίν.

NOTE.—Arc. 146. 2; 140. 1; Herod. π. ε. μ. 1149; Schol. Ven. B. 28; Π. 207.
When followed by a monosyllabic enclitic, such words as φοῖνιξ κῆρυξ probably
remain unaffected, as φοῖνιξ τε, κῆρυξ τε, not φοῖνίξ τε, though I find no clear
direction in the grammarians to that effect.

972. After a perispomenon enclitics lose their accent, as ἦσ-
τινος: ὦντινων: φῶς ἐστι: Ἑρμῆς ἐστι.

NOTE.—Apoll. de Pron. 54 A; Herod. π. ε. μ. 1143; Charax, 1150: ἄλλοι δέ
τινες συγχέουσιν, ὡς καὶ Ῥωμανὸς λέγων, εἰ περισπωμένη προηγεῖται, οὐ παρέχουσι τὸν
τόνον αὐτῇ, οἷον καλοῦ μοῦ· εἰ δὲ ἄλλος τόνος εἴη, παρέχουσι τὸν τόνον, οἷον πόθεν τις,
ὅθεν με. ψευδὲς δὲ λίαν ἐστίν: Charax, 1157. Hermann, de emend. rat. Gr. Gr.
p. 71, contends that φῶς μοῦ, οἷον τινῶν are alone correct. They may be so, but
our only authorities, the native grammarians, say that they are not.

973. When several enclitics follow each other they are all
oxytone except the last, which is unaccented, as ἤ νύ σέ που
δέος ἴσχει: εἴ πέρ τίς σέ μοί φησί ποτε.

974. NOTE I.—Apoll. de Conj. 517. 5: πάμπολλοι δέ εἰσιν οἱ παραπληρωματικοὶ
ἐν ἐγκλίσει, ὡς ὁ γέ, ὁ ῥά, ὁ θήν, ὁ νύ. δύο λέξεων ἢ τριῶν οὐσῶν ἀκώλυτον τὸ
ἐπάλληλον τῆς ὀξείας· καὶ κατὰ τοῦτο οὖν λέξεις τὰ προκείμενα μόρια· ἰδοὺ γὰρ
ἐν τῷ

ἤ νύ σέ που δέος ἴσχει

κάθ' ἐν ἕκαστον μέρος λόγου ἡ ὀξεῖα ἀνέστη: Herod. π. ε. μ. 1142: συνεγκλιτικὸν
δέ ἐστι σύνταξις δυοῖν ἢ πλειόνων μορίων ἐγκλιτικῶν ἐπαλλήλων ὀξυνομένων, ὡς ἔχει
τὰ τοιαῦτα

ἤ νύ σέ που δέος ἴσχει

ὁ μὲν γὰρ ἢ ὀξύνεται διὰ τὸ νύ ἐγκλιτικόν, τὸ δὲ νύ διὰ τὴν ἀντωνυμίαν τὴν σέ, ἡ

δὲ σέ ἀντωνυμία διὰ τὸν τοῦ παραπληρωματικὸν σύνδεσμον. εἴρηται δὲ συνεγκλιτικὸν
διὰ τὸ σὺν ἐγκλιτικῷ παραλαμβανόμενον διεγείρειν τὴν ὑπερκειμένην ἐν τῷ τέλει
τῆς λέξεως ὀξεῖαν: Charax, 1157: ἐὰν οὖν πλείονα συμβῇ ἐφεξῆς ἐγκλιτικὰ εἶναι
πολλαὶ ἔσονται καὶ αἱ ὀξεῖαι, ἤ νύ σέ που δέος ἴσχει ἀκήρων· τρεῖς εἰσὶν ἐφεξῆς αἱ
ὀξεῖαι. δύνατον δὲ καὶ πλείονας ἐπινοῆσαι, εἴ πέρ τίς σέ μοί φησί ποτε· τὸ μὲν γὰρ
εἰ ὀξύνεται διὰ τὴν ἐπιφορὰν τοῦ ἐγκλιτικοῦ πέρ, τὸ δὲ πέρ διὰ τὸ τίς, τὸ δὲ τίς διὰ
τὸ σέ, τὸ δὲ σέ διὰ τὸ μοί, τὸ δὲ μοί διὰ τὸ φησί, τὸ δὲ φησί διὰ τὸ ποτέ, ὥστε
ἐφεξῆς ὀξεῖαι ἕξ καὶ σπάνιον διὰ τὴν τοῦ πνεύματος συνέχειαν. These same words,
with one or two unimportant variations, are also found in Arc. 146. 10; Schol.
Ven. E. 812: ἤ νύ σε· ὁ ἤ ὀξύνεται· διαζευκτικὸς γάρ· φυλάσσεται δὲ ἡ ὀξεῖα διὰ
τὸ ἐπιφερόμενον νύ ἐγκλιτικόν, ὁ καὶ αὐτὸ ἔσχεν ὀξεῖαν διὰ τὴν σέ ἐγκλιτικὴν οὖσαν:
Schol. Ven. N. 15: ἔνθ᾽ ἄρ᾽ ὅγ᾽. τρεῖς παράλληλοι ὀξεῖαι, μία μὲν ἡ ἄρχουσα, δευτέρα
ἡ τοῦ ἄρα, τρίτη δὲ ἡ τοῦ ὅγε: Schol. Ven. Υ. 464: ἡ εὖ ἀντωνυμία ἐν τῇ συντάξει
ἐνέκλινε τὸν τόνον· ἔστι γὰρ ἀπόλυτος, οὐχ ὃν τρόπον δ᾽ οἴεται ὁ Ἀσκαλωνίτης τὸ
πῶς πάντως ὀξυτονηθήσεται, ἐπεὶ ἤδη ἐμελέτησε καὶ ἄλλων ἐγκλιτικῶν ἐπιφερομένων
τὸ πῶ καὶ τὸ πῶς τοῦτο μὴ πάσχειν· οὔπως ἔστ᾽, Ἀγέλαε διοτρεφές (Od.
22. 136)· μήπως με προϊδών (Od. 4. 396)· μήπω μ᾽ ἐς θρόνον ἵζε,
διοτρεφές (Il. 24. 553)· οὔπω μίν φασι φαγέμεν (Od. 16. 143). οὕτως
οὖν καὶ τὸ εἴ πως εὖ πεφίδοιτο οὐκ ἀναγκαστικὴν ἕξει τὴν ἐπὶ τοῦ πώς
ὀξεῖαν. ὁ μέντοι Ἀρίσταρχος γενόμενος κατὰ ταύτην τὴν προσῳδίαν τοῦτο μόνον
ἀπεφήνατο, ἐγκλίνοντα δεῖν τῷ τόνῳ καὶ δασύνοντα λέγειν τὴν τρίτην συλλαβήν·
σημαίνει γὰρ εἴ πως αὐτοῦ: E. M. 638. 15: οὔ θήν μιν· Πόσοι τόνοι; Δύο. Διατί;
Ἡνίκα εὑρεθῇ ἐγκλιτικὰ ἐφεξῆς ἀλλήλων κείμενα, πολλαὶ ἔσονται καὶ παράλληλοι αἱ
ὀξεῖαι, Ἤ ῥά νύ μοί τι πίθοιο (sic), where the printed accents contradict the written
rule; they should be ἤ ῥά νύ μοί τι πίθοιο, as in A. G. Oxon. 1. 323. 26.

975. NOTE 2.—Though this rule regarding the accentuation of a succession
of enclitics is enunciated by all the native grammarians, from Apollonius down-
wards, several modern writers reject it as absurd; for instance, Hermann, de
emend. rat. Gr. gr. p. 74; Göttling, Accent. p. 405; Kühner, G. G. 1. 267, who
all determine to accent two or more successive enclitics after a fashion of their
own devising. Kühner declares that this new-fangled way is not new, that it is
justified by the manner in which such combinations are accented in the Codex
Venetus B of the Iliad, a manuscript written by a learned scribe of the eleventh
century, and he quotes from it six instances, in which the old rule is not observed:
they are δέ τε μιν Il. χ. 94; οὐδέ τε μιν, φ. 322; μή ποτέ τις, χ. 106; ἄρα πώ τι,
279; ὄφρα τί μιν, 329; οὐδέ νυ πώ με. Of these two (μή ποτέ τις and ἄρα πώ τι) are
not in point. If I rightly understand Kühner, he maintains that the scribe of
Codex B objected to write two or more oxytone monosyllables in succession; but
in the leaf photographed for Dindorf's edition, containing Il. H. 395–443, we find
μή τ᾽ ἄρ τις, and that he has no objection to two acute accents on successive
syllables is clear from the same page· where we have οἵ δ᾽ ἄρα (sic) twice running.
But Kühner further urges that manuscripts and old editions of the Bible also
depart from the ancient rule. Even if all these statements were strictly accurate,
I fail to see how the practice of a scribe of the eleventh century can be evidence
against the clear and express words of Apollonius and Herodian. The writer of
Codex B was as far from Apollonius as we are from King Canute; the pronunciation of English has changed a good deal since his day.

976. NOTE 3.—The new-fashioned rule is thus stated by Dr. Donaldson,
Greek Grammar, p. 43: 'If two or more *enclitics* occur in succession, an accent
may be added for every three syllables: as εἴ πέρ τίς σε μοί φησίν ποτέ, where
εἴ περ τις and τίς σε μοι are considered to be successive *proparoxytona*.' Göttling,
Greek Accent. p. 104, expresses it thus: 'If several enclitics follow one another

they must all be regarded as forming *one* word with the preceding orthotone, and the accentuation must be proceeded with according to III [a rule stating that "two syllables standing immediately next each other in the same word cannot be accented"]. Thus e. g. πλούσιος τις ἐστιν; here τις unites to πλούσιος πλούσιόστις; this word obtains now as paroxytone; hence ἐστιν must be accented on the last syllable, πλούσιός τις ἐστίν, or ἤ νυ σε που δέος ἴσχει; here νυ and σε are joined to the now oxytone ἤ: ἤνυσε; but σε as the third syllable of ἤνυσε, which now obtains as a proparoxytone, receives the acute, because που follows it: ἤ νυ σέ που δέος ἴσχει.' This very example Kühner G. G. I. 267 insists upon writing ἤ νυ σε πού, and appeals to Göttling, Accent. 405, to bear him out, which Göttling by no means does. Thus it appears that the new rule is one which its inventors find hard to manage: modern editors generally disobey the old rule, and follow their grammatical instincts;—the result is what might be expected.

977. All the rules laid down by the ancient grammarians, for the accentuation of words when standing in a sentence, have been either quoted or referred to in the preceding sections. That they fully provide for all the combinations which actually occur can hardly be asserted. To mention a simple matter which perpetually meets us, there are difficulties arising from punctuation, from crasis and other forms of synaloephe, for which the extant rules of the grammarians appear to be insufficient. For instance, it may be asked how φησι is to be accented in such passages as ἤκω γὰρ εἰς γῆν, φησι, καὶ κατέρχομαι, or τὸ πρᾶγμα αὐτό, φησι, δείξει. Is a mere parenthetic *inquit* to be treated, as it is here written, strictly according to the old rules, or is it not more reasonable to write φησὶ or φησί in such passages? How is μοι to be accented in such a position as ἔρμαιον τὸ βιβλίον, ἔφη, μοι γέγονε? Are we obliged to write 'μοὶ, or may we say that a real enclitic actually begins a clause and write μοὶ? Or consider a verse which is divided between two speakers, e. g. Eurip. Orest. 1345, where Hermione speaks one half and Electra the other:

Herm. σώθηθ' ὅσον γε τοὐπ' ἔμ'. *Elect.* ὦ κατὰ στέγας.

To exhibit the scansion to the eye editors so write it; but can anything be more absurd than to suppose, as the grammarians must, that Hermione's prophetic soul knows that Electra will begin her reply with a vowel, and therefore, to accommodate her sister, she gracefully elides the last letter of her personal pronoun and alters her accent accordingly? Editors do as well as they can in such awkward cases. Sometimes perhaps they reproduce the accents of a manuscript, and when they do, they

print what may be the faint echo of a tradition going back
to the best ages of classical antiquity, but which probably represents no more than the practice of the scribe's own times. The
oldest manuscript of any classical author continuously accented
is comparatively modern. When manuscripts are not followed,
theories of what the Greek accents must have been are generally
acted on, and the result is an amount of variety in the accentuation of printed books which could hardly have been reached in
any other manner. The curious reader should by all means
peruse Lobeck's unfinished essay, ' De interpunctione cum enclisi
et synalœphe conjuncta,' in the Pathologiæ Græci Sermonis
Elementa. Pars posterior, pp. 321–337.

Ἄν τ' εἴπῃ τις ἀξιῶν προπερισπᾶν, ὡς ἂν ἐκεῖνος ἐθελήσῃ καὶ σὺ φθέγγου, καὶ πάλιν ἂν ἑτέρῳ συντύχῃς ὀξυτονεῖν ἐθέλοντι, καὶ αὐτὸς οὕτως πρᾶττε καταφρονῶν καὶ τόνων καὶ ὀνομάτων, ὡς οὔτε πρὸς φιλοσοφίαν συντελούντων, πολύ γε μᾶλλον οὔτε πρὸς γεωμετρίαν ἢ ἀριθμητικὴν ἢ μουσικὴν ἢ ἀστρονομικήν, ὥστε εἰ μηδεμία τέχνη δέεται πρὸς τὸ ἑαυτῆς τέλος τῆς τῶν ἐπιτρίπτων τούτων ὀνομάτων μακρολογίας, οὐ μόνον οὐ χρὴ προσίεσθαι τὸ ἐπιτήδευμα τῶν ἀνδρῶν, ἀλλὰ καὶ καταγελᾶν ὡς μάλιστα.

INDEX OF TERMINATIONS.

Those words only are inserted which could not easily be found by the Table of Contents. The references are to the Sections.

-ᾰ, masc. subst. of the first decl., 56.
-α, fem. of the first decl., monosyllables, 65; hypermonosyllables, 66-201; contracted from -αα, fem. of the first decl., 67.
-α, fem. of adj. in os, 561.
-α, fem. of adj. of the third decl., 695.
-α, adv., 833-839.
-α, interject., 892.
-ᾶ = έα, acc., 681.
-αα, fem. first decl., 66.
ἀβληχρός, 405.
ἀβρίξ, 724.
ἀβρογόος, 528.
ἀβροδαίς, 724.
ἀγασός = ἀγαθός, 406.
ἀγενείς, Bœot., 26.
-αγος (ἄγω), compd. adj., 430.
-αγος (ἄγνυμι), compd. adj., 431.
-αγρος, comp. adj., 432.
ἀγυιᾶς, ἀγυιᾷ, 112. 211.
-αγωγος, compd. adj., 433.
ἄδελφε, voc. of ἀδελφός, 330.
-αδελφεος, compd. subst., 422.
-αδελφη, compd. subst., 193.
-αδελφος, compd. subst., 425.
-αδις, adv., 877.
ἀδράνεος, 528.
ἀδρογόος, 528.
ἄεισι, 800.
ἀεισκώψ, 621.
-αη, fem. of the first decl., 66.
Ἄθοως, 547.
αι, when short for the accent, 16; its quantity in Doric, 17.
-αι, adv., 854; interjects., 896.
-αια, fem. of the first decl., 89.
-αια, neut. pl. of the second decl., names of festivals, etc., 358.

ἀϊδνός, 399.
-αιετος, compd. subst., 424.
-αιον, neut. subst., 355; temenica, 360.
-αιος, simple subst. of the second decl., 250-253; simple adj., 378-380; compd. adj., 536.
Αἶπυ, 695.
-αις, Doric part., 779.
αἰσχροπράγος, 528.
-αιων, subst. of the third decl., 594.
-ακης, 701.
-ακι, adv., 862.
-ακις, adv., 871.
ἀκλεᾶ, 712.
-ακουος, compd. adj., 434.
ἀλαός, 535.
-αλγος, comp. adj., 435.
ἀλικράς, 725.
ἀλκί, 683.
-αμοιβος, compd. adj., 436.
-αν = ων, Doric gen., 217. 795.
-αν, subst. of the third decl., 578.
ἀνάκλεις, 575.
-ανδις, adv., 877.
ἀνδραπόδεσσι, 683.
-ανεψιος, 422.
ἀνθρωποφλόγος, 528.
-αντης, compd. adj. of the third decl., 696. 700.
ἀντίκλεις, 575.
ἀντίσφην, 575.
-αο, gen. sing. of the first decl., 209. 210.
-αοιδος, compd. adj., 437.
-αος, simple subst. of the second decl., 221-225; simple adj., 364.
-αος = αιος, Æolic subst. of the second decl., 225.
ἀπαφών, 779.
ἀπέσται, 811.

ἀποδασμός, 419.

ἀπορρώξ, 727.

-αρ = ηs, Lacedæmonian nouns of the first decl., 58.

-αρ, subst. of the third decl., 623.

Ἀραρώς, 779.

-αρηs, 701.

ἀριγνώς, 724.

ἀρχιεταῖρος, 423.

ἀρχιμῖμος, 419.

ἀρχιφώρ, 575.

-αρωγος, compd. adj, 438.

-as, masc. nouns of the first decl., 27–58.

-ᾶs = άas, έas, proper names of the first decl., 30. 32; common substantives and adjectives, 33.

-ᾶs = αεις, adj. of the third decl., 691.

-ᾰs, acc. pl., Doric, 218.

-as, subst. of the third decl., 630–633.

-as, gen. αδος, compd. adj. of the third decl., 713.

-as, adv., 871.

-ασκος, compd. adj., 439.

-άτηs, subst. of the first decl., 51.

ἀτταγᾶs, 31. 33.

-αυγος, compd. adj., 440.

αὐθάδης, 698.

αὐτ- or αὐτο-, words beginning with, of the first decl., 28; neuters of the third decl., 575.

αὐτάρκης, 698.

αὐτογραμμή, 131.

αὐτοζωή, 204.

-αυων, subst. of the third decl., 604.

Ἀφρόδιτα, Æolic, 14.

Ἀχηός, 373.

ἄψορρος, 423.

-αων, subst. of the third decl., 585; masc. proper names, 613.

-βα, fem. of the first decl., 68–70.

-βαλος, compd. adj., 464.

-βας, compd. adj. of the third decl., 720.

-βασταξ, compd. adj. of the third decl., 717.

-βαφος, compd. adj., 463.

-βαψ, compd. adj. of the third decl., 721.

-βη, fem. of the first decl., 68–70.

βιβάσθων, 779.

βιβλιοτάφος, 528.

-βλεψ, compd. adj. of the third decl., 721.

-βληs, compd. adj. of the third decl., 722. 724.

-βλως, 724.

-βλωψ, compd. adj. of the third decl., 722. 724.

-βοηθος, compd. adj., 441.

-βολος, compd. adj., 464.

-βορος, compd. adj., 465.

-βος, subst. of the second decl., 226–228; simple adj., 365.

-βοσκος, compd. adj., 442.

βουλιμός, 419.

-βρως, compd. adj. of the third decl., 722. 724.

-βων, subst. of the third decl., 586.

-γα, fem. of the first decl., 71–74.

γαμέτης, 38.

-γε, 744.

γελαῖμι, 793. 802.

-γη, fem. of the first decl., 71–74.

-γηθης, compd. adj. of the third decl., 700.

-γηρως, compd. adj., 546. 680.

-γλυφος, compd. adj., 466.

-γνως, compd. adj. of the third decl., 722. 724.

-γονος, compd. adj., 467.

-γος, subst. of the second decl., 229–232; simple adj., 366.

-γραφος, compd. adj., 468.

γυνή, 670.

-γων, subst. of the third decl., 587.

-δα, fem. of the first decl., 75.

-δα, adv., 835.

δαινῦτο, 795.

-δαπος, adj., 737.

-δε, adv., 846. 849.

-δε, 748.

δεῖνα, 742.

-δεσμος, compd. subst., 419.

δέσποτα, 57. 212.

-δεψος, compd. adj., 443.

-δη, fem. of the first decl., 77; pron., 746.

διασφάξ, 575.

δίδοισθα, 793.

διοικοδομή, 131.

-δμης, comp. adj. of the third decl., 722. 725.

δοκιμῶμι, 793.

-δοκος, compd. adj., 469.

-δομος, compd. adj., 470.

-δονος, compd. adj., 471.

-δορος, compd. adj., 472.

-δos, subst. of the second decl., 233–235 ; simple adj , 367.

-δoχos, compd. adj., 473.

-δρas, 724.

-δρηs, 724.

-δρομos, compd. adj., 474.

-δροπos, compd. adj., 475.

δυσκλέα, 712.

-δων, subst. of the third decl., 588.

δωρουμένοι, Doric, 17.

-ε, adv., 840 ; interject., 894.

-εα, fem. of the first decl., 79–82.

-εα, adv., 834.

-έαι = έεαι, verbs in, 799.

έγχελυs, 686.

-εγχηs, 704.

έγωγε, έμοιγε, 730.

έηs, 739.

-ει, adv., 854 ; interject., 898.

-εια and -ειη, fem. of the first decl., 99–106.

-εια, neut. pl. of the second decl., names of festivals, etc., 358.

εἰδῶ, 802.

εἰκώ, 678.

-ειον, neut. subst. of the second decl., 344. 353-4 ; Temenica, 357–362.

-ειοs, subst. of the second decl., 254–256 ; simple adj., 381 ; compd. adj., 537.

εἰπόν, 775.

-ειρ, subst. of the third decl., 627.

εἰρῦτο, 781.

-ειs, subst. of the third decl., 640.

-είω, gen. sing. of the first decl., 209–210.

-ειων, subst. of the third decl., 594.

ἑκών, 779.

ἐλαιοτρυγητόs, 424.

ἐλάχεια, 695.

ἐλεμθερῶμι, Æolic, 793.

Ἑλένη, Bœot., 14.

ἐμύ, Bœot., 26.

-εν, Doric infin., 778. 801.

-εν = ησαν, 782.

ἐνειπεῖν, 777.

ἐνίσπειν, 777.

ἐξανέψιος, 422.

-εο = έεο, verbs in, 799.

-εos, subst. of the second decl., 236–238 ; simple adj., 368–371.

-εos = os, Ionic adj. of the second decl., 368.

ἑός, 368. 371.

ἐπέσται, 803.

ἐπιβλής, 575.

ἐπιπλάξ, 575.

ἐπισχοῖες, 786.

ἐπιτήθη, 87.

-ερ, voc. of the third decl., 670. 676.

-εργos, compd. adj., 444–446.

ἐρυγών, 779.

ἐρυοῦσιν, 773.

-εs, voc. of the third decl., 670. 706.

-εs, adv., 872.

-εσσι, dative pl. of the third decl., 574.

-εταιρos, 423.

ἐτεοδμώς, 575.

-ετηs, compd. adj. of the third decl., 703. 709.

-ευ, second aor. mid. imp., 783.

εὐγενείs, Bœot., 26.

εὐκλέας, 712.

εὐζωή, 204.

εὑρέτις, 38.

εὐρυχωρήs, 702.

-ευs, subst. of the third decl., 655.

-ευs, comp. adj. of the third decl., 697.

εὐτείχης, 698.

-ευτηs, masc. of the first decl., 48.

εὐωδόs, 528.

ἐχρῆν, 772.

-εψos, compd. adj., 447.

-έω, gen. sing. of the first decl., 210.

ἑῶμεν, 794.

-εων, subst. of the third decl., 589.

ἐών = ὤν, 779. 798.

-ζα, fem. of the first decl., 83.

-ζε, adv., 846. 848.

-ζos, subst. of the second decl., 239 ; simple adj., 372.

-ζων, subst. of the third decl., 590.

-η, fem. of the first decl., 65–204.

-η, adv., 851 ; interject., 895.

-η, pron., 747.

-ῆ = εα, fem. of the first decl, 82.

-ηα, fem. of the first decl., 85.

-ηγοροs, compd. adj., 476.

-ηη, fem. of the first decl., 85.

-ηθηs, compd. adj. of the third decl., 698. 700.

-ηκηs, compd. adj. of the third decl., 698. 701.

ἧμαι, its compds., 813.

ἡμιθῆτα, 575.

ἡμικρήs, 575.

ἡμιμῦ, 575.

ἡμιφῖ, 575.

-ην, subst. of the third decl., 580.

-ην, Doric inf. in, 778.

-ηξ, compd. adj. of the third decl., 725–728.

-ηος, subst. of the second decl., 241; simple adj., 373.

-ηος = ειος, 241.

-ηρ = ης, Lacedæmonian masc. of the first decl., 58.

-ηρ, subst. of the third decl., 624–626; syncopated words in, 672.

-ηρης, compd. adj. of the third decl., 701.

-ης, masc. of the first decl., 27–58.

-ης, subst. of the third decl., 634–639.

-ης, contracted subst. of the third decl., 673.

-ης, gen. εος, simple adj., 688; compd. adj. 696. 705.

-ης, gen. in ος impure, 690.

-ῆς, adj. of the third decl., 691.

-ης, adv., 873.

-ητης, masc. of the first decl., 51.

-ηων, subst. of the third decl., 591.

-θα, fem. of the first decl., 86.

-θα, adv , 836.

-θε, cases in, 219. 555. 682; adv., 841–845.

θέραπες, 683.

-θη, fem. of the first decl., 86.

-θην, Æolic pass. aor. inf., 787.

-θηξ, compd. adj. of the third decl., 722. 725.

-θι, adv., 841–845.

θιγεῖν, 777.

-θλιψ, 725.

-θνης, compd. adj. of the third decl., 722. 725.

-θοος, compd. adj., 477.

-θορος, compd. adj., 478.

-θος, subst. of the second decl., 242–243; simple adj., 374.

-θων, subst. of the third decl., 592.

-ι, adv., 854–863.

-ι, pron., 747.

-ια, fem. of the first decl., 95–97.

-ια, neut. pl. of the second decl., names of festivals, 358.

ἰαμβεῖον, 382.

ἴαρυ, Bœot., 14.

λᾶς, ιᾷ, 211.

-ιατρος, compd. subst., 423.

ἰάχων, 779.

ἰδού, 784.

ἵημι, subj. act. of, 794.

-ιλος, 276.

-ιν, 582.

-ινδα, adv., 835.

-ινς, subst. of the third decl., 654.

-ιον, dim. of the second decl., 343. 347–352.

-ιος, subst. of the second decl., 244–249; simple adj., 357–377.

-ις, subst. of the third decl., 641–653.

-ις, fem. from masc. in ης, 646.

-ις, simple adj., 688; comp. adj., 697. 713.

-ις, adv , 874–875.

-ισκος, compd. subst., 420.

ἴσχων, 779.

-ιτης, masc. of the first decl., 39.

-ιῶ = ίσω, fut., 773.

-ιω, gen. sing. of the first decl., 209.

ἰῶκα, 683.

-ιων, subst. of the third decl., 635.

ἰών, 779. 798.

-κα, fem. of the first decl., 114–119.

καθεύδω, 817.

καθίζω, 817.

κακκᾶν, 33.

καλοκἀγαθύς, 535.

καλουμένοι, Doric, 17.

καλύ, Bœot., 26.

κάρ, 564.

καταδαρθεῖν, 777.

κατακλῶθες, 575. 725.

κεῖμαι, compd. of, 813.

κελάδων, 779.

Κερεᾶτε or Κερεᾶτε, 181.

κέρως, 679.

-κη, fem. of the first decl., 114–119.

-κητης, compd. adj. of the third decl., 698. 702.

κιών, 779.

κλάδεσι, 683.

κλαδί, 683.

-κλειτος, compd. adj., 532.

-κλεψ, compd. adj. of the third decl., 721.

-κλοπος, compd. adj., 479.

-κλυτος, compd. adj., 532.

-κλωψ, compd. adj. of the third decl., 725.

-κμης, compd. adj. of the third decl., 722. 725.
-κολλα, 121.
-κολος, compd. adj., 480.
-κομος, compd. adj., 481.
-κοος, compd. adj., 482.
-κοπος, compd. adj., 483.
-κορος, compd. adj., 484.
-κος, subst. of the second decl., 260–273; simple adj., 387; compd. adj., 538.
-κουρος, compd. adj., 448.
κραγόν, 867.
-κρας, compd. adj. of the third decl., 722. 725.
κρέως, 679.
κρόκα, 683.
-κροκος, compd. adj., 485.
-κτης, masc. of the first decl., 41–44.
-κτονος, compd. adj., 486.
-κτυπος, compd. adj., 520.
-κων, subst. of the third decl., 595.

-λα, fem. of the first decl., 120–122.
-λαβος, compd. adj., 487.
-λαλία, 96.
-λαλος, compd. adj., 488.
λελῦτο, 795.
λευκερινεός, 422.
λευκερωδιός, 422.
-λη, fem. of the first decl., 123–130.
λίγεια, 695.
λῖτα, 683.
λιτί, 683.
-λογος, compd. adj., 489.
-λοιγος, compd. adj., 449.
-λοιχος, compd. adj., 450.
-λος, subst. of the second decl., 274–283; simple adj., 389. 392; compd. adj., 539.
-λοχος, compd. adj., 490.
-λτης, masc. of the first decl., 41–45.
-λων, subst. of the third decl., 596.

-μα, fem. of the first decl., 131–134.
-μα, adv., 837.
μαμμᾶν, 33.
μαντομάγος, 421.
-μαχος, compd. adj., 491.
-μεγεθης, compd. adj. of the third decl., 698. 702.
μέθιεν, 793.
μειλίχιν, Bœot. 14.
Μενελάοι, Doric, 17.

-μη, fem. of the first decl., 131 134.
Μήδεια, 7.
-μηδης, compd. adj. of the third decl., 704.
-μηκης, compd. adj. of the third decl., 698. 702.
-μητις, compd. adj. of the third decl., 717.
-μι, verbs in, 765–767. 793–798. 818.
-μολγος, compd. adj., 451.
μολιβδοτήξ, 728.
μονόρρηξ, 728.
-μορος, compd. adj., 492.
-μος, subst. of the second decl., 284–287; simple adj., 393; compd. subst., 419.
-μων, subst. of the third decl., 597.

-ν, adv., 864–867; interject., 900.
-να, fem. of the first decl., 135–139.
νεωρής, 702.
-νη, fem. of the first decl., 140–146.
νίφα, 683.
-νομος, compd. adj., 493.
-νος, subst. of the second decl., 288–302; simple adj., 395–399; compd. adj., 540.
-ντης, masc. of the first decl., 41. 46.
-ντι = εισι, Doric, 800.
-νυμφιος, 422.
-νων, subst. of the third decl., 598.

-ξ, subst. of the third decl., 620; compd. adj., 713.
-ξ, adv., 868; interject., 901.
-ξα, fem. of the first decl., 147.
-ξα, adv., 837.
-ξη, fem. of the first decl., 147.
-ξοος, compd. adj., 494.
-ξος, subst. of the second decl., 303–305, simple adj., 400.
-ξων, subst. of the third decl., 599.

-ο, adv., 869; interject., 901.
-οα, and οη, fem. of the first decl., 149–152.
ὀγκοτράφος, 528.
-οι, quantity of, 16; in Doric, 17.
-οι, adv., 854–858; interject., 899.
-οια, fem. of the first decl., 107–110.
-οιγος, comp. adj., 452.
-οιη, fem. of the first decl., 107–110.
οἰκοδομή, 131.

οἰκοσκευή, 190.
-οιο = ου, gen. sing. of the second decl., 556.
-οιος, subst. of the second decl., 257–259 ; simple adj., 384–385.
ὀλίος, 366.
-ολκος, compd. adj., 453.
ὀλοοίτροχος, 425. 528.
Ὅμηρυ, Bœot., 14.
-ον, neut. of the second decl., 340–345. 357.
-ον, voc. sing. of the third decl., 670.
-οος, subst. of the second decl., 306 ; simple adj., 401 ; compd. adj., 541.
δου, 739.
-οπαδος, compd. adj., 454.
-οπωρινος, compd. adj., 540.
-οργος, compd. adj., 445.
ὀρειπέλαργος, 421.
ὀρεσσιπάτος, 528.
ὀρνέων, 686.
-os, adv., 880.
ὅστις, 743.
ὅτου, 743.
-ου, adv., 886.
-ουλκος, compd. adj., 453.
-ουργος, compd. adj., 445 ; proper names, 231.
-ουρος, compd. adj., 331. 455. 495.
-ους, subst. of the second decl., 306 ; simple adj., 415 ; subst. of the third decl., 656–657.
οὗτος, 407.
ὀφλεῖν, 777.
-οχος, compd. adj., 495.

-π, interject., 901.
-πα, fem. of the first decl., 153–156.
παληός, 373.
Πάν, 565 ; oblique cases, 568.
πάρολκος, 453.
πᾶς, 692.
-περ, pron., 750.
περιγλώξ, 719.
περιστίξ, 719.
περιχθών, 575.
πέφνειν, 777.
-πη, fem. of the first decl., 153–156.
-πηγος, compd. adj., 456.
Πηνέλοπη, Bœot., 14.
-πηξ, compd. adj. of the third decl., 722. 726.
-πηχης, compd. adj. of the third decl., 698. 702.

πιέ, 774.
πίτνειν, 777.
-πλαθος, compd. adj., 496.
-πλανος, compd. adj., 497.
-πληθης, compd. adj. of the third decl., 700.
-πληξ, compd. adj. of the third decl., 722. 726.
-πλης, compd. adj. of the third decl., 722.
-πλοκος, compd. adj., 498.
ποδάρκης, 698 : ποδαρκές, 708.
ποδώκης, 698.
-ποιος, compd. adj., 457.
-ποκος, compd. adj., 499.
-πολος, compd. adj., 500.
-πομπος, compd. adj., 458.
-πονος, compd. adj., 501.
-ποπος, 503.
-πορος, compd. adj., 504.
-πος, subst. of the second decl., 308–310 ; simple adj., 403 ; compd. adj., 541.
πούλιμος, 419.
πρόβασι, 683.
-προπος, compd. adj., 505.
προσφδία, 4.
προτήθη, 87.
πρών, 607.
-πτην, compd. adj. of the third decl., 722. 726.
-πτως, compd. adj. of the third decl., 722. 726.
-πτωξ, 726.
πωλουμένοι, Doric, 17.
-πων, subst. of the third decl., 600.

-ρ, adv., 870.
-ρα, fem. of the first decl., 157–171.
-ρα, adv., 834.
-ραιστης, compd. subst. of the first decl., 36.
-ραφος, compd. adj., 506.
-ρη = ρα, Ionic, 168.
-ρηξ, 727.
-ρος, subst. of the second decl., 311–314 ; simple adj., 404 ; compd. adj., 542.
-ροφος, compd. adj., 507.
-ρτης, masc. of the first decl., 41. 47.
-ρων, subst. of the third decl., 601.
-ρωξ, compd. adj. of the third decl., 722–727.

-s, adv., 871-885.
-σα, fem. of the first decl., 172-176.
σαμπῖ, 575.
σάν, 564.
-σε, adv., 850.
-ση, fem. of the first decl., 177.
-σι, adv., 859.
-σκαφος, compd. adj., 508.
-σκηθης, compd. adj. of the third decl., 700.
-σκοπος, compd. adj., 509.
-σκωψ, compd. adj. of the third decl., 722. 727.
-σοος, compd. adj., 510.
-σος, subst. of the second decl., 315-319; simple adj., 406.
-σπαξ, compd. adj. of the third decl., 721.
-σπας, compd. adj. of the third decl., 720.
-σπορος, compd. adj., 511.
-σταθμος, compd. subst., 419.
-στελεχης, compd. adj. of the third decl., 698. 702.
-στην, compd. adj. of the third decl., 722. 727.
-στης, masc. of the first decl., 49.
-στολος, compd. adj., 512.
-στροφος, compd. adj., 513.
-στρως, compd. adj. of the third decl., 727.
συγκορυφαῖος, 422.
Συοβοιωτοί, 424.
συρίσδες, Doric, 770.
-σφαγος, compd. adj., 514.
-σφαξ, compd. adj. of the third decl., 720.
σχεθεῖν, 777.
-σων, subst. of the third decl., 602.

-τ, interject., 901.
-τα, fem. of the first decl., 179-181.
ταυροθρύος, 528.
τεθνᾶναι, 797.
-τεος, verbal adj., 368.
τεός. 368. 371.
-τη, fem. of the first decl., 182-186.
τηλύγετος, 408.
-τηξ, 728.
-τηρης, compd. adj. of the third decl., 698.
-της, masc. of the first decl., 35-55.
-τιμηξ, compd. adj. of the third decl., 722.

-ημης, compd. adj. of the third decl., 722. 728.
τοῖσδεσι and τοῖσδεσσι, 15. 741.
-τοκος, compd. adj., 515.
-τομος, compd. adj., 516.
-τον, neut. with a corresponding masc. in τος, 342.
τόνος, 4.
-τορος, compd. adj., 517.
-τος, subst. of the second decl., 320-326; simple adj., 407; verbal derivatives, 529-531.
-τραγος, compd. adj., 518.
-τρης, compd. adj. of the third decl., 722. 728.
τριήρων, 674.
τριχοβρώς, 725.
-τριψ, compd. adj. of the third decl., 720.
-τροφος, compd. adj., 519.
-τρωξ, compd. adj. of the third decl., 722. 725. 728.
-τρως, compd. adj. of the third decl., 722. 728.
-τυπος, compd. adj., 520.
τύπτομη, Bœot., 14.
-των, subst. of the third decl., 603.

-υ, adv., 886; interject., 902.
-υα, fem. of the first decl., 187-191.
ὑγία, 712.
-υδις, adv., 878.
-υη, fem. of the first decl., 187-191.
-υια, fem. of the first decl., 111-113.
-υιος, simple adj., 386.
-ὔλος, 276.
-υν, subst. of the third decl., 583.
-υνς, subst. of the third decl., 654.
-υος, subst. of the second decl., 327-328; simple adj., 409.
ὑποδράς, 725.
-υρ, subst. of the third decl., 628.
-υς, subst. of the third decl., 658-664; simple adj. of the third decl., 688; compd. adj., 697.
-υς, adv., 881.
ὑσμῖνι, 683.
-ὕτης, masc. of the first decl., 51.
-υων, subst. of the third decl., 604.

-φα, fem. of the first decl., 192-196.
φαγέ, 774.
-φαγος, compd. adj., 521.
-φη, fem. of the first decl., 192-196.

THE END.

December 1885.

Clarendon Press, Oxford

A SELECTION OF

BOOKS

PUBLISHED FOR THE UNIVERSITY BY

HENRY FROWDE,

AT THE OXFORD UNIVERSITY PRESS WAREHOUSE, AMEN CORNER, LONDON.

ALSO TO BE HAD AT THE

CLARENDON PRESS DEPOSITORY, OXFORD.

[*Every book is bound in cloth, unless otherwise described.*]

LEXICONS, GRAMMARS, &c.

ANGLO-SAXON.—*An Anglo-Saxon Dictionary*, based on the MS. Collections of the late Joseph Bosworth, D.D., Professor of Anglo-Saxon, Oxford. Edited and enlarged by Prof. T. N. Toller, M.A. (To be completed in four parts.) Parts I and II. A—HWISTLIAN (pp. vi, 576). 1882. 4to. 15*s.* each.

CHINESE.—*A Handbook of the Chinese Language.* By James Summers. 1863. 8vo. half bound, 1*l.* 8*s.*

ENGLISH.—*A New English Dictionary, on Historical Principles:* founded mainly on the materials collected by the Philological Society. Edited by James A. H. Murray, LL.D., President of the Philological Society; with the assistance of many Scholars and men of Science. Part I. A—ANT (pp. xvi, 352). Part II. ANT—BATTEN (pp. viii, 353-704). Imperial 4to. 12*s.* 6*d.* each.

—— *An Etymological Dictionary of the English Language.* By W. W. Skeat, M.A. *Second Edition.* 1884. 4to. 2*l.* 4*s.*

——Supplement to the First Edition of the above. 1884. 4to. 2*s.* 6*d.*

—— *A Concise Etymological Dictionary of the English Language.* By W. W. Skeat, M.A. *Second Edition.* 1885. Crown 8vo. 5*s.* 6*d.*

GREEK.—*A Greek-English Lexicon*, by Henry George Liddell, D.D., and Robert Scott, D.D. Seventh Edition, Revised and Augmented throughout. 1883. 4to. 1*l.* 16*s.*

—— *A Greek-English Lexicon*, abridged from Liddell and Scott's 4to. edition, chiefly for the use of Schools. Twenty-first Edition. 1884. Square 12mo. 7*s.* 6*d.*

—— *A copious Greek-English Vocabulary*, compiled from the best authorities. 1850. 24mo. 3*s.*

—— *A Practical Introduction to Greek Accentuation*, by H. W. Chandler, M.A. Second Edition. 1881. 8vo. 10*s.* 6*d.*

[9]   B

HEBREW.—*The Book of Hebrew Roots*, by Abu 'l-Walid
Marwân ibn Janâh, otherwise called Rabbi Yônâh. Now first edited, with an
Appendix, by Ad. Neubauer. 1875. 4to. 2*l.* 7*s.* 6*d.*

—— *A Treatise on the use of the Tenses in Hebrew.* By
S. R. Driver, D.D. Second Edition, Revised and Enlarged. 1881. Extra
fcap. 8vo. 7*s.* 6*d.*

—— *Hebrew Accentuation of Psalms, Proverbs, and Job.*
By William Wickes, D.D. 1881. Demy 8vo. stiff covers, 5*s.*

ICELANDIC.—*An Icelandic-English Dictionary*, based on the
MS. collections of the late Richard Cleasby. Enlarged and completed by
G. Vigfússon, M.A. With an Introduction, and Life of Richard Cleasby, by
G. Wehbe Dasent, D.C.L. 1874. 4to. 3*l.* 7*s.*

—— *A List of English Words the Etymology of which is
illustrated by comparison with Icelandic.* Prepared in the form of an
APPENDIX to the above. By W. W. Skeat, M.A. 1876. stitched, 2*s.*

—— *An Icelandic Prose Reader*, with Notes, Grammar and
Glossary, by Dr. Gudbrand Vigfússon and F. York Powell, M.A. 1879.
Extra fcap. 8vo. 10*s.* 6*d.*

LATIN.—*A Latin Dictionary*, founded on Andrews' edition
of Freund's Latin Dictionary, revised, enlarged, and in great part rewritten
by Charlton T. Lewis, Ph.D., and Charles Short, LL.D. 1879. 4to. 1*l.* 5*s.*

MELANESIAN.—*The Melanesian Languages.* By R. H.
Codrington, D.D., of the Melanesian Mission, Fellow of Wadham College,
Oxford. 8vo. 18*s.* *Just Published.*

SANSKRIT.—*A Practical Grammar of the Sanskrit Language*,
arranged with reference to the Classical Languages of Europe, for the use of
English Students, by Monier Williams, M.A. Fourth Edition, 1877. 8vo. 15*s.*

—— *A Sanskrit-English Dictionary*, Etymologically and
Philologically arranged, with special reference to Greek, Latin, German, Anglo-
Saxon, English, and other cognate Indo-European Languages. By Monier
Williams, M.A. 1872. 4to. 4*l.* 14*s.* 6*d.*

—— *Nalopákhyánam.* Story of Nala, an Episode of the
Mahá-Bhárata: the Sanskrit text, with a copious Vocabulary, and an improved
version of Dean Milman's Translation, by Monier Williams, M.A. Second
Edition, Revised and Improved. 1879. 8vo. 15*s.*

—— *Sakuntalá.* A Sanskrit Drama, in Seven Acts. Edited
by Monier Williams, M.A. Second Edition, 1876. 8vo. 21*s.*

SYRIAC.—*Thesaurus Syriacus:* collegerunt Quatremère, Bern-
stein, Lorsbach, Arnoldi, Agrell, Field, Roediger: edidit R. Payne Smith,
S.T.P. Fasc. I-VI. 1868–83. sm. fol. each, 1*l.* 1*s.* Vol. I, containing
Fasc. I-V, sm. fol. 5*l.* 5*s.*

—— *The Book of Kalīlah and Dimnah.* Translated from Arabic
into Syriac. Edited by W. Wright, LL.D. 1884. 8vo. 21*s.*

GREEK CLASSICS, &c.

Aristophanes: A Complete Concordance to the Comedies
and Fragments. By Henry Dunbar, M.D. 4to. 1*l.* 1*s.*

Aristotle: The Politics, translated into English, with Introduction, Marginal Analysis, Notes, and Indices, by B. Jowett, M.A. Medium
8vo. 2 vols. 21*s.* *Just Published.*

Heracliti Ephesii Reliquiae. Recensuit I. Bywater, M.A.
Appendicis loco additae sunt Diogenis Laertii Vita Heracliti, Particulae Hip-
pocratei De Diaeta Libri Primi, Epistolae Heracliteae. 1877. 8vo. 6*s.*

Herculanensium Voluminum. Partes II. 1824. 8vo. 10*s.*

Fragmenta Herculanensia. A Descriptive Catalogue of the
Oxford copies of the Herculanean Rolls, together with the texts of several
papyri, accompanied by facsimiles. Edited by Walter Scott, M.A., Fellow
of Merton College, Oxford. Royal 8vo. *cloth,* 21*s.* *Just Published.*

Homer: A Complete Concordance to the Odyssey and
Hymns of Homer; to which is added a Concordance to the Parallel Passages
in the Iliad, Odyssey, and Hymns. By Henry Dunbar, M.D. 1880. 4to. 1*l.* 1*s.*

—— *Scholia Graeca in Iliadem.* Edited by Professor W.
Dindorf, after a new collation of the Venetian MSS. by D. B. Monro M.A.,
Provost of Oriel College. 4 vols. 8vo. 2*l.* 10*s.* Vols. V and VI. *In the Press.*

—— *Scholia Graeca in Odysseam.* Edidit Guil. Dindorfius.
Tomi II. 1855. 8vo. 15*s.* 6*d.*

Plato: Apology, with a revised Text and English Notes, and
a Digest of Platonic Idioms, by James Riddell, M.A. 1878. 8vo. 8*s.* 6*d.*

—— *Philebus,* with a revised Text and English Notes, by
Edward Poste, M.A. 1860. 8vo. 7*s.* 6*d.*

—— *Sophistes and Politicus,* with a revised Text and English
Notes, by L. Campbell, M.A. 1867. 8vo. 18*s.*

—— *Theaetetus,* with a revised Text and English Notes,
by L. Campbell, M.A. Second Edition. 8vo. 10*s.* 6*d.*

—— *The Dialogues,* translated into English, with Analyses
and Introductions, by B. Jowett, M.A. A new Edition in 5 volumes, medium
8vo. 1875. 3*l.* 10*s.*

—— *The Republic,* translated into English, with an Analysis
and Introduction, by B. Jowett, M.A. Medium 8vo. 12*s.* 6*d.*

Thucydides: Translated into English, with Introduction,
Marginal Analysis, Notes, and Indices. By B. Jowett, M.A. 2 vols. 1881.
Medium 8vo. 1*l.* 12*s.*

B 2

THE HOLY SCRIPTURES, &c.

STUDIA BIBLICA.—Essays in Biblical Archæology and Criticism, and kindred subjects. By Members of the University of Oxford. 8vo. 10s. 6d. *Just Published.*

ENGLISH.—*The Holy Bible in the earliest English Versions,* made from the Latin Vulgate by John Wycliffe and his followers : edited by the Rev. J. Forshall and Sir F. Madden. 4 vols. 1850. Royal 4to. 3l. 3s.

[Also reprinted from the above, with Introduction and Glossary by W. W. Skeat, M.A.

——— *The Books of Job, Psalms, Proverbs, Ecclesiastes, and the Song of Solomon:* according to the Wycliffite Version made by Nicholas de Hereford, about A.D. 1381, and Revised by John Purvey, about A.D. 1388. Extra fcap. 8vo. 3s. 6d.

——— *The New Testament in English,* according to the Version by John Wycliffe, about A.D. 1380, and Revised by John Purvey, about A.D. 1388. Extra fcap. 8vo. 6s.]

——— *The Holy Bible:* an exact reprint, page for page, of the Authorised Version published in the year 1611. Demy 4to. half bound, 1l. 1s.

——— *The Psalter, or Psalms of David, and certain Canticles,* with a Translation and Exposition in English, by Richard Rolle of Hampole. Edited by H. R. Bramley, M.A., Fellow of S. M. Magdalen College, Oxford. With an Introduction and Glossary. Demy 8vo. 1l. 1s.

——— *Lectures on Ecclesiastes.* Delivered in Westminster Abbey by the Very Rev. George Granville Bradley, D.D., Dean of Westminster. Crown 8vo. 4s. 6d. *Just Published.*

GOTHIC.—*The Gospel of St. Mark in Gothic,* according to the translation made by Wulfila in the Fourth Century. Edited with a Grammatical Introduction and Glossarial Index by W. W. Skeat, M.A. Extra fcap. 8vo. 4s.

GREEK.—*Vetus Testamentum* ex Versione Septuaginta Interpretum secundum exemplar Vaticanum Romae editum. Accedit potior varietas Codicis Alexandrini. Tomi III. Editio Altera. 18mo. 18s.

——— *Origenis Hexaplorum* quae supersunt ; sive, Veterum Interpretum Graecorum in totum Vetus Testamentum Fragmenta. Edidit Fridericus Field, A.M. 2 vols. 1875. 4to. 5l. 5s.

——— *The Book of Wisdom:* the Greek Text, the Latin Vulgate, and the Authorised English Version; with an Introduction, Critical Apparatus, and a Commentary. By William J. Deane, M.A. Small 4to. 12s. 6d.

——— *Novum Testamentum Graece.* Antiquissimorum Codicum Textus in ordine parallelo dispositi. Accedit collatio Codicis Sinaitici. Edidit E. H. Hansell, S.T.B. Tomi III. 1864. 8vo. half morocco, 2l. 12s. 6d.

GREEK.—*Novum Testamentum Graece.* Accedunt parallela
S. Scripturae loca, necnon vetus capitulorum notatio et canones Eusebii. Edidit
Carolus Lloyd, S. T. P. R. 18mo. 3*s.*

The same on writing paper, with large margin, 10*s.*

—— *Novum Testamentum Graece* juxta Exemplar Millianum.
18mo. 2*s.* 6*d.*

The same on writing paper, with large margin, 9*s.*

—— *Evangelia Sacra Graece.* Fcap. 8vo. limp, 1*s.* 6*d.*

—— *The Greek Testament*, with the Readings adopted by
the Revisers of the Authorised Version:—

(1) Pica type, with Marginal References. Demy 8vo. 10*s.* 6*d.*

(2) Long Primer type. Fcap. 8vo. 4*s.* 6*d.*

(3) The same, on writing paper, with wide margin, 15*s.*

—— *The Parallel New Testament*, Greek and English; being
the Authorised Version, 1611; the Revised Version, 1881; and the Greek
Text followed in the Revised Version. 8vo. 12*s.* 6*d.*

The Revised Version is the joint property of the Universities of Oxford and Cambridge.

—— *Canon Muratorianus:* the earliest Catalogue of the
Books of the New Testament. Edited with Notes and a Facsimile of the
MS. in the Ambrosian Library at Milan, by S. P. Tregelles, LL.D. 1867.
4to. 10*s.* 6*d.*

—— *Outlines of Textual Criticism applied to the New Testament.* By C. E. Hammond, M.A. Fourth Edition. Extra fcap. 8vo. 3*s.* 6*d.*

HEBREW, etc.—*The Psalms in Hebrew without points.* 1879.
Crown 8vo. 3*s.* 6*d.*

—— *A Commentary on the Book of Proverbs.* Attributed
to Abraham Ibn Ezra. Edited from a MS. in the Bodleian Library by
S. R. Driver, M.A. Crown 8vo. paper covers, 3*s.* 6*d.*

—— *The Book of Tobit.* A Chaldee Text, from a unique
MS. in the Bodleian Library; with other Rabbinical Texts, English Transla-
tions, and the Itala. Edited by Ad. Neubauer, M.A. 1878. Crown 8vo. 6*s.*

—— *Horae Hebraicae et Talmudicae*, a J. Lightfoot. A new
Edition, by R. Gandell, M.A. 4 vols. 1859. 8vo. 1*l.* 1*s.*

LATIN.—*Libri Psalmorum* Versio antiqua Latina, cum Para-
phrasi Anglo-Saxonica. Edidit B. Thorpe, F.A.S. 1835. 8vo. 10*s.* 6*d.*

—— *Old-Latin Biblical Texts: No. I.* The Gospel according
to St. Matthew from the St. Germain MS. (g_1). Edited with Introduction
and Appendices by John Wordsworth, M.A. Small 4to., stiff covers, 6*s.*

OLD-FRENCH.—*Libri Psalmorum* Versio antiqua Gallica e
Cod. MS. in Bibl. Bodleiana adservato, una cum Versione Metrica aiiisque
Monumentis pervetustis. Nunc primum descripsit et edidit Franciscus Michel,
Phil. Doc. 1860. 8vo. 10*s.* 6*d.*

FATHERS OF THE CHURCH, &c.

St. Athanasius: Historical Writings, according to the Benedictine Text. With an Introduction by William Bright, D.D. 1881. Crown 8vo. 10s. 6d.

—— *Orations against the Arians.* With an Account of his Life by William Bright, D.D. 1873. Crown 8vo. 9s.

St. Augustine: Select Anti-Pelagian Treatises, and the Acts of the Second Council of Orange. With an Introduction by William Bright, D.D. Crown 8vo. 9s.

Canons of the First Four General Councils of Nicaea, Constantinople, Ephesus, and Chalcedon. 1877. Crown 8vo. 2s. 6d.

—— *Notes on the Canons of the First Four General Councils.* By William Bright, D.D. 1882. Crown 8vo. 5s. 6d.

Cyrilli Archiepiscopi Alexandrini in XII Prophetas. Edidit P. E. Pusey, A.M. Tomi II. 1868. 8vo. cloth, 2l. 2s.

—— *in D. Joannis Evangelium.* Accedunt Fragmenta varia necnon Tractatus ad Tiberium Diaconum duo. Edidit post Aubertum P. E. Pusey, A.M. Tomi III. 1872. 8vo. 2l. 5s.

—— *Commentarii in Lucae Evangelium* quae supersunt Syriace. E MSS. apud Mus. Britan. edidit R. Payne Smith, A.M. 1858. 4to. 1l. 2s.

—— Translated by R. Payne Smith, M.A. 2 vols. 1859. 8vo. 14s.

Ephraemi Syri, Rabulae Episcopi Edesseni, Balaei, aliorumque Opera Selecta. E Codd. Syriacis MSS. in Museo Britannico et Bibliotheca Bodleiana asservatis primus edidit J. J. Overbeck. 1865. 8vo. 1l. 1s.

Eusebius' Ecclesiastical History, according to the text of Burton, with an Introduction by William Bright, D.D. 1881. Crown 8vo. 8s. 6d.

Irenaeus: The Third Book of St. Irenaeus, Bishop of Lyons, against Heresies. With short Notes and a Glossary by H. Deane, B.D. 1874. Crown 8vo. 5s. 6d.

Patrum Apostolicorum, S. Clementis Romani, S. Ignatii, S. Polycarpi, quae supersunt. Edidit Guil. Jacobson, S.T.P.R. Tomi II. Fourth Edition, 1863. 8vo. 1l. 1s.

Socrates' Ecclesiastical History, according to the Text of Hussey, with an Introduction by William Bright, D.D. 1878. Crown 8vo. 7s. 6d.

ECCLESIASTICAL HISTORY, BIOGRAPHY, &c.

Ancient Liturgy of the Church of England, according to the uses of Sarum, York, Hereford, and Bangor, and the Roman Liturgy arranged in parallel columns, with preface and notes. By William Maskell, M.A. Third Edition. 1882. 8vo. 15*s.*

Baedae Historia Ecclesiastica. Edited, with English Notes, by G. H. Moberly, M.A. 1881. Crown 8vo. 10*s.* 6*d.*

Bright (W.). *Chapters of Early English Church History.* 1878. 8vo. 12*s.*

Burnet's History of the Reformation of the Church of England. A new Edition. Carefully revised, and the Records collated with the originals, by N. Pocock, M.A. 7 vols. 1865. 8vo. *Price reduced to* 1*l.* 10*s.*

Councils and Ecclesiastical Documents relating to Great Britain and Ireland. Edited, after Spelman and Wilkins, by A. W. Haddan, B.D., and W. Stubbs, M.A. Vols. I. and III. 1869–71. Medium 8vo. each 1*l.* 1*s.*

Vol. II. Part I. 1873. Medium 8vo. 10*s.* 6*d.*

Vol. II. Part II. 1878. Church of Ireland; Memorials of St. Patrick. Stiff covers, 3*s.* 6*d.*

Hamilton (John, Archbishop of St. Andrews), The Catechism of. Edited, with Introduction and Glossary, by Thomas Graves Law. With a Preface by the Right Hon. W. E. Gladstone. 8vo. 12*s.* 6*d.*

Hammond (C. E.). Liturgies, Eastern and Western. Edited, with Introduction, Notes, and Liturgical Glossary. 1878. Crown 8vo. 10*s.* 6*d.*

An Appendix to the above. 1879. Crown 8vo. paper covers, 1*s.* 6*d.*

John, Bishop of Ephesus. The Third Part of his Ecclesiastical History. [In Syriac.] Now first edited by William Cureton, M.A. 1853. 4to. 1*l.* 12*s.*

—— Translated by R. Payne Smith, M.A. 1860. 8vo. 10*s.*

Leofric Missal, The, as used in the Cathedral of Exeter during the Episcopate of its first Bishop, A.D. 1050–1072; together with some Account of the Red Book of Derby, the Missal of Robert of Jumièges, and a few other early MS. Service Books of the English Church. Edited, with Introduction and Notes, by F. E. Warren, B.D. 4to. half morocco, 35*s.*

Monumenta Ritualia Ecclesiae Anglicanae. The occasional Offices of the Church of England according to the old use of Salisbury, the Prymer in English, and other prayers and forms, with dissertations and notes. By William Maskell, M.A. Second Edition. 1882. 3 vols. 8vo. 2*l.* 10*s.*

Records of the Reformation. The Divorce, 1527–1533. Mostly now for the first time printed from MSS. in the British Museum and other libraries. Collected and arranged by N. Pocock, M.A. 1870. 2 vols. 8vo. 1*l.* 16*s.*

Shirley (W. W.). Some Account of the Church in the Apostolic Age. Second Edition, 1874. Fcap. 8vo. 3s. 6d.

Stubbs (W.). Registrum Sacrum Anglicanum. An attempt to exhibit the course of Episcopal Succession in England. 1858. Small 4to. 8s. 6d.

Warren (F. E.). Liturgy and Ritual of the Celtic Church. 1881. 8vo. 14s.

ENGLISH THEOLOGY.

Butler's Works, with an Index to the Analogy. 2 vols. 1874. 8vo. 11s.

Also separately,

Sermons, 5s. 6d.   *Analogy of Religion, 5s. 6d.*

Greswell's Harmonia Evangelica. Fifth Edition. 8vo. 1855. 9s. 6d.

Heurtley's Harmonia Symbolica: Creeds of the Western Church. 1858. 8vo. 6s. 6d.

Homilies appointed to be read in Churches. Edited by J. Griffiths, M.A. 1859. 8vo. 7s. 6d.

Hooker's Works, with his life by Walton, arranged by John Keble, M.A. Sixth Edition, 1874. 3 vols. 8vo. 1l. 11s. 6d.

—— the text as arranged by John Keble, M.A. 2 vols. 1875. 8vo. 11s.

Jewel's Works. Edited by R. W. Jelf, D.D. 8 vols. 1848. 8vo. 1l. 10s.

Pearson's Exposition of the Creed. Revised and corrected by E. Burton, D.D. Sixth Edition, 1877. 8vo. 10s. 6d.

Waterland's Review of the Doctrine of the Eucharist, with a Preface by the late Bishop of London. Crown 8vo. 6s. 6d.

—— *Works*, with Life, by Bp. Van Mildert. A new Edition, with copious Indexes. 6 vols. 1856. 8vo. 2l. 11s.

Wheatly's Illustration of the Book of Common Prayer. A new Edition, 1846. 8vo. 5s.

Wyclif. A Catalogue of the Original Works of John Wyclif, by W. W. Shirley, D.D. 1865. 8vo. 3s. 6d.

—— *Select English Works.* By T. Arnold, M.A. 3 vols. 1869–1871. 8vo. *Price reduced to 1l. 1s.*

—— *Trialogus.* With the Supplement now first edited. By Gotthard Lechler. 1869. 8vo. *Price reduced to 7s.*

HISTORICAL AND DOCUMENTARY WORKS.

British Barrows, a Record of the Examination of Sepulchral
Mounds in various parts of England. By William Greenwell, M.A., F.S.A.
Together with Description of Figures of Skulls, General Remarks on Pre-
historic Crania, and an Appendix by George Rolleston, M.D., F.R.S. 1877.
Medium 8vo. 25*s*.

Britton. A Treatise upon the Common Law of England,
composed by order of King Edward I. The French Text carefully revised,
with an English Translation, Introduction, and Notes, by F. M. Nichols, M.A.
2 vols. 1865. Royal 8vo. 1*l*. 16*s*.

Clarendon's History of the Rebellion and Civil Wars in
England. 7 vols. 1839. 18mo. 1*l*. 1*s*.   •

Clarendon's History of the Rebellion and Civil Wars in
England. Also his Life, written by himself, in which is included a Con-
tinuation of his History of the Grand Rebellion. With copious Indexes.
In one volume, royal 8vo. 1842. 1*l*. 2*s*.

Clinton's Epitome of the Fasti Hellenici. 1851. 8vo. 6*s*. 6*d*.

—— *Epitome of the Fasti Romani.* 1854. 8vo. 7*s*.

Corpvs Poeticvm Boreale. The Poetry of the Old Northern
Tongue, from the Earliest Times to the Thirteenth Century. Edited, clas-
sified, and translated. with Introduction, Excursus, and Notes, by Gudbrand
Vigfússon, M.A., and F. York Powell, M.A. 2 vols. 1883. 8vo. 42*s*.

*Freeman (E. A.). History of the Norman Conquest of Eng-
land;* its Causes and Results. In Six Volumes. 8vo. 5*l*. 9*s*. 6*d*.

Freeman (E. A.). The Reign of William Rufus and the
Accession of Henry the First. 2 vols. 8vo. 1*l*. 16*s*.

Gascoigne's Theological Dictionary ("Liber Veritatum"):
Selected Passages, illustrating the condition of Church and State, 1403-1458.
With an Introduction by James E. Thorold Rogers, M.P. Small 4to. 10*s*. 6*d*.

Magna Carta, a careful Reprint. Edited by W. Stubbs, M.A.
1879. 4to. stitched, 1*s*.

Passio et Miracula Beati Olaui. Edited from a Twelfth-
Century MS. in the Library of Corpus Christi College, Oxford, with an Introduction and Notes, by Frederick Metcalfe, M.A. Small 4to. stiff covers, 6*s*.

Protests of the Lords, including those which have been expunged, from 1624 to 1874; with Historical Introductions. Edited by James
E. Thorold Rogers, M.A. 1875. 3 vols. 8vo. 2*l*. 2*s*.

Rogers (J. E. T.). History of Agriculture and Prices in
England, A.D. 1259-1793.
    Vols. I and II (1259-1400). 1866. 8vo. 2*l*. 2*s*.
    Vols. III and IV (1401-1582). 1882. 8vo. 2*l* 10*s*.

Saxon Chronicles (Two of the) parallel, with Supplementary
Extracts from the Others. Edited, with Introduction, Notes, and a Glossarial Index, by J. Earle, M.A. 1865. 8vo. 16s.

Sturlunga Saga, including the Islendinga Saga of Lawman
Sturla Thordsson and other works. Edited by Dr. Gudbrand Vigfússon.
In 2 vols. 1878. 8vo. 2l. 2s.

York Plays. The Plays performed by the Crafts or Mysteries
of York on the day of Corpus Christi in the 14th, 15th, and 16th centuries.
Now first printed from the unique manuscript in the Library of Lord Ashburn-
ham. Edited with Introduction and Glossary by Lucy Toulmin Smith. 8vo.
21s. *Just Published.*

Statutes made for the University of Oxford, and for the Colleges
and Halls therein, by the University of Oxford Commissioners. 1882. 8vo.
12s. 6d.

Statuta Universitatis Oxoniensis. 1885. 8vo. 5s.

The Examination Statutes for the Degrees of B.A., B. Mus.,
B.C.L., and B.M. Revised to Trinity Term, 1885. 8vo. sewed, 1s.

The Student's Handbook to the University and Colleges of
Oxford. Extra fcap. 8vo. 2s. 6d.

The Oxford University Calendar for the year 1885. Crown
8vo. 4s. 6d.
The present Edition includes all Class Lists and other University distinctions for
the five years ending with 1884.

Also, supplementary to the above, price 5s. (pp. 606),

The Honours Register of the University of Oxford. A complete
Record of University Honours, Officers, Distinctions, and Class Lists; of the
Heads of Colleges, &c., &c., from the Thirteenth Century to 1883.

MATHEMATICS, PHYSICAL SCIENCE, &c.

Acland (H. W., M.D., F.R.S.). Synopsis of the Pathological
Series in the Oxford Museum. 1867. 8vo. 2s. 6d.

Astronomical Observations made at the University Observ-
atory, Oxford, under the direction of C. Pritchard, M.A. No. 1. 1878.
Royal 8vo. paper covers, 3s. 6d.

De Bary (Dr. A.) Comparative Anatomy of the Vegetative
Organs of the Phanerogams and Ferns. Translated and Annotated by F. O.
Bower, M.A., F.L.S., and D. H. Scott, M.A., Ph.D., F.L.S. With two
hundred and forty-one woodcuts and an Index. Royal 8vo., half morocco,
1l. 2s. 6d.

Müller (J.). On certain Variations in the Vocal Organs of
the Passeres that have hitherto escaped notice. Translated by F. J. Bell, B.A.,
and edited, with an Appendix, by A. H. Garrod, M.A., F.R.S. With Plates.
1878. 4to. paper covers, 7s. 6d.

Phillips (John, M.A., F.R.S.). Geology of Oxford and the
Valley of the Thames. 1871. 8vo. 21s.

—— *Vesuvius.* 1869. Crown 8vo. 10s. 6d.

Price (Bartholomew, M.A., F.R.S.). Treatise on Infinitesimal
Calculus.

   Vol. I. Differential Calculus. Second Edition. 8vo. 14s. 6d.

   Vol. II. Integral Calculus, Calculus of Variations, and Differential Equations.
   Second Edition, 1865. 8vo. 18s.

   Vol. III. Statics, including Attractions; Dynamics of a Material Particle.
   Second Edition, 1868. 8vo. 16s.

   Vol. IV. Dynamics of Material Systems; together with a chapter on Theoretical Dynamics, by W. F. Donkin, M.A., F.R.S. 1862. 8vo. 16s.

Rigaud's Correspondence of Scientific Men of the 17th Century,
with Table of Contents by A. de Morgan. and Index by the Rev. J. Rigaud,
M.A. 2 vols. 1841–1862. 8vo. 18s. 6d.

Rolleston (George, M.D., F.R.S.). Scientific Papers and Ad-
dresses. Arranged and Edited by William Turner, M.B., F.R.S. With a
Biographical Sketch by Edward Tylor, F.R.S. With Portrait, Plates, and
Woodcuts. 2 vols. 8vo. 1l. 4s.

Sachs' Text-Book of Botany, Morphological and Physiological.
A New Edition. Translated by S. H. Vines, M.A. 1882. Royal 8vo., half
morocco, 1l. 11s. 6d.

Westwood (J. O., M.A., F.R.S.). Thesaurus Entomologicus
Hopeianus, or a Description of the rarest Insects in the Collection given to
the University by the Rev. William Hope. With 40 Plates. 1874. Small
folio, half morocco, 7l. 10s.

The Sacred Books of the East.

TRANSLATED BY VARIOUS ORIENTAL SCHOLARS, AND EDITED BY
F. MAX MÜLLER.

[Demy 8vo. cloth.]

Vol. I. The Upanishads. Translated by F. Max Müller.
Part I. The Khândogya-upanishad, The Talavakâra-upanishad, The Aitareya-
âranyaka, The Kaushîtaki-brâhmana-upanishad, and The Vâgasaneyi-samhitâ-
upanishad. 10s. 6d.

Vol. II. The Sacred Laws of the Âryas, as taught in the
Schools of Apastamba, Gautama, Vâsishtha, and Baudhâyana. Translated by
Prof. Georg Bühler. Part I. Apastamba and Gautama. 10s. 6d.

Vol. III. The Sacred Books of China. The Texts of Con-
fucianism. Translated by James Legge. Part I. The Shû King, The Reli-
gious portions of the Shih King, and The Hsiâo King. 12*s.* 6*d.*

Vol. IV. The Zend-Avesta. Translated by James Darme-
steter. Part I. The Vendîdâd. 10*s.* 6*d.*

Vol. V. The Pahlavi Texts. Translated by E. W. West.
Part I. The Bundahis, Bahman Vast, and Shâyast lâ-shâyast. 12*s.* 6*d.*

Vols. VI and IX. The Qur'ân. Parts I and II. Translated
by E. H. Palmer. 21*s.*

Vol. VII. The Institutes of Vishnu. Translated by Julius
Jolly. 10*s.* 6*d.*

Vol. VIII. The Bhagavadgîtâ, with The Sanatsugâtîya, and
The Anugîtâ. Translated by Kâshinâth Trimbak Telang. 10*s.* 6*d.*

Vol. X. The Dhammapada, translated from Pâli by F. Max
Müller; and The Sutta-Nipâta, translated from Pâli by V. Fausböll; being
Canonical Books of the Buddhists. 10*s.* 6*d.*

Vol. XI. Buddhist Suttas. Translated from Pâli by T. W.
Rhys Davids. 1. The Mahâparinibbâna Suttanta ; 2. The Dhamma-*k*akka-
ppavattana Sutta ; 3. The Tevi*gg*a Suttanta ; 4. The Akankheyya Sutta ;
5. The *K*etokhila Sutta ; 6. The Mahâ-sudassana Suttanta ; 7. The Sabbâsava
Sutta. 10*s.* 6*d.*

Vol. XII. The Satapatha-Brâhmana, according to the Text
of the Mâdhyandina School. Translated by Julius Eggeling. Part I.
Books I and II. 12*s.* 6*d.*

Vol. XIII. Vinaya Texts. Translated from the Pâli by
T. W. Rhys Davids and Hermann Oldenberg. Part I. The Pâtimokkha.
The Mahâvagga, I–IV. 10*s.* 6*d.*

Vol. XIV. The Sacred Laws of the Âryas, as taught in the
Schools of Apastamba, Gautama, Vâsishtha and Baudhâyana. Translated
by Georg Bühler. Part II. Vasishtha and Baudhâyana. 10*s.* 6*d.*

Vol. XV. The Upanishads. Translated by F. Max Müller.
Part II. The Katha-upanishad, The Mundaka-upanishad, The Taittirîyaka-
upanishad, The Brihadâranyaka-upanishad, The Svetasvatara-upanishad, The
Prasña-upanishad, and The Maitrâyana-Brâhmana-upanishad. 10*s.* 6*d.*

Vol. XVI. The Sacred Books of China. The Texts of Con-
fucianism. Translated by James Legge. Part II. The Yî King. 10*s.* 6*d.*

Vol. XVII. Vinaya Texts. Translated from the Pâli by
T. W. Rhys Davids and Hermann Oldenberg. Part II. The Mahâvagga,
V–X. The *K*ullavagga, I–III. 10*s.* 6*d.*

Vol. XVIII. Pahlavi Texts. Translated by E. W. West.
Part II. The Dâ*d*istân-î Dinîk and The Epistles of Mânû*sk*îhar. 12*s*. 6*d*.

Vol. XIX. The Fo-sho-hing-tsan-king. A Life of Buddha
by A*s*vaghosha Bodhisattva, translated from Sanskrit into Chinese by Dhar-
maraksha, A.D. 420, and from Chinese into English by Samuel Beal. 10*s*. 6*d*.

Vol. XX. Vinaya Texts. Translated from the Pâli by T. W.
Rhys Davids and Hermann Oldenberg. Part III. The *K*ullavagga, IV–XII.
10*s*. 6*d*.

Vol. XXI. The Saddharma-pu*nd*arîka; or, the Lotus of the
True Law. Translated by H. Kern. 12*s*. 6*d*.

Vol. XXII. *G*aina-Sûtras. Translated from Prâkrit by Hermann Jacobi. Part I. The Â*k*ârâṅga-Sûtra. The Kalpa-Sûtra. 10*s*. 6*d*.

Vol. XXIII. The Zend-Avesta. Translated by James Dar-
mesteter. Part II. The Sîrôzahs, Va*s*ts, and Nyâyi*s*. 10*s*. 6*d*.

Vol. XXIV. Pahlavi Texts. Translated by E. W. West.
Part III. Dinâ-î Maînôg-î Khirad, *S*îkand-gûmânîk, and Sad-Dar. 10*s*. 6*d*.

Second Series.

The following Volumes are in the Press:—

Vol. XXV. Manu. Translated by Georg Bühler.

Vol. XXVI. The *S*atapatha-Brâhma*n*a. Translated by
Julius Eggeling. Part II.

Vols. XXVII and XXVIII. The Sacred Books of China.
The Texts of Confucianism. Translated by James Legge. Parts III and IV.
The Lî *K*î, or Collection of Treatises on the Rules of Propriety, or Ceremonial
Usages.

Vols. XXIX and XXX. The G*ri*hya-sûtras, Rules of Vedic
Domestic Ceremonies. Translated by Hermann Oldenberg. Parts I and II.

Vol. XXXI. The Zend-Avesta. Part III. The Yazna,
Visparad, Afrîgân, and Gâhs. Translated by the Rev. L. H. Mills.

Vol. XXXII. Vedic Hymns. Translated by F. Max Müller.
Part I.

** *The Second Series will consist of Twenty-Four Volumes*

Clarendon Press Series

I. ENGLISH.

A First Reading Book. By Marie Eichens of Berlin ; and edited by Anne J. Clough. Extra fcap. 8vo. stiff covers, 4*d.*

Oxford Reading Book, Part I. For Little Children. Extra fcap. 8vo. stiff covers, 6*d.*

Oxford Reading Book, Part II. For Junior Classes. Extra fcap. 8vo. stiff covers, 6*d.*

An Elementary English Grammar and Exercise Book. By O. W. Tancock, M.A. Second Edition. Extra fcap. 8vo. 1*s.* 6*d.*

An English Grammar and Reading Book, for Lower Forms in Classical Schools. By O. W. Tancock, M.A. Fourth Edition. Extra fcap. 8vo. 3*s.* 6*d.*

Typical Selections from the best English Writers, with Introductory Notices. Second Edition. In Two Volumes. Extra fcap. 8vo. 3*s.* 6*d.* each.

    Vol. I. Latimer to Berkeley.   Vol. II. Pope to Macaulay.

Shairp (J. C., LL.D.). *Aspects of Poetry;* being Lectures delivered at Oxford. Crown 8vo. 10*s.* 6*d.*

A Book for the Beginner in Anglo-Saxon. By John Earle, M.A. Third Edition. Extra fcap. 8vo. 2*s.* 6*d.*

An Anglo-Saxon Reader. In Prose and Verse. With Grammatical Introduction, Notes, and Glossary. By Henry Sweet, M.A. Fourth Edition, Revised and Enlarged. Extra fcap. 8vo. 8*s.* 6*d.*

An Anglo-Saxon Primer, with Grammar, Notes, and Glossary. By the same Author. Second Edition. Extra fcap. 8vo. 2*s.* 6*d.*

Old English Reading Primers; edited by Henry Sweet, M.A.

    I.   Selected Homilies of Ælfric. Extra fcap. 8vo., stiff covers, 1*s.* 6*d.*

    II. Extracts from Alfred's Orosius. Extra fcap. 8vo., stiff covers, 1*s.* 6*d.*

First Middle English Primer, with Grammar and Glossary. By the same Author. Extra fcap. 8vo. 2*s.*

The Philology of the English Tongue. By J. Earle, M.A. Third Edition. Extra fcap. 8vo. 7*s.* 6*d.*

A Handbook of Phonetics, including a Popular Exposition of the Principles of Spelling Reform. By H. Sweet, M.A. Extra fcap. 8vo. 4*s.* 6*d.*

Elementarbuch des Gesprochenen Englisch. Grammatik, Texte und Glossar. Von Henry Sweet. Extra fcap. 8vo., stiff covers, 2*s.* 6*d.*

The Ormulum; with the Notes and Glossary of Dr. R. M.
White. Edited by R. Holt, M.A. 1878. 2 vols. Extra fcap. 8vo. 21s.

English Plant Names from the Tenth to the Fifteenth
Century. By J. Earle, M.A. Small fcap. 8vo. 5s.

Specimens of Early English. A New and Revised Edition.
With Introduction, Notes, and Glossarial Index. By R. Morris, LL.D., and
W˙. W. Skeat, M.A.

> Part I. From Old English Homilies to King Horn (A.D. 1150 to A.D. 1300).
> Second Edition. Extra fcap. 8vo. 9s.

> Part II. From Robert of Gloucester to Gower (A.D. 1298 to A.D. 1393).
> Second Edition. Extra fcap. 8vo. 7s. 6d.

Specimens of English Literature, from the 'Ploughmans
Crede' to the 'Shepheardes Calender' (A.D. 1394 to A.D. 1579). With Introduction, Notes, and Glossarial Index. By W. W. Skeat, M.A. Extra fcap.
8vo. 7s. 6d.

The Vision of William concerning Piers the Plowman, by
William Langland. Edited, with Notes, by W. W. Skeat, M.A. Third
Edition. Extra fcap. 8vo. 4s. 6d.

Chaucer. I. *The Prologue to the Canterbury Tales;* the
Knightes Tale; The Nonne Prestes Tale. Edited by R. Morris, Editor of
Specimens of Early English, &c., &c. Fifty-first Thousand. Extra fcap. 8vo.
2s. 6d.

—— II. *The Prioresses Tale; Sir Thopas;* The Monkes
Tale; The Clerkes Tale; The Squieres Tale, &c. Edited by W. W. Skeat,
M.A. Second Edition. Extra fcap. 8vo. 4s. 6d.

—— III. *The Tale of the Man of Lawe;* The Pardoneres
Tale; The Second Nonnes Tale; The Chanouns Yemannes Tale. By the
same Editor. Second Edition. Extra fcap. 8vo. 4s. 6d.

Gamelyn, The Tale of. Edited with Notes, Glossary, &c., by
W. W. Skeat, M.A. Extra fcap. 8vo. Stiff covers, 1s. 6d.

Spenser's Faery Queene. Books I and II. Designed chiefly
for the use of Schools. With Introduction, Notes, and Glossary. By G. W.
Kitchin, D.D.

> Book I. Tenth Edition. Extra fcap. 8vo. 2s. 6d.

> Book II. Sixth Edition. Extra fcap. 8vo. 2s. 6d.

Hooker. Ecclesiastical Polity, Book I. Edited by R. W.
Church, M.A. Second Edition. Extra fcap. 8vo. 2s.

*Marlowe and Greene. Marlowe's Tragical History of Dr.
Faustus, and Greene's Honourable History of Friar Bacon and Friar Bungay.*
Edited by A. W. Ward, M.A. 1878. Extra fcap. 8vo. 5s. 6d.

Marlowe. Edward II. With Introduction, Notes, &c. By
O. W˙. Tancock, M.A. Extra fcap. 8vo. 3s.

Shakespeare. Select Plays. Edited by W. G. Clark, M.A., and W. Aldis Wright, M.A. Extra fcap. 8vo. stiff covers.

The Merchant of Venice. 1*s*.	Macbeth. 1*s*. 6*d*.
Richard the Second. 1*s*. 6*d*.	Hamlet. 2*s*.

Edited by W. Aldis Wright, M.A.

The Tempest. 1*s*. 6*d*.	A Midsummer Night's Dream.
As You Like It. 1*s*. 6*d*.	1*s*. 6*d*.
Julius Cæsar. 2*s*.	Coriolanus. 2*s*. 6*d*.
Richard the Third. 2*s*. 6*d*.	Henry the Fifth. 2*s*.
King Lear. 1*s*. 6*d*.	Twelfth Night. 1*s*. 6*d*.

King John. *Just Ready.*

Shakespeare as a Dramatic Artist; a popular Illustration of the Principles of Scientific Criticism. By Richard G. Moulton, M.A. Crown 8vo. 5*s*.

Bacon. I. *Advancement of Learning.* Edited by W. Aldis Wright, M.A. Second Edition. Extra fcap. 8vo. 4*s*. 6*d*.

—— II. *The Essays.* With Introduction and Notes. By S. H. Reynolds, M.A., late Fellow of Brasenose College. *In Preparation.*

Milton. I. *Areopagitica.* With Introduction and Notes. By John W. Hales, M.A. Third Edition. Extra fcap. 8vo. 3*s*.

—— II. *Poems.* Edited by R. C. Browne, M.A. 2 vols. Fifth Edition. Extra fcap. 8vo. 6*s*. 6*d*. Sold separately, Vol. I. 4*s*.; Vol. II. 3*s*.

In paper covers :—

Lycidas, 3*d*.   L'Allegro, 3*d*.   Il Penseroso, 4*d*.   Comus, 6*d*. Samson Agonistes, 6*d*.

—— III. *Samson Agonistes.* Edited with Introduction and Notes by John Churton Collins. Extra fcap. 8vo. stiff covers, 1*s*.

Bunyan. I. *The Pilgrim's Progress, Grace Abounding, Relation of the Imprisonment of Mr. John Bunyan.* Edited, with Biographical Introduction and Notes, by E. Venables, M.A. 1879. Extra fcap. 8vo. 5*s*.

—— II. *Holy War, &c.* Edited by E. Venables, M.A. In the Press.

Dryden. Select *Poems.* Stanzas on the Death of Oliver Cromwell; Astræa Redux; Annus Mirabilis; Absalom and Achitophel; Religio Laici; The Hind and the Panther. Edited by W. D. Christie, M.A. Second Edition. Extra fcap. 8vo. 3*s*. 6*d*.

Locke's Conduct of the Understanding. Edited, with Introduction, Notes, &c., by T. Fowler, M.A. Second Edition. Extra fcap. 8vo. 2*s*.

Addison. Selections from Papers in the Spectator. With Notes. By T. Arnold, M.A. Extra fcap. 8vo. 4*s.* 6*d.*

Steele. Selections from the Tatler, Spectator, and Guardian. Edited by Austin Dobson. Extra fcap. 8vo. 4*s.* 6*d.* In white Parchment, 7*s.* 6*d.*

Pope. With Introduction and Notes. By Mark Pattison, B.D.

—— I. *Essay on Man.* Extra fcap. 8vo. 1*s.* 6*d.*

—— II. *Satires and Epistles.* Extra fcap. 8vo. 2*s.*

Parnell. The Hermit. Paper covers, 2*d.*

Johnson. I. *Rasselas; Lives of Dryden and Pope.* Edited by Alfred Milnes, M.A. (London). Extra fcap. 8vo. 4*s* 6*d.*

—— *Lives of Pope and Dryden.* Stiff covers, 2*s.* 6*d.*

—— II. *Vanity of Human Wishes.* With Notes, by E. J. Payne, M.A. Paper covers, 4*d.*

Gray. Selected Poems. Edited by Edmund Gosse, Clark Lecturer in English Literature at the University of Cambridge. Extra fcap. 8vo. Stiff covers, 1*s.* 6*d.* In white Parchment, 3*s.*

—— *Elegy and Ode on Eton College.* Paper covers, 2*d.*

Goldsmith. The Deserted Village. Paper covers, 2*d.*

Cowper. Edited, with Life, Introductions, and Notes, by H. T. Griffith, B.A.

—— I. *The Didactic Poems of* 1782, with Selections from the Minor Pieces. A.D. 1779–1783. Extra fcap 8vo. 3*s.*

—— II. *The Task, with Tirocinium,* and Selections from the Minor Poems. A.D. 1784–1799. Second Edition. Extra fcap. 8vo. 3*s.*

Burke. Select Works. Edited, with Introduction and Notes, by E. J. Payne. M.A.

—— I. *Thoughts on the Present Discontents; the two Speeches on America* Second Edition. Extra fcap. 8vo. 4*s.* 6*d.*

—— II. *Reflections on the French Revolution.* Second Edition. Extra fcap. 8vo. 5*s.*

—— III. *Four Letters on the Proposals for Peace with the* Regicide Directory of France. Second Edition. Extra fcap. 8vo. 5*s.*

Keats. Hyperion, Book I. With Notes by W. T. Arnold, B.A. Paper covers. 4*d.*

Byron. Childe Harold. Edited, with Introduction and Notes, by H. F. Tozer, M.A. Extra fcap. 8vo. Cloth, 3*s.* 6*d.* In white Parchment, 5*s. Just Published.*

Scott. Lay of the Last Minstrel. Introduction and Canto I, with Preface and Notes by W. Minto, M.A. Paper covers, 6*d.*

II. LATIN.

Rudimenta Latina. Comprising Accidence, and Exercises of
a very Elementary Character, for the use of Beginners. By John Barrow
Allen, M.A. Extra fcap. 8vo. *2s.*

An Elementary Latin Grammar. By the same Author.
Forty-second Thousand. Extra fcap. 8vo. *2s. 6d.*

A First Latin Exercise Book. By the same Author. Fourth
Edition. Extra fcap. 8vo. *2s. 6d.*

A Second Latin Exercise Book. By the same Author. Extra
fcap. 8vo. *3s. 6d.*

Reddenda Minora, or Easy Passages, Latin and Greek, for
Unseen Translation. For the use of Lower Forms. Composed and selected
by C. S. Jerram, M.A. Extra fcap. 8vo. *1s. 6d.*

Anglice Reddenda, or Easy Extracts, Latin and Greek, for
Unseen Translation. By C. S. Jerram, M.A. Third Edition, Revised and
Enlarged. Extra fcap. 8vo. *2s. 6d.*

Passages for Translation into Latin. For the use of Passmen
and others. Selected by J. Y. Sargent, M.A. Fifth Edition. Extra fcap.
8vo. *2s. 6d.*

Exercises in Latin Prose Composition; with Introduction,
Notes, and Passages of Graduated Difficulty for Translation into Latin. By
G. G. Ramsay, M.A., LL.D. Second Edition. Extra fcap. 8vo. *4s. 6d.*

Hints and Helps for Latin Elegiacs. By H. Lee-Warner, M.A.,
late Fellow of St. John's College, Cambridge, Assistant Master at Rugby
School. Extra fcap. 8vo. *3s. 6d. Just Published.*

First Latin Reader. By T. J. Nunns, M.A. Third Edition.
Extra fcap. 8vo. *2s.*

Caesar. The Commentaries (for Schools). With Notes and
Maps. By Charles E. Moberly, M.A.

     Part I. *The Gallic War.* Second Edition. Extra fcap. 8vo. *4s. 6d.*
     Part II. *The Civil War.* Extra fcap. 8vo. *3s. 6d.*
     The Civil War. Book I. Second Edition. Extra fcap. 8vo. *2s.*

Cicero. Selection of interesting and descriptive passages. With
Notes. By Henry Walford, M.A. In three Parts. Extra fcap. 8vo. *4s. 6d.*
         Each Part separately, limp, *1s. 6d.*

    Part I.   Anecdotes from Grecian and Roman History. Third Edition.
    Part II.   Omens and Dreams: Beauties of Nature. Third Edition.
    Part III. Rome's Rule of her Provinces. Third Edition.

Cicero. Selected Letters (for Schools). With Notes. By the
late C. E. Prichard, M.A., and E. R. Bernard, M.A. Second Edition.
Extra fcap. 8vo. *3s.*

Cicero. Select Orations (for Schools). In Verrem I. De
Imperio Gn. Pompeii. Pro Archia. Philippica IX. With Introduction and
Notes by J. R. King, M.A. Second Edition. Extra fcap. 8vo. 2*s.* 6*d.*

Cornelius Nepos. With Notes. By Oscar Browning, M.A.
Second Edition. Extra fcap. 8vo. 2*s.* 6*d.*

Livy. Selections (for Schools). With Notes and Maps. By
H. Lee-Warner, M.A. Extra fcap. 8vo. In Parts, limp, each 1*s.* 6*d.*

        Part I. The Caudine Disaster.

        Part II. Hannibal's Campaign in Italy.

        Part III. The Macedonian War.

Livy. Books V–VII. With Introduction and Notes. By
A. R. Cluer, B.A. Extra fcap. 8vo. 3*s.* 6*d.*

Ovid. Selections for the use of Schools. With Introductions
and Notes, and an Appendix on the Roman Calendar. By W. Ramsay, M.A.
Edited by G. G. Ramsay, M.A. Second Edition. Extra fcap. 8vo. 5*s.* 6*d.*

Ovid. Tristia. Book I. The Text revised, with an Introduction and Notes. By S. G. Owen, B.A. Extra fcap. 8vo. 3*s.* 6*d.*

Pliny. Selected Letters (for Schools). With Notes. By the
late C. E. Prichard, M.A., and E. R. Bernard, M.A. Second Edition. Extra
fcap. 8vo. 3*s.*

Tacitus. The Annals. Books I–IV. Edited, with Introduction and Notes for the use of Schools and Junior Students, by H. Furneaux,
M.A. Extra fcap. 8vo. 5*s.*

Terence. Andria. With Notes and Introductions. By C.
E. Freeman, M.A., and A. Sloman, M.A. Extra fcap. 8vo. 3*s.*

Catulli Veronensis Liber. Iterum recognovit, apparatum cri-
ticum prolegomena appendices addidit, Robinson Ellis, A.M. 1878. Demy
8vo. 16*s.*

—— *A Commentary on Catullus.* By Robinson Ellis, M.A.
1876. Demy 8vo. 16*s.*

—— *Veronensis Carmina Selecta,* secundum recognitionem
Robinson Ellis, A.M. Extra fcap. 8vo. 3*s.* 6*d.*

Cicero de Oratore. With Introduction and Notes. By A. S.
Wilkins, M.A.

        Book I. 1879. 8vo. 6*s.*   Book II. 1881. 8vo. 5*s.*

—— *Philippic Orations.* With Notes. By J. R. King, M.A.
Second Edition. 1879. 8vo. 10*s.* 6*d.*

Cicero. Select Letters. With English Introductions, Notes, and Appendices. By Albert Watson, M.A. Third Edition. 1881. Demy 8vo. 18s.

—— *Select Letters.* Text. By the same Editor. Second Edition Extra fcap. 8vo. 4s.

—— *pro Cluentio.* With Introduction and Notes. By W. Ramsay, M.A. Edited by G. G. Ramsay, M.A. Second Edition. Extra fcap. 8vo. 3s. 6d.

Horace. With a Commentary. Volume I. The Odes, Carmen Seculare, and Epodes. By Edward C. Wickham, M.A. Second Edition. 1877. Demy 8vo. 12s.

—— A reprint of the above, in a size suitable for the use of Schools. Extra fcap. 8vo. 5s. 6d.

Livy, Book I. With Introduction, Historical Examination, and Notes. By J. R. Seeley, M.A. Second Edition. 1881. 8vo. 6s.

Ovid. P. Ovidii Nasonis Ibis. Ex Novis Codicibus edidit, Scholia Vetera Commentarium cum Prolegomenis Appendice Indice addidit, R. Ellis, A.M. 8vo. 10s. 6d.

Persius. The Satires. With a Translation and Commentary. By John Conington, M.A. Edited by Henry Nettleship, M.A. Second Edition. 1874. 8vo. 7s. 6d.

Plautus. The Trinummus. With Notes and Introductions. Intended for the Higher Forms of Public Schools. By C. E. Freeman, M.A., and A. Sloman, M.A. Extra fcap. 8vo. 3s.

Sallust. With Introduction and Notes. By W. W. Capes, M.A. Extra fcap. 8vo. 4s. 6d.

Tacitus. The Annals. Books I–VI. Edited, with Introduction and Notes, by H. Furneaux, M.A. 8vo. 18s.

Virgil. With Introduction and Notes. By T. L. Papillon, M A. Two vols. Crown 8vo. 10s. 6d.

Nettleship (H., M.A.). Lectures and Essays on Subjects connected with Latin Scholarship and Literature. Crown 8vo. 7s. 6d.

—— *The Roman Satura:* its original form in connection with its literary development. 8vo. sewed, 1s.

—— *Ancient Lives of Vergil.* With an Essay on the Poems of Vergil, in connection with his Life and Times. 8vo. sewed, 2s.

Papillon (T. L., M.A.). A Manual of Comparative Philology. Third Edition, Revised and Corrected. 1882. Crown 8vo. 6s.

Pinder (North, M.A.). Selections from the less known Latin Poets. 1869. 8vo. 15s.

Sellar (W. Y., M.A.). Roman Poets of the Augustan Age.
VIRGIL. New Edition. 1883. Crown 8vo. 9*s.*

—— *Roman Poets of the Republic.* New Edition, Revised and Enlarged. 1881. 8vo. 14*s.*

Wordsworth (J., M.A.). Fragments and Specimens of Early Latin. With Introductions and Notes. 1874. 8vo. 18*s.*

III. GREEK.

A Greek Primer, for the use of beginners in that Language. By the Right Rev. Charles Wordsworth, D.C.L. Seventh Edition. Extra fcap. 8vo. 1*s.* 6*d.*

Graecae Grammaticae Rudimenta in usum Scholarum. Auctore Carolo Wordsworth, D.C.L. Nineteenth Edition, 1882. 12mo. 4*s.*

A Greek-English Lexicon, abridged from Liddell and Scott's 4to. edition, chiefly for the use of Schools. Twenty-first Edition. 1884. Square 12mo. 7*s.* 6*d.*

Greek Verbs, Irregular and Defective; their forms, meaning, and quantity; embracing all the Tenses used by Greek writers, with references to the passages in which they are found. By W. Veitch. Fourth Edition. Crown 8vo. 10*s.* 6*d.*

The Elements of Greek Accentuation (for Schools): abridged from his larger work by H. W. Chandler, M.A. Extra fcap. 8vo. 2*s.* 6*d.*

A SERIES OF GRADUATED GREEK READERS:——

First Greek Reader. By W. G. Rushbrooke, M.L. Second Edition. Extra fcap. 8vo. 2*s.* 6*d.*

Second Greek Reader. By A. M. Bell, M.A. Extra fcap. 8vo. 3*s.* 6*d.*

Fourth Greek Reader; being Specimens of Greek Dialects. With Introductions and Notes. By W. W. Merry, M.A. Extra fcap. 8vo. 4*s.* 6*d.*

Fifth Greek Reader. Selections from Greek Epic and Dramatic Poetry, with Introductions and Notes. By Evelyn Abbott, M.A. Extra fcap. 8vo. 4*s.* 6*d.*

The Golden Treasury of Ancient Greek Poetry: being a Collection of the finest passages in the Greek Classic Poets with Introductory Notices and Notes. By R. S. Wright M.A. Extra fcap. 8vo. 8*s.* 6*d.*

A Golden Treasury of Greek Prose, being a Collection of the finest passages in the principal Greek Prose Writers, with Introductory Notices and Notes. By R. S. Wright, M.A., and J. E. L. Shadwell, M.A. Extra fcap. 8vo. 4*s.* 6*d.*

Aeschylus. Prometheus Bound (for Schools). With Introduction and Notes, by A. O. Prickard, M.A. Second Edition. Extra fcap. 8vo. 2s.

―― *Agamemnon.* With Introduction and Notes, by Arthur Sidgwick, M.A. Second Edition. Extra fcap. 8vo. 3s.

―― *Choephoroi.* With Introduction and Notes by the same Editor. Extra fcap. 8vo. 3s.

Aristophanes. In Single Plays. Edited, with English Notes, Introductions, &c., by W. W. Merry, M.A. Extra fcap. 8vo.

    I. The Clouds, Second Edition, 2s.

    II. The Acharnians, 2s.   III. The Frogs, 2s.

Cebes. Tabula. With Introduction and Notes. By C. S. Jerram, M.A. Extra fcap. 8vo. 2s. 6d.

Euripides. Alcestis (for Schools). By C. S. Jerram, M.A. Extra fcap. 8vo. 2s. 6d.

――― *Helena.* Edited, with Introduction, Notes, and Critical Appendix, for Upper and Middle Forms. By C. S. Jerram, M.A. Extra fcap. 8vo. 3s.

―― *Iphigenia in Tauris.* Edited, with Introduction, Notes, and Critical Appendix, for Upper and Middle Forms. By C. S. Jerram, M.A. Extra fcap. 8vo. cloth, 3s.

Herodotus, Selections from. Edited, with Introduction, Notes, and a Map, by W. W. Merry, M.A. Extra fcap. 8vo. 2s. 6d.

Homer. Odyssey, Books I–XII (for Schools). By W. W. Merry, M.A. Twenty-seventh Thousand. Extra fcap. 8vo. 4s. 6d.

    Book II, separately, 1s. 6d.

―― *Odyssey,* Books XIII–XXIV (for Schools). By the same Editor. Second Edition. Extra fcap. 8vo. 5s.

―― *Iliad,* Book I (for Schools). By D. B. Monro, M.A. Second Edition. Extra fcap. 8vo. 2s.

―― *Iliad,* Books I–XII (for Schools). With an Introduction, a brief Homeric Grammar, and Notes. By D. B. Monro, M.A. Extra fcap. 8vo. 6s.

―― *Iliad,* Books VI and XXI. With Introduction and Notes. By Herbert Hailstone, M.A. Extra fcap. 8vo. 1s. 6d. each.

Lucian. Vera Historia (for Schools). By C. S. Jerram, M.A. Second Edition. Extra fcap. 8vo. 1s. 6d.

Plato. Selections from the Dialogues [including the whole of the *Apology* and *Crito*]. With Introduction and Notes by John Purves, M.A., and a Preface by the Rev. B. Jowett, M.A. Extra fcap. 8vo. 6s. 6d.

Sophocles. In Single Plays, with English Notes, &c. By
Lewis Campbell, M.A., and Evelyn Abbott, M.A. Extra fcap. 8vo. limp.

Oedipus Tyrannus, Philoctetes. New and Revised Edition, 2*s.* each.
Oedipus Coloneus, Antigone, 1*s.* 9*d.* each.
Ajax, Electra, Trachiniae, 2*s.* each.

—— *Oedipus Rex:* Dindorf's Text, with Notes by the
present Bishop of St. David's. Extra fcap. 8vo. limp, 1*s.* 6*d.*

Theocritus (for Schools). With Notes. By H. Kynaston,
D.D. (late Snow). Third Edition. Extra fcap. 8vo. 4*s.* 6*d.*

Xenophon. Easy Selections. (for Junior Classes). With a
Vocabulary, Notes, and Map. By J. S. Phillpotts, B.C.L., and C. S. Jerram,
M.A. Third Edition. Extra fcap. 8vo. 3*s.* 6*d.*

—— *Selections* (for Schools). With Notes and Maps. By
J. S. Phillpotts, B.C.L. Fourth Edition. Extra fcap. 8vo. 3*s.* 6*d.*

—— *Anabasis*, Book I. Edited for the use of Junior Classes
and Private Students. With Introduction, Notes, and Index. By J. Mar-
shall, M.A., Rector of the Royal High School, Edinburgh. Extra fcap. 8vo.
2*s.* 6*d. Just Published.*

—— *Anabasis*, Book II. With Notes and Map. By C. S.
Jerram, M.A. Extra fcap. 8vo. 2*s.*

—— *Cyropaedia*, Books IV and V. With Introduction and
Notes by C. Bigg, D.D. Extra fcap. 8vo. 2*s.* 6*d.*

———————

Aristotle's Politics. By W. L. Newman, M.A. [*In preparation.*]

Aristotelian Studies. I. On the Structure of the Seventh
Book of the Nicomachean Ethics. By J. C. Wilson, M.A. 1879. Medium 8vo.
stiff, 5*s.*

Demosthenes and Aeschines. The Orations of Demosthenes
and Æschines on the Crown. With Introductory Essays and Notes. By
G. A. Simcox, M.A., and W. H. Simcox, M.A. 1872. 8vo. 12*s.*

Geldart (*E. M., B.A.*). *The Modern Greek Language* in its
relation to Ancient Greek. Extra fcap. 8vo. 4*s.* 6*d.*

Hicks (*E. L., M.A.*). *A Manual of Greek Historical Inscrip-
tions.* Demy 8vo. 10*s.* 6*d.*

Homer. Odyssey, Books I–XII. Edited with English Notes,
Appendices, etc. By W. W. Merry, M.A., and the late James Riddell, M.A.
1876. Demy 8vo. 16*s.*

—— *A Grammar of the Homeric Dialect.* By D. B. Monro,
M.A. Demy 8vo. 10*s.* 6*d.*

Sophocles. The Plays and Fragments. With English Notes
and Introductions, by Lewis Campbell. M.A. 2 vols.

> Vol. I. Oedipus Tyrannus. Oedipus Coloneus. Antigone. Second
> Edition. 1879. 8vo. 16s.

> Vol. II. Ajax. Electra. Trachiniae. Philoctetes. Fragments. 1881.
> 8vo. 16s. '

Sophocles. The Text of the Seven Plays. By the same
Editor. Extra fcap. 8vo. 4s. 6d.

IV. FRENCH AND ITALIAN.

Brachet's Etymological Dictionary of the French Language,
with a Preface on the Principles of French Etymology. Translated into
English by G. W. Kitchin, D D. Third Edition. Crown 8vo. 7s. 6d.

—— *Historical Grammar of the French Language.* Translated into English by G. W. Kitchin, D.D. Fourth Edition. Extra fcap.
8vo. 3s. 6d.

Works by GEORGE SAINTSBURY, M.A.

Primer of French Literature. Extra fcap. 8vo. 2s.

Short History of French Literature. Crown 8vo. 10s. 6d.

Specimens of French Literature, from Villon to Hugo. Crown
8vo. 9s.

Corneille's Horace. Edited, with Introduction and Notes, by
George Saintsbury, M.A. Extra fcap. 8vo. 2s. 6d.

Molière's Les Précieuses Ridicules. Edited, with Introduction
and Notes, by Andrew Lang, M.A. Extra fcap. 8vo. 1s. 6d.

Beaumarchais' Le Barbier de Séville. Edited, with Introduction
and Notes, by Austin Dobson. Extra fcap. 8vo. 2s. 6d.

Voltaire's Mérope. Edited, with Introduction and Notes, by
George Saintsbury. Extra fcap. 8vo. cloth, 2s. *Just Published.*

Musset's On ne badine pas avec l'Amour, and *Fantasio.* Edited,
with Prolegomena, Notes, etc., by Walter Herries Pollock. Extra fcap.
8vo. 2s.

Sainte-Beuve. Selections from the Causeries du Lundi. Edited
by George Saintsbury. Extra fcap. 8vo. 2s.

Quinet's Lettres à sa Mère. Selected and edited by George
Saintsbury. Extra fcap. 8vo. cloth, 2s.

L'Éloquence de la Chaire et de la Tribune Françaises. Edited
by Paul Blouët, B.A. (Univ. Gallic.). Vol. I. Fiench Sacred Oratory
Extra fcap. 8vo. 2*s.* 6*d.*

Edited by GUSTAVE MASSON, B.A.

Corneille's Cinna, and *Molière's Les Femmes Savantes.* With
Introduction and Notes. Extra fcap. 8vo. 2*s.* 6*d.*

Louis XIV and his Contemporaries; as described in Extracts
from the best Memoirs of the Seventeenth Century. With English Notes,
Genealogical Tables, &c. Extra fcap. 8vo. 2*s.* 6*d.*

Maistre, Xavier de. Voyage autour de ma Chambre. Ourika,
by *Madame de Duras;* La Dot de Suzette, by *Fievée;* Les Jumeaux de
l'Hôtel Corneille. by *Edmond About;* Mésaventures d'un Écolier, by *Rodolphe
Töpffer.* Second Edition. Extra fcap. 8vo. 2*s.* 6*d.*

Molière's Les Fourberies de Scapin. With Voltaire's Life of
Molière. Extra fcap. 8vo. stiff covers, 1*s.* 6*d.*

Molière's Les Fourberies de Scapin, and *Racine's Athalie.*
With Voltaire's Life of Molière. Extra fcap. 8vo. 2*s.* 6*d.*

Racine's Andromaque, and *Corneille's Le Menteur.* With
Louis Racine's Life of his Father. Extra fcap. 8vo. 2*s.* 6*d.*

Regnard's Le Joueur, and *Brueys and Palaprat's Le Grondeur.*
Extra fcap 8vo. 2*s.* 6*d.*

*Sévigné, Madame de, and her chief Contemporaries, Selections
from the Correspondence of.* Intended more especially for Girls' Schools.
Extra fcap. 8vo. 3*s.*

Dante. Selections from the Inferno. With Introduction and
Notes. By H. B. Cotterill, B.A. Extra fcap. 8vo. 4*s.* 6*d.*

Tasso. La. Gerusalemme Liberata. Cantos i, ii. With Introduction and Notes. By the same Editor. Extra fcap. 8vo. 2*s.* 6*d.*

V. GERMAN.

Scherer (W.). A History of German Literature. Translated
from the Thiid German Edition by Mrs. F. Conybeare. Edited by F. Max
Müller. 2 vols. 8vo. 21*s. Just Published.*

GERMAN COURSE. By HERMANN LANGE.

The Germans at Home; a Practical Introduction to German
Conversation, with an Appendix containing the Essentials of German Grammar.
Second Edition. 8vo. 2*s.* 6*d.*

The German Manual; a German Grammar, Reading Book,
and a Handbook of German Conversation. 8vo. 7*s.* 6*d.*

Grammar of the German Language. 8vo. *3s. 6d.*

This 'Grammar' is a reprint of the Grammar contained in 'The German Manual,' and, in this separate form, is intended for the use of Students who wish to make themselves acquainted with German Grammar chiefly for the purpose of being able to read German books.

German Composition ; A Theoretical and Practical Guide to the Art of Translating English Prose into German. 8vo. *4s. 6d.*

Lessing's Laokoon. With Introduction, English Notes, etc. By A. Hamann, Phil. Doc., M.A. Extra fcap. 8vo. *4s. 6d.*

Schiller's Wilhelm Tell. Translated into English Verse by E. Massie, M.A. Extra fcap. 8vo. *5s.*

Also, Edited by C. A. BUCHHEIM, Phil. Doc.

Goethe's Egmont. With a Life of Goethe, &c. Third Edition. Extra fcap. 8vo. *3s.*

—— *Iphigenie auf Tauris.* A Drama. With a Critical Introduction and Notes. Second Edition. · Extra fcap. 8vo. *3s.*

Heine's Prosa, being Selections from his Prose Works. With English Notes, etc. Extra fcap. 8vo. *4s. 6d.*

Lessing's Minna von Barnhelm. A Comedy. With a Life of Lessing, Critical Analysis, Complete Commentary, &c. Fourth Edition. Extra fcap. 8vo. *3s. 6d.*

—— *Nathan der Weise.* With Introduction, Notes, etc. Extra fcap. 8vo. *4s. 6d.*

Schiller's Historische Skizzen ; Egmont's Leben und Tod, and *Belagerung von Antwerpen.* Second Edition. Extra fcap. 8vo. *2s. 6d.*

—— *Wilhelm Tell.* With a Life of Schiller ; an historical and critical Introduction, Arguments, and a complete Commentary, and Map. Sixth Edition. Extra fcap. 8vo. *3s. 6d.*

—— *Wilhelm Tell.* School Edition. With Map. Extra fcap. 8vo. *2s.*

Halm's Griseldis. In Preparation.

Modern German Reader. A Graduated Collection of Extracts in Prose and Poetry from Modern German writers :—

Part I. With English Notes, a Grammatical Appendix, and a complete Vocabulary. Fourth Edition. Extra fcap. 8vo. *2s. 6d.*

Part II. With English Notes and an Index. Extra fcap. 8vo. *2s. 6d. Just Published.*

Part III in Preparation.

VI. MATHEMATICS, PHYSICAL SCIENCE, &c.

By LEWIS HENSLEY, M.A.

Figures made Easy : a first Arithmetic Book. (Introductory to 'The Scholar's Arithmetic.') Crown 8vo. 6*d.*

Answers to the Examples in Figures made Easy, together with two thousand additional Examples formed from the Tables in the same, with Answers. Crown 8vo. 1*s.*

The Scholar's Arithmetic : with Answers to the Examples. Crown 8vo. 4*s.* 6*d.*

The Scholar's Algebra. An Introductory work on Algebra. Crown 8vo. 4*s.* 6*d.*

Baynes (R. E., M.A.). Lessons on Thermodynamics. 1878. Crown 8vo. 7*s.* 6*d.*

Chambers (G. F., F.R.A.S.). A Handbook of Descriptive Astronomy. Third Edition. 1877. Demy 8vo. 28*s.*

Clarke (Col. A. R., C.B., R.E.). Geodesy. 1880. 8vo. 12*s.* 6*d.*

Cremona (Luigi). Elements of Projective Geometry. Translated by C. Leudesdorf, M.A.. 8vo. 12*s.* 6*d.*

Donkin (W. F., M.A., F.R.S.). Acoustics. Second Edition. Crown 8vo. 7*s.* 6*d.*

Galton (Douglas, C.B., F.R.S.). The Construction of Healthy Dwellings ; namely Houses, Hospitals, Barracks, Asylums, &c. Demy 8vo. 10*s.* 6*d.*

Hamilton (Sir R. G. C.), and J. Ball. Book-keeping. New and enlarged Edition. Extra fcap. 8vo. limp cloth, 2*s.*

Harcourt (A. G. Vernon, M.A.), and *H. G. Madan, M.A. Exercises in Practical Chemistry.* Vol. I. Elementary Exercises. Third Edition. Crown 8vo. 9*s.*

Maclaren (Archibald). A System of Physical Education : Theoretical and Practical. Extra fcap. 8vo. 7*s.* 6*d.*

Madan (H. G., M.A.). Tables of Qualitative Analysis. Large 4to. paper, 4*s.* 6*d.*

Maxwell (J. Clerk, M.A., F.R.S.). A Treatise on Electricity and Magnetism. Second Edition. 2 vols. Demy 8vo. 1*l.* 11*s.* 6*d.*

—— *An Elementary Treatise on Electricity.* Edited by William Garnett, M.A. Demy 8vo. 7*s.* 6*d.*

Minchin (*G. M., M.A.*). *A Treatise on Statics.* Third Edition, Corrected and Enlarged. Vol. I. *Equilibrium of Coplanar Forces.* 8vo. 9*s. Just Published.* Vol. II. *In the Press.*

—— *Uniplanar Kinematics of Solids and Fluids.* Crown 8vo. 7*s* 6*d.*

Rolleston (*G., M.D., F.R.S.*). *Forms of Animal Life.* Illustrated by Descriptions and Drawings of Dissections. A New Edition in the Press.

Smyth. A Cycle of Celestial Objects. Observed, Reduced, and Discussed by Admiral W. H. Smyth, R. N. Revised, condensed and greatly enlarged by G. F. Chambers, F.R.A.S. 1881. 8vo. *Price reduced to* 12*s.*

Stewart (*Balfour, LL.D., F.R.S.*). *A Treatise on Heat,* with numerous Woodcuts and Diagrams. Fourth Edition. 1881. Extra fcap. 8vo. 7*s.* 6*d.*

Story-Maskelyne (*M. H. N., M.A.*). *Crystallography.* In the Press.

Vernon-Harcourt (*L. F., M.A.*). *A Treatise on Rivers and Canals,* relating to the Control and Improvement of Rivers, and the Design, Construction, and Development of Canals. 2 vols. (Vol. I, Text. Vol. II, Plates.). 8vo. 21*s.*

—— *Harbours and Docks;* their Physical Features, History, Construction, Equipment, and Maintenance; with Statistics as to their Commercial Development. 2 vols. 8vo. 25*s.*

Watson (*H. W., M.A.*). *A Treatise on the Kinetic Theory of Gases.* 1876. 8vo. 3*s.* 6*d.*

Watson (*H. W., D. Sc., F.R.S.*), *and S. H. Burbury, M.A.*

I. *A Treatise on the Application of Generalised Coordinates to the Kinetics of a Material System.* 1879. 8vo. 6*s.*

II. *The Mathematical Theory of Electricity and Magnetism.* Vol. I. Electrostatics. 8vo. 10*s.* 6*d. Just Published.*

Williamson (*A. W., Phil. Doc., F.R.S.*). *Chemistry for Students.* A new Edition, with Solutions. 1873. Extra fcap. 8vo. 8*s.* 6*d.*

VII. HISTORY.

Bluntschli (*J. K.*). *The Theory of the State.* By J. K. Bluntschli, late Professor of Political Sciences in the University of Heidelberg. Authorised English Translation from the Sixth German Edition. Demy 8vo. half-bound, 12*s.* 6*d. Just Published.*

Finlay (*George, LL.D.*). *A History of Greece* from its Conquest by the Romans to the present time, B.C. 146 to A.D. 1864. A new Edition, revised throughout, and in part re-written, with considerable additions, by the Author, and edited by H. F. Tozer, M.A. 1877. 7 vols. 8vo. 3*l.* 10*s.*

Fortescue (Sir John, Kt.). The Governance of England:
otherwise called The Difference between an Absolute and a Limited Mon-
archy. A Revised Text. Edited, with Introduction, Notes, and Appendices,
by Charles Plummer, M.A. 8vo. half-bound, 12s. 6d. *Just Published.*

Freeman (E.A., D.C.L.). A Short History of the Norman
Conquest of England. Second Edition. Extra fcap. 8vo. 2s. 6d.

—— A History of Greece. In preparation.

George (H. B., M.A.). Genealogical Tables illustrative of Modern
History. Second Edition, Revised and Enlarged. Small 4to. 12s.

Hodgkin (T.). Italy and her Invaders. Illustrated with
Plates and Maps. Vols. I and II., A.D. 376–476. 8vo. 1l. 12s

Vols. III. and IV. *The Ostrogothic Invasion,* and *The Imperial Restoration.*
8vo. 1l. 16s. *Just Published.*

Kitchin (G. W., D.D.). A History of France. With numerous
Maps, Plans, and Tables. In Three Volumes. *Second Edition.* Crown 8vo.
each 10s. 6d.

Vol. 1. Down to the Year 1453.

Vol. 2. From 1453–1624. Vol. 3. From 1624–1793.

Payne (E. J., M.A.). A History of the United States of
America. In the Press.

Ranke (L. von). A History of England, principally in the
Seventeenth Century. Translated by Resident Members of the University of
Oxford, under the superintendence of G. W. Kitchin, D.D., and C. W. Boase,
M.A. 1875. 6 vols. 8vo. 3l. 3s.

Rawlinson (George, M.A.). A Manual of Ancient History.
Second Edition. Demy 8vo. 14s.

Select Charters and other Illustrations of English Constitutional
History, from the Earliest Times to the Reign of Edward I. Arranged and
edited by W. Stubbs, D.D. Fifth Edition. 1883. Crown 8vo. 8s. 6d.

Stubbs (W., D.D.). The Constitutional History of England,
in its Origin and Development. Library Edition. 3 vols. demy 8vo. 2l. 8s.

Also in 3 vols. crown 8vo. price 12s. each.

Wellesley. A Selection from the Despatches, Treaties, and
other Papers of the Marquess Wellesley. K.G., during his Government
of India. Edited by S. J. Owen, M.A. 1877. 8vo. 1l. 4s.

Wellington. A Selection from the Despatches, Treaties, and
other Papers relating to India of Field-Marshal the Duke of Wellington, K.G.
Edited by S. J. Owen, M.A. 1880. 8vo. 24s.

A History of British India. By S. J. Owen, M.A., Reader
in Indian History in the University of Oxford. In preparation.

VIII. LAW.

Alberici Gentilis, I.C.D., I.C. Professoris Regii, De Iure Belli
Libri Tres. Edidit Thomas Erskine Holland, I.C.D. 1877. Small 4to.
half morocco, 21*s.*

Anson (Sir William R., Bart., D.C.L.). Principles of the
English Law of Contract, and of Agency in its Relation to Contract. Second
Edition. Demy 8vo. 10*s.* 6*d.*

Bentham (Jeremy). An Introduction to the Principles of
Morals and Legislation. Crown 8vo. 6*s.* 6*d.*

Digby (Kenelm E., M.A.). An Introduction to the History of
the Law of Real Property. Third Edition. Demy 8vo. 10*s.* 6*d.*

Gaii Institutionum Juris Civilis Commentarii Quattuor; or,
Elements of Roman Law by Gaius. With a Translation and Commentary
by Edward Poste, M.A. Second Edition. 1875. 8vo. 18*s.*

Hall (W. E., M.A.). International Law. Second Edition.
Demy 8vo. 21*s.*

Holland (T. E., D.C.L.). The Elements of Jurisprudence.
Second Edition. Demy 8vo. 10*s.* 6*d.*

—— *The European Concert in the Eastern Question,* a Collection of Treaties and other Public Acts. Edited, with Introductions and
Notes, by Thomas Erskine Holland, D.C.L. 8vo. 12*s.* 6*d.*

Imperatoris Iustiniani Institutionum Libri Quattuor; with
Introductions, Commentary, Excursus and Translation. By J. B. Moyle, B.C.L.,
M.A. 2 vols. Demy 8vo. 21*s.*

Justinian, The Institutes of, edited as a recension of the
Institutes of Gaius, by Thomas Erskine Holland, D.C.L. Second Edition,
1881. Extra fcap. 8vo. 5*s.*

Justinian, Select Titles from the Digest of. By T. E. Holland,
D.C.L., and C. L. Shadwell, B.C.L. 8vo. 14*s.*

Also sold in Parts, in paper covers, as follows :—

Part I. Introductory Titles. 2*s.* 6*d.*   Part II. Family Law.   1*s.*
Part III. Property Law.   2*s.* 6*d.*   Part IV. Law of Obligations (No. 1).   3*s.* 6*d.*
Part IV. Law of Obligations (No. 2).   4*s.* 6*d.*

Markby (W., D.C.L.). Elements of Law considered with refer-
ence to Principles of General Jurisprudence. Third Edition. Demy 8vo. 12*s.*6*d.*

Twiss (Sir Travers, D.C.L.). The Law of Nations considered
as Independent Political Communities.
Part I. On the Rights and Duties of Nations in time of Peace. A new Edition,
Revised and Enlarged. 1884. Demy 8vo. 15*s.*
Part II. On the Rights and Duties of Nations in Time of War. Second Edition
Revised. 1875. Demy 8vo. 21*s.*

IX. MENTAL AND MORAL PHILOSOPHY, &c.

Bacon's Novum Organum. Edited, with English Notes, by
G. W. Kitchin, D.D. 1855. 8vo. 9s. 6d.

—— Translated by G. W. Kitchin, D.D. 1855. 8vo. 9s. 6d.

Berkeley. The Works of George Berkeley, D.D., formerly
Bishop of Cloyne; including many of his writings hitherto unpublished.
With Prefaces, Annotations, and an Account of his Life and Philosophy,
by Alexander Campbell Fraser, M.A. 4 vols. 1871. 8vo. 2l. 18s.

The Life, Letters, &c. 1 vol. 16s.

—— *Selections from.* With an Introduction and Notes.
For the use of Students in the Universities. By Alexander Campbell Fraser,
LL.D. Second Edition. Crown 8vo. 7s. 6d.

Fowler (T., M.A.). The Elements of Deductive Logic, designed
mainly for the use of Junior Students in the Universities. Eighth Edition,
with a Collection of Examples. Extra fcap. 8vo. 3s. 6d.

—— *The Elements of Inductive Logic*, designed mainly for
the use of Students in the Universities. Fourth Edition. Extra fcap. 8vo. 6s.

Edited by T. FOWLER, M.A.

Bacon. Novum Organum. With Introduction, Notes, &c.
1878. 8vo. 14s.

Locke's Conduct of the Understanding. Second Edition.
Extra fcap. 8vo. 2s.

——————

Green (T. H., M.A.). Prolegomena to Ethics. Edited by
A. C. Bradley, M.A. Demy 8vo. 12s. 6d.

Hegel. The Logic of Hegel; translated from the Encyclo-
paedia of the Philosophical Sciences. With Prolegomena by William
Wallace, M.A. 1874. 8vo. 14s.

Lotze's Logic, in Three Books; of Thought, of Investigation,
and of Knowledge. English Translation; Edited by B. Bosanquet, M.A.,
Fellow of University College, Oxford. 8vo. *cloth,* 12s. 6d.

—— *Metaphysic*, in Three Books; Ontology, Cosmology,
and Psychology. English Translation; Edited by B. Bosanquet, M.A.
8vo. *cloth,* 12s. 6d.

Martineau (James, D.D.). Types of Ethical Theory. 2 vols.
8vo. 24s.

Rogers (J. E. Thorold, M.A.). A Manual of Political Economy,
for the use of Schools. Third Edition. Extra fcap. 8vo. 4s. 6d.

Smith's Wealth of Nations. A new Edition, with Notes, by
J. E. Thorold Rogers, M.A. 2 vols. 8vo. 1880. 21s.

X. ART, &c.

Hullah (John). The Cultivation of the Speaking Voice.
Second Edition. Extra fcap. 8vo. 2s. 6d.

Ouseley (Sir F. A. Gore, Bart.). A Treatise on Harmony.
Third Edition. 4to. 10s.

—— *A Treatise on Counterpoint, Canon, and Fugue,* based
upon that of Cherubini. Second Edition. 4to. 16s.

—— *A Treatise on Musical Form and General Composition.*
4to. 10s.

Robinson (J. C., F.S.A.). A Critical Account of the Drawings
by Michel Angelo and Raffaello in the University Galleries, Oxford. 1870.
Crown 8vo. 4s.

Ruskin (John, M.A.). A Course of Lectures on Art, delivered
before the University of Oxford in Hilary Term, 1870. 8vo. 6s.

Troutbeck (J., M.A.) and R. F. Dale, M.A. A Music Primer
(for Schools). Second Edition. Crown 8vo. 1s. 6d.

Tyrwhitt (R. St. J., M.A.). A Handbook of Pictorial Art.
With coloured Illustrations, Photographs, and a chapter on Perspective by
A. Macdonald. Second Edition. 1875. 8vo. half morocco, 18s.

Vaux (W. S. W., M.A., F.R.S.). Catalogue of the Castellani
Collection of Antiquities in the University Galleries, Oxford. Crown 8vo.
stiff cover, 1s.

The Oxford Bible for Teachers, containing supplementary HELPS TO THE STUDY OF THE BIBLE, including Summaries
of the several Books, with copious Explanatory Notes and Tables
illustrative of Scripture History and the characteristics of Bible
Lands; with a complete Index of Subjects, a Concordance, a Dictionary of Proper Names, and a series of Maps. Prices in various sizes
and bindings from 3s. to 2l. 5s.

Helps to the Study of the Bible, taken from the
OXFORD BIBLE FOR TEACHERS, comprising Summaries of the
several Books, with copious Explanatory Notes and Tables illustrative of Scripture History and the Characteristics of Bible Lands;
with a complete Index of Subjects, a Concordance, a Dictionary
of Proper Names, and a series of Maps. Crown 8vo. *cloth,* 3s. 6d.;
16mo. *cloth,* 1s.

———+———

LONDON: HENRY FROWDE,
OXFORD UNIVERSITY PRESS WAREHOUSE, AMEN CORNER,

OXFORD: CLARENDON PRESS DEPOSITORY,
116 HIGH STREET.

The DELEGATES OF THE PRESS *invite suggestions and advice from all persons*
interested in education; and will be thankful for hints, &c. addressed to the
SECRETARY TO THE DELEGATES, *Clarendon Press, Oxford.*

SD - #0021 - 010524 - C0 - 229/152/20 - PB - 9781332786152 - Gloss Lamination